RUSSIAN POETICS

UCLA SLAVIC STUDIES
Volume 4

Published under the auspices of
the Department of Slavic Languages and Literatures,
University of California, Los Angeles

RUSSIAN POETICS

Proceedings of the
International Colloquium
At UCLA, September 22-26, 1975

edited by

THOMAS EEKMAN   DEAN S. WORTH

UCLA

SLAVICA

Slavica publishes a wide variety of books and journals dealing with the peoples, languages, literatures, history, folklore, and culture of the peoples of Eastern Europe and the USSR. For a complete catalog with prices and ordering information, please write to:

Slavica Publishers, Inc.
P.O. Box 14388
Columbus, Ohio 43214
USA

ISBN: 0-89357-101-6.

Text set by Randy Bowlus, Andrew Corin, and Kathleen McDermott at the East European Composition Center, supported by the Department of Slavic Languages and Literatures and the Center for Russian and East European Studies at UCLA with grants from the Joint Committee on Eastern Europe of the American Council of Learned Societies and Social Sciences Research Council and the Research and Development Committee of the American Association for the Advancement of Slavic Studies.

Printed in the United States of America.

In memory of

PROFESSOR ROMAN JAKOBSON

CONTENTS

8 CONTENTS

FOREWORD

This volume contains papers prepared for the fourth in a series of international Slavistic colloquia at the University of California, Los Angeles. Held on the University of California, Los Angeles campus and at the Lake Arrowhead Conference Center in the nearby San Bernadino Mountains, the colloquium brought together some forty scholars from a dozen American universities and ten foreign countries (several other scholars, regrettably, were unable to attend because of illness or other exigencies). While no such meeting can present an adequate view of the current state of research in a broad and complex field, the 1975 colloquium seemed to point out at least some of the trends in poetic research of the seventies: continuing concern for statistical evidence rather than impressionistic vagaries, increasing interest in rhyme and in the interrelation of folk genres to literary texts, a movement toward micro- rather than macro-analyses in metrics, the poetics of poetry as a special instance of general poetics, etc.

After some discussion, the organizers reluctantly decided to restrict the colloquium to Russian, rather than Slavic poetics. In spite of the important work being done e.g. in Poland and Czechoslovakia, our resources — generous as our sponsors were — simply did not permit a meeting of the scope that would have been necessary to do justice to poetic research on several different Slavic languages. On the other hand — by way of relief from the detail of metrical counts and rhyme types — we did include a few papers of general theoretic orientation, and, as always happens, not all the papers received conformed as closely to the announced thematics as we might have wished. Still and all, there was no reason to be dissatisfied with the overall profile of the meeting.

As is customary at the UCLA colloquia, papers were solicited and pre-printed in advance of the meetings, at which the authors then merely summarized their views as an introduction to the ensuing discussion. The debates themselves were extensive and incisive, without becoming unpleasant; the cutting edge of intellect was tempered — without being dulled — by humor. The full range and flavor of discussion is, regrettably, reflected only partially in the written comments printed in this volume (as the number of "additional discussants" listed after most papers makes clear); most of us apparently found talking easier than writing.

The colloquium would not have been possible without the financial, logistic, secretarial and even social assistance of a number of organizations and individuals. The International Research and Exchanges Board and the American Council of Learned Societies generously provided financial aid for participants from Eastern and Western Europe respectively, while the bulk of the conference funding was contributed by UCLA's James Duke Endowment Fund via the Center for Russian and East European Studies (Professor Henrik Birnbaum, Director). CREES Administrative Assistants, the late Mrs. Lucille Liets, and especially Dr. Marsha Gauntt took charge of the complex logistic, financial and editorial tasks of our meeting with the able student assistance of S. Tabata, J. de Varon, D. Woodruff, J. Zelenák, and in particular D. Ponomareff. The Lake Arrowhead Center staff provided an ambiance catering to the palate as well as to the mind. To all these people and organizations, our sincere thanks for having done most of the work for which we take most of the credit.

The appearance of *Russian Poetics* has been delayed for years, due to a series of publishing problems beyond the editors' control. We are thankful to those participants (all but two) who shared our hope that this volume would indeed appear; many, no doubt, would have preferred to update or modify their views of 1975, but technical problems have prevented this in all but the most minor instances. Death has taken two of the colleagues represented here (Professors Isačenko and Meijer). Death, too, has caused us to change our original dedication: *Russian Poetics* was to have been offered to Professor Roman Jakobson on his eightieth birthday, but now, alas, it can be dedicated only to his memory.

October 1982   THOMAS EEKMAN
                                                DEAN S. WORTH

THE EARLIEST EXAMPLES
OF RUSSIAN FOLK METERS

JAMES BAILEY

Russian folk poetry can be divided into three broad categories according to the mode of performance: spoken (proverbs and riddles), sung (lyric), and recitative verse (epic and lament). Each type is also distinguished by its own forms of organization.[1] Spoken verse (*skazovyj stix*) is based on syntactic prosody and is usually rhymed. Trediakovskij first pointed out that trochaic meters are employed in lyric songs and he founded his partial reform of syllabic verse on them.[2] Vostokov, however, asserted that trochaic meters were not native to Russian folk poetry and that they appeared only in new city songs.[3] Controversy over the nature and kinds of meters appearing in epic verse continues to the present day. Vostokov, for instance, stated that the basic epic meter constitutes what today would be termed accentual verse, that is, verse having a constant number of metrical stresses per line and a varying number of syllables between them.[4] Gil'ferding maintained that five- and six-foot trochaic verse forms the chief epic meter.[5] Jakobson and Taranovsky analyzed the trochaic meters in a number of epics (as well as lamentations), and demonstrated that their prosodic features are nearly the same as those found in literary binary meters.[6] Gasparov has concluded that accentual verse (*taktovik*) represents the main epic meter and that trochaic songs constitute a regularized variant.[7]

The earliest extant instances of folk verse are important because they offer some insights into the nature of indigenous Russian versification. In this paper, three groups of works will be examined: (1) the historical song about Griška Otrep'ev, "Ty Bože moj, Bože, Spas milostivyj", (2) the six songs of Richard James, and (3) two poems by S. I. Pazuxin. Bessonov, the editor of the first issue of P. Kireevskij's folk song compilation, initially published the poem about Otrep'ev and noted that the manuscript bears the date 1688. The text was undoubtedly written much earlier because the date was added by a second hand.[8] Since Bessonov's time, collectors have recorded about twenty variants of this song, which some scholars believe may have originally been a literary creation.[9] In the middle of the nineteenth century, Gamel' discovered

and published the six songs taken down for the English clergyman Richard
James during his stay in Russia from 1619 to 1620.[10] Some investigators
consider these poems to be authentic folk songs, while others deny any folk
origin and deem them literary;[11] only one lyric, "Berežoček zybletsja", was
eventually collected by folklorists.[12] Pazuxin's two poems were found on
documents in his family archives; they have been dated about 1680.[13] Several
other early texts of folk songs have been discovered, but the meters in them are
poorly preserved.[14]

Analyzing folk versification is much more complex than literary meters,
partly because one never knows how accurately the text has been recorded;
collectors do not always indicate archaic stressing, arbitrary rhythmical
stresses, morphological variants, particles, and hypocoristics. Dealing with
texts from the seventeenth century is even more difficult because less is known
about Russian accentuation at that time. Nevertheless, the tenacity of some
features of the folk style permits the utilization of stress variants appearing in
later, more reliable recordings as one basis for coping with this problem.
Investigations of Russian accentuation in various written works from this
period as well as information about dialects offer further aids.

Rhythmical analysis in this paper will be based on the texts edited by
Adrianova-Peretc in the volume *Demokratičeskaja poèzija XVII veka*;[15] most
suggested textual emendations will not be utilized. When a word has stress
variants, the alternate best fitting the meter will be selected. James' lyric
"Berežoček zybletsja" is in trochaic trimeter; the other poems are composed
in epic three-stress accentual verse. Korš studied James' songs and made many
pertinent observations about their rhythm;[16] however, he based his recon-
structions on an outdated musical theory of poetic rhythm. To a large extent,
the method developed by Bobrov, Kolmogorov, and Gasparov for analyzing
literary and folk accentual verse will be applied here.[17]

The following stressing differing from present-day norms will be assumed in
the accentual songs. Poem of 1688: line 8 – *drúgogo* (dialectical and common in
folk songs), 14 – *v prokljatój Litve* (variant which preserves the dactylic
ending), 52, 66 – *pjatý kladet*[18] (archaic, dactylic ending), 67, 76 – *zgóvorit*
(folk), and 97 – *dó veku*[19] (archaic and folk). In line 70 the emendation of *i* will
be accepted as will the word *rjad* in line 95. Lines 15, 43, 48, 55, 57, and 78 will
be excluded because they lack clarity, or have two or four stresses. The rhythm
of James' songs is the least clear and their stressing is most subject to doubt;
many of the stresses Korš suggests will be utilized. Song II, line 2 – *s polunóči*
(variant), II-3 – *moskovíči*[20] (archaic), II-11 – *vysóko sókol podnjálsja*[21] (all
variants), II-12 – *syrú*, II-17 – *v Nové-gorode*[22] (archaic) and *zaperlísja* (variant), III-2, 9 – *molodý* (folk variant), III-8 – *ná Moskve*,[23] III-10 – *k Móskve*[24]

(archaic), III-18 – *molodcóv*,[25] IV-1 – *zradoválosja*,[26] IV-11 – *bójarja* (folk variant, dactylic ending), V-1 – *ná Moskve*, V-19 – *k Móskve*, VI-8 – *belý šatry* (archaic formula), VI-9 – *s celá uma* (formula), VI-15 – *Nové-gorode* and VI-23 – *Novým-gorodom*. Korš's placement of a stress on the first syllable of the noun *žit'e* in lines III-21, 25, V-9, 16, seems unsupported and will not be employed;[27] even so, his supposition may be correct since these are the only lines in James' songs with a masculine ending. Line III-1 will be divided into two lines. The preposition *u* emendated in line VI-7 (*u Oki*) will be utilized; since all other instances of the noun *žit'e* are disyllabic, this word in III-25 (*žitie*) will also be considered disyllabic. Nine lines will be omitted (IV-12, 22-24, V-7, VI-8, 18, 21-22). Pazuxin: I-3-5, 7-10 = milá druga (a frequent formula), II-3 – *daléče* (variant) and *v čísto póle* (feminine ending), II-4-5, 7 – *lúgi*[28] (archaic), II-6,8 – *cvéty*[29] (archaic), and II-7 – *v čistóm pole* (formula within the line).

The rhythmical features for each group of songs will be studied separately and then those for all songs will be presented. In order that some comparison may be made with later three-stress accentual folk verse, the characteristics of fifteen songs about Griška Otrep'ev will also be cited.[30] In the first table are given the mean figures for the number of syllables in the anacrusis, stem, clausula, interval between the first and second ictuses (I), and interval between the second and third ictuses (II). The anacrusis varies from zero to three syllables, but mainly has one or two syllables. The results for the clausula are distorted because the type of line ending changes from song to song. In the poem from 1688, the endings have one to three syllables, but most are dactylic; two of James' songs mainly have dactylic endings while three have feminine; all but one line in Pazuxin's poems have feminine clausula. The characteristics of the songs about Otrep'ev are fairly close to those for the other songs except that the clausula and the line are somewhat larger.

	Anacrusis	Stem	Clausula	Line	Intervals I	Intervals II	Lines
1688	1.12	7.02	2.08	10.22	2.07	2.05	91
James	1.64	7.24	1.48	10.36	2.10	2.18	130
Pazuxin	1.78	8.11	0.96	10.85	2.41	2.70	27
All songs	1.46	7.26	1.64	10.36	2.13	2.20	248
"Otrep'ev"	1.40	7.35	2.11	10.86	2.08	2.29	694

Although some zero- or four-syllable intervals appear in the intervals between fulfilled ictuses, usually the number of syllables ranges from one to three ($x = 1\text{-}3$); most but not all the longer intervals having four to six syllables result from an unstressed second ictus (20 lines). In Pazuxin's lyrics, all intervals correspond to the syllabic grid; the least agreement appears in James' songs (92.0%).

Syllables	0	1	2	3	4	5	6	$x = 1\text{-}3$
1688	—	13.9	60.5	19.8	4.6	1.2	—	94.2
James	0.4	17.6	50.0	24.4	4.8	2.0	0.8	92.0
Pazuxin	—	3.7	37.0	59.3	—	—	—	100
All songs	0.2	14.7	52.3	26.7	4.2	1.5	0.4	93.7
"Otrep'ev"	0.2	12.8	57.2	27.3	2.5	—	—	97.3

In the following table, the rhythmical variations which fit the paradigm $x = 1\text{-}3$ are presented; lines not corresponding are included under 'other lines'. In variations ten through twelve, the second ictus is unstressed. Taking the possibility of unfulfilled ictuses into consideration, lines having either one- or three-syllable intervals resemble binary meters (B), those displaying one-or

Variation	Type	1688	James	Pazuxin	All songs	"Otrep'ev"
1. -1-1-[31]	B	3.3	3.1	3.7	3.2	1.7
2. -1-2-	D	6.6	10.8	—	8.1	10.4
3. -1-3-	B	2.2	6.2	—	4.0	6.9
4. -2-1-	D	6.6	8.4	—	6.9	2.9
5. -2-2-	T	38.4	26.1	11.1	29.0	34.9
6. -2-3-	A	13.2	11.5	40.8	15.3	15.3
7. -3-1-	B	4.4	2.3	—	2.8	1.7
8. -3-2-	A	11.0	10.0	11.1	10.5	13.4
9. -3-3-	B	3.3	6.9	33.3	8.5	7.7
10. - 4 -	D	8.8	3.1	—	4.9	0.9
11. - 5 -	T	2.2	3.1	—	2.4	—
12. - 6	A	—	1.5	—	0.8	—
13. other	A	—	7.0	—	3.6	4.2
Total		100.0	100.0	100.0	100.0	100.0

two-syllable intervals are like the *dol'nik* (D), those possessing two-syllable intervals are similar to ternary meters (T), and those with other combinations constitute 'pure' accentual verse (A). In regard to the fulfillment of ictuses, the first and third are constants, while the second is occasionally unstressed: I-100, II-91.9, III-100. This indicates that the law of regressive accentual dissimilation acts to some extent in the rhythm of these poems in three-stress accentual verse. No 'other lines' appear in the poem of 1688 or in Pazuxin's lyrics; James' songs have the most (7.0%), while the "Otrep'ev" group evinces 4.2%.

So that a more generalized notion of the rhythmical variety in the songs may be obtained, the total percentage for each line type will be cited. This reveals not only the predominant kind of line but also the rhythmical differences which emerge in each instance of accentual verse. In the song of 1688, ternary type lines prevail, in James' songs all types are mixed and in Pazuxin's poems accentual and binary type lines are the most common. In the "Otrep'ev" group ternary and accentual type lines form the majority, a relationship which is nearly the same for the poem of 1688.

Line type	B	D	T	A	Main types
1688	13.2	22.0	40.6	24.2	T
James	19.3	22.3	29.2	29.2	mixed
Pazuxin	37.0	—	11.1	51.9	AB
All songs	19.0	19.8	31.4	29.8	mixed
"Otrep'ev"	18.0	14.1	34.9	33.0	TA

Lines twenty through thirty-one from the song of 1688 will be quoted to illustrate epic three-stress accentual verse. Lines twenty and twenty-three do not stress the second ictus; the anacrusis ranges from zero to two syllables, the clausula has two or three syllables, and the intervals vary from one to three syllables.

20	Ста́ли бла́говестить к зау́трене	2- 4 -2
	у свято́го Миха́йла арха́нгела,	2-2-2-2
	гдѐ кладу́тся цари́ благове́рные,	2-2-2-2
	благове́рные, благочести́вые.	2- 5 -2
	Боя́ра пошли́ до зау́трене,	1-2-2-2
25	ко свято́му Миха́йлу арха́нгелу,	2-2-2-2

а Гри́шка Ростри́га в ба́ню пошел	1-2-1-3
с своею Мари́нкою до̀чь Ю́рьевой,	1-2-3-2
бояра иду́т от зау́трени,	1-2-2-2
а Гри́шка Ростри́га из ба́ни идет,	1-2-2-3
30 шу́ба на не́м соболи́ная,	0-2-2-2
на Мари́нке сая̀н кра̀сного зо́лота.	2-2-3-2

In the trochaic lyric from James' collection, this stressing will be employed: line – *berežóček*, 5, 14, 19 – *mólodcy*, 10, 17-18, 29 – *vesnovój*, 12-13 – *zimovój*, 22, 26 – *járovy*, and 24 – *vetljanój*. Korš supplies a missing syllable in the beginning of lines three and twenty; these added syllables will be excluded because syllabic variation in the line opening occasionally occurs in trochaic folk verse (see further on). As a means of explaining the trochaic rhythm of James' song, reference will be made to this meter's features in literary poetry and to those in later recordings of folk lyrics.

Two structural variants are found in the literary trochaic trimeter. In the one with level or rising fulfillment of the first two ictuses and a constant third ictus, the law of the stabilization of the first ictus after the first weak position in the line determines the rhythm. In the other, the first and third ictuses are fulfilled more often, while the second is less frequently stressed; in this bipartite form, the law of regressive accentual dissimilation affects the structure. In literary binary meters, non-metrical stressing is limited to monosyllabic words; however, when poets stylize their trochaic poems after folk verse, they may employ non-metrical stresses on polysyllabic words.[32] Kol'cov's folk song stylizations offer numerous instances of such stressing; in his trochaic trimeter poems, for example, non-metrical stressing on the second position falls on words having from one to four syllables, while on the fourth position such words have one or two syllables.[33]

Fifty songs having 1824 lines have been analyzed in order to demonstrate the rhythmical structure of the trochaic trimeter in folk lyrics. This meter is not especially common, partly because collectors may often combine two lines into one hexameter line. Texts have been selected from a number of collections which were made from the beginning of the nineteenth century to the present (see the Appendix). Such diversity in recorders and chronology serves to confirm the existence of the trochaic trimeter as one folk meter. Although this type of verse occurs in a number of genres, all are essentially lyric: agricultural, wedding, dance, everyday (*bytovaja*), round dance (*xorovodnaja*), game, and satirical songs. It does not appear to be utilized in narrative songs, epics, or lamentations. Among the lyrics studied, eighteen have refrains which are repeated after every pair of lines; refrains will be omitted in analysis.

The same two above rhythmical structures develop in the folk trochaic trimeter. Since the type of clausula affects their stressing profile, these songs will be examined according to the main kind of line ending, that is, feminine (F), dactylic (D), or mixed. For the sake of conciseness, stressing on each syllable of the line will be presented. From the standpoint of literary binary meters, the rhythm of these lyrics is extremely rough because of the large amount of non-metrical stressing. However, one should judge folk meters on their own merits and not on those of more restrictive literary verse; the final ictus remains a constant and the number of syllables in the stem tends to be fixed (see further on). The difference between literary and folk trochaic meters may be explained by the fact that the former observes strict placement of word stress since the stresses of polysyllabic words always correspond to an ictus; in the latter phrase stress usually coincides with an ictus, while the position of word stress is freer so that polysyllabic words may receive a non-metrical stress. The short trochaic trimeter line (feminine ending — six syllables, dactylic — seven) usually consists of a single phrase whose stress falls on the fifth syllable or final ictus; the line is so cramped syllabically that a preceding word stress may occur on any of the first four syllables. Consequently the opening of the trochaic trimeter line is unstable. The large degree of non-metrical stressing on the second syllable may also result from the general tendency of all Russian verse to avoid strong fulfillment of the first syllable in the line. The total stressing for the first two syllables for all categories is about 90%, so that a kind of trade-off develops between these two positions.

Ictus	I		II		III		
Syllable	1	2	3	4	5	Average	Lines
I. Rising							
F	30.4	59.0	40.7	8.0	100	57.0	273
D	19.0	68.1	27.6	16.4	100	48.9	116
mixed	39.9	52.9	42.0	3.1	100	60.6	193
All verse	31.3	58.8	38.5	8.1	100	56.6	586
II. Bipartite							
F	54.3	38.4	32.5	5.2	100	62.3	890
D	49.3	42.9	32.2	11.7	100	60.5	205
mixed	48.3	44.2	23.8	12.9	100	57.4	147
All verse	52.7	39.9	31.4	7.2	100	61.4	1242

Approximately two-thirds of the lines display the dominant bipartite structure, while one-third have the minor rising movement. As in Kol'cov's trochaic
trimeter, words bearing a non-metrical stress on the second position consist of
one to four syllables, while on the fourth position they have one or two
syllables.

In the table below, the percentage of all non-metrical stressing on polysyllabic words is given; most occurs on the second syllable, and it is higher in the
rising form (54%) than in the bipartite form (35%).

	I. Rising		II. Bipartite	
Syllable	2	4	2	4
F	53.1	4.0	33.2	3.4
D	62.9	12.9	41.0	10.2
mixed	48.7	3.1	38.8	10.2
All verse	53.6	5.5	35.2	5.3

The anacrusis occasionally varies in these trochaic songs, a feature which is
largely non-existent in literary binary meters.

Syllables	−1	0	+1	+2
All verse	2.0	94.5	3.2	0.3

Even in the poems which have mainly a feminine or dactylic ending, the
number of syllables in the clausula occasionally oscillates. 'Classical' rhyme is
not at all infrequent in the folk trochaic trimeter, although it is usually
grammatical or tautological. Ordinarily rhymes occur only sporadically,
chiefly in couplets and sometimes in strings of three to ten. Almost half the
lines with a feminine ending are rhymed, but far fewer are rhymed in the other
types; about two-thirds of the lines have a feminine clausula.

	Clausula				Rhymed	Lines
Syllables	0	1	2	3		
All F	0.9	98.4	0.7	—	47.2	1163
All D	0.9	0.9	97.6	0.6	17.8	321
All mixed	2.6	46.8	50.6	—	21.5	340

Many 'modern' rhymes are also encountered; when they are also considered,
the percentage of rhymed lines increases: F – 55.9, D – 29.6, mixed – 27.1.

Rhymes have been included which differ by one consonant, voiced and unvoiced pairs of consonants, truncation of one final consonant, and one unstressed final vowel. The following rhymes are examples: širókoe : veséloe, golóvušku : storónušku, oxápku : lávku, oréxam : uéxal, ščúka : belúga, pokátitsja : srjáditsja, xoróšij : prigóžij, édja : séja, sísti : čísti', na réčke : doséčka.

A song recorded not long ago in the Kaluga region[34] will be cited to exemplify the folk trochaic trimeter. All twenty-four lines have a feminine ending and zero anacrusis so that they are isosyllabic (six syllables); fifteen lines are rhymed. Non-metrical stressing on the second position falls on words having one to three syllables, and on the fourth position it involves words with two syllables. The rhythm of this lyric displays the rising structural variant for this meter. The 'unusual' stresses for the words *muravýe, alýe, devóčku,* and *vovrémja* are marked in the original.

Ictus	I		II		III
Syllable	1	2	3	4	5
Times stressed	6	10	9	3	24
Percentage	25.0	41.7	37.5	12.5	100

Тра́вы, мои́ тра́вы,	x́ x x x̀ x́ x	Хороша́, учли́ва,	x x x́ x x́ x
Тра́вы муравы́е.	x́ x x x x́ x	Ре́чи говори́ла:	x́ x x x x́ x
Тра́вы муравы́е,	x́ x x x x́ x	15 –Ты́ ли, моя́ ра́дость,	x́ x x x̀ x́ x
Цвето́чки алы́е.	x x̀ x x x́ x	Я́ ли твое́ се́рдце.	x́ x x x̀ x́ x
5 По э́тим по тра́вам	x x̀ x x x́ x	Мое́ се́рдце бье́тся,	x x̀ x́ x x́ x
Не бу́ду ходи́ти.	x x̀ x x x́ x	На ча̀с не уйме́тся.	x x̀ x x́ x x
Не бу́ду ходи́ти,	x x̀ x x x́ x	Хоть оно́ уйме́тся,	x x x́ x x́ x
Не бу́ду люби́ти.	x x̀ x x x́ x	20 А всѐ не воврё́ма.	x x̀ x x x́ x
Полюблю́ дево́чку	x x x́ x x́ x	Не воврё́ма, врё́ма,	x x x́ x x́ x
10 Купѐческу до́чку.	x x̀ x x x́ x	Не в таку́ю по́ру.	x x x́ x x́ x
Купѐческа до́чка	x x̀ x x x́ x	А меня́, девчо́нку,	x x x́ x x́ x
Хороша́, учли́ва.	x x x́ x x́ x	Обуя́ло го́ре.	x x x́ x x́ x

The rhythm in James' song belongs to the variant with a rising structure. The trochaic meter is fairly well formed because non-metrical stressing on the second and fourth syllables is relatively low. The words whose stress non-metrically falls on the second position have from two to four syllables, while on the fourth position such words have only one syllable. Lines three and twenty omit the first syllable; the first three lines have dactylic endings, but the remainder have feminine clausula.

JAMES BAILEY

Ictus	I		II		III
Syllable	1	2	3	4	5
Times stressed	9	3	21	3	29
Percentage	31.0	10.3	72.4	10.3	100

Бережо́чек зы́блется,	x x x́ x x́ x x	Йно да́й же, Бо́же,	x́ x x́ x x х́ x x
да песо́чек сы́плется,	x x x́ x x́ x x	весновꙋ́ю слꙋ́жбу,	x x х́ x х́ x x
ледо́чек ло́мится,	x х́ x x х́ x x	весновꙋ́я слꙋ́жба	x x х́ x х́ x x
до́бры ко́ни то́нут,	x́ x x x́ x х́ x́	мо́лодцам весе́лье,	x́ x x x x́ x x
5 мо́лодцы томя́тся.	x́ x x x x́ x	20 сѐрдцу ꙋте́ха.	x̀ x x x́ x
Йно, Бо́же, Бо́же,	x́ x х́ x x х́ x	А емли́те, бра́тцы,	x x х́ x x х́ x x
сотвори́л Ты́, Бо́же,	x x х́ x х́ x́ x	Я́ровы весе́льца,	x́ x x x x́ x x
да и не́бо-зе́млю	x x x х́ x х́ x	а сади́мся, бра́тцы,	x x х́ x x х́ x x
сотвори́л же, Бо́же,	x x х́ x х́ x x	в ветляны́ струже́чки,	x x х́ x х́ x x
10 весновꙋ́ю слꙋ́жбу.	x x х́ x х́ x x	25 да грѐнемте, бра́тцы,	x х̀ x x x́ x x
Не дава́й Ты́ Бо́же,	x x х́ x х́ x́ x	в я́ровы весе́льца,	x́ x x x x́ x x
зимовы́е слꙋ́жбы,	x x х́ x х́ x x	йно вни́з по Во́лге.	x́ x х́ x х́ x x
зимова́я слꙋ́жба	x x х́ x х́ x x	Сотвори́л на̀м, Бо́же,	x x х́ x х̀ x́ x
мо́лодцам кручи́нно	x́ x x x x́ x x	29 весновꙋ́ю слꙋ́жбу.	x x х́ x х́ x x
15 да сѐрдцу надса́дно	x х̀ x x x́ x		

Considering the difficulty involved in analyzing these earliest examples of Russian folk meters, one can make several tentative conclusions about folk versification in the seventeenth century. The epic accentual verse has three metrical stresses per line, mainly one to three syllables between ictuses, and either feminine or dactylic ending. Trochaic trimeter consisting chiefly of six-syllable lines with feminine endings appears in one lyric, the sole song from James' collection which folklorists later recorded. The existence of both these types of epic and lyric verse is confirmed in subsequent compilations of folk songs. One may conclude that Vostokov's assertion about trochaic meters being used only in new city songs is not substantiated.

Trubeckoj advanced the theory that the original Russian epic verse was syllabic, a characteristic which was disrupted after the loss of the weak jers and the establishment of stress as the main prosodic feature in the Russian language.[35] On the basis of comparative Slavic metrics, Jakobson and Taranovsky deduced that the trochaic pentameter constitutes the initial Russian epic line and that accentual verse developed later from a modification of the syllabic organization in the trochaic line.[36] Gasparov, through his study of epics collected from the eighteenth through the twentieth centuries, concluded that accentual verse represents the chief epic meter and that the trochaic verse appearing in the songs of such a singer as T. G. Rjabinin amounts to a regularization of accentual verse.[37] However, he does not take into consideration the results of research into comparative Slavic metrics or the diachronic evolution of folk epic verse. Analysis offered in the present investigation permits one to state only that epic accentual and lyric trochaic verse were already well established by the beginning of the seventeenth century.

The last question concerns the 'folk authenticity' of the meters of the songs being studied. As has been pointed out, the song of 1688, the poems of Pazuxin, and perhaps all but one of the songs from James' collection are literary. What is important is not whether these works are 'true' folk songs or 'author's songs', but how accurately they preserve attested folk meters. Comparison of the rhythmical characteristics of these poems with those of later recordings indicates that the folk meters have been reasonably well reproduced. If the songs examined here are indeed literary, then one should remark that they were very much a part of their contemporary literary environment because a number of works in the seventeenth century were composed partially or entirely in the oral style.[38] The songs investigated in this paper may be a reflection of an epoch when the boundary between written and oral poetry was not so clear-cut, and when writers deliberately chose to express themselves through the folk style in works which may have been absorbed later into what today is termed folklore.[39] It would be interesting to speculate what course the history of Russian literary versification would have taken if literary poets had continued exploiting the possibilities of folk meters rather than turning to syllabic verse in the seventeenth century.[40]

The University of Wisconsin, Madison

APPENDIX

Trochaic Trimeter Folk Songs

Reference will be made by page or song number. P. V. Kireevskij, *Pesni, novaja serija*, I-II (M., 1911), No. 313, 793, 1345; A. I. Sobolevskij, *Velikorusskie narodnye pesni* (P., 1895-1902), III, No. 282-3, 407, 428, IV, No. 8, V, No. 614, VI, No. 601; P. V. Šejn, *Velikoruss v svoix pesnjax ...*, I-II (P., 1898, 1900), No. 369, 419, 468, 534, 816, 938, 1224; *Russkie narodnye pesni*, A. M. Novikova, ed. (M., 1957), p. 284; A. V. Ermačenko, *Pesennoe tvorčestvo Kalužskogo kraja* (Kaluga, 1959), No. 67, 82, 104, 148; *Narodnye liričeskie pesni*, V. Ja. Propp, ed. (L., 1961), pp. 331, 374, 378, 389; N. Kotikova, *Narodnye pesni Pskovskoj oblasti* (M., 1966), No. 80-82, 155, 223, 227, 249; *Narodnye pesni Permskogo kraja,* M. A. Genkeľ, ed., I (Perm', 1966), No. 68, 200, 241; *Pesennyj foľklor Mezeni,* N. P. Kolpakova, ed. (L., 1967), No. 96; I. I. Zemcovskij, *Toropeckie pesni* (L., 1967), No. 16; *Pesni, sobrannye pisateljami, Literaturnoe nasledstvo,* 79 (M., 1968), p. 194, No. 16, 302, No. 14, 308, No. 22, 614, No. 25; G. Pavlova, *Narodnye pesni Smolenskoj oblasti* (M., 1969), No. 61; *Poèzija kresťjanskix prazdnikov,* I. I. Zemcovskij, ed. (L., 1970), No. 107, 479, 525, 664, 686; A. Nesterov, *Narodnye pesni Gorʹkovskoj oblasti* (M., 1972), No. 56; *Lirika russkoj svaďby,* N. P. Kolpakova, ed. (L., 1973), No. 292.

NOTES

[1]   Roman Jakobson, "Studies in Comparative Slavic Metrics," *Oxford Slavonic Papers,* 3 (1952), 21-61; Kiril Taranovsky, "Roman Jakobson, 'Studies in Comparative Slavic Metrics,'" *Prilozi za književnost, jezik, istoriju i folklor,* 20, No. 3-4 (1954), 350-60, "M. P. Štokmar, 'Issledovanija v oblasti russkogo narodnogo stixosloženija,'" *Južnoslovenski Filolog,* 21 (1955-56), 335-63.

[2]   V. K. Trediakovskij, *Stixotvorenija* (Leningrad, 1935), 351-3, 390, 412.

[3]   A. X. Vostokov, *Opyt o russkom stixosloženii,* 2nd ed. (Petersburg, 1817), 136.

[4]   Vostokov, 100-7.

[5]   A. F. Gilʹferding, *Onežskie byliny* (Petersburg, 1873), xxxiii.

[6]   See the items in footnote 1 and: Taranovsky, "The Identity of the Prosodic Bases of Russian Folk and Literary Verse," in *For Roman Jakobson* (The Hague, 1956), 553-8.

[7]   M. L. Gasparov, "Statističeskoe obsledovanie russkogo bylinnogo stixa," in *Problemy prikladnoj lingvistiki,* 1 (Moscow, 1969), 82-6. Also see: James Bailey, "The Epic Meters of T. G. Rjabinin as Collected by A. F. Gilʹferding," *American Contributions to the Seventh International Congress of Slavists,* I (The Hague, 1973), 9-32. For a survey of works about Russian folk versification, see: M. P. Štokmar, *Issledovanija v oblasti russkogo narodnogo stixosloženija* (Moscow, 1952), 17-135.

[8]   P. V. Kireevskij, *Pesni,* VII, No. 2 (Moscow, 1868), 61-6.

[9]   P. A. Bessonov, in Kireevskij, *Pesni,* VII, No. 2, 61; Carl Stief, *Studies in the Russian Historical Song* (Copenhagen, 1953), 63-95; A. P. Evgenʹeva, *Očerki po jazyku russkoj ustnoj poèzii* (Moscow-Leningrad, 1963), 335-6.'

[10]   Stief cites most information about these songs, 11-17.

[11]   F. I. Buslaev, *Istoričeskie očerki russkoj narodnoj slovesnosti i iskusstva,* I (Petersburg, 1861), 470, 517-543; L. Majkov, "O starinnyx rukopisnyx sbornikax narodnyx pesen i bylin," *Žurnal Ministerstva Narodnogo Prosveščenija,* 212 (November, 1880), 197-216; Vs. I. Miller, *Očerki russkoj narodnoj slovesnosti,* II (Moscow, 1910), 267-8, III (Moscow-Leningrad, 1924), 242-5; V. V. Danilov, "Sborniki pesen XVII stoletija — Ričarda Džemsa i P. A. Kvašina," *Trudy otdela drevne-russkoj literatury* (henceforth *TODRL*), 2 (1935), 165-80; *Russkoe narodnoe poètičeskoe tvorčestvo,* V. P. Adrianova-Peretc, ed., I (Moscow-Leningrad, 1953), 455-6; L. S. Šeptaev, "Zametki o pesnjax, zapisannyx dlja Ričarda Džemsa," *TODRL,* 14 (1958), 304-8; V. P. Adrianova-Peretc, D. S. Lixačev, Introduction to the volume edited by them, *Demokratičeskaja poèzija XVII veka* (Moscow-Leningrad, 1962), 23-5; Evgenʹeva, 335; A. V. Pozdneev, "Èvoljucija stixosloženija v narodnoj lirike XVI-XVIII vekov," *Russkij foľklor,* 12 (1971), 37-46; A. I. Stender-Petersen, "Stixi moskovskogo poèta-anonima načala XVII-go veka, soxranennye Ričardom Džemsom," *Scando-Slavica,* 3 (1957), 112-136.

[12]   Šeptaev, "Zametki," 305; N. A. Usov, *Russkie pesni* (Gorʹkij, 1940), 58.

[13]   I. M. Kudrjavcev, "Dve liričeskie pesni, zapisannye v XVII veke," *TODRL,* 9 (1953), 380-6.

[14] M. N. Speranskij, "Iz materialov dlja istorii ustnoj pesni," *Izvestija Akademii Nauk SSSR, otdelenie obščestvennyx nauk,* 10 (1932), 913-34; Pozdneev, "Liričeskie pesni XVII veka," *Russkij fol'klor,* 1 (1956), 78-96; Šeptaev, "O repertuare russkoj narodnoj bytovoj pesni XVII veka," *Učenye zapiski leningradskogo gosudarstvennogo pedagogičeskogo instituta, kafedra russkoj literatury,* 134 (1957), 91-111; I. S. Filippova, "Pesni P. A. Samarina-Kvašina, *Izvestija Akademii Nauk SSSR, serija literatury i jazyka,* 31, No. 1 (1972), 62-6. Most of the texts appear in the collection *Demokratičeskaja poèzija XVII veka,* 91-112.

[15] References to James' songs will be made by song and line number: I — "Berežoček zybletsja", II — "Ino čto u nas v Moskve učinilosja", III — "Splačetsja mala ptička", IV — "Zradovalosja carstvo moskovskoe", V — "A splačetsja na Moskve carevna", VI — "A ne sil'naja tuča zatučilasja". The same will be done for Pazuxin's poems: I — "Da oj ne plačte moi jasnye oči", II — "Pojdu ja, mladen'ka, poguljaju". The song of 1688 will be mentioned by 1688 and line number.

[16] F. E. Korš, "Čtenie", *Sbornik otdelenija russkogo jazyka i slovesnosti,* 82, No. 7 (1907), 16-29.

[17] S. Bobrov, "K voprosu o podlinnom stixotvornom razmere puškinskix 'Pesen zapadnyx slavjan'", *Russkaja literatura* (1964), 3, 119-137; A. Kolmogorov, "O metre puškinskix 'Pesen zapadnyx slavjan'," *Russkaja literatura* (1966), 1, 98-111; Gasparov, "Taktovik v russkom stixosloženii XX v.", *Voprosy jazykoznanija* (1968), 5, 79-90, "Narodnyj stix A. Vostokova", in *Poètika i stilistika russkoj literatury,* M. P. Alekseev, ed. (Leningrad, 1971), 437-443. For details about the method of analysis employed here, see: Bailey, "The Epic Meters", 22-8, and "The Early Development of Accentual Verse in Russian Literary Poetry", *Russian Literature,* 9 (1975), 87-109.

[18] V. Kiparsky, *Der Wortakzent der russischen Schriftsprache* (Heidelberg, 1962), 207.

[19] V. V. Kolesov, *Istorija russkogo udarenija* (Leningrad, 1962), 132; A. Orlov, *Domostroj* (Moscow, 1908), 88.

[20] P. Ja. Černyx, *Jazyk Uloženija 1649 goda* (Moscow, 1953), 246.

[21] Several stressing combinations are possible for this ambiguous line.

[22] L. Vasil'ev, "K istorii zvuka ѣ v moskovskom govore v XIV-XVII vekax", *Izvestija otdelenija russkogo jazyka i slovesnosti,* 10, No. 2 (1905), 208; C. S. Stang, *Slavonic Accentuation* (Oslo, 1957), 103; Roman Jakobson, Dean S. Worth, *Sofonija's Tale of the Russian-Tatar Battle on the Kulikovo Field* (The Hague, 1963), 68-9.

[23] This stressing is not attested, but it is given by Korš and best preserves the meter.

[24] Jakobson and Worth, 67; Kiparsky, 198; Černyx, 281; Vasil'ev, 213.

[25] The stressing *mólodec* is normal in folklore; however, singers may occasionally employ the variant *molodéc* for rhythmical reasons. For example, see two songs by T. G. Rjabinin in Gil'ferding's collection: song No. 89, lines 20, 24, and song No. 90, lines 95-96. The meter is better perserved in James' line with the stress on the third syllable.

[26] Korš surmises this stressing which occurs in two epics recorded by Gil'ferding: song No. 3, line 30, song No. 6, line 296.

[27] L. A. Bulaxovskij, "Sravnitel'no-istoričeskie kommentarii k vostočnoslavjanskomu udareniju", *Voprosy slavjanskogo jazykoznanija,* 4 (1955), 30-1. In three lines (IV-18, VI-19-20), the pronouns *svóego* and *tvóemu* may have been stressed on the first syllable; such stressing is frequently met in northern epics and is also archaic. See: Jakobson and Worth, 31, 70.

[28] Černyx, 123; Kiparsky, 39; Jakobson and Worth, 68; Kolesov, 143.

[29] Stang, 77; Kiparsky, 53; Kolesov, 145, 152.

[30] *Istoričeskie pesni XVII veka,* A. M. Astaxova, ed. (Moscow-Leningrad, 1966), songs No. 5 (omit lines 39, 44, 53-55, 58, 65-67), 6 (omit 8, 12), 7 (omit 34, 40, 46, 48-9), 8 (omit 35, 51), 9, 10 (omit 39-40), 11 (omit 29), 12 (omit 12-13, 15, 20, 22, 28, 42, 45, 49, 51), 15 (omit 31, 49, 56, 60), 16, 17 (omit 11, 45, 49-50), 18, 22 (omit 2); A. M. Astaxova, *Byliny severa,* II (Moscow-Leningrad, 1951), song No. 143 (rerecording of No. 16 above), *priloženie* I, No. 6 (omit 44, 56).

[31] In notation, the first number designates the syllables in the anacrusis and the last the syllables in the clausula; a hyphen indicates a stressed ictus and the other numerals the syllables between ictuses. These other symbols may also be used: ´ = stressed ictus, ` = non-metrical stress, and x = syllable.

[32]   Taranovsky, "O ritmičeskoj strukture russkix dvusložnyx razmerov", in *Poètika i stilistika russkoj literatury,* 420-9, *Ruski dvodelni ritmovi,* I-II (Belgrade, 1953), 298-304.

[33]   Bailey, "The Trochaic Song Meters of Kol'cov and Kašin", *Russian Literature,* 12 (1975), 5-27.

[34]   A. V. Ermačenko, *Pesennoe tvorčestvo Kalužskogo kraja* (Kaluga, 1959), No. 104.

[35]   N. S. Trubeckoj, "W sprawie wiersza byliny rosyjskiej", *Prace ofiarowane Kazimierzowi Wójcickiemu, Z zagadnień poetyki,* 6 (1937), 100-110.

[36]   See the articles by Jakobson and Taranovsky in footnote 1, and V. V. Ivanov, V. N. Toporov, "K rekonstrukcii praslavjanskogo teksta", *Slavjanskoe jazykoznanie, V Meždunarodnyj s"ezd slavistov* (Moscow, 1963), 94-100.

[37]   Gasparov, "Statističeskoe obsledovanie".

[38]   V. Ržiga, "Povesť o Gore i Zločastii i pesni o Gore", *Slavia,* 10, No. 1 (1931), 53-5; Adrianova-Peretc, *Očerki po istorii russkoj satiričeskoj literatury XVII v.* (Moscow-Leningrad, 1937), 116, 231, 258-9; Adrianova-Peretc, Lixačev, *Demokratičeskaja poèzija,* 6-25; Lixačev, *Razvitie russkoj literatury X-XVII vekov* (Leningrad, 1973), 163.

[39]   A. N. Robinson, "K voprosu o narodno-poètičeskix istokax stilja 'voinskix' povestej drevnej Rusi", in *Osnovnye problemy èposa vostočnyx slavjan,* V. V. Vinogradov, ed. (Moscow, 1958), 131-157; V. K. Sokolova, *Russkie istoričeskie pesni XVI-XVIII vv.* (Moscow, 1960), 19, 29, 35; Jakobson, "Die Folklore als eine besondere Form des Schaffens", *Selected Writings,* IV (The Hague, 1966), 1-15.

[40]   A. M. Pančenko, *Russkaja stixotvornaja kul'tura XVII veka* (Leningrad, 1973), 3-33.

COMMENTS

(McLean) Is it correct to speak of the following as a historical change? In the Puškin era, when the first syllable in an iambic line was stressed and the second was not, there was a tendency to require that the first word should be monosyllabic, of the type "Boj barabannyj, kliki, skrežet". In the twentieth century, however, it became permissible to use two-syllable words in such cases (e.g., "Xolod i mrak grjaduščix dnej"). Or is this wrong: I note that Unbegaun cites a contrary example from I. Dolgorukij (1902): "So vremenem sej dom, ja znaju. / Krásen mne budet platežem." However, Unbegaun's example assumes the accentuation *krásen,* whereas the form *krasën* may be intended here, as attested in the proverb *Velik zvon, da ne krasën*; the latter stress would not only make the line a conventional iambic, but would provide an internal semi-rhyme with *platežom.*

(Pszczołowska) In your paper you have considered the sources of transaccentuation in Russian folk verse. It seems to me that the cases of transaccentuation may be connected also with melody. These poems were sung. E.g., in the history of the Gregorian choral there were periods when word stress and musical stress coincided and other periods when transaccentuation was accepted.

As far as the trochaic structure of folk verse is concerned your own tables and comparisons seem to lead to a different conclusion than the one given in the paper. The difference between the accentual structure of literary trochaic meters and of these which you call "folk trochaic meters" is rather considerable. Perhaps in folk verse no trochaic meter was realised; there only existed a tendency to a trochaic structure due to the linguistic factors.

(Smith) I agree completely that "one should judge folk metres on their own merits and not on those of more restrictive literary verse", and it seems to me that in accordance with this principle one should not describe as 'trochaic trimeter' and compare with the literary trochaic trimeter the folk metre analysed and exemplified on pp. 7-10. The differences outweigh the similarities between the two metres. The crux of the problem is the interpretation of the stressing of the 2nd and 3rd syllables in the line. In the literary metre, the 3rd syllable is overwhelmingly more strongly stressed than the 2nd; in the folk metre, however, the 2nd syllable is in all six types presented here stronger than the 3rd. Under these circumstances, can the 3rd syllable really be regarded as an ictus in the same sense as this term is understood in the analysis of literary metres? Perhaps it would be more reasonable to describe both types I and II of the 'folk trochaic trimeter' as a two-stress accentual metre. At any rate, the rhythmical movement of Type I seems to have a more clearly developed ternary than binary structure.

Additional discussion: Heim, Hrushovsky, Stankiewicz

AUTHOR'S REPLY

(to McLean) Tomaševskij, Jakobson, Žirmunskij, and Taranovsky have shown in detail that Russian binary meters in the eighteenth and nineteenth centuries overwhelmingly limit non-metrical stressing to monosyllabic words. Jakobson and Taranovsky have interpreted this trait from the standpoint of phonemic theory by pointing out that monosyllables in Russian do not have phonemic stress — whereas disyllables do. I have often wondered, however, if this characteristic was not due, at least in part, to the fact that Russian literary meters first were developed during the classical period when by and large everything should be neatly arranged according to extremely rationalistic categories. In other words, did this feature arise because of the nature of the Russian language or because Lomonosov established it through his poetic practice and theory? Russian folk trochaic verse is much more flexible in regard to non-metrical stressing of polysyllabic words than is, for example,

English iambic verse. Here and there instances of such stressing appear in
Russian verse of the eighteenth and nineteenth centuries, but actually only in
blank verse: Tomaševskij in his study of Puškin's iambic pentameter, Taranovsky in the introduction to his book on Russian binary meters, and I in my
article about the iambic pentameter from 1880-1920 cite examples. However,
as you state, in the twentieth century at least some Russian poets more freely
use non-metrical stressing of disyllabic words, particularly when they are
function words. I would not, however, use the line you cite from Blok as an
example because it occurs in a very experimental poem. As you indicate, one
must be very careful to be aware of possible stress variants, which may today
be archaic but which poets may occasionally employ.

(to Pszczołowska) My response to Mr. Smith's question in part answers your
query. I am not quite certain what you mean by 'transaccentuation'. I assume
you may have *perestanovka udarenija* in mind. This term as you use it may
refer to what I call non-metrical stressing, or stressing which does not coincide
with an ictus. Another meaning concerns purely arbitrary shifts of a stress to
make it correspond to an ictus or to ensure a stressed rhyme, as, for example,
several scholars have done in regard to Polockij's rhymes. Stressing in Russian
folk verse can be divided into four categories: 1) literary, 2) dialectical, 3)
archaic, and 4) arbitrary. Many stresses marked by collectors in texts appear
to be purely arbitrary; however, when one goes into the history of Russian
accentuation it frequently turns out that these 'strange' stresses really are
archaic. Nevertheless, arbitrary stresses exist and in many cases they may
result from a singer's attempt to make the musical rhythm and the linguistic
rhythm coincide. This problem is very complex and as yet little of a positive
nature has been elucidated. In effect, what I said in regard to Mr. Smith's
question concerns the fact that it is precisely linguistic factors which do
determine the structure of the folk trochaic trimeter.

(to Smith) You have hit on the crux of the problem in explaining this type of
folk meter when you point out that many lines have a stress on the second
syllable and consequently resemble the amphibrach dimeter (xx́xxx́). The
difficulty is that a Russian amphibrach meter in the reverse fashion does not
have shifts in which the stress of a polysyllabic word falls on the first syllable of
the line. Insofar as accentual verse is concerned, only rarely does one find it in
isosyllabic lines; the type of line I discuss in my paper is essentially isosyllabic,
exluding the clausula. Actually one has to consider the rhythmical features of
what I have termed the trochaic trimeter on the background of all other folk

trochaic meters. Non-metrical stressing does occur fairly often on disyllabic words in four, five, and six-foot lines, and occasionally even on trisyllables. In an article of mine which has not yet appeared I found just these characteristics to occur in Koľcov's trochaic verse and in that of the song book of Daniil Kašin. The same type of non-metrical stressing appears in their trochaic trimeter as I have presented in my paper here. But all of this must be viewed in the larger context of the rhythmical vocabulary of the Russian language, that is, number of syllables in a word, place of stress, and frequency of each type. As you know, the average Russian word consists of about three syllables, or slightly less. Furthermore, words of three syllables or more, as Nikonov has demonstrated, tend to have their stress on a mid syllable. Stressing the second syllable of the trochaic trimeter avoids strong fulfillment of the first syllable in the line. This is the general reason why all Russian meters tend to leave the first syllable of the line in a meter unfulfilled when an ictus corresponds to that syllable. It seems to me that the rhythmical structures I have described represent precisely what one could expect to find in the folk trochaic trimeter.

ON XLEBNIKOV'S LOVE LYRICS:
I. ANALYSIS OF "O, ČERVI ZEMLJANYE"

HENRYK BARAN

Velimir Xlebnikov's literary works can no longer be automatically regarded as chaotic, fragmentary or semantically impenetrable. Within the last decade, several studies of individual poetic texts have brought about a new degree of understanding of his art. A brief review of these studies in the first part of this paper will describe what has been learned about the contents and organization of each poem. Certain general conclusions regarding Xlebnikov's poetic system will follow this review. In the main portion of the paper these observations will be highlighted in an analysis of "O, červi zemljanye", a short love lyric.

This discussion is the first in a series of studies devoted to Xlebnikov's love poems, a category of texts which until now has remained underemphasized in the critical literature. Here and in my subsequent papers I shall show that Xlebnikov is as much a remarkable lyric poet as a utopian thinker and creator of epics.

The conception of the 'incomprehensible' Xlebnikov was first called into question by V. Ivanov, who showed that the central image of "Menja pronosjat na slonovyx ..." derives from an Indian miniature of the god Vishnu. The poem's structure, seemingly illogical and distorted, reflects the dual nature of the representation of Vishnu's 'vehicle' — maidens who have arranged themselves into the outline of an elephant.[1]

Independently of Ivanov, A. Parnis demonstrated the possibility of successfully deciphering the meaning of a Xlebnikov text by analyzing "Ispaganskij verbljud", a work from the poet's 'Persian period'. Parnis showed that two levels of meaning are present in this poem: a concrete one, in which details of a specific object, an inkwell in the shape of a camel, are conveyed, and a theoretical one, in which the poet speaks of his conception of the historical relationship between East and West.[2]

In her monograph on Formalism and Futurism, K. Pomorska analyzed "Gonimyj — kem, počem ja znaju". She pointed out that an important feature of many Xlebnikov texts is the use of a changing point of view in narration. In discussing the poem she focussed on Xlebnikov's use of the so-called 'shifted image' technique (derived from Cubism), showing that one of the two parts of the text develops the image of Lermontov's Demon, the other — a love scene drawn from folklore.[3]

Emphasis on the simultaneous autonomy and interaction of different semantic planes characterizes M. Grygar's discussion of "V ètot den' golubyx medvedej". The tension within the poem, Grygar suggests, involves two separate sets of images. One of these describes a spring scene, the second — the birth and passing of feelings of love.[4]

In a previous paper, I analyzed the fable "Bex". I showed that the semantics of this text is made deliberately difficult. The author turns a legend associated with the name of a plant into what is essentially a poetic riddle and uses this riddle to make a broad political-historical comment.[5]

Most recently, R. Duganov has discussed the quatrain "O dostoevskijmo beguščej tuči". He has shown that this seemingly simple work is based on a stanza from Verlaine's "L'art poètique", and that its ternary structure, manifested on several levels of the text, conveys a mythopoeic vision of the cosmos in its esthetic aspect.[6]

Without exception, the studies reviewed above support Ivanov's concluding remark: "... po durnoj tradicii upominaemaja maloponjatnost' mnogix veščej Xlebnikova pri bližajšem rassmotrenii okazyvaetsja glubočajšim zabluždeniem kritikov. Xlebnikovu (kak i Mandel'štamu) bylo svojstvenno preimuščestvennoe vnimanie k značenijam otdel'nyx èlementov poètičeskogo jazyka (načinaja s fonem) i k značeniju vsego teksta."[7] Consequently, in approaching a Xlebnikov work, we may take as a working hypothesis that its semantics are consciously shaped and that each of its individual elements is motivated on some level of the text.

The texts studied exemplify three related features of Xlebnikov's poetic system which have made his work difficult for the general reader. These include:

1. Choice of poetic materials. Xlebnikov uses images and themes drawn from widely differing spheres of human experience as 'building blocks' in his works. In particular, these images and themes come from diverse cultural texts with which the general reader is not, as a rule, familiar. Moreover, given that the poet frequently treats his sources quite freely, even the specialist encounters difficulties in his search for a code appropriate to a given text.

2. The manner in which texts are constructed from such materials. Xlebnikov regularly uses techniques of composition, such as absence of an overall frame in a work, unmotivated shifts of point of view, and montage, which violate the requirements for producing a coherent text.[8] Thus, even where the reader has identified the code which the poet relies on in a given work, he frequently must carry out special operations on the text which will permit him to comprehend the manner in which this code is applied. These operations include, for example, 'rearranging' portions of the text so as to produce a proper chronological and/or causal order, establishing the intellectual framework for a montage, etc.

3. The function of these materials. The poet uses unfamiliar proper names, fragments of archaic or primitive myths, references to obscure rituals, etc. to convey complex trains of thought. This is true not only of works devoted to 'major' subjects (historical, political, philosophical), but also of texts dealing with intimate thoughts, feelings and situations.

These three characteristics of Xlebnikov's poetic system will be further illustrated below in the analysis of "O, červi zemljanye". The discussion will concentrate on the poem's semantics. Elements of lower levels of the text will be considered as required.

The text of "O, červi zemljanye" is found in: Velimir Xlebnikov, *Neizdannye proizvedenija* (henceforth *NP*), N. Xardžiev and T. Gric (eds.), (Moskva, 1940), p. 153:

> О, черви земляные,
> В барвиночном напитке
> Зажгите водяные
> Два камня в черной нитке.
> 5 Темной славы головня,
> Не пустой и не постылый,
> Но усталый и остылый,
> Я сижу. Согрей меня.
> На утесе моих плеч
> 10 Пусть лицо не шелохнется,
> Но пусть рук поющих речь
> Слуха рук моих коснется.
> Ведь водою из барвинка
> Я узнаю, все узнаю,
> 15 Надсмеялась ли косынка,
> Что зима, растаяв с краю.

In the commentary to the poem, N. Xardžiev provides the following information about its autograph: "Tekst zapisan na liste togo že formata i tem že počerkom, čto i stixotvorenija 'I smelyj tovarišč šipovnika' i 'Bex'. Nad tekstom stix. 'I smelyj tovarišč šipovnika' — sledujuščaja zapis': 'D<eti> Vydry — Kamenskomu'" (*NP,* 406). Since the 'supertale' (*sverxpovest'*) *Deti Vydry* was completed in 1913, Xardžiev suggests that the three poems were written during that same year. However, in view of the fact that Xlebnikov's note does not specify which text of *Deti Vydry* (the MS or the printed version) is to be sent or given to V. Kamenskij, it is possible to assume that the poems were written in early 1914, subsequent to the January publication of *Deti Vydry* in the collection *Rykajuščij Parnas.*

A comparison of the text published in *NP* with the autograph permits us to correct a mistake in the printed version: in line 2, the epithet is *barvinočnom,* and not *barvičnom.*[9]

The text of the poem consists of 16 lines. Although there are no graphic divisions into strophes, it is easily segmented into four distinct quatrains according to the rhyme scheme (discussed below). The unity of each quatrain is reinforced syntactically in that the end of each quatrain's final line coincides with the end of a full sentence (in quatrains I, III and IV the sentence extends over the entire unit; in quatrain II the end of the main sentence comes in the middle of line 8, but is supplemented by the brief "Sogrej menja").

From the outset, the first quatrain stands out as the most confusing portion of the poem. Its imagery is complex and apparently without roots in the real world: an unseen speaker expresses the desire for an action in which earthworms (*zemljanye červi, Lumbricus*), two stones, and a solution of the periwinkle flower (*Vinca minor L.*: ₂*v barvinočnom napitke*) all participate.

The meaning of the middle quatrains is more easily discerned. Their subject is a potential love relationship between the speaker (the "I" of the poem) and an unidentified woman.

Both themes — that of the periwinkle solution and that of the love relationship — appear in the fourth quatrain. Although the imagery is much simpler than in quatrain I, the claim put forward by the speaker — that he will be able to learn certain things by means of the periwinkle solution (₁₃*vodoju iz barvinka*) — brings back some of the initial uncertainty.

On the basis of distribution of themes by quatrain, two distinct relationships may be isolated within the poem. First, the outer quatrains (I, IV) are united by the presence of the periwinkle theme and are opposed to the inner quatrains (II, III), which are characterized by its absence. Second, the absence of the theme of the love relationship from the first quatrain and its presence elsewhere in the poem establishes an opposition between quatrain I and quatrains II-IV.

The two oppositions are reflected on lower levels of verse organization.

A change of meter within the poem underscores the I vs. II-IV asymmetry. The first quatrain is written in iambic trimeter, while the remaining quatrains are written in trochaic tetrameter.

The outer/inner dichotomy within the poem is seen in the rhyme scheme: ABABcDDceFeFGHGH. The first and fourth quatrains contain only feminine rhymes, while the second and third each contain a masculine and a feminine rhyme. Because of the change in meter, this distribution is reflected in the distribution of lines by length: quatrains I and IV are composed of, respectively, 7- and 8-syllable lines, and are in contrast to quatrains II and III, each of which contains two 7- and two 8-syllable lines.

Words in rhyming position also reflect the I vs. II-IV asymmetry. The first quatrain contains only grammatical rhymes ($_1$zemljanye-$_3$vodjanye, $_2$napitke-$_4$nitke), while each of the remaining quatrains contains both grammatical and antigrammatical rhymes. Similarly, only in the first quatrain is the same stressed vowel phoneme (/i/) maintained in all rhyme words; in the other quatrains the stressed vowels vary (II – /a-i-i-a/; III – /e-o-e-o/; IV – /i-a-i-a/).

It follows from the remarks made thus far that the first quatrain and, to a lesser extent, the fourth quatrain, occupy a special position within the poem. On the surface, in spite of a thematic link with the fourth quatrain, there is no apparent motivation for the imagery of the first quatrain. However, this violation of semantic coherence of the text is only superficial, since a logical explanation of the role of the first quatrain does exist.

The solution to the problem is provided by an annotation to line 2 found in the poem's autograph. Xlebnikov writes: "Nastoj iz barvinka služit dlja celej vorožei" (NP, 406). His statement, in particular the reference to a vorožeja (a seeress, a wise-woman), suggests that the periwinkle theme has been borrowed from folklore — more precisely, from ethnobotany and ethnomedicine.

Such an inference is not surprising. As I have shown in the article mentioned previously, an origin legend of the Cicuta virosa plant served as the point of departure for the development of "Bex", the companion poem to "O, červi zemljanye".[10] Names of plants, descriptions of their physical appearance, and references to beliefs and practices associated with them are likewise found in a very large number of other Xlebnikov texts. The most notable concentration of such elements occurs in "V lesu" (subtitled "Slovar' cvetov"). Botanical names and images are also present in "Kak bystro nosjatsja leta", "Černyj ljubir'", "Ljutikov želtyj pučok", "Usad'ba nočju – Čingisxan'!", etc.

Some aspects of this large-scale introduction of ethnobotanical lexicon and subject matter into Xlebnikov's literary works may be considered briefly. To begin with, the process was neither spontaneous nor haphazard. An express declaration of the poet's interest in such materials is found in a letter he wrote to A. Kručenyx sometime during August-September, 1912. In this letter, which on a number of points anticipates his important programmatic article "O rasširenii predelov russkoj slovesnosti" (publ. 1913), Xlebnikov proposes several possible poetic tasks for himself and his fellow-*budetljane*. These include: "6) Vospeť rastenija. Èto vse šagi vpered".[11]

An important reason for Xlebnikov's concern with plant names was his desire to extend and shift the boundaries of the Russian poetic language. In this endeavor, his primary tool was the formation of neologisms modelled on verbal creations current among village folk. He wonders in "Kurgan Svjatogora" (1908), his first declarative article: "Russkoe umnečestvo, vsegda alčuščee prav, otkažetsja li ot togo, kotoroe emu vručaet sama volja narodnaja: prava slovotvorčestva. Kto znaet russkuju derevnju, znaet o slovax obrazovannyx na čas i živuščix vekom motyľka" (*NP*, 323). The same thought appears more than a decade later, in the article "Naša osnova" (1919): "Slovotvorčestvo — vrag knižnogo okamenenija jazyka, i, opirajas' na to, čto v derevne okolo rek i lesov do six por jazyk tvoritsja, každoe mgnovenie sozdavaja slova, kotorye to umirajut, to polučajut pravo bessmertija, perenosit èto pravo v žizn' pisem" (*SP* V, 233).

His own original verbal creations are supplemented by Xlebnikov with borrowings from other languages, dialects, children's speech, etc. These are functionally equivalent to neologisms: they have the same effect of reviving an automatized poetic language and, within a given text, of enriching the work's semantics.[12] Their potential leads Xlebnikov to include the following point in the previously mentioned letter to Kručenyx: "8) Zagljadyvať v slovari slavjan, černogorcev i dr. — sobiranie russkogo jazyka ne okončeno — i vybirať mnogie prekrasnye slova, imenno te, kotorye prekrasny" (*SP* V, 298). Similarly, in a letter to Kručenyx from August 31, 1913, following a discussion of his friend's poetry, he notes:

> Мое мнение о стихах сводится к напоминанию о родстве стиха и стихии.
> Это гневное солнце, ударяющее мечом или хлопушкой по людским волнам. Вообще молния (разряд) может пройти во всех направлениях, но на самом деле она пройдет там, где соединит две стихии. Эти разряды пересекали русский язык в сельско-земледе<льческом> быту. Быт Пушкина думал и говорил на иностр<анном>, переводя на русский. Отсюда многих слов нет. Другие в плену томятся славянских наречий (*NP*, 367).

A poetic version of such a program of collecting new words, confined to the domain of plant names, is found in an undated poetic fragment:

Я и Саири мы вместе гуляли
Слова собирая для ласковой Ляли.
Они растут среди мощных дубов
Друзьями черники, друзьями грибов,
Словесными чарами громко чаруясь,
Наполнили мы весь березовый туес.[13]

(SP II, 294)

Another reason for Xlebnikov's interest in the literary potential of the Russian flora and its nomenclature was his training and experience as a naturalist.[14] Although his principal concerns were ornithology and phenology, allusions to plants in his literary works frequently reveal an accuracy of detail possible only to a practiced observer of the plant kingdom. One example of this precision is found in "Vesny poslovicy i skorogovorki" (1919):

Весны пословицы и скороговорки
По книгам зимним проползли.
Глазами синими увидел зоркий
Записки стыдесной земли.

Сквозь полет золотистого мячика
Прямо в сеть тополевых тенет
В эти дни золотая мать-мачеха
Золотой черепашкой ползет.

(SP III, 31)

A remarkable aspect of this description of nature at the moment of transition from winter to spring is that the details emphasized by the poet are entirely realistic. In the second quatrain, the contrast between the image of the sun, seemingly in rapid motion ("polet zolotistogo mjačika") and the turtle-like mať-mačexa (coltsfoot, Tussilago farfara) is well motivated. The coltsfoot flower, which also appears in "Rus' pevučaja v mesjace Aj" ("Na ovragax mať-mačexa / Zolotymi zvezdočkami. / I ona ot vodki boga / Oxmelela i p'jana" [NP, 191]), is associated with the earliest part of spring and does indeed have a golden appearance: "Pod tajavšimi snegami ja s udovoľstviem uvidel samye rannie cvety našej russkoj sarmatskoj ravniny — svetlo-želtye cvety mať-i-mačexi".[15]

In contrast to the emphasis on description in "Vesny poslovicy i skorogovorki" and in other texts, the external appearance of the periwinkle plays no role in "O, červi zemljanye"; instead, the question of the possible uses of this flower must be considered.

Xlebnikov's remark that the periwinkle is used by a *vorožeja,* with its suggestion of magical purposes, finds only limited support in Slavic ethnographic literature. The compilative entry in N. I. Annenkov's dictionary — a work with which Xlebnikov was familiar — emphasizes the periwinkle's medicinal potential:[16]

Прежде употр. при поносах, кровотечениях, чахотке, шкорбуте и снаружи при ранах. В народной медицине уптр. от боли горла в виде полосканья (Ворон.). В Беловежской пуще крестьяне от колтуна употребл. отвар барвинки (sic!), которую и разводят у себя в огородах; она служит и наружным средством от колтуна, для чего смачивают голову тем же отваром.[17]

A rare instance of the periwinkle's involvement in a magical operation is reported:

Barwinku używają czarownice, ażeby kogo przywołać do siebie. Wiedma chcąc kogo przywołać, gotuje korzeń z tego ziela. Gdy woda zacznie kipieć, to wciąż bulkoce: "Hryciu, Hryciu", czy jak tam się ten człowiek nazywa. A ten podnosi się do góry i leci jak ptak do wiedmy. Dobrze, jeżeli nie zawadzi o nic; lecz gdy napotka drzewo w drodze lub cobądź twardego, to się zabija na śmierć. (Rohatyn).[18]

In the Ukraine, the periwinkle is associated with a young girl falling in love or with a young bride. N. I. Sumcov notes: "Barvinok na malorusskix svaďbax samoe ljubimoe rastenie. V pesnjax barvinok — simvol sostojanija nevesty, krasoty i nevinnosti. Barvinok idet na venki; v Galicii ego prišivajut k uglam poduški pri raspletenii kosy".[19] A slightly varied interpretation is offered by N. I. Kostomarov: "Barvinok ... bolee vsego simvol bračnogo toržestva — svaďby, no takže neredko voobšče ljubvi i udovoľstvij, približajuščix k ljubvi"; "Necvetenie barvinka — obraz izmeny, a uvjadanie — nesčastnogo braka i durnogo obraščenija muža s ženoju ili ljubovniceju".[20]

It is possible that some other Slavic ethnographic source containing information about the periwinkle which would correspond precisely to the contents of quatrain I may yet be found. However, at the present time it appears more likely that the treatment of the periwinkle theme in the first quatrain is based on Western herbal traditions which regarded this flower as particularly potent in the preparation of charms and love philtres.[21] Specifically, although it is not known how he became acquainted with it, Xlebnikov's source seems to have been a prescription for a love philtre which originally appeared in the so-called *Liber secretorum Alberti Magni de virtutibus herbarum,* a work from the end of the 13th c. which was spuriously attributed to the great theologian and naturalist Albertus Magnus (c. 1200-1280).

When it [i.e. the periwinkle — H. B.] is beaten unto powder with worms of the earth wrapped about it, and with an herb called *Semperviva*, in English House-leek, it induceth love between man and wife, if it be used in their meats.[22]

That earthworms and the periwinkle are both necessary for the magical prescription explains their being conjoined in quatrain I. At the same time, Xlebnikov modifies his source to a significant extent. New components — the stones and the thread — are added to the magical operation, while the periwinkle powder mentioned in the prescription becomes a solution of periwinkle, probably due to the influence of the previously described popular medical practices. More important, while the sentence which constitutes quatrain I may describe a portion of a ritual, its primary function is not prescriptive — it is a *love incantation,* a verbal text designed to achieve a certain object.

Two elements of the sentence combine to give it the form proper to a love incantation. First, there is the emphasis on communication with non-sentient creatures which cannot enter into a communicative relationship: earthworms (₁*červi zemljanye*) become the addressee of a conative message.[23] The speaker commands them to set alight the two stones, apparently thought of as being held by loops within a black thread, the entire assemblage being immersed in the periwinkle solution. As Jurij Levin has noted, such a use in lyric poetry of the category termed by him "2-nd non-proper person" (*II nesobstvennoe lico*), brings the given text close to the texts of spells and incantations.[24] Second, there is the use of the verb ₃*zažgite.* Its presence in a text intended as a love incantation is consistent with what is found in Russian love charms (*prisuški*): the onset or the experience of the love passion is frequently conveyed in them by verbs expressing the idea of heat or burning.[25] Some examples from Majkov's collection: "... i tak by o mne, rabe Božem (imja rek), rabica Božja (imja rek) serdcem kipela, krov'ju gorela, telom soxla" (#1); "Goj vy esi, tri brata ... podite vy, sxodite, poslužite mne, kogda ja vas pošlju, rab Božij, zažgite vy retivoe serdce u raby Božiej (i.r.), čtoby gorelo po rabe Božiem" (#2); "Goj, esi ty, ognennyj zmej! ... zažgi ty krasnu devicu (i.r.), v sem'desjat-sem' sostavov, i sem'desjat-sem' žil i v edinuju žilu stanovuju, vo vsju eja xoč" (#7); '... Podi, tolstaja baba, razožgi u krasnoj devicy serdce po mne, rabe (i.r.)" (#23).[26]

An important feature of the medieval prescription is that it is designed to engender mutual love in a married couple. Similarly, the alteration of a man's and a woman's mutual negative feelings into love appears to be the object of the incantation in quatrain I. The condition which is to be transformed is expressed through the imagery of the stones and the thread. The presence of the former suggests the well-known analogy between a *stone* and an *unfeeling heart,* which is reflected, for example, in various folk sayings: "Serdce ne kamen'"; "Rovno kamen' na serdce naleg"; "Kamen' ot serdca otvalilsja"; "Moe serdce v tebe, a tvoe v kameni" (Dal''s dictionary). The thread connecting the stones may be interpreted as a metaphor of the emotional linkage; given its black color, this linkage may be assumed to be a negative one. Support for such an interpretation is provided by an analogous image in the *poèma* "I i È". Repeated twice, this image emphasizes the love between the hero and the heroine: "Čistyx serdc svjataja nit' / Vse voľna soedinit', / Žizni vse protivorečja!" (*SP* I, 89); "Tam, gde rokot vodopada / Duš ljubvi svjazuet nit'" (*SP* I, 90).

One detail of the imagery in the first quatrain is somewhat ambiguous. The adjective $_3vodjanye$ may be interpreted in two ways. On the one hand, in spite of it not being set off by commas, it could be a reference to the earthworms, presumably derived from *doždevye červi,* another term for *Lumbricus* in Russian. On the other hand, it could be an epithet modifying $_4kamnja$; if so, it would reflect the conception of the two stones being immersed in the periwinkle solution. Whatever the reading intended by Xlebnikov, the two rhyme words, *zemljanye–doždevye,* help create the kind of logically contradictory situation which is frequently encountered in charms and incantations. They also set up a contrast between the two elements of 'fire' and 'water' which has strong mythological associations and is not out of place in an incantatory text.

In sum, the first quatrain makes manifest the speaker's wish that feelings of love awake in himself and in some woman. This desire is presented through a verbal form capable of effecting a magical transformation.[27]

The conception of the use of the periwinkle found in quatrain IV is also associated with the realms of love and sorcery. This time, however, the magical operation contemplated by the speaker is not an active one: it is not intended to alter some aspect of reality, but is to be used in a passive acquisition of information. Taking up the motif of a solution of periwinkle Xlebnikov places it within the widespread Slavic tradition of divination through water.[28] The speaker claims that by using the infusion of periwinkle in soothsaying he will learn the truth about a certain woman's feelings. He will find out whether what must have been an admission of love, made at some point in the past, was genuine, or whether the woman, represented metonymically by a kerchief (*kosynka*),[29] mocked him, as winter sometimes mocks men with a false promise of spring ("Nadsmejalas' li kosynka / Čto zima, rastajav s kraju").

With the imagery of the outer quatrains clarified, we may now turn to quatrains II and III, in which the speaker reveals the situation which prompted his thoughts about sorcery.

In quatrain II the speaker makes himself manifest to the reader for the first time. However, before he refers to himself directly in line 8, he describes himself in a series of clauses in ll. 5-7.

His initial self-characterization is *Temnoj slavy golovnja*. The motivation for this image appears to be two-fold. As the speaker indicates in the subsequent two lines, he has a rather negative view of his own emotional and physical state, and so the metaphor of a torch from which a dark substance emanates is quite apt. A parallel to this usage is found in the short story "Učimica", in a construction (termed by Jakobson *obraščennyj parallelizm*)[30] which is developed around the figure of an old sorcerer:

> Может быть, текла вниз борода сребровитой куделью. Может быть, это было морозное утро над заброшенными в степи огнеокими избушками.
> Если это не было сивое зимнее утро, видимое откуда-нибудь из узкого места, из затянутого бычачьим пузырем окна, то это могла еще быть охладевшая, посизелая головня, в которой мелькали злобные вишнево-желтые огоньки-очи под отяжелевшими ховунскими веками. (*SP* IV, 22)

The torch metaphors in the two texts may have been influenced by proverbs contrasting loneliness and companionship: "Odna golovnja ni gorit, ni gasnet"; "Odna golovnja i v peči gasnet, a dve i v pole kurjatsja" (Dal''s dictionary).

As for the expression *temnaja slava,* it suggests the dubious reputation of someone who deals in sorcery: in using it the speaker may be echoing a potential remark about himself. An analogous expression occurs in a somewhat similar overall context in "Smugol, temen i izjaščen". A girl and a young stranger have the following brief exchange: "O, sudar', s krasnoju perčatkoj, / O vas očen' *durnaja slava?*' // '— Ja ne *znaxar'*, ne *kudesnik,* / Verit' možno li molve?'" (*SP* II, 28).

The speaker's self-characterization is developed in greater detail in lines 6-7. The initial two epithets (6*pustoj,* 6*postylyj*) are rejected while they are being presented; *pustoj* would indicate a permanent spiritual and/or emotional vacuity, while *postylyj* would imply a serious turning away from the speaker by his beloved (cf. the unfinished short story "Žiteli gor", in which the heroine applies the epithet to her would-be lover: "Idi, postylyj" [*NP*, 308]). In their place, he uses epithets which would suggest weariness (7*ustalyj*) and emotional drainage (7*ostylyj*) — conditions which are serious but temporary. The contrast between the two sets of epithets is reinforced by grammatical parallelism and paronomasia.

In line 8, the speaker at first continues to focus his attention on himself. He begins by stating that he is sitting still ("Ja sižu") and follows this with a command "Sogrej menja". The imperative sentence is directed at someone who is apparently not far from the speaker. Since the addressee is undoubtedly a woman, the command must be read as an appeal for love.

The development of the contents of quatrain III parallels that of quatrain II. The speaker describes himself (lines 9-10) and then turns his attention back to the figure of the woman (lines 11-12).

Initially, the speaker uses a 3rd person imperative construction to indicate his wish that his face remain impassive: "Na utese moix pleč / Pusť lico ne šeloxnetsja". While the major thought expressed in this statement is quite unambiguous, the significance of the image is enhanced by connotations of the metaphor *utes pleč*. One of these is purely descriptive: *utes pleč* suggests greater than normal physical dimensions. This association is supported by a parallel from the *poèma* "Perevorot v Vladivostoke", a passage describing a Japanese soldier's skill in judo: "Odnim liš znan'em tajn silač, / S uprugim mjačikom lovkač. / Igraet telom velikana. / Umeet brosiť na zem' mjaso, / Čužoj utes kostej i mjas" (*SP* I, 281). On another level, the metaphor suggests that the speaker is conscious of both his loneliness and pride. These connotations are also reflected elsewhere in Xlebnikov; for example, in the play "Asparux", the hero declares in the face of death: "Ja budu stojať kak večernij utes" (*SP* IV, 199).

The 3rd person imperative construction in lines 11-12, "No pusť ruk pojuščix reč / Sluxa ruk moix kosnetsja", is potentially ambiguous. To clarify it we must deal separately with its two components, the epithet 11*pojuščix* and the twin metaphors *reč' ruk* and *slux ruk*. The former is also metaphoric: its real plane could be a woman's hands moving so swiftly and gracefully as to appear to be playing a stringed instrument and, by extension, singing. The latter may be read as a request for tactile contact, with the images of speech and hearing conveying the hero's hope that the woman's hands will touch his own.

There is some evidence that the two parallel metaphors, which transfer the idea of touching into an auditory channel, derive from a deeper level of Xlebnikov's model of the world. In one of his earliest articles, "Pusť na mogiľnoj plite" (1904), the poet raises the question of the nature of the five senses, suggesting that they are merely intelligible discontinuous segments of a higher-order, continous, multidimensional reality, and that transformations of one sense into another are perfectly possible:

Есть некоторое много, неопределенно протяженное многообразие, непрерывно изменяющееся, которое по отношению к нашим пяти чувствам находится в том же положении, в каком двупротяженное пространство находится по отношению к треугольнику, кругу, разрезу яйца, прямоугольнику.

То есть, как треугольник, круг, восьмиугольник суть части плоскости, так и наши слуховые, зрительные, вкусовые, обонятельные ощущения суть части, случайные обмолвки этого одного великого, протяженного многообразия.

Оно подняло львиную голову и смотрит на нас, но уста его сомкнуты.

Далее, точно так, как непрерывным изменением круга можно получить треугольник, а треугольник непрерывно превратить в восьмиугольник, как из шара в трехпротяженном пространстве можно непрерывным изменением получить яйцо, яблоко, рог, боченок, точно так же есть некоторые величины, независимые переменные, с изменением которых ощущения разных рядов — например слуховое и зрительное или обонятельное — переходит одно в другое.

Так есть величины, с изменением которых синий цвет василька (я беру чистое ощущение), непрерывно изменяясь, проходя через неведомые нам, людям, области разрыва, превратится в звук кукования кукушки или в плач ребенка, станет им.

При этом, непрерывно изменяясь, он образует некоторое одно протяженное многообразие, все точки которого, кроме близких к первой и последней, будут относиться к области неведомых ощущений, они будут как бы из другого мира. (*NP*, 319-320)

The preceding analysis reveals a rather striking feature of the text. It becomes apparent that in selecting words, expressions and images and juxtaposing them within the poem Xlebnikov follows a well-defined semantic model. Chosen on a conscious or subconscious basis, the lexicon and imagery of "O, červi zemlja-nye" revolve around the opposition between two sets of closely associated semantic features: I) *cold, dark, static, stone-like,* and II) *warm, bright, mobile.* The terms of the opposition are realized in the poem as follows: in quatrain I: "Zažgite vodjanye / Dva kamnja v černoj nitke"; in quatrain II: "Temnoj slavy golovnja", "No ustalyj i ostylyj, / Ja sižu. Sogrej menja"; in quatrain III: "Na utese moix pleč / Pust' lico ne šeloxnetsja / No pust' ruk pojuščix reč"; in quatrain IV: "Nadsmejalas' li kosynka, / Čto zima, rastajav s kraju".

A question arises: are the several instances of direct speech found in the text to be interpreted as being actually voiced by the speaker? Since, as quatrains II and III suggest, the speaker finds himself in the presence of a woman, this question must be answered in the negative. In a real-life situation, an incantation such as that given in quatrain I is not likely to be uttered aloud. The appeal to the woman in quatrain II follows the speaker's thoughts about himself, and this makes the presumption of a sudden shift to an actual utterance difficult to accept. Neither the command directed at a portion of the speaker's body in quatrain III nor the desire to have the woman's hands touch those of the speaker can be realistically seen as being voiced in public. Finally, in quatrain IV, the speaker's own thoughts are clearly being given.

We may now recreate in logical order the events indicated in the poem. In essence, the text directly presents the thoughts and inner speech of a lyrical hero. The few details provided suggest that the "I" of the poem is physically near a woman whom he has loved, but from whom he now feels estranged. Tongue-tied, he functions within his own consciousness.

The poem begins forcefully with a magical attempt to reestablish the earlier, happier relationship between the lyrical hero and his beloved. However, the incantation is only a fantasy. The real situation reasserts itself in the second quatrain and the hero can only appeal to the woman. His wish not to reveal his feelings in front of the woman is noted in the third quatrain; even now, however, although his desire is less direct than previously and its scope more limited, the hero wishes for some contact with her. In the final quatrain, the hero isolates himself fully in his imagination and plans to verify magically the suspicion that he has been betrayed. His hopes have apparently collapsed and have been replaced by self-inflicted pain.

A concluding remark: as a rule, the lack of biographical materials on Xlebnikov makes it difficult to correlate events in his life with his love lyrics. Fortunately, the poem we have discussed appears to be an exception in this regard. An entry for December 9, 1913 in his "Dnevnik" describes a quarrel between Xlebnikov and an unnamed woman: "9-XII-1913: 7-XII — самый короткий день, его я провел на даче Куокалла у Пуни. День был безотрадный и ... (моя Солодка) разгневана. 1-я ссора. Ссора и гнев на меня. Дни будут расти? Ссора или мир. Три дня сидел, не выходя из комнаты. Солнцестояние осени, мрачное настроение" (*SP* V, 327). Even though this diary entry may spring from a different set of circumstances than "O, červi zemljanye", it offers a suggestive parallel and commentary to the events hinted at in this text.

State University of New York at Albany

NOTES

[1]   V. V. Ivanov, "Struktura stixotvorenija Xlebnikova 'Menja pronosjat na slonovyx ...'," *Trudy po znakovym sistemam* III (1967), pp. 156-71. Prose parallels to the poem discussed by Ivanov are found in the drafts for the *sverxpovest' Deti Vydry*. The following passage is included in a 1913 rough draft (RO IMLI, f. 139, op. 1. ed. xr. 6): "Сын выдры с пером в руке идет один через зеленую чащу Индии [где в ветка<х> прячутся обезьяны. Очковая змея залегла на его пути.] Толпа служанок храма с велики<ми> очам<и>, у них большие смелые рты, сплетаясь руками в нечто напоминающее слона и покрытые довром, зовет его к себе знаками. Он садится на ковер покрывающ<ий> живого, но не подлин<ного> <?> слона и трогается дальше, держа в одн<ой> руке свяшенну<ю> к<н>игу и лотос в другой, <нрзб.>

<нрзб.> черепаху на слоне. Обезьяны криками зависти провожают его шествие и бросают плоды и шелуху орехов. Но те храбро идут дальше." A variant of this passage appears in the fair copy of a draft which may have been intended as a section of the final text of *Deti Vydry*.

² A. E. Parnis, "V. Xlebnikov v revoljucionnom Giljane (novye materialy)", *Narody Azii i Afriki* 5 (1967), pp. 156-64.

³ K. Pomorska, *Russian Formalist Theory and its Poetic Ambiance* (The Hague-Paris, 1968), pp. 101-06.

⁴ M. Grygar, "Remarques sur la dénomination poétique chez Khlebnikov", *Poetics* 4 (1972), pp. 109-18. In dealing with the poem Grygar neglects contextual parallels and fails to consider the origin of some of the expressions found in the text. To take the most striking example: the last two lines, "No za to v beznadežnoe kanut / Pervyj grom i puť dalše vesennij", originate in folk omens such as "Pervyj grom pri severnom vetre, xolodnaja vesna, pri vostočnom, suxaja i teplaja; pri zapadnom, mokraja; pri južnom, teplaja, no mnogo budet červja, nasekomyx" (Daľ's dictionary). For other omens (*primety*) relating to 'first thunder' see A. S. Ermolov, *Narodnaja seľsko-xozjajstvennaja mudrosť* IV (SPB, 1905), pp. 185-87.

⁵ H. Baran, "Chlebnikov's Poem 'Bech'", *Russian Literature* 6 (1974), pp. 5-19.

⁶ R. V. Duganov, "Kratkoe 'Iskusstvo poèzii' Xlebnikova", *Izvestija Akademii Nauk. Serija literatury i jazyka,* t. 33, No. 5 (1974), pp. 418-27.

⁷ Ivanov, pp. 170-71.

⁸ On Xlebnikov's composition, see: R. Jakobson, *Novejšaja russkaja poèzija* (Praga, 1921), pp. 6-30; B. A. Uspenskij, "K poètike Xlebnikova: problemy kompozicii", *Sbornik statej po vtoričnym modelirujuščim sistemam* (Tartu 1973), pp. 122-27; M. Grygar, "Kubizm i poèzija russkogo i češskogo avangarda", *Structure of Texts and Semiotics of Culture,* J. van der Eng & M. Grygar, eds. (The Hague-Paris 1973), pp. 59-101.

⁹ The autograph is in the personal archive of N. I. Xardžiev, whom I wish to thank for permitting me to consult it.

¹⁰ Baran, *op cit.*

¹¹ Velimir Xlebnikov, *Sobranie proizvedenij* (henceforth *SP*), N. Stepanov, ed. (Leningrad 1928-33) V, p. 298.

¹² Pomorska, p. 100.

¹³ Cf. in "V lesu": "Ljubite nosiť vse te imena, / Čto mogut onežiťsja v Ljalju" (*SP* II, 211).

¹⁴ See N. Xardžiev, "Novoe o Velimire Xlebnikove", *Russian Literature* 9 (1975), pp. 8-10.

¹⁵ S. Tjan-Šanskij, "Putešestvie" (cited in the entry for *mať-i-mačexa* in the 17-volume Academy of Sciences dictionary).

¹⁶ Baran, pp. 12-13.

¹⁷ N. I. Annenkov, *Botaničeskij slovar'* (SPB, 1878), p. 380. Similar information is found in E. R. Romanov, *Belorusskij sbornik* III, p. 492.

¹⁸ B. Gustawicz, "Podania, przesądy, gadki i nazwy ludowe w dziedzinie przyrody", *Zbiór Wiadomości do Antropologii Krajowej* VI (Kraków 1882), p. 307.

¹⁹ N. F. Sumcov, *O svadebnyx obrjadax, preimuščestvenno russkix* (Xarʹkov 1891), p. 184. See also P. P. Čubinskij, *Trudy ètnografičesko-statističeskoj èkspedicii v zapadno-russkij kraj* (SPB, 1872) I, p. 83.

²⁰ N. I. Kostomarov, "Istoričeskoe značenie južnorusskogo pesennogo tvorčestva", *Sobranie sočinenij N. I. Kostomarova* 8, Tomy XIX-XXI (SPB, 1906), pp. 522, 525.

²¹ M. Grieve, *A Modern Herbal* II (New York 1971), p. 630. I wish to thank Mrs. Laura Petrochko for bringing to my attention the information found in this volume.

²² *The Book of Secrets of Albertus Magnus,* M. R. Best and F. H. Brightman, eds. (Oxford 1973), p. 8. The prescription is cited in Grieve, *op. cit.,* p. 630; it is also referred to in the article on the periwinkle in the *Funk and Wagnalls Standard Dictionary of Folklore, Mythology and Legend,* M. Leach and J. Fried, eds. New York 1972), p. 857.

²³ R. Jakobson, "Linguistics and Poetics", *Style in Language,* T. A. Sebeok, ed. (Cambridge, Mass., 1966), p. 355.

[24]   Ju. I. Levin, "Lirika s kommunikativnoj točki zrenija", *Structure of Texts and Semiotics of Culture,* p. 193.

[25]   See I. Černov, "O strukture russkix ljubovnyx zagovorov. I", *Trudy po znakovym sistemam* II (1965), pp. 163-65.

[26]   L. N. Majkov, "Velikorusskie zaklinanija", *Zapiski Russkogo Geografičeskogo Obščestva* II (SPB, 1869), pp. 424-35.

[27]   The impact of the first quatrain is reinforced by the anagrammatization of the root morpheme *červ-*: [1]*červi,* [2]*v barvinočnom,* [4]*v černoj.*

[28]   See K. Moszyński, *Kultura ludowa słowian* II/1 (Warszawa 1967), pp. 369-71, 374-75, 389-92, 396-98.

[29]   An interesting metaphoric use of the word *kosynka* is found in the second part of "Vy pomnite o gorode", a work dealing with the city of Moscow:

> В тебе, любимый город,
> Старушки что-то есть.
> Уселась на свой короб
> И думает поесть.
> Косынкой замахнулась — косынка
>   не простая:
> От и до края летит птиц черных
>   стая. (*SP* II, 27)

Parallels to (and perhaps the source of) the image of Moscow as a bent old woman are found in two folk sayings: "Moskva gorbitsja", "Moskva — gorbataja staruška". These are thought to reflect the fact that Moscow is spread out over hills (B. Šejdlin, *Moskva v poslovicax i pogovorkax* [Moskva 1929], p. 21).

[30]   R. Jakobson, *Novejšaja russkaja poèzija,* pp. 18-20.

THE SUPPLICATION OF DANIEL THE EXILE
AND THE PROBLEM OF
POETIC FORM IN OLD RUSSIAN LITERATURE

HENRIK BIRNBAUM

0. The perennial question of where prose (including rhythmized prose) ends and poetry or verse (including free verse) begins, a problem which in various contexts has troubled so many students of poetics, is eminently relevant also to Slavic verbal art of the Middle Ages and to Old Russian literature in particular.[1] It is further complicated by the frequent need, felt to a varying extent also concerning medieval textual material from other language areas, first to draw a clear line between writing in general, that is, in the broad sense of serving primarily the conveyance of more or less material information only (inherent in terms such as R *pis'mennost'* G *Schrifttum*, etc.), and literature proper, that is, in the narrow and more precise meaning of verbal art or poetic language, written or oral and, as a rule, only secondarily recorded (suggested, for example, by the Russian terms *slovesnost'*, cf. G *Wortkunst*, and, when applicable merely to its written form, *xudožestvennaja literatura* or by the French-English expression *belles lettres*, cf. G *schöne Literatur*, if the latter is not limited to its more specific connotation of 'light entertaining literature', cf. R *belletristika*, G *Belletristik*, E *fiction*). Reference to works such as the so-called Nestor (also Primary) or Galician-Volynian Chronicles and many pieces of Old Russian hagiography and semi-secular biography will suffice to bring to mind the intricate problems attendant on making, in as unambiguous a fashion as possible, this often fine and occasionally difficult distinction.

However, in this paper I will not be concerned with the preliminary difficulty of drawing this sometimes fine line between the non-literary and literary usage of Old Russian and/or Russianized Church Slavic. Nor will I here address myself except in passing to the much-debated issue of whether to consider the written language of medieval Russia essentially Common East Slavic with a substantial admixture of interspersed Slavonisms which enriched it — not in the least as a tool of artistic expression — or, on the contrary, to conceive of it as made up of a Church Slavic base (transplanted onto Russian soil from early medieval Bulgaria and only insignificantly adapted to the local vernacular in some such instances as the replacement of *št* by *šč* or of *ę* by *ja/a* more in tune with East Slavic phonology) to become increasingly overlayered, at all levels of linguistic structure, with elements of genuinely Russian (in the broad sense) origin; or whether to adopt, perhaps, a compromise view amounting to a synthesis of the two aforementioned more extreme stand-points. Some of these questions recently surveyed by me elsewhere[2] bear on the problem of poetic form in Old Russian literature only insofar as certain of the formal poetic devices utilized in this body of texts are held to be of folkloric East Slavic (and, in the final analysis, Common Slavic) provenience, whereas others appear to have originated in the Church Slavic (and, in large part, ultimately Byzantine or even classic) literary tradition. Instead, the chief point to be raised in this paper will be the question of whether a few unequivocally poetic texts of the Old Russian period (the term 'poetic' here taken in its broad meaning of 'artistic') should be interpreted as written in prose — a prose shaped and arranged according to some aesthetic principle, of course — or whether they should rather be considered as being versified, that is, as display-ing some kind of meter, with various formal characterizations suggested for such presumed prosodic-rhythmic regularization (occasionally enhanced, moreover, by some further poetic means such as alliteration, assonance/con-sonance, or rhyme, including grammatical rhyme — all used in a fairly unsystematic way, however), as has been claimed particularly in recent years.

The mystifying though undoubtedly highly artistic and stylistically sophis-ticated piece, dating most probably from the final phase of the pre-Mongol period, usually known as the Supplication of Daniel the Exile (*Molenie,* also *Poslanie,* and its generally assumed earlier version, *Slovo Daniila Zatočnika*), will serve here as a case in point. Note that nearly identical claims could be made and quite similar conclusions drawn, too, on the basis of a parallel analysis of some other poetically endowed and in part equally controversial Old Russian texts. This, to mention just a few works falling into this category, would be true of, say, the famous Igor Tale (*Slovo o polku Igoreve*), of its imitation, model, or parallel counterpart — the proper definition depending on where one stands on the still hotly debated issue of the authenticity of the "Igor' Tale"[3] — the Tale of the Battle Beyond the Don (lately, since the new edition by R. Jakobson and D. S. Worth, often referred to as Sofonija's Tale but better known under its Russian name, *Zadonščina,* to be used here), or of the perhaps only fragmentarily preserved lyrical Tale of the Destruction of the Russian Land (by some also quoted as Discourse on the Ruin of the Land of Rus', *Slovo o pogibeli Ruskyja zemli*), all of which, incidentally, are related to a degree in the sense that they in some — more or less — frequent instances echo each other.[4] Certain poetic, or here rather perhaps mnemotechnic, devices (for example, alliteration, rhyme, and some measure of rhythmicization) were used occasionally even in works with less or no particular aesthetic concern such as the *Izbornik Svjatoslava* of 1076 or the *Russkaja Pravda* (with some instances of rhythmized diction, facilitating the memorization of the originally recited customary law, especially in its so-called Expanded Version).[5]

Admittedly my own point of departure in discussing the problem of prose vs. poetry in Old Russian literature is one of guarded skepticism about "reading verse and poetry proper into a 'poetic' passage of medieval Slavic text where there is none", as I put it on another occasion when summarily discussing some Old Russian (including Russianized Church Slavic) and Old Church Slavic literary works in terms of this fundamental dichotomy of poetic form.[6] A brief stocktaking and assessment of the artistic devices utilized in the Supplication, whether it be considered poetically shaped prose, or in part at least, formally versified, will be the natural by-product of the findings reported below.

1. It is not proposed to deal here other than in brief outline with the many unanswered questions and enigmas which still surround the genesis as well as the social context and literary function of the Supplication of Daniel the Exile — a unique phenomenon of Old Russian literature and one of its most fascinating pieces at the same time. Virtually every standard textbook, theoretical outline, or major reference work of Old Russian literature devotes a chapter, a section, or at least a paragraph or two to the *Molenie,*[7] and only where the coverage is deliberately selective, an introductory text in this field may contain no discussion or even mention of the Supplication.[8] Its language has been the subject of a thorough if biased analysis by Obnorskij.[9] The overall implication of this analysis, claiming, on the one hand, the *Molenie* as another proof of the alleged purely East Slavic beginnings of the Old Russian literary language while, on the other hand, dating it, on linguistic grounds, to as late as the 13th-14th centuries, was subsequently modified by Vinogradov, among others, to the effect that a "profound and close interlacement of East Slavic features and Slavonisms is characteristic also for those monuments of earliest Russian writing" singled out by Obnorskij to corroborate his theory.[10] This statement assumes particular significance in the light of K. Taranovsky's recent attempt to ascertain both indigenous folkloric "narrative" (*skazovyj*) and Church Slavic "prayer" (*molitvoslovnyj*) verse in our text; for details and criticism of this view, see below. The social and psychological setting of the Supplication and its likely prototype, the *Slovo* — though some experts still believe in a reverse dependency as once did V. N. Peretc and N. K. Gudzij,

among others — was again discussed by literary scholars like Lixačev (1954; cf. also 1970, 42, and 44) and by historians such as Romanov (17-38, under the telling title "'Mizantrop' XII-XIII vekov"); and numerous are the special studies devoted in their entirety to this literary work, its two basic redactions and their relationship, or some of its particular aspects.[11]

In terms of its specific genre the *Molenie* stands alone, having no immediate match in Old Russian literature. While sharing some characteristics, as was already hinted, with such highly poetic works as the Igor' Tale, the *Zadon-ščina* (though it should be remembered that the latter marks the final phase of the Mongol period whereas the Supplication in its original form clearly falls into the late pre-Mongol epoch) and the *Slovo o pogibeli,* because of its largely gnomic-aphoristic contents Daniel's enigmatic work can, in a broader sense, be conceived of as belonging to the same category of instructive 'common wisdom' literature (though hardly constituting a genre of its own) as, say, the *Izbornik Svjatoslava* of 1076 and the early — probably 12th century — translation or adaptation of a Byzantine florilegium known by the name *Pčela* (Gk *Melissa*) and containing quotations, sayings, proverbs, and whole small tales which all serve a moralizing and edifying purpose, of both religious (mostly biblical and patristic) and secular provenience.[12]

As was noted by Voronin (and many previous students of our text have made the same observation), the "popularity of the monument and the movable character of its mosaic text determined the ease with which subsequent 'coauthors' would rework it and add to it".[13] None of the preserved manuscripts of either the redaction usually referred to as the *Slovo* (but as the testimony of one relatively recently discovered copy suggests also known as the *Napisanie Daniila Zatočnika*)[14] or that represented by the *Molenie* (or *Poslanie Daniila Zatočnika,* also *Danila Zatočenogo*) goes beyond the 16th-17th centuries, thus further obscuring the genesis of this piece.[15] Whereas a majority of scholars today see in the *Slovo* an earlier redaction from the 12th century (in a version which was probably reworked as early as the end of that very century), the longer *Molenie* (*Poslanie*) variant is less controversial as to its presumed origin and dating: it was probably written in Perejaslavl' Suz-dal'skij (Zalesskij) or some place on the shores of Lake Lača between 1223 and 1236 (at any rate between 1213 and 1238/42) and was addressed to Jaroslav Vsevolodovič, the son of Vsevolod III Bol'šoe Gnezdo (the first prince of Suzdal' to assume the title grand prince, *velikij knjaz'*, var. *car'*, referred to in the text of the *Molenie*), who during those years ruled simultaneously over Perejaslavl' (subsequently, Perejaslav) Južnyj (southeast of Kiev) and Nov-gorod, in addition to having Perejaslavl' Suzdal'skij as his appanage.[16] As to the identity of the addressee of the (original) *Slovo,* the son of a not further

specified "grand prince Vladimer", it is usually thought that he was Jaroslav
Vladimirovič, son of Vladimir Mstislavič and great-grandson of Vladimir
Monomax, who between 1181/2 and 1199 on several occasions was the ruler
of Novgorod. However, other potential addressees have been considered as
well, especially one of the sons of Vladimir Monomax, Jurij Dolgorukij or
Andrej Dobryj. Traditionally, the *Slovo* is believed to have been written
somewhere on the shores of Lake Lača, the presumed place of the original
Daniel's exile or involuntary residence. As was made clear by Obnorksij, the
language of the *Molenie* points to the Russian North, not the South, which
squares with the historians' and the literary scholars' attempts to seek its
origin in the Suzdaľ or Novgorod area. From a literary point of view, the
question of identifying the addressee of our text loses some of its significance,
as was already indicated, if we see in the *Molenie* (as well as in the *Slovo*)
primarily a literary piece, disguising an anthology of the *Pčela* type, an
instructive-moralizing work, a "didactic poem", or even, as has also been
suggested, the outpouring in bitter jest of a deprived literary genius rather
than a true and seriously meant appeal to a ruling prince from an exiled
person, founded in historical reality.[17] In view of the obvious folkloric component in the *Molenie* (both as an influence and an effect), it may be worth
mentioning that Lixačev and others have considered the possibility of its
originating in the milieu of the so-called *skomoroxi*, the minstrels and jocula-
tors of medieval Russia.[18]

2. In considering the poetic form of the *Molenie* from a structural point of
view and, in particular, the question of whether we are dealing here with a
specimen of artistic prose or metric poetry, the complex and far from defini-
tively solved problems of its origin and various modifications throughout the
centuries of its popular life are of secondary import at most. In other words, I
can only agree with K. Taranovsky's approach when, in his formal analysis of
parts of this literary text, he feels free to view the monument as a whole and
"qualifiedly will speak about its author (although it would be appropriate to
speak about its 'authors'), and freely will adduce quotations from its various
redactions".[19] Whether I will see fit, as others have done,[20] to subscribe to the
upshot of his findings is another matter.

According to Taranovsky, the *Molenie* is a perfect example of the happy
combination of the two meters available to the Old Russian poet, the two verse
forms designated by Taranovsky, following others, prayer and narrative verse
(*molitvoslovnyj* and *skazovyj stix*).[21] While rightly, of course, noting that the
so-called Insertion about Iosif Prekrasnyj (found in the Nikoľskij copy of the
Slovo) is written in plain prose,[22] Taranovsky considers the "imploring

appeals" (*molitvennye obraščenija*) to be composed in prayer verse. This, therefore, would be true of such passages as the following:

(1) Темъ же вопию к тобѣ, одержимъ нищетою:
     Помилуи мя, сыне великаго царя Владимера,
     Да не восплачюся, рыдая, аки Адамъ рая,
     Пусти тучю на землю художества моего.

(2) Княже мои, господине!
     Яви ми зракъ лица своего,
     Яко гласъ твои сладокъ и образ твои красенъ;
     Медъ истачають устнѣ твои,
     И послание твое аки раи [с] плодом.
     Но егда веселишися многими брашны,
     А мене помяни, сух хлѣбъ ядуща,
     Или пиеши сладкое питие,
     А мене помяни, теплу воду пиюща от мѣста незавѣтрена;
     Егда лежиши на мяккых постелях под собольими одѣялы,
     А мене помяни, под единым платом лежаща и зимою умирающа,
     И каплями дождевыми аки стрѣлами сердце пронизающе.

(3) Но боюся, господине, похулениа твоего на мя.
     Азъ бо есмь, аки она смоковница проклятая:
     Не имѣю плода покаянию;
     Имѣю бо сердце, аки лице безъ очию;
     И бысть умъ мои, аки нощныи вранъ на нырищи, забдѣх;
     И расыпася животъ мои, аки Ханаонскыи царь буестию;
     И покры мя нищета, аки Чермное море фараона.

There can naturally be no doubt that we have to do here with a highly poetic, artistically formed and rhythmized language. But are we really entitled to call this verse? Are these specimens of verbal art governed by an ascertainable meter that would lend them a clearly perceivable, regularized prosodic-rhythmic structure? My own answer can only be in the negative. The graphic arrangement is, needless to say, deceptive: not only will a hexameter (by Žukovskij) disguised in the printed format of a regular prose text be even more difficult to identify as verse,[23] but also a prosaic text, particularly if it is indeed endowed with a high measure of rhythm and, moreover, adorned with many stylistic embellishments, can occasionally lure us into interpreting it as poetry proper if printed — or written — in this vein (as is the case with the samples cited by Taranovsky; the late manuscripts of the *Molenie* do not, of course, display any such graphic arrangements).[24] However, it would certainly not be fair to claim that Taranovsky's poetic, *sensu stricto,* interpretation of the *Molenie* and other Old Russian literary texts is merely predicated on their graphic rendition.

At the outset of his contribution to the Prague Congress of Slavists, the Harvard scholar offers a tentative definition of his understanding of the specifics of the prayer meter. Thus we read there (377) that: "the basic determinant of the prayer verse is the system of rhythmic signals marking the beginning of the lines. Primarily, two grammatical forms assume this function — the vocative and the imperative" which not only constitute altogether separate grammatical categories (not subjectable to the truth test) but also frequently carry particularly strong, expressive stress. Another way of marking the beginning of the line in the prayer verse is said to be achieved by syntactic inversion, for example, by placing the direct object before the predicate verb; here, too, the word thus singled out will often attract particular, logical stress. However, such line-initial strong emphasis can also be automatized and need therefore not always be syntactically motivated. "Thus", we read further (378), "the rhythmic movement of the prayer verse is primarily built on the expectation of the markedness of the beginning of the lines. Having registered the repeated coming of the initial signal we expect also its continued appearance: the speech flows in two dimensions, as it were (from one word unit to the other and from line to line), i.e., it turns into verse".[25] It seems to me that this descriptive analysis is not, in fact, sufficient to define a particular meter, here the assumed prayer verse of Church Slavic origin, but that, at best, it can serve as a proper description of one possible mechanism (among several conceivable) that will accomplish one particular kind of rhythmization of speech, that is, the process of converting non-rhythmic into rhythmic prose.[26] Without the support of other poetic devices, it does not seem possible, at least to me, to speak here of any form of regularized verse proper. Such devices could be alliteration, assonance/consonance, and/or rhyme — and, in particular, isosyllabicity, available to Old Church Slavic and Early Old Russian prior to the loss of the weak jers but no longer usable for the same poetic text once the syllabic structure of the word had been drastically altered as a result of that phonetic change. Nor was the thus lost early isosyllabic structure at that time compensated for by any strict isotonic pattern capable of achieving the same or a similar rhythmic-euphonic effect. Isosyllabicity was, as is well known, artificially — and ultimately unsuccessfully — (re)introduced in Russian poetic language only by the 17th century under the influence of Polish and Ruthenian syllabic poetry (*virši,* Simeon Polockij *et al.*).

To illustrate the structure of the prayer verse Taranovsky quotes (378-9) the Russian Church Slavic form of the Lord's Prayer (*Otče naš*), and, as a typical — and, incidentally, the earliest — example of its application in Old Russian writing he adduces a passage from Ilarion's famous *Slovo o zakone i blagodati* (380). However, both here and in the excerpts from the *Molenie* quoted above there are quite a few lines (even given that we accept the suggested particular breakdown into lines) that in no way comply with Taranovsky's own criteria defining the prayer meter. Thus, the first line in excerpt one, not marked by either a vocative form, the imperative, or inversed, emphatic word order, cannot, being the first line of that section, very well be considered rhythmically automatized, i.e., marked for particular line-initial stress without syntactic motivation. And also line three of the same excerpt does not adhere to the prerequisites of the prayer meter but rather, as noted by Taranovsky himself, is reminiscent of some other rhythmic pattern, the narrative verse.[27] Similarly, in excerpt two, of the imperative forms said to distinctly signal the beginning of the lines only one actually opens the line (2) while in three other lines of this passage (7, 9, and 11) the imperative *pomjani* is preceded by the recurrent *A mene*. The vocative occurs here only once (in line 1: *Knjaže moi*) and just one line has reversed word order (4: *Medъ istačajutь ustně tvoi*). In the third excerpt where the structure of the prayer verse is said to be less evident the beginnings of the lines are supposedly marked by verbal forms; but, again, only one line opens with the verb (4: *Iměju*) while in all other lines the verb form is preceded by one (mostly monosyllabic) word.

The other verse form thought by Taranovsky to be found in the *Molenie* is the so-called narrative verse (*skazovyj stix*), a variety and descendant of the Common Slavic spoken (as opposed to sung) verse expertly described by Jakobson and based on syntactic (sentential) rather than word prosody.[28] It is not my intention to scrutinize and argue here about the validity of each detail of the definition of this inherited Slavic folk-meter given by Jakobson (and the findings of his predecessors on which he draws) though I have some doubt whether even without the "similar close" or rhyme as a supportive device, holding cola and/or lines together, we could still speak here of some form of full-fledged metric verse in the traditional sense.[29] Also much of the illustrative relevant material cited by Taranovsky does indeed display rhyme (though not always perfect rhyme), in many instances monosyllabic (masculine) rhyme under stress, linking cola or lines.[30] However, notwithstanding a remote resemblance in rhythmic structure — and, here too, the proposed graphic decomposition of the text, closely following that of A. V. Solov'ev, may be suggestively deceptive! — I cannot find Taranovsky's attempt to interpret the highly lyrical and contemplative *Slovo o pogibeli* as also written in narrative

verse all too persuasive (granted that Taranovsky himself notes the great
number of incomplete lines, consisting of the second colon only, and is aware
of the arguable division into cola).[31] Recognizing, of course, the presence of a
high degree of rhythmization inherent in this poetic piece, particularly perceivable when read aloud, I nonetheless feel that it is much more realistic to
consider, with a majority of scholars,[32] the *Slovo,* so different in content from
the facetious, jocular, and gnomic sayings and formulas of folkloric nature
and origin for which the narrative verse was the appropriate form of artistic
expression, to be written in a highly poetic, rhythmic prose rather than in any
strictly versified meter.

But how about certain passages of the *Molenie* and, in particular, those
aphoristic maxims referred to by its author(s) under the somewhat obscure
term *mirskie pritči?*[33] Again, while there is in the following sentences an
obvious, particular rhythm, here and there enhanced by grammatical end
rhyme — though not masculine rhyme — and some other euphonic means
(such as alliteration and partial internal rhyme), it is hard to perceive in them
anything like a fully regularized metric pattern even when they are graphically
arranged as if written in narrative verse:

Ни птица во птицах сычь,	ни в звѣрех звѣрь еж;
Ни рыба в рыбах рак.	ни скот в скотех коза;
Ни холоп в холопех,	хто у холопа работает;
Ни муж в мужехъ,	которыи жены слушает;
Ни жена в женах,	которая от мужа блядетъ;
Ни работа в работех	под женами повозничати.

or:

Доброму бо господину служа,	дослужится слободы,
А злу господину служа,	дослужится болшеи работы.
Как в утелъ мех лити,	так безумнаго учити;
Псомъ бо и свиниамъ	не надобѣ злато, ни сребро,
Ни безумному	драгии словеса
Ни мертвеца росмѣшити,	ни безумнаго наказати.
Дѣвиця бо погубляеть	красу свою блядею,
А мужь	свое мужество татбою ...

It is therefore difficult for me to follow Taranovsky when in a number of
instances he sees an artistically purposeful combination and/or contrasting
not only of two different rhythmic patterns with some skillfully managed
switching from one to the other (and line 10 of the last passage quoted by
Taranovsky undoubtedly explicitly draws attention to such a rhythm

switching: *No uže ostavim/ rěči i rcem sice* — in addition to being a formula frequently used also in Old Russian hagiography, for example) but actually conceives of these turns and contrasts of rhythmization as changes and combinations of two formal verse meters. In this context it is of course impossible to comprehend the oft-cited lines

Кому Переславль,	а мнѣ гореславль;
Кому Боголюбиво,	а мнѣ горе лютое;
Кому Белоозеро,	а мнѣ чернѣе смолы;
Кому Лаче озеро,	а мнѣ много плача исполнено ...

as anything but the work of a talented punster, regardless of whether this punning was done in jest (and therefore is perhaps attributable to the original *skomoroxi* milieu of the *Molenie* as some scholars tend to believe; cf. above) or whether it was meant in bitter earnest and thus has a passionate, almost desperate ring. But even this masterful playing with names, words, and sounds can hardly be considered verse in any precise meaning of the term!

See now also the relevant views of Sazonova (32-4) on the "principle of the rhythmic organization" of artistically formed Old Russian prose works such as Ilarion's *Slovo,* the Igor' Tale, and the *Molenie*, with particular attention paid to the first one (comparing it to the rhythmized prose of the Old Serbian panegyrist and hagiographer Domentijan), and arguing against Taranovsky's and Pozdneev's recent attempts to interpret these and some kindred works of Old Russian literature as versified poetry.

3. While acknowledging the significant accomplishments of K. Taranovsky, as well as those of R. Jakobson, in the field of Old Russian (and generally Slavic) poetics, R. Picchio in his recent contribution to the volume honoring Taranovsky takes a different view of the formal structure of some of the Old Russian poetic texts previously discussed by Taranovsky.[34] As indicated already by the title of his essay, in which he also deals at some length with the inherent difficulties of neatly separating prose from poetry in Old Russian writing, Picchio, with some qualifications, obviously considers the texts cited by him for exemplification as written in prose. Thus, Picchio notes that "apparently, in Taranovsky's opinion, as well as in that of other scholars" — undoubtedly having in mind primarily Jakobson — "there is a considerable number of genuine poems, i.e., of literary works written in verse, still hiding behind the prosaic facade of a but superficially explored edifice of Old Russian literature". And he goes on to caution that "while the existence of a prosodic tradition in Russia, and more generally in the whole of the Orthodox Slavic area, in the Middle Ages, could hardly be denied by any heedful reader of

medieval Slavic texts, the fact remains that this poetic patrimony is still neither simple to detect nor easy to define".[35] He then compliments Taranovsky for squarely facing "the problem from a clearly. defined notion of the poetic structures which he tries to recognize in Old Russian works", in contradistinction to "the prosodic units which are impressionistically indicated, without any preliminary definition of the very object of the research, for example in Stender-Petersen's *Anthology*". Calling for first making sure "that we know exactly what we mean by both 'Old Russian *poetry*' and 'Old Russian *prose*'", Picchio states that the purpose of his own contribution is "to provide ... more information concerning some rhetorical patterns, which seem peculiar to Old Russian prose".[36] Some objections to his aprioristic wording (if not reasoning) and questionable method of quoting Old Russian texts notwithstanding, I find myself substantially in agreement with Picchio's approach and with his interpretation of the "isocolic principle" as expounded in some detail on the following pages. In his understanding, this is a recurrent poetic-stylistic device characteristic of rhythmized prose but not by itself constituting a means of converting prose into poetry proper (verse). For the isocolic structure does not cut across the boundaries of the syntactic (or, rather, syntagmatic, i.e., "natural") segmentation of the text in the sense of redistributing its prosodic units in a fashion that systematically — though not necessarily consistently — would run counter to the syntactic segmentation. Thus, by not super-imposing any new, "marked", i.e., poetically "distorted", articulation of the text, it fails to establish the most fundamental, viz., only universal, criterion defining versified, metric speech, as conceived, for example, in Buxštab's incisive if broad formulation regarding the "dual segmentation" of the text, quoted above.[37] Instead, the "isocolic principle" coincides with or merely further subdivides already existing larger syntactic units (or, more precisely, sequentially contiguous syntagms) into smaller prosodic entities producing a rhythmic ring in this artistically shaped and on occasion additionally poetically embroidered prose. While this analysis and interpretation obviously presuppose keen observation, it should be noted that a generalizing statement such as the following, although in fact capturing an essential perception, is bound rather to convey the impression of a certain lack of precision and objectivity: "Everyone familiar with Old Russian works sooner or later becomes subjugated by a kind of persistent melody resounding throughout hundreds of pages, which belong to different works and still seem to be following the same leading symphonic theme".[38] And, although specifically stating his awareness of "the problems which can rise in connection with the critical establishment of a given text" (so much in evidence, say, in Taranovsky's many references to Zarubin's scholarly edition of the *Molenie!*), Picchio by his decision to cite his textual excerpts from anthologies "for the reader's convenience" [?] cannot but raise some methodological doubts rather than giving us any reassurance about his relevant mode of procedure. For only modern critical editions reflect more or less adequately, of course, the actual state of preservation of a given literary text and its specific philological tradition.

Whether one in each and every instance will agree with Picchio's suggested breakdown of the prose texts adduced as illustrative material into the recurrent accentual units (cola) of two to five stressed syllables (or, where occurring in combination, of up to seven stresses) achieving the clearly perceivable rhythmization of these portions of prose text is another matter, to be sure. But I would like to state that I, for one, have few if any reservations regarding the way in which he suggests that the five passages selected from the Supplication of Daniel the Exile should be analyzed into isocolic sequences or alternations of such sequences.[39]

The conclusions which Picchio himself draws from his analysis and argumentation, while enlightening, seem at the same time to blur, in some respects, the basic problematics addressed in his paper. For after once more paying tribute to Jakobson and Taranovsky and speaking, now apparently metaphorically, of a "poetic treasury which still hides in many medieval Slavic works", Picchio closes with the following remarks: "In my opinion, the basic question still consists in how to reach a right definition of the poetic forms peculiar to Old Russian literature. What I call the 'isocolic principle' seems to pertain to a large section of Old Russian *prose*". And after having stated that in his view the text samples adduced by him cannot qualify as poems in the narrow sense, Picchio immediately adds that "this does not mean ... that specimens of genuine *poetry* are not to be found in the rhetorical context of some prose writings". And he goes even further to say that "the prosodic devices which I have tried to describe seem to entangle our problem even more, since the limits between prose and poetry very often are failing, because of the persistent prosodic structure of prose writing". And as a future task to consider he then mentions "that precisely this characterizing feature of Old Russian literature can give an answer to the question why a good deal of Old Russian poetry, apparently, was absorbed in the prose writing. Therefore", Picchio concludes, "one should not limit himself to attempting to extract neglected poems from prose, but should rather try to recognize the system of mutual prose-poetry relations conditioning the various poetic forms of Old Russian literature".[40] Similar views were voiced by Picchio also in another article written at about the same time (Picchio 1972).

While not all too fortunately phrased, and voicing an almost unexpected note of despondence as to the prospects of future research in the field, in my view there is nonetheless some obvious merit in Picchio's conclusions quoted above. For if we accept, as I think there is good reason to do, his "isocolic principle" as an organizing force of rhythm in Old Russian literature characteristic of artistic prose as well as poetry proper, it is easy to see how this accentual (tonic) patterning of a text, allowing, to be sure, for a fairly large degree of elasticity, could have been mistaken for a criterion *per se* of versification; yet it is not. It takes greater and more strict regularization, the organization of speech into more rigidly marked recurrent accentual units to achieve poetry proper, i.e., verse. Other poetic devices, and rhyme foremost among them (in Old Russian, as in Slavic generally, often grammatical or morphological and in particular verb rhyme), will frequently add to our perception of bound poetic speech as verse. Picchio is right, I would think, when he claims that a good deal of — original — Old Russian poetry may subsequently have been absorbed in, or rather submerged by, prose. However, see now the recent article by Zykov, on a particularly instructive instance of an adaptation and modification of an Old Church Slavic poem (the *Acrostic* or *Alphabet Prayer* by Constantine the Priest, subsequently bishop of Preslav). Dated toward the end of the Old Russian period — probably during the second half of the 17th century — this adaptation retained the verse form of the original poem. (See further the *Postscript* at the end of this paper).

In its earlier phase, Kievan Rus' is likely to have known at least two major genuine verse meters. One was indeed the imported prayer meter (*molitvoslovnyj stix*) which the Eastern Slavs had taken over from Old Church Slavic where, as relevant research by Sobolevskij, Trubeckoj, Nahtigal, and, in particular, Jakobson as well as some others has shown, it flourished in emulation of corresponding Byzantine meters to a considerable extent (Constantine-Cyril himself being the first outstanding Slavic poet).[41] While, to borrow Jakobson's phrase, Old Church Slavic versification constituted "the Slavic Reponse to Byzantine Poetry", this verbal art in metric form was originally entirely based on syllabification; cf. the artificial introduction of syllabic verse (*virši*) in Russian literature patterned on Polish and Ukrainian-Belorussian models in the 17th century. Echoes of Church Slavic poetry, ultimately going back to Byzantine models such as the hymns of a Romanus Melodus or adapted to and imitating the less sophisticated and occasionally somewhat monotonous patterns of medieval Latin hymnography, resound in early West Slavic — Czech and Polish — religious songs typically represented by the archaic *Hospodine pomiluj ny!* and the no less ancient, controversial *Bogurodzica*.[42] But only a few traces of it can be found in Old Russian writing. Even the grandiose — and much too little studied — *Kanon Moleben* by Kirill Turovskij (12th c.) turns out, upon closer scrutiny, to be but a masterful and undoubtedly highly poetic prose adaptation of a Byzantine prototype in verse; and his other great canon, *Kanon Pokajannyj,* supposedly written in the form of a Greek acrostic, has not come down to us, as far as is known.[43] What actually has been preserved of Russian Church Slavic poetry (as opposed to Russianized versions of earlier Old Church Slavic religious verse) does not amount to much and is not overly impressive; Čiževsky has counted some thirty such poems.[44] But the bulk of Russian Church Slavic poetry proper seems to have fallen victim to the ultimate dissolution of Slavic linguistic unity and to the remodeling of the syllabic structure of the Russian language resulting from the loss of the reduced vowels.

The other chief meter which in all likelihood was used in ancient Russia during the pre-Mongol period was presumably a predecessor of the epic (or 'heroic') *bylina* or *starina* verse (*bylinnyj stix*), known in several varieties which, although of folkloric origin and based on the tonic, not the syllabic principle, should not be confused with the narrative verse (*skazovyj stix*) recently discussed again by Taranovsky.[45] Of course, we can only tentatively reconstruct its original metric structure on the basis of later recordings and by resorting to comparative evidence.[46] At any rate, we must not conceive of the *bylina* verse as nearly as rigidly structured and displaying the same regularity as some epic meters from other language areas of medieval Europe such as, say, the *Nibelungenstrophe* (consistently made up of four lines having 6 + 6 + 6 + 7 stressed syllables).

4. Returning now to the *Molenie Daniila Zatočnika,* it is my opinion, therefore, that we have to do here with a piece (or, to be exact, a number of variant pieces) of rhythmized prose dominated by a prosodic poetic device referred to in Picchio's terminology as the "isocolic principle". But, needless to say, this rhythmization, though important and prominent, is not the only means by which this text is marked as eminently artistic. Other devices are attributable to its mixed (or "syncretic") stylistic genre, a genre of both didactic and rhetoric prose, gnomic and oratorical at the same time, even though this term in the narrow sense is perhaps somewhat inadequate when applied to such a rather unique literary work as the *Molenie.* Thus, for example, the Supplication abounds in metaphoric symbols, as noted by Adrianova-Peretc in her fine study on the poetic style of ancient Rus'.[47] Here are just a few of such symbolic similes used in various ways by Daniel the Exile:

> Вижу, господине, вся человѣки, яко солнцем, грѣеми
> милостию твоею, точию аз единъ яко трава, в застѣни
> израстущи, на нюже ни солнце сияетъ, ни дождь идетъ.[48]

Яко же дубъ крепится множеством корения,
тако и град нашь твоею державою.[49]

Вода мати рыбамъ, а ты, княже нашь, людем своимъ,
Весна украшает землю цветы, а ты насъ, княже,
украшаеши милостию своею.[50]

Обрати тучю милости твоея на землю худости моея
(var.: художества моего).[51]

Орел птица царь надо всѣми птицами, а осетръ над рыбами, а
лев над зверми, а ты, княже, над переславцы (var.: переа-
славцы). Левъ рыкнетъ, кто не устрашится; а ты, княже,
речеши, кто не убоится. Яко же бо змии страшен свистанием
своимъ, тако и ты, княже нашь, грозенъ множеством (силных,
var.) вои. Злато красота женам, а ты, княже, людемъ своимъ.
Тѣло крепится жилами, а мы, княже, твоею державою. Птен-
цы радуются веснѣ, а младенцы матери, а мы, княже, тебѣ.
Гусли строятся персты, а град нашь твоею державою.[52]

And, as Adrianova-Peretc points out,[53] Daniel likens a man humbled by fate,
a human failure, to a *древо сухо при пути, смоковница она бесплодная
проклятая* — the latter a simile borrowed from the parables of the gospels,
while he calls a cunning man *змея лукавая* — a metaphor later applied to the
woman seducing a youth (in the 17th century story *Povest' o Savve Grudcyne*).

Hand in hand with these symbolic metaphors and similes runs an antithetic
composition through a good portion of the *Molenie.* Down to the syntactic
structure of the text, where sentences are either strung together by means of
the coordinating-contrasting conjunction *a* or subordinate clauses are introduced by a conditional or concessive conjunction, the rhetoric of this literary
work is to a very large extent built on antitheses. The linguistic sophistication
expressing itself in a feeling for punning and playing with words, their sound
and meaning, was exemplified above with the famous passage where clauses
beginning with *komu ... a mně ...* contrast with each other.[54] And the author
demonstrates his learning not only with numerous quotes and echoes from the
Bible, especially the Psalter, the Book of Proverbs, the Wisdom of Solomon,
and the Gospels as well as from Byzantine sources (such as the Sayings of
Menander, cf. n. 33), but also by resorting to the classic humility topos of
Byzantine literature (used widely also, for example, in Old Russian
hagiography):

Аз бо не во Афинех ростох, ни от философ научихся, но бых
падая аки пчела по различным цветомъ и оттуду избирая
сладость словесную, и совокупляя мудрость, яко в мѣхъ воду
морскую.[55]

The literary *Melissa/Pčela* theme is also clearly echoed in these lines marked by a consciously euphonic selection and combination of words, thus being something of an early harbinger of the both learned and emotional "sweet new style" of the Second South Slavic Influence and its Byzantine models. A sophisticated combination of learned and euphonic style also characterizes the proud and exuberant openings lines of the *Molenie*:

> Вострубим убо, братие, аки в златокованную трубу, въ разумъ ума своего и начнемъ бити в сребреныя арганы во извѣстие мудрости, и ударимъ в бубны ума своего, поюще в богодохновенныя свирѣли, да восплачются в нас душеполезныя помыслы. Востани слава моя, востани псалтыр и гусли.[56]

As Lixačev has noted, both the simile and the antithesis are further developments of the poetic means of "stylistic symmetry" anchored in and best illustrated with examples from the Psalter. For both modifications of stylistic symmetry (viz., to the device of the simile, leading to a violation of the principle of symmetry, and to that of the antithesis) he quotes examples from the *Slovo Daniila Zatočnika.*[57]

A further strong argument against considering the Supplication to be written in some sort of uniform verse (of two kinds, in the narrow technical sense of the term) is of course the well-known fact that, to a large, though not yet fully determined, extent, it consists of secondary integrated material of quite heterogeneous origin — direct or only slightly reworked quotations from other translated as well as original Slavic literary texts. (As communicated to me by Professor J. Holthusen, Munich, a former student of his, Mr. B. Enck, Bochum, working on the *Molenie,* has established a remarkably high share of direct quotations and literary paraphrases in the text of the Supplication, a share approaching as much as 50 percent.) As just one further example of such inclusion of bits and pieces from other, partly much earlier Slavic textual material, one could point to the close paraphrase in the *Molenie* of a passage encountered in the *Besěda na novojavivšuju sja eresь Bogumilu* by the 10th century Bulgarian writer Kozma Presviter (Cosmas the Priest), recently noted by Begunov (1973:38-41).

The passage quoted and the observations they suggest should suffice, I would think, to leave no doubt whatsoever that the Supplication of Daniel the Exile, though written in prose, is a work of great poetic value and power. One may ask, in closing, whether the fact that it, like some kindred works of Old Russian literature, is written in rhythmic prose and, as I have tried to show, not regular meter[58] detracts from its artistic qualities, from its eminent poeticity. To this my own answer can only be unequivocally negative. For I believe that Ju. Lotman is right when, following Hegel, he characterizes artistic prose as the secondary, derived, and — one may add — marked category of verbal art in relation to poetry proper, verse being the primary and "natural" category of poetic language, both historically and typologically.[59] Also, in this connection. A. Belyj's pertinent remark of 1919 comes to mind: "Proza — trudnejšaja forma poèzii".[60]

Postscript. Only after this paper was completed was I able to familiarize myself with the article "Le strutture prosodiche dello *Slovo Daniila Zatočnika*" by Professor Michele Colucci, Bologna, a former student of Professor Picchio, appearing in *Ricerche Slavistiche* XX (1973), 1-41 (to be released in January, 1975). I am indebted to Professor Picchio for bringing this article to my attention and for making a preprint of it available to me. Applying to the *Slovo* of Daniel the Exile his teacher's "isocolic principle" (by Picchio further elaborated in his Warsaw Congress contribution; see Picchio 1973b: esp. 457-64 and 467, *sub* 5), Colucci demonstrates convincingly, in my view, and in detail the validity and indeed applicability of the proposed interpretation of prosodic patterning to this particular Old Russian literary text. Some conceivable minor points of difference of opinion as regards the actual scansion, yielding in part slightly different groupings of cola — a possibility acknowledged, incidentally, also by Picchio; cf. esp 1973b: 462 — do not, it would seem to me, detract from the overall relevance of the prosodic principle first clearly discerned and defined for medieval Slavic literature by Picchio.

University of California, Los Angeles

NOTES

[1] Cf., e.g., the acute statement by B. Ja. Buxštab (110-11) recently: "Вопрос о разграничении стиха и прозы не решен в науке, требует дальнейшего исследования. Скажу здесь лишь тезисно, что основной признак стиха удобнее всего, по моему мнению, определить, как признак двойной сегментации текста. Любой текст членится на соподчиненные синтаксические отрезки, но в стихотворном тексте с этим членением сочетается членение на стихотворные строки и на более крупные и мелкие, чем строка, стиховые единства. Это второе членение то совпадает, то расходится с первым, создавая бесчисленные возможности ритмико-синтаксических соотношений. Эта двойственность, эта соотнесенность двух членений — основной признак стиха. Поэт и членит стихотворение на стиховые строки так, чтобы создавались нужные соотношения, — но там, где второе членение не маркировано (графикой, рифмовкой и т.п.) — мы не можем утверждать, что имеем дело со стихами; так обстоит дело, скажем, со *Словом о полку Игореве*. ... Немало споров велось и ведется о признаках *свободного стиха*. Я думаю, что свободный стих — это стих, в котором нет

никаких постоянных признаков стиха, кроме общего признака двойной сегментации текста. Присоединим свободный стих к уже рассмотренным в качестве особого типа." I will in the following return to this cautious and tentative definition of verse. For a detailed discussion of the specifics of poetry proper (verse) as opposed to prose, see in particular Lotman 1970:120-242, esp. 120-32 and 191-4; 1972:23-33. On the prose/poetry distinction and its problematics in Old Russian literature, see further the pertinent work by Jakobson, Pančenko, Pozdneev, and, in particular, Taranovsky and Picchio to be discussed below.

² Cf. Birnbaum 1975.

³ For a sober account of the controversy regarding the relationship of the Igor' Tale and the *Zadonščina,* particularly in its more recent phase (centered around the views of A. A. Zimin and the discussion they evoked), cf. Fennell, 191-206, who without himself taking a definite stand does not rule out the possibility of the *Slovo* being a late 18th c. forgery, to be sure, by "a man of singular genius and almost superhuman knowledge"; see also *ibid.,* 97-107, for an assessment of the *Zadonščina* and its artistic qualities, acknowledged also, e.g., by D. S. Worth who considers it a "self-contained work of artistic *prose*" [emphasis added, H.B.]. For a strongly worded plea for the 12th c. origin of the Igor' Tale (and a vehement attack on latter-day skeptics, esp. A. Mazon and A. A. Zimin), see the arguments adduced by one of the most passionate believers in the authenticity of the *Slovo,* R. Jakobson 1966:654-704 and 738-51. For a recent attempt to ascribe the authorship of the Igor' Tale to Karamzin (or at any rate to a "Karamzinist" of the *novyj slog*) see now Trost.

⁴ If the Igor' Tale is indeed an authentic original of the late 12th c., the frequent echoes of the *Zadonščina* and the more rare traces of the *Molenie* and of the *Slovo o pogibeli* can all be considered secondary literary reminiscences; otherwise such parallels, where not coincidental, may point to various, in part perhaps as yet unknown common sources. Assuming the first alternative, cf. also Solov'ev and Jakobson 1966:50, 150, 158-9, 226, 234-5 (fnn. 95-6), 282-3, 402-3 (fn. 7), 656. Generally on the *Slovo o pogibeli* and its problematics, see Begunov 1965 who in discussing the rhythmic structure of this work (123-34) mentions that, contrary to the findings of, e.g., R. Abicht and E. Hofmann, a majority of contemporary scholars (D. S. Lixačev and I. P. Eremin, among them) consider the Igor' Tale written in rhythmic prose, not in verse, and arrives at the conclusion that the *Slovo o pogibeli,* too, is composed in rhythmic prose rather than in verse, as, e.g., A. V. Solov'ev and A. Stender-Petersen would have it (133). Among recent proponents of the *Slovo o pogibeli* as "entirely built on the syntactic-intonational model of the narrative verse", see Taranovsky 1968:387-9. For some echoes of this text in the Kirillo-Belozersky (KB) copy of the *Zadonščina,* cf. Begunov 1965:135-7. The *Slovo o pogibeli* and the Igor' Tale (if an authentic 12th c. text) are also unique in sharing an early pan-Russian ideology. On the poetic form of the Igor' Tale (rhythmized prose vs. verse), see also Dmitriev, 135, critical of the renewed attempt by Timofeev to read versification into the rhythmic structure of the *Slovo.* For some valid criticism of Timofeev's position, cf. further Lotman 1970:374 (n. 26), pointing to the metric organization of a poetic text as a potent mechanism for preserving it from distortion. And, as Lotman also indicates, an imcomprehensible word of a versified text would normally be replaced by a copyist with an isometric one. Also Picchio (1972) considers the Igor' Tale written in — rhythmically structured — prose.

⁵ Cf. Birnbaum 1974a:242-8 (with further references in particular to work by D. Čiževsky in fn. 45).

⁶ See Birnbaum 1974a:29-30. Cf. further also Čiževksy 1948:96-8 (where the section headed "Die Versdichtung" opens with the sweeping statement: "Es sieht so aus, als ob die altrussische Literatur überhaupt keine Versdichtung besaß!").

⁷ By way of exemplification reference can be made here to Čiževsky 1948:374-81; 1960:131-5; 1968:70; Stender-Petersen 1957:150-3; Picchio 1959:122-8 (aptly characterizing the *Molenie* as representing "il sotrato ritmico popolare dello stile dotto" and as shedding light on the "origini del ritmo nella prosa anticorussa"); Skripil' 1958:151-6; Gudzij, 178-88; Eremin, 128-33; Pereverzev, 103-13; Jakubowski, 68-71 (explicitly labeling our text a "zabytek staroruskiej świeckiej prozy oratorskiej"); Lixačev 1973:57-8.

[8] This applies, for example, to Trubeckoy and Fennell. In view of the exceptional literary qualities of the *Molenie* I cannot always find such omission justified, however. Thus, in my review of Trubeckoy's posthumously published "Lectures on Old Russian Literature" (Birnbaum 1974b), I expressed my surprise that the author had not also discussed the *Molenie* which, in all probability, is a product of the same refined literary court tradition (cf. esp. also Budovnic) to which Trubeckoy is inclined to attribute the Igor' Tale, the latter, in his opinion, "kein Gedicht im gewöhnlichen Sinne des Wortes, sondern ein Werk in Prosa, freilich in einer deutlich rhythmischen Prosa" and "ein Produkt nicht der volkstümlichen, sondern der künstlichen [read: *kunstvollen, H.B.*] Fürstenhofpoesie"; cf. Trubeckoy 1973:61-76, esp. 64-5 and 73. For a somewhat different view, once more stressing the close ties of the *Slovo* with literary folklore, see, e.g., Dmitriev, 133-4, where, in addition, the rhetoric character of the Igor' Tale and the classic as well as Byzantine parallels (studied in detail by I. P. Eremin) are pointed out.

[9] Cf. Obnorskij, 81-131.

[10] Cf. Vinogradov 1961:53.

[11] Cf., to cite just a few examples, the studies by Budovnic, Skripi' 1955, and Voronin, with references to much of the earlier relevant literature. See now also Colucci.

[12] On some of the sources of the *Izbornik* of 1076, see most recently Meščerskij (with further bibliography); on the aphorisms of that text and their relation to Russian proverbs, cf. Adrianova-Peretc 1970. For some reinterpreted secular (erotic) sources of the *Pčela*, see Egunov.

[13] Cf. Voronin, 54.

[14] Cf. Tixomirov.

[15] Cf. Zarubin, iv and ix-x.

[16] Cf. Zarubin, ix, and Voronin, 55 and 84; see also Eremin, 132-3.

[17] Cf. Zarubin, iii-iv.

[18] See Lixačev 1973:57-8 (and in previous relevant writing by him); cf. also Pereverzev, 111-12, and, on the other hand, "declining to see in it traces *skomoroš'ego balagurstva*", Taranovsky 1968:393.

[19] See Taranovsky 1968:390.

[20] Cf., among others, Vinogradov 1969:10-14, esp. 12-14; see further also, e.g., Bartoszewicz, 72-3.

[21] Note that Taranovsky's "prayer verse" corresponds to what otherwise is frequently referred to as "contacarium verse" (R *kondakarnyj stix*), a term which Taranovsky (1968:377, fn. 1) prefers to reserve for a particular — which? — variety of the prayer verse. Yet another term roughly corresponding to "prayer verse" is "psalm verse" (Cz *žalmový verš*); cf. Birnbaum 1974a:30 (with further references in fn. 28).

[22] Cf. Taranovsky 1968:390; see also Zarubin, 36.

[23] Taranovsky 1968:389-90.

[24] Although in the introduction to his *Anthology of Old Russian Literature* (1954:viii) Stender-Petersen explicitly states that "the driest prosaist may suddenly shift to the most delicate lyricism; *but this lyricism never assumes the form of versified poetry*" [emphasis added, H.B.], it is hard to believe that the Danish Slavist by his freely exercised graphic rendition of the texts selected by him was not occasionally implying a poetic interpretation as — perhaps free — verse.

[25] Cf. the broad definition of verse as marked, primarily, by the dual segmentation of the text, suggested by Buxštab (quoted in n. 1, above). On the "two dimensions" constituting the essence of versified poetry, see also Taranovsky 1966:180-1.

[26] I can therefore also not quite agree with Taranovsky when he claims (168:379, fn. 5) that it is only the presence of end rhyme that will make those who otherwise tend to characterize non-rhyming prayer verse as merely rhythmic prose accept it as versified speech.

[27] Cf. *ibid.*, 391.

[28] Cf. Jakobson 1966:455-9.

[29] Cf. Jakobson's statement (*ibid.*, 455-6): "Some kind of homœoteleuton or rhyme usually links either the two colons or a part of consecutive lines; masculine rhymes with the word accent on the end-syllable of the line are favored for this purpose...."

30   Cf. Taranovsky 1968:383-7.

31   Cf. *ibid.*, 388, fn. 18.

32   See the references quoted in n. 4, above; cf. further also Picchio 1973a:320-2.

33   It should be noted, incidentally, that the term *mirskie pritči* is used not only, as indicated by Taranovsky 1968:392, on pp. 69, 72, 95 (and elsewhere, e.g., p. 26) in Zarubin's edition within the text, but, in addition, it also appears in the heading of one reworked and abridged version of the *Slovo*, represented by two manuscripts, the Pogodin and Vladimir copies, the *Slovo o mirskix pritčax i bytejskix veščex*, which besides extracts from the *Slovo Daniila Zatočnika* also contains some of the sayings found in Menander's Περὶ γυναικῶν. Cf. Zarubin, viii-ix and 39-48; for bibliography on Menander's aphorisms and their early Slavic versions, see Krumbacher, 601-2. Whatever the rhythmization of these sayings, it was not the "rhythmic system" as such that the Old Russian author labeled *mirskie pritči* as one would gather from Taranovsky's wording.

34   Cf. Picchio 1973a, esp. 320-1 and 324-5. Notice that in his reluctance to openly disagree with Taranovsky's "skillful interpretation" of the Discourse, Picchio contemplates the possibility of "consider[ing] this fragment a poem" but suggests that "we should not underestimate the possibility of also putting this *Slovo* into a regular isocolic context ..."; but cf. also Picchio's remark in the closing section of his essay (331): "In fact, I don't see how one could qualify as 'poems' the examples of rhythmically organized prose which I have cited in this paper.". As indicated above, I, for my part, see no need to interpret the *Slovo o pogibeli* as poetry proper but would rather think that its undoubtedly very poetic language and lyrical tone have induced some scholars to detect a formalized meter in a literary piece which in actuality is merely highly rhythmized, artistic prose; see also n. 4, above.

35   See Picchio 1973a:300.

36   Cf. *ibid.*, 301. For a similar assessment of Stender-Petersen's somewhat impressionistic approach to identifying, at will, Old Russian poetry and rhythmic prose, partly by the purely mechanical device of suggestive typesetting, see above, n. 24.

37   Cf. n. 1. For some further thoughts on the specifics of verse (in contradistinction to prose), see also, e.g., Cohen, esp. 53-104 (ch. II: "Niveau phonique: la versification"). For some earlier discussion by Picchio of the "isocolic principle" or "isocolic structure", see Picchio 1970/72 with additional references, esp. in n. 1 (p. 491), and a tentative definition in n. 3 (pp. 419-20). For some further, more recent reasoning in support of his "isocolic principle", see now also Picchio 1973b.

38   Cf. Picchio 1973a:301.

39   See *ibid.*, 324-5, cf. now also Colucci, esp. 26-41, and *Postscript.*

40   Cf. *ibid.*, 331.

41   For a fairly rich set of references, see Birnbaum 1974a:30-1 (fn.. 28 and 29) and 365. Of basic relevant literature, cf. also Jakobson 1953, esp. 37-55.

42   Cf. Birnbaum 1974a:260-98 and 368-9, with ample further references.

43   Cf. Stender-Petersen 1957:58-63, esp. 62-3; Čiževsky 1948:98.

44   See Čiževsky 1948:98.

45   In fact, as was pointed out by Taranovsky 1968:381, n. 8, the *bylina* verse and the prayer meter can combine, in a reincarnated form, in the *vers libre* of the Symbolists, shown with a stanza taken from a poem by A. Dobroljubov.

46   Cf. Jakobson 1953:23-36; 1966:434-44. Of more recent work, see now also Jones. For a somewhat different view of the evolution of poetry in the Old Russian period (11th through 17th cc.), see also Pozdneev who points to the origins of Russian poetry in ecclesiastic chant rather than in formal versification and who also suggests some modifications in the current notions concerning the tonic *bylina* verse and its relationship to the prayer (or, in his terminology, *contacarium*) meter (23-4); cf. further also Pančenko.

47   Cf. Andrianova-Peretc 1947: 21, 44, 51, 84, 87, and 94. Note that Lixačev 1971 distinguishes between symbolic metaphors (R *metafory-simvoly,* the same term as that used by Adrianova-Peretc) and similes (or simply comparisons, R *sravnenija*) in Old Russian literature. Cf. 175-84 and 193-202; for the use of the latter literary device in the *Molenie,* see 196-7.

[48]   See Zarubin, 54.
[49]   *Ibid.*, 59.
[50]   *Ibid.*, 60.
[51]   *Ibid.*, 62-4.
[52]   *Ibid.*, 66.
[53]   Cf. Adrianova-Peretc 1947:121.
[54]   See Zarubin, 61.
[55]   *Ibid.*, 59. The last portion of the quotation echoes Psalms 34,7; cf. *Ps. Sin.* (ed. S. Sever'janov), 39: *Sъbirajęi ěko vъ měxъ vody morъskyję.* (I am indebted to Prof. J. Holthusen for bringing this parallelism to my attention.)
[56]   *Ibid.*, 53; cf. also the *Slovo* variant; *ibid.*, 4. On the latter, see also Lixačev 1971:191.
[57]   Cf. Lixačev 1971:185-92, esp. 191-2.
[58]   It should be noted that Taranovsky is not the only one to recently detect verse in the *Molenie*. Thus, for example, reflexes of a "declamatory verse" (*deklamacionnyj stix*) are claimed to be ascertainable in our text by Pančenko, 170-1.
[59]   Cf. Lotman 1970:128 where he states, "художественная проза возникла на фоне определенной поэтической системы как ее отрицание"; and 1972:23-33, where (23-4) we read: "стихотворная речь (равно как и распев, пение) была первоначально единственно возможной речью словесного искусства. Этим достигалось 'расподобление' языка художественной литературы, отделение его от обычной речи. И лишь затем начиналось 'уподобление': из этого — уже относительно резко 'непохожего' — материала создавалась картина действительности, средствами человеческого языка строилась модель-знак. Если язык по отношению к действительности выступал как некая воспроизводящая структура, то литература представляла собой структуру структур." And *ibid.*, 26, Lotman declares: "эстетическое восприятие прозы оказалось возможным лишь на фоне поэтической культуры. Проза — явление более позднее, чем поэзия, возникшее в эпоху хронологически более зрелого эстетического сознания." And though Lotman applies this particular reasoning to the period of Puškin with whom prose in the modern sense of the word is said to take its beginning in Russian literature, it is, I would contend, *mutatis mutandis* also true of the medieval period of Russian verbal art. Much earlier already, Hegel stated: "Die *Poesie* ist älter als das kunstreich ausgebildete prosaische Sprechen" (1970:240; original posthumous edition, based on lectures read in Berlin in the 1820s, 1838:239).
[60]   See Belyj, 55 (quoted by Sazonova, 35).

REFERENCES

Andrianova-Peretc, V. P.
    1947   *Očerki poètičeskogo stilja drevnej Rusi.* Moscow & Leningrad: Izd-vo AN SSSR.
    1970   "Aforizmy Izbornika Svjatoslava 1076 g. i russkie poslovicy", *TODRL* XXV, 3-19.
Bartoszewicz, A.
    1973   *Istorija russkogo literaturnogo jazyka*, I (*Donacional'nyj period*). Warsaw: PWN.
Begunov, Ju. K.
    1965   *Pamjatnik russkoj literatury XIII veka: "Slovo o pogibeli Russkoj zemli".* Moscow & Leningrad: Nauka.
    1973   *Kozma Presviter v slavjanskix literaturax.* Sofia: Izd-vo BAN.
Belyj, A.
    1919   "O xudožestvennoj proze", *Gorn* 2-3, 49-55.

Birnbaum, H.
    1974a *On Medieval and Renaissance Slavic Writing: Selected Essays.* The Hague & Paris:
           Mouton (= *SPR* 266).
    1974b [Review of] N. S. Trubeckoy, *Vorlesungen über die altrussische Literatur, WdSl* (in press).
    1975   "On the Significance of the Second South Slavic Influence for the Evolution of the
           Russian Literary Language", *IJSLP* (in press).
Budovnic, I. U.
    1951   "Pamjatnik rannej dvorjanskoj publicistiki (Molenie Daniila Zatočnika)", *TODRL* VIII,
           138-57.
Buxštab, B. Ja.
    1973   "Ob osnovax i tipax russkogo stixa", *IJSLP* XVI, 96-118.
Cohen, Jean
    1966   *Structure du langage poétique.* Paris: Flammarion.
Colucci, M.
    1973   "Le strutture prosodiche dello *Slovo Daniila Zatočnika*", *RicSlav* XX [1975], 1-11.
Čiževsky, D.
    1948   *Geschichte der altrussischen Literatur im 11., 12. und 13. Jahrhundert: Kiever Epoche,*
           Frankfurt/M: Klostermann.
    1960   *History of Russian Literature: From the Eleventh Century to the End of the Baroque.* The
           Hague: Mouton (= *SPR* 12).
    1968   *Abriss der altrussischen Literatur.* Munich: Fink (= *Forum·Slavicum* 9).
Dmitriev, L. A.
    1964   "Važnejšie problemy issledovanija 'Slova o polku Igoreve'", *TODRL* XX, 120-38.
Egunov, A. N.
    1969   "Erotici scriptores v drevnerusskoj 'Pčele'", *TODRL* XXIV, 101-4.
Eremin, I. P.
    1968   *Lekcii po drevnej russkoj literature.* Leningrad: Izd-vo LU.
Fennell, J., and A. Stokes
    1974   *Early Russian Literature.* Berkeley & Los Angeles: UC Press.
Gudzij, N. K.
    1966   *Istorija drevnej russkoj literatury.* 7th ed. Moscow: Prosveščenie.
Hegel, G. W. F.
    1970   *Werke* 15: *Vorlesungen über Ästhetik* III. Frankfurt/M: Suhrkamp (first edition: Berlin:
           Dunckel und Humblot, 1838).
Jakobson, R.
    1953   "The Kernel of Comparative Slavic Literature", *Harvard Slavic Studies* I, 1-71.
    1966   *Selected Writings, IV: Slavic Epic Studies.* The Hague & Paris: Mouton.
Jakubowski, W.
    1970   "Piśmiennictwo państwa kijowskiego (XI-XIII w.)", ch. 1 (31-72) of: *Literatura
           rosyjska. Podręcznik,* I. Warsaw: PWN.
Jones, R. G.
    1972   *Language and Prosody of the Russian Folk Epic.* The Hague & Paris: Mouton (= *SPR*
           275).
Krumbacher, K.
    1897   *Geschichte der byzantinischen Litteratur* ..., I. 2nd ed. Munich, 1897 (= *Hb. d. klass.
           Altertumswiss.* 9) [Reprint: New York: Burt Franklin, 1958].
Lixačev, D. S.
    1954   "Social'nye osnovy stilja 'Molenija' Daniila Zatočnika", *TODRL* X, 106-19.
    1970   *Čelovek v literature drevnej Rusi.* 2nd ed. Moscow: Nauka.
    1971   *Poètika drevnerusskoj literatury.* 2nd ed. Leningrad: Xudožestvennaja Literatura.
    1973   *Razvitie russkoj literatury X-XVII vekov: Èpoxi i stili.* Leningrad: Nauka.

Lotman, Ju. M.
1970   *Struktura xudožestvennogo teksta.* Moscow: Iskusstvo.
1972   *Analiz poètičeskogo teksta: Struktura stixa.* Leningrad: Prosveščenie.
Meščerskij, N. A.
1972   "K voprosu ob istočnikax 'Izbornika 1076 goda'", *TODRL* XXVII, 321-8.
Obnorskij, S. P.
1946   *Očerki po istorii russkogo literaturnogo jazyka staršego perioda.* Moscow & Leningrad: Izd-vo AN SSSR.
Pančenko, A. M.
1964   "Perspektivy issledovanija istorii drevnerusskogo stixotvorstva", *TODRL* XX, 256-73.
Pereverzev, V. F.
1971   *Literatura drevnej Rusi.* Moscow: Nauka.
Picchio, R.
1959   *Storia della letteratura russa antica.* Milan: Nuova Accademia Editrice.
1970/72 "Strutture isocoliche e poesia slava medievale: A proposito dei capitoli III e XIII della *Vita Constantini*", *RicSlav* XVII-XIX [1973], 419-45.
1972   "On the Prosodic Structure of the *Igor Tale*", *SEEJ* 16, 147-62.
1973a   "The Isocolic Principle in Old Russian Prose", *Slavic Poetics: Essays in honor of Kiril Taranovsky,* R. Jakobson, C. H. van Schooneveld, D. S. Worth, eds., 299-331, The Hague & Paris: Mouton.
1973b   "Models and Patterns in the Literary Tradition of Medieval Orthodox Slavdom", *American Contributions to the Seventh International Congress of Slavists, II: Literature and Folklore,* V. Terras, ed., 439-67. The Hague & Paris: Mouton.
Pozdneev, A. V.
196   "Stixosloženie drevnej russkoj poèzii", *ScSl* XI, 5-24.
Romanov, B. A.
1966   *Ljudi i˘ nravy drevnej Rusi: Istoriko-bytovye očerki XI-XIII vv.* 2nd ed. Moscow & Leningrad: Nauka.
Sazonova, L. I.
1974   "Princip ritmičeskoj organizacii v proizvedenijax tvorčestvennogo krasnorečija staršej pory ('Slovo o zakone i blagodati' Ilariona, 'Poxvala sv. Simeonu i sv. Savve' Domentiana)", *TODRL* XXVIII, 30-46.
Skripil', M. O.
1955   "'Slovo Daniila Zatočnika'", *TODRL* XI, 72-95.
1958   "Literatura vtoroj četverti XIII veka — 1380-x godov. Veduščaja rol' v literature nacional'no osvoboditel'noj temy", ch. 4 (134-67) of: *Istorija russkoj literatury, I (Literatura X-XVIII vekov).* Moscow & Leningrad: Izd-vo AN SSSR.
Solov'ev, A. V.
1953   "New Traces of the *Igor Tale* in Old Russian Literature", *Harvard Slavic Studies* I, 73-81.
Stender-Petersen, A. (ed.)
1954   *Anthology of Old Russian Literature,* in collaboration with S. Congrat-Butlar. New York & London: Columbia University Press (3rd printing, 1966).
Stender-Petersen, A.
1957   *Geschichte der russischen Literatur, I.* Munich: Beck.
Taranovsky, K.
1966   "Osnovnye zadači statističeskogo izučenija slavjanskogo stixa", *Poetics — Poetyka — Poètika,* II, 173-96. Warsaw & the Hague: PWN & Mouton.
1968   "Formy obščeslavjanskogo i cerkovnoslavjanskogo stixa v drevnerusskoj literature XI-XIII vv.", *American Contributions to the Sixth International Congress of Slavists, I: Linguistic Contributions,* H. Kučera, ed., 377-94. The Hague & Paris: Mouton.
Timofeev, L. I.
1963   "Ritmika 'Slova o polku Igoreve'", *Russkaja literatura* 1963: 1, 88-104.

Tixomirov, M. N.
1954 "'Napisanie' Daniila Zatočnika", *TODRL* X, 269-79.
Trost, K.
1974 "Karamzin und das Igorlied", *AnzfslPh* VII, 128-45.
Trubeckoy, N. S.
1973 *Vorlesungen über die altrussische Literatur.* Florence: Licosa (= *SHPh, Sectio Slavica* 1).
Tschiževskij *see* Čiževsky
Vinogradov, V. V.
1961 "Osnovnye problemy izučenija obrazovanija i razvitija drevnerusskogo literaturnogo jazyka", *Issledovanija po slavjanskomu jazykoznaniju,* 4-113. Moscow: Izd-vo AN SSSR.
1969 "Osnovnye voprosy i zadači izučenija istorii russkogo jazyka do XVIII v.", *VJa* 6, 3-34.
Voronin, N. N.
1967 "Daniil Zatočnik", *Drevnerusskaja literatura i ee svjazi s novym vremenem,* 54-101. Moscow: Nauka.
Zarubin, N. N.
1932 *Slovo Daniila Zatočnika po redakcijam XII i XIII vv. i ix peredelkam.* Leningrad: Izd-vo AN SSSR (= *PDRL* 3).
Zykov, E. G.
1974 "Russkaja peredelka drevnebolgarskogo stixotvorenija", *TODRL* XXVIII, 308-16.

COMMENTS

(Bailey) I do not think that your criticism of Taranovsky's innovative and perceptive elucidation of *molitvoslovnyj stix* is based on valid principles. Poetry does not have to be 'metric' for it to be considered poetry. Actually a number of organizing elements may be regarded as contributing to the structure of a poem: meter, rhyme, stanzaic form, various kinds of parallelism, the intonational unity of each line, and alliteration. A poet, in a given poem, may choose to make one or any combination of these features fixed, or he may even vary them. Viewed from this broader standpoint, some types of free verse may be very tightly organized but still be without meter; blank verse, which is unrhymed and may have a large amount of enjambement, is relatively 'free' in many respects but it still retains meter, the iambic pentameter. Your definition of poetry as being only metrical would exclude much Biblical poetry, medieval liturgical chants in which the end of the line is marked by a special type of performance clausula, and modern free verse. Even free verse, as Žovtis has shown in his book *Stixi nužny,* may furthermore consist of a variety of organizing elements which vary from one section to another. You also seem to imply that *skazovyj stix* also does not represent verse since it has no meter. Actually such verse, particularly in proverbs, sayings, and riddles, often is metrical. But even when this verse is not metrical it usually still has two fixed elements: rhyme and the intonational independence of each line. The last element is a typical feature of folk verse in general. One needs only to leaf

through the volume *Narodno-poètičeskaja satira* to find numerous examples of *skazovyj stix*. I would not translate this term as 'narrative verse' but simply 'spoken verse' to indicate its spoken form of performance as opposed to true folk narrative verse (epics, ballads, and lamentations) which basically are recitative, and sung verse which essentially includes lyric songs. Furthermore, the *bylinnyj stix* really consists of several meters, including trochaic, and it is not just tonic. In origin, some of these meters were isosyllabic as well. I think that Taranovsky has made a first step in expanding our knowledge and understanding of medieval poetry, but you in essence have taken a step backwards by insisting, as scholars so often did in the eighteenth and nineteenth centuries, that poetry was not poetry unless it was also metric.

(de Mallac)   I do not wish to address myself to the more specific aspects of Professor Birnbaum's paper, but only to raise a point in connection with an assumption underlying it — i.e. the assumption that there necessarily exists a straight poetry/prose polarity, according to an obvious binary pattern.

It seems to me that such a simplified bipolarity was a helpful generalization in Hegel's time, while now (with all due respect to Hegel) this scheme requires to be somewhat refined. From a historical standpoint, the complex genealogy of the *Poème en prose,* of poetic prose should be taken into account. From a generic viewpoint, in various passages (notably the opening sections) of his *The Bow and the Lyre* (Austin, 1973) Octavio Paz gives an interesting picture (in an essayistic rather than scholarly vein) of the complex plurality of types and genres that exist under the general rubric of what is (often and conveniently, but much too loosely) referred to as 'poetry'. All of this militates against too univocal or uncritical a use of the term 'poetry' viewed as a self-evident major category or type of literature. Finally, at what may be viewed — genetically — as the near-terminal or terminal point of a process, Max Bense's "theory of the text" (as developed in his *Aesthetica: Eine Einführung in die Ästhetik,* Baden-Baden, 1965) points out a *Jenseits* of the contradistinction between prose and poetry. All of this does, in my opinion, call for a revision of the 'simple' prose/poetry polarity used as a methodological assumption. I do not see that Lotman has adequately addressed himself to this problem.

(Marvan)   1. In connection with your paper I would like to mention some specific methodological problems of old texts. Their formal poetic investigation must start (or terminate) with establishing (or disproving) the deep system (poetic *langue*). The system, however, can be approached only through the concrete texts, i.e. its surface realization (poetic parole). In older literature

— besides the problems connected with our limited knowledge of the language — we also face the problem of much higher probability of channel disturbances between the depth and surface (intention and implementation). Thus the text which was intended to be poetic might be perceived by us (but not usually by its original addressees) as formally non-poetic. If we have enough data (more substantial texts, school, generation) representing the underlying system, the chances of reconstructing it are rather good, but such a task can be next to impossible if the surface data are limited, as the intention and unintentional interferences cannot be properly separated. I think that some Russian texts, esp. those without any considerable radiation, belong to the latter category.

2. A brief remark on 'Constantinian' poetry: I agree that Constantine-Cyril was a key personality in creating Slavic poetry. But his primary importance is his 'radiation'. If it could be claimed that he created a school and tradition (which in my opinion was the case), his activity would not be depreciated but more properly and more highly appreciated, although the question of his authorship would remain open for further investigation and specification.

(Meijer)   Agreed that the *Supplication* is not poetry, but highly stylized prose. But is the cause for that not to be found in the sources? Proverbs etc. are highly rhythmicized. An author working with such material in a rhetorical framework can hardly fail to be influenced by this rhythmization.

(Winner)   You raised very important issues of poetic language in your theoretical discussions of the boundary between poetry and prose. I believe this is a question that must be approached historically. I believe it is futile to look for absolute and timeless definitions which would mark prose as distinct from poetry. We could establish formal criteria which could tell us with absolute certainty: this is verse/this is prose. Since, I believe, we all agree that prose is the marked form, it is natural that in the period of its early development the marked form should exhibit many features of the unmarked form. Hence in your *Molenie* ... you find strongly marked rhythmic elements. But this changes. In 19th-century prose, we find few of the types of equivalents which we usually associate with verse — rhythm, rhyme, etc. In the prose of symbolism, and already in that of Čexov, we again find elements of poetry — but these are a result already of breaking the norms of prose established in the 19th century.

Additional discussion: Issatschenko, Markov, Shapiro, Worth

AUTHOR'S REPLY

I would like to express my appreciation for the thoughtful comments made concerning my paper. As regards the broader theoretical issue of how to distinguish between prose and poetry (artistic prose and poetry proper, to be exact), and whether any universal, absolute and timeless definitions are possible and appropriate here, I would tend to agree with Professor Winner that this question can indeed perhaps only be approached historically; in other words, every (broadly defined) period probably has to be examined in terms of its own criteria for drawing the sometimes fine line between what is to be considered prose and what poetry. Still, for my specific purpose I feel that using as general a formal definition of poetry as that proposed by Buxštab makes reasonably good sense. And, of course, I am convinced that precisely in terms of the Old Russian (or, generally, medieval Slavic) poetic system the *Molenie* does not qualify as poetry proper. I cannot but agree, at least in general, also with the point raised by Professor de Mallac — noting, however, the inherent lack of clarity and precision in the term 'poetic', either referring to a particular, formally definable organization of speech and texts for aesthetic purposes or used merely as a synonym for 'aesthetic' or 'artistic' (or, more precisely, 'aesthetically' or 'artistically motivated'). While I am pleased to find myself in agreement with Professor Meijer that the Supplication is, in fact, not poetry proper but highly stylized prose, I would think that the nature of many — but not all — of its identifiable (or presumed) sources, themselves frequently being rhythmized, may very well be a factor responsible, in part at least, for its, broadly speaking, 'poetic', i.e., largely artistically structured form. But, in addition, the various authors (or, rather, compilers and editors) of the many extant variants have probably contributed to further perfecting some of its passages, including some, as it were, connecting passages, also from an artistic point of view. As for Professor Marvan's interesting comments, I must confess that I am a bit skeptical when it comes to applying such notions as 'deep system' and 'surface realization' (whose equivalence to poetic *langue* and *parole*, moreover, seems at least problematic to me) to the domain of verbal art (and aesthetics). As for Constantine's contribution to Early Slavic poetry, only in passing touched upon in my paper, I am not quite sure that I see the relevance of your remarks to the substance of my paper.

OSIP MANDEL'ŠTAM'S "TRISTIA"

STEVEN BROYDE

TRISTIA

Я изучил науку расставанья
В простоволосых жалобах ночных.
Жуют волы, и длится ожиданье,
Последний час вигилий городских,
И чту обряд той петушиной ночи,
Когда, подняв дорожной скорби груз,
Глядели вдаль заплаканные очи,
И женский плач мешался с пеньем муз.

Кто может знать при слове — расставанье,
Какая нам разлука предстоит,
Что нам сулит петушье восклицанье,
Когда огонь в акрополе горит,
И на заре какой-то новой жизни,
Когда в сенях лениво вол жует,
Зачем петух, глашатай новой жизни,
На городской стене крылами бьет?

И я люблю обыкновенье пряжи:
Снует челнок, веретено жужжит,
Смотри, навстречу, словно пух лебяжий,
Уже босая Делия летит!
О, нашей жизни скудная основа,
Куда как беден радости язык!
Всё было встарь, всё повторится снова,
И сладок нам лишь узнаванья миг.

Да будет так: прозрачная фигурка
На чистом блюде глиняном лежит,
Как беличья распластанная шкурка,
Склонясь над воском, девушка глядит.
Не нам гадать о греческом Эребе,
Для женщин воск, что для мужчины медь.
Нам только в битвах выпадает жребий,
А им дано гадая умереть.

1918.

The essential role that subtexts play in interpreting Mandel'štam's poetry is becoming more and more widely recognized. Careful attention to the literary sources upon which the poet draws often provides necessary information for understanding the total poetic meaning. In his dense, allusive texts, a reference to another literary source may be present as a significant similarity in imagery or phrasing, as an almost exact quotation of a line or group of words, or a more generalized evocation of a literary situation. Ideally, his reader recognizes not only the original source, but its new function in the fresh poetic environment which Mandel'štam provides. The shared community of knowledge which he presupposes may include, besides familiarity with a vast literary heritage, a shared awareness of the topics and phrases peculiar to the contemporary moment. The scholar's task is both to recover the source of the citation and to elucidate the vital interaction of all these elements, the ways in which they illuminate each other, and the complex manner in which they participate in Mandel'štam's own statement. A particularly fertile ground for undertaking such a study is Mandel'štam's poem "Tristia" (1918). It is a well-known poem whose subtexts have largely been identified; but no coherent statement of the poem's total meaning has yet been made. It is also particularly worthwhile to investigate the use of subtexts in this poem, because "Tristia," as we shall see, concerns Mandel'štam's relationship to literature.

The title, "Tristia," immediately alerts the reader to anticipate that some kind of literary reminiscences will figure in the poem to follow. Mandel'štam sometimes provides such signals in the title itself, e.g. "Silentium" (1910), "Ljuteranin" (1912), "Dombi i syn" (1913), "Našedšij podkovu (Pindaričeskij otryvok)" (1923), "Ariost" (1933). In "Tristia" the reader's expectations are rewarded; echoes from Ovid's *Tristia* can be heard in Mandel'štam's poem. Yet to expect a simple maintained parallel between Mandel'štam and Ovid would result in a loss of the essential complexity with which Mandel'štam manipulates his subtexts. Mandel'štam is not, like Ovid, lamenting his own exile, separation from wife, friends, beloved city. He is, however, at least in part, examining literature whose theme is, broadly speaking, parting. Having alerted the reader to the presence of literary antecedents in the title, he then in the first line establishes the perspective in which the poet views Ovid's *Tristia*, and thus the framework in which we, as readers, should consider the title: Ovid's poem is only one part of the "science of separation" which has been studied. By referring to separation, which clearly in Ovid's poem is a highly personal and emotional experience, with the unexpected term "science," Mandel'štam is suggesting from the outset a complex understanding of poetic creation which will be further explored subsequently. The term "science" itself implies an articulated, codified body of knowledge which deals with observed phenomena that recur in time and which thus have the potential to be predictive. The noun *nauka*, coupled with a seemingly unlikely complement, appears several times in Puškin as well. One example occurs in *Evgenij Onegin*, where, interestingly, it is juxtaposed with the name of Ovid:

> Čto zanimalo celyj den'
> Ego toskujuščuju len' −
> Byla *nauka strasti nežnoj*,
> Kotoruju vospel Nazon,
> Za čto stradal'cem končil on
> Svoj vek blestjaščij i mjatežnyj
> V Moldavii, v gluši stepej,
> Vdali Italii svoej.
>
> (I, VIII)[1]

Likewise its appearance in "Vsevoložskomu" (1819): "I dokaži, čto ty znatok/ V nevedomoj *nauke sčast'ja*."; "Poltava" (I, 142): "Surovyj byl v *nauke slavy*/Ej [Rossii] dan učitel'. . ."; and "Gavriliada" (1. 272): "Ja videl ix! ljubvi − moej nauki − / Prekrasnoe načalo videl ja." Analogously, again in *Evgenij Onegin*, we read: "Kak učat slaboe ditja,/Ty dušu nežnuju, mutja,/*Učila goresti glubokoj*".[2] Thus, in addition to *nauka ljubvi, sčast'ja, slavy, goresti glubokoj*, we have added by Mandel'štam a "nauka rasstavan'ja" as well. The verb *izučil* emphasizes that the speaker's familiarity with this subject, far from being accidental, is a careful and self-conscious act. The root "uk" meaning teach/ learn further links these two words.

The rather abstract opening statement is immediately juxtaposed to the very specific, emotionally charged situation of the second line. The image of bareheaded women lamenting at night again reminds us of Ovid's separation from his wife (*Tristia*, I, iii, 43, 89). But as the rest of this stanza makes clear, this is not an isolated experience, but a recurring literary situation in a number of poems which provides the empirical data from which the speaker's science of separation is constructed. Quite clearly, the oxen in 1.3 are a familiar topos in classical poetry. In several of his own poems, Mandel'štam depends upon our recognition of this classical fixture to establish a non-modern setting (e.g. "Est' ivolgi v lesax, i glasnyx dolgota," 1914: "Voly na pastbišče, i zolotaja len'/ Iz trostnika izvleč' bogatstvo celoj noty "; "Zverinec," 1916: "Poka jagnjata i voly/Na tučnyx pastbiščax vodilis'. . . .").[3] It is also significant that the image of oxen chewing is repeated, but in an altered context, in the second stanza of this poem. Here the measured rumination of these oxen which remains constant through long periods of poetic time helps to draw out the duration of the speaker's "expectation." This expectation seems to be a premonition of parting, but this is not specified, and certain elements in the third stanza would suggest that the expectation created by a study of literature has additional significance.

The time of this premonition is well worth noting. It is, the speaker tells us, "the final hour of the city's vigils," the last moment in a night of attentive watchfulness, either dawn or a time right before daybreak. This detail, as others in this stanza, reinforces our sense of the presence here of a historic or literary past. The speaker's relationship to this past is not as coldly analytical as the first line might imply. He introduces the sharply particularized final image of parting in this stanza with an expression of reverential solemnity: "I čtu obrjad. . ." This is not a common expression; more normal is *sobljudat' obrjady*, or *ispolnjat'*, *soveršat'*. Blok uses it in "Na ostrovax" (Nov. 22, 1909): "Ja čtu obrjad: legko zapravit'/ Medvež'ju polost' na letu,/I, tonkij stan obnjav, lukavit',/ I mčat'sja v sneg i temnotu".[4] Here the expression has a definite suggestion of irony. This phrase occurs with no irony in Axmatova's poem "Ved' gde-to est' prostaja žizn' i svet" (1915), written during the war about living in "granitnyj gorod slavy i bedy": "A my živem toržestvenno i trudno/I čtim obrjady našix gor'kix vstreč."[5] Axmatova's, most probably, is the principal subtext for Mandel'štam.

The moment itself is portentous. The pairing of the cock with night, rather than with dawn, emphasizes that the actual moment of separation has yet to come. Other elements in this image reveal that the intensity of emotion arises from the knowledge that parting is fully and painfully expected, but has yet to be endured ("gruz skorbi," "zaplakannye oči," "ženskij plač"). The burden of the sorrow of the road is yet to be shouldered, and the distance is yet to be travelled, but this does nothing to lessen the shared sorrow of the present moment.

However it is not only the authenticity and intensity of human emotions which the speaker reveres. The "ceremony" which he admires involves not only the age-old human response to sorrow, but also his awareness that other poets have given expression to this feeling before him. The image is certainly appropriate to the general situation of Ovid's departure from Rome in *Tristia*. In addition, this reference can be further specified by looking at a poem of Tibullus in Batjuškov's translation. In the Tibullus poem, the speaker remembers his parting from Delia in phrases which Mandel'štam incorporates into his own poem:

> Net druga moego, net Delii so mnoj, —
> Ona v samyj čas razluki rokovoj
> Obrjady tajnye i čary soveršala:
> V svjaščennom užase bessmertnyx voprošala —
> I žrebij sčastlivyj nam otrok vynimal.
> Čto pol'zy ot togo? Čas gibel'nyj nastal,
> I snova Delija, pečal'na i unyla,

Slezami polnyj vzor nevol'no obratila
Na dal'nyj put'.
("Èlegija iz Tibula. Vol'nyj perevod")[6]

The final line of the first stanza of Mandel'štam's poem affirms by the poet's careful balance of "woman's *lament*" with "*singing* of the muses" that human sorrow can generate poetry, and, equally important, that through his study of literature these emotions remain permanently and vitally available to him.

The clear echo in this stanza of certain images from Tibullus' poem indicates that rather than a single literary source which one might expect from the title, what is more important to Mandel'štam's meaning is the repeated pattern of both human experience and poetic expression. Not only Ovid, but Tibullus and Batjuškov are present in this rich overlay, and are manipulated by Mandel'štam in his own evocation of parting.

The speaker moves from this detailed description of a man leaving a woman to speculate in the second stanza on the broader implications of parting. His focus now is not on past instances preserved in literature, but on the unknown consequences of the present act of parting. He couches his speculation in an elaborate three-part rhetorical question in which he asks to know what the abstract term means, not for himself alone, but for a larger and more inclusive "us." That the poet shares his sense of separation with others and speaks for them seems to suggest that parting is no longer, in this stanza, a private act, such as Ovid's departure from Rome or Tibullus' from Delia, but a more general condition. Not only is the incident less specified, the nature of the outcome is less precisely implied. The expectation in the first stanza was uniformly negative and sorrowful. Here the questions emphasize doubt rather than dread. The speaker asks three times what these recognized signs of parting can tell us about the experience ahead.

In the first line of stanza two, he repeats the same word, "rasstavan'e," he used in the opening line of the poem, but here he questions what it means. What can the abstract term, he asks, reveal of the concrete state of being separated? The implication seems to be that the intellectual label without the lived experience can tell us nothing. He also repeats in the second question the image of the cock.[7] In the first stanza ("obrjad toj petušinoj noči"), the cock presaged an imminent painful departure. Here what the cock's crow promises is entirely unknown. The cock is associated with the "dawn of some new life" rather than the night, and the speaker calls it the "herald of a new life" in l. 15. But whether this new life contains joy or sorrow remains unspecified. The speaker's final question in this stanza reinforces rather than resolves the ambiguity, "Začem petux, glašataj novoj žizni,/Na gorodskoj stene krylami b'et? "

The repetition of the crucial phrase "new life" in the terminal rhyme position in lines 13 and 15 offers some clue for identifying the sense of separation which the speaker and others confront (11. 10-11: "Kakaja *nam* razluka predstoit,/Čto *nam* sulit petuš'e vosklican'e," my italics), and whose outcome is so uncertain. "Tristia" was written in 1918, the same year as the equally well-known poem "Sumerki svobody." In the latter poem Mandel'štam utilized the image of the rising sun ("Vosxodiš' ty v gluxie gody,/O solnce, sudija, narod.") as a way of polemicizing against those who expressed blind optimism in the future. To the bright revolutionary sun, a familiar cliché in the poetry of the Proletarian poets, he opposes a state of half-light, dawn, and a sun which is obscured. In "Tristia," the phrases "at the dawn of some new life" and "herald of a new life" are similarly manipulated. In traditional revolutionary literature these images unambiguously refer to the era inaugurated by the revolution.[8] While such imagery evoked predictably positive responses in the pro-revolutionary poems of the period, the context in which Mandel'štam places it in "Tristia" produces an ambiguous or ironic effect. He does not celebrate this new life, but instead repeatedly questions its significance.

Whatever significance the present moment has must be determined, for lack of any certain knowledge of the future, by its relation to the past. If the historical moment of separation considered in this stanza is 1918, clearly several details mentioned here are anachronistic. The setting very closely parallels the classical literary atmosphere of the first stanza. Besides the cock, the chewing oxen reappear. While neither of these elements in themselves refers unequivocally to a historically distant past, the repeated pattern of this complex of images, plus the reference in 1. 12 to a "fire [which] burns in the acropolis" strongly suggests a classical framework. But our sense of a classical ambience in this stanza in no way excludes the reality of a contemporary Russian moment. The ox in 1. 14 seems immediately present to the speaker, lazily chewing in the passageway: "v senjax lenivo vol žuet." Clearly the rooster is as much a herald of the future in Russia as in ancient Greece and Rome.[9] Yet it is the speaker's awareness that these signs he now observes repeat a literary and historical past which thus furnish the proper context through which he can evaluate the present instance. Mandel'štam describes this phenomenon of having a composite sense of time in his essay "Slovo i kul'tura" (1921):

Itak, ni odnogo poèta ešče ne bylo. My svobodny ot gruza vospomina-nij. Zato skol'ko redkostnyx predčuvstvij: Puškin, Ovidij, Gomer. Ko-gda ljubovnik v tišine putaetsja v nežnyx imenax i vdrug vspominaet, čto èto uže bylo: i slova i volosy, i petux, kotoryj prokričal za oknom, kričal uže v Ovidievyx tristijax, glubokaja radost' povtoren'ja oxvaty-vaet ego, golovokružitel'naja radost'. . . (II, 266-267)

Mandel'štam's meaning in this stanza depends on his reader's realization of the interrelationship of present and past time: the pattern from the past aids in interpreting the present, while the present recognition revitalizes the past. Mandel'štam praises the type of poetry in which such a coincidence yields new resonance:

No veršina istoričeskoj poètiki Bloka, toržestvo evropejskogo mifa, kotoryj dvižetsja v tradicionnyx formax, no boitsja anaxronizma i sovremennosti — èto "Šagi Komandora". Zdes' plasty vremeni legli drug na druga v zanovo vspaxannom poètičeskom soznanii, i zerna starogo sjužeta dali obil'nye vsxody (Tixij černyj, kak sova, motor. . . Iz strany blažennoj, neznakomoj, dal'nej, slyšno pen'e petuxa). (II, 314)

This quotation ends with an implicit allusion to one of Mandel'štam's most notable earlier uses of this device, "Peterburgskie strofy" (1913). Other examples of such mixed "strata of time" can be seen in "O vremenax prostyx i grubyx" (1914), "Kogda v temnoj noči zamiraet" (1918), "Čut' mercaet prizračnaja scena" (1920), "Jazyk bulyžnika mne golubja ponjatnej" (1924).[10]

In the third stanza, the speaker returns to a statement of personal preference, "I ja ljublju obyknoven'e prjaži," which recalls two statements from the first stanza: "Ja izučil nauku rasstavan'ja," "I čtu obrjad toj petušinoj noči." The three statements are alike in that the speaker stresses in each his sensitivity to repeated action. But if the first statement records a careful study of repeated partings, and the second reveals a solemn reverence for ritual, this last seems at first merely to acknowledge a fondness for the repetition of daily routines. The reference to spinning here seems only a homely detail. Yet the speaker's transition from watching the spindle to seeing Delia seems unexpected and unexplained unless we explore more fully the significance of spinning. The hypnotic motions of spinning may produce a trance in the attentive watcher during which his imagination takes flight. In an earlier poem, Mandel'štam describes a similar phenomenon:

Na perlomutrovyj čelnok
Natjagivaja šelka niti,
O, pal'cy gibkie, načnite
Očarovatel'nyj urok!

Prilivy i otlivy ruk —
Odnoobraznye dvižen'ja,
Ty zaklinaeš', bez somnen'ja,
Kakoj-to solnečnyj ispug, —

Kogda širokaja ladon',
Kak rakovina plameneja,
To gasnet, k tenjam tjagoteja,
To v rozovyj ujdet ogon'![11]

But more than the physical movements of the spinner are repeated in "Tristia."
Spinning, like the chewing oxen, the bare-headed women, and the fire in the
acropolis, seems one of the generalized references to the classical tradition which
are so essential to the texture of this poem. Spinning was not an uncommon
pursuit among classical women of either noble or lowly birth; cf. Ovid, *Met.*, IV,
34; *Iliad*, VI, 323: Livy, I, 57, 7. In Mandel'štam's own poetry, "Zolotistogo
meda struja iz butylka tekla" (1917): "Nu, a v komnate beloj kak prjalka stoit
tišina./... Pomniš', v grečeskom dome: ljubimaja vsemi žena — /Ne Elena —
drugaja — kak dolgo ona vyšivala? "

But to comprehend the full significance of the image, and the progression of
this stanza, we must appreciate an even more specific repetition in Mandel'štam's
reference to spinning. The conjunction of spinning with a vision of Delia is
almost a verbatim transcription from Batjuškov's translation of Tibullus' poem:

Pri šume zimnix v'jug, pod sen'ju bezopasnoj,
Podruga v temnu noč' zažžet svetil'nik jasnyj
I, tixo vreteno kruža v ruke svoej,
Rasskažet povesti i byli staryx dnej.
A ty, sklonjaja slux na sladki nebylicy,
Zabudeš'sja, moj drug, i tomnye zenicy

Zakroet tixij son, i prjaslica iz ruk
Padet... i u dverej predstanet tvoj suprug,
Kak nebom poslannyj vnezapno dobryj genij.
Begi navstreču mne, begi iz mirnoj seni,
V prelestnoj nagote javis' moim očam:
Vlasy razvejanny nebrežno po plečam,
Vsja grud' lilejnaja i nogi obnaženny....

In Tibullus, the sight of Delia is also an act of imagination. By remembering her
engaged in a traditional domestic task, the speaker in Tibullus' poem is able to
visualize clearly the absent Delia. In Mandel'štam's poem, another layer of
complexity is present. While contemplating the familiar habit of spinning, the
speaker recognizes the literary antecedents of such a setting, which in turn
generates a vision of Delia. This concatenation of events arising from a domestic
situation aptly demonstrates Mandel'štam's definition of the vital reality of
Hellenism: "Èllinizm, — èto sistema v Bergsonovskom smysle slova, kotoruju

čelovek razvertyvaet vokrug sebja, kak veer javlenij, osvoboždaemyx ot vremennoj zavisimosti, sopodčinennyx vnutrennej svjazi čerez čelovečeskoe ja." (II, 296).

The second quatrain of this stanza comments on the experience just related. In the vocative, "našej žizni skudnaja osnova," the word *osnova* suggests two complementary meanings, basis and warp.[12] He exclaims abruptly that the very basis of life is meagre; yet if "osnova" is understood as warp, the vocative is a metaphoric outgrowth of the earlier image of spinning. Since warp is the lengthwise thread in fabric, this metaphor suggests life in its daily linear unfolding. Perhaps as a consequence of the meagre experience of life, the language of joy is poor, which may imply by contrast that the language of sorrow is rich. However the speaker's emotional declaration in these two lines is entirely unexpected and cannot have been motivated by the profoundly complex moment of insight he has just experienced. The stanza ends with a cryptic aphorism which if understood fully will explain the apparent contradiction: "Vse bylo vstar', vse povtoritsja snova,/I sladok nam liš' uznavan'ja mig".[13] The speaker realizes here the endless and inevitable repetition in life: the future is linked to the past by a continuous series of repeated phenomena. Yet in a flash of intuition, the individual may recognize, in certain precious moments like the one just felt, his own immediate involvement in the pattern. This perception represents a momentary intersection of the individual life (the meagre warp) with the inherited tradition. In experiencing this felt correspondence, the individual's life is enriched through his contact with the pattern of tradition which is so unexpectedly alive and available to him. It is worth noting in this context, that the particular source through which Delia comes alive for Mandel'štam in this poem is the translation of Batjuškov.[14] In "Čut' mercaet prizračnaja scena" (1920), he claims that his sense of the original may in fact be intensified by having it accessible in his native language:

> Slašče pen'ja ital'janskoj reči
> Dlja menja rodnoj jazyk,
> Ibo v nem tainstvenno lepečet
> Čužezemnyx arf rodnik.

The sweetness of Russian in part arises from the poet's recognition that his own language now contains as an integral part the beauty of the original sources. Ideally in the present poem the reader will also experience a moment of recognition in which he is aware of the classical poem, through Batjuškov's translation, as well as Mandel'štam's reworking of this source in a new poetic context.

The final stanza opens with the words "Da budet tak." With this ritualized expression of agreement, the speaker affirms the recognized validity of the aphorism in the preceding stanza. What follows is directly related to the acceptance of this truth. But the focus shifts to an image of a girl using wax to tell the future. An initial and valid response is to link this method of divination with the already established network of classical elements in this poem. But just as the complex of images in the second stanza was at once classical and Russian, ancient and contemporary, this girl's attempt to foretell the future is rooted in a Russian reality as well. Other poetic references to this native custom include (*topit' vosk*) "Svetlana," *Evgenij Onegin*, and Mandel'štam's own "Na strašnoj vysote bluždajuščij ogon'" (1918; "Prozračnaja vesna nad černoju Nevoj/Slomalas', vosk bessmert'ja taet"). Although the custom itself may belong to either culture, the line, "Kak belič'ja rasplastannaja škurka," points directly to a contemporary Russian source, Axmatova's poem "Vysoko v nebe oblako sere-lo."[15] Significantly, in Axmatova's poem this act of divination is associated with the parting of lovers. Thus her poem is also part of the subtle pattern of recurrence which Mandel'štam in the opening line calls the "science of separation." The image of the girl divining relates not only to Axmatova's poem, but Mandel'štam's description in line four of this stanza recalls line seven of the first stanza: "Sklonjas' nad voskom, devuška gljadit", "Gljadeli v dal' zaplakannye oči." In both instances an attempt is made to see into the future. But in the very next line, the speaker explicitly rejects this course: the verb "gljadet'" is paranomastically transformed to "gadat'" ("Ne nam gadat' o grečeskom Èrebe").

In making this declaration, the speaker again assumes a public voice. One should note that this alternation between private and public statements has occurred repeatedly throughout the poem. In the first stanza, the outlook is purely personal, the speaker employs the first person singular ("Ja izučil," "I čtu"). The second stanza opens with the inclusive interrogative pronoun "kto," and the rhetorical questions have a generalized frame of reference and are asked on behalf of us ("Kakaja nam razluka predstoit,/Čto nam sulit petuš'e voskli-can'e"). Clearly the speaker's more abstract concern with separation develops logically from his own study of the science of parting in the opening stanza. A similar alternation is repeated and condensed in the two quatrains of the third stanza: his metaphor "warp of life" is an outgrowth of the spinning image in the first line of the stanza. From the personally experienced moment of recognition in the first quatrain, the speaker moves to an aphoristic statement of its universal validity. Here, in the final stanza, the sharply realized image of the girl appears to prompt the speaker's rejection of fortune-telling. Again, the speaker couches the general truth in the form of an aphorism: "Dlja ženščin vosk, čto dlja mužčiny med'." What the speaker appears to propose through this analogy are two antithetical ways of responding to the future. *Vosk* clearly is a metonymy for the means of divination just described. *Med'* is also a metonymic image. *Bitvy* in the next line suggests that, by contiguity, it is connected with war. Here, the primary reference is classical: in Homeric poetry, "chalkos" (copper, bronze)[16] was a frequent metonymy for the tools of war – axes, shields, spears. Examples from *The Iliad* and *The Odyssey* (in Gnedič's and Žukovskij's translations) illustrate this:

> Meges Filíd, na nego stremjasja, kopejščik mogučij,
> V golovu okolo tyla kop'em porazil izoščrennym –
> Med', mež zubov proletevši, podsekla jazyk u Pedeja,
> Grjanulsja v prax on i med' xolodnuju stisnul zubami.[17]
>
> ... sideli
> Ljudi trojanskie, bylo mež nimi trojakoe mnen'e:
> Ili gubitel'noj med'ju gromadu pronzit' i razrušit'...[18]

Med' thus implies active, assertive confrontation. The verb, *vypadaet*, is imperfective, used in the timeless sense of the present tense (*voobšče, vsegda*, formerly, now, and in the future).

The speaker's preference for active engagement is reinforced by the image of the final line of the poem in which death is unexpectedly linked to the passive diviners rather than with the conflict of battle. Clearly, Mandel'štam's model for action is an epic, heroic image of man. In a later essay, "O prirode slova," the poet asserts that such an ideal must be recreated to serve the present age:

> Obščestvennyj pafos russkoj poèzii do six por podnimalsja tol'ko do "graždanina", no est' bolee vysokoe načalo, čem "graždanin", – ponjatie "muža".
>
> V otličie ot staroj graždanskoj poèzii, novaja russkaja poèzija dolžna vospityvat' ne tol'ko graždan, no i "muža". Ideal soveršennoj mužestvennosti podgotovlen stilem i praktičeskimi trebovanijami našej èpoxi. Vse stalo tjažele i gromadnee, potomu čelovek dolžen stat' tverže, tak kak čelovek dolžen byt' tverže vsego na zemle i otnosit'sja k nej, kak almaz k steklu.

(II, 300)

The ending of the poem, with its setting, its tone, and final injunction, recalls similar features in the conclusion of "Sumerki svobody." Both poems look toward an uncertain future (cf. "ogromnyj, neukljužij,/Skripučij povorot rulja"). In the face of uncertainty, both call for courage: in "Tristia" this is implied by the speaker's preference for confronting one's lot in battle; in "Sumerki svobody," this imperative is directly stated, "Mužajtes', muži," a phrase suggesting a battlecry from an older tradition.[19] If these poems counsel a similar response to the future in 1918, "Tristia" is much more explicit in demonstrating the sources from which such courage is derived. Clearly, throughout the poem, knowledge of the past informs the present moment. We have seen in stanza three how an awareness of the literary past illuminates an ordinary moment with a flash of recognition. However, a sense of the past not only adds sweetness to the meagre warp of our daily existence, but it can provide a moral framework as well (cf. "gieratičeskij, to est' svjaščennyj, xarakter poèzii," II 300). If, as the speaker insists, it is futile to try to guess the future, the lack of foreknowledge should not exclude action. Instead, one's guide for the future is the knowledge of the repeated pattern of the past. Mandel'štam's reverence for the past clearly was a liberating force, and produced not, as one might have hypothesized, hostility toward the revolution, but a stable set of positive values on which to base his response.

Amherst College

NOTES

1. All Puškin quotations are cited from *Polnoe sobranie sočinenij v desjati tomax*, M., 1963. All italics mine.
2. *P.s.s*, V, 538, "Iz rannix redakcij".
3. Poetry and prose quotations are cited from Osip Mandel'štam, *Sobranie sočinenij v trex tomax*, ed. G. V. Struve, B. A. Filippov (Inter-Language Literary Associates, 1966). One might note the different but analogous use of the horse in "Našedšij podkovu".
4. *Sočinenija v dvux tomax*, M., 1955, I, 346.
5. *Sočinenija*, Inter-Library Literary Associates, 1967, I, 149.
6. The Tibullus subtext has been mentioned by Victor Terras, "Classical Motives in the Poetry of Osip Mandel'štam," *The Slavic and East European Journal*, 1966, X, no. 3. Boris Bukhshtab ("The Poetry of Mandelstam," *Russian Literature Triquarterly*, 1971, no. 1) and Nikolaj Xardžiev (ed., O. Mandel'štam, *Stixotvorenija*, Biblioteka poèta, 1973) indicate specifically Batjuškov's translation as well. See also, N. V. Fridman, *Poèzija Batjuškova*, M., 1971, p. 371. Batjuškov's poem is cited from *Polnoe sobranie sočinenij*, Biblioteka poèta, M.-L., 1964.
7. In Annenskij's translation from Leconte de Lisle, "Nad sinim mrakom noči dlinnoj", *rasstavan'e* and *petušij krik* are juxtaposed. *Stixotvorenija i tragedii*, Biblioteka poèta, L., 1959, p. 255.
8. For example, M. P. Gerasimov, "Divites' vse, kak vsadnik mednyj/K zare zovuščej voznesen!" (1918); V. T. Kirillov, "I v ètot mig zari grjaduščej lik čudesnyj razgadal" (1917); A. P. Krasnyj, "V novuju, svetluju žizn' golubaja/Vxodit 'Avrora', podnjav jakorja/ Gorodu, miru – zarja! zarja!" (1917); Ivan Kuznecov, "Vrag trepeščet,/Vidja svet inoj zari" (1918), etc. (Examples from *Proletarskie poèty pervyx let sovetskoj èpoxi*, Biblioteka poèta, 1959, pp. 197, 227, 400, 410.) Cf. Z. Papernyj, "Možno bylo by privesti desjatki podobnyx primerov, gde govoritsja o rassejavšejsja t'me, mrake, noči, o rassvete, o vosxode, o načale radostnogo dnja" (*Poètičeskij obraz u Majakovskogo*, Moscow, 1961, p. 239). I discuss

Mandel'štam's use of such current imagery in "Sumerki svobody" and "Vojna. Opjat' raznogolosica" in my Harvard dissertation, "Osip Mandel'štam and His Age: A Commentary of the Themes of War and Revolution in the Poetry, 1913-1923", pp. 54ff, 106ff.

9. Afanas'ev notes, "narod nazyvaet ego (petuxa) prorokom." (*Poètičeskie vozzrenija slavjan na prirodu*, Moscow, 1865, I, 519; "Kak s drugimi pticami,provozvestnicami burnyx groz, soedinjalis' primety o vojne i soprovoždajuščix ee bedstvijax, tak teže primety prilagalis' i k petuxu i kuram," I, 524). The cock appears in at least one *skazka* in connection with divination: "Na tu poru pribežal v izbu petux, zaxlopal kryl'jami i zakričal: "Kukureku!" – "Èkoj golosistyj kakoj! – skazal kupec. – Xotel by ja znat', pro čto ty gorlaniš'? " – "Požaluj, ja tebe skažu, – promolvil mal'čik, – petux veščuet, čto pridet vremja – budeš' ty v bednosti, a ja stanu vladet' tvoimi bogatstvami." ("Veščij son," A. A. Afanas'ev, *Narodnye russkie skazki v trex tomax*, ed. V. Ja. Propp, M. 1957, II, 266-268). The Greeks used the cock as a mode of divination in the rite of alectryomantia: "The letters of the alphabet were written in a circle. A grain of wheat or barley was laid on each letter, a cock, consecrated or provided for the occasion,was placed within the circle. The required information was obtained by putting together those letters off which the cock picked the grains of corn." (Harry T. Peck, ed., *Harper's Dictionary of Classical Literature and Antiquity*, N.Y., 1898, p. 53). Note, too, "the Romans' practice of taking fowls with the army or navy in hostile expeditions, (for divination) (Cicero, de Nat. Deor., II, iii). A real war-omen, however, was the foretelling of the Theban victory, by the oracle of Trophonius at Lebadea, from the crowing of cocks, 'quia galli victi silere solent, canere victores' (Cicero, de Divinat. II. xxvi)." (James Hastings, ed., *Encyclopedia of Religion and Ethics*, N.Y., 1908, III, 697). Perhaps in Mandel'štam's 1922 poem, "Komu zima, arak, i punš goluboglazyj," the cock is connected with *gadan'e*, "I s petuxom v gorške pridti na dvor k gadalke."

10. It might conceivably be argued that no anachronism exists in this stanza, and that the entire action takes place in the past. However, if this is so, the rhetorical questions would seem irrelevant or merely coy, since the speaker would already know the outcome of past action.

11. Cf. too Mandel'štam's early poem "Besšumnoe vereteno" (1909-1910?) which is perhaps in part literary polemics with Merežkovskij's well-known "Parki."

12. The word "osnova" occurs only twice in Mandel'štam's poetry. In both instances this dual meaning is present. Cf. in "Umyvalsja noč'ju na dvore" (1921), "Čišče pravdy svežego xolsta/Vrjad li gde otyščetsja osnova." Ju. I. Levin's insightful analysis is worth citing: "Značimo i slovo *osnova*, priobretajuščee osobuju rol' blagodarja svoej dvuznačnosti v kontekste stixotvorenija (tkackaja osnova – v svjazi s *xolstom*, i nravstvennaja, žiznennaja osnova – v svjazi s *pravdoj* i *sovest'ju*). Dvuznačno i slovo *čišče* (vo vtoroj strofe), takže svjazannoe i s *xolstom*, i s *pravdoj*. Funkcija ètoj dvuznačnosti v tom, čto blagodarja ej tesno do nerazličimosti slivajutsja 'bytovoj' i 'nravstvennyj' sloi stixotvorenija, tak čto 'nravstvennoe' estestvenno vyrastaet iz 'byta'." ("Razbor odnogo stixotvorenija Mandel'štama", *Slavic Poetics: Essays in Honor of Kiril Taranovsky*, ed. Roman Jakobson, et al., The Hague, Paris, 1973, 271-272.)

13. There are many possible sources for Mandel'štam's aphorism. Perhaps he is engaging in polemics with the pessimism of Blok's "Noč', ulica, fonar', apteka": "Umreš' – načneš' opjat' snačala,/I povtoritsja vse kak vstar'. . . ." In Professor K. Taranovsky's 1971 seminar on Mandel'štam at Harvard, Peggy Troupin cited as a possibility Puškin's review "Frakijskie èlegii. Stixotvorenija Viktora Tepljakova, 1836," where Puškin cites long excerpts of Tepljakov's poetry, including the following lines, "Ty prav, božestvennyj pevec:/ Veká vekov liš' povtoren'e!" (*Polnoe sobranie sočinenij*, M., 1964, VII, 429). Also noteworthy is Baratynskij's "Na čto vy, dni! Judol'nyj mir javlenij": "Vse vedomy, i tol'ko povtoren'ja/ Grjaduščee sulit."

14. See similarly Vjačeslav Ivanov's translations of Sapho: K. F. Taranovsky, "Pčely i osy v poèzii Mandel'štama: k voprosu o vlijanii Vjačeslava Ivanova na Mandel'štama," *To Honor Roman Jakobson*, The Hague-Paris, 1967.
15. See I, 444. The punctuation in the first four lines of the last stanza of Mandel'štam's poem is not precise; the simile, "kak belič'ja rasplastannaja škurka," can seemingly refer either to "figurka" or "devuška." I understand it as describing the configuration of the girl as she bends over the wax: Prozračnaja figurka na čistom bljude glinjanom ležit. (or[;]) Devuška, sklonjajas' nad voskom, kak belič'ja rasplastannaja škurka, gljadit.
16. "Both Greeks and Romans use only one term for copper and for that mixture of copper and tin which we call bronze." *Harper's Dictionary*, p. 33.
17. Gnedič, *Iliada*, V, 72-75; see also III, 348; V, 292, etc. (N. I. Gnedič, *Stixotvorenija*, Biblioteka poèta, Malaja serija, Moskva-Leningrad, 1963).
18. Žukovskij, *Odisseja*, VIII, 505-507; see also IV, 743; V, 244; etc. (Va. Žukovskij, *Sobranie sočinenij v četyrex tomax*, Moscow-Leningrad, 1960). For a multitude of examples, see any concordance to Homer. The concordances consulted in this paper were Guy Lushington Prendergast, *A Complete Concordance to the Iliad of Homer*, new edition by Benedetto Marzullo, Darmstadt, 1962; Harry Dunbar, *A Complete Concordance to the Odyssey of Homer*, new edition by Benedetto Marzullo, Darmstadt, 1962. *Med'* can be associated with battle in various ways in a Russian context as well. For example, in "Ruslan i Ljudmila" (I, 222): "Na brovi mednyj šlem nadvinuv"; (VI, 323) "Struitsja krov' s kol'čugi mednoj." Other possibilities include *mednyj kolokol*, a tocsin announcing danger in general, war in particular; *mednaja truba*, a musical instrument used in war.
19. See Nils Åke Nilsson, " 'Mužajtes', muži!': On the History of a Poetism," *Scando-Slavica*, No. 12.

COMMENTS

de Mallac Problems raised in Professor Broyde's excellent paper call for the following observations:

1. It would be very helpful for Professor Broyde to attempt making a distinction between the terms *rasstavan'e* (perhaps a more general concept of 'separation'?) and *razluka* (apparently the more concrete, specific parting?) — insofar as the beginning of stanza 2 of this poem allows us to see a difference between the two.

2. Does Mr. Broyde really think that '*science* of separation' is the best translation of *nauka rasstavan'ja*? I would suggest that he consider 'the *art* of separation' — since the latter word, it seems to me, would better convey the semantic value of Latin *ars*, to which *nauka* corresponds.

3. When he refers to Mandel'štam's poem "Est' ivolgi v lesax" (p. 75), Mr. Broyde might want to keep in mind the metonymic as well as the metaphoric functions of the image of the oxen in that poem, as was stressed by Nils Åke Nilsson in his interpretation (cf. Nils Åke Nilsson, *Osip Mandel'štam: Five Poems*, Stockholm: Almqvist and Wiksell, 1974, p. 28).

4. I am not altogether convinced by the arguments used by the author to

establish the subtexts of "I čtu obrjad. ..." (p. 76). I think that he is less convincing here than when he is establishing other subtexts (Annenskij, Tibullus, ...). This brings up the delicate (and to my knowledge, as yet unsolved) question of which the sound criteria should be for identifying a subtext with any measure of convincingness.

5. Labeling the statement "Vsë bylo vstar' ..." as an aphorism (p. 81, l. 2) may be misleading in so far as aphorisms are fragments that are 'detached' by definition, and are uttered in a context that is unrelated to further treatment of the topic. I realize Mr. Broyde is aware that this statement is not casual or unconnected with the rest of the poem. It should nonetheless be stressed that the last two lines of stanza 3 both relate closely to the **whole** mood of the poem, and represent a key formula for Mandel'štam's **philosophy** as expressed both in this poem and elsewhere − a philosophy which might best be labeled as Alexandrinistic.

6. While he is endeavoring to pay attention to certain very delicate textual problems − e.g. the unclear punctuation discussed in footnote 15 − Mr. Broyde might simultaneously keep in mind the possibility that in at least certain instances (such as here?) syntactic ambiguity in Mandel'štam may well, like in Mallarmé, be clearly **intentional** and aesthetically motivated.

7. Drawing parallels with the treatment of themes of separation in other poets might yield worthwhile results. Thus, a cursory comparison with Pasternak's famous poem "Razluka" (from "The Poems of Jurij Živago") reveals that Pasternak's approach to the same theme (at least during his mature period) is clearly highly concrete (focusing on one concrete separation of two specific individuals), as opposed to Mandel'štam's tendency towards abstraction, and that Pasternak uses chiefly similes and very plain metaphors, in contrast to the far more complex structure of Mandel'štam's imagery.

Meijer 1. I agree with other speakers that *Nauka* should be rendered by *ars*, τεκνη. This means not a body of codified knowledge, but a way of going about separation.

2. In general I think that you somewhat overemphasize the subtext. Thus I think that bringing in associations with the revolution is not convincing. But there may be a common ground between our general views if we both agree that for Mandel'štam, the pristine word was impossible, that for better or for worse the word carries traces of anterior usage: but what this brings out is brought out in the context.

Nilsson Tristia was published in 1918, the same year as the well known "Proslavim, brat'ja, sumerki svobody". This poem appeared under the ambiguous title of "Gimn", which at that particular time referred not only to a classical genre but also to a topical genre of poems praising the revolution. Could we suggest a similar ambiguity in the title of *Tristia* in the sense that it refers to a classical genre and at the same time evokes an impression of a present situation? A similar ambiguity seems to characterize the poem as a whole. It would be read as a poem of love but also as a comment on the time when it was written, the theme of parting being the common denominator. It also seems to me that some key words of the poem could be grouped under an opposition of movement and change on the one hand, and routine and staticness on the other. *Petux* represents the first part of this opposition while *voly, ogon', prjaža* represent the other part. Evidently this opposition constitutes a major theme of the whole poem.

Additional discussion: Segal, Shapiro, Vickery

AUTHOR'S REPLY

Although Mr. Meijer and Mr. de Mallac may validly propose that *nauka* might be rendered in English as 'art' rather than 'science', I believe the significance and connotations of the term remain those I have fully developed in the paper.

Both Mr. Meijer's and Mr. Nilsson's comments on the relevance of certain subtexts, in counterpoint provide support for my major premise, that many subtle implied references to the Revolutionary period as well as to the classical era are present in the poem and a proper appreciation of Mandel'štam's art demands hearing the fine nuances of each.

I would disagree with Mr. Nilsson's reference to the classical poem *Tristia* as constituting a genre comparable to that of 'hymns'.

Points 1 through 4 of Mr. de Mallac's comments are more than adequately explored in my paper. I would disagree with his understanding of the term 'aphorism'. As I used it in the paper, and as it is generally defined, an aphorism is a terse statement of truth notable for its stylistic effectiveness, which therefore provides an especially appropriate comment on or summary of the entire context. The question he raises about intentional syntactic ambiguity is premature now, since we do not yet have a definitive text of this poem. The parallels drawn in point 7 are interesting but hardly within the scope of my paper.

SOME QUESTIONS OF INVERSION IN RUSSIAN POETRY

Thomas Eekman

Ljublju tebja, Petra tvoren'e,
Ljublju tvoj strogij, strojnyj vid,
Nevy deržavnoe tečen'e,
Beregovoj ee granit,
Tvoix ograd uzor čugunnyj,
Tvoix zadumčivyx nočej
Prozračnyj sumrak, blesk bezlunnyj...

Puškin's lines are, from a syntactic and stylistic point of view, characterized by constructions where one noun is dependent on another noun (as expressed by the genitive case), the dependent (appositive) noun being placed before the other (dominant) noun instead of behind it, as is considered normal in the everyday spoken and written language. V. Žirmunskij, discussing this type of inversion (which we shall call here anteposition), of which there are no less than four examples in these seven lines, remarks that it "stimulates a syntactic detachment, creating better noticeable boundaries between the joined elements of a syntactic group".[1] In other words, a syntagm or syntactic combination is conceived by the reader as a whole, but this unusual reversion of the order draws attention to the component parts.

B. V. Tomaševskij, analyzing the text of *Cygane*, notes that inversions "are possible when the rhythmic movement dominates over the syntactic movement". He pays special attention to more complicated inversions, where one or more words are interpolated between the two inverted nouns. In them "the poetical rhythm assumes its rights and the musicality of the language is revealed".[2]

N. S. Pospelov subjected the very lines quoted above and the other three *ljublju* passages of *Mednyj vsadnik* to an elaborate analysis. He put the lines in a 'normal', prosaic order and concluded that this complex syntactic structure, acceptable in a poem, would be clearly 'overladen' (*peregružennyj*) in prose.[3] These inversions, he points out, "play a significant role in the structure of complicated syntactic units in the poetic language and stimulate its expressiveness. In that language a deviation from the usual word order, subject to the rhythmic movement of the verse, appears to be less striking than in prose".[4]

So, according to Pospelov, the inversion under consideration plays a structural role and heightens the expressiveness. All three studies quoted here give the impression that Puškin was consciously looking for and applying these unusual syntactic figures in order to let the reader notice the separate elements of a syntagm and make him aware of their expressive value. They do not consider the possibility that the reader (and especially the early 19th century reader) was not struck at all by these inversions, since they were rather habitual in the classical poetical language; and that the poet did not construct or use them with special, subtle stylistic purposes, but simply accepted and followed (consciously or unconsciously) a long established tradition, a method or license which facilitated the creation of his metrical and rime patterns.

In the entire text of *Mednyj vsadnik* (478 lines) there are some eighty instances in which one noun, in the genitive case, is dependent on another (dominant) noun. Of these, about 74% have the normal order ("Na beregu pustynnyx voln"), about 26% the reversed order ("Petra tvoren'e"). There appear to be more genitive constructions, and consequently more antepositions, in the first, predominantly static, contemplative part of the poem and fewer in the more dynamic, narrative second part. This is a fact we should bear in mind when discussing the phenomenon of anteposition: it appears mainly where a substantial number of genitive and other dependent noun relations occur; and this is rarely the case in more primitive texts: a certain level of sophistication seems to be required. Narrative texts will show fewer constructions with 'of'; in lyrical verse they will also be relatively rare. Their highest frequency is reached in philosophical, reflective, reasoning, or rhetorical poetry. An extreme instance of the former type is the 'folkish' verse of the Ukrainian poet P. Hulak-Arte-movs'kyj, in which practically no instances of dependent genitive nouns occur at all and, consequently, no antepositions are to be found. In Tjutčev's poetry, on the other hand, I found an average of one such construction to every 3.7 lines.

The phenomenon is not restricted to poetry, to be sure: there is an abundant occurrence in all kinds of prose texts, notably during the 17th and 18th centuries, the period when anteposition was part of a general habit or fashion of rhetorical expression – a trend of clearly international character. It seems not without interest for the study of the Russian literary language and poetical style (and for those of the other Slavs as well) to ascertain how the phenomenon of anteposition came into existence and developed.

The question then arises whether the figure of noun inversion occurred in Old Russian texts and in folk literature. In the *Slovo o polku Igoreve* there are dependent genitives in the usual, postpositive order, but almost no antepositions – except in just a few cases: "ne xuda gnězda šestokrilci" (birds, apparently falcons,[5] but here used for men: "people of a good stock"); "na moeja lady voi" ("against the warriors of my beloved"), repeated a few lines further with a possessive dative: "na ladě voi"; and "(Rek Bojan i Xodyna ...), Ol'gova koganja xoti" (probably to be read: "... the favorites of prince Oleg",[6] constructed with a possessive adjective next to an antepositioned substantive). These cases are rare, and they occur only with *persons*: this appears usually to be the case 'in older texts.

In the *byliny* and the older *istoričeskie pesni* hardly any antepositions occur, because the whole figure of a noun dependent on another noun is hardly ever used in them, neither with a genitive nor with a possessive dative case. These old epic songs consist of short sentences coinciding with the verse line, sentences of a dynamic narrative nature that do not admit dependent structures.[7] What we do occasionally find is anteposition of a noun before a numeral, a frequent type of inversion in all Slavic languages on all levels: "A-j stojalo tatar vse desjat' tysjačej", "Da ostalos' dubinočki-to vse odin oblomoček" (next to "Vse oblomoček našel ètoj dubinočki"). Even in historical songs of much more recent times anteposition is rare: "Čto prijut-gorod Moskva vsej Rossii čest'-xvala" (in "Razorena put'-dorožka", early 19th century; this can also be understood as a dative); or in a revolutionary song from the late 19th-early 20th century: "Vsex stran proletarii, idite vpered" (here the text is strongly influenced by the literary language).

There is some anteposition in the lyrical folk songs, but there, too, the genitive constructions are rare and usually in the postpositioned order. In the lines "Oj da v mogile ležit telo beloe/ S Donu kazaka" the words "S Donu" are simply substituted for *donskogo*. In love songs lines or syntagms like "Moego družka konja vedut", "Kak uvižu mila druga oči", "Vinograda visit vetka", "Gorela b u devicy vosku jarogo sveča" occur, and in a song about Sten'ka Razin the words "Sten'ki Razina my rabotnički". Most of these inversions are called for by the requirements of the meter and especially of the rime – a factor not relevant in the unrimed epic songs. The constructions are simple and sound natural, not as mannered as in many texts of the 18th century. In proverbs the cases are equally rare: there is a rime parallel in "Nagoty-bosoty navešany šesty".

Only few instances of noun anteposition are to be found in Old Church Slavic and Old Russian texts, whether translated from the Greek or original. I came across one in the "Poxvala Grigoriju Nazianzinu", a text, clearly of a verse character, restored by N. S. Trubeckoj, which was included in the so called *Pannonskoe žitie Konstantina-Kirilla* and supposedly written by Konstantin himself: "Pravyę věry kazaniemь". This might well be the oldest example in Slavic of the phenomenon under discussion; even though it may be a single instance, it does show that this figure was not unknown to the early Slavic scribes. In the acrostic "Prolog o Xristě" by Konstantin Preslavskij, from the late ninth or early tenth century, the peculiar form of the poem requires some inversion; therefore we find, next to numerous instances of normal word order, sentences like "Vidimyja i nevidimyja vseja tvari sodětelju, nebesnyja i zemnyja", or the double anteposition "I letit bo nyně slovenskago jazyka plemen upovanie pravoslavnyja xristijanskija věry".[8] Otherwise we meet anteposition only in combinations with nouns used as prepositions: "vь obidy město" (*Sbornik Svjatoslavov*), (pravdy d(ě)lę", "Boga radi". Even in the 17th century narrative poems, like *Povest' o Gorě i Zločastii*, no inversions of this type occur, although there are rather numerous adjective inversions ("kružku ... piva p'janogo"). One could, of course, call the possessive adjective a veiled form of noun anteposition ("carev kabak"); but it can be used in a limited number of instances only. There are many denominative adjectives: *božestvennoe pisanie, kun'ja šuba, sobolina šapka*, in *Gore i Zločastie*: *spasennyj put'* for *put' spasenija*; cf. the proverb "odin volk gonjaet ovečej polk".

The picture changes when we consider other types and genres of the 17th century literary production as well as written documents in which a new rhetorical style was applied. As early as 1581 this style appears in the Ukrainian Ondrej Rymša's *Xronologija*, the title of which was an extended anteposition: *Kotorogo sja mesjaca čto za staryx věkov děelo korotko opisanie*. In innumerable texts, letters, petitions and supplications, deeds and contracts, etc., examples of inversion can be found. "Kak Tebe, Gosudarju, Vyšnjago promysl izvěstit ..." ("Poslanie kn. Šaxovskogo kn. Požarskomu");[9] "I krasnago sego mira mudrost' Bogu neprijatna", "Vostočnyja cerkvi božestvennuju dobrotu" (Ivan Xvorostinin's "Molitva Xristu Bogu"), "aki sladkago pittija zlataja čara" ("Poslanie d'jaku V. S. Prokof'evu" by the *spravščik* Savvatij), "Bog vsjakoj duši zritel'" ("Poslanie kn. Alipiju Nikitiču"); "na prositelej otvět", "Drevnix bo knjažat ustavy otvergoša" ("Deklaracija moskovskomu posol'stvu" by Timofej Akundinov), "Kieva načalo" (Arximandrit Tixon), "Vašego carskago velikago miloserdija, presvětloj i bogatoj ščedrosti ... istinno userdnyj želatel'" (Sil'vestr Medvedev's "Vručenie ... carevne ... Sofii Aleksievne, privilija na akademiju"), etc.

Sometimes the genitive case is replaced by the dative, both in the proper and the possessive sense: "No ereticy tvorjat prisnyja Bogu ofery", "No vsemu miru velikija mučiteli". And sometimes other cases are used with prepositions – instances that can be likewise classified as nouns dependent on other nouns: "Gorě v nebě derznovenie, Obščij zemli mir, smirenie/ Daeši vsěm ..." (in a eulogy by monax German).

Not all writers of the 17th century indulged in the stylistic exuberance of which the anteposition was but a part. Karion Istomin's *Domostroj* is written in a simple language, in which almost no inversions occur; in Avvakum's *Žitie* antepositions are very rare ("... ikonnago pisma nepodobnago izugrafy"); in

Peresvetov's writings they are absent, whereas Kotošixin has some. In Avraam Palicyn's *Skazanie* the regular order of dominant plus dependent noun is often used, the anteposition only exceptionally, and not in the narrative parts, but only where the author occasionally speaks in a more ceremonial tone – for example in the introductory words: "Istorija v pamjat' predyduščim rodom ... spisano byst toja že velikija obiteli – troica sergieva monastyrja kelarem inokom Avramiem Palicynym"; and: "Semu že skazaniju načalo sicevo": or in phrases like "vsěx načal'nejšix vel'mož sovětom", "velikim bědam zamyšlenicy". Cf. this construction, with parallelism of verbal nouns: "... daet po togo izvoleniju nemjatěžno zemli Rustěj prebyvanie i vsex blagix preizobilovanie". The third chapter ends with: "Směxu dostojno skazanie, plača že veliko dělo byst' ".

The figure occurs in poetry even more frequently than in prose. An additional and important reason for its use in verse is the rime requirement. The *raešnye stixi* often have grammatical rimes, for a large part consisting of verbal forms, and notably verbal nouns (mostly with the ending *-nie*), which necessitates anteposition of the dependent noun: "oka tvoego blistanie" (*Artakserksovo dejstvo*), "... no božiim pomoženiem/ I bogonosnyx i čjudotvornyx otec k nemu moleniem". This order is part of a tendency to place verbal forms at the end of a sentence in the poetry of this period.[10] On the other hand, a striving after parallelism, not the necessity of riming, explains lines like this one: "No v urok xristijanom, svjatyx ikon poklonnikom, predloženy". There are also antepositions of nouns preceded by a preposition: "... krepkix i nelestnyx po věrě pobaratelej", "naše pred Bogom velie i sogrěšenie", "naše malo sie k Tebě, Gosudarju, prošenie", or, in Simeon Polockij: "Jako bez světa solnce ne byvaet".

As was indicated in the above, the phenomenon under discussion is part of a general endeavor to widen the stylistic means, to express oneself in an intricate, flowery way. It is not surprising that anteposition became one of the favorite stylistic devices: after all, the Slavic languages have, thanks to their flectional character, a freedom of word order within the sentence that is much greater than in the Germanic and Romance languages; and this freedom was being further and further exploited. Simeon Polockij, for example, varied the word order by frequent dislocations, placing a verb between the two nouns: "v čislo napisati bogov i xotjaxu", "župel ognja est' pišča, vino poxoti" (in this syllabic line with the cesura after the seventh syllable there was no rime or meter requirement calling for this order: "župel est' pišča ognja" would have been just as possible and correct). He also liked to separate the substantive from the possessive or demonstrative pronoun ("Six serdce moe blag tebě želaet"). In his poem "Bogatyx obyčaj" the first line starts: "Bogatym est' obyčaj ščedro razdajati", which shows that the possessive dative was equivalent with the genitive.

Anteposition was sometimes used to construct chiasms ("na utverždenie že věrnyx i na zabluždajuščix ispravlenie", Stefan Javorskij).[11] There are numerous transitional cases, which one hesitates whether or not to classify as antepositions: "To vsěm nam nadeža i upovanie", for example, or: "na vsja vidimyja vragi naša nepobědimyj progonitel' ", "ne ostalos' by ix v zemli našej slědu".

In the early 18th century we come across examples in Petr Buslaev's, Stefan Javorskij's, Feofan Prokopovič's writings ("otčestva vrag velij..."), but they are not numerous. A much wider use of the device is found in the Ukrainian poet Klimentij Zinoviïv, in whose *virši* (early 18th century) 51% of various sorts of anteposition occur, as an early example of baroque *Formenfreude* in East Slavic poetry. In Russia, the situation changes with the emergence of Trediakovskij as one of the leading poets, who employed inversions, and notably the type we are discussing, to a degree never attained before or after him by any other Russian poet. Counting the antepositions in a number of his poems and plays, including only the genitive cases in our calculations, and only nouns (no antepositions with numerals and quantitative nouns or adverbs, as these constitute separate categories used more frequently in Russian of all levels, styles, and periods), we arrive at a percentage of 54 of antepositions; adding the dative antepositions and those with a preposition (if they are not separate syntagms, but clearly an apposition to the dominant noun: "s samym serdečnym k Anne duxom") it is no less than 74. A second calculation, which included a different group of poems by Trediakovskij, yielded a lower percentage, 60; but even this is considerably more than half of all the pertinent cases.

Lomonosov also has a high frequency of noun inversions: 49%, or 44% if we exclusively count the genitive cases. In Ozerov's tragedies the antepositions practically match the instances of normal order (49.8%). M. M. Xeraskov's antepositions amount to 46.6% (45% of the genitives only); Deržavin's to 45% (44% of the genitives); Sumarokov's to 38% (35% of the genitives), which is about half of Trediakovskij's percentage.

Very close to Sumarokov as to the measure in which they use anteposition are the classical poets of the 19th century. This might well be an indication that, although the extravagances of a baroque or a classicist style were rejected in the subsequent era, some characteristics of poetic expression of the 18th century were firmly anchored in the literary tradition and survived all changes of literary schools, trends, and styles. Only the antepositions with the dative case or with prepositions and the cases they govern decrease, their percentage becomes rather insignificant in the 19th century.

Žukovskij's average of noun inversion (with the genitive case) is 38.5%, Puškin's 32.5%, but, as I indicated, only 26% in a later work of a partly reflexive and descriptive, partly narrative character like *Mednyj vsadnik*. Tjutčev was even more inclined to use noun inversions: he did it in 42% of the instances in his verse. With Fet the percentage is lower: 24%. In his contemplative lyrical verse the amount of dependent genitive constructions is relatively large (approximately one in every four lines), but it decreases in his later works. However, the proportion of antepositions undergoes little change. The fact that the line from Deržavin's "Arfa": "Otečestva i dym nam sladok i prijaten" was modified in *Gore ot uma* into "I dym otečestva nam sladok i prijaten" seems not to indicate that anteposition was less usual or less wanted in 19th century poetry, but rather that Deržavin's sentence did not fit the colloquial style of Griboedov's comedy.

As could be expected, in Nekrasov's poetry the antepositions are much rarer: they cover merely 15% of the dependent genitive constructions. He wrote in a simple idiom, his style is unadorned, based on the folk song and the way of expression of the Russian peasant. But this tone is not typical of Russian poetic expression during the first part of the 19th century. Most normal in this poetry is an alternation of the regular and the transposed order of nouns — partly because this was the way of writing handed down by previous poets, and partly because it was a most useful license, facilitating the creation of metrical, rimed, stanzaic verse. This is particularly true of the (often abstract) verbal nouns, that were put at the end of the line, just as the 18th century poets had done, albeit less frequently than the latter used to do. As an example Lermontov's poem "Rodina" could serve:

> Ni polnyj gordogo doverija pokoj,
> Ni temnoj stariny zavetnye predan'ja,
> Ne ševeljat vo mne otradnogo mečtan'ja.
>
> No ja ljublju — za čto, ne znaju sam —
> Ee stepej xolodnoe molčan'e,
> Ee lesov bezbrežnyx kolyxan'e,
> Razlivy rek ee, podobnye morjam ...", etc.

In the next lines there is "noči ten' ", "v stepi nočujuščij oboz", "s raznymi stavnjami okno".

One would anticipate that the period of symbolizm should cause significant shifts in this pattern. However, the picture remains virtually unchanged. Brjusov has 25% of his dependent genitives in the reversed order, Bal'mont 21%, Blok 22% — at least in the lyrical poetry of his early career, later, for example in the long poem "Vozmezdie", we find only 12%, although the number of genitive constructions in this largely reflexive work is high (one case of a dependent genitive construction in each 4.5 lines). In addition to the nouns, there are numerous numerals and quantitative nouns and adverbs with a dependent genitive noun in the verse of these poets, both antepositioned and postpositioned (*mnogo, malo, t'ma, tolpa*, etc.; as was mentioned, these are not included in our statistics).

In the course of the 20th century several poetic schools succeeded each other or coexisted, but the anteposition retained its place. In Majakovskij's verse it averages 26.5% of his genitive noun constructions ("Izbavlenija srok" — it sounds like an old Russian religious text); in Pasternak's 20%; and in Vinokurov's (to take a contemporary example) likewise 20%. Obviously there is a reduction from Tjutčev's 42% to Vinokurov's 20%, and the anteposition figure is certainly less customary now than a century and a half ago. In Pasternak's line "I tixoju zarej, — verxi derev gorjat" he could have written just as well, so it seems to us: "... derev verxi gorjat", but he did not — maybe for compositional reasons, maybe because it would sound old-fashioned; but then, he has "Gde šepčet jabloni priboj", "Kogda za liry labirint", "treščal i tajal kresel šelk", "Vselennoj nebyvalost'/ I žizni novizna", etc.

Thus we may conclude that the apposition of a noun to another noun in the reversed order is a usual and generally employed variety of the genitive noun dependence in Russian poetry from the 17th century onwards up to this time. It survived all evolutions and revolutions in the development of the Russian literary language and of poetic expression: those of Polockij, Lomonosov, Karamzin, Puškin, Blok, Majakovskij, and others. However, it should be borne in mind that the usage is not restricted to poetry. As we have seen, it was very fashionable in the prose language of the 17th and 18th centuries, whether of a purely literary character or not. It lost its attraction in the 19th century, even though it continued to be occasionally applied, either for special reasons of style or emphasis or because the case in point was a traditional turn of phrase.[12] One can find occasional instances even in realistic, not particularly stylized prose: "generala Žukova dvorovyj" (Čexov), "zamečatel'nogo uma francuz" (Gor'kij).[13]

In the first quarter of this century some writers paid special attention to their language and literary style. The most original among them was probably A. Remizov. However, he did not use antepositions: his style was patterned after the language of old popular legends — not a source for style figures like the anteposition. A. Belyj rather followed the literary tradition of the 18th and 19th centuries; he saw noun inversion as one of the means of heightening the expressiveness and the rhythm of his prose. Anton Hönig in his book on Belyj's novels writes: "No prose writer of the 20th century has the genitive object as often antepositioned as Belyj: in the novel *Serebrjanyj golub'* fifty times. ... And it happens with insignificant words as well. Decisive here is not the meaning — what decides about the position of the genitive is the rhythm".[14] The author calculates that there are, in *Serebrjanyj golub'*, twice as many genitive antepositions as in all Belyj's other novels taken together. Here are some of the examples he quotes: "polosatogo kanifasa čexly", "ruki vozloženie", "šei svoej xudobinu", "milovatogo večera grust' ". It should be added that in *Peterburg*, his next novel, anteposition is only occasionally used, but these instances, together with other types of inversions, contribute to the special style of this book: "zolotogo venka i lavry, i rozany", "svoi krasnogo laka korobočki", "Sergeja Sergeeviča lico". However, this innovation, or rather revival of an old figure, did not take root: it was evidently too archaic and stylish to be usable in Soviet prose.

I. I. Kovtunova, in her book on word order in the Russian literary language, points to the influence of Latin syntax on Russian in the early 18th century, when large numbers of books were translated;[15] and likewise to the influence of German syntax – translations from German were also very numerous.[16] She does not enlarge upon these aspects. There is no doubt that in classical Latin prose and poetry anteposition was frequently used, as one of the possibilities of stylistic variation in a strongly flectional language: "... Troiae qui primus ab oris" (Virgil), "accusare de epistolarum negligentia" (Cicero), "Flaminii tamen recens casus" (Livius), etc. The same habit of inversion was followed in Medieval Latin, the literary language all over Europe up to the time when it was supplanted by the national languages. On Slavic territory Latin was frequently used by the Poles, Czechs, Dalmatians, etc., in all kinds of texts, from laws, treaties, and contracts to poetry and philosophical treatises, from their earliest written documents up to the 17th, partly the 18th century. The poem "Epistola ad Dominicellam", which is probably the oldest Polish love poem (15th century; 46 stanzas) has both anteposition and the 'normal' order,[17] and so do other Latin verse and prose texts emanating from West Slavic territory. In a country like Poland, where 'Liberum veto' was a household word, the syntax of the official and literary language was imbued with Latin elements, including inversions.

The knowledge of Latin spread to Southwest Russia in the early 17th century; in the Kievan Academy it was intensively studied. Only toward the end of the century Muscovy discovered the value of Latin; through the numerous Ukrainians who came to and worked in Russia, and later through the direct contacts with the West and through Russian translations from Latin, elements of Latin vocabulary, idiom, and syntax must have penetrated into the Russian literary language, as was the case with the Ukrainian language. This whole question has not yet been sufficiently investigated.

The Greek language had a position of much longer standing in Russia and the other Orthodox Slavic regions: it had dominated literary activity since its beginnings, just as Latin had done in the rest of Europe. Greek texts were copied and used as models by many generations of monks. This must have left strong imprints on the literary languages of the East Slavs. In classical Greek the freedom of word order, though not as great as in Latin, was quite considerable and inversions of various kinds were not uncommon. One finds anteposition both in poetry and in prose ("Messaniou gerontis... frèn", Pindar; "tous tou Aisōpon logous", Plato), although less frequently than in Latin literature. The same liberty can also be found in the Greek Bible texts and other religious literature ("hè eis to theion blasfèmia", Ezekiel (O.T.); "iatrōn paides", "ho tou Dios outōs huios", N.T.). Just as in the case of Latin, an exact measurement of the influence upon Old Church Slavic and Russian can hardly be made, but it is more than likely that certain Greek stylistic and syntactic peculiarities, including anteposition, were copied from Greek originals and entered the literary language.

A third external factor which may have contributed to the wide usage of the antepositioned substantive in the Russian literary language is the influence of German, as was suggested by I. Kovtunova. In German, structured differently from the Slavic languages, inversions cannot be applied as freely and with such variety as in Slavic, but the anteposition is a widely used device — again, not in the spoken or simple written language, but as a rhetorical figure in prose and as a poetic license; probably the Latin example played a certain role in German, too. In Goethe's works 46% of the dependent genitive noun constructions have this form, in Schiller's no less than 72%. The majority of the cases has an inversion of two substantives with the article or possessive or demonstrative pronoun of the dependent, antepositioned noun, but omission of those attributives of the dominant noun ("deš Jünglings Mund", "deiner Waffen Schalle"). Sometimes an adjective would be added to either one of these nouns. Grammatical dependence can in some cases be expressed, instead of the genitive case, by the preposition *von* ("Der Herr vom Haus"); here no inversion takes place.

As is well known, many German books came to Russia and many translations from German were made, especially under Peter the Great's reign. We can also think of the influence German poetry had on, for example, Lomonosov. This influence came at a time when various literary rhetorical devices, among them also inversions, had already become well known and rather common in the Russian written language. To establish the degree of direct influence of the German model is again impossible; but one can imagine that the presence of this syntactic figure in German texts encouraged Russian writers to apply it in their works. The same can be said of the French and English usage: in French classical literature the occurrence is low (Molière used 22% of antepositions among his dependent genitive cases); in English it is high (Byron's antepositions amount to 60% of the cases, i.e. in 40% he uses *of*, in 60% the anteposition with the genitive -*s*), but this is the normal sentence structure in English; anteposition is not used here as a poetic device or stylistic figure. Yet the fact that in so many languages the dependent noun could be placed before the dominant one may have had a certain effect upon Russian writers and poets.

Anteposition should not be studied as an isolated phenomenon in Russian poetry. In the first place, it is obvious that it is connected with other types of inversion, also frequent in the Russian written language and also reaching their culmination point in the 18th century: various kinds of dislocation, interpolation of the verb ("suxoe tlelo leto", M. Šoloxov), the postposition of the attribute (adjective, participle, possessive and demonstrative pronoun), the postposition of the verb (any verbal form) ("muk věčnyx svobodi mja", "Iz Persidy volxvov prišedšix" in 17th century texts); the anteposition of a noun dependent on an adjective (for example, with *dostojnyj, polnyj*: I refer again to *Mednyj vsadnik*: "... dum velikix poln"); the anteposition of adverbs and adverbial adjuncts ("V dom novozdannyj ašče kto vselitsja"); the anteposition of *kotoryj* in the possessive genitive form ("smotritel', kotorogo deti"). The latter example is from A. Belyj, in whose work this figure is certainly an archaic feature; in the 18th and 19th centuries it was relatively frequent (in Polish the equivalent is more common: "X., w którego książkach...").

It should be clear that anteposition is not just a rhetorical device invented or imitated by 17th and 18th century stylists. The idea of placing the dependent noun (without preposition in the genitive and sometimes dative case, or with a preposition in the required case) ahead of the dominant noun is much more familiar to the Russians, and the Slavs in general, than to most other European peoples. In the modern Russian spoken and prose language it occurs rather infrequently, usually for reasons of special emphasis or when it is required by the context, as in a sentence like: "so spinkoj divan mne ne nravitsja, ja xoču kupit' divan bez spinki"; somewhat more often when the dominant noun has an attribute preceding the construction: "šerstjanuju, radužnyx cvetov kosynku".[18] As a reminiscence of poetic language or as a rhetorical device it is sometimes employed in newspaper headings etc.: "Kommuny doma prorastajut".[19]

It is comprehensible that in a language with such a facility of varying the word order of individual morphemes and syntagms within a sentence the type of inversion discussed here is bound to appear, even without any stylistic purposes. When it is normal to say "černoe pal'to", then why not "temnogo cveta pal'to"? When "analogičnye predloženija" is the norm, why should "analogičnogo xaraktera predloženija" be so unusual? When "ego druz'ja" is the most common order, then why not "Kuzneckogo druz'ja"? And if "Ivanov dom" exists, why not "Ivana (Dmitrieviča) dom"? (As mentioned above, very many antepositions are formed with a personal name or a person.) Sometimes such syntagms would become fixed turns of phrase, for example, in the case of "(pušečnyx) del master". The reversed order is common with numerals (where it has acquired a special semantic function, indicating approximation: "čelovek desjat' ") and with quantitative nouns and adverbs, as mentioned above.[20] But it is clear that the inversion in poetry, as I briefly discussed in these pages, is a stylistic device of a different order than this purely syntactic, semantically and stylistically neutral (as a rule) construction in the Russian language.

University of California, Los Angeles

NOTES

1. V. Žirmunskij, *Vvedenie v metriku. Teorija stixa* (Moscow, 1925) (Voprosy poètiki, VI), p. 125.
2. B. V. Tomaševskij, *Puškin* I (Moscow-Leningrad, 1956), p. 657.
3. N. S. Pospelov, *Sintaktičeskij stroj stixotvornyx proizvedenij Puškina* (Moscow: AN SSSR, 1960), p. 7. Pospelov also quotes Žirmunskij (note 1).
4. *Ibid.*, p. 22. The analysis referred to is on pp. 194-97.
5. Cf. D. S. Lixačev, "Kommentarij istoričeskij i geografičeskij", *Slovo o polku Igoreve*, red. V. P. Adrianova-Peretc (Moscow-Leningrad: AN SSSR, 1950), p. 447.
6. *Ibid.*, p. 465.
7. There is one instance in the bylina "Aleša Popovič i Tugarin Zmaevič": "Nalej čaru... / za Tugarina Zmeeviča zdravie". The dependent noun is again a personal name, it is almost a possessive adjective, which it might have been (Tugarinovo) if the patronymic had not been added.
8. The quotations are from the Russian version. See È. T. Zykov, "Russkaja peredelka drevnebolgarskogo stixotvorenija", *Issledovanija po istorii russkoj literatury XI-XVIII vv.* (Trudy Otdela Drevnerusskoj Literatury, XXVIII) (Leningrad, 1974), pp. 308-15 (the text is reproduced on pp. 314-15).
9. Many of the following examples are taken from the volume *Russkaja sillabičeskaja poèzija 17-18 vv.* (Biblioteka poèta, Bol'šaja serija; Leningrad, 1970).
10. Cf. I. I. Kovtunova, *Porjadok slov v russkom literaturnom jazyke XVIII – pervoj treti XIX v.* (Moscow, 1969), p. 83 among other places.
11. Cf. I. I. Kovtunova, *op. cit.*, p. 78, from where the example is taken.
12. *Ibid.*, pp. 42-43 and 51: inversion can be motivated by expressive intentions or can be neutral; in most cases it gives a phrase an "opredelennuju stilističeskuju okrasku". See the discussion of the problem in the Academy of Sciences *Grammatika russkogo jazyka* II: *Sintaksis* 1 (Moscow, 1954), pp. 681-83.
13. The examples are taken from *Grammatika russkogo jazyka* (see previous note), pp. 682-83.
14. Anton Hönig, *Andrej Belyjs Romane: Stil und Gestalt* (München, 1965), p. 16 (my translation, T. E.).
15. *Op. cit.*, pp. 76-77, 80.
16. *Ibid.*, p. 81.
17. See *Sredniowieczna poezja polska świecka* (opr. S. Vrtel-Wierczyński) (Wrocław: Bibl. Narodowa, 1952), pp. 70-76.
18. The examples are taken from *Grammatika russkogo jazyka* (see note No. 12).
19. I. I. Kovtunova, *op. cit.*, pp. 53-54.
20. One could include here the type "Srednej veličiny medved' " (Gogol'; adduced in *Grammatika russkogo jazyka, ibid.*), although not the dominant, but the dependent noun is a quantitative noun.

COMMENTS

de Mallac Considering that the significance of inversion in Russian poetic speech can hardly be exaggerated, it would be highly worthwhile for Professor Eekman to pursue certain aspects of the important research he has undertaken, so as to come to even more specific conclusions.

He might find it profitable not only to consider differentiating — as far as is compatible with his personal interests as an investigator — between the different literary genres in which inversion occurs (as was already suggested to him), but also to keep in mind the potential helpfulness for his investigation of material contained both in treatises on rhetoric used in the Ukraine in the 17th century *and* in similar treatises from Western Europe — which might yield significant suggestions for **typology** relevant to his subject.

I believe it would also be most worthwhile for Mr. Eekman to consider more frankly some of the **semantic-esthetic** implications of the uses of inversion in Russian poetic speech. The considerable (and necessary) statistical survey he has undertaken seems to provide a rich basis for further interesting deductions and conclusions.

Lilly Did you find a smaller percentage of examples of inversion in blank than in rhymed verse?

Marvan It is quite tempting to consider the external origin of the genitive preposition. The Finnic languages in which such a construction is regular and whose substrate elements in Russian are often claimed would be such a case. Yet it seems obvious that this construction has primarily common Slavic sources as indicated by both the data of other (even old) Slavic languages and their syntactic typology (relaxed word order).

Additional discussion: Abernathy, Grossman, Hrushovsky, Issatschenko, Nilsson, Segal, Stankiewicz, Vickery, Worth

AUTHOR'S REPLY

The theme is not exhaustively dealt with in this paper; some of the unsolved or untouched problems I bring up in another paper, soon to be published. In it, I show, a.o., that inversion is less frequent in blank than in rhymed verse. The aspects mentioned by Professor de Mallac should certainly be investigated. The same is true of Dr. Pszczołowska's oral comments: one should try to differentiate between anteposition as a mere style figure and as an expressive means: it is often semantically and stylistically marked. This difference is hard to catch in statistics, though! Also, as was remarked in the discussion, the question of addition of adjectives and pronouns to either one of the two nouns should be given more attention, as well as the question of a different frequency of anteposition in the 18th century Russian 'high' and 'low' styles.

К АНАЛИЗУ РУССКОЙ НЕТОЧНОЙ РИФМЫ

М. Л. ГАСПАРОВ

1. Стиховедам хорошо знакома диаграмма Р. Якобсона в статье "Лингвистика и поэзия",[1] показывающая тремя волнообразными линиями ритм русского стиха на трех уровнях: чередование согласных и гласных в слоге, чередование ударных и безударных слогов в стопе, чередование сильноударных и слабоударных стоп в стихе (можно добавить и четвертый уровень: чередование необлегченных и облегченных стихов в строфе[2]). Исследование стиха обычно сосредоточивалось на средних уровнях, на слоге и стопе; до низшего уровня — до согласных и гласных — исследователям случалось проникать очень редко.[3] Однако в стихе есть место, где этот низший уровень ритмичности текста как бы сам обнажается и становится непосредственно ощутим. Это место — рифма.

С помощью точных методов русская рифма по существу не исследовалась вплоть до самого недавнего времени. В. Жирмунский в своей классической книге опирался на подсчеты, но не публиковал их. В. Тренин и Н. Харджиев, М. Штокмар в своих работах о рифме Маяковского подсчетами не пользовались. Д. Самойлов, собрав богатейший и интересно осмысленний материал по фольклорной и литературной рифме XVIII-начала XX вв., подошел к тому самому рубежу, на котором подсчеты становятся неизбежны, но там и остановился. Едва ли не первыми попытками ввести статистику в изучение русской рифмы были статьи С. Толстой — с проектом учета (пожалуй, слишком тонкого) точности рифм по числу совпадающих дифференциальных признаков в составляющих ее фонемах, и А. Кондратова — с опытом учета (пожалуй, слишком грубого) точных и неточных, грамматических и неграмматических рифм. Уже после этого появились работы Д. Уорса с подсчетами звукового богатства русской рифмы XVIII в. и, наконец, исключительно ценная по содержательности и тонкости анализа статья А. Исаченко, после которой возврат к прежним приблизительным определениям точности и неточности рифмы уже, по-видимому, невозможен.[4]

Предлагаемое сообщение представляет собой попытку дальнейшего уточнения приемов анализа русской рифмы с помощью простейших подсчетов. Оно не притязает на открытие новых фактов — почти все приводимые здесь примеры (или аналогичные им) уже рассматривались В. Жирмунским, Д. Самойловым или А. Исаченко. Мы лишь пытались более последовательно, чем это обычно делалось, дифференцировать точность созвучия *на отдельных позициях,* занимаемых звуками в рифме.

2. Под рифмой здесь и далее имеется в виду созвучие окончаний стиха, начиная с последнего обязательно-ударного слога (константы). Рифма состоит из ряда чередующихся вокальных (V) и консонантных (С) позиций. Схема мужской рифмы — СV (открытая рифма) или VC (закрытая рифма); женской — VCVC, дактилической — VCVCVC. Консонантные позиции различаются: предвокальная (в мужской рифме), интервокальные и финальная. Каждая консонантная позиция может быть занята одним согласным ("мало-ломало"), группой согласных (царство-лекарство") или нулем звука (последнее чаще всего в финальной позиции — "мало-ломало", "царство-лекарство" — но возможно и в интервокальной позиции: "какао-хаос").

Фонемы, занимающие аналогичные позиции в двух рифмующих словах (членах рифмы) могут находиться в трояком отношении друг к другу: тождества (Т), прибавления-убавления (П) и замены (М). Рифмы, в которых все элементы тождественны, называются точными. Рифмы, в которых имеется хоть один П-элемент, называются пополненными. Рифмы, в которых имеется хоть один М-элемент, называются измененными.[5]

Здесь будет рассматриваться только консонантное строение рифмы, т.е. соотношение согласных фонем на аналогичных позициях. Вокальное строение рифмы — предмет для рассмотрения в будущем. Соответственно в дальнейшем в формулах рифм знаками Т, П и М будут отмечаться только консонантные позиции; вокальные же позиции будут отмечаться черточками.

3. Классификация рифм.

Мужские:

                    Т-: топора-пора;
                    -Т: завод-зовет;
        П- : табуНы-бунТы;   М- : себЯ-сПя;
        Т-П: урагаН-врага;   М-П: заГиБ-казаКи;
         -П: наш-маРш;   -М: собоР-боЙ;

Ж е н с к и е :

Т-Т : разом-приказом;   П-Т : веским-КереНским;

Т-П : КалиниН-клине;   П-П : рыскаЛ-СимбиРска;

Т-М: грабастаЛ-горбастыЙ;   П-М: ВеНчиК-человечиЙ;

М-Т : раДость-припара/Д′/ясь;

М-П : теСно-протеЗный;

М-М: затыРкаЛ-затыЛкоМ;

Д а к т и л и ч е с к и е :

Т-Т-Т : Ульянова-заново;   П-Т-Т : найДена-громадина;

Т-Т-П : лохматого-выматываЛ;   П-Т-П : поД вечеР-Прокоповича;

Т-Т-М : выпачкаВ-на цыпочкаХ;   П-Т-М : (поД вечеР-ПрокоповычеЙ);

Т-П-Т : преснеНцы-треснется;   П-П-Т : селень/J/ице-лениНцы;

Т-П-П : начисто-кулачестВоМ;   П-П-П : спокоеН каК-χокой/Н′/ика;

Т-П-М : хлынуВшеЙ-клинышеК;   П-П-М : (спокоеН каК-покой/Н′/икаМ);

Т-М-Т : представиТели-виДели;   П-М-Т : ДездеМо/Н′/е-звезде оНа;

Т-М-П : береГоМ-АмериКа;   П-М-П : уделитьЛи ВаМ-удивитеЛьНа;

Т-М-М: наигрыВаЙ-эпиграФоМ;   П-М-М: (уделить Ли ВаМ-

                                                                         удивитеЛьНоЙ);

М-Т-Т : выКовки-ЛиГовке;

М-Т-П : сиВого-разизнасиЛоваЛ;

М-Т-М : оБухоМ-оПухоЛь;

М-П-Т : сляКоти-за ЛоКти;

М-П-П : иНаче-вы/Н′/яНчиЛ;

М-П-М : (иНаче-С — вы/Н′/яНчиЛ);

М-М-Т : трансПоРТы-ас/П′/иДы;

М-М-П : боМ/Б′/иЩеЙ-оБЩу/J/ю;

М-М-М: плаМеНеМ-правиЛеН.

Мы исходим из предположения, что ощутимость неточной рифмы вырастает в последовательности Т - П - М: восприятие созвучия П требует одного психического акта (прибавление-убавление звука), восприятие созвучия М — двух (убавление одного звука и появление другого звука). В таком случае пропорция Т:П:М будет удобным *показателем неточности рифмы* — как в целом, в данном произведении или у данного поэта, так и в частности, для каждой отдельной звуковой позиции в рифме.

4. Материалом для настоящего предварительного обследования взяты следующие произведения: 1) Блок, II том лирики (1904-1908); 2) Брюсов, "Urbi et orbi" (1901-1904); 3) Брюсов, "Mea" (1922-1924); 4-7) Маяковский,

“Облако в штанах” (1915); “Война и мир” (1916); “Владимир Ильич Ленин” (1924); “Хорошо!” (1927); 8) Пастернак, “Сестра моя жизнь” (1917); 9) Есенин, “Пугачев” (1920); 10) Асеев, “Семен Проскаков” (1927); 11-12) Сельвинский, “Улялаевщина” в редакциях 1924 г. (гл. 1-4) и 1956 г. (гл. 1-2); 13) Евтушенко, 12 стихотворений 1965-1968 гг. и поэма “Коррида”; 14) Вознесенский, 125 стихотворений 1964-1968 гг. и поэма “Оза”; 15) для сравнения — пословицы и поговорки конца XVII-начала XVIII в. по изданию П. Симони (Сб. ОРЯС, т. 66 (1899), № 7), по три первых страницы на каждую букву до “П”. Для дактилических рифм у Асеева обследована дополнительно лирика 1926-1928 гг., у Сельвинского — полный текст обеих редакций “Улялаевщины”.

5. Вот показатель неточности рифмы Т:П:М отдельно для мужских, женских и дактилических рифм в нашем материале. Под рубрикой ‘в целом’ дается общее соотношение ‘точных’, ‘пополненных’ и ‘измененных’ рифм, под остальными рубриками — соотношение Т:П:М для отдельных позиций. Так как для финальной позиции в точных рифмах может быть существенно, заполнена она согласным звуком или нет (закрытая перед нами рифма или открытая), то при показателе Т в скобках указывается соотношение открытых и закрытых рифм в данном виде: так, ‘61(18+43):24:15’ означает, что в данном тексте из 61% точных созвучий в финальной позиции 18% представляют собой созвучие нуля звука с нулем звука, а 43% — созвучие согласного с согласным.

Для Блока и раннего Брюсова, у которых неточных рифм мало, указано только общее соотношение точных, пополненных и измененных рифм.

МУЖСКИЕ:	в целом	предвок.	финал.	Число рифм
Блок	: 99: 0 :1			1288
Брюсов, 1901-04	: 97: 1 :2			757
Брюсов, 1922-24	: 87(68+19): 8: 5	92:2 : 6	85:10: 5	260
Маяковск., 1915	: 61(18+43):24:15	79:4 :17	81: 6:13	61
Маяковск., 1916	: 44(16+28):55: 1	100:0 : 0	79:17: 4	68
Маяковск., 1924	: 59(16+43):35: 6	93:0 : 7	78:16: 6	201
Маяковск., 1927	: 47(19+28):42:11	88:1 :11	76:12:12	249
Пастернак, 1917	: 49(15+34):33:18	89:5,5:5,5	41:39:20	309
Есенин, 1920	: 62(26+36):27:11	74:7 :19	58:33: 9	195
Асеев, 1927	: 46(19+27):36:18	74:5 :21	36:47:17	164
Сельвинск., 1924	: 22(10+12):42:36	84:1 :15	26:10:64	243
Сельвинск., 1956	: 93(39+54): 3: 4	97:0 : 3	94: 0: 6	182
Евтушенко	: 78(29+49): 4:18	74:4 :22	81: 4:15	253
Вознесенский	: 61(26+35): 4:35	70:7 :23	58: 2:40	162
Нар. пословицы	: 81(20+61): 2:17	62:5 :33	90: 0:10	240

ЖЕНСКИЕ:	в целом	интервок.	финал.	Число рифм
Блок	: 86:11: 3			1034
Брюсов, 1901-04	: 82:17: 1			720
Брюсов, 1922-24	: 51:32:17	86: 5: 9	61(41+20):32: 7	265
Маяковск., 1915	: 48:45: 7	85: 9: 6	61(40+21):37: 2	104
Маяковск., 1916	: 42:52: 6	92: 5: 3	48(27+21):48: 4	102
Маяковск., 1924	: 41:51: 8	85:10: 5	48(34+14):49: 3	248
Маяковск., 1927	: 26:57:17	67:20:13	46(42+ 4):48: 6	187
Пастернак, 1917	: 32:41:27	66:19:15	48(35+13):39:13	212
Есенин, 1920	: 42:32:26	78: 8:14	51(40+11):34:15	131
Асеев, 1927	: 38:29:33	64: 9:27	60(40+20):32: 8	106
Сельвинск., 1924	: 23:38:39	60:13:27	44(37+ 7):41:15	238
Сельвинск., 1956	: 62:23:15	80: 7:13	75(61+14):21: 4	150
Евтушенко	: 45:12:43	48:11:41	88(71+17): 6: 7	259
Вознесенский	: 26:24:50	36:21:43	70(59+11):16:14	182
Нар. пословицы	: 75: 3:22	78: 2:20	96(68+28): 2: 2	255

ДАКТИЛИ-ЧЕСКИЕ:	в целом	1-инт-вок.	2 инт-вок.	финал.	Число рифм
Блок	: 75: 6:19				109
Брюсов, 1901-04	: 88:10: 2				59
Брюсов, 1922-24	: 53:20:27	75: 9:15	75:14:11	88(80+ 8):10: 2	112
Маяковск., 1915	: 63:28: 9	79:12: 9	91: 7: 2	81(74+ 7):19: 0	43
Маяковск., 1916	: 52:35:13	85: 9: 6	94: 2: 4	72(63+ 9):26: 2	46
Маяковск., 1924	: 39:33:28	72:12:16	81: 6:13	69(66+ 3):31: 0	64
Маяковск., 1927	: 36:29:35	67:12:21	77: 6:17	67(62+ 5):32: 1	66
Пастернак, 1917	: 9:30:61	64:11:25	42:19:39	36(31+ 5):47:17	64
Есенин, 1920	: 31:21:48	72: 7:21	52:10:38	62(48+14):34: 4	29
Асеев, 1927	: 34:18:48	64: 8:28	69:10:21	78(70+ 8):18: 4	106
Сельвинск., 1924	: 27:18:55	70:10:20	39:18:43	78(76+ 2):20: 2	49
Сельвинск., 1956	: 35:17:48	61: 4:35	65: 9:26	83(83+ 0):17: 2	23
Евтушенко	: 24: 4:72	29: 7:64	44:10:46	87(80+ 7): 6: 7	83
Вознесенский	: 3:28:69	28:30:42	30:25:45	75(72+ 3):22: 3	36
Нар. пословицы	: 47: 3:50	57: 3:40	83: 0:17	97(84+13): 0: 3	30

6. Из таблицы видно: наиболее устойчивыми по точности являются мужские рифмы, наиболее расшатанными — дактилические. Отчасти это зависит от того простого факта, что длинная дактилическая рифма предоставляет гораздо больше разнообразных возможностей дефор-мации, чем короткая мужская; отчасти же, несомненно, сами поэты стараются точностью мужских рифм оттенить и компенсировать неточ-ность рифм женских и дактилических. Наибольшая степень точности мужских рифм — у Брюсова и Евтушенко (стихи Евтушенко обычно

представляют собой чередование более или менее традиционных мужских рифм с резко нетрадиционными женскими или дактилическими); наименьшая степень точности дактилических — у Пастернака и Вознесенского. Исключение представляет Сельвинский, в ранних стихах сознательно экспериментирующий с расшатыванием мужской рифмы, а в поздних стихах возвращающийся к почти классической строгости.

Внутри рифмы самая слабая позиция — финальная. Прибавление-убавление фонем происходит преимущественно именно здесь. Только в поэзии последнего десятилетия происходит сдвиг экспериментов с финальной на интервокальные позиции — у Евтушенко, Вознесенского. Неожиданным прообразом этой манеры оказывается рифмовка народного стиха, для которого характерна именно интервокальная, а не финальная неточность (57 случаев типа "пиВо-миМо", "ЕреМку-вереВку" на 11 случаев типа "голоД-ГолоС", "гороД-вороГ").

Интервокальная позиция в женских рифмах сильнее финальной у всех авторов, кроме Евтушенко и Вознесенского. В дактилических рифмах у Маяковского вторая интервокальная позиция сильнее первой, у Сельвинского (1924) — слабее первой; у Асеева точность дактилической рифмы к концу все больше, у Пастернака — все меньше. Иными словами, для Маяковского характернее рифмы типа "поРтятся-безработица", чем "выстеГать-публицистиКа", для Сельвинского — наоборот; для Асеева характернее тип "окоЛыша-такоГо же", для Пастернака — тип "наигрыВай-эпиграФом". Мы видим, что неточные рифмы неточны у каждого по-своему; смешиваться в понятии 'неточных рифм вообще' они могут разве лишь в противопоставлении традиционным рифмам XIX в. Современники очень хорошо чувствовали разницу индивидуальных манер рифмования; отсюда — возможность таких пародий как "Рифма-пифма на 'любовь'" в "Записках поэта" Сельвинского.

Соотношение закрытых и открытых точных рифм в нашем материале было нами сопоставлено с таким же соотношением рифм в "Евгении Онегине" (по 500 рифм) и слов в прозе "Пиковой дамы" (по 500 слов). Результаты:

	муж.	жен.	дакт.
Рифмы XX в.:	59:41	25:75	14:86
Рифмы "Онегина":	66:34	45:55	—
Слова в прозе:	55:45	34:66	18:82

Соотношения "Онегина" сильно отклоняются от прозы в сторону преобладания закрытых рифм: несомненно, это результат дополнительных словарных ограничений, связанных с традицией грамматической рифмы. В стихах XX в. пропорции мужских и дактилических рифм не отклоняются от аналогичных пропорций в прозе, в женских же рифмах заметно усиление открытых слов — не для контраста ли с преимущественно закрытыми мужскими рифмами?

7. Общее направление эволюции неточной рифмы, насколько можно судить по нашему материалу — это сокращение тождественных созвучий и нарастание измененных созвучий. Первый рубеж в ходе этой эволюции лежит между Блоком и Маяковским, второй — между Сельвинским и Евтушенко.

В экспериментах Блока были заложены возможности для обоих путей развития: и к пополненной рифме с расшатанной финальной позицией ("шепчет-крепче", "стуже-кружев", "море-Теодорих") и к измененной рифме с расшатанной интервокальной позицией ("ветер-вечер", "купол-слушал", "пепел-светел"). Первое из этих направлений шло от традиционной для русского стиха дозволенности прибавления-убавления йота в рифме ("могилы-унылый" и т.п.; заметим, что в пополненных рифмах Блока из отмеченных 11% не менее 7% приходится на традиционные йотированные рифмы, а у раннего Брюсова еще того больше: из 17% - 16,5%); второе — от традиционных для народного стиха вольных созвучий ("кормит-колет" и т.п.). Рифм первого типа (Т-П, за исключением йотированных) во II томе Блока — 31, второго типа (М-Т) — 25, почти поровну. Любопытно, что у Брюсова соотношение совсем другое: в его дореволюционных стихах рифм Т-П — 13, рифм М-Т — 32, в 2,5 раза больше.

После Блока и Брюсова Ахматова, Маяковский и другие ближайшие к ним по времени преемники предпочитали разрабатывать первое направление ("колени-Ленин", "Калинин-клине"), Евтушенко, Вознесенский и другие современные поэты — второе направление ("ловко-Лорка", "базы-бабы"). Прямой преемственности между рифмой Маяковского и рифмой современных поэтов, повидимому, нет: влияние Маяковского на современную поэзию в этом отношении обычно преувеличивается, оно сказывалось преимущественно в других областях поэтики. Другие поэты 1920-х гг. оказываются гораздо ближе к теперешнему культу измненной рифмы — и Асеев, и Пастернак, и Сельвинский, не говоря уже об их предтече — Брюсове.

Любопытна эволюция манер Маяковского и Сельвинского: Маяковский от поэмы к поэме постепенно и неуклонно сокращает созвучия Т и усиливает созвучия М, то есть следует в направлении общего развития неточной рифмы XX в.; Сельвинский начинает с предельного для своего времени усиления созвучий М, а затем решительно сворачивает к традиционной, почти 'классической' рифме на созвучиях Т, то есть следует в направлении, обратном общему развитию неточной рифмы XX в. Этапы этой 'антиэволюции' Сельвинского, может быть, вскроются при более детальном обследовании его творчества 1930-40-х гг.; можно думать, что подобные изменения происходили и в творчестве некоторых других поэтов, например, Пастернака с его движением от 'футуристической' к классической манере.

8. Отношение прибавления-убавления звука в рифме (П) может реализоваться с помощью различных фонем. Мы подсчитали, какие фонемы прибавляются-убавляются в наиболее характерной для этого отношения позиции — финальной, для мужских и женских рифм отдельно. Результаты выражены в виде пропорции трех категорий согласных: "йот" : "сонорные" : "шумные".

	мужские	Число рифм	женские	Число рифм
Маяковский, 1915 :	13: 0:87	(15)	22:33:45	(27)
Маяковский, 1916 :	6:30:64	(33)	26:29:45	(49)
Маяковский, 1924 :	11:57:32	(53)	27:35:38	(120)
Маяковский, 1927 :	7:42:49	(99)	25:38:37	(87)
Асеев, 1927 :	10:20:70	(59)	29:21:50	(34)
Пастернак, 1917 :	12:33:55	(92)	23:26:51	(80)
Сельвинск., 1924 :	10:36:54	(102)	32:28:40	(95)
Сельвинск., 1956 :	20:40:40	(5)	79:17: 4	(23)

Подлинное значение этих цифр прояснится лишь из сопоставления с естественным языковым соотношением йота, сонорных и шумных согласных в мужских и женских окончаниях слов, которое еще предстоит рассчитать. Пока можно лишь отметить явное нарастание сонорных от ранних к поздним произведениям Маяковского: ранний Маяковский играл контрастом традиционного йота ("грубый-губы") и резко ощутимых шумных ("в Одессе-десять"), поздний Маяковский нейтрализует и то и другое промежуточным фоном сонорных ("Калинин-клине"). Ранний Сельвинский держится ближе к раннему Маяковскому, чем к позднему; поздний Сельвинский и здесь возвращается к традиционной точности рифмы, преумущественно пользуясь издавна дозволенным йотом ("задушевней-деревни").

Распределение в таких рифмах 'прибавленного' звука по членам рифмы (т.е. соотношение случаев "Калинин-клине" и "клине-Калинин") более или менее равномерно: отклонение от среднего соотношения 50:50 нигде не превышает 10%.

Следует отметить особый тип рифмы, пополненной за счет вставного сонорного ("наш-марш", "щелк-щек", "сметь-смерть"), характерный для Маяковского (5 случаев в "Ленине", 8 в "Хорошо!") и чуждый всем остальним поэтам (у Сельвинского — только 1 случай в "Улялаевщине": "орд-рот").

9. Отношение замены звука (М) в рифме также может реализоваться за счет различных фонем. Здесь также выявляется разница между сдержанной манерой позднего Маяковского и резкой — других поэтов. В "Ленине" и "Хорошо!" на 150 случаев замены в 70 случаях происходит лишь замена однородного твердого согласного мягким ("радость-припарадясь", "Плеханов-лохани") и в 34 случаях — однородного звонкого глухим ("высясь-кризис", "тесно-протезный"); в "Улялаевщине" 1924 г. на 227 случаев замены это происходит соответственно лишь 72 и 11 раз. Таким образом, на более резко ощутимые случаи замены ("басом-Дубасов", "негде-дэнди") у Маяковского остается около одной трети всех замен (30,6%), у Сельвинского — около двух третей (63,6%); у Пастернака резкие замены составляют еще того больше, 72,5%, у Евтушенко — 83%. Народный стих в этом случае дает показатель 76,5%.

Наиболее часто вступают в замену у Маяковского следующие звуки (в убывающем порядке): Н, Н′, С, М - Р, С′ - Т - К; у Сельвинского: Й, К, Н, Т, Л - С, Н′, Р; у Пастернака: Й - Т, К, М, С, С′, Х - М′, Ф; в народных рифмах — Н, Л, Д, Т, Р, М, В, Н′.

10. Расшатывание точности послеударного созвучия, как известно, может компенсироваться различными способами:

а) использованием в пополнении или замене уже наличных в рифме звуков ("воронье-заронен", "копит-тропик", "мошкой-намокший"); частным случаем этого приема является так называемая рифма с 'перемещением' или 'перестановкой' ("тише-пишите");

б) совпадением пополнения с начальным звуком следующего стиха ("Перехожу от казни к казни *Ш*ирокой полосой огня; Ты только невозможным дразни*шь*, Зовешь неведомым меня ..." — А. Блок; "Один взойду на помо*ст Р*осистым утром я, Пока спокоен дома *Ст*рогий судия ..." — Ф. Сологуб; "Сверху хозяин, европее*ц*, Завоеватель, бог, пилот, Тучи подмяв, под небом рее*т*, *С*ам направляя птичий лет ..." — Н. Оцуп);

в) чаще всего — совпадением предрифменных опорных согласных

('левизна рифмы', в терминологии В. Брюсова); по существу, именно распространение этого приема помогло неточной рифме стать из эксперимента Брюсова и Блока массовым и общеупотребительным средством в русской поэзии.

Подсчеты здесь затруднительны, потому что эти опорные согласные могут довольно далеко отодвигаться от своего предрифменного места, размывая границу между рифменным созвучием и общеэвфоническим созвучием стихов (классический пример: "*наши* отходят *на Ковно-нашинковано*", Маяковский). Поэтому для начала мы учитывали здесь лишь самые бесспорные случаи: совпадение непрерывной последовательности предрифменных согласных фонем (так, в рифме "посторонним - с троном" учитывались три опорные согласные С, Т, Р, а в рифме "грозе-газет" только одна З'). В эту последовательность включались не только полностью тождественные фонемы (С-С, З-З), но и наиболее близкие из нетождественных (твердые-мягкие, глухие-звонкие, как выше, §9).

Показателем предударной рифменной опоры считалось частное от деления числа опорных согласных на число рифм: так, показатель 0,17 (0,21) означает, что на 100 рифм данного вида в рассматриваемом произведении приходится 17 полностью тождественных и 4 неполностью тождественных опорных согласных, всего 21. В таблице для экономии места вместо 0,17, 1,02 и т.д. печатается 17, 102 и т.д.

Подсчеты делались раздельно для следующих видов рифм: 1) точные женские, 2) точные мужские закрытые, 3) точные мужские открытые, 4) неточные мужские, 5) неточные женские с Т в интервокальной позиции (Т-П, Т-М), 6) неточные женские с П и М в интервокальной позиции (П-Т, П-П, П-М, М-Т, М-П, М-М), 7) точные и неточные дактилические. Для Маяковского рассматривались "Облако в штанах" и "Ленин", для Сельвинского — "Улялаевщина" 1924; для сравнения по точным рифмам был взят "Евгений Онегин" Пушкина, гл. 2-3.

	"Оне-гин"	"Обла-ко"	"Ленин"	Асеев	Пастер-нак	Сель-винский
ТОЧНЫЕ:						
1) женские	17(21)	28(36)	46 (65)	60 (80)	52 (72)	45 (59)
2) муж. закр.	15(20)	62(77)	76(102)	61 (89)	66 (86)	86 (93)
3) муж. откр.	9(11)	82(91)	53 (75)	31 (56)	38 (48)	96(121)
НЕТОЧНЫЕ:						
4) мужские		50(58)	57 (69)	77 (98)	92(110)	93(106)
5) жен. с -Т-		34(45)	60 (74)	71 (86)	73 (79)	46 (52)
6) жен. с -П, М-		38(50)	45 (63)	103(116)	79 (90)	61 (69)
ТОЧНЫЕ И НЕТОЧНЫЕ:						
7) дактилические		42(49)	33(45)	40 (57)	41 (53)	—

Женские и мужские рифмы подкреплены опорными согласными приблизительно в одинаковой степени (с разными особенностями у разных поэтов), дактилические — в несколько меньшей: по-видимому, длинная послеударная часть позволяет обойтись более короткой предударной. Неточные рифмы почты всюду подкреплены опорными звуками больше, чем точные.

Разница показателей Пушкина и поэтов XX в. разительна: здесь в цифрах выражено то "полевение" рифмы, о котором говорил Брюсов. Интересна в этом отношении эволюция рифмы самого Брюсова: в раннем его стихе ("Urbi et orbi") показатели предударной опоры близки к пушкинским и даже ниже их (вместе с неполностью тождественными созвучиями: 16 для женских, 25 для мужских закрытых, 8 для мужских открытых), в позднем его стихе ("Mea") — близки к показателям поэтов-футуристов и даже выше их (в точных рифмах: 106 для женских, 116 для мужских закрытых, 72 для мужских открытых; в неточных рифмах: 175 для мужских, 112 для женских; в дактилических рифмах — 72). Можно сказать, что в известной статье "Левизна Пушкина в рифмах"[6] Брюсов вместо портрета Пушкина дал собственный автопортрет.

Разница индивидуальных показателей поэтов XX в. интерпретируется труднее. Можно заметить, что у Маяковского обычно выше показатели по женским рифмам, у Сельвинского по мужским (еще одно свидетельство, что именно мужские были для Сельвинского главной областью эксперимента); можно заметить, что у Маяковского в "Ленине" из трех видов мужских рифм максимальные показатели дает вид (2), минимальные вид (3), а из трех видов женских рифм максимальные — вид (5), минимальные — вид (6), тогда как у Сельвинского в обоих случаях как раз наоборот.

Для Сельвинского, Пастернака и отчасти Асеева были отдельно подсчитаны показатели опоры для неточных рифм с элементом П и с элементом М:

	Сельвинский	Пастернак	Асеев
4) мужские-П	67 (80)	64 (82)	47 (68)
мужские-М	134(152)	146(163)	148(168)
5) женские Т-П	46 (51)	72 (76)	
женские Т-М	48 (56)	74 (87)	
6) женские П-(Т, П, М)	84 (94)	68 (85)	
женские М-(Т, П, М)	51 (57)	96 (97)	

В мужских рифмах резко заметное несоответствие М требует заметно большей компенсации с помощью предударной опоры; может быть, можно сказать, что в мужских измененных рифмах опорный согласный так же обязателен, как и в мужских пополненных рифмах ("могу-уйду" в русской традиции, в отличие от немецкой и французской, не считается достаточной рифмой; соответственно, пополненная рифма "могу-уйдут" также не употребительна; можно думать, что уникальную даже у Сельвинского рифму 'рук-шум' следует считать аномалией). Эксперименты с ослабленными рифмами типа "дыша-коротка" были характерны в XVIII в. для раннего Ломоносова (до 1743 г.), в XIX в. для А. Тимофеева, в XX в. для С. Боброва и отчасти для имажинистов; они еще требуют исследования.

11. Вокальная структура неточной рифмы, как сказано, не рассматривалась. В принципе она поддается анализу при помощи тех же категорий: "Т" на вокальных позициях дает 'точную рифму', "М" на вокальных безударных — 'приблизительную рифму' (в терминологии В. Жирмунского, т.е. "пустыню-отныне", "отраду-стадо" и т.п.), "М" на вокальных ударных — 'диссонансную' или 'консонансную' рифму ("стеная-стеною", "итак-итог" и т.п.), "П" на различных позициях — 'неравносложную' рифму. Ограничимся некоторыми замечаниями об этой последней.

Нарастание добавочного гласного в неравносложной рифме может иметь место, как известно, (1) между двумя согласными из которых один обычно сонорный ("убыль-рубль", "охало-заглохло", "Англию-евангелии") или (2) в конце слова ("ниц-казнится", "хамелеона-охмеленная", "папахи-попахивая"); (3) прочие случаи сравнительно менее употребительны ("власть-влажность", "пористый-просто"). Соотношение этих трех случаев у Маяковского ("Облако в штанах", "Война и мир", "Ленин") — 75:23:2; у Асеева, Пастернака, раннего Сельвинского вместе взятых (индивидуальные различия невелики) — 30:55:15; у Есенина — 15:83:2; у Вознесенского — 4:77:19. Таким образом, Маяковский предпочитает 'межсогласное', а другие поэты — 'надставное' наращение рифмы: опять-таки манера Маяковского оказывается не общехарактерной для всего XX в., а индивидуальной его чертой.

12. Все приведенные выше цифры еще требуют тщательной проверки их значимости, требуют привлечения более широкого материала по рифме XIX-XX вв. и народной поэзии, требуют сопоставления с естественными языковыми показателями (в частности — сопоставления фоники рифмующих и нерифмующих слов в одних и тех же произведениях). Интересно также влияние рифмующих звуков (особенно ударных гласных)

на подбор звуков внутри строки. Но думается, что уже сейчас можно сказать: применение точных методов исследования к рифме обещает быть не менее перспективным, чем оно оказалось для метрики и ритмики.

Москва

NOTES

[1] В кн. *Style in language,* ed. by Th. A. Sebeok (Cambridge, Mass., 1960), стр. 363.
[2] М. Гаспаров, *Современный русский стих: метрика и ритмика* (Москва, 1974), стр. 470.
[3] Исключение составляют в русском стиховедении разве лишь некоторые работы С. И. Бернштейна, например: "О методологическом значении фонетического изучения рифм", *Пушкинский сборник памяти С. А. Венгерова* (Москва-Ленинград, 1922), стр. 329-54; "Опыт анализа словесной инструментовки", *Поэтика* 5 (Ленинград, 1929), стр. 156-92; "Художественная структура стихотворения А. Блока 'Пляски осенние'", *Семиотика* 6 (Тарту, 1973), стр. 521-45.
[4] В. М. Жирмунский, *Рифма, ее история и теория* (Петроград, 1923); В. Тренин и Н. Харджиев, *В мастерской стиха Маяковского* (Москва, 1937); М. Штокмар, *Рифма Маяковского* (Москва, 1958); Д. Самойлов, *Книга о русской рифме* (Москва, 1973); А. Кондратов, "Статистика типов русской рифмы", *Вопросы языкознания* 1963, 6, стр. 96-106; С. Толстая, "О фонологии рифмы", *Семиотика* 2 (Тарту, 1965), стр. 300-05; D. S. Worth, "On 18th-century Russian rhyme", *Russian literature* 3, стр. 47-74; D. S. Worth, "Remarks on 18th-century Russian rhyme", *Slavic poetics: Essays in honor of K. Taranovsky* (The Hague, 1973), стр. 525-29; А. В. Исаченко, "Из наблюдений над 'новой рифмой'", *там же,* стр. 203-29. Даже исследователи, с сомнением относящиеся к точным методам в стиховедении, начинают обращаться к подсчетам: см., например, Б. Гончаров, *Звуковая организация стиха и проблемы рифмы* (Москва, 1973), стр. 155-56. Образец широкого и последовательного применения подсчетов ко всем аспектам исследования рифмы представляет собой исследование о польском стихе: L. Pszczołowska, *Rym (Poetyka: Zarys encyklopedyczny* III, t. 2, cz. 2, zesz. 1) (Wrocław etc., 1972). Наша работа была выполнена до публикации исследований Исаченко и Пщоловской, поэтому некоторые рассматриваемые явления выделяются и учитываются нами иначе.
[5] Наше 'прибавление-убавление' соответствует 'отсечению' и 'выпадению' звука в терминологии В. Жирмунского и 'усечению' в терминологии Д. Самойлова; наша 'замена' — 'чередованию' по В. Жирмунскому и 'замещению' по Д. Самойлову (см. В. Жирмунский, *ук. соч.,* стр. 74-77; Д. Самойлов, *ук. соч.,* стр. 36). Так называемую 'перестановку' (В. Жирмунский) или 'перемещение' (Д. Самойлов) мы предпочитаем не выделять в особый род рифмы — см. об этом ниже. §10.
[6] В. Брюсов, "Левизна Пушкина в рифмах", *Печать и революция,* 1924, 2, стр. 81-92; перепечатано в В. Брюсов, *Избранные сочинения* 2 (Москва, 1955), стр. 499-514.

SEGMENTATION AND MOTIVATION IN THE TEXT CONTINUUM OF LITERARY PROSE:
THE FIRST EPISODE OF *WAR AND PEACE*

BENJAMIN HRUSHOVSKI

1. SOME PRINCIPLES OF A GENERAL THEORY OF THE LITERARY TEXT

1.0 This paper is based on a study of the text continuum, or the unfolding of the text, in the first episode of *War and Peace*. It aims, however, not merely at describing the structure of the opening of *War and Peace*, but at a contribution towards the development of a theory of the text continuum which, it seems, was rarely discussed in literary theories. Moreover, it should provide an example for the analysis of 'non-narrative' prose, which is organized not along the lines of plot or a story told.

I shall dwell primarily on aspects of segmentation and motivation in the prose continuum. I do not aim here at presenting a comprehensive theory of the prose continuum but rather at a contribution towards such a theory from whatever the material of our example may illustrate. This theory is imbedded in a wider framework, "a unified theory of the literary text". In order to be able to discuss the issue at hand I shall have to outline at least some of the major principles of the general theory of the literary text, which will be presented in detail elsewhere.[1]

1.1. *The Text and the Reader*

1.1.1 Everything we experience in literature or say about it is based on texts. A work of literature, however, is not to be identified with a text as a fixed object. As we know, primarily from Roman Ingarden and from endless interpretations of texts, there are many things readers have to add to the actual language presented on the pages of a book. A work of literature is a text to be read by a reader. The reader 'realizes' the text, links up things which are not explicitly connected, makes guesses, fills in gaps, constructs points of view, creates tensions, etc.

1.1.2 When speaking about the reader we should not give up the study of literature for a subjectivist anarchy. We can certainly discuss what should be a 'proper' reading, what additions and interpolations the text itself requires, what norms are imposed upon us by the language of the period, the author's possible intentions, the tendencies of his time and genre, etc.; or what kind of different reading-hypotheses may be posited in a given case.

1.1.3 In the 'realization' of a text by a reader there are two major aspects: **understanding** of the **meanings** presented in the text and **experience** of the non-semantic, rhetorical, or poetic effects of the text. In both respects a realization of the text as an aesthetic object involves linking up of numerous elements within the text: sounds which are repeated and make alliterations or rhyme patterns, word or scene repetitions, events in a chain of plot, behavior, incidents of characters, comic or tragic qualities, etc.

1.1.4 The linking done by a reader is based either on specific 'instructions' of the text such as rhymes in a regular rhyme pattern, or on various principles of 'understanding', for example the construction of a hypothesis that a character is afraid based on an interpretation of a certain situation in which the character is presented. To **linking** (in the process of realization by the reader) there is an equivalent in the text which we may call a **pattern**. Patterns may be certain or ambiguous, formalized or free, etc. If we want, however, to talk about observable facts rather than about the psyche of the reader we have to discuss such possible or plausible patterns, rather than the reader's linkings.

1.1.5 We must distinguish between the psychological act of actual understanding or experiencing literature, which may be largely intuitive, and the reasoned **accounting for** and justification of specific structures and meanings understood and realized in a text. Actual understanding proceeds usually through guesses and approximations; it is not a final act and does not usually exhaust all possible meanings and effects of a work of literature. Even very well trained readers are not immediately aware of all the meanings and poetic patterns which they perceived in the text. If we want, however, to account for a certain impression we must link up all those elements which are relevant to support the impression-hypothesis. The analysis of a literary text by literary critics is, in a sense, an interference. They make explicit what is not necessarily so in the process of reading.

1.1.6 I shall not go here into the very difficult problem of what kind of reader or readers we may construct for a specific text. I shall proceed on two assumptions:

a. that we may speak of an ideal 'maximal' meaning of a text, based on the assumption that all possible interconnected and uncontradicted constructions of meaning are necessary and that there is a maximal functionality of all elements and all orders of elements in a text;

b. that no matter which is a better reading or on what grounds we may accept a certain reading, all readings, 'right' or 'wrong', even 'misunderstandings', as well as 'partial' readings, employ similar techniques. That is, even if we may disagree on specific particular readings, we may construct a general theory of how readings proceed. Furthermore, we may construct a general theory of how texts are built, in conjunction with an understanding of the processes of reading, which such texts require.

1.2 *The Hierarchy of Patterns*

1.2.1 A text is a highly complex network of patterns of all kinds. Any element of an aspect of language as well as any element from anything that may be presented in language (the so-called 'secondary modelling systems') may serve as a basis for a pattern. We link up dispersed elements in the text in order to construct plot, character A and character B, the writer's view of peasant society, style, parallelism of various kinds, etc. Within such larger patterns there are numerous smaller sub-patterns, little chains of things repeated or linked up in various ways.

1.2.2 A pattern is, in short, a link of two or more elements in a text (continuous or discontinuous to each other), constructed by any means whatsoever. The principles of pattern construction, which cannot be discussed in detail here, may be largely classified into two kinds: a) principles of equivalence; b) reality-like principles (such as the nature of human psychology, or the order of a setting). Literary theories usually discuss the first kind rather than the second. The enormous variety of structures in prose, however, is based precisely on the endless variety of the real world and possible worlds which are used as principles for pattern constructions in literature. The important point here is that we not only use literature to understand the world, but we use the world, as well as all possible worlds, to understand and construct literary texts.

We may also speak of a third kind, based on a mixture of the two, namely principles of literary institutions, e.g., literary genres, which use aspects from both kinds, such as the rigid strophic structure of a sonnet on one hand and the thematic pattern of a tragedy on the other.

1.2.3 A more formal way of dividing patterns may be the threefold division: elements are linked by principles of **equivalence** (a is parallel to b in the sense of p); **inclusion** (a, b, c may be perceived as parts of M); or **extension** (b is an extension of a in the sense p [such as cause, space, time]). Of course, for each of these principles, we shall have to employ either norms from the literary tradition or from knowledge of the world. Thus, equivalence of repeated sounds or grammatical forms is one thing, and equivalence of two presented situations from the point of view of a character's behavior is quite another thing.

1.2.4 Patterns may be built of homogeneous or heterogeneous material. Thus, rhymes or alliterations are made of homogeneous elements: 'inherent' aspects of sound. But if we take plot, it is a highly complex construct made by a reader from a rather large variety of heterogeneous elements. Thus, one event may be presented directly in an event sentence: "A killed B". Another event may be presented as a chain of sentences in a whole chapter, such as "The phone rang. She picked up the receiver. Her hand trembled. She ran to the closet. She took her coat. She ran out of the door", etc.; the reader may conclude from the whole chapter that there was a threat, or that she left Chicago. In spite of the fact that many of the sentences in such a chapter present, in their linguistic form, event statements, they do not serve as events on the level of the reconstructed plot; in the construct of plot we receive a statement from the process of interpretation, a sentence which was not presented as such in the text but has to be constructed by the reader. Furthermore, an event may be based on non-event material. For example, in an argument between two lovers about the weather or about whether to close or open a window, a reader may detect a crucial point in the story, a crisis in their mutual relationship.

1.2.4.1 In heterogeneous patterns, we may distinguish between 'proper' elements and 'extrinsic' elements. Thus, events are 'proper' material for the construction of plot, but the reconstructed plot will be based on extrinsic material as well, such as dialogue, character description, mood, ethical and behavioral norms of a society etc.

1.2.4.2 As a further example may serve the issue of who makes history: the leaders or the people? Clearly, at a certain point in *War and Peace* the reader is led to be interested in this historiosophic question. The reader has to scan the whole text for answers. He will construct a pattern which runs throughout *War and Peace* and is not less important and not different in structure from plot patterns. This pattern, too, will be based on 'proper' elements, such as ideas expressed by the narrator or by characters (i.e., to be qualified by the reader from whatever he constructed as the position of the given speaker-character), but also from material extrinsic to ideas such as the general plot of the novel, the characterization and behavior of leaders such as Kutuzov, Napoleon as compared to the behavior of representatives of the people, etc.

Any question whatsoever may send us back to the text to collect material dispersed throughout it which may contribute to an answer to the given question. Linking up of such elements is not simply a passive process, the reader has to readjust the various information he gets and reunderstand and reorganize it.

1.2.5 The patterns of a text create a complex network of hierarchies. Without such hierarchical constructs it would be impossible to grasp a work of literature as large and complex as *War and Peace*. Such hierarchies, however, are not stable and architectonic, but are reversible. I shall not go into this very complex issue here. An example may suffice. In order for the reader to realize properly a certain point in the development of plot or create the correct tensions at this point, he cannot simply link up the events which lead up to this point. He has to construct as well the characters of the persons involved in the event, the social and moral norms which regulate their behavior, etc. Such patterns as character or norms of behavior are subordinated here to the single point in the pattern of plot. But at a later point we may wish to construct a certain character and then an abstraction from the whole plot in which the character participated may be subordinated to a conclusion about this character. The availability of a whole network of patterns which may at any point be subordinated to any pattern which interests the reader at the moment is a very characteristic feature of literary texts.

1.3 *Two Levels of Organization of a Text*

1.3.0 It is a basic principle of this model of the literary text that the patterns in any text are organized on **two levels**: the level of the text continuum and the reconstructed level.

1.3.1 Characters, plot, ideas, time, space, style, etc. are built by the reader from discontinuous elements in the text and are reorganized according to their inherent principles (e.g., time elements are reorganized in their chronological order, ideas in their logical order, etc.). This reconstructed level is the one that is usually discussed in interpretations of a text and in literary theories. Unfortunately, in many theories and interpretations it is not always clear whether the scholar discusses something given in the text or something constructed or understood by himself as a reader.

1.3.2 A writer, however, does not present us with plots, ideas, rhyme patterns, etc. but with a text which unfolds step after step before the reader. He has to shift from sentence to sentence, from paragraph to paragraph, from scene to scene, and he has to justify such shiftings. Any close observation of a text will show a high degree of organization of the text continuum which is separate from the organization of the reconstructed level. We know, of course, the formal means of text segmentation, such as the division of a novel into chapters or of a poem into strophic groups. Much more interesting and complex is the segmentation of a text based on semantic groupings, as we shall see in this paper. A long text cannot possibly be of one piece. It is usually divided into many small segments with a whole network of motivations for the introduction of such segments and for their closure, shifters from one segment to another, transitions from one semantic focus to another, etc.

1.4 *The Concept of Junction*

1.4.1 As we observe the typical patterns of literature, such as rhyme, meter, plot, ideas, characters, etc., we find that there is no language material which is purely of one of these kinds. A rhyme for example is a pattern of sounds, but we have no sounds without words in language (I do not discuss here the extreme cases of *заумный язык*), words have other aspects as well: meaning, syntactic qualities, concrete qualities, etc. When a poet finds a second word to match his rhyme this second word has to fit at the same time several patterns: with some of its inherent sounds it has to fit the rhyme pattern according to the rhyming norms of this poet; with its syllabic and prosodic features, it has to fit the metrical pattern of the line in which it is imbedded; with its syntactic properties, it has to fit the sentence; with its semantic properties, it has to fit the imagery and the ideas of the poem. In short, a rhyming word is a **junction** in which several patterns meet. The rhyming word has to link up and contribute something to all of those patterns, within the norms proper to each kind of pattern, and at the same time contribute something new and interesting, again within the norms required by this poet or genre.

    The same could be said for an event. There is no pure event material in language. Each passage presenting an event has to contribute at the same time to a number of other patterns: the characters participating in this event, the setting in which the event occurs, etc. Such a passage is, clearly, a **junction** in which several heterogeneous patterns meet, intersect, and interact.

    1.4.2 Let me take an example of a rhyme from Majakovskij:

> Ведь для себя не важно
> и то, что бронзовый,

и то, что сердце — холодной железкою.
Ночью хочется звон свой
спрятать в мягкое,
в женское.

(Облако в штанах)

It is not enough to say in this case that Majakovskij likes such rhymes as *железкою—женское* or *бронзовый—звон свой*. Each rhyming word here fits into the rhyme pattern according to the norms which were prevalent in Majakovskij's poetry at the time, such as the discontinuous rhymeme (based on a number of sounds throughout the word which are not continuous to each other), the diverging endings of the rhyming words, the use of a compound rhyme member, the use of rhyme with members not equal in their number of syllables (*бронзовый—звон свой*), the linking of two semantically very remote words, such as iron and feminine. All this is true but not enough. Majakovskij has to find a way of including his rhyming words in the lines of his poem. We have to consider the norms of his elliptical syntax and futurist metaphors in order to account for that. Thus, *железкою* would not be possible without the metaphor using the instrumental. And the word *женское* is introduced due to the concretization of a non-concrete noun and the nominalization of an adjective. *Звон*, a concretization of a non-concrete metonymy of metal, can then be hidden in a concretized softness, linking in one image the two semantic domains.

Now we can say that a rhyming word is a junction at least on two levels. It is a junction of concrete patterns within the given context as well as a junction of norms pertaining in the domains of these patterns. The task of the poet is not a simple one as it would seem from the technique of rhyming or the outline of a simple plot. He cannot simply add a rhyme. He has to unfold the text in such a way as to present new junctions which link up with several patterns in the text, according to the norms of his poetics and the logic of the poem's theme.

1.4.3 Quite a different case, but similar in structure, is the case of what is called traditionally a scene. Let us look at the following example.

Prince Bagration screwed up his eyes, glanced back over his shoulder and seeing the cause of the confusion turned his head again indifferently, as much as to say: "Is it worth while bothering with trifles?" He reined in his horse with the ease of a good rider, and slightly bending over disengaged his sabre which had caught in his cloak. It was an old-fashioned one, of a kind no longer in general use. Prince Andrey remembered the story of how Suvorov had presented his sabre to Bagration in Italy, and the recollection was particularly agreeable to him at this moment. They reached the battery from which Prince Andrey had surveyed the field of battle.

This may be called the episode with the sword. It is one unit of the text based on a semantic principle; nothing before or after speaks about this sword. However, on the reconstructed level, the episode of the sword is a junction: it contributes to a number of heterogeneous discontinuous patterns: the characterization of Bagration; the characterization of Andrej; Andrej's relationship towards Bagration; Tolstoy's meticulous attention to the changes in armament and warfare; the question of whether Russians can beat the French, asked during a battle of defeat but recalling a period when the Russians did beat the French (Suvorov). It is interesting to note how this semantic material was introduced. In the previous sentence a Cossack was killed and his horse still trembled. The confusion ensuing called for Bagration's attention. He moved his head and by moving it caused his sword to be caught in the sabre, thus the reader's attention was called to this unusual sword through the eyes of an observer: Prince Andrej. Andrej, paying attention to this peculiar sword, recalls then that it stems from a previous war in which Prince Bagration participated with Suvorov. One continuous chain leading from one event to another in a rather realistic procession and emphasizing the point of view of Andrej, created this minor scene. Then, as a whole, the scene functions as a junction for patterns on the reconstructed level, each of them abstracts from the scene such elements or conclusions which fit its nature or its set of questions.

1.4.4 There is a considerable difference between our two examples: the rhyming word and the scene. In the first case, the unit which served as a junction was a unit of language, a word, whereas in the second case it was a piece of the text constituted by a semantic principle. The difference between these two kinds of junctions is one of the basic reasons for the differences between poetry and prose.

1.4.5 We see now that higher constructs in literature are not like the simple architectonic model we have of the smaller units of language. In language we may say that a number of phonemes link up to make a morpheme, and a number of morphemes link up to make a sentence. Each higher pattern is an exhaustive summary of the lower ones. And each lower element enters as a whole unit into the higher pattern. (Of course, even in language there are much more complex things such as supra-segmentals, transformations of deep structures in sentences, etc.) In literature, however, no pattern is based on units which enter completely this particular pattern, but rather a pattern abstracts from the elements linked to it those aspects which are relevant to its nature. A rhyme abstracts from the rhyming words those sounds which may be considered parallel. Plot will abstract from specific scenes or situations their event-aspect rather than their setting or ideas.

1.4.6 In literature, unlike language, not all existing elements belong to the literary organization. Thus, all sounds belong to the phonology of a language, but not all sounds belong to the structure of a poem. Only such sounds which may be linked into patterns of rhyme or alliteration or sound orchestration will be activated, but the same sounds in other places, if they cannot be linked in such a way, will be considered neutral from the point of view of literary organization. Such neutral or irrelevant material to a given pattern dominating a passage will appear throughout any prose text.

1.4.7 Seeing segments of the text as junctions, as units which have their own continuous consistency, rather than serving directly plot or any other kind of structure of the text, is very different from the accepted description of the text continuum. Thus, the concept of 'motif' implies that a certain plot (fabula) consists of a chain of such units which have merely been presented in a different order (*sjužet*) in a text. But as we see from the notion of the junction, a piece of the text may serve as 'motif' for several heterogeneous patterns. Similarly misleading is the description of narrative as a deep structure, which is then mapped onto a rather accidental surface structure: if a piece of a text serves as surface for some 'deep' structure (e.g., of plot), it serves at the same time for other, heterogeneous, 'deep' structures. A text is not merely a reshuffling of elements for a structure of plot or ideas, or whatever, but the presentation of an unfolded text continuum which has its own logic and its own organization and from which a reader is led to construct both form and meaning, plot, style, structure, ideas, world view, genre properties, and so on. Mallarmé's famous saying that poems are made not of ideas but of words could be directed against rhymes and meter as well: poems are not made of rhymes or meter either, but of words. The only material used are words, rather than events, meter, rhyme or ideas. The writer has to present his words, however, in such an order as to enable the construction of those other patterns.

1.4.8 We can observe a typical example from our passage from the opening of the first chapter of *War and Peace*: "Анна Павловна кашляла несколько дней, у нее был *грипп*, как она говорила (*грипп* был тогда новое слово, употреблявшееся только редкими"). (7/15)[2] This passage serves as a characterization of Anna Pavlovna, as a concrete description of the period, as an observation of the language, as well as a contribution to creating a distance of time (and attitude) between the writer and the reader on one hand and the characters presented on the other hand. Of course, each of these things constructed from the given sentence will be strengthened and repeated or developed in other parts of the text. Thus, the distance in time between the readers and the characters, illustrated through the language of the characters, can be seen a few lines later: "он говорил на том изысканном французском языке, на котором не только говорили, но и думали наши деды." (8/8)

1.5 *The Three-Story Construct of Meaning*

1.5.1 The two levels of patterning of a literary text involve both semantic and non-semantic material. Whenever semantic material is organized, a **three story construct** is involved. The three stories are: the level of 'sense', a Field of Reference, and Regulating Principles. If meaning is to be taken as anything which may be understood by a reader, meaning is a resultant of the interaction of these three stories.

1.5.2 While using a language we know the senses (designations) of words and the resultant senses of sentences. We apply these senses of words and of sentences to a Field of Reference (FR). From the Field of Reference we obtain further information about the referents discussed, specification of the meanings presented, as well as justification or falsification of the truth values of the sentence. Thus, if I say "it was a gray day", those who were there could see whether I meant that the sky was clouded or that my mood was bad. Metaphors exist precisely as an interaction between the sense of a word and the field of reference. In everyday life we save a lot of what we want to say by simply relating our words to existing frames of reference and to information which our listener has or may easily obtain from those frames of reference.

1.5.3 I would like to make a distinction between a large **Field of Reference** (FR) and specific **frames of reference** (fr) within it. A **frame of reference** is a continuum of any kind, in time and space, or in theme, or in ideas, which may accommodate a number of referents. A room about which I speak is an fr, but so is a scientific theory. When speaking about one or the other, or applying sentences to them, I rely on the reader's knowledge of a certain continuum of referents within each framework. In real life as well as in literature, we encounter numerous small fr's. A Field of Reference (FR) is a theoretical continuum of a large number of such fr's. Thus, in a novel we have a number of fr's in which a character appears when he was two years old, when he was 20 and 70, but not in-between. We nevertheless assume a hypothetical Field of Reference (FR), only parts of which were actually presented in the text, which comprises one continuous lifetime of this character. The same holds for a science, such as physics, where not all details are discussed in one continuous field, but there are developed specific frames which we assume to belong to one larger field.

1.5.4 **Regulating Principles** present the attitudes of the speaker or producer of a text. Such phenomena as irony, point of view, set, etc. belong to this domain. The Regulating Principles tell us in what sense to take the senses of the words. They are not merely based on the nature of the speaker, his position vis-à-vis the topic at hand, but also on his present position, for example: whether he may be excited because of a recent event which influenced his exaggerating in the information he tells us.

1.6 *The Internal Field of Reference*

1.6.1 The one exclusive feature of a literary text is that it is a text which creates an **Internal Field of Reference** (IFR), that is, at least part of the sentences create a Field of Reference to which the same sentences refer. Within this IFR we know only what the sentences relating to it have presented us. We cannot go beyond the text to find out whether the speaker lied or didn't lie, whether there was such a Natasha, whether she loved, what tint the redness of the roof was, etc. In any other text we can, in principle, find additional texts or sources of information about the same FR to which the given words relate.

This is not to say that sentences and words in a literary text refer only to the Internal FR. They (or some of them) may refer at the same time to an External Field of Reference (ExFR) as well. Clearly, in *War and Peace* many words and sentences refer at the same time to places in Europe or dates in modern history. General sentences about human nature refer certainly inside as well as outside the literary text. Moreover, many general constructs made by the reader on the basis of a text will refer to an External Field of Reference: generalizations and images of a society, of history, of man, of Russia. This double relationship is crucial, for example, in Solzhenitsyn's novels, where we relate not only the internal information to the ExFR (Soviet Russia under a certain regime) but vice versa, information from the ExFR is brought in to illuminate the Internal FR.

1.6.2 In the use of language in everyday life we have an illusion that only the level of sense is given by means of language; the Field of Reference is presented in external reality; and the Regulating Principles are given in the social conditions of the speech situation. In a literary text, however, we have to reconstruct both the Field of Reference and the Regulating Principles from the same body of language which carries the senses of words and sentences. Since this is the case, there is an interdependence (if not a circularity) between these three stories. For example, the assumption that a certain passage is ironic influences the meanings of the sentences to be taken by the reader, but only such an understanding of the sentences approves of the hypothesis that the passage is indeed ironic. As soon as we get a sentence which does not seem to be ironic we may have ro revise or discontinue the Regulating Principle (irony) which we constructed previously.

1.6.2.1 For example, in our chapter, after having told us that the Vicomte tells his story, Tolstoy writes:

15   Рассказ был очень мил и интересен, особенно в том месте, где соперники вдруг узнают друг друга, и дамы, казалось, были в волнении.
        — Charmant[3], — сказала Анна Павловна, оглядываясь вопросительно на маленькую княгиню.
20   — Charmant, — прошептала маленькая княгиня, втыкая иголку в работу, как будто в знак того, что интерес и прелесть рассказа мешают ей продолжать работу.

In this case we assume that the story was pleasant and interesting only through half of the first sentence. In the second half, and especially in what follows, we start doubting whether Tolstoy meant it seriously or ironically. We may say that this passage underlies two Regulating Principles. From the point of view of the women listening to the story, it was indeed literally a pleasant and interesting story, but from the narrator's point of view who mocks at these women and who presents a very different seriousness of political issues, the words are certainly meant ironically. Thus, the resultant meaning of the sentence is interdependent with the Regulating Principles under which the sentence should be read.

2. INTERNAL AND EXTERNAL FR IN *WAR AND PEACE*

2.1 *Referential grounding*

2.1.0 In daily life we use words applying them to a Field of Reference about which we know a lot, to a world in which we live for years. We do not present entirely new information, but take a position on or reshuffle some elements of previous knowledge. One of the difficulties of a text of fiction is that it presents words as if they were said in such a real life situation, but the writer had no opportunity beforehand to present all the details of a frame of reference to which these words apply. In short, the Internal Field of Reference created in a work of literature needs **referential grounding**. Thus, major characters may be introduced only after minor characters have appeared and some setting has been presented; major places will be presented only as a continuation of minor places which have been detailed in the beginning; etc. Exposition, known to traditional theories of literature, is only one way of referential grounding — by presenting the past of characters and events which are central to the story — but this is by no means the only possible technique. Grounding is a metonymic rather than a chronological-causal dimension given to referents in the IFR.

2.1.1 The party thrown by Anna Pavlovna which makes the first large episode of *War and Peace* serves, among others, for several purposes of such grounding. Thus, the major characters are introduced through it, though only after the reader's having a rather full image of the fr which is the party and after several minor characters have been presented to which these major characters are linked by several links.

2.1.2 This, however, is not sufficient. Tolstoy links his Internal FR in turn to the External FR known to the reader from history. He uses a famous chapter in history much as a Greek tragedy uses myth. Indeed, the IFR of the party did not exist in history. It is, as it were, a plane parallel to the plane of real life in historical time. But in literature parallel planes may meet and overlap at several points, quite unlike Euclidian geometry. A number of places, names of persons and dates pertain at the same time to the ExFR in history and to the IFR which is discontinued from it. By this device the reader brings in a wealth of information and attitudes in order to grasp the party and the situation in which the characters are set, in spite of the fact that he is confronted right away with a large number of characters, all of them presented rather sketchily in a kaleidoscopic party.

2.1.3 As is well known, Tolstoy worked on this chapter for a whole year. E. Zajdenšnur has published fifteen versions of the opening of *War and Peace*.[3] In all of them Tolstoy tried to find a place where many people of various origins and attitudes could meet together. He preferred the party to a battlefield. In order to have not a one-family novel but what he called an *èpopeja*, he had to make many people meet. A party provides an excellent motivation for that purpose.

The specific party is conveniently chosen because it is given by a person at the same time linked to the court and opening a store of information from higher circles and low enough to invite aristocrats of lesser importance.

The party has to be presented in such a way that many people express themselves briefly and we move on to other characters. This is achieved through a special technique, as we shall see below.

In order for such characters, unknown to the reader and not related to each other by any obvious plot, to be palpable, they have to say something about something very important. For this purpose, we have a crucial political event, reopening the question of 'war or peace' to which the characters may take issue and thereby reveal their positions. For this purpose, the novel starts in July after the Russians have learned of Napoleon's annexation of Genoa and Lucca, though towards the end of the same evening we hear that it is a June night (June being apparently the last possibility of a white night in Petersburg).

2.2 *Three Planes of Reality*

2.2.1 There are in this episode three Fields of Reference or, as it were, three planes, to which the words refer. There is, basically, the Internal Field of Reference: the party, a definite place and time and a group of characters meeting there. There is, then, the External Field of Reference: Europe in 1805. The relationship between IFR and ExFR is a peculiar one. Clearly the time and place of IFR are continuous to the time and place of ExFR, though they are disconnected. Thus, the party is held specifically in July 1805, though it is not clear when exactly in July; it is held somewhere in Petersburg, but not exactly clear where. Even it it were clear, it would be impossible to demand truth values of a continuum in time and space between ExFR and IFR. It is, however, a basic assumption of the semantics of the text that the characters and the ideas the characters speak of are continuous in both fields. The characters speak to each other and about each other as well as about referents in the ExFR.

2.2.2 In addition to the **presented present** in the IFR, there is a **projected future** and a **projected past**. This is due to the quasi-realistic assumption of a character as a semantic unit which has a past and probably a future or that such past and future are presupposed.

The party is an fr based on a continuum of time and space: fr(t, p). We may consider each character as an fr in its own right, based on the unity of a person, without any unity of time and place: fr(-t, -p). Thus words in this chapter may refer not only to the basic fr of the chapter itself, but to other places and times which are located in fr's of the characters. Moreover, such characters may meet in the projected past or in the projected future, some points of which, again, coincide with points in time and space of the ExFR.

2.2.3 The third, the highest, plane or FR is the time and place of the narrator. Though no sentences refer directly to him, and his nature is a zero if accounted for by direct semantic descriptions, nevertheless he plays an important role in the chapter. His different time is established by such remarks as the one on the French language of our grandfathers or on the word *grippe* which was 'then' (i.e., in Anna Pavlovna's time) a fashionable word (cf. 1.4.8 above). Clearly many understandings of the situation are necessarily related by the reader to the position, point of view and understanding of the narrator and his time. Moreover, the text is interspersed with remarks by the narrator on the events narrated.

2.2.4 One obvious means of segmenting the text is the mechanism of the narrator's interference. Thus, one way of cutting the text into pieces is the shifting from one to another of these three planes: from the narrator to the characters to the outside world and back again. This three-fold referential structure may be seen in the following diagram:

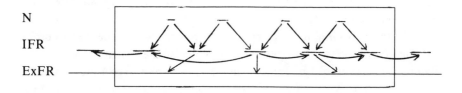

N — narrator; IFR — the Internal Field of Reference: the characters at A. P.'s party; ExFR — the External Field of Reference: the political situation in Europe. Within the frame — the presented present; outside — on the level of IFR — the projected past and future of the characters. Arrows indicate referring: the narrator refers to the characters; the characters speak about each other as well as about the ExFR.

2.3 Information and Segmentation Through Interaction of the Three Planes

2.3.1 The reader is presented within the IFR with a stock of information from the ExFR: (1) Some facts and dates (actually it is of no consequence which dates and facts are mentioned as long as they create the connection between the internal and external historical situation); (2) Some abstractions, e.g., the general situation of hesitation between war and peace; (3) Norms of relating to this general situation, both in its specific historical details (such as Napoleon, the French Revolution) and in the general ideological dimensions of society, war and peace.

The ExFR is used as a store of information and as a point of departure for orientations within the IFR. For example, if Pierre says something about Napoleon it is clear immediately that Pierre is a 'revolutionary', simply through our understanding of the political positions of that period.

2.3.2 A number of specific links connect the three planes of reference of the text. Thus, the first sentence establishes right away the dependence of a personal relationship on the issues of war and peace: Anna Pavlovna declares, though of course jokingly, that if Prince Vasilij will not admit that it is war he will not be her friend. This basic dependence of personal positions and relationships on the state of the "World" is well established throughout the episode, winding up in Andrej's abandoning his pregnant wife.

2.3.3 Shifting between the three planes enables not merely one kind of segmentation of the text but also the shifting from minor issues to major issues, from concrete details to generalizations, and vice versa. We could say that the shifting semantic perspective is enhanced or enabled by this mechanism. Thus, long political speeches are not presented here at all, though the reader is constantly being prepared to listen to them with the audience of the party. We simply shift from the political issues referring to the ExFR to the characters within the IFR.

2.3.4 In the beginning of the episode segmentation is achieved by cutting off the stream of the dialogue by comments of the narrator. At first the comments seem to be presented, as it were, in parentheses: our story starts with a speech by Anna Pavlovna, after her talk the narrator comments on it, explains how the whole thing came about, and only then Vasilij answers, but he answers as if no break occurred between her part of the dialogue and his.

On another occasion (9/20) the narrator's comment is used to skip parts of the dialogue: "В середине разговора про политические действия Анна Павловна разгорячилась."

2.3.5 The bulk of the chapter consists of dialogues of characters. Tolstoy presents them, as it were, in a scenic way. He lets his characters talk but then he observes their way of talking and subsequently remarks on his observation, explaining it through characterization and description of the speaker. The general direction of this procedure is as follows:

Speech → Observation → Characterization (Description)

Cutting across this gradual transition there is another semantic transition: from a detail (D) to a generalization (G) in the domain of this detail. We may observe the following passage of the narrator's commenting on Prince Vasilij's speech:

> Он говорил на том изысканном французском языке (D_1)
> на котором не только говорили, но и думали наши деды (G_2)
> и с теми тихими, покровительственными интонациями, (D_2)
> которые свойственны состаревшемуся в свете и при дворе
> значительному человеку (G_4). Он подошел к Анне Павловне,
> (D_3) поцеловал ее руку, (D_4) и покойно уселся на диване, (D_5)
> подставив ей свою надушенную и сияющую лысину. (D_6) (8/8)[4]

The following diagram represents roughly the structure of transitions from Details to Generalizations in this passage:

N → *Sentence 1*   *Sentence 2*

  Obs: $G_1 = D_1$ $G_3 = D_2$ Anaphora ("он") → D_3 → D_4 D_6

  Char: G_2 G_4 *Descr:* D_5

G — generalization; D — detail; N — narrator;
Obs — observation; *Descr* — description; *Char* — characterization

Each generalization may express several things and carry several functions. Thus G_3 expresses the time distance between the narrator and the characters, the social status, and the character of Prince Vasilij.[5]

2.3.6 Thus, instead of unfolding the IFR in a logical manner which would have taken a great deal of space, Tolstoy starts *in medias res*, shows the reader directly speeches of some characters unknown to him yet, and then, through the narrator's comments, enlarges the semantic framework and the amount of information. This technique enables creating a very wide network (of time, characters, society, places) in merely hinted threads. For the sake of concreteness one would have needed a much greater detailing of each of the presented generalizations. But if some concreteness within each generalization (representing a different fr) is embedded not in the framework of the semantics of the particular generalization but in the fr of the party, an fr in which all such fr's intersect, the effect of concreteness is achieved.

3. MOTIVATIONS FOR SEGMENTATION

3.0 In addition to the three-plane division which contributes to segmentation of the text, there is a further mechanism for segmentation. Since the bulk of the semantic material is within the second plane, i.e., on the level of the characters (presented in the front fr), the author needs a further device to cut their dialogue into small pieces. Indeed, no dialogue is allowed to be unfolded and developed in detail and length as Dostoyevsky would have done it. The reader is led from one circle of people to another.

I shall first show some specific devices of this segmentation and then summarize the principles of segmentation and motivation in the whole episode.

3.1 *Local Motivation*

3.1.1 In the first part of the episode we have only two characters: Anna Pavlovna and Prince Vasilij. Here the dialogue is not simply rambling from one issue to another but concentrates around changing topics in shifting segments. For example:

> — Ne me tourmentez pas. Eh bien, qu'a-t-on décidé par rapport à la dépêche de Novosilzoff? Vous savez tout.
> — Как вам сказать? — сказал князь холодным, скучающим тоном.—Qu'a-t-on décidé? On a décidé que Bonaparte a brûlé
> 5 ses vaisseaux, et je crois que nous sommes en train de brûler les notres.
> Князь Василий говорил всегда лениво, как актер говорит роль старой пьесы. Анна Павловна Шерер, напротив, несмотря на свои сорок лет, была преисполнена оживления и порывов.
> 10   (9/I 10)

This passage starts with a dialogue continuing the previous tension between the two characters: Anna Pavlovna tries to lead the discussion into political questions, whereas Prince Vasilij is bored and, as we shall see later, intends to shift the interest to his own personal affairs. The passage opens with a dialogue: she asks a political question and he answers. The reader gets from the dialogue some information on the ExFR as well as some implicit information of the IFR. He grasps implicitly the contrast of positions of the two persons, the contrast of tone, emotional involvement, etc. The text takes up this implicit level, leading the reader from the explicit referential semantics relating to world affairs to the implicit semantics of the IFR. In lines 7-10 the narrator gives a description of his speech and her speech. The narrator's remarks parallel the structure of the preceding dialogue. However, since the unfolding of the text is done not in a logical order, but rather in a way of concatenation, the description of *his* speech proceeds, being linked directly to *his* replica. (*She → He.* N: *He, She*) From the description of her speech we shift to a generalization on her character (according to the principles described in 2.2.8).

3.1.2 The next passage starts with a new theme linked directly to the subsidiary theme of the previous sentence: the nature of her excitement. What has been a third level subordinated topic became the main topic not only of the sentence but of a whole segment of the text: "Быть энтузиасткой сделалось ее общественным положением (9/11)". Again, there is a shifting of topic within the passage: from the nature of her excitement with its contradictions we turn to her own awareness of this situation and then to other features of her character and age. The next passage uses this by-now well-established feature of Anna Pavlovna's character, her being an 'enthusiast' and her excitability, to introduce a whole long passage on the political situation in Europe: "В середине разговора про политические действия Анна Павловна разгорячилась: — Ах, не говорите мне про Австрию! ..." etc. (9/20).

3.1.3 The general principle of this technique could be formulated as follows: **any point in the text continuum may be used as supra-segmental.** Thus, information on A. P.'s character is used as a motivation for the introduction of a new passage. Indeed, Tolstoy uses Anna Pavlovna to present the reader with at least a summary of the whole political situation of Europe, though this summary is presented in an almost parodic manner through the naive and excited talk of Anna Pavlovna.

3.1.4 Now, since Anna Pavlovna was, as previously established, self-conscious of the advantages and defects of her nature, she herself discontinues the same segment by means of the same motivation: "Она вдруг поостановилась с улыбкой насмешки над своею горячностью." (10/10)

3.1.5 One should stress that Tolstoy never uses new semantic themes all of a sudden. The excitement of Anna Pavlovna has been well established in previous passages in something that could be called a **semantic chain**: various remarks in this direction have accumulated throughout the first pages of the chapter: "Dieu, quelle virulente sortie!" (8/4); "Разве можно, имея чувства, оставаться спокойною в наше время?" (8/21); "Ne me tourmentez pas" (9/1); "... была преисполнена оживления и порывов. Быть энтузиасткой сделалось ее общественным положением ...", etc. (9/9).

3.1.6 The principle of concatenation has led us from polite talk to a political dialogue to characterization of the persons involved in the dialogue to a presentation of the political situation in Europe. Logically it is a reversed order.

3.2 *Long-Range Motivation*

3.2.1 In addition to such local motivations for the introduction and the discontinuation of specific segments there are also **long-range** or **global motivations**. The shifting from a dialogue of some persons to other persons, from one topic to another topic, from political to personal affairs and vice versa, is enabled by the general semantic conditions of the fr of the party. Such global motivations are: the nature of a party, the political situation referred to, the social basis of the participants, the use of known historical information, etc.

3.2.2 There are, however, in addition to the features of the typical fr some specific long-range motivations as well. Thus, the functions of a hostess carried out by Anna Pavlovna are elaborated into an image of a manager of a spinning factory:

И, отделавшись от молодого человека, не умеющего жить, она возвратилась к своим занятиям хозяйки дома и продол-
5   жала прислушиваться и приглядываться, готовая подать помощь на тот пункт, где ослабевал разговор. Как хозяин прядильной мастерской, посадив работников по местам, прохаживается по заведению, замечая неподвижность или
10   непривычный, скрипящий, слишком громкий звук веретена, торопливо идет, сдерживает или пускает его в надлежащий ход, — так и Анна Павловна, прохаживаясь по своей гостиной, подходила к замолкнувшему или слишком много говорившему кружку и одним словом или перемещением опять заводила
15   равномерную, приличную разговорную машину (17/3)

This image is developed further too: "Вечер Анны Павловны был пущен. Веретена с разных сторон равномерно и не умолкая шумели." (17/31).

The image fulfills several functions in the text: (1) It serves the characterization of Anna Pavlovna; (2) It serves as a device of irony; (3) It is connected to the pattern of similar images of the mechanical wheel as opposed to the natural principle which divides characters in Tolstoy's work; (4) It serves as a metaphor, i.e., a stylistic device. Thus, the same image serves as a symbol, an irony, a characterization, as well as a suprasegmental principle for motivating the composition of the chapter.

3.2.3 Indeed, the guests are divided into three groups. Anna Pavlovna goes from one group to another, tries to link such groups and to take care of the normal humming of her machinery.

Her function in this respect clashes with the one of Pierre. Pierre is, on the one hand, a bastard, i.e., a lower character, and on the other hand he is the son of a rich and influential person, i.e., a potentially higher character. Pierre is a newcomer and, as any newcomer, wants to receive information; he is young and revolutionary and clumsy and therefore does not know the rules of the polite game. Thus, Pierre's character serves, too, as a motivating force for the introduction of new things or for the disruption of the polite flow of dialogue.

3.2.4 In addition to the image of the spinning factory, there are minor motivations for continuing or discontinuing, linking groups of people, etc. Thus, Anna Pavlovna presents the Vicomte as an expensive dish to her guests: "... и виконт был подан обществу в самом изящном и выгодном для него свете, как ростбиф на горячем блюде, посыпанный зеленью." (18/30)

3.2.5 On the other hand, there are several disturbances of a rather silly nature like the Princess's knitting, Hippolyte's silly jokes, Prince Vasilij's having to go to the British ambassador, and so on. As a result of all such disturbances made of semantically minor or irrelevant material, the dialogues are kept very short and lively, are actually purposeless and simply used for the sake of characterization of a society. There is no time for serious political discussion.

3.3 On Classifying Motivations

3.3.1 We may now summarize. Motivations may be classified as to their extension: there may be immediate motivations, long-range or global (for a certain part of a text). Global motivations depend on the nature of the FR of the given text. Immediate motivations are responsible for the introduction of one specific segment (such as the introduction of Anna Pavlovna's political outburst). Long-range motivations are such which establish a principle repeated many times within a given text. Such a principle is not necessarily used throughout the text and may be used in conjunction with several other principles.

3.3.2 Motivations may also be classified by the material used for their construction. There may be formal motivations, such as divisions of a text into chapters or strophes; and motivations of a semantic nature. The latter may be built of local material, such as the unfolding of a secondary topic of a previous sentence to become the main topic of a following paragraph; or of a reconstructed pattern, such as the constructed psychology of a character which is responsible for his behavior and speech.

3.3.3 Furthermore, we may distinguish between motivations for introducing a segment and motivations for its nature. Thus, the image of Anna Pavlovna as a foreman of a spinning factory is responsible for the mere introduction of segments presenting groups of people talking at a party; but Anna Pavlovna's excitement is responsible for the nature of the segment serving the political situation.

3.3.4 A similar example, though a more complex one, is the story to be told by the Vicomte de Mortemart after a rather elaborate preparation, throughout which the reader and the participants at the party are promised to be served the interesting Vicomte. Finally we hear that the Vicomte is going to tell a story about the Duc d'Enghien (18/15). The story is, however, delayed several times until page 21/6.

When, finally, the Vicomte is given his turn to tell the story he does not talk at all. We are presented merely with a very brief summary of the topic of his story, shifting immediately to gossip about the personal aspects of it. This abbreviation is motivated by the listeners, the ladies of the evening who have no interest in politics as such. In this case motivation for the introduction of a certain story, even after an elaborate build-up, is not enough to have the story presented unless it has a good motivation for the nature of the presentation.

4.   ORDER AND DYNAMIZATION
4.1 *Logical order*

4.1.1 Besides the principles of segmentation discussed above, there is also a logical order imposed upon the fluid text. One obvious division is the division of the party into three circles. This, of course, helps to break up the discussion into separate discussions of groups. Nevertheless, it is clearly an artificial device, since Anna Pavlovna takes all the trouble to bring these groups together.

4.1.2 A further device of ordering is the summary statement at the beginning of chapter II:

> Гостиная Анны Павловны начала понемногу наполняться. Приехала высшая знать Петербурга, люди самые разнородные по возрастам и характерам, но одинаковые по обществу, в каком все жили;
>
> (13/28)

Here the technique is reversed as compared to the first chapter: first a generalization about the society as a whole and then a detailing, by groups and individuals. The middle part of the whole episode looks like a list of such characters belonging to Peterburg's aristocracy (see Table 1). Segments are clearly devoted to particular characters, then transferring the lead to another character in a new segment.

Nevertheless, as we observe closely the opening passage of Chapter 2 we see that all the names mentioned here: Prince Vasilij, his daughter, the beautiful Hélène, the young Princess Bolkonskij, Prince Hippolyte, Mortemart, the Abbé Morio have been introduced in the previous chapter, not systematically but a propos of other matters. Thus each of them separately has had his own referential grounding.

4.1.3 The symmetrical order of the structure of the second to fourth chapters is not easily felt, due to the large number of disturbances, caused by rather silly things, in the concatenations and associative transitions from one topic to another topic abounding here as in the first chapter.

As Table 1 shows, the whole episode is very well planned and rather schematically divided into large segments centered on particular characters or

TABLE 1: A SCHEMATIC OUTLINE OF THE EPISODE

Semantic parts	chapters	segments
A. *Prologue* *to the party:* *Prince Vasilij* *+ Anna P.*	*(I)*	*1) Phatic function (+ characterization)* *2) Politics* *3) The problem of his children*
B. Characters	(II)	4) Everybody arrives → a list → presentation to aunt 5) Princess B. 6) Pierre 7) The hostess
	(III)	8) 3 circles: 9) (a) Vicomte 10) (b) Hélène 11) Her circle: the Princess + Hippolyte 12) The Vicomte's story 13) (c) Abbé + Pierre
[as all are gathered enters:]		14) Andrej [Vasilij gets up] 15) Vasilij + Hélène are leaving
	(IV)	16) The mother of Boris [returns to circle]
C. *Political Argument*		17) Opening resumed: Genoa + Lucca 18) Andrej + Vicomte 19) Pierre — the argument about Napoleon 20) Hippolyte
D. *Epilogue*	(V)	21) Leaving: Pierre 22) Andrej, Hippolyte, the Princess
After the party:		23) Hippolyte + Vicomte 24) Pierre at Andrej's

topics. Nevertheless, the impression is of a disorderly party and of a natural flow of associations without any backbone of plot. This impression is due both to the associative and, as it were, unplanned transitions from one theme to another, to the fact that a segment will start with one theme and shift into another towards its end or provide towards its end a lead for the next segment, as well as to the nature of the planning itself: planned segmentation does not overlap exactly with chapter divisions, motivations and headings of divisions are not necessarily given at their head.

4.1.4 The logical order is not a framing order, it is not given from the beginning. The fact of the party is introduced only after the first dialogue has been presented to the reader. The image of the hostess as a manager of a spinning factory is presented much later than she actually behaves in this manner. The generalization about the kind of society attending the party is given only at the beginning of Chapter II. The division into three circles is given even later, at the beginning of Chapter III.

Nevertheless, the list of characters is presented to the reader in a continuous way: in the first chapter, they are referred to only in the words of the two speaking characters, i.e., outside the presented fr. Throughout Chapters II and III the list continues, disregarding the formal overall different structures of the respective chapters.

4.2 *Dynamization*

4.2.0 In sum, a number of overlapping principles of segmentation work throughout the whole episode. The author picks up once one, another time another, or uses several of them together, in order to shift from one segment to another, without seeming to be systematic.

4.2.1 The episode is very well planned out as we can see. The impression of a fluid irregular and natural situation, the rousseauist element in Tolstoy, is enhanced by the principles of dynamization. The major forms of dynamization are: (1) Disruption of an established logical order; (2) Shifting of theme in the text continuum; (3) Little threads of plot; (4) Semantic chains running throughout parts of a text discontinuously.

4.2.2 The first category is easily seen throughout the episode in the large number of disruptions of announced themes. It works also in such a planned matter as the three circles. There is, first, a generalization about the three circles, then one after the other is presented. The little thread of plot, however, which created an anticipation for Mortemart's story is led into the third part of the second circle (9). Thus, this part becomes disproportionately conspicuous above the others, and the first two circles are from this point of view conceived as corridors leading up to the 'point'.

4.2.3 The second category, **shifting**, too, can be seen throughout the text. We have shown above how a secondary topic becomes a primary in a following segment. A different kind of concatenation is caused by a logical unfolding of a disrupting theme. Thus, the pregnant princess, having caused a disturbance in the story and having delayed further the long expected story of the Vicomte, sits finally down.

> Княгиня, улыбаясь и говоря со всеми, вдруг произвела пере-
> становку и, усевшись, весело оправилась.
> Теперь мне хорошо, приговаривала она и, попросив начи-
> нать, принялась за работу.   10
>
> (20/7)

Now, there is bound to be a gentleman who pays attention to her and of all people it is Hippolyte:

> Князь Ипполит перенес ей ридикюль, перешел за нею и,
> близко придвинув к ней кресло, сел подле нее.
>
> (20/11)

This is cause enough for Tolstoy to switch to the description of Hippolyte (segment 11).

4.2.3.1 A chain of such shifting may be illustrated in the dialogue between Anna Pavlovna and Prince Vasilij. The political tirade of Anna Pavlovna which we have analyzed above starts with a bursting out on the issue of Austria. Before her tirade there was a cut in the scene motivated by the narrator's interference. He says clearly: "В середине разговора про полити-ческие действия Анна Павловна разгорячилась: — Ах, не говорите мне про Австрию!" etc. (9/20). The reader has no idea what Prince Vasilij said that could have caused such an outburst on her part. Moreover, it seems at first that Prince Vasilij is bored and uninterested in Anna Pavlovna's politics. He is simply polite and plans to leave soon for the party of the British Ambassador. Then, after more than a page, the name Vienna pops up again.

> — А! Я очень рад буду, — сказал князь. — Скажите, — при-
> бавил он, как будто только что вспомнив что-то и особенно-   25
> небрежно, тогда как то, о чем он спрашивал, было главной
> целью его посещения, — правда, что l'impératrice-mère желает
> назначение барона Функе первым секретарем в Вену? C'est
> un pauvre sire, ce baron, à ce qu'il paraît. — Князь Василий желал   30
> определить сына на это место, которое через императрицу
> Марию Феодоровну старались доставить барону.
>
> (10/24)

It turns out that Prince Vasilij has a family matter to discuss with the hostess. The issue is not introduced directly but through mentioning Baron Funke, as if he were another person in the line of persons mentioned earlier in Anna Pavlovna's gossip. In what follows Anna Pavlovna is used by the author for skillful manoeuvres to shift aside from the topic of interest to Prince Vasilij. Eventually, when she returns to the topic of his family, she talks about his daughter rather than the son, and only afterwards she mentions the two children and the third (the disturbing one), thus shifting to the third son, Anatole, and from here to the issue of finding a match for this Anatole. Through this match for Anatole we are led into a discussion of the Princess Bolkonskij, the old Bolkonskij, then her brother who is not yet mentioned by name (though later he will be introduced as Prince Andrej, to become the major character of the book), his wife, Lise, and even Kutuzov.

The listing of this chain does not at all exhaust all motives discussed or touched upon in the coextensive text. It is rather one chain running through a certain text, while at each point there are chains or patterns intersecting with the one listed here.

4.2.4 The little tensions of plot created in this story are rather harmless. They cannot become semantically dominating patterns of the chapter. The rest of the material cannot possibly be subordinated to them. They are used, however, for the sake of creating little anticipations and leading the reader by the nose on rather uninteresting matters of no consequence. Prince Vasilij announces right away that he will leave the soiree later, for the British Ambassador's party (8/23). This is a reason good enough to try to influence him so he stays on, which Anna Pavlovna does skillfully, using his interest in a match for his son. Prince Vasilij's departure later, also executed in several installments, actually serves as a frame to close the noisy party, leaving in the end only a few people who resume the real discussion of politics, announced at the very beginnning.

4.2.4.1 A similar anticipation is built up around: the two interesting Frenchmen who are to come to the party (10/18); Bolkonskij, the son, will come too (13/12); Lise, his wife, mentions that her husband leaves her, which reopens the whole issue of war and personal destiny, and the issue of the relationship between her and her husband (15/25).

With such little anticipations built up, a number of delaying techniques are used to disrupt the promised result. It is easy for Tolstoy to pick up one principle in order to disrupt another one, using primarily characterization and behavior or the misunderstanding in dialogue for that purpose.

4.2.5 A large number of semantic threads are spread throughout the episode. As we saw, when the narrator lists a whole list of people of the Petersburg aristocracy coming to the party, all of them have been introduced previously. Practically no important information is given without any grounding at all. Typically, Andrej Bolkonskij's name is not mentioned with his first mentioning in the story. In a similar way the information on other persons is spread out through the skillful brief and dispersed introductions of such persons in stories of other persons.

This is true for a large number of semantic elements in the story. Thus: "Пьер сделал обратную неучтивость" (16/33). Pierre's misbehavior, used clearly as a motivation for the nature of a new segment, is built upon his previous misbehavior and upon a whole pattern of conventional behavior well developed in the episode.

4.2.5.1 Anna Pavlovna's attempt at finding a match for Prince Vasilij's son uses a repetition of the issue of a match-maker. It opens with the following sentence: "Говорят, — сказала она, что старые девицы ont la manie de marriage. Я еще не чувствую за собой этой слабости, но у меня есть одна petite personne ..." (12/28), and it closes with resuming the same theme: "Ce sera dans votre famille, que je ferai mon apprentissage de vieille fille" (13/25).

4.2.5.2 Despite the extremely condensed amount of information in this episode there are numerous repetitions; one more example: "Вы думаете? ... — сказала Анна Павловна, чтобы сказать что-нибудь и вновь обратиться к своим занятиям хозяйки дома" (16/31). And in the next paragraph: "Она возвратилась к своим занятиям хозяйки дома" (17/4).

5. MULTIPLICITY OF INFORMATION

5.1 *Shifts of Theme*

Beside the external means of segmentation, such as the dramatic technique of dividing a chapter into scenes by introducing a new character or making a character exit, there are also shifts within the text of a speaker or within one theme.

We have mentioned a number of those above and we may now summarize the major types: (1) A piece of speech by a character is presented, then the narrator comments on the character's intonation and behavior, then he shifts from that to a general characterization, in some parts a brief biographical note on that character. (2) Most of the interlocutors speak at cross purposes. This is not done in the mode of absurd drama emphasizing the lack of communication between people, but rather well motivated as a clash of interests of the two speakers, e.g., Anna Pavlovna leading into political matters and Prince Vasilij trying to shift the discussion to his personal concerns. (3) A large number of thematic shifts has a global motivation, the major motivation being the interdependence of politics and the issue of war and peace with the personal affairs of the characters. (4) The introduction of a secondary topic, embellishing or explaining the main topic, which then becomes a major topic for the following passage.

5.2 *Diverted Concreteness*

This shifting, multi-directioned, fluid text continuum built by means of a number of well-defined and well-organized principles of motivation and along a well-planned and well-disguised schematic order, enables the inclusion of a great amount of information. Interestingly enough, the major topics introduced are not developed at all. They are merely openings for future great themes of the novel. It seems in the chapter itself that Tolstoy is interested more in the way people react to important information, both on a political and a personal level, rather than in the information itself.

Moreover, this technique enables Tolstoy to make many remarks of a general nature, which are introduced simply as explanations of concrete observations. If the order were reversed, such a generalization would need a great deal of elaborating and detailing to be acceptable by the reader. The realistic effect is achieved due to the fr of the party, in which all such concrete details are embedded, though the bulk of information relates to other fr's, both political and personal, about which the characters speak and think. Thus, we can say that the party serves for purposes of **diverted concreteness** much in the way a metaphor serves in poetry to present concreteness in an fr other than the one of the topic of the information.

5.3 *Point of View*

5.3.1 We shall not discuss here the intricate issue of point of view in this episode and in Tolstoy's work in general, mentioning its importance merely in order to explain the technique of shiftings throughout the discussed text.

Clearly, the overall effect is of an omniscient author, not only omniscient but also omnipotent. He manipulates the division of information throughout the chapter, the concatenations, the cuttings or introduction of new segments, ironization of the characters, and so on.

This is achieved without making the narrator obvious. Only in the beginning a distance between the characters presented and their time, and the time and position of the narrator and his readers is clearly established. It is a distance of two generations. Later, however, within this framework of an omniscient narrator, Tolstoy uses his omniscience extremely sparingly. The reader never moves from one character to another without being led by a character, e.g., by the hostess. The reader is never presented with a view of the behavior and position of a character but through the eyes of other characters present at the situation. The omniscient framework enables Tolstoy simply to shift the point of observation from one character to another, from one circle to another.

5.3.2 On the whole, we could say that point of view in this text is divided into three aspects: (1) The point of judgement is in the present (of the narrator and his readers); (2) The point of observation is moving from one character to another, from one circle to another; (3) The selection of information is given from the speaker's point of view, and motivated by the speaker's character. This is a threefold network of point of view used interchangeably throughout.

5.3.3 This technique is well represented on the level of language. Thus, in some cases the narrator has general information on "our grandfathers" or on human nature. But in most cases he does not know exactly what the characters feel, he simply formulates their feelings from the point of view of an external observer who imagines:

> [...] сказал князь Ипполит таким тоном, что *видно было*, — он сказал эти слова, а потом уже понял, что они значили, (20/32); из всех же прискучивших ему лиц лицо его хорошенькой жены, *казалось*, больше всех ему надоело (22/27); Элен была так хороша, что не только не было в ней *заметно* и тени кокетства, но, напротив, ей *как будто* совестно было за свою [...] красоту (19/14); *как будто* пораженный чем-то необычайным, виконт пожал плечами [...] (19/21)

In such cases the narrator does not know exactly what the characters feel and think but has external impressions of them or suspicions. In other cases, however, Tolstoy is not shy of telling clearly what the feelings of a character are:

> Князь Василий *знал это, и, раз сообразив,* что ежели бы он стал просить за всех, кто его просит, то вскоре ему нельзя было бы просить за себя, *он редко употреблял* свое влияние. В деле княгини Друбецкой он *почувствовал*, однако, после ее нового призыва, что-то вроде укора совести. Она напомнила ему правду [...] *Это последнее соображение поколебало его.* (25/14)

6. OUTLOOK

As we have seen, there are basically two kinds of techniques of presenting the text continuum: (1) Overall principles of segmentation, overlapping with each other but dividing the whole text into smaller parts; (2) A number of principles of step after step transitions and dynamic uses of chains of semantic material of one form or another. This provides for the high degree of linkage to which each semantic detail is connected. It is a technique which leads the reader in a number of simultaneous ways step after step throughout the several chapters. It is not, however, based on building up a major pattern on the level of the reconstructed text (such as plot).

Actually there is only one major pattern for the whole episode: the nature of the party and the nature of the society participating in such a party. In addition to that, there is a large number of patterns opened up, to be used in large or small degrees throughout the novel: characters, relationships between characters, political circumstances, ideas and attitudes. But none of those has been built up throughout the episode in a sufficient degree to be able to take over any hierarchy either in the sense of dominating the meaning of this episode or in the sense of dominating its structure. The composition of the whole part is based primarily on the level of segmentation.

Tel-Aviv

NOTES

[1]   A brief summary of this theory can be found in Ziva Ben-Porat & B. Hrushovski, *Structuralist Poetics in Israel (= Papers on Poetics and Semiotics 1)*, Institute for Poetics & Semiotics, Tel-Aviv University, 1974, p. 13-23. In the meantime the author published several papers in English, discussing various aspects of the theory: 1) "The Structure of Semiotic Objects" (*Poetics Today* 1:1-2 (1979), 363-76; and in: Steiner, Wendy, ed., *The Sign in Music and Literature*, Texas UP, 1981). 2) "The Meaning of Sound Patterns in Poetry," *Poetics Today* 2:1a (1980), 39-56. 3) "Poetic Metaphor and Frames of Reference," *Poetics Today* 3:4 (1982). 4) "Fictionality, Reference, and Re-Presentation," *Poetics Today* 4:1 (1983). 5) "Integrational Semantics," in: Byrnes, Heidi, ed., *Contemporary Perceptions of Language: Interdisciplinary Dimensions* (= GURT 1982), Washington, D.C., Georgetown UP, 1982.

[2]   Throughout this paper I am using the text of *Vojna i mir* from L. N. Tolstoy, *Sobranie sočinenij v dvadcati tomax* 4 (Moscow 1961). In quotations the first number indicates the page, the second the line, e.g., (7/15) refers to p. 7 line 15 (of the running text).

[3]   E. E. Zajdenšnur, "Poiski načala romana «Vojna i mir»: pjatnadcat' nabroskov (1863-1864)", *Literaturnoe nasledstvo* 69: Lev Tolstoj I (Moscow: AN SSSR, 1961), 291-396.

[4]   This technique is reflected in language: *Так говорила* (7/10); *он говорил на том* (8/8); *сказал он* (8/17); *князь В. говорил* (12/12) — all introducing the speaker's manner of speech.

[5]   Explanations of gestures of the speaker by means of a generalization, which is believed to be known to the reader but is actually introduced and motivated by this device, appear elsewhere: *несмотря на свои сорок лет* (9/9); *и он с теми свободными и фамильярными грациозными движениями, которые его отличали* (13/19); *как это бывает, у вполне привлекательных женщин* (14/35).

РИФМА И СЛОВО

А. В. ИСАЧЕНКО†

1. В науке нет споров о том, что феномен 'рифмы' основан на 'созвучии', т.е. на совпадении ('тождестве') фонетических элементов двух (или нескольких) сопоставляемых ритмических единиц (строк, полустиший). В 17-ти-томном Словаре СРЛЯ (1961) *рифма* толкуется как "созвучие концов стихотворных строк".[1] Русские теоретики рифмы, начиная В. Брюсовым, подчеркивали метрическую функцию рифмы, отказываясь рассматривать ее как дополнительное эвфоническое 'украшение' стиха. Напомним в этой связи слова Б. В. Томашевского: "Под рифмой обычно понимают концевые созвучия стихов. В этом определении — два признака: 1) концевое положение созвучных слов и 2) звуковые условия созвучия" (1959:70). Анна Ахматова сравнивала стих со строчкой, печатаемой на пишущей машинке: "Рифм сигнальные звоночки".

В своей компетентно написанной и местами очаровательно сформулированной книге о русской рифме поэт Д. Самойлов (1973) всячески подчеркивает "ассоциативную, конструктивную, композиционную роль рифмы". Изолирование рифмы, как фонического явления, от знаковости того материала, которым она оперирует, подчеркивание лишь "звукового тождества", ведет неизбежно к бесплодной ориентации рифмоведения на изучение отклонений от принципа тождества. Да и сам термин 'созвучие', "тождество рифмующихся отрезков" гораздо сложнее, чем это казалось классикам русского стиховедения полстолетия тому назад.

1.1 Во всех известных нам стихотворных системах наблюдаются постоянные сдвиги и переоценки самого понятия, 'тождественности' рифмующих сегментов, причем речь идет не только и не столько о степени акустической близости 'созвучий', сколько о единицах других языковых ярусов, таких как слог, морфема, слово, значимое выделение которых и определяет выбор, объем, некую минимальную 'точность' участвующих в рифмовке единиц.

1.2 Исследования последних лет в области истории русской рифмы обнаружили совершенно неожиданные факты, связанные с развитием того измерения, которое принято называть 'богатостью' рифмы. Д. С.

Ворт убедительно показал, что рифмы многих поэтов XVIII в. гораздо сложнее и требовательнее рифм поэтов 'Золотого века'. Так в "Илиаде" Е. И. Кострова (1755-92) Вортом были отмечены многочисленные случаи 'левой' рифмы, явления, считающегося достижением XX века. В переводе Кострова поражает обилие повторов, стоящих налево от последнего ударного гласного: *прекРАТится : возвРАТится, колЕСНица : дЕСНица, нагРАЖду : сию вРАЖду*. Поражает также использование не тождественных, а 'эквивалентных' звуков, таких как парные по глухости/звонкости шумные согласные: *Не ГЛаГОЛи Сице : На КОЛеСнице* и т.п. (Worth 1973:528-29). Эти наблюдения коренным образом меняют господствующее до сих пор представление об однонаправленности развития русской рифмы от 'элементарных' к более сложным формам.

1.3 Дальнейшим сюрпризом в истории русского стихосложения является опубликованный недавно в журнале *Russian Linguistics* II/1-2 (1975) "Акафист. Предисловие стихами изложенное". М. Альтбауэр, нашедший и опубликовавший этот интереснейший текст, подчеркивает целый ряд совершенно неожиданных в виршевом стихосложении отклонений от известных нам норм. Из 118 рифм по крайней мере 55 (т.е. почти половина) в том или ином отношении являются нетривиальными. Историки русской рифмы, обобщившие и теоретически обосновавшие результаты своих наблюдений над современной рифмой, вне всякого сомнения найдут в ранних стадиях русского (и церковнославянского) стихосложения целый ряд характерных явлений, не отмеченных их предшественниками ввиду односторонней и теоретически недостаточно обоснованной общей установки рифмоведения на процессы 'деканонизации'.

2. В европейской литературе появление конечной рифмы генетически и причинно связано с одним из наиболее общих принципов построения поэтического текста, с принципом параллелизма, ср. основополагающее исследование В. Штейница (1934). Два смежных предложения или две смежных фразы строятся на основании тождественных или близких синтаксических моделей, так что в конце строки почти неизбежно появляются одни и те же классы слов с тождественным морфологическим оформлением. Вот несколько примеров, приводимых А. М. Панченко в его прекрасной книге о русской стихотворной культуре XVII века (1973, 41):

> Есть некто твоей милости проситель,
> а к нам грешным всегдашний исходитель …

где бы мне бедному глава своя прокормити
и женишко и детишек гладом не поморити ...   (40)
Люто убо есть зело надолзе в печали пребывати,
и бедно есть виному казни ожидати ...   (45)

Синтаксический, а отсюда и морфологический параллелизм и связанная с ним незамысловатая рифмовочная техника наглядно прислеживается особенно в ранних образцах виршей. В качестве примера приведем 'моноримичную' запись, помещенную в конце перевода Тропика папы Иннокентия. Запись относится к 1607 г. и принадлежит перу Федора Говзинского:

В премудростех славимый
И в разуме хвалимый,
Честностию же чести честно почитаемый,
Во своих бо сих делех художно познаваемый,
Понеже трудолюбно подвизаемый
И усердно совершаемый,
Богом же самем наставляемый ...
                                (Панченко 1973:31)

Трудно сказать с уверенностью: является ли морфологическое тождество результатом синтаксического параллелизма, или же автор, находящийся под гнетом поэтической константы, прибегает к синтаксическому параллелизму как к наиболее простому способу реализации 'звукового повтора'.

В начальных стадиях развития рифмовочной техники нет почти ограничений в выборе тех или иных рифмующихся пар. Панченко приводит следующие строки, написанные в 1613 году:

Безначальному отцу, без отца, без матери не рожденну,
Сыну сначальному [...] цу, от отца без матери порожденну.   (29)

Любопытно, что автор не прибегает к, казалось бы, наиболее простому приему создания абсолютного звукового повтора — к механическому воспроизведению последнего слова первого стиха в конце второго. Очевидно с самого начала в рифмованных текстах соблюдается чрезвычайно важный запрет не допускать в рифме идентичных по звучанию и по значению пар слов. В данном случае рифмуются два слова с одинаковой основой, но второе (*порожденну*) является префиксальным образованием и, следовательно, формально не идентично с первым (*рожденну*). Аналогичные факты наблюдаются и в вышеупомянутом рифмованном Акафисте: *бу́деть* : преизбу́деть, немогу : несмогу, пока́йся : *раскайся*, *недостойный* : достойнымъ. Проверка значительного материала (начиная с второй половины XVIII в.) приводит нас к заключению, что правило, запрещающее рифмовку слова 'с самим собой', является, очевидно, константой русского стихосложения (да и не только русского!), причем константой весьма устойчивой во времени.[2] Этим самым феномен рифмы перестает быть чисто звуковым: с самого начала основная единица языка поэзии — слово — участвует (пусть пока негативно) в определении и в реализации рифмы, ибо рифмовать можно любые сегменты, кроме идентичных слов.

2.1 Если отвлечься от вопросов семантики, то в области метрической организации стихотворного языка надо будет выделить два (взаимосвязанных) ряда единиц:

(1) незнаковые единицы: звуки, слоги, просодические свойства;

(2) знаковые единицы: морфемы, слова, конструкции, фразы, предложения (ср. эффект *enjambement*), синтаксически значимые интонации.

Необходимо подчеркнуть, что слово в русском стихосложении является не только семантической, но чрезвычайно важной метрической единицей. Напомним, что цезура в русском (и не только русском) стихосложении осуществляется не при помощи каких-то мнимых 'пауз',[3] а исключительно в силу соблюдения словораздела в определенном месте строки. Такие словоразделы маркируют цезуру не в произносительном, а в метрическом плане, чаще всего не имея никаких фонетических эквивалентов. В белом стихе русской классической драмы словораздел приходится перед пятым слогом пятистопной строки, причем этот словораздел обычно не совпадает с 'фразой' или 'синтагмой', а проходит внутри конструкции (или, если угодно, внутри 'экспираторной единицы'):

> Как я люблю | его спокойный вид,
> Когда, душой | в минувшем погруженный
> Он летопись | свою ведет; и часто
> Я угадать | хотел, о чем он пишет?
> О темном ли | владычестве татар?
> О казнях ли | свирепых Иоанна?
> О бурном ли | новогородском Вече?
>
> (Борис Годунов)

2.2 Еще в 1923 г. Р. О. Якобсон раскрыл роль слова в организации анакрузы классического ямбического стиха (1923:29). Первый (метрически слабый) слог ямба может быть реализован исключительно только односложными словами, ср. из "Евгения Онегина":

> *Мой* модный дом и вечера ...
> *Весь* этот блеск, и шум, и чад ...

Где нынче крест и тень ветвей ...
Так близко! ...
Уж решена ...

В недавно опубликованной статье Р. О. Якобсон возвращается к проблеме односложных слов в анакрузе. Вот два ad hoc придуманных стиха, фонетическая реализация которых совершенно идентична:

(1) С ней убежать мечтал гусар.
(2) С нею бежать мечтал гусар.

Только тип (1) вошел в обиход русского ямба, тогда как (2) явно противоречит наследственному канону (1973:242). Данное ограничение связано не с появлением ударяемого слога в анакрузе, а с появлением хореического слова в этом положении, или, вернее, с отсутствием словораздела перед вторым слогом.

3. Созвучие, реализируемое рифмой, существует не само по себе, не ограничивается чисто фоническим планом и уж конечно не имеет ничего общего с так называемой 'инструментовкой' стиха. Рифма — это чрезвычайно комплексная величина.

В своей замечательной статье "Об усилении" А. К. Жолковский определяет любой художественный эффект как искусство "найти и продемонстрировать такую комбинацию элементов действительности, которая позволяла бы достигать каких-либо существенных целей с помощью минимальных данных" (1962:170). При такой установке рифма оказывается типичным 'усилителем'. В ней художественный эффект достигается с помощью сочетания звуковых, слоговых, морфемных, словесных и метрических элементов, используемых одновременно в иерархически разных планах. Рифма, функционирующая как метрический прием сигнализации конца строки, использует на самом 'поверхностном' уровне фонический материал, но этот фонический материал подчиняется знаковым элементам разных ярусов (морфемам, словам, даже словосочетаниям) и допускает одновременно определенное семантическое и семиотическое толкование рифмующихся единиц, т.е. во всяком случае не просто звуковых цепочек, а 'рифмующихся слов'.

3.1 Рассматривая рифму как осуществление звуковых повторов структурно связанных с категорией слова и (негативно или позитивно) зависящих от нее, мы вынуждены будем вернуться к истокам русского стихотворного искусства и выяснить, когда общий запрет механического повтора того же слова (см. 2), являющийся чисто негативной 'связью' созвучия и слова, превращается в 'положительный' прием возможности (или даже желательности) повторять не только конечные сегменты последних слов в строке, а целые, причем не-идентичные, слова.

Приведенный нами рифмованный Акафист содержит несколько случаев, в которых рифмовка целых слов между собою маркирована идентичным анлаутом рифмующихся слов: *(на) ВоСто́къ : (островъ) Высо́къ, Освяще́нъ : Открове́нъ, МОлю́ : МО́ю, Умоли́ : Ускори́, Живу́ще : Жду́ще, ПРошу́ : ПРиношу́.* Можно привести ряд случаев, когда начало рифмующих слов маркирована звуками, считающимиси эквивалентными с точки зрения современной поэзии: *ТЕ́ломъ : ДЕ́ломъ, Мо́щи : Но́щи, Зову́тъ : Живу́тъ.* Прекрасным примером рифмовки целых слов является следующая строфа:

> Вознеси́ гласъ твой *молбы́*
> Ни́лу преподо́бну
> та изба́вы мя *молвы́*
> сотвори́ть свобо́дна.

Заметную тенденцию к рифмовке целых слов можно заметить и в переводе Кострова. Среди приводимых у Ворта примеров отметим явно 'словесные' рифмы: *ПОрази́л : ПОчти́л, ВОЗврати́те : ВОСпри́мите, ПРОстира́ет : ПРОрица́ет, ОБлада́тель : ОБита́тель, Спо́ром : Ско́ром, ПРо́стер : ПРимѣ́ръ,* и т.д. Мы полностью присоединяемся к мнению Д. Самойлова, что "случайных рифм не бывает". Если это так, то исследователя ожидает большая работа по обследованию рифмо-вочной техники поэзии XVIII в., явно отличающейся от преимущественно 'грамматической' рифмовочной техники классиков XIX в.

4. Как известно, запрет рифмовки заударных *а : о,* а также *е : и, -ье : ья* в классической поэзии XIX в. объяснялся по-разному. Жирмунский ссылался на графику, Томашевский объяснял это явление "высоким стилем" стихопроизношения, Якобсон связывал этот запрет с "установкой поэтов на грамматическую рифму, исключающую в течение XVIII — начала XIX вв. антиграмматическую ориентацию" (1962:6).

Тут Р. О. Якобсон вплотную подходит к нашей теме: в его понимании рифма перестает быть автономным звуковым явлением, она соотносится с величиной грамматической (т.е. значимой) — с морфемой. Можно утверждать, что в XIX в. преобладает ориентация на дериваци-онную, формообразующую или флективную морфему (или цепочку таких морфем). Взять хотя бы последние стихи Державина (1816):

> Река времен в своем *стремленьи*
> Уносит все дела *людей*

И топит в пропасти забве*нья*
Народы, царства и цар*ей*.
А если что и оста*ется*
Чрез звуки лиры и труд*ы*,
То вечности жерлом пож*рется*
И общей не уйдет судьб*ы*!

И у Державина, и у его современников встречаются, разумеется, многочисленные рифмы, не связанные с тождеством аффиксов: *пирамид : сокрушит, Урал : стал, эту : нету* и т.п. Но нельзя не заметить у Державина явного преобладания морфемных, в том числе и 'деривационных' рифм типа *птичка : певичка, младость : радость.*

4.1 Морфемный принцип рифмовки, столь характерный для поэтов конца XVIII — начала XIX вв. 'изнашивается', становится тривиальным, дешевым, непривлекательным, исчезает эффект усиления. Достигнуть 'богатого' созвучия за счет механического повтора аффиксов почти так же легко, как рифмовать слово с самим собой. Ни один русский поэт (до Маяковского), вероятно, так сознательно и требовательно не относился к рифме, как Пушкин. В замечательном своем произведении "Домик в Коломне" (которое почему-то в изданиях приводится в рубрике "Поэмы") Пушкин в целом ряде октав обыгрывает проблему рифмы, создает как бы новую поэтику рифмы, построенную однако на устарелых принципах: он якобы не хочет "гнушаться рифмой наглагольной" и заявляет:

Отныне в рифму буду брать глаголы.

Мы подсчитали общее число морфемных рифм в "Домике в Коломне" и сопоставили их с неморфемными. К первым мы отнесли все рифмы, в которых рифмующие отрезки отражают идентичные морфологические (флективные или деривационные) категории, например *надоел : хотел : совладел; резвушка : старушка.* Ко вторым отнесены все остальные: *браковать : плохую стать, наречья : беречь я.* Морфологических рифм в данном произведении несколько меньше половины; соотношение выражается цифрами 92 : 108. В составе неморфемных рифм выделяются для нас особенно интересные словесные рифмы *ВЗОРУ : ВЗДОРУ, припала СТРАСТЬ* ('passion') *: какая СТРАСТЬ* ('how awful').

Вообще у Пушкина можно найти целый ряд формально выраженных словесных рифм (типа *боливáр : бульвáр*), а также несколько бравурных рифм-омофонов:

А что же делает *супрýга*
Одна в отсутствии *супрýга?*

(Граф Нулин)

Вы, щенки! за мной ступайте!
Будет вам *по калачу́*,
Да смотрите ж, не болтайте,
А не то *поколочу́*.

(Утопленник)

5. В поэтике Пушкина и его современников словесная рифма сводилась к повтору абсолютно идентичных звуковых отрезков, границы которых совпадали с границами слова (не только в чисто лексическом, но и в акцентуационном отношении, например *по калачу́*). Естественно, что такие рифмы могли появляться лишь в определенных жанрах и неизбежно были связаны с эффектом виртуозной игры слов. Для того, чтобы словесная рифма стала массовой, должна была измениться вся поэтика русской рифмы, как таковая.

В составе рифмы игнорируется ('нейтрализируется') дистинктивность безударных гласных. Можно утверждать, что из всех отличительных признаков остается лишь один: [+ безударность]. В безударном слоге игнорируются конечные согласные и *х* (*ми́лый : си́лы, пору́ка : му́ках, хоро́ший : кало́ши*, А. Блок), Маяковский вводит разносложные рифмы (типа *а́втора : за́втра*). В 'авангардной' поэзии намечаются еще многочисленные сдвиги, о которых речь будет ниже.

И вот у молодого Маяковского мы встречаемся с словесной рифмой, как с массовым и вполне канонизованным явлением. В одном только "Облаке в штанах" появляются словесные рифмы, эксплицитно маркированные идентичными анлаутами: *гру́бый : гу́бы, маляри́я : Мари́я, желе́зкою : же́нское, чёткий : чечёткой, замш : за́муж, Джек Ло́ндон : Джиоко́нда, вы́качу : вы́скочу, чета́ : чита́ть, сно́ва : сло́во, подря́дчики : пода́чки, кисе́ль : карусе́ль*. Как видно, словесные рифмы не ограничены мужскими (типа *кисе́ль : карусе́ль*), а широко применяются в стихах с женскими и дактилическими концовками (*гру́бый : гу́бы, желе́зкою : же́нское*).

У ранней Марины Цветаевой встречаем такие рифмы: *врозь : вёрст, до пя́т : плат, глото́к : глубо́к, реко́й : руко́й, жила́ : ждала́, кляч : кума́ч, сло́ва : сно́ва* (1921), *труды́ : трубы́* (1921), *шерсти́ : шести́, спи́те : спи́сок, па́шущий : пля́шущий* (1918), *бе́дную : бле́дную* (1918), *просто́й : посто́й*. Эти словесные рифмы формально маркированны идентичным анлаутом.

Лишь в общих рамках 'поэтики словесной рифмы' становятся возможными рифмовки слов с переменной ударной г л а с н о й:

Было:
  Социализм —
     восторженное *сло́во*!
С флагом,
   с песней
     становились *сле́ва,*
и сама
   на головы
     спускалась *сла́ва.*
Сквозь огонь прошли,
     сквозь пушечные *ду́ла.*
Вместо гор восторга
    горе *до́ла*
Стало:
  коммунизм —
    обычнейшее *де́ло*
     (Маяковский)

В том же стихотворении (1928 г.) встречаются такие словесные рифмы: *жар : ржа, мота́ло : мета́лла, гео́лог : го́ло, перега́р : берега́* ('эквивалентные' анлауты, см. ниже), *гул : ни гу-гу́, кус : Курск, нагни́ : магни́т* ('эквивал.'), *до́чки : то́чки* ('эквивал.'), *то́мной : до́мны, лития́ : литья́, хвост : хао́с, совко́м : завко́м.*

5.1 Массовой словесная рифма становится у современных поэтов, причем далеко не у всех. Современная поэтика допускает самые 'авангардные', нетривиальные и даже иногда просто 'шокирующие' формы рифмовки, но одновременно относится чрезвычайно терпимо ко всем формам традиционных рифм, вплоть до *ра́дость : сла́дость.*

Чтобы не быть голословным, приведем список эксплицитно маркированных словесных рифм в сборнике Евгения Винокурова "Жест" (1969): *стреля́л : столя́р, пери́л : пари́л, реча́х : рыча́г, водоём : вдвоём, спрос : сплошь, сердца́ : самца́, Рамайа́на : румя́на, миры́ : милы́, дыша́ : душа́, наставле́ния : настрое́ние, полоса́ : паруса́, наступле́ние : настрое́ние, на вы́нос : неви́нность, гулево́ю : голово́ю, проста́ : пласта́, сложны́ : слоны́, обессу́дьте : абсу́рде, глу́би : гу́бы, держа́ : душа́, причу́д : плечу́, живо́т : живёт, сара́я : сыра́я, то́лка : то́лько, по́стно : по́здно, рома́нтик : ревма́тик, "Пролета́рка" : Плута́рха, дух : двух.*

У Евтушенко ("Братская ГЭС") находим: *бадаму́т : было му́к, изво́дит : исхо́дит, кро́ме : кро́вью, волшбе́ : вообще́, спина́ : спала́, вруно́в : враго́в, у́мник : у́мер, мудрю́ : мою́, невёжд : надёжд, повалится : повадится, покажется : пока еще, завёртится : заве́сится, кали́тки : кали́ки, по ноча́м : палача́м, простира́ю : повторя́ю, скрипа : скры́тно, сыро́ю : сестро́ю, бра́ков : бра́тьев, жару́ : шару́, развя́зка : рома́нса,* преступле́нье : представле́нье, зве́нье : зе́млю, бале́т : биле́т, за́ руку : за́говор, Мохо́вым : молоды́м, застыжу́ : засажу́, перчёной : Печо́рой, котелке́ : катерке́, гомони́вшем : говори́вшем.

Мастер рифмы Александр Галич реже прибегает к словесной рифме: жале́ю : шале́ю, во́лки : "Во́лги", свети́л : следи́л, жа́рко : жа́лко, быль : пыль, не те́ло : не де́ло, урожа́ю : уезжа́ю, да́мою : да́нную, вы́дано-переви́дано : вы́дано-перевы́дано, кры́лья : кли́нья, промета́лся : прометейство.

У Р. Рождественского ("Реквием" 1969) находим: жа́рко : ша́ра, пря́мо : пра́во, вы́ше : вы́жить, смешки́ : снежки́, побе́ги : побе́да, давно́ : дано́.

В любом сборнике стихов начинающих поэтов можно найти словесные рифмы типа сире́ни : смире́ный, лучи́ : лечи́ть, не́бом : не́ был, во́лком : Во́лхову (Ольга Берггольц), береди́ : Беренде́й, дома́ми : дыма́ми, ста́ли : ста́вен, поги́кал : поги́бель, плеча́ми : печа́ли, роня́я : роя́ля, и т.п.

6. Установив структурную связь между звуковым повтором в конце стиха и значимыми единицами, в рамках которых этот повтор осуществляется, перейдем в проблематике самого звукового повтора.

В литературе сложилось убеждение, что повторяющиеся в рифме единицы — фонемы. Исследователи фонологии русского языка любят ссылаться на рифмы типа испи́ть : забы́ть, миг : язы́к, якобы объективно доказывающие отнесенность звуков [i] и [ɨ] к одной фонеме. Авторы, интересовавшиеся 'инструментовкой' ('sound texture') русского стиха, по-разному интерпретировали участвующие в этой 'инструментовке' элементы (ср. К. Тарановский 1965).

Оставим в стороне вопросы 'инструментовки', не подлежащие пока строго системному описанию, и ограничимся теми звуковыми явлениями, которые следует отнести к проблематике конечной рифмы.

6.1 Совершенно очевидно, что 'эхо', коим по существу является любая рифма, явление не механическое, а художественное. Поэтому рифма не является повтором акустически тождественных отрезков, а воспринимается на фоне целого ряда условностей, меняющихся в ходе развития каждого национального стихосложения. Однако можно, кажется, привести и такие свойства русской рифмы, которые не изменились с самого появления рифмованных текстов на русском языке, т.е. с XVIII в. до наших дней. К таким устойчивым условностям относится тождество последней ударной гласной. Приведенные выше эксперименты Маяковского и единично встречающиеся отклонения от этого принципа в современной поэзии дела не меняют. О проблеме разноударных рифм с большим знанием дела пишет В. Ф. Марков в этом сборнике.

Следует подчеркнуть, что вводя в нашу аргументацию понятие фонемы, мы имеем в виду единицу, выделяемую в работах Пражской школы, а не глубинные морфофонемы генеративистов. Глубинные (абстрактные) единицы, плодотворно применяемые в формо- и словообразовании, не имеют ничего общего с теми единицами, которые участвуют в рифмах. Как бы мы ни транскрибировали 'исходные формы' таких слов как *день* и *тень*, не о каком 'созвучии' между {d,#n,} и {t,en,}, *dini* и *t̃ni* не может быть и речи. Из этого следует, что сам феномен рифмовки является в значительной мере феноменом 'поверхностным', связанным с фактическим произношением, со 'сходством' скорее перцептивным, чем системным.

6.2 В пределах безударного вокализма справа от последнего икта принцип фонематического тождества, как мы уже знаем, неприменим. Нет ни полного фонетического, ни, тем менее, фонологического тождества в рифмах *у́жин : ну́жен* (Граф Нулин), *нера́вен : Держа́вин* (Цветаева), *пятака́ми : пла́мя* (Цвет.), *удосто́юсь : по́яс* (Цвет.), *чёрной : одёрну, кра́ску : па́сха* (Цвет.) и т.п. В рифмующихся позициях здесь появляются гласные [ɨ : ə], [ə : i], [i : ə], [u : i], [ə : u], [u : ə].

С точки зрения *системы* такой 'либерализм' предполагает полный отказ от фонемного тождества в безударных слогах рифмующихся слов, т.е. замену принципа 'тождества' принципом 'эквивалентности'. Об эквивалентных звуках в рифме см. Исаченко 1973.

Освоение этой новой условности в плане системы (т.е. в плане допустимых в данный отрезок времени типов рифмовки) сопровождается в плане текста дополнительными, чисто произносительными адаптациями. Совершенно очевидно, что безударный вокализм подвергается в определенных случаях такой степени 'редукции', которая, вообще говоря, не соответствует нормам литературного чтения и приближается к типам редукции, свойственным даже не 'разговорному языку', а подчас прямо стилю скороговорок.

Именно на принципе радикальной редукции безударного вокализма построены неравносложные рифмы типа *замш : за́муж, Ну́жно : жемчу́жиной, а́втора : за́втра,* и т.п. 'Созвучие' может быть осуществлено лишь при условии, что под влиянием слова *ну́жно* рифмующееся слово *жемчу́жина* будет произнесено как *жемчу́жна*, хотя такое произношение вовсе не свойственно какому-либо из существующих 'произносительных стилей' русского языка. Точно также достигается 'созвучие' в неравносложных рифмах Маяковского *по́здно : ро́зданы,* на́гло : на́голо, теа́тры : гладиа́торов, нама́ренней : на Ма́рне, и т.п. Отметим вскользь, что подобного рода произносительные модификации свойствены не только 'риторическому' стиху Маяковского (чрезвычайно неудачный термин), но и любому 'говорному' или 'напевному' стиху, если эти категории вообще еще применимы к современной поэзии.

6.3 Исключительно на фонетическом (и притом далеко не полном) созвучии основаны рифмы типа цари́ца : весели́ться, сёрдца : терёться (Маяк.) и т.п. Эти рифмы построены на фонетическом сходстве, а не на фонологическом тождестве согласных [с] и [с:].

6.4 В настоящем докладе мы не можем проследить эволюцию тех процессов, которые отражают постепенную замену звуковых 'тождеств' звуковыми 'эквивалентностями'. Автор этих строк исходит из того, что классическая русская поэзия строго соблюдает требование 'опорных согласных', т.е. идентичных неслоговых звуков в положении перед последней гласной в мужской рифме на открытый слог: колдуна́ : княжна́ : одна́, не буди́ : на груди́, стопе́ : канапе́. Положение 'опорной согласной' можно считать 'сильным'. И если в современном стихосложении допускаются рифмы типа корабля́ : моря́, столбы́ : тропы́, глазу́ : росу́, петухи́ : пятаки́ (Евт.) и т.п., то можно считать стоящие в этой 'сильной' позиции нетождественные звуки — квази-тождественными, т.е. эквивалентными (Исаченко, 1973).

6.5 В ряде случаев эквивалентные звуки отличаются друг от друга лишь одним единственным признаком. Рифмы, в которых участвуют единицы, отстоящие друг от друга лишь на один признак, иногда называются по-английски feature rhyme. Наиболее распространенным типом таких рифм в современной русской поэзии являются рифмы парных глухих и звонких; ограничиваемся здесь случаями, в которых эквивалентные звуки стоят в 'сильной' позиции, т.е. выступают в качестве опорных согласных: уСы́ : аЗы́ (Винокуров), листКе́ : тайГе́ (Возн.). Еще у Лермонтова имеется рифма глаЗа́ : роСа́, но в классической поэзии такие рифмы единичны.

6.6 Эквивалентность носовых — явление, известное не только в русской версификации, ср. ладо́Ни : в до́Ме (Ахмад.), да́мой : да́нной (Галич). В английском языке попадаются рифмы типа dame : lane, dream : screen. В словацком, где вообще все сонорные являются эквивалентными, находим рифмы типа

Dobrá piecka na zimu,   (хороша печка на зиму,
    Nemá každý perinu.   не у всякого есть перина).

6.7 В русском стихосложении рифмы, содержащие только глухие [p t k] или только звонкие [b d g] весьма редки: *ноГú : груДú* (Цвет.), *теБé : беДé* (Возн.). Зато в германских языках губные, зубные и велярные взрывные могут входить в правильные рифмы при условии, что все участвующие в рифме звуки будут либо глухими, либо звонкими. J. P. Maher (1969) приводит следующие детские стишки:

> Little Tommy Tucker
> Sings for his supper
> What shall we give him?
> Bread and butter.

Или в старой ирландской песне:

> She was a fish monger,
> and sure 't was no wonder.

Эквивалентность звуков [p t k] или [b d g] в рифмах английских детских стишков очевидна. Интересно, однако, что эти звуки объединяются признаками звонкость/глухость и мгновенность/длительность, в то время как признаки места артикуляции (лабиальность, дентальность, велярность) или их акустические эквиваленты игнорируются. Как бы то ни было, разница между [p t k] может быть выражена в бинарной системе не менее чем д в у м я признаками.[5] В литературе указывалось, что сборник детских стишков *Mother Goose* не содержит ни одной рифмы типа [p:b], [t:d], [k:g]. Очевидно, что с точки зрения английского языка звуки (или, если угодно, фонемы) [p t k] более 'похожи' друг на друга, акустически более 'близки', чем звуки (или фонемы) [p:b], [t:d], [k:g], хотя эквивалентность звуков [p t k] или [b d g] соответственно требует 'отказа' от д в у х отличительных признаков, а эквивалентность звуков [p:b] и т.д. — лишь одного. Столь удобный термин *feature rhyme* на поверку оказывается применимым далеко не всегда.

6.8 В австрийском фольклоре широко распространены рифмы типа *hobN* (= haben) : *sogN* (= sagen), *kšri:bN* (geschrieben) : *li:gN* (= liegen) : *cfri:dN* (= zufrieden), причем *N* выражает слоговую носовую, место артикуляции которой зависит от места артикуляции предшествующей взрывной. Приношу свою благодарность проф. Махеру за ценные указания (ср. Maher 1972).

В русском стихосложении рифмы этого типа, как уже было сказано, крайне редки. Однако в церковнославянской поэтике, находящейся под решающим влиянием польской рифмовочной техники, имеются случаи эквивалентности звуков [b:d]. В цитированном выше Акафисте находим: Столо́бно : свобо́дно, в одно́мъ : в Столобно́мъ, преподо́бну :

свобо́дна, ра́дость : сла́бость. Как известно, в польском стихосложении звонкие взрывные являются вполне эквивалентными (Nitsch 1912/1954).

6.9 К эквивалентным звукам относятся также 'тупые' и 'острые' фрикативы типа š : s, ž : z, ср. *роСа́ : хороШа́, ноЖа́ : глаЗа́, туЗы́ : туЖи́* (Возн.).

6.10 Довольно четко намечается эквивалентность взрывных и соответствующих щелинных, ср. *петуХи́ : пятаКи́* (Евт.), *труБы́ : уВы́* (Матвеев) и др.

6.11 Наиболее распространенной еще у поэтов XIX в. является эквивалентность звуков [n m l r n, m, l, r, v v, j]. В существующих фонологических классификациях эти единицы не объединены общим признаком; 'сонорными' обычно признаются лишь плавные, носовые почему-то в этот класс не включаются, а звуки [j v] в некоторых классификационных системах рассматриваются как 'глайды', т.е. ни гласные, ни согласные. Эквивалентность этих звуков не только в русской, но и в польской или словацкой рифмовочной технике дает основания для того, чтобы объединить все приведенные звуки (или, если угодно, фонемы) под единым вполне объективным признаком 'наличие голоса' и вытекаюшая из этого 'формантная структура' (Исаченко, 1973, 219). Затруднительность преодолеть противоречия между традиционными классификациями и функционированием эквивалентных звуков в рифме была подвергнута критике со стороны М. Шапиро, оперирующего понятиями 'семиотических значимостей' (semiotic values) и 'значимостей маркированности' (markedness values). Эквивалентность в рифмах объясняется как идентичность маркировки, причем М. Шапиро принимает тезис Андерсена (1969), согласно которому основным признаком праславянского консонантизма было противопоставление tense/lax а не глухость/звонкость. Доводы, приводимые М. Шапиро, — если только нам удалось их правильно проинтерпретировать, — не объясняют всех известных нам случаев эквивалентности в русских рифмах. Отказ от фонологической интерпретации явлений рифмы М. Шапиро считает отказом от системности языка вообще. Нам представляется, однако, что звуковая эквивалентность, наблюдаемая в современной русской рифмовочной технике, безусловно так или иначе опирается о фонологическую, но сам эффект 'эхо', 'повтора', 'созвучия' осуществляется в фонетическом, т.е. чисто произносительном плане.

7. Появление в русской рифме эквивалентных согласных значительно расширило возможность словесной рифмовки. Начало слова может сигнализироваться не только идентичными, но и эквивалентными

анлаутами. Так мы находим у Маяковского: *звезд : съезд, Босфор : про-сфор, безу́мий : Везу́вий, вы́сморкал : Би́смарка*; у Винокурова: *за́ло : са́ло, сорт : шорт, спор : шпор*; у Евтушенко: *жару́ : шару́*; у Нины Альтовской: *стиль : штиль*; у Рождественского: *жа́рко : ша́ра, ме́ркнут : бе́ркут* ("Реквием", 1969), причем [m:b] рифмуются на основании общих признаков 'лабиальность' и 'наличие голоса'.

7.1 Установка рифмы не на морфему, а на целое слово, подготовляет возврат именно к морфемной рифме. Но если в поэзии XIX в. риф-мующими отрезками были исключительно только аффиксы (типа лю-би́ла : говори́ла), то в современной рифме аффиксы являются лишь составной частью более крупной рифмующей единицы — слова, ср. у Евтушенко: *изво́дит : исхо́дит, простира́ю : повторя́ю, сыро́ю : сес-тро́ю, вруно́в : враго́в, преступле́нье : представле́нье, пова́лится : пова́дится, гомони́вшем : говори́вшем*, и т.п.

8. Даже крупные специалисты по русскому стихосложению не всегда отдают себе отчет в массовости словесной рифмы в современной поэзии. "В формировании созвучия н а ч и н а е т участвовать слово в целом, а то и группы слов (см. обилие составных рифм у раннего Мая-ковского) взамен прежнего слога", пишет Д. Самойлов (1973:19; раз-рядка моя). Совершенно справедливо и с большим знанием дела расценивая рифмовочную технику Маяковского, раннего Асеева, ран-него Пастернака, Д. Самойлов оставляет в стороне творчество совре-менных нам поэтов 60-х и 70-х годов.

Чтобы с предельной наглядностью продемонстрировать удельный вес словесной рифмы в современной поэтике, мы выбрали творчество Андрея Вознесенского, яркого представителя 'новой рифмы'. Анализу был подвергнут сборник "Тень звука" (Молодая гвардия, 1970), в который вошли разные произведения и целые сборники начиная с 60-х годов. Из общего количества 1114 рифм (на 258 страницах текста) мы насчитали 330 формально маркированных словесных рифм, т.е. рифм с идентичным или эквивалентным анлаутом типа *рассы́льный : Росси́и, мину́ем : нему́ю, рожде́ние : разде́лено, лабрадо́ры : лаборато́риях*. Мы умышленно не включали в общее число такие явно словесные рифмы, в которых общий анлаут, как формальный признак границы рифмы, отсутствует, например *заи́к : язы́к, туга́ : утюга́, смешне́й : мише́нь, гво́здики : во́здуха, отбре́хивались : штрайкбре́хершу*. Число сло-весных рифм в данном сборнике составляет 30% всех рифм, т.е. немного меньше одной трети. Из 10 рифм три — словесные. Нередко встре-чаются накопления словесных рифм в смежных стихах:

> В банкетах пре́сных
> нас хвалят го́сти,
>   мы нежно кро́тки.
> Но наши пе́сни
> вонзятся ко́стью
> в чужие гло́тки!

Это уже не 'эксперименты', не 'модные штучки', это — плоть от плоти современной русской поэзии. И замечательно то, что ни одна из этих 330 словесных рифм ни разу не повторяется (ср., с другой стороны, набившие оскомину рифмы *мла́дость : ра́дость, ро́зы : грёзы : моро́зы, век : челове́к, оче́й : рече́й*).

9. *Заключение.* Звуковые характеристики поэтического языка, в частности такие константы, как цезура (в определенных жанрах) или конечная рифма не представляют собой автономных, чисто звуковых 'надстроек' над семантически интерпретируемым и, следовательно, семантически сегментируемым текстом. В рифме участвуют не просто 'звуки' и не просто 'слоги', а звуки и слоги, входящие в состав значимых единиц — морфем (флективных, деривационных, корневых), целых слов и групп слов. Преобладание и удельный вес тех или иных форм рифмовки является важной характеристикой рифмовочной техники эпохи или литературной школы.

Если в 'классической' русской поэзии XIX в. явно преобладают морфологические рифмы (типа молод-*о́е* : ин-*о́е*, сад-*а́ми* : замка́ми, черн-*е́-ют* : рд-*е́-ют*) а также созвучия корней и флексий (подков : луго́в, душо́й : стро́й), то в 'авангардной' поэзии XX в. начинает распространяться словесная рифма. В наши дни словесная рифма построена на следующих принципах:

(1) граница рифмы маркируется идентичным или эквивалентным анлаутом, хотя это требование необязательно, ср. *до су́ти : сосу́да* (Возн.);

(2) ударные гласные, как правило, идентичны;

(3) минимальное число идентичных или эквивалентных звуков рифмующихся слов, включая сюда ударную гласную — три.

Эти минимальные условия налицо в таких рифмах как *лбу : люблю́, ценя́ : себя́, бой : боль, мглы : миры́, сто : что, хмырь : мир, миг : мо́их, наст : нас, у́же : у́шки, дух : двух*. Такие рифмы, однако, являются исключениями; гораздо чаще созвучие осуществляется четырьмя или пятью звуками, ср. *пле́нных : поле́нья, колю́ч : ключ, го́рдо : го́рло, тро́их : тари́ф, тракти́рную : дегради́рую, заво́да : зево́той, остре́л : остре́й, горлово́й : голово́й,* и т.п.

На протяжении всего развития поэзии на русском языке рифма оставалась структурно связанной с основной единицей речи — со словом. Но если эта структурная связь в прошлом носила чисто негативный характер запрета рифмовать идентичное слово 'с самим собой', то в настоящее время корреляция слово — рифма проявляется положительно. Давно назревший, но до сих пор не нашедший удовлетворительного ответа вопрос о семиотической нагрузке рифмы у разных поэтов, в разные эпохи и в разных жанрах предстает ныне в несколько новом и, казалось бы, более обнадеживающем аспекте.

В нашем докладе мы побочно пытались показать, что далеко не все звуковые характеристики современной русской рифмы сводимы к упрощенным фонологическим моделям и что необходимое для понимания современной рифмы понятие звуковой эквивалентности в ряде случаев связано с весьма 'поверхностной' реализацией заданного звукоряда в стихопроизношении. Именно в умышленном пренебрежении обязательными (вне поэтического языка) дистинктивными признаками и заключается сопоставление и условная идентификация неидентичных сегментов, на которых построена современная русская рифма.

Клагенфурт / Лос Анджелес

ПРИМЕЧАНИЯ

[1]   В *Словаре лингвистических терминов* О. С. Ахмановой слово 'рифма' отсутствует. М. Шапиро (1973:1) приводит довольно неудачное определение рифмы из *Princeton Encyclopedia of Poetry and Poetics:* "a metrical-rhetorical device based on sound identities of words" (Alex Preminger, ed., 1965:705).

[2]   Как всякая художественная условность, запрет рифмовать слово 'с самим собой' не является абсолютным. Во всякого рода рефренах, при повторении целого стиха, в позиции рифмующих элементов могут оказаться идентичные слова. Ср. у Марины Цветаевой:

> Леса не сдам,
> Дома не сдам,
> Края не сдам,
> *Пяди* не сдам!

где улавливается сочетание свободного употребления слово *сдам* с фразеологизмом *пяди не сдам* (выделено автором). Намек на противопоставление связанного и свободного (т.е. не вполне идентичного) употребления слова находим у того же автора:

> Поэт — издалекá заводит речь,
> Поэта — далеко заводит речь.

Ср. "заводить речь" и "далеко заводить кого-л.".

[3] 'Организующую роль' пауз до абсурда доводит Б. П. Гончаров (1973:48 сл.). Т.к. свое мнение об этой публикации мы подробно изложили в рецензии, напечатанной в журнале *Russian Linguistics,* I (1973), 177-82, в данной статье мы к взглядам Гончарова не возвращаемся.

[4] Среди многочисленных работ, посвященных вопросам так наз. 'инструментовки' стиха, особого внимания заслуживает статья А. Л. Жовтиса (1969).

[5] М. Халле (1959, 45) приводит следующую классификацию взрывных:

	t	p	k
compact	—	—	+
low tonality	—	+	+

На основании данных, полученных при обследовании словацкого консонантизма, мало чем отличающегося от консонантизма русского, автор этих слов не обнаружил объективно измеримой 'компактности' у велярных взрывных; как можно легко убедиться сравнением сонограмм лабиальных звуков с дентальными, палатальными и велярными, звуки типа [p b f] отличаются именно весьма 'плоским' спектром, не дающим никаких оснований для выделения 'низкой тональности', ср. Isačenko 1968:202, 225.

ИСПОЛЬЗОВАННАЯ ЛИТЕРАТУРА

Альтбауэр, М.
1975　"Рифмованный акафист в честь Нила Столбенского", *Russian Linguistics,* II, 1-2, 1-9.
Гончаров, Б. П.
1973　*Звуковая организация стиха и проблемы рифмы.* Москва: Наука.
Жирмунский, В. М.
1966　"О русской рифме XVIII в.", *Роль и значение литературы XVIII века в истории русской культуры. К 70-летию со дня рождения члена-корреспондента АН СССР П. Н. Беркова. XVIII век,* Сб. 7, 419-27. Ленинград: Наука.
1959　*Стих и язык.* Москва-Ленинград.
Жовтис, А. Л.
1969　"О способах рифмования в русской поэзии", *ВЯ,* вып. 2, 64-75.
Жолковский, А.
1962　"Об усилении", *Структурно-типологические исследования,* 167-72. Москва: Изд. АН СССР.
Isačenko, A. V.
1968　*Spektrografická analýza slovenských hlások.* Bratislava: Slovenská akadémia vied.
1973　"Из наблюдений над 'новой рифмой'", *Slavic Poetics: Essays in honor of Kiril Taranovsky,* R. Jakobson, C. H. van Schooneveld, Dean S. Worth, eds. The Hague-Paris: Mouton.
Maher, J. P.
1969　"English-speakers' awareness of the distinctive features", *Language Sciences,* 5.14 (April 1969).
1972　"Distinctive feature rhyme in German Folk versification", *Language Sciences,* February, 1972, 19-20.
Nitsch, K.
1912　"Z historii polskich rymów", *Studium językowe,* 1912. [Reprinted in: K. Nitsch, *Wybór pism polonistycznych,* Wrocław, 1954. II, 33-77.]
Панченко, А. М.
1973　*Русская стихотворная культура XVII века.* Ленинград: Наука.

Самойлов, Д.
1973 *Книга о русской рифме.* Москва: Художественная литература.
Taranovsky, K.
1965 "The sound texture of Russian verse in the light of phonemic distinctive features",
       IJSLP, IX, 114-51.
Томашевский, Б. М.
1948 "К истории русской рифмы", *Труды Отдела новой русской литератруы*, I, 233-
       80. Москва-Ленинград: Институт литературы (Пушкинский дом) АН СССР.
Shapiro, M.
1973 (?) "The linguistic analysis of rhyme and its semiotic facet" [preprint]
Steinitz, W.
1934 *Der Parallelismus in der finnisch-karelischen Volksdichtung, untersucht an den Liedern des
       karelischen Sängers Arhippa Perttunen.* Helsinki.
Worth, D. S.
1973 "Remarks on eighteenth-century Russian rhyme (Kostrov's translation of the *Iliad*)",
       Slavic Poetics ..., 525-29.
Якобсон, Р.
1923 *О чешском стихе, преимущественно в сопоставлении с русским.* ОПОЯЗ-МЛК.
1962 "Toward a linguistic analysis of Russian rhyme" [К лингвистическому анализу
       русской рифмы], *Studies in Russian Philology*, 1-13. (Michigan Slavic Materials, 1, L.
       Matejka, ed.). Ann Arbor.
1973 "Об односложных словах в русском стихе", *Slavic Poetics ...*, 239-52.

COMMENTS

(Bailey) I have a number of comments to make about your paper. First of all,
we should realize that there is no such thing as an 'absolute' rhyme, that is,
what phonetically constitutes an acceptable rhyme is a matter of convention.
These conventions of acceptability change from one period to another. Consequently, one should always view a rhyme within a given historical context
and only then compare the historical evolution of rhyme from different
periods. It seems to me that you do not always carefully distinguish between a
synchronic and diachronic approach to this aspect of rhyme. I wonder if you
perhaps are not viewing Russian rhyme as a whole too much from the
viewpoint of the practice of some ultra-modern twentieth-century poets when
you speak of rhyme as an 'intensifier'. Poets such as Majakovskij and Voznesenskij like to use 'shock' rhymes in which they sharply juxtapose the meaning
of the rhyming words, thereby increasing the semantic load of the rhymes. But
this should not become an absolute criterium for evaluating all rhymes from
all periods. The 'pure' rhymes used around the turn of the nineteenth century
might seem 'trivial' to us today, but were they for the poets of that time?
Besides this, many present-day poets continue to use such 'quiet' rhymes. As I
remember, Jakobson's full definition of rhyme concerns the phonetic similarity of the rhyming words and their semantic dissimilarity. In speaking of the

rhyme used in the beginning of the nineteenth century he uses the term 'morphophonemic' and not just phonemic. So far no one has really applied his ideas to specific analysis to verify it. While you do mention 'compound rhyme' or 'mosaic rhyme' (*sostavnaja rifma*), you lay most emphasis on what you call *slovesnaja rifma*, which apparently might be rendered in English as 'word rhyme'. Correct me if I am wrong. It seems to me that compound rhyme is far too common in Russian poetry to limit the domain of rhyme just to the word; such rhyme is used by poets beginning with the seventeenth century and it also appears in folk verse. The constant rhymes you cite from Majakovskij (*slovo, sleva, slava*) also constitute what Jakobson called 'poetic etymologies' in Xlebnikov's poetry, if I recall rightly. Poets basically are limited to using the givens of their language; they cannot use what does not exist in their language already. For this reason I doubt very much that poets may reverse this situation and influence the phonetics of their language. I doubt very much that usage of rhymes with a different number of syllables (*raznosložnaja rifma*) would lead to a non-existent pronunciation of the words involved. Have you studied poets' recordings of their verse to verify this, one way or another? In the beginning of your paper, you quite rightly emphasize that rhyme is far more than just sound texture because it also performs an organizing function in verse structure to signal the ends of the lines. However, one trait of many 'loud' twentieth-century poets is the fact they use a large amount of internal rhyme, so much that at times this older function of rhyme becomes obscured. The poem you cite by Voznesenskij on p. 162 is a good example because it actually is basically written in iambic hexameter with double caesura (xx́xx́ / xx́xx́ / xx́xx́). In this instance he employs internal rhymes to mark the caesura. One must always take care not to confuse the graphic layout of a poem's lines with the actual metrical lines. In general, the papers by you, Dean Worth, Vladimir Markov and Edward Stankiewicz reflect the intense present-day interest in rhyme, and an attempt to reexamine many commonly accepted ideas about the evolution of Russian rhyme. This is a welcome development, but I think it indicates how much remains to be studied. One needs to investigate not only literary rhyme, but also rhymes in popular plays from the eighteenth century, the song books, and folklore, particularly in satirical verse, the *raešnik*, and the folk tales appearing in *lubok*. To date little attention has been paid to émigré poetry.

(*Marvan*) 1. The ideas contained in this paper might account for many mysteries. Clearly, the surface elements (phones, words) besides their traditional linguistic depth (phonemes, morphemes) possess another set of underlying elements, i.e., poetic deep structure. The phonologically irrelevant or even non-existing features become highly relevant, in fact the cumulation of surface (antisystematic) disturbances equals the cumulation of poetic message. The traditional phonemic analysis is definitely outdated, the new second deep structure must be defined and constructed in the poetic language.

2. The practical application of your views is quite promising. Here I mention the Old Czech *Píseň Ostrovská* (ab. 1280) which until now had no proper context. The suggested approach might make this oldest, yet traditionally marginal poem one of the key works of the oldest Czech literature.

(Pszczołowska) Рифмовка слов с одинаковой основой, но с различными префиксами (или одно слово с префиксом, другое без него) не является обязательно прямой реализацией запрета "не допускать к рифме идентичных по звучанию пар слов" (стр. 149). Это явление может быть связано с употреблением в рифме т.н. *figura ethymologica*, известной как прием поэтического языка еще в античной и средневековой литературах. В Польше например упомянутый способ сочетания слов применялся — не только в рифме впрочем, но и внутри строк — в XVI и XVII ст. Интересно, что в конце XVII ст., может быть в связи с уходом от грамматической рифмы, созвучие слов с одинаковой основой начинает приниматься теоретиками как нечто, чего надо избегать.

(Žovtis) В связи с чрезвычайно интересным докладом А. В. Исаченко хотелось бы заметить: В наше время рифмы оказываются не просто воспринимаемыми на слух 'сходствами' и 'несходствами', а функционируют в числе многих приемов эквивалентовки рядов. В современной поэзии очевидна установочная гетероморфность механизма создания двухмерной речи (какой является любой стих). На уровне рифменных связей смена средств непрерывна — они варьируют от сквозного рифмования строки со строкой до утери границы между рифмой и вертикальной (внешней — по Брику) инструментовкой или до исчезновения всякой звуковой симметрии. В последнем случае строки корреспондируют уже на других уровнях. Грань между собственно рифмой (с точки зрения Жирмунского) и 'нерифмой' становится почти неуловимой. Так, в примере из Цветаевой (примечание первое к докладу) релевантна уже не звуковая соотнесенность, а грамматическая эквивалентность начал строк. Надо обратить также внимание на то, что 'словесная рифма' часто ограничивается тождественностью одного гласного в субъединицах повтора (например, *ястреб : явор* у Б. Слуцкого). До сих пор считалось, что "русская рифма не может свестись к одному только гласному" (Якобсон).

Additional discussion: Abernathy, Hrushovsky, Markov, Segal, Segert, Shapiro, Stankiewicz, Timberlake

К ИССЛЕДОВАНИЮ ПОЭТИКИ БЛОКА
("ШАГИ КОМАНДОРА")

ВЯЧ. ВС. ИВАНОВ

0. Предметом настоящей работы служат некоторые вопросы поэтики Блока (преимущественно 10-х годов), важные и для исследования крупных русских поэтов следующих поколений, испытавших его влияние. В этом отношении особый интерес представляет стихотворение "Шаги командора", высоко ценившееся в "Цехе поэтов" и прямо воздействовавшее на самых больших поэтов-акмеистов.

1. МЕТР И РИТМ

"Шаги командора" написаны разностопным 'вольным хореем' (Гаспаров 1965:87-88, 1974:395; Рундев 1972:242 и 61), но по отношению к этому стихотворению такое обозначение условно: по характеру чередования числа стоп (или метрически сильных слогов-иктов) "Шаги командора", состоящие из 10 хореических четверостиший, распадаются на 3 части (A, B, C) по 3 строфы каждая (ниже обозначаются соответственно A-I, A-II и т.д.) с одной промежуточной строфой (A') между A и B. Различия между частями определяются схемами:

$$
\begin{array}{ll}
\text{A-I, A-II, A-III:} & 5\ 4\ 6\ 4 \\
\text{A'} & :\ 5\ 4\ 5\ 5 \\
\text{B-I, B-II, B-III:} & 5\ 5\ 5\ 4 \\
\text{C-I, C-II, C-III:} & 5\ 4\ 5\ 4 \\
\end{array}
$$

Предположение о том, что "в основе стихотворения хореическая строфа 5 4 5 4, но с вариациями" (Гаспаров 1974:395) оправдано в том отношении, что схема 5 4 определяет не только обе половины четверостиший C, но и вторые половины четверостиший B и первые половины четверостиший A и A'. Только в A' четверостишие завершается не четырехстопной, а пятистопной строкой ("Сладко ль видеть неземные сны?"), что образует трансформацию 5 4 → 5 5; результирующая схема 5 5 повторяется в первых половинах четверостиший В. Во вторых половинах четверостиший А обнаруживается трансформация 5 4 → 6 4. Таким образом, метрические отступления от основной строфы, выдержанной в С, всегда наблюдаются только в одной из строк: в 3-й в А, в 4-й в А', во 2-й в В.

Деление стихотворения на описанные метрические части согласуется с тематической его структурой. В строфах А-I, А-II, А-III дается экспозиция темы: пустая спальня со спящей Донной Анной и испуганным Дон Жуаном. В А' вводится в явном виде существенный для стихотворения (и отличающая его от других вариаций на ту же тему в европейской традиции) мотив мертвой Донны Анны. В строфах В-I, В-II, В-III приход командора сопоставляется с цепью равнозначных ему образов, по самой сути своей звуковых — рожка автомобиля, боя часов, — что особенно существенно для ритма. В строфах С-I, С-II, С-III осуществляется возврат к теме строф А, завершаемой последним боем часов в С-III. Это тематическое членение, объединяющее А и С и выделяющее В, может быть прослежено не только на уровне метра, но и на уровне ритмической структуры.

1.1 Немного менее половины строк стихотворения (16 из 40) написаны 4-стопным хореем, ритмические особенности которого видны из табл. 1, где скудость объема выборки искупается отчетливостью ритмической тенденции.

Табл. 1

| | Стопы | | |
	I	II	III	IV
Число ударных иктов	14	16	6	16
в %	87,5	100	37,5	100

При сопоставлении со статистическими данными по другим поэтам XX в. и с языковой теоретической моделью (Гаспаров 1974:96–97, табл. 10 и 10а) обращает на себя внимание крайне повышенная (в том числе и по сравнению с другими стихами самого Блока) ударность первого метрически сильного слога; точную аналогию обнаруживает только ритм четырехстопных хореев пьесы Цветаевой "Ариадна" (ударность первого икта 88,5). Пропуск ударения на этом слоге наблюдается только в 2-й (т.е. первой с этим размером) строке стихотворения ("За ночным окном туман"), сигнализирующей начало А, и в симметрично по отношению к ней расположенной 2-й строке А', где (единственный раз в

4-стопной строке во всем стихотворении) наблюдается пропуск двух метрических ударений ("В зеркалах отражены", $-\cup \stackrel{\angle}{} \mid \cup - \cup \stackrel{\angle}{} \parallel$), что подчеркивает ритмическую необычность А'. Несколько пониженной по сравнению с другими поэтами (за исключением раннего Клюева, Городецкого и Мандельштама) является ударность 3-го метрически сильного слога, которая, однако, при этом точно совпадает с теоретической языковой моделью, предполагающей его ударность 37,6. Пропуски ударений на этом слоге в конце А-II и начале А-III, в А', а также в конце В-II согласуются с отмеченными ниже аналогичными пропусками ударений в смежных 6- и 5-стопных строках в А-II и А-III, а также в В-II и начале В-III и позволяют говорить о ритмическом единстве этих трех групп строк.

1.2 Около половины стихотворения (21 строка из 40) написано 5-стопным хореем, ритм которого представлен на табл. 2.

Табл. 2

	Стопы				
	I	II	III	IV	V
Число ударных иктов	17	19	17	14	21
в %		80,9	90,5	80,9	66,6	100

При сопоставлении со статистическими данными по другим поэтам XX в. и с теоретической языковой моделью (Гаспаров 1974:110-11, табл. 12 и 12а) обращает на себя внимание повышенная ударность 1-го слога, сопоставимая только со стилистическими характеристиками 5-стопного хорея позднего Брюсова (ударность 1-го слога 80,5 в стихах 1916-1918 гг., но не ранее, т.е. для периода, существенно более позднего по сравнению с разбираемым стихотворением). Из четырех пропусков начального метрического ударения три сгруппированы в смежных строках В-I ("Выходи на битву, старый рок!", "И в ответ — победно и влюбленно") и в начальной строке В-II ("Пролетает, брызнув в ночь огнями"); автор признателен М. Л. Гаспарову, обратившему его внимание на эту и некоторые другие особенности ритма стихотворения. 4-й аналогичный пропуск ударения в начале 5-стопной строки знаменует начало С ("На вопрос жестокий нет ответа"), симметричное по отношению к В-I.

Три строки стихотворения, написанные 6-стопным хореем, характеризуются полноударностью 2-го и 3-го метрически сильного слогов при наличии одинаковых пропусков ударений на каждом из остальных слогов. На фоне преимущественно повышенной ударности существен-

ный интерес представляет шестистопная строка А-II "Из страны блаженной, незнакомой, дальней", характеризующаяся одновременным
пропуском ударений на 1-м и 4-м метрически сильных слогах. Для 5- и
6-стопных строк стихотворения пропуски ударений не на предпоследнем сильном слоге могут считаться показательными (Иванов 1975:33).
Кроме только что приведенной 6-стопной строки А-II такой пропуск
обнаруживается в рифмующейся с ней первой 5-стопной строке того же
четверостишия ("Холодно и пусто в пышной спальне"), в тематически
и лексически связанной с нею же первой строке следующего четверостишия А-III ("Что изменнику блаженства звуки?") и в завершающей
5-стопной строке А', а также в смежных друг с другом строках В-II,
соединенных повтором слова "тихий" ("Черный, тихий как сова мотор",
"Тихими, тяжелыми шагами"), и В-III ("Настежь дверь. Из непомерной
стужи").

Во всех указанных группах строк пропуски ударений на одних и тех
же или симметрично расположенных слогах объединяют тематически и
синтагматически связанные между собой строки. Вместе с тем насыщенность ударениями на метрически сильных слогах сама по себе
является иконической. Отсутствие пропусков метрических ударений
выделяет строки А, А' и С, прямо относящиеся к Донне Анне и содержащие ее имя. В строфах, где непосредственно передается образ боя
часов — в В-III и С-III — только по одному разу встречается пропуск
метрического ударения. Напротив, наибольшее число пропусков метрических ударений — 5 — выделяет строфу В-II, где речь идет о вступлении
в дом командора. В А-III, С-I и С-II — по два пропуска, в А-I (т.е. в
начале стихотворения) — 3 пропуска, в А-II, А' и В-I — по 4 пропуска.

1.3 Взаимосвязь разобранных пропусков метрических ударений и особенности их размещения видны на ритмической схеме, см. табл. 3:

Табл. 3

```
A-I   ́⌣ | ́⌣ | ́⌣ – | ⌣ ́∩ ||
      – ⌣ ́ | ⌣ ́ | ⌣ ́ ||
      ́ | ⌣ ́ | ⌣ ́ | ⌣ ́ ⌣ – | ⌣ ́ O ||
      ́ | ⌣ ́ ⌣ | ́ | ⌣ ́ ||

A-II  ́⌣ – | ⌣ ́ ⌣ | ́⌣ | ́ O ||
      ́⌣ | ́ || ⌣ ́ | ⌣ ́ ||
      – ⌣ ́ | ⌣ ́ ⌣ | – ⌣ ́ ⌣ | ́ O |
      ́⌣ | ́⌣ | – ⌣ ́ ||
```

```
A-III   ∸ | U ∸ U – | U ∸ U | ∸ O ‖
        ∸ U | ∸ U | – U ∸ ‖
        ∸ U | ∸ U | ∸ | U ∸ | U ∸ U | ∸ O ‖
        ∸ U | ∸ U | ∸ U | ∸ |
   A'   ∸ | U ∸ | U ∸ U – | U ∸ O ‖
        – U ∸ | U – U ∸ ‖
        ∸ U | ∸ U | ∸ U | ∸ | U ∸ O ‖
        ∸ U | ∸ U | – U ∸ U | ∸ ‖
  B-I   ∸ | U ∸ | U ∸ U | – U ∸ O ‖
        – U ∸ | U ∸ U | ∸ U | ∸ ‖
        – U ∸ | U ∸ U | – U ∸ O |
        ∸ U | ∸ | U ∸ | U ∸ ‖
 B-II   – U ∸ U | ∸ U | ∸ | U ∸ O |
        ∸ U | ∸ U | – U ∸ | U ∸ ‖
        ∸ U – | U ∸ U – | U ∸ O |
        ∸ | U ∸ U | – U ∸ ‖
B-III   ∸ U | ∸ ‖ U – U ∸ U | ∸ O |
        ∸ U | ∸ U | ∸ | U ∸ | U ∸ ‖
        ∸ | U ∸ ‖ U ∸ | U ∸ | U ∸ O ‖
        ∸ | U ∸ ‖ U ∸ | U ∸ ‖
  C-I   – U ∸ | U ∸ U | ∸ | U ∸ O ‖
        ∸ | U ∸ U | – U ∸ ‖
        ∸ U | ∸ U | ∸ U | ∸ | U ∸ O ‖
        ∸ U | ∸ ‖ U ∸ | U ∸ ‖
 C-II   ∸ | U ∸ U | ∸ U – | U ∸ O ‖
        ∸ | U ∸ U | ∸ | U ∸ ‖
        ∸ U | ∸ U | ∸ U | ∸ U | ∸ O ‖
        ∸ U | ∸ U ‖ – U ∸ ‖
C-III   ∸ U | ∸ U | ∸ U – | U ∸ O |
        ∸ | U ∸ | U ∸ U | ∸ ‖
        ∸ U | ∸ U | ∸ U | ∸ U | ∸ U ‖
        ∸ U | ∸ U | ∸ U | ∸ ‖
```

Несовпадение ритмического членения с синтаксическим в качестве особого приема выразительности используется только в B-III (в трех строках) — в строфе, вводящей слова Командора — "бой часов", и в повторяющихся формулах в A-II, C-I и C-II.

1.4 Две характерные черты метрической и ритмической организации стихотворения — строгость строфической структуры с фиксированными вариациями и насыщенность ударениями на метрически сильных слогах — отчетливо обнаруживаются при сопоставлении с более ранними опытами Блока, написанными разностопным хореем, где наблюдаются лексические и семантические переклички с разбираемым текстом. Особенно показательно сравнение "Шагов командора" (1910-1912 гг.) со стихотворением 1904 г. "День поблек, изящный и невинный", где при наличии таких сходств, как тема смерти женщины, отражаемой в *зеркале, портьера* (ср. *занавес у входа*; к строке "Тихо дрогнула портьера" обнаруживается ритмическая и лексическая параллель во "Втором рождении" Пастернака: "Но нежданно по портьера Пробежит вторженья дрожь", ср. у раннего Пастернака в 6-стопном хорее "Никого не ждут, но наглухо портьеру"), *шаги* (*кавалера,* ср. *командора*), *слуги — услыхала* (ср. *слуги — слышно*), обнаруживаются и близкие хореические схемы 5 5 4 4 (в 1-й строфе), 4 5 (в начале 3-й строфы), но характер чередований хореических строк (от 5-стопных до 2-стопных) значительно более свободен, а число пропусков метрических ударений весьма значительно (как и в метрически сходном разностопном хорее стихотворения 1907 г. "Насмешница", заключительная строфа которого содержит формулу "Ночь глуха", которая с той же рифмой — *петуха* повторяется в "Шагах командора"). Для сопоставления с метром "Шагов командора" значительный интерес представляет последнее четверостишие "Осенняя воля" (1905 г.), где схема 5 4 5 5 совпадает с А. Сходные метры при обилии ударений на метрически сильных слогах характерны и для последних строф хореического стихотворения 1906 г. "Шлейф, забрызганный звезда́ми"; но единственная строка этого последнего, имеющая явное синтаксическое соответствие в разбираемом тексте ("Ты — рукою узкой, белой, странной", ср. "Из страны блаженной, незнакомой, дальней") отличается от соответствующей строки "Шагов командора" существенно бо́льшей перегруженностью ударениями. Поэтому можно утверждать, что после перечисленных опытов разностопного хорея II-го тома Блок впервые в "Шагах командора" пришел к описанной ритмической форме. С некоторыми видоизменениями она воспроизводится и в стихотворении 1914 г. "Ветер стих, и слава заревая", но бо́льшая свобода вариаций длины строк (включающая строки от 3-стопных до 5-стопных без жесткой строфической организации всего стихотворения) и меньшая отягченность ударениями на метрически сильных слогах объединяет и это стихотворение не с "Шагами командора", а с названными более ранними стихотворениями.

1.5 В этом же смысле не столько с ритмом, сколько с метром "Шагов командора" можно сблизить цикл из трех стихотворений Мандельштама, законченных не позднее осени (октября-ноября) 1920 г.: "Веницейской жизни мрачной и бесплодной", "В Петербурге мы сойдемся снова", "Чуть мерцает призрачная сцена" и обнаруживающих как отмеченные несколькими исследователями семантические и лексические сходства с "Шагами командора" (см. о строках "Только злой мотор во мгле промчится И кукушкой прокричит" во втором стихотворении Харджиев 1973:279, ср. образы занавеса, смерти, ночи, спальни, зеркал, роль прилагательного *блаженный* и т.д.), так и стилистические и метрические (на что указали М. Б. Мейлах и М. Л. Гаспаров при обсуждении первого варианта настоящей работы). Но для метра мандельштамовского цикла существенно наличие 6-стопных нечетных строк, у Блока представленных лишь в трех строках из 40. В первом стихотворении ("Веницейской жизни ..."), отмеченном в записной книжке Блока, у Мандельштама преобладает схема 6 5 с дальнейшими трансформациями, хотя бы и единичными, 6 5 → 6 6 и даже 6 5 → 6 7 (см. о строке "Тяжелее платины Сатурново кольцо" Гаспаров 1974:395, ср. 7-стопные хореические строки в составе полиметрического стихотворения 1932 г. "Там где купальни, бумагопрядильни"). Нечетные 5- (а не 6-)-стопные строки выступают только в 3-ей строфе и в 1-х строках двух последних строф (трансформация 6 → 5 в схеме 6 5), тогда как четные 4-(а не 5-)-стопные строки — только в завершающих строках 3-й и 4-й строф (трансформация 5 → 4 в той же схеме). Поэтому строфа 5 5 5 4, непосредственно сопоставимая с метром части В "Шагов командора", представлена только в 3-й строфе стихотворения, которая тем не менее благодаря обычному для хорея Мандельштама (Тарановский 1962) значительному числу пропусков метрических ударений отличается от ритма стихотворения Блока (при некотором сходстве ритма первых 2 строк с B-II):

> И горят, горят в корзинах свечи,
> Словно голубь залетел в ковчег.
> На театре и на праздном вече
> Умирает человек.

Сопоставление с двумя другими стихотворениями цикла позволяет предположить, что и разбираемый текст Мандельштама состоял из четырех восьмистиший, но позднее одно четверостишие было опущено. Поскольку 3-я и 4-я строфы, а также две последние объединяются описанными метрическими трансформациями, вероятным кажется пропуск одного четверостишия, парного по отношению к стоящему особняком 5-му, но следовавшего за 4-м. Причиной пропуска, в частности, могло быть то, что в предшествовавшем четверостишии строка "Черным бархатом завешенная плаха" намечает тему, продолженную (в том же метре) во втором стихотворении цикла в строках "В черном бархате всемирной пустоты" (ср. 5-стопную строку "В черном бархате советской ночи", внешне близкую к "Черным табором стоят кареты" в 3-м стихотворении цикла): это сопоставление согласуется и с одинаковым образом свеч в обоих стихотворениях.

В стихотворении "В Петербурге мы сойдемся снова" строфа схемы 5 4 5 4 повторяется (с единственной трансформацией 4 → 5 в конце второго восьмистишия) во втором и третьем восьмистишиях, составляющих половину всего стихотворения. Первое же и четвертое восьмистишия строятся на основе той же схемы 6 5, что и первое стихотворение, но с частой инверсией 6 5 → 5 6, что описывается трансформациями 6 → 5 (в 1-х строках первых двух четверостиший стихотворения и в первых трех нечетных строках последнего восьмистишия), 5 → 6 (во 2-й строке стихотворения и в последних двух четных строках последнего восьмистишия, где образуется инвертированная схема 5 6 6 6, в первоначальном варианте следовавшая за 5 5 5 6, ср. последовательность 5 6 6 в первых трех строках стихотворения), ср. также единичное 5 → 4 (в 4-й строке стихотворения, тем самым предвосхищающей метр срединных восьмистиший). Схема 5 4 5 4 бесперебойно выдерживается в начальных двух восьмистишиях третьего стихотворения Мандельштама "Чуть мерцает призрачная сцена", но в двух следующих восьмистишиях осуществляются трансформации 4 → 5 (в первых двух четных строках 3-го и 4-го восьмистиший), 4 → 6 (в предпоследней четной строке), 5 → 6 (в 3-й строке последнего восьмистишия, где прилагательное "блаженного" явственно говорит о связи со 2-м стихотворением). Помимо существенного тяготения к шестистопности (в "Шагах командора" еле намеченного) стихи Мандельштама отличаются от блоковского текста значительной облегченностью метрически сильных слогов (в соответствии с общей тенденцией хорея Мандельштама, Тарановский 1962:109). Для Мандельштама также чрезвычайно характерно регулярное двучастное синтаксическое деление строки, почти не встречающееся в стихотворении Блока, где синтаксические паузы среди строки в А-II, В-III, С-I и С-II служат исключительными приемами выразительности. Эти характерные черты указанной стихотворной формы у Мандельштама обнаруживаются и в конце стихотворения воронежского цикла

(1936 г.) "Мой щегол, я голову закину" (ср. также разностопный 5- и 6-стопный хорей в стихотворении того же времени "Я живу на важных огородах" 1935 г.). Третья (последняя) строфа стихотворения "Мой щегол …", в целом написанного по схеме 5 4, отвечает схеме 5 4 6 4, совпадающей с метром части А "Шагов командора":

> Что за воздух у него в надлобье —
> Черн и красен, желт и бел!
> В обе стороны он в оба смотрит — в обе!
> Не посмотрит — улетел!

2. АНАГРАММАТИЧЕСКАЯ СТРУКТУРА И РИФМЫ

Можно предположить, что звуковую структуру "Шагов командора" задают анаграмматически осмысляемые имена *Дóнна Áнна* и *(Дóн-) Жуáн*. Поэтому стихотворение представляет значительный интерес как один из наиболее наглядных примеров обнаружения в поэзии XX в. действия той "основополагающей и архаичной" закономерности, которой можно объяснить появление анаграмм (Lévi-Strauss 1971:581-82; Иванов 1972:86; Ivanov 1974:837). Характерно, что и при анализе звуковой организации более ранних стихотворений Блока было выявлено, что небольшие звуковые единицы, такие как отдельные фонемы или группы фонем, внутри стихотворения могут семантизироваться "по принципу pars pro toto, благодаря их введению в аффективно насыщенные и стратегически размещенные в главных позициях ключевые слова" (Abernathy 1963 и 1967:8, примеч. 23); например, в стихотворении "Ночная фиалка" сочетание *от,* связанное с темой "болота" в 10 строках (240-249) повторяется 11 раз. В докладе В. С. Баевского и А. Д. Кошелева "Поэтика Блока: Анаграммы" на III Блоковской конференции в Тарту в апреле 1975 г. было показано, что анаграмматическая структура обнаруживается и во многих стихах I тома.

2.1 Звуковая организация стихотворения "Шаги командора" на фонемном уровне характеризуется явным преобладанием гласных *á* (всего 52 из 159, т.е. 32.8%) и *ó* (всего 41 при частотах других ударных гласных: *э́* – 25, *ы́* – 17, *и́* – 14, *у́* – 10 при 11 безударных нередуцируемых *у*). Комбинации ударных гласных *á – ó, ó – á* начинают стихотворение, в частности, в анаграмматических сочетаниях с *н* (ср. *зáнавес* в 1-й строке, где содержится костяк имени *Áнна*; всего в первых двух строках 6 *н*; Иванов 1975:34; статистическая значимость накопления *н* в стихотворении отмечена в упомянутом докладе В. С. Баевского и А. Д. Кошелева) и *д*. В А' повторение имени *Áнна* включено в строку, где 4 раза подряд повторено ударное *á*: "*Áнна, Áнна*, слáдко ль спáть в могиле?", ср. сходное трехчленное построение в конце предпоследней строфы с инверсией сочетания *áн → ná*: "*Áнна, Áнна!* Тишинá!", которая сходна с обнаруживаемой в конце первого четверостишия: "Страх познáвший Дон Жуáн". Вероятной представляется анаграмма имени *Дóнна* в сочетании *нó*чь бле*дná* (с аналогичной инверсией *нó → óн*).

Сочетание *у – а*, повторяющееся в стихотворении 10 раз, представляется анаграммой имени *Жуан*; в частности, такое толкование можно дать звуковой структуре повторяющегося сочетания *слýги спя́т*, ср. также *ýтреннем тумáне* в последней строфе. Согласные этого же имени воспроизводятся в повторяющейся основе *блаженный, блаженство* (которая, по гипотезе В. С. Баевского и А. Д. Кошелева, как и некоторые другие упомянутые слова — *занавес, ночь*, — сама может быть гипограммой, шифрующейся другими соседними звуковыми комбинациями).

Возможно, что при изменении признака звонкости первых двух согласных на признак глухости последовательность *т ... ш ... н* в *тишина, страшно* можно соотнести с именем **Дон Жуан**а. Слово *тишина*, повторяющееся в стихотворении, анаграмматически связано с предикативным наречием *страшно* и словообразовательно соотнесено с повторяющимся в другой строфе прилагательным *тихий* (ср. словообразовательную связь прилагательного *блаженный* и последующего существительного *блаженство* в ритмически сходных друг с другом строках).

В двух последних строфах в явном виде наличествует звукопись, основанная на имени и символическом обозначении Донны Анны (**Дéва свéта! Гдé ты** ...); всего в В-I и В-II 10 *э* из общего числа 25, т.е. 40%, Иванов 1975:34 (В. С. Баевский и А. Д. Кошелев отмечают гипограммы *свет* и *смерть* в этих строфах).

2.2 Существенной особенностью звуковой организации стихотворения является то, что его рифмы в основном включены в ту же сеть анаграмматических повторов.

Анаграмматически осмысляемые рифмы первых двух строф (А-I и А-II) явным образом соотносятся с рифмами трех последних строф С (которые отчасти и лексически их повторяют, ср. в начале стихотворения в А-I *туман* и *тумане* в конце стихотворения в С-III). С точки зрения анаграмматической особенно показательны первые рифмы

входа – свобода с инверсией анаграмматического сочетания *дó → óд* ...
Анаграмматическая последовательность гласных *у ... а* выдерживается
в первых четырех мужских рифмах в А-I (где в рифме выступает и само
слово — анаграмма *Дон-Жуан*). В А-II все рифмы (как и в двух
последних строфах — С-II и С-III) строятся на гласной *á*. В женской
рифме за *á* следует (не в контактной позиции) сочетание /н'ь/:/спáл'н'ь/
— /дáл'н'ьĭ/, дающее гипограмму /áн'ь/, развиваемую в С-III. В
мужской рифме этому *á* предшествует безударное *у*, тогда как в
следующей женской рифме в А-III выступает ударное *у*, в предшествующей строфе дважды встречающееся под ударением (*пýсто, слýги*, ср.
отчасти созвучную и грамматически однотипную рифму *звýки – рýки*).
А-III и А-IV соединены одинаковой мужской рифмой, включающей
анаграмматическое *н* и связанной с повторением формы *сны* (в одинако-
вом сочетании с глаголом *видеть*) в конце обоих четверостиший:
сочтены́ – сны́ – отражены́ – сны́. Наиболее изолировано в сети анаграмматических рифм стихотворения стоит женская рифма *застыли –
могиле* в А', как бы подчеркивающая особое место этой строфы. С В-I
начинается цикл рифм, включающих ударное *ó* (все рифмы В-I, мужские
рифмы С-II и С-III). В В-I первая рифма *бездóнно* содержит слово
Дóнна. Женская рифма В-II /ɑгн'áм'ь/ – /шɑгáм'ь/ содержит в транс-
формированном виде анаграмматическое сочетание *á* + носовой согласный (*м' ← н'*). От других рифм стихотворения резко отличается глубокая
рифма (*как ...*) *мотóр – Командор* (в строфе и строке, исходной для
всего стихотворения), где второе слово содержит анаграмматические
последовательности *ан* и *дó* (слово *Командóр* предварено созвучным с
ним *дóм* с перестановкой *м*; фонема *м* наличествует и в женской рифме
этой строфы).

В В-III приход Командора и бой часов сигнализируется первой (если
не считать более обычной *спальне – дальней*) неточной женской рифмой
усеченного (пополненного) типа (ср. Самойлов 1973:219; Гаспаров
1975:74-75): *стужи* (состав согласных этого слова предвосхищен в
слове *настежь* в начале строки) — *ужин*; в последней рифме содержится
бóльшая часть анаграммы *Жуан*. Вторая неточная женская рифма того
же типа в С-III *тумане – встанет* завершает стихотворение. Все
остальные рифмы в С точные, мужские рифмы все строятся на ударном
á. Строфы С-I и С-II объединяются одной мужской рифмой, связанной с
повторением слова *тишина* в качестве первого рифмующегося мужского слова в С-I и второго рифмующегося мужского слова в С-II с
повторением однотипной формулы: *тишина – (ночь) бледна – (ночь)
мутна – тишина*. В тех же четверостишиях повторяются и внутренние

рифмы *нет ответа – нет ответа – рассвета; рассвета – Дева Света!*
Где ты. В С-II и женские и мужские рифмы строятся на анаграмматическом сочетании *а* с носовым *н*, продолжающемся и в конечной женской рифме С-III.

2.3 Общая структура стихотворения задается повтором, связывающим А-II:

> Холодно и пусто в пышной спальне,
> Слуги спят, и ночь глуха

и С-I:

> В пышной спальне страшно в час рассвета,
> Слуги спят, и ночь бледна.

Звуковые и лексические вариации в этих формулах (ср. также *ночь мутна* в следующей строфе, продолжающей и нагнетающей композиционные повторы) представляют интерес для выяснения характера синтагматических связей. В первом употреблении формулы *глуха* в конце строки соотносится по звуковому составу со *слуги* в начале строки. Во втором употреблении *бледна* (которое в сочетании с *ночь* толкуется анаграмматически) в то же время воспроизводит состав согласных слова *холодна* из первой формулы (повторяющейся и в следующей строфе), тогда как слово *мутна* содержит звуковую тему *у – а* (ср. *Жуан*).

Второе употребление формулы характеризуется увеличением числа ударных *á* (5 при 3 в первом употреблении), хотя в рифме появляется *э́*, характерное именно для С.

2.4 Характерные особенности описанной звуковой структуры стихотворения видны из схемы решетки гласных, см. табл. 4.

Табл. 4

А-I   á – ó – á – ó
    ы́ – ó – у – á
    ó – э́ – á – ы́ – ó
    á – á – ó – у – á

А-II   ó – ý – ы́ – á
    ý – á – ó – у – á
    { ы́ – э́ – ó – á
    { ы́ – э́ – у – á

A-III   ó – э́ – ý
      и́ – и́ – ы́
      ó – á – и́ – и́ – э́ – ý
      ó – á – и́ – ы́
A'   и́ – ы́ – ó – ы́
      á – ы́
      á – á – á – á – и́
      á – и́ – ы́ – ы́
B-I   и́ – á – ý – ó
      и́ – и́ – á – ó
      { э́ – э́ – ó
       { э́ – э́ – ó – ó
B-II   á – ы́ – у – ó – á
      ó – и́ – á – ó
      и́ – ó – á
      ó – у – á – ó
B-II   á – э́ – э́ – ý
      ó – и́ – ó – ы́ – ó
      ó – ó – á – á – ý
      á – ó – ы́ – ó
C-I   ó – ó – э́ – э́
      э́ – э́ – á
      ы́ – á – á – á – э́
      ý – á – ó – á
C-II   á – э́ – ó – á
      á – э́ – ó – á
      э́ – э́ – э́ – ó – á
      á – á – á
C-III   ó – ó – ý – у – á
      ý – ы́ – э́ – á
      ó – á – э́ – á – á
      á – á – э́ – á

3. ПОЭТИЧЕСКАЯ ГРАММАТИКА

На уровне поэтической грамматики самой приметной чертой этого стихотворения (как и ряда других лирических стихотворений Блока этого времени) является скупость употребления личных форм глагола при преобладании чисто именных предложений или предложений с именными формами предиката: с краткими формами прилагательных

— *глуха, пуста, безумна, бездонна, бледна, мутна; готов;* причастиями
— *сочтены, отражены,* предикативными наречиями, относящимися к
"категории состояния" — *холодно, пусто, сладко, страшно, странно*
(формально к этой группе приближается и согласованное с существительным среднего рода причастие *слышно—пенье),* ср. также преди-
кативное употребление *настежь.* Поскольку все стихотворение (кроме
прямой речи) написано в плане настоящего времени (единственное
исключение — форма совершенного вида — *застыли* в А' понимается не
столько во временном, сколько в видовом плане), во всех этих случаях
отсутствует глагол–связка (ср. ее присутствие в ряду глагольных предложений прошедшего времени в начале стихотворения разностопного
хорея II тома "А под маской *было* звездно"). Поэтому предложения
с указанными видами именных предикатов совпадают по признаку
отсутствия личных форм глагола с собственно именными предложениями как в утвердительном статусе (ср. уже в А-I: *Тяжкий, плотный
занавес у входа),* так и в вопросительном (ср. в А-I: *Что теперь твоя
постылая свобода)* и отрицательном *(нет ответа).* В А-I и С-II личные
формы глаголов отсутствуют, в А-II и С-I единственной личной глагольной формой является непереходный глагол *спят* (в повторяющейся
формуле *слуги спят),* обозначающий состояние; этот же глагол выступает в словоформе *спит* А-III, где к тождественному подлежащему
(Донна Анна) относится и форма *видит* в сочетании *видит сны,*
семантически связанном с *спит.* Обе эти формы трансформируются в А'
(где употреблена и личная глагольная форма *застыли)* в инфинитивные
конструкции с предикативным *сладко* (ср. такую же конструкцию
Сладко ль спать тебе, матрос? в финале стихотворения того же периода — 1909 г. "Поздней осенью из гавани", а также скопление подобных
инфинитивных конструкций в близком к именному стилю стихотворении 1908 г. "Май жестокий с белыми ночами!", где личные формы
встречаются только в повелительном наклонении, ср. *выходи* во 2-й
строке этого стихотворения и во 2-й строке В-I). Строфы В-I и В-II
характеризуются наличием связанных друг с другом личных форм настоящего времени *(поет — пролетает — вступает);* в В-II (как и в
А-III) встречается деепричастный оборот *(брызнув,* ср. *скрестив).* На
этом фоне особенно отчетливо выступает подчеркнутая неглагольность
повествовательного текста в первых строках В-III, контрастирующая с
личными глагольными формами прошедшего времени в конце той же
строфы в прямой речи:

> Настежь дверь. Из непомерной стужи,
> Словно хриплый бой ночных часов —

Бой часов: "Ты звал меня на ужин,
Я пришел ..."

Синтаксически сходные построения, начинающиеся предложной кон-
струкцией с предлогом *из* без личного глагола, встречаются в начале
стихотворения 1909 г. "Из хрустального тумана".

Каждый вечер — запах мяты,
Месяц узкий и щербатый,
Тишь и мгла.
... На траве, едва примятой,
Легкий след.
Свежий запах дикой мяты,
Неживой голубоватый
Ночи свет.

Несколько наиболее характерных лирических стихотворений III тома
характеризуется преимущественным использованием именного стиля:
"Ночь. Улица. Фонарь. Аптека" (1912 г., по времени близко к дате
завершения "Шагов командора"), "Черный ворон в сумраке снежном"
(1910 г.), "Ночь — как века, и томный трепет" (1913 г.), "Была ты всех
ярче, верней и прелестней" (1914 г.). Начальные части, характеризуемые
именным стилем (как в "Шагах командора") представлены в стихотворениях "Вновь оснеженные колонны" (1909 г.), "Из хрустального
тумана" (1909 г.; четвертая строфа стихотворения тоже выдержана в
именном стиле), "Унижение" (1911 г.), "Старый, старый сон. Из мрака"
(1914 г.), "На улице — дождик и слякоть" (1915 г.), "Вот он — ветер" (1908
г.; глагольная личная форма выступает только в предпоследней строке,
контрастирующей с именным стилем 6-и предшествующих строк). Некоторые стихотворения и начинаются и кончаются именными конструкциями: "Перуджия" (1909 г.); "Весь день — как день: трудов исполнен
малых" (1914 г.); "Вербы — это весенняя таль" (1914 г.; кажется возможным установить связь синтаксической конструкции начальной
строки и трех последних — "Это — рыжая ночь твоих кос?..." и т.д. — с
известным весенним стихотворением Фета — "Это утро, радость эта" —
"Это все — весна"; к Фету восходит и собственно именной стиль Блока,
ср. "Шопот. Робкое дыханье"). Из других стихотворений III тома
характерные вкрапления именного стиля представлены в стихотворениях "Демон" (1910 г.; четверостишие "И в горном закатном пожаре"),
"Авиатор" (1910-1912 гг.; по времени написания почти совпадает с
"Шагами командора"; строки "В бинокле, вскинутом высоко"), "Когда

невзначай в воскресенье" (1913 г.; конец последнего четверостишия); "Похоронят, зароют глубоко" (1915 г.; вторая половина 2-й строфы); "Уж вечер хладной полосою" (1909 г.; последнее четверостишие); "Ветр налетит, завоет снег" (1912 г.; вторая и третья строфы), "Ты — как отзвук забытого гимна" (1914 г.; начало и 2-я строфа, ср. выше о стихотворении этого же цикла "Вербы — это весенняя таль" и первую строку "На небе — празелень" в том же цикле), "Посещение" (1910 г., четверостишие "Я сквозь ночи, сквозь долгие ночи").

3.2 Из стихотворений II-го тома, обнаруживающих сходные именные конструкции, в особенности в начале стихотворения, для сопоставления с "Шагами командора" особый интерес представляет написанное разностопным хореем "Шлейф, забрызганный звездáми" (1906 г.; две первых строфы состоят из именных конструкций), ср. также "В синем небе, в темной глуби" (1906 г.), "Невидимка" (1905 г.), "Улица, улица" (1905 г.). Но в этот период именные конструкции значительно чаще выступают в составе восклицательных предложений — обращений, вводимых междометием О! (первые две строфы "Корабли идут", 1904 г.; заключительное двустишие стихотворения "Снежная вязь", 1907 г.; последние строки стихотворения "На серые камни ложилась дремота", 1906 г.; начало и конец стихотворения "О, что мне закатный румянец", 1907 г.; начало стихотворения "О, весна без конца и без краю", 1907 г. и т.п.). Для становления именного стиля у Блока особенно существенно представляется стихотворения "Обман" (1904 г.), где наряду с именными предложениями типа "Ночь. Улица. Фонарь. Аптека" ("Хохот. Всплески, Брызги ...", "Утро. Тучки. Дымы. Опрокинутые кадки", "Блестки солнца. Струйки. Брызги. Весна") есть и именные предикативные конструкции, по семантике совпадающие с соответствующими местами в III томе ("Как страшно! Как бездомно!"). Характерные черты именного стиля обнаруживаются с достаточной отчетливостью уже в последних стихах I-го тома (первое и последнее четверостишие стихотворения "В час, когда пьянеют нарциссы").

Если согласиться с передаваемыми В. Б. Шкловским словами Блока о том, что ему самому писание стихотворения представлялось как перевод (иногда не доводившийся до конца, как в стихах "Там, в ночной завывающей стуже") текста на его собственном языке в русский текст, то можно высказать гипотезу, что именным стилем часто писались наиболее индивидуально-лирические фрагменты, как бы сохраняющие часть структуры первоначального текста. Вместе с тем возможно и отражение в этих именных конструкциях реальных различий между именем и глаголом, позволяющих говорить об их конфликте в разговорном языке (несмотря на несогласие с этим некоторых языковедов, Виноградов 1947:424) и частичной победе именных конструкций над глагольными в некоторых стилях.

3.3 Значительный интерес представляет выяснение того, в какой степени именной стиль Блока оказал влияние на крупнейших поэтов следующего поколения. Пока можно ограничиться предварительными беглыми замечаниями. В этом отношении показательны начальные именные конструкции в целом ряде стихов Цветаевой в ее цикле, посвященном Блоку ("Имя твое", "Зверю — берлога", "И тучи оводов", "Не проломанное ребро"), что может удостоверить связь с традицией Блока именного стиля некоторых главок "Поэмы конца" и отдельных ее лирических стихотворений (вплоть до поздних: "Ледяная тиара гор"). У Мандельштама именные конструкции обнаруживаются, в частности, и в трех стихотворениях, метрически связанных с "Шагами командора" (на что обратил внимание М. Б. Мейлах при обсуждении настоящей работы). У Пастернака при композиционной значимости фрагментов именного стиля в отдельных лирических стихах (уже в "Марбурге", в стихотворениях "Скрипка Паганини" (2), "Ты в ветре, веткой пробующем", "Определение поэзии", "Поэзия, я буду клясться", "Может статься так, может иначе" и т.п.; из более поздних стихотворений следует отметить две первые строфы "Мертвецкая мгла" и "Окно, пюпитр, и как овраги эхом" во "Втором рождении") можно найти интересный пример использования именного стиля для передачи ощущения времени (1905-го года), в сознании Пастернака явственно соотносившегося с Блоком; имеется в виду главка "Октябрь. Кольцо забастовок" в "Лейтенанте Шмидте" (где употребляется специфический для второго тома Блока, то-есть для его стихов эпохи 1905-го года, вариант восклицательного именного стиля с повторяющимся междометием О!; ср. в самом этом отрывке: "Щадящий из связей на свете Одни междометья"; этот же тип с опорой на стихи Блока использован и в стихах Пастернака о Блоке "Широко, широко, широко", Баевский 1975:67). Для раннего Маяковского продолжение блоковского именного стиля (в начале таких стихотворений, как "Улица. Лица ...") явно связано с развитием урбанистической темы, намеченной уже в "Обмане" и других стихах II-го тома.

4. ВОПРОСНО-ОТВЕТНАЯ КОМПОЗИЦИЯ И ЗВУКОВОЙ КОД

Для "Шагов командора" характерна последовательная вопросно-ответная композиция. 1-я и 3-я строфы А (A-I и A-II), последняя строфа B

(В-III) и вторая строфа С (С-II) содержат вопросы, первая половина 1-й строфы В (В-I) содержит обращение ("Выходи на битву"). В тех же строфах и строках, где нет вопросов, есть как бы ответы на них — звуковые знаки (пенье петуха во 2-й строфе А, рожок в последней части В-I — "И в ответ … поет рожок", шаги командора в следующей строфе В, бой часов в последней строфе С-III, предваренный боем часов в последней строфе В, где он одновременно и звуковой знак-ответ, и вопрос) или нулевой знак — тишина ("Нет ответа — тишина" в С-I). Обозначая вопросы как Q, ответы, звуковые знаки и их эквиваленты как S, формальную структуру можно изобразить следующим образом, см. табл. 5.

Табл. 5

А-I	Q
А-II	S
А-III	Q
А'	Q
В-I	S
В-II	S
В-III	$\begin{cases} S \\ Q \end{cases}$
С-I	S
С-II	Q
С-III	S

Таким образом, в стихотворении обнаруживается та вопросно-ответная композиция, которая характерна для самых ранних образцов словесного искусства (Фрейденберг 1963; Топоров 1971; как заметил В. С. Баевский при обсуждении настоящей работы, чередование 5-стопных и 4-стопных строк напоминает и формальную структуру амебейной композиции, которая по А. Н. Веселовскому и О. М. Фрейденберг предстает как особо архаичная).

4.1 Как черту, сопоставимую с текстами архаического типа, можно отметить то, что в основную вопросно-ответную композицию включены разные звуковые знаки — не только обращения, вопросы и ответы, исходящие от людей, но и пение петуха, песнь рожка-мотора, бой часов. Переплетение всех этих звуковых знаков, сигнализируемых описанными выше приемами ритма и звукописи, с тишиной (так же передаваемой звуковой структурой стихотворения) определяет структуру текста на уровне звукового кода; см. табл. 6.

Табл. 6

A-I	Вопрос, обращенный к Дон-Жуану
A-II	{ Тишина в спальне / Пение петуха
A-III	Молчание спящей Донны Анны
A'	Вопрос, обращенный к мертвой Донне Анне
B-I	{ Обращение к року / Пение рожка
B-II	{ Тихий звук мотора / Тихие шаги командора
B-III	{ Бой часов / Вопрос командора Дон-Жуану
C-I	Тишина в спальне
C-II	{ Тишина в спальне / Вопрос, обращенный к Донне Анне
C-III	Бой часов

Рассмотренные выше чередования строк с пропусками метрических ударений и без пропусков, анаграмматические сочетания звуков (самой своей структурой передающие и бой часов) и чередования именных и глагольных конструкций прямо соотносимы с описанной структурой текста на уровне звукового кода.

4.2 По сравнению с этим звуковым кодом зрительный код отступает на задний план. Зрительные образы стихотворения (соответствующие зрительным образам других стихов того же времени) либо воссоздают помехи, мешающие зрительному восприятию (занавес, туман, снежная мгла, мутная ночь), либо переводят зрительные восприятия во вторичные образы — отражения в зеркалах (ср. Минц 1969) и сны. Единственный предмет, описываемый согласно его зрительному восприятию, одновременно характеризуется и звуковым эпитетом, раскрытым в метафоре: ***Черный, тихий, как сова,*** *мотор.* Этот зрительный образ пролетающей ночной черной птицы соответствует тому же ночному зрительному колориту. Через все стихотворение на уровне осязательного кода проходит тема холода, стужи.

5. ЛЕКСИЧЕСКАЯ И СЕМАНТИЧЕСКАЯ СТРУКТУРА

Для лексики характерно значительное число прилагательных, бóльшая часть которых встречается и во многих других текстах Блока (ср. Минц 1969). Предикативные формы прилагательных и наречий, как и глаголы, рассмотрены в разделе 3. Прилагательные в атрибутивной функции относятся главным образом к числу оценочных (*жестокий*, повторенное дважды, *грозный, непомерный, постылый, блаженный*) или же переосмысленных как таковые (*незнакомый, дальний*). Остальные атрибуты являются описательными (*утренний, ночной, снежный, тяжкий, тяжелый, черный, тихий, плотный, пышный, старый, хриплый*). Группа их относится к смерти (*неземной, смертный, последний*). Существительные относятся к действующим лицам и их характеристикам (*изменник, Дева Света*), к названиям птиц (*петух, сова*) звучащих предметов (*рожок, моторы*), описаниям места, дома и его частей (*страна, дом, спальня, вход, дверь, окно*) или убранства (*занавес, зеркала*), к времени (*час, миги, ночь, рассвет, ужин*) и его измерению (*часы*), световым и осязательным характеристикам (*туман, мгла, стужа, огни*), звукам (*вопрос, ответ, звуки, пенье, тишина, рожок, шаги, бой*), описанию состояний (*сны, страх*). Очень невелико число абстрактных существительных (*жизнь, битва, блаженство, свобода*, ср. *могила*), притом часть их персонифицирована (*рок*).

5.1 Малое число глагольных личных форм (см. раздел 3) согласуется с тем, что в стихотворении очень мало приглагольных наречий — всего 2. Оба эти наречия — *победно* и *влюбленно*, относящиеся к глагольной форме *поет* — представляют исключительный интерес, потому что они объединяют строфу В-I с двумя другими стихотворениями Блока, написанными 11 февраля 1910 г. и по первоначальному замыслу связанными с "Шагами командора". Две заключительные строки первого четверостишия стихотворения "Седые сумерки легли" содержат тот же образ и те же слова -*петь, рожок, победный* (трансформированное из прилагательного в наречие в "Шагах командора"):

> Автомобиль про*пел* вдали
> В *рожок победный*.

Второе приглагольное наречие в В-I — *влюбленно* — соответствует прилагательному, использованному в предпоследней строке стихотворения "С мирным счастьем покончены счеты", второе четверостишие которого в существенной степени совпадает и с В-II, ср. в В-II "Жизнь пуста, безумна и бездонна" и начало второго четверостишия этого стихотворения:

> Жизнь пустынна, бездомна, бездонна,
> Да, я в это поверил с тех пор,
> Как пропел мне сиреной влюбленной
> Тот, сквозь ночь пролетевший мотор.

В черновиках этого стихотворения (III, 503) сохранилась строфа 5-стопного хорея, в которой размер, 1-я строка и сочетание двух приглагольных наречий совпадает с В-I, но глагол выступает в форме *пропел,* как в цитированном окончательном тексте стихотворения:

> Жизнь пуста, безумна и бездонна,
> Дай забыть, дай вспомнить об ином.
> Он *пропел* — победно и влюбленно —
> Твой рожок в ... голубом.

5.2 Для семантического истолкования стихотворения центральной представляется проблема соотнесения использованной Блоком традиционной символики европейской легенды с мотивами его собственного творчества. Это соотнесение очень отчетливо выступает в прозаическом наброске, следующем в черновике (III, 519) за первоначальным вариантом В-II, который размером (5-стопным хореем во всех строках), отнесенностью к прошедшему времени и наличием притяжательного *твой* при слове *мотор* (ср. *твой рожок* и *твой дурак* в черновике В-III) совпадает с приведенным черновиком В-I и служит его продолжением:

> Пролетел, сверкнув сквозь мглу огнями,
> Твой бесшумный, черный твой мотор.
> Тихими, тяжелыми шагами
> В дом вступил старинный командор.

По первоначальному замыслу Блока стихотворение строилось на соположении образа рожка-мотора и символики "Каменного гостя": "Я кощунствовал и услыхал рожок. Пролетел мотор, и командор вошел в мой дом. — Ты звал меня на пир? — Налейте вина командору" (III, 519). В окончательном тексте стихотворения этому прозаическому плану соответствуют строфы В-I, где тема кощунства героя выражена в обращении "Выходи на битву, *старый* рок" (ср. *"старинный* командор" в черновике В-II), В-II и В-III. Последняя строфа В содержит наиболее явную отсылку к тексту пушкинского "Каменного гостя" в прямой речи Командора (Минц 1973).

Приход Командора как образ *возмездия*, согласующийся со "старинной" европейской легендой и с ее развитием у Пушкина (Jakobson 1973:159; Чумаков 1975), у Блока подчеркнут тем, что "Шаги командора" включены в цикл "Возмездие". Возмездие связано с темой смерти и ограниченности жизни ("миги жизни сочтены"), переданной боем часов. Другой специфический для Блока аспект темы связан с *изменой*, о которой говорится и в "Шагах командора" ("Что *изменнику* блаженства звуки?"), и в стихотворении "Седые сумерки легли" ("Ты *изменил* давно, Бесповоротно", "с изменой" соответственно связывается и "мотор", см. Минц 1975:50; к указанному там же сопоставлению пенья петуха и пенья рожка: следует иметь в виду и образ мотора как совы — другой, ночной птицы, ср. о петухе Выготский 1968). Для того чтобы понять, о какой измене идет речь, необходимо учитывать и другие стихи III-го тома об измене, в частности, помещенное в цикле "Возмездие" одним стихотворением раньше "Шагов командора" программное стихотворение "Кольцо существования тесно" (1909 г.) с формулой:

> Опять — любить Ее на небе
> И изменить ей на земле.

Правильность интерпретации измены в "Шагах командора" как измены Ей — главной лирической героине блоковского творчества подтверждается обозначением Донны Анны в С-II: "Дева Света" — обозначение Прекрасной Дамы в таких стихах I-го тома, как "Вот снова пошатнулись дали" (1902 г.: характерно, что *Дева Света* рифмуется с *просвета*, ср. *рассвета* в "Шагах командора"). Эта интерпретация "Шагов командора" согласуется и с явной близостью стихотворения к "Песне ада" (1909 г.), где "чудесная жена" изображена почти как Донна Анна, спящая в спальне в В-III:

> в далеком мраке спальной,
> Где спит она …

Эти сближения позволяют понять и основную особенность блоковской трактовки темы Дон Жуана, отличающей ее от всех предшествующих: у Блока Донна Анна мертва еще до прихода в дом командора, она встанет из могилы в час смерти Дон Жуана. Возмездие приходит после смерти Донны Анны. Главная тема стихотворения — пустота и холод, вызванные отсутствием Девы Света. Стихотворение это, если переиначить название раннего блоковского цикла, — "после света".

Поэтому личное начало в "Шагах командора" следует понимать не столько в плане традиционного в семье Бекетовых сравнения Блока с

Дон Жуаном (ср. Топоров 1975:121, примеч. 1), сколько как подведение итогов движения основной лирической темы, к 10-м годам себя исчерпавшей (если не говорить о ее сублимации в теме Родины). Поэтому естественным представляется и устранение из стихотворения "я", наличествовавшего в приведенном прозаическом плане. В окончательном тексте стихотворения Дон Жуан выступает только как 2-е лицо, к которому обращаются на *ты*. Как и "Каменный гость" Пушкина в блистательной интерпретации Ахматовой (Ахматова 1958 и 1970), развитой и в недавних исследованиях (Чумаков 1975:8; Топоров 1975:120-22), "Шаги командора" воплощают внутреннюю личность поэта, его собственный жизненный опыт, но в форме претворенной, исключающей простое автобиографическое чтение. Недаром почти все эмоции Дон Жуана в "Шагах командора" переданы безличными оборотами типа "холодно", "странно", "страшно" (ср. "Страх познавший Дон-Жуан").

Амбивалентность образов легенды о Дон Жуане выявляется при разборе ее воплощений у Тирсо де Молины, Мольера, Моцарта (с философской интерпретацией оперы которого у Кьеркегора в "Или-или", ср. Vetter 1963, Блок мог быть знаком по докладу о Кьеркегоре, отмеченном в его дневнике, 18 октября 1912 г., VII, 166), Гормана, Байрона, Пушкина, см. также из более поздних интерпретаций пьесу Фриша и произведения, в бóльшей степени ориентирующиеся на ироническую поэму Байрона, как роман "Juan in America" Линклатера, ср. Gendarme de Bévottes 1907, 1912; Schröder 1912; Нусинов 1941; Кржевский 1960; Чумаков 1975.) У Блока не только развивается многозначность образов (Донна Анна как Дева Света; Дон Жуан, вызывающий на битву рок и выражающий блоковское отношение к безумной жизни), но и виден фрагментарный характер их представления. Традиционная легенда нарушена смертью Донны Анны и искажена наложением на нее собственной символики и тем Блока: описание пустой ночной спальни с мертвой Донной Анной и испуганным Дон Жуаном вообще не соотносимо с хронологически точным изложением легенды. У Блока передан эмоциональный фон легенды и отдельные ее детали при смещении всех соотношений между ними и другими деталями, ассоциативно с ними связанными (пение петуха, мотор, бой часов). В этом Блок оказывается предвестником позднейших течений поэзии XX века.

5.3 Соотнесением собственной символики творчества Блока с образами традиционной европейской легенды определяется и "контрапункт" более новой лексики с традиционной (в том числе и для символизма, см. приведенный в 5 список прилагательных). В этом отношении особенно характерно критическое замечание в письме Брюсова (III, 520) о слове *мотор*, имеющем первостепенное значение для всего цикла трех стихотворений. Напротив для Гумилева (свидетельства, относящиеся к 1916 г.; любезно сообщено автору Р. Д. Тименчиком), раннего Мандельштама (статья о Блоке, где "Шаги командора" характеризуются как вершина его исторической поэтики) и Ахматовой (по сообщению В. Берестова, Ахматова в Ташкенте в 1942-1943 гг. называла строки "Из страны блаженной, незнакомой, дальней Слышно пенье петуха" лучшими в русской поэзии) "Шаги командора" были стихотворением, наиболее близким к их творчеству. Это подтверждается тем, что метр, стиль и символика "Шагов командора" отразились в рассмотренном выше цикле стихов Мандельштама. Самый характер ассоциативного соположения образов этих стихотворений Мандельштама явственно следует принципам поэтики блоковского стихотворения. Мандельштаму было близко именно усвоение традиционного языка европейской культуры (о чем Блок пишет в письме матери по поводу "Песни Ада"), на котором поэт говорит о собственной своей теме. Использование образов "Орфея" Глюка, поставленного Мейерхольдом, в двух стихотворениях из указанного цикла Мандельштама можно сопоставить с такой "театральной" интерпретацией "Шагов командора", которая видит в них спор с постановкой Мейерхольдом "Дон-Жуана" Мольера в 1910 г. в Александринском театре, ср. Родина 1972.

У Ахматовой "Шаги командора" отразились в "Поэме без героя", в частности, в связи с Блоком, и в стихотворении "Я гашу заветные свечи", см. об этом подробно Топоров 1975:120-22; вместе с тем и сама ее интерпретация "Каменного гостя" (Ахматова 1958 и 1970) ставится в один ряд с ее собственным продолжением пушкинской темы, развитой Блоком. По сообщению В. Б. Шкловского Маяковский в 20-х годах написал автобиографическую поэму "Дон Жуан", позднее им уничтоженную.

Сплав традиционной символики европейской легенды и соответствующей лексики с собственной блоковской отличает "Шаги командора" от более ранних опытов обращения к теме Дон Жуана в европейском символизме (Бодлер) и делает это стихотворение особенно созвучным последующим вариациям на темы общеевропейских мифов (что представляет особый интерес для архетипической критики, ср. Frye 1969; White 1971, и др.) в поэзии конца 10-х и 20-х годов и ее позднейших продолжениях. Так, наложение на символику легенды о Дон Жуане традиционной евангельской (пение петуха, ср. Минц 1975:50) при введении новой лексики, обозначающей предметы современного технического мира (*мотор*) непосредственно сближается с аналогичным наложением друг на друга символики Гамлета и евангельских образов в стихотворении Пастернака "Гамлет"; "бинокли на оси" в этом последнем стихотворении сходны с "мотором" в "Шагах командора" (последний предваряет и такие позднейшие примеры использования символа автомобиля в архаизирующем мифологическом искусстве XX в., как автомашина, за рулем которой сидит грач, в "Мастере и Маргарите" и автомобиль — образ смерти в фильме Кокто "Орфей").

Автор признателен В. С. Баевскому, М. Л. Гаспарову, С. И. Гиндину, Ю. М. Лотману, М. Б. Мейлаху, З. Г. Минц, З. С. Паперному, Т. М. Родиной, Р. Д. Тименчику за критические замечания, советы и дополнения.

Москва

ЛИТЕРАТУРА

Ахматова, А. А.
   1958   "'Каменный гость' Пушкина", *Пушкин: Исследования и материалы* т. 2, Москва-Ленинград.
   1970   "Неизданные заметки Анны Ахматовой о Пушкине", *Вопросы литературы* №1.
Баевский, В. С.
   1975   "Стихи Блока как текст и подтекст", Тезисы I Всесоюзной (III) конференции *Творчество А. А. Блока и русская культура XX века*. Тарту, 63-68.
Виноградов, В. В.
   1947   *Русский язык (грамматическое учение о слове)*. Москва-Ленинград.
Выготский, Л. С.
   1968   *Психология искусства*. Примечания В. В. Иванова. 2 изд. Москва.
Гаспаров, М. Л.
   1965   "Вольный хорей и вольный ямб Маяковского", *Вопросы языкознания* №3.
   1974   *Современный русский стих: Метрика и ритмика*. Москва.
   1975   "Рифма Блока", Тезисы I Всесоюзной (III) Конференции *Творчество Блока и русская культура XX века*. Тарту, 74-75.
Иванов, В. В.
   1972   "Два примера анаграмматических построений в стихах позднего Мандельштама", *Russian Literature* 3, 81-87.
   1975   "Структура стихотворения Блока 'Шаги командора'", Тезисы I Всесоюзной (III) конференции *Творчество А. А. Блока и русская культура XX века*. Тарту, 33-38.
Кржевский, Б. А.
   1960   "Об образе Дон Жуана у Пушкина, Мольера и Тирсо де Молины", Б. А. Кржевский, *Статьи о зарубежной литературе*. Москва-Ленинград.
Минц, З. Г.
   1969   *Лирика Александра Блока (1907-1911)* II. Тарту.
   1973   "Блок и Пушкин", *Труды по русской и славянской филологии*, XXI: *Литературоведение*. Тарту.
   1975   "Из поэтической мифологии 'Третьего тома': II. Поезд и 'мотор'", Тезисы I Всесоюзной (III) конференции *Творчество А. А. Блока и русская культура XX века*. Тарту, 49-50.

Нусинов, И. М.
 1941 "История образа Дон Жуана", И. М. Нусинов, *Пушкин и мировая литература.* Москва.
Родина, Т. М.
 1972 *Александр Блок и русский театр начала XX века.* Москва.
Руднев, П. А.
 1972 "Метрический репертуар А. Блока", *Блоковский сборник* II. Тарту.
Самойлов, Д.
 1973 *Книга о русской рифме.* Москва.
Тарановский, К.
 1962 "Стихосложение Осипа Мандельштама", *International Journal of Slavic Linguistics and Poetics* V. 97-125.
Топоров, В. Н.
 1971 "О структуре некоторых архаических текстов, соотносимых с концепцией 'мирового дерева'", *Труды по знаковым системам* 5. Tartu.
 1975 "Об одном аспекте 'испанской' темы у Блока", Тезисы I Всесоюзной (III) конференции *Творчество А. А. Блока и русская культура XX века.* Тарту, 118-123.
Фрейденберг, О. М.
 1936 *Поэтика сюжета и жанра.* Ленинград.
Харджиев, Н. И.
 1973 "Примечания", в кн.: О. Мандельштам, *Стихотворения (Библиотека поэта).* Ленинград.
Чумаков, Ю. Н.
 1975 "Дон Жуан Пушкина", *Проблемы пушкиноведения: Сборник научных трудов.* Ленинград.

Abernathy, R.
 1963 "A Vowel Fugue in Blok", *International Journal of Slavic Linguistics and Poetics* VII.88-107.
 1967 "Rhymes, Non-rhymes and Antirhyme", *To honor Roman Jakobson.* The Hague-Paris.
Frye, N.
 1969 *Anatomy of Criticism.* New York.
Gendarme de Bévottes, G.
 1907 *La légende de Don Juan, son évolution dans la littérature des origines au romantisme.*
 1912 *La légende de Don Juan,* I-II.
Ivanov, V. V.
 1974 "Growth of the Theoretical Framework of Modern Poetics", *Current Trends in Linguistics* 12; *Linguistics and Adjacent Arts and Sciences,* 835-61. The Hague-Paris.
Jakobson, R.
 1973 "La statue dans la symbolique de Pouchkine", R. Jakobson, *Questions de poétique,* Paris (= R. Jakobson, *Studies in Verbal Art: Texts in Czech and Slovak,* Ann Arbor 1971, 307-42).
Lévi-Strauss, C.
 1971 *Mythologiques,* IV. *L'homme nu.* Paris.
Schröder, Th.
 1912 *Die dramatischen Bearbeitungen der Don Juan Sage in Spanien, Italien, Frankreich bis auf Molière einschliesslich.* Halle.
Vetter, A.
 1963 *Frömmigkeit als Leidenschaft.* Freiburg-München.
White, J. J.
 1971 *Mythology in the Modern Novel: A Study of Prefigurative Techniques.* Princeton.

DISTINCTIVE FEATURES AND SOUND TROPES IN RUSSIAN VERSE

LAWRENCE G. JONES

0. INTRODUCTION

0.1 One of the most useful aspects of Jakobson's system of distinctive features for describing the phonemic units of a language is that it consists of a uniform set of terms which can be applied for all members of the phonemic inventory. Previously, when articulatory descriptions of phonetic and phonemic units were the norm, if not the only available means of description, it was customary to describe the vowels of a language in one set of terms and the consonants in terms of another. But now that a uniform set of terms is available and for the most part corroborated through research in acoustic phonetics, it is possible to make statements about the phonological properties of linguistic structures which had been hitherto unnoticed, obscured or neglected. In the realm of verbal art, for instance, it is now possible to look at entire texts for uniformity of sound texture since the same set of terms can serve as the basis for the description. The following study is a first step in that direction. It attempts to examine the interplay of certain distinctive features in Russian phonemes, primarily the so-called tonality features, in poetic texts. Although most of the emphasis is on the rhyme structures of the texts, some attention is given to more pervasive patterning of the features in the sound texture of the text as a whole.

0.2 Table I shows an analysis of the (morpho)phonemes of Russian into distinctive features. This distribution of features is based on, but differs considerably from, the analysis by Halle[1] as well as from various treatments of this system by Jakobson himself. In this table the phonemes are ordered vertically according to the high/low tonality feature (originally called acute/grave) since this particular feature is highly pertinent to the configurations of sounds in verbal art. The acoustic phonetic qualities of the Russian vowels serve as the basis for this particular order. It is a readily observable acoustic fact that the second formant of a vowel indicates the marking of the high-low feature. The phoneme /i/ shows the highest frequency resonance for

TABLE 1   *The (Morpho)phonemes of Russian and Their Distinctive Features*

	j	i	e	a	o	u	n	ṇ	r	ṛ	l	ḷ	m	ṃ	s	ş	š	šč	x	z	ẓ	ž	žž	t	ţ	k	ḳ	p	p̣	c	č	d	ḍ	b	ḅ	g
High (H)																																				
Diffuse (D)																																				
Compact (C)																																				
Vocalic	−	+	+	+	+	+	+	+	+	+	+	+	+	+	−	−	−	−	−	−	−	−	−	−	−	−	−	−	−	−	−	−	−	−	−	−
Consonantal	−	−	−	−	−	−	+	+	+	+	+	+	+	+	+	+	+	+	+	+	+	+	+	+	+	+	+	+	+	+	+	+	+	+	+	+
Continuous	0	0	0	0	0	0	0	0	0	0	0	0	0	0	+	+	+	+	+	+	+	+	+	−	−	−	−	−	−	−	−	−	−	−	−	−
Voiced	0	0	0	0	0	0	0	0	0	0	0	0	0	0	−	−	−	−	0	+	+	+	+	−	−	−	−	−	−	0	0	+	+	+	+	+
Sharp	−	0	0	0	0	0	−	+	−	+	−	+	−	+	−	+	0	0	0	−	+	+	0	−	+	−	+	−	+	0	0	−	+	−	+	0

this second formant and the vowel /u/ the lowest. The second formant shows a step by step lowering through the sequence /i e a o u/.[2] Similar resonance characteristics can be found for most all of the non-vowels and their relative positions with respect to the feature structure of the vowels as presented in Table I. Thus, *e.g.*, the same relations of high/low tonality appear to hold for the sequence /t c k č p/ as for the vowel sequence mentioned above. It should be noticed, incidentally, that the diffuse/non-diffuse feature is distinctive only in the two sequences just mentioned, that is, for the vowels and the unvoiced stops. In all other cases the feature compact/non-compact is sufficient to produce a unique coding of the phonemes. This situation also holds, of course, for the unstressed vowels. For this reason the diffuse feature will rarely be adverted to in the structures described below. Emphasis rather will be given chiefly to the high and compact features. The sharp/plain feature (indicating what is usually called the 'hard' vs. 'soft' or palatalized vs. non-palatalized oppositions in the consonants) is left out of consideration since it does not appear to play as dominant a role in patterning as do the two features just mentioned.

0.3 The high/low feature might be designated the 'synaesthetic' feature since it reflects the oppositions of light/dark, happy/sad, small/large which are often associated with just the opposing values of this feature, *e.g.*, vowels with high tonality such as /i/ and /e/ are felt to carry feelings of lightness, happiness as opposed to the vowels having low tonality such as /u/ or /o/ which are felt to transmit feelings of darkness or sadness. As noted above, it is now possible to look at the distribution of this feature in consonants to see how it patterns in terms of such synaesthetic values. One might also say that this is the most 'melodic' of the features since acoustically it represents the most extensive oppositions in terms of frequency resonance. That is, the second formant of the vowel /i/ tends to occur at about 2000 cps. whereas the second formant of /u/ averages about 600 cps. Differences in resonances in the sharp/plain feature would necessarily be much less in comparison and hence less 'melodic'. As was demonstrated in "The Tonality Structure of Russian Verse", very often just the stressed vowels in Russian poems show more or less abstract patterning of this feature primarily in terms of bilateral or terminal symmetry in which latter case the vowel tonality of the first and last stanza of a poem will be similar to one another but markedly different from that of the intervening stanzas. It will be shown below that in addition to this feature the diffuse feature also plays an interesting role in the sound texture of poetic texts, especially in the pretonic consonant(s) of the rhyme, the so-called supporting (*opornye*) consonant(s).

0.4 In the texts dealt with below, the structures are given in a pure phonemic, as opposed to morphophonemic, transcription. Hence, all non-diffuse
unstressed posttonic vowels are reduced to /a/, which in most cases would
have the phonetic value /ə/, e.g., /možat/ for možet, etc. Similarly, devoiced
final consonants and assimilated prevocalic consonants are represented as
manifested phonetically, thus xod is written /xot/.

1. RHYME TONALITIES

1.0 From a structuralist point of view the phenomenon of rhyme in poetry,
which seems to be an ancient and pervasive kind of sound trope in verbal art
no matter where or when poetical structures occur, poses a number of interesting analytical problems which appear to have been either neglected or left
unnoticed in the traditional treatment of the subject where primary attention
is given to rhyme schemes in a rather abstract way as opposed to the makeup
of the phonemic sequences involved, their interrelationships and their
uniformity wherever the latter occurs. For instance, one of the most important
aspects of rhyme, especially from the psychological and probably aesthetic
point of view is the choice of the consonant or consonant cluster immediately
preceding the stressed vowel of the rhyme. It is just this structure of oppositions which produces unusual juxtapositions of morphemes or semantic pairs
of linguistic structures in the verse. Furthermore, this pretonic sequence often
shows rather deep interrelationships across rhymes in a poem. As will be
shown below, it sometimes happens that in an alternating rhyme sequence
such as $A_1b_1A_2b_2$ the pretonic consonant(s) may be the same for A_1 and b_2
and/or the same situation may hold for the pretonic consonants of b_1 and A_2,
thus yielding, if all these relationships hold, the following pattern:

$$C_1 \ A_1$$
$$C_2 \ b_1$$
$$C_2 \ A_2$$
$$C_1 \ b_2$$

Many other such patterns are obviously possible and deserve further attention. In addition to this, the composition and patterning of the posttonic
consonants (indeed, the entire unstressed syllable sequence in the case of
feminine or hyperfeminine rhymes) deserve some attention. These sequences,
of course, are that part of the rhyme, which in most of the poetic canons of
nineteenth-century European poetry is the identical part of the rhyme. But it
often happens that even here there is obvious patterning across rhyme

sequences. In all of these cases the distinctive feature components of the phonemes, particularly the tonality features, frequently show extensive patterning within a text, several examples of which are present in the texts analyzed below.

1.1 Puškin's *Ja vas ljubil*. This short poem serves as a good introduction to the patterning of features in rhyme structures although these structures are not as striking as those in most of the other examples presented below. Table II shows the rhyme syllables (in phonemic transcription) and their tonality markings for the compact (Cp.) and high (Hi.) features for the pretonic consonant sequences and the stressed rhyme vowel.

In the case of all feminine rhymes the value of the high feature is the same for both the pretonic consonant and the associated stressed vowel: A_1: /mo/ A_2: /vo/, C_1: /ḍe/ C_2: /ṇe/ and the compact marking is always the opposite, *e.g.*, /m/ and /v/ are non-compact but /o/ is compact; similarly, /ḍ/ and /ṇ/ are non-compact while /e/ is compact. Using the 'alpha' notation of generative grammar, this structure follows the formula:

$$\begin{array}{ccc} & C & \acute{V} \\ \text{Compact:} & \alpha & -\alpha \end{array}$$

for all four occurrences of feminine rhymes.

For the masculine rhymes the pretonic consonant(s) of the first instance of the rhyme is non-compact and the second compact, and hence the 'alpha' notation cannot be as concise as the one for the feminine rhymes:

$$\begin{array}{ccc} & C & \acute{V} \\ \text{Compact} & & \\ R_1 & -\alpha & \alpha \\ R_2 & \alpha & -\alpha \end{array}$$

But this shows the chiastic relationship of the features in this rhyme structure where consonant and vowel always have the opposite marking.

On the level of the total consonantal structure of the rhymes the masculine occurrences, with only one exception, contain only non-high consonants: /fsem/ (where /s/ is the exception mentioned), /čem/, /mim/, /gim/. This pattern is also carried into the pretonic consonants of the feminine rhymes /mo/ and /vo/. In the unstressed syllable of both feminine rhymes this pattern of low tonality is taken up in the first (or only) pretonic consonant which is /ž/. Finally, from the viewpoint of tonality, these unstressed syllables show an interesting reversal in that the sequences /at/ and /na/ have exactly the same distribution of compact and high features in their respective vowels and consonants (/t/ and /n/ being both non-compact and high) but the main difference being in the source feature vocalic/non-vocalic. In other words, this pattern follows the same alpha formula as the one given above for masculine rhymes but with C and V generalized to phonemic sequence:

$$P_1 \quad P_2$$
$$\alpha \quad -\alpha$$

Thus the entire rhyme scheme exhibits a number of interrelated patterns of a very general nature.

TABLE II

Rhyme Structure of Puškin's "Ja vas ljubil"

Rhyme	CC	V́	Syllable(s) CC	CC	V	CC	CC Cp.	Hi.	V́ Cp.	Hi.
A₁	m	o		ž	a	t	-	-	+	-
b₁	fṣ	e	m				--	-+	+	+
A₂	v	o		ž	a	t	-	-	+	-
b₂	č	e	m				+	-	+	-
C₁	ḍ	e		žn	a		-	+	+	+
d₁	m	i	m				-	-	-	+
C₂	ŋ	e		žn	a		-	+	+	+
d₂	g	i	m				+	0	-	+

1.2 Lermontov's *Vyxožu odin ja na dorogu*. Table III presents the rhyme tonalities for this poem. Again, as in the Puškin example above, the pretonic consonants show clear patterning in the tonality features but in a different distribution of tonality markings. For instance the masculine and feminine rhymes of each stanza are connected by the fact that the first or only pretonic consonant has the same compact value in both b_2 and A_1, e.g., in stanza I: b_1/st/ A_2/b/; stanza II b_1/b/ A_2/tr/, etc. The central stanza III is the only stanza in which these pairs of rhyme consonants are marked plus for compact. All of the other pairs are minus. Remarkably, another pattern which includes all of the other rhyme consonants follows a contrasting pattern to this one. This pattern, however, has one exception. Except for the very last pretonic rhyme consonant in the poem: V b_2/m/, the first and last pretonic rhyme consonant in each stanza has the same compact marking and it is always the reverse of the marking for the corresponding consonants of two inner lines. Hence each stanza follows the alpha formula:

$$A_1 \quad b_1 \quad A_2 \quad b_2$$
$$\text{Compact:} \quad \alpha \quad -\alpha \quad -\alpha \quad \alpha$$

where $\alpha = +$ in all stanzas except III where it assumes the minus value. This means, of course, that the pattern is symmetrically disposed among the

TABLE III
Rhyme Structure of Lermontov's "Vyxožu odin ja na dorogu"

Stanza	Rhyme	Syllable(s)						C		V́	
		CC	V	CC	CC	V	CC	Cp.	Hi.	Cp.	Hi.
I	A₁	r	o		g	u		+	+	+	−
	b₁	s̨t	i	t				−	+	−	+
	A₂	b	o		g	u		−	−	+	−
	b₂	r̨	i	t				+	+	−	+
II	A₁	č	u		dn	a		+	−	−	−
	b₁	b	o	m				−	−	+	−
	A₂	tr	u		dn	a		−+	+	−	−
	b₂	č	o	m				+	−	+	−
III	A₁	v	o		j	a		−	−	+	−
	b₁	č	u	t̨				+	−	−	−
	A₂	k	o		j	a		+	0	+	−
	b₂	sn	u	t̨				−	+	−	−
IV	A₁	g	i		l	i		+	0	−	+
	b₁	sn	u	t̨				−	+	−	−
	A₂	ş	i		l	i		−	+	−	+
	b₂	gr	u	d̨				+	0+	−	
V	A₁	l̨	e		j	a		+	−	+	+
	b₁	p̨	e	l				−	−	+	+
	A₂	ŋ	e		j	a		−	+	+	+
	b₂	m	e	l				+	−	+	+

stanzas since it is only the central stanza which has the opposite or reversed structure.

The patterning of the high feature in the pretonic consonants, although not as striking as the above, is correlated with the separate rhyme genders.

	Stanza				
	I	II	III	IV	V
High marking of					
A₁	+	−	−	0	−
A₂	−	+	0	+	+
b₁	+	−	−	+	−
b₂	+	−	−	+	−

Here it can be seen that for the feminine rhymes the two outside stanzas, I and V have opposite values in respect to one another. The masculine rhymes each have + for I and − and V and hence follow this general pattern. However, these masculine rhymes in this respect show a parallelism in that the values in I and II are repeated in IV and V.

Finally it should be noticed that all of the final unstressed syllables end in a vowel which was not the case in the previous example and is not the case in following examples. A non-symmetrical pattern can be seen among these syllables: where the prevocalic consonant is compact the vowel is diffuse. In all other cases the vowel is /a/. That is, in I and IV the consonant is /g/ and /l/ respectively and the associated vowels are /u/ and /i/. In all other cases the consonant(s) are either non-compact (/dn/) or unmarked (/j/).

1.3 Puškin's *Prorok*. The rhyme scheme of *Prorok* has a rather complex and even sophisticated structure which comes to light even before it is analyzed according to the tonality markings of its constituents. The rhyme genders or rhyme alternations in this thirty-line poem show a very strong tendency toward bilateral symmetry. To make this tendency clear the rhyme scheme is displayed in Table IV with the second half of the poem presented in reverse order so that potentially symmetrical pairs are immediately across from one another. The rhyme gender alternations are symmetrically disposed at the beginning and end of the poem in lines 1-6 paired with lines 30-25:

a masc. n
B fem. M
a masc. n
B fem. M
c masc. l
c masc. l

Similarly, lines 10-15 pair up with lines 21-16. Thus, of 15 pairs of rhyme words only four do not enter into this symmetrical relationship. It is a further curious fact that this section contains another kind of symmetry as well as some clear contrasts which are not present elsewhere in the poem. Lines 6 and 9 are identical except for the second word in the line:

6: *zenic*
Moix *kosnulsja on*
9: *užej*

The word *on* in this rhyme pair is the only true *rime riche* in the entire poem and forms part of the only rhyme in the poem which has four occurrences. Furthermore, the word *on* makes up the two innermost members of this sequence and hence there is a symmetry about *rime riche* as well as of the presence or absence of pretonic consonant(s):

/s/ ⧣ ⧣ /zv/

(Notice that the consonants are all diffuse and the only or initial consonant is high.)

The high tonality feature for the stressed vowels shows aspects of symmetry which are only in part related to the symmetry of rhyme gender. Lines 1-4

TABLE IV

The Rhyme Structure of Puškin's "Prorok"

Line	Rhyme Scheme	Rhyme Syllable(s) C V̌ C C V	C (Cp. Hi.)	V̌ (Cp. Hi.)	Symmetry of High Tonality of V̌	C (Cp. Hi.)	V̌ (Cp. Hi.)	Rhyme Syllable(s) C V̌ C C V C	Rhyme Scheme	Line
1	a	m i m	– –	– +	=	– –	+ +	d e j	n	30
2	B	č i l s a	– –	– +	=	# #	+ +	ž e mļ i	M	29
3	a	f i m	– –	+ +	=	+ +	+ +	#e j	n	28
4	B	v i l s a	– –	+ +	=	– –	+ +	vņ e mļ i	M	27
5	c	s o n	# #	+ –	≠	+ –	+ –	zv a l	–	26
6	c	#o n	# #	+ –	≠	– –	– +	ž a l	l	25
7	D	ņ i c a	# –	+ –	≠	+ –	– +	ď i nul	K	24
8	D	ļ i c a	# #	– +	≠	– –	+ +	gņ o m	j	23
9	c	zv o n	+ –	+ –	≠	+ –	– +	vi nul	K	22
10	c	zv o n	+ –	+ –	=	+ –	+ –	čo m	–	21
11	E	g a ņ j a	+ 0	+ 0	=	– –	+ 0	va vaj	H	20
12	f	ļ o t	+ –	+ –	≠	# #	+ +	#i	i	19
13	f	x o t	+ 0	+ –	≠	# #	+ +	#i	i	18
14	E	b a ņ j a	+ 0	+ 0	=	– –	+ 0	ka vaj	H	17
15	g	ņ i k	– +	– +	–	– +	– +	z i k	g	16

share high tonality with their paired sequence 30-27. Lines 7 and 24 have identical stressed vowels as do 10 and 21; 11 and 20; 14 and 17; 15 and 16 (this last, of course being the central rhyming couplet in the poem). Within the centralized portion of this whole rhyme symmetry, that is, in lines 7 through 10 and their paired lines 24-21, there is a chiastic structure in the non-symmetrically disposed vowels and which are immediately bounded by symmetrically paired vowels:

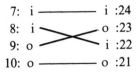

```
7:  i ———————— i :24
8:  i ⟩⟨ o :23
9:  o ⟩⟨ i :22
10: o ———————— o :21
```

These particular vowels appear in the next non-symmetrical sequence 12-13 paired with 19-18. Finally, the vowel /o/ which figures in all of these sequences is one of the members of the non-symmetrical sequence 5-6 paired with 26-25.

The supporting consonants in this long rhyme structure do not exhibit any strong tendency toward patterning except for the rather remarkable fact that in the central couplet the supporting consonants and stressed vowels have the same pattern of features: they are noncompact and high. Beyond that the next strongest patterning trend comes in the terminal lines 1-4 paired with 30-27 where the supporting consonants in 1-4 are all low tonality in contrast with the high tonality of the corresponding consonants in 30-27 (with the exception of the initial consonant in 27).

The post accentual phonemic sequences in the rhyme structure show patterning which forms a kind of contrast to the symmetries of the pretonic section. In the first half of the poem all of the unstressed final syllables end in /a/. In terms of the features under discussion the prevocalic consonants in rhymes B and D differ only in the compactness feature. (They also differ in the feature of continuous/non-continuous but that is a source feature as opposed to a tonality feature and hence plays no role in this description.) The /ja/ sequence in rhyme E appears in reversed form as /aj/ in rhyme H. The last feminine rhyme (M) in the poem is the only feminine rhyme in the second half of the poem which ends with a vowel and hence shares this fact with rhyme B with which it is symmetrically paired.

The posttonic consonants in the masculine rhymes show certain tendencies toward patterning. Rhymes a, c, j and l all end in a consonant which is both consonantal and vocalic, i.e., nasal or lateral. In their symmetrical pairs most of these show a contrast of high tonality in the first half of the poem to low tonality in the second:

| 5,6 | /n/ | /l/ | 26,25 |
| 10 | /ŋ/ | /m/ | 21 |

There is a more unstructured similarity in the general consonantal structure of this poem with respect to the symmetrical pairing of the lines. In rhymes a and B the consonants /m/, /l/ and the vowel /i/ make up the identical (posttonic) section of the rhyme, together with the sequence /sa/. These consonants are then repeated in the corresponding terminal part of the poem where they figure as the structure of the posttonic section of the rhyme, e.g., the syllable /mļi/ of rhyme M. Furthermore, the pretonic consonants in D /n/ and /l/ make up the consonants of the posttonic syllable in the symmetrically corresponding rhyme K. As in the case of the other texts discussed above the various structures contribute to a strong tendency to terminal symmetry where a significant portion of the beginning of a poem shares feature distribution with a corresponding section at the end of the text.

1.4 Axmatova's *Pamjat' o solnce v serdce slabeet.* In the rhyme structure of this poem presented in Table V, wherever # or 0 do not occur in the markings for the compact and high features for the innermost supporting consonant and the following stressed vowel, the consonant always has the opposite marking as does the vowel and hence follows the alpha formula:

	C	V́
Compact	α	-α
High	β	-β

The first and last stanzas have low tonality in the only or innermost consonant before the stressed vowel. The masculine rhymes, in addition to this pattern have consonants marked with high tonality in the other, inner, stanzas.

The stressed vowels of the rhyme set up a pattern in stanzas II and III which is symmetrical for the diffuse feature which has not played any distinctive role in the structures of the other poems under consideration:

	II		III	
	A	b	A	b
V́				
Diffuse	+	—	—	+

Stanzas I and V must stand outside this pattern since these two stanzas share the same first lines and hence the same rhyme vowel thus making bilateral symmetry impossible unless both rhymes in the stanza were to have the same stressed vowel.

The unstressed posttonic syllables of the feminine rhymes fall into a pattern. The vowel is /a/ in all cases. Stanzas I and IV have the sequence VC whereas the inner stanzas II and III have the reverse CV. With the exception of stanza IV where /l/ is compact and non-high, all of these consonants are non-compact and high. It is perhaps significant that this fourth stanza contains what appears to be the climactic statement of the poem and which contains one of the instances of this rhyme:

Možet byť lučše, čto ja ne stala
Vašej ženoj.

TABLE V
Rhyme Structure of Axmatova's "Pamjat' o solnce v serdce slabeet"

Stanza	Rhyme	Syllable(s) CC	Vę	CC	CC	V	CC	C Cp.	Hi.	Vę Cp.	Hi.
I	A	b	e			a	t	—	—	+	+
	b	v	a					—	+	+	0
	A	ÿ	e			a	t	—	—	+	+
	b	dv	a					——	+—	+	0
II	A		i		s	a		#	#	—	+
	b	d	a					—	+	+	0
	A	č	i		ts	a		+	—	—	+
	b	d	a					—	+	+	0
III	A	st	a	l	a			——	++	+	0
	b	zn	o	j				——	++	+	—
	A	st	a	l	a			——	++	+	0
	b	n	o	j				—	+	+	—
IV	A	ḅ	e			a	t	—	—	+	+
	b	ţm	a					——	+—	+	0
	A	sp̦	e			a	t	——	+—	+	+
	b	m	a					—	—	+	0

2. DISCUSSION

All of the analyses above have been carried out on a restricted portion of the poetic text, its rhyme structure. The tonality features, as well as the source features, need to be explored for their patterning into other opposing types of configurations in verbal art. The first is the uniform distribution of a feature or features through the entire line, stanza and complete text. This is an extremely cumbersome undertaking which, although it sorely needs to be done, requires a great deal of clarification. One of the problems that immediately arises is whether consonants and vowels should be treated on a level with one another as equally contributing members to the tonality of the line or text. On the one hand, intuitively one feels that this should not be the case but on the other there arises the problem of weighting the values if one proceeds in the opposite direction. For instance, one could assign values to the phonemes as they are ordered in Table I in such a way that high tonality features in phonemes would have some plus value and low tonality value minus. Then vowels could be given some such value as 5, sonorants 4, fricatives 3, stops 2 and /j/ 1 and these values multiplied by the tonality values. This has been tried and leads to fairly interesting results but the main problem is that assigning these values is an entirely arbitrary procedure and cannot be based on the phonetic facts to any satisfactory degree.

On the other hand, it is often quite interesting and revealing to look at the tonality structure of individual words or lines within a poem. For instance, in the Axmatova poem just discussed, the consonants of the first two nouns in the first line show an interesting contrast:

$$p. \quad m.\underline{t} \quad s. \quad (\,1\,) \quad n \quad c.$$
$$\text{High.} \quad - \quad - \quad + \quad + \quad (-) \quad + \quad +$$

The low, synaesthetically dark or sad, component of *pamjat'* is contrasted to the high, synaesthetically bright values of *solnce* and then the low values of the consonants in *pamjat'* recur again in the first syllable of the word *slabeet* at the end of the line:

$$s \quad l. \quad b. \quad .t$$
$$\text{High.} \quad + \quad - \quad - \quad +$$

where /l/ and /b/ are related to /m/ and /b/ both in the feature of high tonality and vocalic/non-vocalic. Or, to take another example from Axmatova, in *Nastojaščuju nežnost'*, the key word *nežnost'* figures throughout the sound texture of the poem and is contrasted to the line

Govoriš' o pervoj ljubvi

and rapid inspection shows that whereas *nežnost'* contains a large number of high tonality among its phonemes, the opposite is true for the line just quoted. It is an interesting and perhaps sad fact that in Russian the word *ljubov'* has not a single instance of high tonality among its phonemes. Curiously enough the same is true for the English word *love* when it is viewed in the tonality features of English. As a final example in this regard, one might consider such structures as the closing word in Pasternak's Razluka. At the very end of the poem, the man has pricked his finger on a needle which stuck out of the embroidery hoop of the woman who has left and whom he loves. This brings memories of her back and he cries:

... i plačet vtixomolku.

This is the very end of the poem and the last word is entirely low in tonality after the first three phonemes (the /x/ having 0 for this feature), so that the crying can be said to be mirrored in the low or sad tonality of the word which expresses the emotion. In any event, the tonalities and phonological structure of rhyme needs much further investigation as well as all other aspects of the poetic text from the point of distinctive features and their distribution.

Boston College

NOTES

[1]   Morris Halle, *The Sound Pattern of Russian* (The Hague: Mouton, 1959).
[2]   See Lawrence G. Jones, "Contextual Restraints in the Russian Vowels", in Halle, *op. cit.*
[3]   See Lawrence G. Jones, "The Tonality Structure of Russian Verse", *International Journal of Slavic Linguistics and Poetics,* IX (1965), 125-51.

COMMENTS

(Pszczołowska)   I would like to know how large was the material you comprised in your research. The results obtained are very interesting, but I suppose that they may be caused by the rules and tendencies existing in the phonological structure of any Russian text. It is known that every text in a given language is built according to some mechanisms of sound organisation.

After all, in Segal's book on the phonological structure of Polish we have some statistical information about the frequency of given phonemes, groups of phonemes, etc., showing many regularities in the sound texture of every text. From my own research I also know how many sound phenemona which seem to be characteristic of one poem are as a matter of fact governed by the rules and tendencies of the phonological organisation of the text. If we have similar information for Russian we will know whether the rhyme tonalities you observed in some poems occur incidentally or whether they are characteristic only of a particular text.

Additional discussion: Abernathy, Broyde, Marvan, Segal, Stankiewicz, Worth

TJUTČEV'S VOCABULARY:
A QUANTITATIVE APPROACH

GEIR KJETSAA

0.1 Poetry is written in words, and no poet has any existence other than in the words he wrote. Outside the words there are no 'feelings' or 'thoughts' in poetry. Poets differ from one another in their choice of words and in their way of putting them together. Once we know which words a poet prefers we have also made a significant step toward a determination of his favourite ideas. No wonder, then, that the poets have always been extremely aware of the value of the word and of the consideration of vocabulary as a significant index to a writer's mind. Thus Baudelaire, commenting on a statement of Sainte-Beuve, once noted: 'Je lis dans un critique: 'Pour deviner l'âme d'un poète, ou du moins sa principale préoccupation, cherchons dans ses œuvres quel est le mot ou quels sont les mots qui s'y représentent avec le plus de fréquence. Le mot traduira l'obsession''.[1]

0.2 The purpose of this paper is to show some features of Tjutčev's "obsession." What are the words he most often uses in his poems? Which of these words are comparatively more used by him than by other poets? In what way does his vocabulary differ from that of his poet contemporaries? These are some of the questions that will be discussed, if not fully answered in the paper.

1.0 The study of vocabulary can be greatly assisted by the use of modern computational techniques. In fact, without the aid of computers scholars would hardly even think of asking the above questions. To answer them would mean spending years only in collecting the necessary materials.

1.1 For the present examination of Tjutčev's lexicon I have used a set of programs written in FORTRAN and run at my university's computer, a CDC 3300.[2]

1.2 The first step in using these programs was to prepare the text for input. Using an IBM 029 keypunch, I had the poems recorded with one line of text on each card. The data from these cards were then transferred to magnetic tape and disk by a utility program, after which I was provided with various indexes, notably one arranged in alphabetical order. The most valuable result of this procedure was a concordance to the poetry of Tjutčev, which is soon to be published by the Institute of Slavic and Baltic Studies at the University of Oslo.

1.3 The text used was the latest edition of Tjutčev's poetry: *Lirika* in two volumes, prepared by K. V. Pigarev and published in Moscow in 1966. Only the final editions of his Russian poems were recorded, altogether 347 poems, containing 30,942 running words or tokens.

1.4 Having lemmatized the words (e.g. *dnja, dni* → *den'*; *skažu, skaži* → *skazat'*; *mil, milo, milaja* → *milyj*) and distinguished homonyms (e.g. *mir*[1] = 'world' and *mir*[2] = 'peace', I compiled lists of the fifty most frequent nouns, verbs, and adjectives used in Tjutčev's poems.[3]

2.0 These lists are now to be published and discussed:

Rank	Noun	Frequency	Verb	Frequency	Adjective	Frequency
1	den'	148	byt'	260	živoj	63
2	duša	136	stojat'	50	svetlyj	50
3	nebo	119	moč'	43	velikij	49
4	mir[1]	112	znat'	38	zemnoj	46
5	žizn'	108	ljubit'	36	rodnoj	43
6	zemlja	86	žit'	34	rokovoj	41
7	bog	78	videt'	32	svjatoj	40
8	serdce	78	dyšat'	31	russkij	36
9	ljubov'	74	gljadet'	30	milyj	34
10	ten'	74	blestet'	27	poslednij	34
11	son	72	stat'	27	čistyj	34
12	luč	62	smotret'	26	božij	32
13	noč'	59	molčat'	25	volšebnyj	32
14	drug[1]	56	pet'	25	polnyj	32
15	svet[1]	56	svetit'	24	vysokij	31
16	volna	55	verit'	23	tichij	31
17	solnce	54	lit'sja	23	mnogij	29
18	pora	52	bežat'	22	nebesnyj	29
19	vzor	50	vejat'	22	večnyj	27
20	ruka	49	idti	21	nočnoj	27
21	kraj	47	chotet'	21	dikij	26
22	čas	45	igrat'	20	pervyj	26
23	vek[1]	43	projti	20	celyj	26
24	krov'	43	slyšat'	20	strašnyj	24
25	sila	43	ujti	19	legkij	23
26	zvezda	41	dat'	18	pozdnij	23
27	duch	40	prijti	18	skoryj	23
28	more	39	skazat'	18	tainstvennyj	23
29	narod	39	goret'	17	morskoj	22
30	slovo	39	šumet'	17	novyj	22
31	grud'	37	letet'	16	sladkij	22
32	vesna	36	pit'	16	temnyj	22
33	leto	36	sijat'	16	vernyj	21

Rank	Noun	Frequency	Verb	Frequency	Adjective	Frequency
34	oko	36	davať	15	lučšij	21
35	sleza	36	pasť	15	bednyj	20
36	priroda	35	sideť	15	byloj	20
37	suďba	34	trevožiť	15	veselyj	20
38	voda	33	govoriť	14	prekrasnyj	20
39	gora	32	ležať	14	čudnyj	20
40	car'	30	ponjať	14	užasnyj	19
41	raz[1]	29	vstavať	13	zolotoj	18
42	vremja	28	zabyť	13	vozdušnyj	17
43	glava[1]	28	služiť	13	dolgij	17
44	breg	27	spať	13	smelyj	17
45	dym	27	brodiť	12	glubokij	16
46	poèt	27	vesti	11	bessmertnyj	15
47	borba	26	zvučať	11	divnyj	15
48	god	26	zvať	11	zloj	15
49	Rossija	26	zreť[2]	11	nezrimyj	15
50	vera	25	iskať	11	svežij	15
1-50	Total = 8.44%	2,611	Total = 4.12%	1,275	Total = 4.34%	1,343

2.1 What we have here, are lists of Tjutčev's most frequent 'thematic words', or *mots-thèmes,* to use the term of the eminent French lingo-statistician Pierre Guiraud.[4] Thus, the list of nouns provides us with some rough idea of what themes Tjutčev is most often occupied with in his poetry, while the list of adjectives gives us some information on the characteristics most often attributed by the poet to his materials. Of course, a word's frequency is an important indication of this word's importance to the poet. However, to argue that a poet's most frequent words are also his most characteristic ones would appear erroneous, due to the fact that most poets seem to be occupied with the same themes, as for instance the themes of love and nature.

2.2 At present we have about half a million Russian words in machine-readable form in our department. Besides Tjutčev the materials include the poems of Lomonosov, Baratynskij, Lermontov, Fet, Annenskij, Achmatova, and Gumilev. A comparison of the lists of the most frequent nouns, verbs, and adjectives in these poets with our lists in 2.0 reveals a striking similarity. For example, of the 50 most frequent nouns in Tjutčev 23 are also found in the list of Lomonosov, 27 in the list of Lermontov, and 28 in the list of Baratynskij. The lists are more or less headed by the same words, which can be shown by ranking lists of the most frequent nouns in poets of different times:

	Lomonosov	Baratynskij	Tjutčev	Lermontov	Fet	Achmatova
1.	ruka	duša	den'	duša	noč'	ruka
2.	svet[2]	den'	duša	ljubov'	duša	den'
3.	den'	serdce	nebo	serdce	serdce	glaza
4.	serdce	drug[1]	mir[1]	žizn'	den'	dom
5.	nebo	ljubov'	žizn'	den'	nebo	golos
6.	delo	žizn'	zemlja	ljudi	žizn'	serdce

Words such as *den', zemlja, serdce, ljubov', noč',* and *ruka* are likely to be represented in most lists of the 50 most frequent nouns in any poet of any time. True, the lists of verbs and, especially, of adjectives, are a bit more dependent on time and poetic individuality. But in them, too, there will always be a high degree of similarity in the frequency lists.

2.3 Thus, a frequent use of a word does not necessarily imply that this word is especially *typical* for the poet in question. It is only an indication that this word occupies a strong position in the poet's system of words. Consequently, information on how many times certain words are used by Tjutčev[5] is not very helpful for the scholar who is primarily concerned with the individuality of the poet's vocabulary. For this scholar one ought to compare the frequencies of the poet's words with the frequencies in a word count dictionary. Only such a procedure can provide us with information on the poet's 'key words', or *mots-clés,* to use Guiraud's term.

3.0 The most comprehensive Russian word frequency dictionary to have appeared until now is *Russian Word Count* by È. Šteinfel'dt. This dictionary, prepared in 1959-1962, was compiled from material of 400,000 words and contains the 2,500 most commonly used words in modern literary Russian. Of course, a comparison of Tjutčev's lists with the materials provided by this dictionary may shed some light on the differences between modern literary Russian and the vocabulary of a 19th century poet. But it is also evident that such a comparison is not very satisfactory from the point of view of poetics. For one thing, the amount of material to be compared is very unequal, both in quantity and in quality; it is very inconvenient to compare Tjutčev's 30,942 words of poetry to Šteinfel'dt's 400,000 words of fiction, plays, radio broadcasts, and articles from periodicals. Besides, a lot of Tjutčev's archaic and typically 'poetic' words are not likely to be represented in Šteinfel'dt at all.

3.1 A better way to show Tjutčev's originality would probably be to compare his vocabulary to a 'norm' of the Russian poetic language of his time. Such a norm or base can only be established by way of taking random samples from poets preferably writing in the same period as the poet in question. In my study of Lermontov's vocabulary (43,315 tokens) this base is given by taking a sample of 2,063 words each from 21 poets writing in the period of 1820-1849. The pages, providing a corpus of 43,323 tokens, were chosen by means of a table of random digits, and the poets were selected on the basis of 'literary importance' and of 'popularity' by using the name-indexes of two authoritative works on the history of Russian literature, and two comprehensive bibliographies.[6] Although these texts cannot be regarded as representative for all that was written in poetry at that time, they do provide a satisfactory norm of the poetic language in the Age of Puškin, being taken from a relatively large number of the most influential poets of the time. To be sure this norm may also be considered very appropriate for comparing Tjutčev's vocabulary. Besides, one of my students has used the same method in his study of the vocabulary in Lomonosov's poems (36,230 tokens), taking a 2,264 word sample from 16 carefully selected poets writing in the period of 1725–1775, thus getting a corpus of 36,224 tokens.[7] This sample may be used for comparing Tjutčev's vocabulary to the most representative Russian poets of the 18th century.

3.2 To measure the degree of originality of the most frequent nouns, verbs, and adjectives in Tjutčev, we have found it convenient to use the coefficient applied in the lexicographical works of Pierre Guiraud. This coefficient is calculated by the formula

$$Q = \frac{o - t}{\sqrt{t}}$$

where o is the observed individual frequency and t is the theoretical frequency. The latter is a value in the population estimated on the basis of a sample. It is found by dividing the individual frequency by the number of tokens in the sample and by multiplying the result by the number of tokens in the text in question. For example, knowing that the word *den'* is 148 times used by Tjutčev, 112 times by the poets of the 18th century, 146 times by the poets of the Age of Puškin, and 816 times in Šteinfeľdt's texts, we shall get the following coefficients:

(a) Tjutčev compared to the poets of the 18th century (Sample 1):

Individual frequency (o)	Theoretical frequency (t)
148	$\dfrac{112 \times 30{,}942}{36{,}224} = 95{,}67$
Difference	Coefficient (Q value)
52,33	$\dfrac{52{,}33}{\sqrt{95{,}67}} = 5{,}35$

(b) Tjutčev compared to the poets of the Age of Puškin (Sample 2):

Individual frequency (o)   Theoretical frequency (t)

148 $\dfrac{146 \times 30{,}942}{43{,}324} = 104{,}28$

Difference   Coefficient (Q value)

43,72 $\dfrac{43{,}72}{\sqrt{104{,}28}} = 4{,}28$

(c) Tjutčev compared to Šteinfeľdt's texts (Sample 3):

Individual frequency (o)   Theoretical frequency (t)

148 $\dfrac{816 \times 30{,}942}{400{,}000} = 63{,}12$

Difference   Coefficient (Q value)

84,88 $\dfrac{84{,}88}{\sqrt{63{,}12}} = 10{,}69$

3.3 The question is now whether Tjutčev's deviations from the frequencies observed in Samples 1, 2, and 3 are sufficiently clear to be called significant. In order to answer this question it is necessary to define what we shall here mean by 'significance'.

3.3.1 The question can be posed in the following way: if we were to take a purely chance selection of 30,942 tokens from the populations represented by Samples 1, 2, and 3, how great is then the probability of getting at least as high or at least as low frequencies as in Tjutčev? If this probability is less than or equal to 0.01 (1%), a rather strict criterion, we shall regard the result as significant.

3.3.2 We can now use Guiraud's coefficient for computing this probability by basing ourselves on the following; if t is the frequency of a word for every 30,942 words in the actual population and o is the frequency in a chance selection of 30,942 words from the population, then o will be approximately normally distributed with an expectation $\approx t$ and a standard deviation $\approx \sqrt{t}$. In this way

$$Q = \frac{o - t}{\sqrt{t}}$$

will be approximately normally distributed $(0,1)$, giving significant results for Q values $\geqslant 2.576$ or $\leqslant -2.576$.[8] More popularly speaking: if a word has a coefficient higher than 2.576 or lower than -2.576 and we draw the conclusion that this word is used comparatively more often or seldom than in the general population, then the chance of making a mistake is less than 1%. Admittedly, the approximations proposed in this model will inevitably lead to some inaccuracy in the calculation of the probability. There is reason to believe, however, that the deficiencies in this respect will be compensated for by a strict significance level of 1%.

3.3.3 In accordance with the above reasoning we can now confidently maintain that the word *den'* is definitely much more often used by Tjutčev than by the poets forming the norm of the poetic language of the 18th century (Sample 1: Q value 5.35). The word *den'* is also a more active — i.e. more frequently used — noun in Tjutčev than in the poets of the Age of Puškin (Sample 2: Q value 4.28), and it is very much more used by Tjutčev than in modern literary Russian (Sample 3: Q value 10.69).

3.4 Let us now compare the occurrences of the most active nouns in Tjutčev's poems (see 2.0) with the occurrences of the similar nouns in the different samples, using Q values to measure the deviations from the norms established.

Nouns less frequently used by Tjutčev

    (a) compared to the poets of the 18th century: none

    (b) compared to the poets of the Age of Puškin: *oko* (—2.73), *ruka* (—2.66)

    (c) compared to modern literary Russian: *god* (—4.63), *vremja* (—3.12)

Nouns having uncertain Q values in Tjutčev

    (a) compared to the poets of the 18th century: *duch* (—2.56), *serdce* (—2.23), *ruka* (—1.88), *vek*[1] (—1.58), *god* (—1.40), *ljubov'* (—0.88), *oko* (0.17), *sila* (0.31), *vremja* (0.35), *krov'* (1.03), *slovo* (1.05), *sleza* (1.12), *bog* (1.28), *priroda* (1.65), *sud'ba* (1.65), *narod* (1.66), *čas* (1.69), *car'* (2.10), *Rossija* (2.42), *voda* (2.52), *gora* (2.54)

    (b) compared to the poets of the Age of Puškin: *sleza* (—2.49), *serdce* (—2.46), *drug*[1] (—1.76), *grud'* (—1.75), *ljubov'* (—1.56), *sila* (—1.00), *noč'* (—0.50), *sud'ba* (—0.17), *vremja* (0.30), *vzor* (0.63), *glava*[1] (0.84), *duša* (0.85), *more* (0.93), *gora* (1.05), *volna* (1.36), *raz*[1] (1.63), *leto* (1.69), *žizn'* (1.80), *god* (1.92), *bog* (2.10), *son* (2.17), *čas* (2.27)

    (c) compared to modern literary Russian: *ruka* (—1.16), *raz*[1] (—1.01), *slovo* (0.57), *leto* (2.32)

Nouns more frequently used by Tjutčev

    (a) compared to the poets of the 18th century: *leto* (2.93), *vzor* (3.47), *grud'* (4.82), *drug*[1] (5.00), *den'* (5.35), *noč'* (5.80), *žizn'* (6.39), *glava*[1] (6.57), *vesna* (6.95), *vera* (6.96), *more* (7.32), *solnce* (8.13), *svet*[1] (8.59), *zemlja* (9.39), *raz*

(9.40), *kraj* (10.78), *luč* (10.90), *breg* (10.98), *dym* (10.98), *nebo* (12.67), *pora*
(13.88), *son* (15.76), *volna* (15.91), *duša* (16.06), *mir*[1] (16.19), *ten'* (17.09), *zvezda*
(17.74), *bor'ba* (27.34) / / *poèt*

(b) compared to the poets of the Age of Puškin: *poèt* (2.60), *car' (2.65), krov'*
(2.69), *vera* (2.83), *pora* (3.03), *priroda* (3.07), *zvezda* (3.19), *kraj* (4.00), *breg*
(4.00), *duch* (4.01), *vek*[1] (4.21), *den'* (4.28), *vesna* (4.28), *narod* (4.49), *zemlja*
(5.09), *nebo* (5.19), *dym* (5.81), *luč* (6.25), *ten'* (6.59), *bor'ba* (7.06), *Rossija*
(7.70), *mir*[1] (7.83), *solnce* (8.22), *svet*[1] (9.02)

(c) compared to modern literary Russian: *voda* (2.81), *narod* (4.31), *sila*
(5.53), *bor'ba* (5.83), *drug*[1] (6.33), *čas* (7.14), *žizn'* (8.98), *vesna* (9.85), *pora*
(10.02), *more* (10.10), *den'* (10.69), *gora* (11.00), *priroda* (12.33), *noč'* (13.01),
zemlja (13.41), *sud'ba* (13.76), *grud'* (15.05), *solnce* (15.06), *poèt* (15.62), *sleza*
(16.52), *kraj* (17.85), *svet*[1] (17.95), *dym* (18.04), *vera* (18.41), *vek*[1] (19.03),
zvezda (21.25), *serdce* (21.97), *duch* (22.60), *volna* (23.17), *krov'* (25.44), *mir*[1]
(29.22), *ljubov'* (30.48), *luč* (33.05), *nebo* (42.25), *bog* (42.56), *duša* (44.17), *son*
(46.51), *ten'* (47.84), / / *vzor, oko, car', breg, Rossija, glava*[1].

3.4.1 That the majority of the most active nouns in Tjutčev is less used by
the authors of the samples is only natural. If we had not limited Tjutčev's list
to the 50 most active nouns and instead taken, say, the first 100, the picture
might have been different. At any rate, the result would probably have been
much higher Q values, both negative and positive. But this would have implied
a comparison of words which are not very often used even by Tjutčev and
consequently not so interesting for a quantitative investigation. Even among
the 50 most active nouns in Tjutčev there are words not used in the samples.
True, in Sample 1 we do not find the word *poèt*; here *piit* is used 5 times, which
would have meant a Q value of 10.98 compared to Tjutčev's 27 occurrences of
poèt. As for Sample 3 we must bear in mind that frequencies lower than 14 are
not registered at all, and that proper names occurring in the texts (e.g. *Rossija*)
have been disregarded. This must be the explanation for the impossibility of
giving Q values for *vzor, oko (oči), car', breg, Rossija,* and *glava*[1], together with
the fact that the frequencies of these, for the most part archaic and 'poetic'
words, are naturally bound to be very modest in modern literary Russian.
Thus by Tjutčev the word *glava*[1] is used 28 times in the meaning of 'head' and
is hardly comparable to *glava*[1] in Šteinfel'dt's texts, where the word is used 30
times in the meaning of 'leader'. On the whole, Q values are much higher in
Samples 1 and 3 than in Sample 2. The reason for this is obviously that the
latter sample consists of texts which are more related to the poems in question,
Tjutčev being one of the poets included in the sample.

3.4.2 Although Tjutčev is represented by his 50 most frequently used
nouns, not all of them can be said to be typical for his poetry. The materials

provided in 3.4 show that words such as *god, oko (oči), vremja, slovo,* and *ruka* are comparatively seldom used in his poetry. This is especially true of *ruka*. Although Tjutčev uses this word as often as 49 times, this is obviously insufficient to call it a key word in his poetry, because it reveals negative coefficients compared to all the samples. The popularity of *ruka* seems otherwise to be rather constant in most poets, independently of literary periods. Interestingly, it is the most frequent noun both in Lomonosov (113 times in 36,230 tokens) and in Achmatova (118 times in 39,530 tokens). As a poet of thought Tjutčev is less concrete and does not feel the need of using it so often. Significant in this respect is also the low frequency of a word signifying another part of the body: *oko (oči),* which shows the lowest Q value compared to the texts of the Age of Puškin. The more so, since the modest frequency of this word is not compensated by a preference of the more modern word *glaz (glaza),* which is used only 19 times and has an even lower Q value compared with the texts of this sample, where it is used 64 times.

3.4.3 Passing on to the nouns definitely more often used by Tjutčev than by the sample authors, we can observe a high degree of correlation between the various samples. Obviously, most of these words are typically 'tjutčevian', regardless of the norm compared to. Several semantic fields could be pointed out; here attention will be drawn only to two of them. First, we have the field 'earth', containing words such as *kraj, breg, zemlja,* and *mir*[1] ('world'). The high Q values for all these words, as well as for *zemnoj,* see 3.6, do not leave any doubt that they are very characteristic of Tjutčev, reminding us of his famous saying: "In order to flourish poetry ought to have its roots in the earth."[9] Even more typical is the semantic field 'light', represented by such words as *luč, solnce,* and *svet.* The latter word is very often met in the Age of Puškin, but usually not so much in the meaning of 'light' as in the meaning of 'world' and 'society'. In this meaning *svet* is a key word both in Lermontov and in Baratynskij, showing a Q value of 7.42 and 6.28 in each poet compared with Sample 2. In Tjutčev, on the other hand, *svet* has the meaning of 'light' in at least 56 out of a total number of 70 occurrences. The extraordinarily high Q value for this word, as well as for *luč* and *solnce,* is a clear indication that Tjutčev is very much a *poet of light,* perhaps more so than any other poet in Russian literature. This impression is confirmed by studying the lists of verbs and adjectives, in which words as *svetit'* and *svetlyj* reveal high Q values compared to all the samples. What is especially revealing in this respect, is Tjutčev's tendency to use words from this semantic field in clusters, thereby increasing the impression of light created by his poetry. Here are a few examples: *Sijaj, sijaj, proščaľnyj svet* (I, 156), *I solnce niti zolotit* (I, 12), *Sijaet solnce, vody bleščut* (I, 152), *Svetit mne otradnyj luč* (II, 59), *Svetit solnce zolotoe* (I, 208).

3.5 Let us now compare the number of the most frequently used verbs in Tjutčev's poems (see 2.0) with the occurrences of the similar verbs in the different samples, using, as before, Q values to measure the deviations from the norms established.

Verbs less frequently used by Tjutčev

(a) compared to the poets of the 18th century: *zret*[2] (—6.63), *skazat'* (—5.82), *moč'* (—5.57), *znat'* (—5.13), *chotet'* (—4.39), *byt'* (—4.01), *stat'* (—3.91), *govorit'* (—3.75), *žit'* (—3.59), *iskat'* (—2.77)

(b) compared to the poets of the Age of Puškin: *skazat'* (—3.95), *govorit'* (—3.38), *ljubit'* (—3.24), *dat'* (—3.23), *moč'* (—3.02), *znat'* (—2.69)

(c) compared to modern literary Russian: *skazat'* (—8.76), *govorit'* (—7.26), *byt'* (—5.19), *moč'* (—4.41), *idti* (—4.00), *znat'* (—3.98), *stat'* (—3.96), *chotet'* (—3.56)

Verbs having uncertain Q values in Tjutčev

(a) compared to the poets of the 18th century: *dat'* (—2.45), *videt'* (—2.08), *prijti* (—1.92), *davat'* (—0.88), *vesti* (—0.28), *slyšat'* (0.28), *ljubit'* (0.31), *sijat'* (0.39), *zvat'* (0.84), *pet'* (0.99), *goret'* (1.17), *past'* (1.48), *zabyt'* (1.53), *bežat'* (2.25), *idti* (2.29), *služit'* (2.36)

(b) compared to the poets of the Age of Puškin: *stat'* (—2.16), *prijti* (—1.98), *žit'* (—1.82), *spat'* (—1.70), *videt'* (—1.56), *zabyt'* (—1.43), *idti* (—1.18), *gljadet'* (—1.07), *chotet'* (—1.06), *sidet'* (—0.97), *projti* (—0.88), *blestet'* (—0.87), *past'* (—0.83), *iskat'* (—0.70), *pet'* (—0.67), *goret'* (—0.53), *smotret'* (—0.36), *bežat'* (—0.04), *ležat'* (0.11), *šumet'* (0.32), *letet'* (0.45), *zvučat'* (0.56), *zvat'* (0.56), *verit'* (1.42), *brodit'* (1.82), *davat'* (1.87), *pit'* (1.90), *slyšat'* (2.02), *byt'* (2.03), *ponjat'* (2.19), *sijat'* (2.20)

(c) compared to modern literary Russian: *davat'* (—1.56), *prijti* (—1.48), *sidet'* (—1.45), *smotret'* (—0.63), *videt'* (—0.56), *dat'* (—0.52), *ponjat'* (—0.10), *ležat'* (0.53), *ujti* (0.60), *spat'* (0.77), *vesti* (0.80), *projti* (0.91), *zvat'* (1.01), *žit'* (1.45), *zabyt'* (1.71), *slyšat'* (1.94), *iskat'* (2.17)

Verbs more frequently used by Tjutčev

(a) compared to the poets of the 18th century: *ležat'* (2.75), *spat'* (2.87), *šumet'* (3.36), *igrat'* (3.92), *ponjat'* (3.92), *smotret'* (4.06), *letet'* (4.09), *projti* (5.05), *sidet'* (5.18), *vstavat'* (5.18), *pit'* (5.67), *molčat'* (6.96), *zvučat'* (7.09), *stojat'* (7.56), *brodit'* (7.85), *verit'* (9.05), *svetit'* (9.53), *ujti* (10.28), *lit'sja* (10.58), *blestet'* (10.98), *dyšat'* (11.45), *gljadet'* (14.37), *trevožit'* (15.38), *vejat'* (22.99)

(b) compared to the poets of the Age of Puškin: *vesti* (2.67), *vstavat'* (3.05), *molčat'* (3.09), *stojat'* (3.48), *ujti* (3.56), *služit'* (3.57), *dyšat'* (3.60), *trevožit'* (3.89), *zret'*[2] (4.84), *igrat'* (5.34), *vejat'* (6.13), *lit'sja* (6.52), *svetit'* (6.92)

(c) compared to modern literary Russian: *igrat'* (3.17), *stojat'* (3.94), *ljubit'* (4.10), *bežat'* (4.30), *zvučat'* (5.17), *molčat'* (5.34), *pet'* (5.45), *pit'* (6.16), *služit'* (6.24), *letet'* (6.26), *vstavat'* (6.40), *goret'* (6.66), *brodit'* (6.69), *verit'* (7.23), *šumet'* (10.09), *gljadet'* (11.80), *blestet'* (18.04), *dyšat'* (19.17) / / *zret'*[2], *trevožit'*, *past'*, *sijat'*, *lit'sja*, *vejat'*, *svetit'*.

3.5.1 As will be seen from 3.5, all the 50 most active verbs in Tjutčev's poems are also represented in Samples 1 and 2. As for Sample 3, comparisons are complicated by Šteinfel'dt's grouping participles and verbal adjectives separately from the verbs and giving no frequencies lower than 14. The result is that no Q values can be given for a number of Tjutčev's verbs: *zret'*[2] ('behold'), *trevožit'*, *past'*, *sijat'*, *lit'sja*, *vejat'*, *svetit'*, of which the first, moreover, is an obvious archaism, not likely to be used in modern literary Russian.

3.5.2 The amount of words showing negative or uncertain Q values is clearly higher for Tjutčev's verbs than for his nouns. This is a clear indication that Tjutčev, being primarily a poet of thought, prefers other parts of speech, especially nouns and adjectives.[10] Taken together, his 50 most active verbs are used 1,275 times, which accounts for 4.12% of all words in his poetry. This is definitely less than for instance in Lermontov, where the 50 most frequent verbs account for 5.87% of the poet's vocabulary.[11] Of the verbs comparatively little used by Tjutčev are some of the most active verbs in the Russian language: *moč'*, *znat'*, *byt'*, and, not at least, the verba dicendi *skazat'* and *govorit'*.

3.5.3 Much more typical for Tjutčev are verbs relatively seldom used in the Russian language. I am here thinking of verbs signifying light (*sijat'*, *blestet'*, *svetit'*) and also of verbs having an obvious 'poetic' flavour, such as *molčat'*, *dyšat'*, *trevožit'*, *vejat'*, *lit'sja*. At the first sight it may seem only natural that a poet should have a preference for verbs which are rarely found outside poetry. However, this is not always the case. In Lermontov, for instance, quite the opposite is true: in his vocabulary the highest Q values compared to Sample 2 are found with commonly used verbs such as *ljubit'*, *moč'*, *byt'*, and *pisat'*.[12] The word *pisat'* is used by Lermontov 20 times, by Tjutčev only once, and the verb *bojat'sja*, having a frequency of 30 in Lermontov, is not used in Tjutčev's poems at all. Of course this makes Tjutčev's originality even more striking. Who would have thought of *lit'sja* as one of Tjutčev's most characteristic verbs? By Baratynskij this verb is only used 5 times, by Lermontov 7 times. In both poets it is generally met in connection with liquids (tears, blood, wine), whereas in Tjutčev it is frequently used also with abstract subjects. Here are a few examples: *Sumrak tichij, sumrak sonnyj, Lejsja v glub' moej duši* (I, 75); *No skvoz' vozdušnyj zaves okon Nedolgo lilsja mrak nočnoj* (I, 86); *I l'etsja čistaja i teplaja lazur' Na otdychajuščee pole* (I, 170). The verb showing the highest Q value compared to the poets of the Age of Puškin is nevertheless *svetit'*, not surprising in this poet of light.

3.6 Lastly we shall compare the occurrences of the most active adjectives (epithets) in Tjutčev's poems (see 2.0) with the occurrences of the similar adjectives in the different samples, using Q values to measure the deviations from the norms established.

Adjectives less frequently used by Tjutčev
   (a) compared to the poets of the 18th century: none
   (b) compared to the poets of the Age of Puškin: *milyj* (—3.29)
   (c) compared to modern literary Russian: *pervyj* (—4.91), *novyj* (—4.43), *mnogij* (—2.94).

Adjectives having uncertain Q values in Tjutčev
   (a) compared to the poets of the 18th century: *zloj* (—1.37); *mnogij* (—1.15), *novyj* (—1.02), *skoryj* (—0.83), *bednyj* (0.29), *lučšij* (0.30), *prekrasnyj* (0.71), *užasnyj* (0.85), *večnyj* (1.02), *vernyj* (1.18), *sladkij* (1.69), *dolgij* (1.77), *bessmertnyj* (1.82), *velikij* (1.86), *glubokij* (2.55)
   (b) compared to the poets of the Age of Puškin: *polnyj* (—1.95), *prekrasnyj* (—1.38), *novyj* (—1.35), *veselyj* (—1.13), *tichij* (—1.01), *dolgij* (—0.82), *glubokij* (—0.60), *sladkij* (—0.47), *divnyj* (—0.37), *zloj* (—0.36), *vernyj* (0.38), *svjatoj* (0.46), *zolotoj* (0.57), *nočnoj* (0.86), *strašnyj* (1.07), *legkij* (1.22), *čudnyj* (1.29), *pervyj* (1.34), *bednyj* (1.51), *dikij* (1.52), *skoryj* (1.62), *mnogij* (1.63), *užasnyj* (1.71), *večnyj* (1.76), *lučšij* (1.78), *temnyj* (1.85), *vysokij* (1.87), *svežij* (1.87)
   (c) compared to modern literary Russian: *lučšij* (—0.92), *dolgij* (0.76), *skoryj* (1.61), *veselyj* (2.22)

Adjectives more frequently used by Tjutčev
   (a) compared to the poets of the 18th century: *milyj* (2.98), *vysokij* (3.09), *celyj* (3.33), *smelyj* (3.36), *strašnyj* (3.87), *divnyj* (4.37), *veselyj* (5.05), *čudnyj* (5.72), *polnyj* (6.28), *nebesnyj* (7.01), *tichij* (7.69), *pozdnij* (7.91), *legkij* (7.91), *pervyj* (8.17), *poslednij* (8.72), *čistyj* (8.72), *temnyj* (10.04), *zemnoj* (10.48), *dikij* (10.50), *svetlyj* (10.99), *morskoj* (12.15), *zolotoj* (12.44), *svjatoj* (12.71), *nezrimyj* (15.38), *vozdušnyj* (17.55), *russkij* (17.61), *nočnoj* (19.31), *živoj* (19.97), *božij* (23.12), *volšebnyj* (33.86), *rodnoj* (45.82) / / *rokovoj, tainstvennyj, byloj, svežij*

(b) compared to the poets of the Age of Puškin: *svetlyj* (2.67), *tainstvennyj* (3.11), *byloj* (3.16), *bessmertnyj* (3.37), *vozdušnyj* (4.16), *celyj* (4.31), *čistyj* (4.32), *živoj* (4.39), *pozdnij* (4.49), *poslednij* (4.60), *smelyj* (4.72), *rodnoj* (4.87), *nebesnyj* (5.20), *morskoj* (5.57), *nezrimyj* (6.05), *zemnoj* (6.36), *russkij* (6.45), *volšebnyj* (6.51), *božij* (7.45), *rokovoj* (9.26), *velikij* (11.12)

(c) compared to modern literary Russian: *vysokij* (2.59), *legkij* (2.93), *vernyj* (3.68), *tichij* (3.77), *poslednij* (4.38), *celyj* (4.57), *glubokij* (4.82), *smelyj* (4.92), *prekrasnyj* (5.42), *zolotoj* (5.85), *strašnyj* (6.07), *svežij* (6.30), *pozdnij* (6.47), *temnyj* (6.66), *polnyj* (6.67), *morskoj* (8.26), *russkij* (8.52), *vozdušnyj* (9.84), *zloj* (10.23), *čistyj* (11.37), *velikij* (12.52), *nočnoj* (12.83), *bednyj* (14.08), *milyj* (14.62), *rodnoj* (15.60), *živoj* (17.53), *svetlyj* (18.05), *zemnoj* (34.94), / / *rokovoj, svjatoj, božij, volšebnyj, nebesnyj, večnyj, dikij, tainstvennyj, sladkij, byloj, čudnyj, užasnyj, bessmertnyj, divnyj, nezrimyj.*

3.6.1 As we can see from 3.6, all the 50 most frequent adjectives in Tjutčev's poems are also represented in Sample 2. There are 4 of Tjutčev's adjectives not to be found in Sample 1, among them such highly romantic epithets as *rokovoj* and *tainstvennyj,* not likely to enjoy popularity in the Age of Reason. Among Tjutčev's adjectives there are 15 which are not represented in Sample 3, either because of a somewhat different system of lemmatization (thus in Šteinfeľdt adverbs have been separated from adjectives), or simply because of too low frequencies. For the most part these are words with a distinctive 'poetic' flavour (*rokovoj, volšebnyj, tainstvennyj*), or else words relatively seldom used in the Soviet Union today because of their religious denotations (*svjatoj, božij, nebesnyj, večnyj*).

3.6.2 On the whole, among Tjutčev's lists of 'thematic words' (see 2.0) the list of adjectives is undoubtedly the one showing the lesser degree of correlation as compared to the samples. The explanation for this seems to be that epithets are much more important keys to a poet's individuality than are nouns and verbs. No Russian poet can avoid using a certain portion of the verb *byt'* and consequently this verb will always be found among the 50 most active verbs in any Russian poet. At the same time poets have different outlooks on life and therefore describe it differently, using epithets more or less of their own. In Tjutčev this feature can be observed already at the level of the 50 most used adjectives, where there are very few negative Q values compared to the samples. As will be seen from 3.6, only 4 adjectives are definitely more used in the samples than in Tjutčev. That *pervyj, novyj,* and *mnogij* are more frequently used in modern literary Russian than in Tjutčev, is not surprising, since all of them are not especially 'poetic' epithets. More striking is the result for *milyj.* Compared to Samples 1 and 3 this epithet is relatively much used by Tjutčev, but a comparison with the number of occurrences in Sample 2 gives a clear negative Q value. The reason for this is the extraordinary popularity of this epithet in the Age of Puškin. *Milyj* is by far the most widely used epithet in the norm established for this period; it occurs 83 times, while *polnyj* rates second with 63 occurrences. Moreover, *milyj* heads the list of adjectives both in Puškin and in Baratynskij, and it rates second after *polnyj* in Lermontov. However, from the 1840's onward a reaction seems to have arisen: poets apparently came to regard *milyj* as being too commonplace. Thus it rates only ninth in Tjutčev and twelfth in Fet, showing in both cases a clear negative Q value as compared to the Age of Puškin. Interestingly, it has later on regained some of its lost popularity, rating first among the epithets in Voznesenskij's *Antimiry*. [13]

3.6.3 In one of his books L. A. Bulachovskij observes that "the favourite epithets of F. I. Tjutčev are those closely connected with the mystic elements of his perception of the world: *rokovoj, tainstvennyj, nezrimyj, bezmolvnyj, nemoj, proročeskij, volšebnyj*".[14] By means of the methodology offered in this paper such intuitive observations can now be easily checked. Thus there is no doubt that *rokovoj, tainstvennyj, nezrimyj*, and *volšebnyj* should be considered favourite epithets of Tjutčev. As will be seen in 3.6, all these epithets do also appear in our lists of the poet's key epithets, showing high Q values compared to the norms established. On the other hand, it is hardly correct to include *nemoj* in the group of Tjutčev's favourite epithets. After all *nemoj* is only used 8 times by the poet, as against 15 times by the poets of the Age of Puškin. The result is that this epithet gets a Q value of —0.83, which gives us no right to consider it typically 'tjutčevian'.

As for Tjutčev's key epithets attention is first of all drawn to *velikij*, showing the highest Q value compared to the poets of the Age of Puškin. This epithet is also very often used by Tjutčev compared to modern literary Russian, but not in comparison with Sample 1, revealing a Q value of only 1.86. It is, therefore, tempting to consider the love for *velikij* an 18th century feature in the poet's vocabulary. This epithet is especially favoured by the later Tjutčev, speaking of the greatness of Russia and the great and holy significance of this country in future history.

4.0 To many scholars a quantitative approach to a poet's vocabulary is a rather unsatisfactory one. True, it may best be compared to studying a country using a map of the world: you cannot, of course, expect to find details such as minor lakes or towns. On the other hand, you do get an idea where the country is situated in relation to other countries, that is, information which is not provided by a map of the country, where nothing else is seen. Admittedly, going from the poems to the vocabulary means an enormous abstraction.

Unlike a dictionary, a poem is a work of art where the words have no independent meaning; the words in a poem always mutually illuminate each other, giving independent meaning to the work of art. An adequate investigation of the poet's word can therefore only take place in the individual poem. However, since the poem is an extremely complex phenomenon, the study of a poet's vocabulary can tell us things which are difficult to notice by examining each poem individually.

In this study only a few features have been pointed out: Tjutčev's occupation with words denoting 'earth' and 'light', his love for verbs that are little used by other poets, his preference for epithets closely connected with the mystic elements of his perception of the world. Thus the counts presented confirm fully satisfactorily some intuitive notions on Tjutčev, formed on the basis of the motifs characteristic of his poetry. But they also show up some new and, in this respect, unexpected features. True, what the vocabulary taken as a whole tells us, is only a help for giving a more comprehensive description of the poems later on. By providing such help, however, the quantitative approach shows the way to the text and opens up a new avenue for exploration.

University of Oslo

NOTES

[1]   Charles Baudelaire, *Œuvres complètes,* 3 (Paris 1966), 599.

[2]   I should like to express my profound gratitude to Ivar Fonnes, consultant at NAVF's Centre for Electronic Data Processing in the Humanities, who has been responsible for writing the necessary programs. Mr. Fonnes has also provided valuable assistance in questions of statistics.

[3]   The rules for lemmatization and distinction of homonyms have already been described in my book *Leksika stichotvorenij Lermontova: Opyt količestvennogo opisanija* (Oslo 1973) (= Universitetet i Oslo, Slavisk-baltisk Institutt, Meddelelser, Nr. 2, 1973).

[4]   See Pierre Guiraud, *Les caractères statistiques du vocabulaire* (Paris 1954).

[5]   Some such counts are provided in an article by Borys Bilokur, "Statistical Observations on Tjutčev's Lexicon", *SEEJ,* XIX, 3 (1970), 302-16.

[6]   For more detailed information on how the samples were taken, see my book on Lermontov's vocabulary, 19-20.

[7]   Ernst Hansen, *Ordforrådet i Lomonosovs dikt: En kvantitativ beskrivelse* [The Vocabulary in Lomonosov's poems: A Quantitative description]. In preparation.

[8]   Cf. the table of the normal distribution, for example in J. L. Hodges, Jr., and E. L. Lehmann, *Basic Concepts of Probability and Statistics,* Second Edition (San Francisco 1970), 416.

[9]   K. Pigarev, *Žizn' i tvorčestvo Tjutčeva* (Moskva 1962), 187.

[10]   The same tendency can be observed in other poets of thought, for instance in Baratynskij. See my book *Evgenij Baratynskij: Žizn' i tvorčestvo* (Oslo 1973), 547-48.

[11]   See *Leksika stichotvorenij Lermontova,* 22.

[12]   *Ibid.,* 26.

[13]   See V. S. Baevskij, *Stich russkoj sovetskoj poèzii* (Smolensk 1972), 113.

[14]   L. A. Bulachovskij, *Russkij literaturnyj jazyk pervoj poloviny XIX veka: Leksika i obščie zamečanija o sloge.* Vtoroe izdanie, peresmotrennoe i dopolnennoe (Kiev 1957), 455.

COMMENTS

(Flier)   Your analytic approach unfortunately by-passes two dimensions of
language design which are of fundamental importance for a true understanding of ideas presented in a poetic text, namely, polysemy and idiomaticity.

As I understand your method of selection (1.4, 2.0), homonyms like *mir*
'world'/*mir* 'peace', *svet* 'light'/*svet* 'world', and *glava* 'head'/*glava* 'chapter'
are treated as separate entries, while polysemous words like *nožka* ('leg of a
human being or animal [dim.]', 'furniture leg', 'mushroom stem'), *kraj* ('edge',
'country, region') and *stat'* ('arise, assume a standing position', 'begin',
'become', etc.) are not. Failure to distinguish such nuances can obviously skew
the results of the analysis or, at best, render them ambiguous.

The poetic use of idioms will create even graver problems for your
approach. If idioms like *vverx nogami* 'upside down, topsy-turvy', *postavit'*
krest na kom/čëm 'give up for lost', *ispytat' na svoëm gorbu* 'learn by bitter
experience', and *i koncy v vodu* 'none will be the wiser' are treated as normal
strings of words in their literal meaning, the entire direction of the poet's
intention will be lost.

(Vickery)   I found this paper very interesting and, differing from some present who have expressed skepticism as to the conclusions on the grounds of the
semantic nuances of different words and differences in the way words are used
in different contexts, I find the results of the study significant and entirely
valid — within the limits laid down by the author himself.

One point of particular interest: the high incidence of adjectives with stress
on the ending (type *zolotój*). The incidence of such adjectives tends to be high
in syllabo-tonic poetry for reasons related to metrical constraints. But in
Tjutčev we go beyond what is normally expected. Of his 50 most frequently
used adjectives 10 are of the *zolotój* type, five of these being in the top seven.
And of Tjutčev's 10 *zolotój*-type adjectives nine are used more frequently than
in the samples from eighteenth-century poets, six more frequently than in the
samples from poets of the Puškin age. This has to have implications either for
Tjutčev's handling of metrical constraints, or for his stylistic proclivities, or
both.

(Winner)   My question concerns the methodology of word count. Is it only
one first step in analyzing poetry? I have some misgiving. For, as you yourself
state in your conclusion, words have meaning only in **context**. Actually there
are **two** contexts: (1) a **textual** context; thus a word can have quite different

meanings in contexts such as *on čestnyj čelovek* and in Puškin's "Moj djadja samyx čestnyx pravil"; (2) a **cultural** context; e.g., a word has different meanings in different cultural and poetic contexts. For instance, the word *oblako* has one prevalent meaning in Romantic poetry, different from that in Majakovskij's "Oblako v štanax". I would disagree with your metaphor of the map: it is not only a question of distance, but also of knowledge of the symbolism of the map. We must know **what** the color 'green' means as opposed to 'blue' in maps, and in different kinds of maps this color symbolism may be quite different. Just so in poetry: it is not only a question of 'micro'-/'macro', but of complex many-levelled relationships.

Additional discussion: Harper, Hrushovsky, Issatschenko, Markov, de Mallac, Segal, Worth

AUTHOR'S REPLY

(to Flier) In accordance with other studies of this kind the selection of homonyms has been made with the help of a dictionary, in my case Ožegov's *Slovar' russkogo jazyka.* Here *mir* ('world', 'peace') is given as *mir*[1] and *mir*[2], whereas *kraj* has got only one entry. I do not agree that this procedure will seriously skew the results in a quantitative investigation based on a considerable amount of words. Idioms like those mentioned by Prof. Flier are comparatively seldom used, and there is no reason to believe that the direction of the poet's intention will be lost if we treat them as normal strings of words in their literal meaning. The idiom *i koncy v vodu,* for example, is not found in Tjutčev at all. It is used once by Puškin, but the word *konec* is used 163 times, and the word *voda* 250 times. Obviously the idiom will have very little influence on the results of the analysis.

(to Winner) The scepticism against word count has been answered so many times that I do not find it necessary to repeat all the arguments here. Let me only point out that language is not only a qualitative phenomenon. It is also a quantitative phenomenon, revealing statistical regularities and leaving comparatively little scope for individual elements. True, these individual elements should always be the main object of our study, but it is useful to study them in relation to a norm. This is what I meant by my metaphor of the map. Naturally, such a map can give us only a rough idea of what the poet is primarily occupied with. Nevertheless, it does provide us with some information of the poet's individuality, information that is often confirmed by intuitive impression. Prof. Winner is right in saying that a word often has different meanings in different cultural and poetic contexts. That is why a poet's vocabulary should preferably be compared to a norm of the poetic language of his time, as I have done in my paper. On the other hand, I do not agree that the word *čestnyj* has "quite different meanings" in the contexts mentioned by Prof. Winner. Neither do the authors of the *Slovar' jazyka Puškina* (see Vol. IV, pp. 907-08).

THE STANZAIC FORMS
OF N. M. JAZYKOV

IAN K. LILLY

Although the research that has been conducted on Russian versification in recent times has been both extensive and intensive, relatively little attention has been paid to the question of stanzaic forms (*strofika*). This is of course an area of investigation which can capitalize on the progress made in studying on the one hand the characteristics of Russian rhyme and on the other the nature of the Russian meters. For the nineteenth century, the period examined most thoroughly in this regard, there are detailed published analyses of the stanzaic forms of three poets — Puškin (by B. V. Tomaševskij), Lermontov (by M. A. Pejsaxovič and K. D. Višnevskij) and Nekrasov (primarily by Pejsaxovič).[1] Nevertheless, an enormous amount of work remains to be done. This brief communication describes the salient features of the stanzaic practice of N. M. Jazykov (1803-46), with comments on them in the light of the comparable data already in print on his most important contemporaries, Puškin and Lermontov. In the latter part of the paper the trends in Jazykov's stanzaic choices are related to trends in other major formal features of his poetry.

The corpus of Jazykov's lyric verse analyzed for this study corresponds almost exactly to the principal section of the 1964 edition of his poetic works.[2] Earlier collections and editions of Jazykov's poetry are not a suitable basis for metrical analyses, above all because of their incompleteness. Somewhat less than two thirds of Jazykov's known lyrics were published during his lifetime, so it is not surprising that the 1934 edition of Jazykov contains as many as 80 previously uncollected and 25 previously unpublished poems.[3] But 4 more poems first appeared in the 1948 edition,[4] and the 1964 edition — the latest — includes 1 poem which was first published in a journal in 1961 and 3 earlier unknown ones. There are however two minor problems with the 1964 edition. One is that "E. A. Sverbeevoj" (1845), a verse letter first published in the 1948 edition,[5] was inadvertently omitted by editor Buxmejer. The other is that 10 poems appear in it — as in all earlier publications — in expurgated form; because it is usually rhyme words which were deleted, these poems could not be analyzed as part of this study.[6] Accordingly, from a basic count of 345 poems, 1 must be added and 10 subtracted, so that the total corpus examined here is 336 poems, representing 12,052 lines of verse material.

As in much of the poetry of his age, there are often difficulties in determining what in Jazykov's poetry constitutes a stanza. Jazykov tended to be
inconsistent if not whimsical in the arrangement of his poems on the printed
page. Thus, a group of lines which can be considered an independent entity by
virtue of its rhyme pattern and intonational organization[7] might not always be
arranged as a graphic unit. Such a group of lines might appear as half a graphic
unit or, on occasion, as two graphic units. The former type is not uncommon in
Jazykov's first collection of lyrics, which was compiled under his personal
supervision.[8] Nevertheless, since Jazykov's rhyme-pattern units rarely lack syntactic unity and since they are almost invariably reduplicated within the same
poem, it was only practical to regard them as the key compositional units of his
verse.

Three further points must be made regarding the stanzaic typology employed in this paper. First, poems with non-repeating rhyme patterns are
considered as stanzaic only if they are composed in a fixed form (*tverdaja
forma*) or if their rhyme pattern is symmetrical. Second, the few (18) poems
under 6 lines in total length were automatically excluded from consideration as
stanzaic forms; their rhyme patterns are of the symmetrical rather than repeating
variety. Finally, there is one construction common in Jazykov's stanzaic repertoire which appears not to have been accommodated in existing systems of
stanzaic notation.[9] It has masculine and feminine clausulae alternating in respective positions from stanza to stanza. In this study this construction is denoted by
an asterisk. Thus, while the plain stanzaic repetition of embracing rhyme in
four-line stanzas beginning with a feminine clausula is represented as AbbA and
rhymes AbbA CddC EffE GhhG ..., the alternating variant is represented as
AbbA* and rhymes AbbA cDDc EffE gHHg ...

Given this poetic corpus and this definition of a stanza, Jazykov's stanzaic
catalogue runs to 182 poems in 80 different compositional forms. In virtually all
cases the rhyme pattern is derived from an alternation of masculine and feminine
clausulae; poems beginning with a masculine clausula do occur, but not with any
consistency. For example, as against 41 iambic tetrameter poems rhyming AbAb
there are only 6 rhyming aBaB. Like most poets of his age, Jazykov wrote little
poetry using dactylic clausulae. This phenomenon occurs in three stanzaic
works, and always in conjunction with masculine clausulae – in his only poems
set in dactylic and amphibrachic dimeters, respectively the songs "Gimn" (1823)
and "Vsemu čelovečestvu ..." (1827), and in an iambic trimeter poem from his
final months, "Ugrjum stoit dremučij les ...", whose rhyme pattern is X´aX´a.
This last poem is one of only two stanzaic compositions in Jazykov's *oeuvre*
with half the clausulae unrhymed, the other being "Ja pomnju: byl vesel i šumen
moj den' ..." (1834-36).

Jazykov wrote as many as 28 poems in rhyming couplets, but his preferred unit of stanzaic composition is 4 lines long, since a total of 104 poems in a wide variety of metrical forms are arranged in 4-line stanzas. Although alternating rhyme (AbAb, or sometimes aBaB) easily dominates in this category, embracing rhyme is also common. In the latter case, of course, the full rhyme pattern may be evident over a single stanza (the types AbbA and aBBa) or, as more often happens in Jazykov's poetry, over two stanzas (the types AbbA* and aBBa*). The other stanzaic patterns up to and including 8 lines in length are noteworthy not so much for their originality as for the diversity of the meters they are used with. Of the 19 different stanzaic patterns in the range of 5 through 8 lines only 3 − AbbAb, AAbCCb, and AbAbAb − recur in the course of Jazykov's poetič career. Most of them can be found in the stanzaic repertoire of Puškin, if not in the same meter as the one Jazykov used them with, then in one close to it.[10] Perhaps the most distinctive are the stanzas in which Jazykov composed two songs early in his student period. They are "Pesnja korolja Regnera" (autumn 1822), in amphibrachic tetrameters and his first effort in ternaries (it rhymes $a^1 BBa^2 Ca^3 Ca^1$), and his drinking song "Ot serdca družnye s vinom ..." (late summer 1823), a poem in iambic tetrameters which rhymes aaBaBcc.

The same metrical diversity can be observed in Jazykov's poems in 9-, 10-, and 12-line stanzas. Only one pattern is used more than once with the same meter − there are three lyrics in trochaic tetrameters rhyming AbAbCdCCd. A comparison with the stanzaic practice of Puškin and Lermontov points to Jazykov's apparent independence in using stanzas of this length, an independence which is even more marked in his longest compositional forms. While Jazykov has 5 poems in 9-line stanzas, Puškin has none and Lermontov, a poet with a remarkable repertoire of stanzaic forms, has only 3. And whereas Jazykov has 2 poems in 12-line stanzas, including "Na smert' barona A. A. Del'viga" (1831), one of his finest works, Puškin has only 1 and Lermontov only 2 as well.[11]

The poems in stanzaic units of 13 lines and above include 5 of Jazykov's 6 poems in non-repeating compositional forms. They are in fact his more successful attempts at writing in elongated stanzas. He has only two fixed-form poems, both sonnets addressed to Karolina Jaenisch (later Pavlova) at the turn of the 1830s ("V bylye dni ot muzy pesnopenij ..." and "Na prazdnik vaš prines ja dva priveta ..."). They are written according to the traditional scheme of AbAbAbAbCCdEdE in lines of iambic pentameters. Then there are two poems in iambic tetrameters whose stanzaic pattern may best be described as symmetrical. Thus, "Mne očen' žal', čto ja segodnja ...", one of the "Zapiski A. S. Dirinoj" (1825), consists of quatrains rhyming in the following sequence − embracing, crossed, crossed, embracing. And the second poem to Katen'ka

Moier, "Blagoslovenny te mgnoven'ja ..." (1827), has 4 quatrains of crossed rhyme and then 4 of embracing rhyme for a total of 32 lines. Finally, Jazykov's longest such poem, "Vodopad" (1830), in trochaic tetrameters, has an opening section that is restated at the end of the poem after 4 sets of crossed-rhyming quatrains. This 'frame' around the central section of the poem is all the more striking for being a 7-line unit with the rhyme scheme of AbbbAAb. Both Puškin and Lermontov appear to have hardly any symmetrically organized poems more than 14 lines long.

All the other long-line stanzas are of the repeating variety. Most of the poems they are employed with were written in 1831, that is, precisely at the time that Jazykov was making his boldest attempts at overcoming his popular image as the 'student poet'. These are experimental works which in most cases fail because it is almost impossible to maintain in such extended compositional forms any sense of coherence either within individual stanzas or in each poem as a whole. Jazykov has one poem in trochaic tetrameters with a 13-line stanza rhyming AbAbAcDDcEfEf, "Vami nekogda plenennyj ..." (1835), and 4 in 16-line units. They are his dactylic tetrameter song of 1822, "Moja rodina", rhyming according to the complex scheme of aBBaCaaCaDDeFeeF; the iambic tetrameter ode of 1830, "Na smert' njani A. S. Puškina", rhyming alternately in double crossed and double embracing quatrains – AbAbCdCdEffEgHHg; the 1831 poem "Vospominanie ob A. A. Voejkovoj", a work in iambic pentameters which rhymes AbAbCdCdEfEfGhhG; and "Poètu", a work of the same year, which rhymes AbAbCddCEfEfGhGh on a base of iambic pentameters for the first through sixth and ninth through fourteenth lines and with iambic tetrameters for the other lines. There is one poem in 17-line units and trochaic tetrameters, "Kubok" (1831), whose rhyme pattern is basically crossed, with one extra line inserted in the third quatrain (AbAbCdCdEfEEfGhGh), and then there are two poems with 18-line stanzas. One of these is in iambic tetrameters with the pattern of 3 crossed quatrains, and 1 embracing one with a couplet interspersed after line 8 ("Radušno rabstvuet poètu ...", 1831), while the other, the trochaic tetrameter poem "Kon' " (also 1831), represents a slight variation on the same stanzaic construction. Lastly, Jazykov has one poem in iambic tetrameters which consists of stanzas each 22 lines in length. This is "Au!" (likewise 1831), a work whose rhyme pattern is made up of a couplet followed by quatrains of embracing and crossed rhyme, as follows – AAbCCbDeDeFggF-hIIhJkJk. Such long repeating stanzas appear not to have been common before the time of Nekrasov, who has compositional units up to 24 lines long;[12] however, the rhyme patterns of Nekrasov's long-line stanzas are far less intricate than Jazykov's.

While both Puškin and Lermontov show no clear pattern of preferences in

the course of their creative development for stanzaic over non-stanzaic compositions,[13] this is one formal characteristic of Jazykov's poetry that is abundantly
clear, since in his case there is a steady increase in frequency as he advanced to
maturity of stanzaic versus non-stanzaic forms. Jazykov had begun verse writing
in 1818 or 1819, but only 60 from among the 190 poems he wrote before
leaving Dorpat at the end of his student life in spring 1829 are organized into
stanzaic forms; of this number no less than 16 come from the 2 cycles of student
songs he wrote in 1823 and early 1829. By contrast, as many as 105 of the 120
poems he wrote from the beginning of 1831 and 72 of the 81 from 1834 are
stanzaic. From this later period (1831-46) there are no song cycles; it is only his
small "Slavophile" cycle of verse letters from 1844-45 that is stanzaically as well
as thematically marked.[14] Such a decisive pattern of evolution must have been
accompanied by changes in other aspects of Jazykov's verse form, or so one
might expect. Was this shift in favor of stanzaic compositions perhaps a response
to or even a consequence of changes in other major formal features of his
poetry?

In an effort to reach at least a tentative answer to this question a study was
undertaken of the clausulae of all 12,052 lines of poetry. The analysis demonstrated that except for a negligible quantity of inexact rhymes Jazykov employed only two categories of rhyme besides 'rimes suffisantes': the correspondence in feminine clausulae of the final j-glide with a zero ending,[15] and rich
rhyme. So as to trace possible changes in the distribution of these rhyme
categories the verse material was divided into units of 100 lines each. The results
indicated that for every 100 lines the frequency of the -j:∅ correspondence lies
between 1.7 and 3.8; for rich rhymes it lies between 3.3 and 5.7. There are
isolated poems in which rich rhymes are more common than in others or in
which the -j:∅ correspondence is more frequent than are rich rhymes, yet no
pattern of distribution could be traced. Thus, it would not be possible to use
rhyming conventions as a criterion for establishing the date of any poems by
Jazykov. Figures for these rhyme types in the work of other poets of Jazykov's
time are scant, but the point has been made more than once that while Puškin
used the -j:∅ correspondence continually up to 1820 he turned to it very
erratically in later years.[16]

In an analysis of the importance of rhyme for Jazykov's stanzaic practice,
one further factor must be considered, namely the manner in which the rhyme
sets occur. While some of his contemporaries often used long rhyme sets, in
particular Puškin,[17] Jazykov rarely has complexes of more than 3 rhymes, and
none of more than 5. Rhyme triplets are a characteristic feature of his non-
stanzaic verse, where they are the principal means of breaking up what might
otherwise be regular stanzaic patterns; consequently, the total number of lines in

such poems is often a prime number.[18] Rhyme triplets are at the same time less than half as frequent in his stanzaic verse. They are a standard component of his odd-line stanzas, but are met with rather seldom in the others. Understandably, the rhyme triplets occur in larger clusters in the stanzaic than in the non-stanzaic poetry: whereas their distribution in the stanzaic works averages out at just over 5 per poem, in the non-stanzaic works it is a little over 3 per poem.[19] Sets of 4 rhymes are almost as common in Jazykov's stanzaic as in his non-stanzaic verse (20 as against 21 examples), and it is only with sets of 5 that the stanzaic forms are ahead (8 versus 3 examples).

In sum, the only rhyming factor which parallels — and even then only marginally — the transition from non-stanzaic to stanzaic compositions is the slight decline in frequency of rhyme triplets in favor of rhyme pairs. If further and more cogent reasons for this transition are to be identified, they must be sought in the first place in other formal features, and especially in changes in Jazykov's metrical preferences.

Like the analysis of Jazykov's stanzaic practice, an analysis of the meters he employed in both his stanzaic and his non-stanzaic poetry provides solid evidence for a shift in his works beginning in the early 1830s in the direction of greater formal consciousness and compositional precision. The basic trend is for the iambic tetrameter to dominate in his early works, which are primarily non-stanzaic, and for other kinds of iambic meters and more especially for trochees and the ternary meters to become more prominent in his mature compositions, almost all of which are stanzaic. Thus, of the 190 poems written by spring 1829, as many as 134 were composed in iambic tetrameters. As already noted, 60 of the 190 are stanzaic compositions; 39 of these were written in iambic tetrameters. By contrast, only 37 of Jazykov's last 120 poems (from the beginning of 1831) are in this meter, 30 of them being stanzaic compositions. Further, only 13 of all the non-iambic poems he ever wrote are also non-stanzaic,[20] while 43 are set in stanzaic forms. Along with these tendencies, the complex iambic meters enjoy considerable currency in Jazykov's later period: until spring 1829 he wrote a number of poems in these meters which are non-stanzaic but only 2 which are stanzaic. In the remaining years of his life he wrote a further 17, and they are used exclusively in stanzaic compositions — in metrical patterns such as alternating 4- and 6-foot lines and 6- and 4-foot lines, quatrains of the 4446, 5554, 6444, and 6664 varieties, and so on. Finally, the use of iambic tetrameters becomes less frequent in proportion to the length of stanzas: of the 26 poems in stanzas ranging from 5 through 8 lines in length, 13 are in iambic tetrameters, but only 3 of the 13 in 9- through 14-line stanzas are in this meter.

The evidence presented in this paper suggests strongly that there are parallel and even consistent developments in Jazykov's stanzaic practice and metrical preferences as he matured. In his post-student period, he diversified his metrical repertoire markedly by writing far fewer iambic tetrameter poems, and wrote at the same time almost exclusively in stanzaic forms. The best single indicator of these two points is that all the poems Jazykov wrote in the complex iambic meters after he left Dorpat are also stanzaic compositions. If a correlation on the formal level is to be sought, then, it is of the stanzaic forms with metrical components rather than with rhymes and rhyming trends. Ostensibly a correlation can be argued regarding Jazykov's shift in favor of stricter verse forms and changes in his poetic themes as he outgrew his student phase. However, the thematic implications of the poet's far greater formal awareness in his mature years are a subject that must await discussion in a further paper.[21]

University of Auckland

NOTES

[1] These are the major contributions. For bibliographical details and for a fuller listing of publications in the area of stanzaic forms, see in particular G. S. Smith, "A Bibliography of Soviet Publications on Russian Versification since 1958", *Russian Literature Triquarterly*, No. 6 (1973), 679-94; and Ian K. Lilly and Barry P. Scherr, "Russian Verse Theory Since 1960: A Bibliography and Commentary", *International Journal of Slavic Linguistics and Poetics*, XXII (1976), 75-116.

[2] K. K. Buxmejer, ed., N. M. Jazykov, *Polnoe sobranie stixotvorenij*, Biblioteka poèta, bol'šaja serija, 2nd ed. (Leningrad: Sovetskij pisatel', 1964), 55-415.

[3] M. K. Azadovskij, ed., N. M. Jazykov, *Polnoe sobranie stixotvorenij* (Moscow-Leningrad: Academia, 1934).

[4] M. K. Azadovskij, ed., N. M. Jazykov, *Sobranie stixotvorenij*, Biblioteka poèta, bol'šaja serija, 1st ed. (Leningrad: Sovetskij pisatel', 1948).

[5] Jazykov, *Sobranie stixotvorenij*, 280-82.

[6] The ten poems are "Platonizm" (probably 1823), "N. D. Kiselevu k novomu, 1824 godu", the romance "Ty vidiš' li barin, vdali dereva? ..." (1824), the elegies "Skaži: kogda ...", "Ax, kak mila ...", "Čto slyšu ja? ...", and "Zvonjat k obedni ...", and the romances "Čto delal s Evoju Adam ..." and "Začem izorvannyj sertuk ..." (all 1823-25), and the epigram of 1831, "Vinovnyj pred sudom parnasskogo zakona ...".

[7] On the determinants of a stanza, see in particular V. E. Xolševnikov, *Osnovy stixovedenija: Russkoe stixosloženie*, 2nd ed. (Leningrad: Izd-vo LGU, 1972), 103-12.

[8] *Stixotvorenija N. Jazykova* (Petersburg: V tipografii vdovy N. Pljušar s synom, 1833).

[9] The most detailed system of stanzaic notation published so far is undoubtedly that of J. Põldmäe, "O ritmiko-kompozicionnoj transkripcii rifmy pri opisanii strofiki", Σημειωτική: *Materialy Vsesojuznogo simpoziuma po vtpričnym modelirujuščim sistemam*, I (5) (1974), 176-80. Except for the use of the starred forms, the notation used in this paper follows that of Xolševnikov, *Osnovy stixovedenija*, where small letters represent masculine rhymes, capitals feminine, and capitals with a prime (´) dactylic rhymes (p. 106, note 1). Non-rhyming clausulae are represented by the letter x.

10 See B. V. Tomaševskij, "Strofika Puškina", *Puškin: Issledovanija i materialy*, II (1958), 49-184, passim.

11 See Tomaševskij, "Strofika Puškina", passim; and K. D. Višnevskij, "Strofika Lermontova", *Učenye zapiski Penzenskogo gos. ped. instituta, Serija filologičeskaja*, vyp. XIV (1965), 3-131, passim.

12 M. A. Pejsaxovič, "Strofika Nekrasova", *Nekrasovskij sbornik*, V (1973), 202-32, table 4 (p. 211).

13 Tomaševskij, "Strofika Puškina", 109-11; and Višnevskij, "Strofika Lermontova", 87-90.

14 For a general study of this cycle, see my article, "N. M. Iazykov as a Slavophile Poet", *Slavic Review*, 31 (1972), No. 4, 797-804.

15 On the -j:∅ correspondence, see above all Roman Jakobson, "K lingvističeskomu analizu russkoj rifmy", in his *Studies in Russian Philology*, Michigan Slavic Materials, No. 1 (Ann Arbor, Mich.: Dept. of Slavic Languages and Literatures, Univ. of Michigan, n.d.), 10-11.

16 Tomaševskij, *Russkoe stixosloženie: Metrika*, Voprosy poètiki, vyp. II (Petrograd: Academia, 1923), 105; V. M. Žirmunskij, *Rifma, ee istorija i teorija*, Voprosy poètiki, vyp. III (Petrograd: Academia, 1923), 136-37; and D. S. Samojlov, *Kniga o russkoj rifme* (Moscow: Izd-vo Xudožestvennaja literatura, 1973), 108-11. The occurrence of this as of other rhyme types in Puškin's works can now be readily identified in J. Thomas Shaw, *Pushkin's Rhymes: A Dictionary* (Madison, Wisc.: Univ. of Wisconsin Press, 1974).

17 See Shaw, *Pushkin's Rhymes*, xx-xxxi; and Shaw, "Large Rhyme Sets and Puškin's Poetry", *Slavic and East European Journal*, 18 (1974), No. 3, 231-51.

18 This aspect of Jazykov's non-stanzaic verse was alluded to by Azadovskij, in Jazykov, *Sobranie stixotvorenij*, xxxv. Unfortunately, he failed to note that non-stanzaic compositions are typical only of the early Jazykov.

19 By my count, 122 triplets occur in 24 stanzaic poems and 276 occur in 89 non-stanzaic poems.

20 This figure excludes Jazykov's three polymetrical poems, all of which must be classed as non-stanzaic once they are viewed as single entities. These poems are "Cuvstvitel'noe putešestvie v Revel' " and "Uslad" (both 1823), and "Mečta" (1824).

21 This discussion can be found in my doctoral dissertation, "The Lyric Poetry of N. M. Jazykov: A Periodization Using Objective Criteria" (University of Washington, 1977). That study includes a more detailed and typologically more sophisticated analysis of the stanzaic forms occurring in Jazykov's poetry (Chapter I, 25-28).

В ЗАЩИТУ РАЗНОУДАРНОЙ РИФМЫ (ИНФОРМАТИВНЫЙ ОБЗОР)

В. Ф. МАРКОВ

Ударение в рифмующих словах может
и не совпадать.

Якобсон

I. К ПРОБЛЕМЕ

Егда во свѣтѣ мысленнаго со́лнца
крилы си царства покрываше конца́
(Симеон Полоцкий.)
Все мужчины подлецы́,
Мы с тобой краса́вицы
(частушка)
Забыли мы, что искони́
Проржали вещие ко́ни
(Хлебников)

Приведенные примеры наглядно показывают, что проблема разноударной рифмы (в дальнейшем р.р.) встает перед исследователем
русского стиха, по меньшей мере, трижды.

Существовала ли реально р.р. у силлабиков, пока трудно сказать
(скорее всего, нет).[1] В частушках рифмовка мужских и 'ложных дактилических' клаузул,[2] повидимому, целиком музыкального происхождения[3]
и идет от частого протяжения в напеве в народных песенных жанрах не
только третьего от конца (иктового) слога, но и последнего (клаузуль-
ного). Интерес к р.р. у поэтов русского авангарда XX в. связан с их
ориентацией на сдвиг, однако общая картина отличается некоторой
сложностью (о чем ниже) и не позволяет сформулировать определения,
которое подходило бы ко всем разновидностям такой рифмы.[4]

В поисках новой, необычной рифмы поэты XX в. наткнулись на три
невозделанных поля — неравносложия, так называемого 'диссонанса'
(или 'консонанса') и разноударности. Рифмы этих трех родов могли
быть простые и составные, могли и смешиваться. Слово "пистоле́т",

например, может неравносложно рифмоваться со "столе́тия", диссонансно с "постула́т" и разноударно со "сто́лик", тогда как рифмуясь с "Песталóцци" оно дает и неравносложность и диссонанс, со "сто́ит ли" — разноударность и неравносложность, а с "по Ста́лину" — разноударность, диссонанс и неравносложность.

Нельзя сказать, чтобы все эти ранее почти не употреблявшиеся рифмы вошли в прочный обиход русского стиха, но их нельзя и сбросить со счетов как редкости.[5] Каждая из них имеет свою историю, оставила в поэзии след и до сих пор встречается. Были поэты, строившие свой стих на одной из этих рифм: Маяковский, в значительной степени, на неравносложной, поздний Шершеневич исключительно на диссонансе, а Мариенгоф, в основном, на разноударной.

История исследования р.р. необъемиста, малоинтересна и не богата ни фактами, ни анализом, хотя в трех имеющихся книгах о рифме (Жирмунского, Штокмара и Самойлова) она не игнорируется,[6] и, может быть, было бы преувеличением назвать ее падчерицей стиховедов. Однако у Жирмунского, по существу, все сводится к вписке в каталог: был, дескать, и такой род рифмы — не совсем ясный уродец (если не считать составной, которую тоже еще рано изучать). Бедный Штокмар явно страдает от присутствия противуприродных р.р. у долженствующего быть безупречным Маяковского: они торчат там и сям из его стихов, как занозы, и никак не позволяют заявить о себе, что это "не абстрактная 'словесная живопись', а идейно направленное мастерство великого пролетарского поэта".[7] Недавний исследователь Самойлов уже относится к р.р. с симпатией, приводит много (не всегда убедительных) примеров из малых фольклорных жанров, но в целом не так уж отличается от Жирмунского, лишь констатируя, что р.р. встречается у современных поэтов, а особенно в фольклоре.

Еще более пестрое зрелище получается, если заглянуть в статьи о рифме или в книги о поэтике. Одни авторы р.р. не замечают,[8] другие замечают лишь ее редкостные разновидности,[9] третьи путают ее с чем-то другим,[10] четвертые чуть ли не отрицают ее существование.[11]

Прежде всего, нельзя все р.р. валить в кучу. Среди них есть различные по природе и происхождению. Под крышей разноударности уживаются разные явления, хотя и есть единичные рифмы, годящиеся и в ту и в другую категорию.[12]

Может быть, в первую очередь надо обратиться к обширной группе р.р., где ударность ясно рифмуется с неударностью (*сжима́ть* : *коллекциони́ровать*). Обыкновенно первое рифмующее слово образует мужскую клаузулу, а второе дактилическую, однако (см. частушечный пример в самом начале доклада) дактилическая клаузула ложная: на самом деле это замаскированная мужская, где нет ударения на последнем, решающем икте. Обратные случаи (сперва ложная дактилическая, потом мужская) редки (чаще других так рифмует Сельвинский, но встречается это и у Маяковского, Есенина, Тихонова и Мариенгофа). Такие рифмы иногда называют неударными,[13] но можно называть и недоударными или хромыми. Есть возможность, хотя и слабая, что они пришли в русский стих от немцев (в XIX в. их нет, но есть такие клаузулы в белом пятистопном ямбе, явная имитация стиха немецкой и английской драмы, особенно Шиллера).[14] Хромые рифмы заметно грамматичны. Часто рифмуются одинаковые грамматические формы, особенно глагольные:

ручейки́ : вса́дники   повы́звездит : возвести́т
темно́ : действи́тельно   за́втракай : отвыка́й
бытия́ : бессме́ртия   встава́ть : короле́вствовать
          вы́плакать : лака́ть

или же разные грамматические окончания обыгрываются и сопоставляются:

не индеве́й : обще́ственней
моя́ : неосуществлённая
вся : соверше́нствуйся
в ра́дости : подрасти́
отчего́ : рабо́чего
простоты́ : ша́хматы.

Однако суть этой рифмы в неосуществленном икте, именно этим она 'шокирует' русского читателя. На эвфоническое качество при этом редко обращается внимание, и поэтому хромые рифмы чаще малоинтересны.

Если р.р. I группы хромали на одну ногу, то во II-ой они хромают на обе. Именно эти рифмы разноударны в полном смысле. Как правило, они омографы или омографоиды, в которых ударения, как правило, падают на соседствующие слоги (чего никогда не бывает в рифмах первой группы),[15] так что достаточно мысленно подвинуть акцент на слог, чтобы получилась рифма-омоним традиционного типа (*Му́ра : мура́*). Если считать, что в первом слове ударение падает на икт, то на втором оно попадает в клаузулу; если наоборот, все равно ударение оказывается на слабом времени и приходит преждевременно. В результате рифмы этой группы 'не звучат'[16] и должны компенсировать звуковое неблагополучие визуальностью-омографичностью (в этом смысле, р.р. такого рода больше других заслуживают название 'глазных'):[17]

а) и ва́ми : и́вами	б) вы́глянет : гля́нец
зареву́ : за́реву	по́езд : пое́сть
о́куни : окуни́	вод : о́вод
пого́да : по года́	из ти́ны : и́стины
ве́дьмы : ведь мы́	ве́щи : в щи
в овсе́ : во́все	по́хоти : погоди́
по́длиннее : подлинне́е	кота́ : ико́та
	хо́лода : коло́да

Конечно, в этой группе достаточно и неомографических рифм (*монастырь : пла́стырь, шары́ : бульва́ры, цвета́х : за́пах, ти́хо : э́тих, челе́ : пу́ле, пусто́го : Шу́стова, провели́ : нове́лл, лёг : по́лог, писк : ро́спись*).

Рифмы второй группы можно было бы назвать 'классическими', если б такое название не стояло в конфликте с их крайней авангардностью. Р.р. этого типа — дитя футуризма и основана на принципе сдвига. Икт здесь разрушен,[18] вывихнут, и два рифмующих слова, наподобие качелей, взмывают то одним, то другим концом вверх, но никогда не вместе, как полагалось бы в порядочной рифме.

Нужно ли затрагивать в этом обзоре рифму составную? Жирмунский не только ответил бы на вопрос утвердительно, но и прибавил бы, что это-то и есть настоящая область разноударности. В своей книге он подробно прослеживает постепенное "утяжеление второго элемента"[19] в составной рифме XIX-начала XX в. от пушкинского *где́ вы : де́вы* до брюсовского *кла́дбище : кла́д ищи́*. Последнюю рифму легко приписать Маяковскому, занимающему, как известно, в истории составной рифмы центральное место. Не он начал,[20] но он 'канонизовал' включение в заударную часть рифмы полноударных слов, что́ не только на первых порах, но и совсем недавно приводило в неудобство даже людей искушенных.[21]

В контексте р.р. нужно прежде всего сказать, что составная[22] принципиально отлична от двух других типов: ее разноударность разыгрывается исключительно в клаузуле (и, в этом смысле, можно видеть близость к народному стиху). Клаузульная ударность может быть трех основных родов:[23]

I при женском окончании
     пря́ность : декабря́ на́ст
II при дактилическом окончании
     а) пря́ности : царя́ насти́г
     б) пря́ности : даря́ На́сте.

IIа наиболее частая разновидность, и ее можно считать р.р. в том смысле, в каком мы считали р.р. хромую. Однако, при всем отличии от традиционной составной со слабой ударностью в клаузуле (типа *Мамáя : кумá я*), IIа самая гладкая, 'симметричная' из разноударных. К ней принадлежит большинство разноударных составных у всех поэтов и, конечно, у таких виртуозов составной, как Маяковский (*кáторги : рекá торгú*) и Сельвинский (*верхáм ствол : хáмство*).[24] Об этой разновидности можно написать книгу. Наиболее редка IIб, где не только получается 'спондей' (как и в I), но и ударение приходится на слабый слог клаузулы при наличии более сильного следующего:[25]

> Рýсь лúки : сýслики (Хлебников)
> тéл сáми : рéльсами (Хлебников)
> глáз, тóчкой : лáсточкой (Маяковский)

II. К ИСТОРИИ

История р.р. развертывается в двадцатом веке.[26] Если не считать брюсовских 'народно-эпических' *лучú : Мономáховичи* и *клич : Ольгович* (обе 1899 г.) и одной пары у Блока (*тóчки : фóрточки* 1904 г.), то эту историю следует начинать с Хлебникова. Н. Харджиев приводит в числе других образчиков 'новой рифмы' семь примеров.[27] Самые ранние можно датировать 1908 г. В более позднем стихотворении (напечатанном в *Дохлой луне* 1913 г.) р.р. даже преподносится Хлебниковым с 'обнажением приема':

> Я нахожу, что очаровательная погода,
> И я прошу милую ручку
> Изящно переставить ударение,
> Чтобы было так: смерть с кузовком идет по годá.

К списку Харджиева можно прибавить *Искáндров : ндрав, хóлод : Рогволод,*[28] *úвы : и вы, вод : óвод, стихóм : гóродом, исконú : кóни, Кáлкою : алкáю : пáлкою.* Составные с сильным ударением в заударной части тоже были пущены в обиход Хлебниковым и приблизительно в то же время, т.е., около 1908 г. (*зéлень : грозé лéнь*), т.е., примерно за четыре года до Маяковского. Тогда же Хлебников начинает экспериментировать с более необычными видами разноударности: *рáк, óвен : рáковина, знáменьи : росáм úней,*[29] *выложен, щú нá! : жéнщина, рáз спрячется : рáспря — чý!*[30] Сам Хлебников продолжал пользоваться р.р. до конца жизни, и от него ее усвоили многие поэты русского футуризма и — шире

— авангарда. Среди исключений[31] Асеев (но и он пользуется составною I — *врагá стúх : Гáстев, лéсть сплéсть : éсли*) и Бобров (пропагандист ассонанса). Штокмар, как мы уже видели, насчитывает у Маяковского 'несколько десятков' р.р. (см. прим. 6), но не перечисляет все.[32] У Каменского р.р. редка (*нажúвам : живы́м*) и чаще — первого, хромого типа (*пикнúк : пáмятник, колоколá : Куóккала*). У Давида Бурлюка она появляется в американский период и чаще всего бывает второго типа, но без сильной тенденции к омографу (*страдáний : прúстани, провелú : новéлл, котá : икóта, океáн : угáдан, цветáх : зáпах, луч : всеóбуч, в овсé : вóвсе, хóлода : колóда, тúке : эрóтике*). У Крученых р.р. нечаста (*пóезд : поéсть, жéмчуг : глух, монасты́рь : плáстырь, вы́глянет : гля́нец*).[33] Неудивительно найти р.р. у временных подражателей Хлебникова или у его посмертных поклонников. К первым относится Тихонов, у которого в 'хлебниковской' поэме "Шахматы" находим *простоты́ : шáхматы, зáвтракай : отвыкáй, вставáть : королéвствовать, рты : пáрты : сáрты, пýли и ещё: жилúща* (большинство из них однако не хлебниковского типа, а скорее предвосхищают Вознесенского); ко вторым — Слуцкий (*óбразов : образóв*). Встречаются р.р. у зарубежных примитивистов, вроде Гингера (*даю́щих : вéрующих*). Есть они у курьезного стихоплета Золотухина, стоявшего в 1915-1916 гг. близко к футуристам (*дóчку : звёздочку, слёз тóчку : звёздочку, зóбу дья́вола : забýдь. Я волá, Травиáт : травé я́д*). У Сельвинского р.р. редка, но подчас интересна, как, например, *стороны́ : стóроны* в *Пуштóрге*, где разноударность (омографическая) выступает в грамматической функции. С конструктивизмом был связан и Ушаков, который рифмовал разноударно, по крайней мере, в течение трех десятилетий (*óкуни : окунú, привелú : мéбели, рекú : пáпоротники, крыльцá : укротúтельница, крыльцá : посетúтельница, моя́ : неувядáемая*).[34] В наши дни к р.р. обратился в последних книгах Вознесенский, у которого заметный перевес имеют хромые рифмы:

ТЗвук	бытия́ : бессмéртия
	вся : совершéнствуйся
Взгляд	скрымтымты́м : вы́полним
	книг : пáмятник
	не индевéй : общéственней
	сжимáть : коллекционúровать
	вращáть : вырáщивать

но есть и *вóды : алаверды́* и *раструбы : я́стреб*.

Символистов лишь с натяжкой можно считать предшественниками футуристов в р.р. (см. выше примеры из Брюсова, Блока и Волошина). Но можно предполагать обратное влияние. Мне известны четыре последовательно разноударных стихотворения символистов (чего нет ни у каких других поэтов), причем все четыре поздние в поэзии каждого. Усилие строить стихотворение от начала до конца на р.р. делает все четыре примера уникальными. Однако на поверку эти эффектные, на первый взгляд, опыты оказываются не такими радикальными, как, видимо, казалось авторам. Самое раннее из них — "Рыбарь" Вячеслава Иванова в *Нежной тайне*, где все стихи 1912 г.[35] Рифмы в нем (*бéрегу : берегý, отчáлена : от челнá*) могут считаться хромыми, но с нехарактерной для этого класса омографичностью, которая и маскирует тот факт, что это, собственно, белые стихи, как это ни парадоксально звучит, и *бéрегу* позиционно (по клаузуле) должно бы рифмоваться с *нéводах* (где ассонанс случаен), а не с *берегý*.[36] Стихотворение Андрея Белого "'Я' и 'ты'" (*Звезда*),[37] датированное 1918 г., все построено на хромых рифмах (которые очень хорошо ложатся в традиционные двудольные размеры).[38] Наконец у Брюсова есть два более ранних[39] (чем у Белого) стихотворения с р.р. в *Опытах* (1918). В одном, "Восторг женщины", рифмы опять-таки хромые, но, как у Иванова, с сильной тенденцией к омографии и даже тавтологии.[40] Более интересно другое (в книге идущее первым), "Закатный театр",[41] рифмы которого Брюсов называет 'укороченными' и которое начинается так:

> В небе — яркость повечерия:
> Реют птиц волшебных перья,
> Гривы странного зверья ...,

т.е., первые две строки рифмуются неравносложно, но третья находится к первым двум в разноударной ситуации.

III. "ВЕЛИКОЛЕПНЫЙ МАРИЕНГОФ"

Положа руку на сердце, р.р. было бы нелегко защищать от упреков в редкости и в том, что она лишь маловажное примечание к русской поэтике, если бы не Анатолий Борисович Мариенгоф (1897-1962). Играет роль она и в практике русского имажинизма в целом. Выше, перечисляя футуристов и близких к ним поэтов, я намеренно не упомянул такого завзятого рифмача как Вадим Шершеневич. В его второй футуристической книге стихов *Экстравагантные флаконы* (1913) можно найти стихотворение ("Solo"), датированное мартом 1913 г. (т.е., после хлебниковских открытий, но до Маяковского), где в нечетных строках последовательно рифмуются разноударные *ме́льниц* : *пе́пельниц, пасте́ли* : *Мефисто́фелю, но́вой* : *сафья́новой, карти́ну* : *и́стину*. В остальных стихах книги р.р. нет, хотя Шершеневич и разрабатывает в них чуть ли не все другие возможности неточной и необычной рифмовки. Большого интереса к этой рифме он не проявлял и впоследствии, хотя в его главном сборнике *Автомобилья поступь* (1916) есть *топора́ми* : *уда́рами, поко́рные* : *чо́порные, небе́сная* : *вы́лез, но я́, сно́ва ла́ком* : *про́волокам и вверх* : *вы́сверк*, а позже, в имажинистский период, в *Лошадь как лошадь* (1920) можно найти *во́здух* : *у́хо* и *заусе́ницы* : *гу́сеницы*, а в *Кооперативах веселья* (1921) найдем *моряки́* : *вся́кие, фа́та* : *фата́* и *тепла́* : *пе́пла* (все в поэме "Амбары памяти"). Еще позже, с 1921 г., Шершеневич становится исключительно поэтом рифмы-диссонанс (или 'консонанс', как ее иногда называют).

В трактате *2 × 2 = 5* (1920) Шершеневич почти не интересуется рифмой, но среди его примечаний к его же переводу *Notes sur la technique poétique* Дюамеля и Вильдрака[42] находим полемику с Бобровым в защиту рифмы. Шершеневич настаивает на необходимости рифмы, но признается, что она переживает "какую-то очень сложную и трудную эволюцию". "В этом направлении", продолжает он, "сейчас очень много работает имажинист А. Мариенгоф, трудолюбиво разрабатывающий рифмы, основанные на переходных ударениях. Вот его рифмовка: *кувшины* : *матершина, каторгу* : *берегут, та* : *рассвета, полосовал* : *волосы, толп* : *хлопал*".[43]

В следующем году Иван Грузинов в трактате *Имажинизма основное* (стр. 7) писал: "Особым покровительством имажинистов пользовались до сих пор рифмы составные и обратные, рифмы и ассонансы на разноударные слова", а Шершеневич в одной из своих лучших критических книг, *Кому я жму руку* (стр. 16; книга писалась, повидимому, во второй половине 1921 г.), обращаясь к Мариенгофу, говорил: "К этой же аритмичности тебя неизбежно влечет твоя манера рифмовки,[44] построенная теперь всегда на разноударниках … Даже … /Есенин/ и тот перешел постепенно от ассонансов и консонансов к разноударникам[45] … Твой рифмический путь лучше других уже тем, что ты первый проложил его". Как мы видели, проложен путь был Хлебниковым больше, чем за десять лет до Мариенгофа. Это однако не снимает заслуг имажиниста — забытого, но значительного и оригинального поэта, в стихах которого р.р. больше, чем у всех других русских поэтов вместе взятых. Изобретательность его в этой области тоже немалая. Его р.р. нельзя сбросить со счетов как "эксперимент и только",[46] на ней стоит прочно почти вся его поэзия.[47]

Мариенгоф начал пользоваться р.р. в 1917 г. (стих. "Дикое кочевье", *кочевы́е* : *Пугачёва*, *ка́док* : *клок*). В первой его книге стихов *Витрина сердца* (1918) их нет.[48] В стихах о революции, написанных в 1917-1919 гг. и напечатанных в альманахах *Явь* и первая *Конница бурь*, можно также найти *вы́греб* : *в игре́*, *рвы* : *гри́вы*, *отца́* : *захлебнётся*, *лафа́* : *Голиа́фа*. По-настоящему р.р. входят в его стихотворческий обиход в 'лирических поэмах' 1919-1921 гг.,[49] причем в 1919 г. их число еще сравнительно невелико, и есть строфы, где они вовсе не появляются. В 1920 г. это число возрастает, и в некоторых поэмах имеются строфы, в которых 3/4 рифм разноударны (остальные рифмы Мариенгофа обычно ассонансы или неравносложные). 1921 год — кульминация, и хотя в некоторых поэмах количество рр. как будто убывает, но зато в трагедии *Заговор дураков* (закончена в августе 1921 г.) бушует настоящая оргия разноударности, и после этого Мариенгоф вроде как выдыхается. В 1922 г. р.р. уже редкость, а в 1923 г. они исчезают из мариенгофовских стихов.

Р.р. Мариенгофа требует более тщательного изучения. Все установленные нами до сих пор типы, конечно, можно найти в его стихах, но они далеко не составляют костяка его рифменной системы, которая усложнена не столько смешанным характером рифм (это случалось и у других поэтов) сколько разной степенью рифмабельности. Подчас Мариенгоф едва касается рифменной клавиши и строит созвучие на минимальных основаниях (*и́бо* : *лба*). Именно поэтому в его системе незарифмованные строки перестают быть исключениями, белыми воронами, а становятся лишь следующим (и последним) шагом к рифменной минимальности. На другом же конце, в максимальности, царит неслыханное разнообразие, в котором еще предстоит разбираться. Если раньше у нас из р.р. всегда 'получалась' обычная рифма, когда мы в уме передвигали ударение на соседний слог (а иногда, особенно при хромой рифме, и через слог), то с Мариенгофом такой метод не помогает. Могут мешать диссонирующие и разъединяющие гласные (*ковры́* : *января́*, *заве́те* : *животе́*, *лу́жи* : *возложу́*, *ковша́* : *взалка́вши*, *Ми́них* : *мне*) или слоговая (и иная) метатеза (*проро́йте же* : *обвяжи́те*). Минимальные рифмы, да еще сдвинутые, конечно, иногда 'не звучат', и при этом Мариенгоф не облегчает положения тем, что расставляет их необычно далеко друг от друга (иногда рифму находишь только на следующей странице).[50] В результате восприятие стиха Мариенгофа становится похожим на разглядывание (расслушивание) загадочной картинки: где рифма? рифма ли это?[51] И частенько, будучи готовым к крайностям, не замечаешь, что две соседствующие строки рифмуют простым, традиционным способом. Чтение Мариенгофа часто становится спортом, охотой за рифмами, которая и увлекает и изматывает, и, пожалуй, нет лучшего упражнения для студентов на розыск рифм. Вот пример — начало поэмы "Друзья":

Улица дохнула вином
И болью.
Чумная или пьяная?
По ней или она шатается?

Девушка, кому несешь в дар
Татарские
Кувшины
Узких грудей?

Чьи
Плечи-фонтаны
Белые струи
Рук
На них прольют?

Кос золотая цепь,
А голова словно мертвый жемчуг.

Писал: не склоню над женщиной мудрого лба.
И вдруг — через ритмические ухабы
По чорному тракту строк
Любовь мчу.

Разве угадаешь?
Дни
Как песок
(Так, кажется, говорил Заратустра).

Город, я верный посох
В твоей асфальтовой ладони.

Р.р. в сочетании с широко понимаемым верлибром, изощренной строфикой и сложной метафорикой[52] делают из поэзии Мариенгофа уникальное явление. Это поэзия в высшей степени динамическая, крайне свободная и неуловимая, где признаки и черты колеблются, на глазах распадаются, исчезают, вновь утверждаются, чтобы опять на глазах сдвинуться и исказиться.

Если Хлебников изготовил р.р. в своей поэтической реторте, а Маяковский пользовался ею как одной из красок, то Мариенгоф строил из нее причудливые здания с меняющимися очертаниями — и в каком-то смысле лучше и нагляднее своих 'врагов'-футуристов осуществил их идею сдвига на практике.

Моей целью было обратить внимание на один как будто малозначительный род рифмы и дать некоторый материал, но вовсе не 'решить проблему'. Картина сложная и требует дальнейшего изучения. Во всяком случае, р.р. и интереснее и, в некоторых случаях, важнее, чем принято думать.

University of California, Los Angeles

ПРИМЕЧАНИЯ

[1] Этот вопрос был задет в разыгравшейся недавно между А. М. Панченко и П. Н. Берковым полемике о способе произношения силлабических стихов (см. Академия Наук СССР, *Теория стиха*, Ленинград, 1968, особенно страницы 285, 286, 289, 292; 304, 310), в которой косвенно — а подчас и посмертно — приняли участие Б. Е. Холшевников (там же, 53-55), И. П. Еремин и Б. В. Томашевский. Панченко находит р.р. (причем, как и другие, часто берет этот термин в кавычки) не только в украинской и русской виршевой поэзии конца XVI-начала XVII в. (а также в 'досиллабических стихах'), но и у Симеона. Берков считает, что ударение в одном из рифмующих разноударных слов передвигалось, так чтобы получалось женское окончание. Впрочем, и не соглашающиеся с Берковым подчеркивают "пренебрежение к ударению" (там же, 293) у силлабиков. Таким образом, вопрос о существовании у них р.р. в нашем смысле (т.е., с ударением, которое не только слышится, но и принимается в расчет) как бы снимается. О влиянии силлабической 'р.р.' на р.р. XX в. говорить не приходится.

[2] Речь идет о второй строке в нашем частушечном примере, где пропущено ударение на последнем икте, но слог может тянуться в пении. Это почти наверняка идет от старых песенных фольклорных жанров, особенно от былины, с той большой разницей, что там дактилическая клаузула реальна и последний икт остается всегда в полной ударной неприкосновенности, в клаузуле же может появиться дополнительное ударение:

> Как подсадит-то он да под сы́рой ду́б ...
> А тут той старинке и славу́ поют ...

Имитаторы народного стиха перенесли это в литературу, и в их стихах с дактилическими окончаниями попадаются 'мужские' строки:

> Обступаются и вни́з летя́т (Карамзин, "Илья Муромец")
> Куда глянешь — всюду на́ша сте́пь (Кольцов, "Перепутье")
> Напоить коня студено́й водо́й (А. К. Толстой, "Кабы знала я ...")
> Рабочий конь соло́му ест (Некрасов, "Кому на Руси жить хорошо").

Отсюда, тем не менее, в поэзии XIX в. не родилось р.р., хотя среди нечастых рифм в былине она и появлялась, как демонстрирует Жирмунский (*Рифма. Ее история и теория,* Петроград 1923, 273) примерами *ры́сью идёт* : *поска́киваёт, Бо́г не да́л* : *не пожа́ловал, переска́кивал* : *промеж но́г пуща́л, в скирды́ скла́ду* : *домо́й вы́волочу, на добро́м кони́* : *у стре́мени, Добры́нюшки* : *во Пуча́й-реки́* и др.

Некоторые слова в этих рифмах — с гипердактилическими окончаниями. Гипердактилическая клаузула в былине — вариант более частой дактилической, что хорошо показывает разноударная рифмовка в раннем подражании Брюсова народному эпосу ("О последнем рязанском князе Иване Ивановиче", *Tertia vigilia*):

> ... Вот в венце он горит, а круго́м — лучи́!
> Поклоняются князья — Монома́ховичи
>
> ...
>
> Не услышит никто уда́лый кли́ч,
> За замком сидит последний О́льгович ...

Но есть и другой род 'народного' гипердактилического окончания — результат безударности последнего икта в двустопном анапесте, который почему-то в русской поэзии ассоциируется с народной песней, видимо, с легкой руки Кольцова ("Оседлаю коня", "Обойми, поцелуй", "За рекой, на горе", "Что ты спишь, мужичок", "Не скажу никому", "Я любила его") и его подражателей ("Ни кола, ни двора", "Сиротой я росла"). Такой размер в песнях встречается уже у Сумарокова ("Не терзай ты себя"). См. также "Старый муж, грозный муж" у Пушкина, "Ах, где те острова" Рылеева, "У приказных ворот" А. К. Толстого. Когда в рифмованных стихах этот анапест терял второе ударение, то такой "пиррихий на последней стопе" давал р.р. К. Ф. Тарановский (*Руски дводелни ритмови,* Белград 1953, 11) приводит два редких примера из поэзии XIX в. — из Вяземского (кстати, поэта с особым интересом к рифме):

> Поклонись ты ему
> Изуве́ченному
>
> ("Поручение в Ревель")

и из пушкинского эпиграфа к "Пиковой даме" (не из Рылеева!):

> Гнули — мать их ети́ —
> От пяти́десяти
>
> (ср. у Маяковского *десяти́н* : *шести́десяти*).

Оба примера — песенного типа.

В подлинном фольклоре такой размер и без пропуска ударения встречается редко (главным образом, в начальных строках "Уж ты сад ты мой сад", "Я на горке стою"), с пропуском же — тоже редко — кажется, только в концовках типа 'приговаривает'.

[3] Есть р.р. и в чисто словесных малых жанрах фольклора. См., например, загадку о кормящей матери: *Два комка́, одна ла́комка.* См. также примеры у Самойлова (Д. Самойлов, *Книга о русской рифме,* Москва 1973, 47). Здесь может быть связь с рифмой раешного стиха. Ср., например, в присказке *Почасту бе́гаешь, помногу ешь.* Панченко (*Теория стиха,* 286) приводит таблицу, в которй указано, что раешное "Сказание о попе Саве и о великой его славе" (см. *Демократическая поэзия XVII в.* п/р В. П. Адриановой-Перетц, Библиотека поэта, Большая серия, Москва-Ленинград 1962, 121-23) содержит 5,9% р.р. Повидимому в эти проценты входят следующие рифмы: *зде́лалося* : *учни́лося, твори́т* : *нало́жит, спало́сь* : *ви́делось, на пери́не* : *на рого́зине, глава́* : *Са́ва, спина́* : *шеле́пина.* Некоторые из этих рифм представляются сомнительными, потому что слова могли иметь диалектное ударение и давать регулярную рифму (ср. Самойлов, op. cit., 47, где он выдвигает гипотезу, что некоторые р.р. могли получаться при переходе в другой говор). Например, Даль дает, наряду с *рого́зина* также *рогози́на.* О необходимости

установить правильное ударение в подобных случаях говорит Тарановский (см. прим. 2, стр. 11), приводя старую форму *от часу́*, не зная которой, Штокмар смутился разноударностью в крыловской рифме с *на носу́*. Не один исследователь давал из Блока пример р.р. *подворо́тни* : *оборотни* (из стих. "Иду — и все мимолетно"); однако последнее собрание сочинений поэта ставит ударение в первом слове на первый слог, ссылаясь на произношение самого Блока (см. прим. на стр. 419 *СС* II, Москва-Ленинград 1960). Есть случаи у Хлебникова и Маяковского, где скорее можно подозревать точную рифмовку со словом, где ударение падает 'неправильно' (см. прим. 29), чем разноударную. Иногда один и тот же поэт употребляет слово то с одним, то с другим ударением. Например, Мариенгоф во "Встрече" рифмует *кувши́ны* : *матерши́ной* (sic), и читатель сперва хочет ударить первое слово 'литературно' как *кувши́ны*. Однако Шершеневич (см. *Теория свободного стиха*, Москва 1920, 43) приводит это как пример р.р., что возможно только с часто слышимой формой *кувшины́*. Тем не менее, в другой поэме ("Друзья") Мариенгоф рифмует то же слово как *кувши́ны* (ср. у Пушкина *мечты́* : *где ты́* и *где́ вы* : *де́вы*).

⁴ Близко к такому определению подходит М. Л. Гаспаров ("Русский силлабический тринадцатисложник" в *Poetics, Poetyka. Поэтика*, The Hague-Paris-Warszawa 1966, 48), говоря о "нарушении ударной константы", хотя он и не имеет в виду только разноударность. Томашевский ("К истории русской рифмы", Академия Наук СССР, *Труды отдела новой русской литературы*, I, Москва-Ленинград 1948, 271) описывает р.р. так: "Здесь слоги соответствуют в обоих словах, но неударному соответствует ударный и обратно". М. П. Штокмар (*Рифма Маяковского*, Москва 1958, 80) пишет: "при более или менее тождественном написании слов, ударения располагаются на разных слогах". Жирмунский (*op. cit.*, 78) описывает то, что я обозначу ниже вторым типом, как "простое перенесение ударения".

⁵ Статистический метод подчас загипнотизирывает исследователей, и они начинают недооценивать исключительное и редкое, которое в поэзии может бывать и решающим. Такой 'демократизм' вряд ли всегда уместен в делах эстетических. Ведь не будем мы игнорировать пушкинских сонетов, потому что их лишь три. Иногда слышишь или читаешь почти пренебрежительные замечания о русских 'логаэдах' (что эта форма, дескать, не привилась), а между тем они писались русскими поэтами в течение двухсот лет (от Тредиаковского до Ходасевича), их интересно применял Вячеслав Иванов, и они занимали важное место в поэзии 'младших' символистов (С. Соловьев, Ю. Верховский).

⁶ Жирмунский (см. прим. 2) о р.р. (которую он, как и Штокмар, как и Томашевский, называет "неравноударной") на стр. 13, 73, 78-79, 210, 211, 215-16, 273; Штокмар (см. прим. 4) на стр. 54, 72, 80-82; Самойлов (см. прим. 3) на стр. 6, 46-47, 197-98, 213, 251-53. Для Жирмунского р.р., наряду с неравносложной, представляет из себя один из двух видов рифмы "с различиями в строении стихового окончания" (стр. 13), и первый пример, который он дает, — *сто́нут* : *жну́т*; это также одна из четырех "категорий неточных рифм" (наряду с ассонансом, консонансом — так Жирмунский называет диссонанс — и неравносложной рифмой). Главной областью р.р. Жирмунский считает составные, а р.р. с "простым перенесением ударения" (которая в этом докладе ниже рассматривается как основной тип) считает редкостью, что извинительно, так как даже Жирмунский во время написания своей книги вряд ли хорошо знал Хлебникова, а Мариенгоф был чем-то слишком уж современным для ученого. У Блока Жирмунский находит два случая, *по́чки* : *фо́рточки* и *подворо́тни* : *оборотни* (о последнем см. прим. 3), у Маяковского четыре (на наш взгляд очень пестрые и не все убедительны, *расти́* : *хра́брости*, *дре́безги* : *в не́бе ни зги́*, *напада́ли* : *па́дали*, *это я сам* : *мя́со*. Сравнительно много (13) примеров Жирмунский дает из былин (см. прим. 2), но и они не все убедительны (*палаты белока́менны* : *во белы́ руки́*). Штокмар называет р.р. Маяковского "неудавшимися экспериментами, навеянными влиянием футуристской поэтики" (стр. 80) (что́, если отвлечься от оценочного элемента, правильно), дает из ранней его поэзии гораздо больше примеров, нежели Жирмунский (см. прим. 32), но тут же винит неназванных 'теоретиков', будто бы преувеличивающих роль

этих рифм, тогда как у Маяковского их "лишь / ! В.М./ несколько десятков" и в зрелые годы поэт ими пользовался реже и лучше. Как и Жирмунский, Штокмар связывает обычную для Маяковского составную рифму (с добавочным ударением в клаузуле) с разноударностью (71-72), которую он также видит и в "звуковых повторах" поэта в таких строках, как "за всех расплачýсь,/ за всех распла́чусь". Дефект р.р. Штокмар видит в том, что в ней "совпадают преимущественно буквы, а не звуки" и "под оболочкой тождественного написания" скрывается "разнобой звуков". Самойлов (см. прим. 3), как и Жирмунский, видит близость р.р. к неравносложной и предлагает две гипотезы ее возникновения в фольклоре: 1) переход пословицы в другой говор с принятием другого ударения и 2) отрыв от песни, где дополнительные ударения "связаны с интонацией напева". В главах о рифме отдельных поэтов у Самойлова есть интересные наблюдения, но есть и важные пропуски; например, разбирая рифму Хлебникова на 15 страницах, он ни разу не упоминает р.р. Кое в чем Самойлов расходится со своими коллегами: он не видит заметного "тяготения к разноударности" у Маяковского, кроме как в составных, и считает р.р. в его ранней поэзии практически отсутствующей.

[7]   Штокмар, стр. 59.

[8]   А. В. Исаченко ("Из наблюдений над 'новой рифмой'", *Slavic Poetics: Essays in Honor of Kiril Taranovsky*, The Hague: Mouton, 1973), даже говоря о ' 'разнообразных вольностях" в §5 своей статьи, р.р. не упоминает. Томашевский (см. прим. 4) лишь упоминает ее в примечании на стр. 271 (а в *Стилистике и стихосложении* и совсем не говорит о ней). А. Квятковский (*Поэтический словарь*, Москва 1966), при всей своей любви к раритетам, не уделяет внимания р.р., хотя и упоминает ее в общей статье о рифме.

[9]   Г. Шенгели, например (*Техника стиха*, Москва 1960, 246), демонстрирует р.р. примером из Вячеслава Иванова (см. об этом стихотворении ниже в докладе, в разделе "К истории") и почему-то видит в его рифмах идентичность ("такие ходы встречаются") с ýлица : лúца у Маяковского, хотя в последнем случае совсем иной метрический контекст, замешан enjambement и вообще разноударность не первична, а результат эксперимента с метатезой слогов. Брюсов в *Науке о стихе* (Москва 1919, 125) различает "по строению" рифмы простые, составные и диастолические. Последним мудреным словом он обозначает р.р., получившиеся от нереализованного ударения на последнем икте (см. ниже, в докладе, о хромых рифмах). Брюсов демонстрирует "диастолу" уже известным нам примером из Вяземского (см. прим. 2) и из себя самого — *невзлеле́яны : медленной весны́.* Мне не удалось найти этой рифмы в брюсовских стихах, но пятое двустишие стихотворения "Холод" читается *Гаснут в сердце невзлеле́янные сны, / Гибнут цветики осмея́нной весны* — никакой "диастолы", и рифма затасканная даже для пушкинского времени. Так эти строки читаются во всех доступных мне публикациях (*Пути и перепутья*, IV т. *ПСС, Опыты*). Неужели Брюсов забыл собственное довольно известное стихотворение, которое он к тому же тогда недавно поместил лишний раз в книгу (*Опыты* вышли в 1918)?

[10]   См. Л. В. Краснова, "Рифма цикла А. Блока 'Стихи о Прекрасной Даме' (Опыт статистического анализа)", *Научные доклады высшей школы, Филологические науки,* 1973/6:83, где в р.р. записаны неравносложные *неве́домо : сле́дом.* Странным образом, даже Жирмунский (стр. 211) говорит о неравноударности в рифмовке 4-го стихотворения цикла "Флоренция" Блока, где некоторые рифмы всего только неравносложны. Повидимому, тут просто опечатка. Впрочем, как уже отмечалось (см. прим. 6), неравносложность и разноударность сближается некоторыми исследователями (Жирмунский), а когда читаешь у Унбегауна (*Russian Versification*, Oxford 1956, 146), о р.р. ничего не говорящего, что "the next step is to rhyme lines in which the final stress does not fall on the same syllable, beginning from the end of the word", то ждешь, что он коснется разноударности. Однако разговор идет только о неравносложных, да и те кажутся Унбегауну странным радикализмом ("The majority of poets, it must be said, refuse to take such a step").

[11]   См. А. М. Кондратов, "Статистика типов русской рифмы", *Вопросы языкознания* 1963/6:97: "в русской поэзии начиная с XVIII в. этот тип рифм практически не встречается".

[12] Например, блоковская рифма *по́чки* : *фо́рточки* ("Последний день") может быть воспринята как неравносложный ассонанс. Однако если мысленно передвинуть ударение во втором слове на один слог, то получится обыкновенная точная рифма и, таким образом, перед нами разноударное явление. Такие рифмы среди р.р. образуют небольшую группу: *то́чек* : *ко́сточек* (Пастернак), *топора́ми* : *уда́рами, бе́режно* : *небре́жно, ме́льниц-пе́пельниц, зло́сти* : *по́лости* (все четыре Шершеневича), *припло́д* : *мо́лод* (Бурлюк), *хвост* : *восто́к* (Перелёшин), *озорно́* : *гро́зно* (Лепок), *мо́чке* : *Дюймо́вочке* (Вознесенский). Условием такой рифмы является наличие двух одинаковых гласных подряд в одном из рифмующих слов.

[13] См., например, James Bailey, "The Verse of Andrej Voznesenskij as an Example of Present-Day Russian Versification", *SEEJ*, 17/2, Summer 1973, 157-58. Бейли включает в это понятие и рифмовые переносы (когда строка кончается на союзе, предлоге или же на половине слова). В том же номере, в рецензии на стр. 220, Бейли порицает Б. Гончарова за несогласие с Колмогоровым, утверждавшим, что предлог "за" в известных строках Маяковского *отку́да, мол,/ и что́ это за́//географи́ческие но́вости?* представляет собой неударный икт. Как ни тяжело мне солидаризироваться с Гончаровым, автором псевдоученой и неприятной книги, мне все-таки кажется, что во всех случаях рифмового enjambement происходит реализация последнего икта. Именно в том и суть такой рифмы, что нормально неударные слоги получают ударение, и в этом рифма-enjambement противоположна "безударной". Делается это для комического эффекта (которого не было бы, если б этот слог не ударялся), как у Маяковского; для чисто технического эксперимента, как у Шершеневича; возможны и иные мотивировки. Здесь нельзя ссылаться на разницу между произношением и произнесением, как, скажем, у Георгия Иванова в рифме *судьбы́* : *пое́хал бы* можно "бы" не ударять, а можно и для тонкого эффекта слегка ударить. Ссылки на "язык" в данном случае не помогают, во-первых, потому что это не первый (и не последний) случай, где стих расходится с языком, а во-вторых, несмотря на нормирующие запреты, предлоги и отрицательные частицы, например, нередко в живой речи ударяются (Он мне этого не́ говорил; Ищи по́д столо́м, а не на́ столе́). Если в строке Маяковского не сделать ударения на "за", теряется весь стиховой смысл этого места. Думается, что и в других случаях так же. Ещё реже "неправильные" ударения встречаются и без enjambement, например, в шуточном стихотворении Сельвинского (*Записки поэта*), который ударение специально обозначает:

Мы пришли к Гальперину́.
Ну?
Дома нет Гальперина́.
На!
Ныть ли о Гальперине́?
Не.

По иному поводу, но к сходному явлению подходит Томашевский (*Стилистика и стихосложение,* Ленинград, 1959, 480), когда говорит: "Последний неударный слог в длинных многосложных словах в стихах Маяковского иногда приобретает особую силу, которая достаточна для того, чтобы считать этот слог для рифмы как бы ударным". Один из его примеров *леса́* : *назюзюкался* (собственно, у Маяковского "на-зю-зю-кался"). Это только внешне хромая рифма, а на самом деле входит в действительно редкую группу рифм, где одно из рифмующих слов должно читаться с ударением на всех слогах (вроде того, как Еремин представлял чтение силлабических стихов). Мне известны следующие —*дру́гом* : *кру́-го́м!* (Аблесимов), *сову́* : *Ко-ко-ре-ву!* (Минаев) и *крыш-ка* : *сорока́* (Вознесенский).

[14] Тарановский (*Руски дводелни...,* стр. 8-10) дает примеры из Пушкина, Кюхельбекера, Лермонтова, Островского, А. К. Толстого и из переводов с немецкого и английского. См. также James Bailey, "The Russian Iambic Pentameter from 1880 to 1922", *IJSLP* XVI (1973):

129-31. Может быть, самые разительные примеры можно привести из юношеской трагедии Герцена "Вильям Пенн", где в изобилии встречаются строки вроде:

> Цветут, — а привиденье мра́чное
> Со впалыми щеками тут как тут.
>
> —
>
> Он пишет предику, он пишет пре́дику!
> А сын мой осьмилетний с хо́лоду ...
>
> —
>
> Желанья вялые. А нам что на
> Замен всего ограбленного дали?

В последнем примере "на" ударения на себе не несет, в противоречие к сказанному мною в предыдущем примечании, но здесь мы имеем дело с настоящим исключением: попыткой воспроизвести немецкий стих по-русски любой ценой.

Проблема иностранных влияний в области поэтики щекотливое дело, хотя и бывали пересадки целых систем из иноязычных поэзий (как с силлабикой). В новое время русские поэты (особенно символисты и имажинисты) усердно занимались созданием свободного стиха на русской почве под влиянием, главным образом, французских теорий, но в результате одни говорили про Фому, другие про Ерему. Их предшественники в XIX в., менее изощренные поэтически переводчики гейневского "Die Nordsee" давали, может быть, нехотя, образцы более соответствующие названию "верлибр". Влияние в области рифмы как будто и совсем исключено, настолько она "внутреннее дело" и тесно связана с национальным поэтическим слухом данного периода (например, мои "честные" попытки посильно воспроизвести по-английски рифму Маяковского встретили, кажется, полное недоумение — если не хуже — "туземцев"). И тем не менее, А. К. Толстой в защиту своих рифм ссылался на гетевскую молитву Гретхен (в письме Маркевичу от 8 декабря 1871 г.), Брюсов указывал футуристам на Эдгара По (*Русская Мысль* 1913/3:132) в связи с рифмой-enjambement, забыв, что в России то же делал Лермонтов, а Шершеневич взял идею своих рифм-диссонансов у Лафорга (см. *Теория свободного стиха,* Москва 1920, 47).

[15]   Рифмы типа о́куни : окуни́ просодически похожи на хромые. Разница в том, что там известно, где икт.

[16]   О неравносложных рифмах Томашевский (*Стилистика и стихосложение,* 477) говорит, что они "возникли у Маяковского в силу определенных законов русского языка". Вряд ли он повторил бы то же о р.р.

[17]   Буквенно-графический элемент здесь не только конкретная компенсация, но и часть более широкого контекста: ср. визуальность поэзии Крученых и Зданевича и течение 'конкретной поэзии' на Западе. Даже в фольклоре, области, по всем определениям, *устного* творчества, в XX в. появляются 'антиформы' письменного порядка. См. шуточные вопросы "Ты съешь огурец с Алёной?" и "От чего утка плавает?" или школьный палиндром "Улыбок тебе пара".

[18]   С большим неудовольствием защищаю эту идею разрушения, столь убедительно дискредитированную А. В. Исаченко, но в данном случае разрушение налицо, да, в конце концов, ведь и на знамени у футуристов было написано 'разрушение' и целиком отрицать этот аспект было бы неразумным.

[19]   Жирмунский, стр. 180.

[20]   Если искать начало в XIX в., то можно эту рифму пока датировать мартом-апрелем 1862 г. — дата "Просьбы" Минаева (*му́ж ино́й* : *Ку́кшиной*). Однако у Феофана Прокоповича ("Ея Императорскому Величеству на пришествие в село подмосковное Владыкино") находим *долготу́ дний́* : *многолю́дный.*

[21]   Главным образом, в женских рифмах. Одно из первых выражений такого неудобства — у Шершеневича (который был сам до революции активным футуристом и придумал немало собственных составных рифм). В *2 × 2 = 5* (Москва 1920, 23-24) он пишет о

"насильственных полуударениях" в рифмах Асеева типа *тропа́ та́* : *Карпа́та* и о том, что слово "Карпата", таким образом, несет на себе два ударения, хотя и является женской рифмой. Для Шенгели (*Техника стиха,* 250) приемлема дактилическая *разжа́л уста́* : *пожа́луйста,* но женская *разбо́йник* : *головой ник* "звучит неприятно". Штокмар чуть ли не извиняется за ударение в клаузуле у Маяковского, когда дополнительное ударение "несколько нарушает акцентное равновесие рифмы" (стр. 71), как в *козе́ ле́нь* : *зе́лень* (ср. у Хлебникова *зе́лень* : *грозе́ ле́нь*). Кстати, интересно было бы установить, что́ чаще предшествует в таких рифмах, составной или несоставной элемент, потому что ситуации эти различные. Наконец, для иллюстрации проблемы составной рифмы на английской почве приводим письмо в редакцию *Saturday Review* (Aug. 9, 1969): "A propos the cartoon ... of the poet having tried for ten years to rhyme 'orange'. I tried for five minutes but could only come up with two women discussing the plays of William Inge. One, of course, said, 'I just adore Inge'."

[22] Может быть, следует сказать о ложной составной, которая иногда принимается за настоящую, как в *удво́им* : *у́д во́ем* (Пушкин), *ска́лам бу́рым* : *с каламбу́ром* (Минаев), *чарова́л* : *ча́ры ва́л* (Хлебников). Здесь 'составность' начинается (иногда задолго) до конечного икта и метрического значения не имеет.

[23] Жирмунский в свое время жаловался, что эта ударность в составной рифме не изучена (*Рифма,* 180). Воз и ныне там. Слегка касается этого вопроса Н. Харджиев (см. Харджиев и В. Тренин, *Поэтическая культура Маяковского,* Москва 1970, 106, 205).

[24] Приводим еще несколько примеров составных рифм Сельвинского: *возрази́шь им* : *ды́шим, почти́ ло́сь* : *тащи́лось, тиф врыть* : *цифры, тала́нт спа́ть* : *тра́нспорт, через ро́в кинь* : *махно́вки, рефра́ктор* : *фра́к? Тррр ..., рыжебри́вый·ро́т* : *навы́рот, развóдами* : *тепло́ ды́ма, подцо́кивая* : *в лицо́ кивáя, си́ний ковы́ль* : *Овчи́нниковых, причи́н каковых* : *Овчи́нниковых, леса́ дыби́* : *усáдьбы, багóр у инъ́іх* : *Махóриных.*

[25] Ср. в былине: *И зовет же он бога́тырей к соби в гости.*

[26] Заманчиво начать эту историю, следуя К. Ф. Тарановскому (*Руски дводелни ...,* стр. 11), с Тредиаковского (24-е четверостишие из *Римской истории*):

Потом рассма́тривай,
Поступки в ней какие,
Все склонности позна́й,
Из тех внутрь все ль драгие.

Однако однотомник Библиотеки поэта (В. К. Тредиаковский, *Избранные произведения,* Москва-Ленинград 1963, 328) дает написание 'рассмотревай', так что здесь почти наверняка ударение падает на последний слог.

[27] См. прим. 23. Стр. 107: *из ти́ны* : *и́стины, из мешка́* : *усме́шка, ве́дьмы* : *ведь мы́, за́реву* : *зареву́, погóда* : *по года́, вéщи* : *в щи, пóхоти* : *погоди́.* Там же, на стр. 123, Харджиев, видимо, "для порядку", перечисляя разного типа хлебниковские составные рифмы с ударением в клаузуле, характеризует их как "подсказанные практикой Маяковского". Все эти рифмы хлебниковского изобретения.

[28] Как ни ударять это имя, Ро́гволод (по образцу Всéволод) или Рогволóд (как поют в опере *Рогнеда* Серова), рифма будет разноударная.

[29] Повидимому Хлебников имел ввиду нелитературное ударение *роса́м* (ср. в "Журавле" *волоса́ми* : *роса́ми*). Для него это типично и, по всей вероятности, следующие его рифмы неразноударны: *сви́стом* : *ли́стом, ше́и* : *ворожéи, тóлько* : *óльха, оборóтни* : *сóтни* : *подворóтни.*

[30] Эта и предыдущая рифмы — из стихотворений, напечатанных в *Помаде* (1913) с примечанием, что они написаны совместно с А. Луневым. Харджиев считает, что это псевдоним Хлебникова, но доказательств особых не приводит. Рифмы могут быть хлебниковскими, крученыховскими или коллективными.

[31] Как ни странно, до р.р. не додумались эго-футуристы, так охотно теоретизировавшие на эту тему. Впрочем, В. Гнедов, например, был против звуковой рифмы вообще и

проповедовал 'рифму понятий' (напр., *коромысло : дуга*).

[32]   Штокмар (80-83) дает *но́ги* : *но ги* /бель фонарей/, *зигза́гом* : *за га́м, в ра́дости* : *подрасти́, о́дури* : *одре́, рот* : *го́род, отчего́* : *рабо́чего, темно́* : *действи́тельно, со стороны́* : *э́кстренный, ум* : *ми́нимум, десяти́н* : *шести́десяти, де́рево* — *во́! : пе́рвого.* Томашевский ("К истории ..., 271) демонстрирует р.р. Маяковского одним примером *рывка́ : непреры́вка.* В списке Штокмара внушает некоторое (может быть, неоснователь-ное) сомнение *о́дури* : *одре́* (Маяковский, для которого, как и для Хлебникова, характерны нелитературные формы, мог произносить *о́дре*) и особенно рифмы с переносным расще-плением слова, где разноударность, даже когда она наличествует, вторична (результат enjambement) и поэтому, в каком-то смысле, иррелевантна. Ср. у Крученых *уста́м* : /глу́/постям, у Вознесенского *ревя́* : *реа*/нима́цию/, у Одоевцевой *творца́* : /почита-тель/*ница.* Так же вторичны р.р., получающиеся в результате слоговой метатезы, как в *бе́се* : *себе́* (Хлебников), *наза́д* : *за́нят* (Бурлюк).

[33]   Может быть, хлебниковская рифма. См. прим. 30.

[34]   Эта рифма идет от волошинской *твоя́* : *неосуществлённая,* в стих. "Родина" (*Демоны глухонемые*), датированном 30 мая 1918 г. Что касается Ушакова, его р.р. были отмечены Бейли в рецензии в *SEEJ,* 17/2 (1973): 200, который добавляет к этому списку еще *ле́сенка* : *лесника́.*

[35]   Приводим текст:

> Поразвешены сети по берегу ...
> В сердце память, как дар, берегу
> Об уловом разорванных не́водах
> И о Встретившем нас на вода́х.
>
> И ладья моя в сумрак отчалена:
> Видишь огненный след от челна?
> Лов зачну, как все небо повызвездит,
> Что помочь ты сошла — возвестит.
>
> Солнце мрежи мне сушит по берегу;
> В сердце память весь день берегу
> О закинутых с вечера неводах,
> О подруге в звездах на водах.

[36]   А то надо видеть р.р. и в двух последних строках из "Другу" Волошина:

> Да не прервутся нити прях,
> Сидящих в пурпурных лоскутьях
> На всех победных перепутьях,
> На всех погибельных путях.

[37]   Приводим текст:

> Говорят, что "я" и "ты" —
> Мы телами столкнуты.
>
> Тепленеет красный ком
> Кровопарным облаком.
>
> Мы — над взмахами косы
> Виснущие хаосы.
>
> Нет, неправда: гладь тиха
> Розового воздуха, —
>
> Где истаял громный век
> В легкий лепет ласточек, —

Где, заяснясь, "я" и "ты" —
Светлых светов яхонты, —

Где и тела красный ком
Духовеет облаком.

[38] Здесь встает вопрос о взаимоотношении метра строки и р.р. Я не касаюсь этого вопроса в докладе. Однако см. прим. 44.

[39] Во всяком случае, "Восторг женщины", первая версия которого датируется 1914 г.

[40] См. *Опыты*, стр. 87. Рифмы *по́логом : поло́гом, зе́лено : зелёной, бе́лая : бела́ я, в го́ре ли : горе́ли, ми́нута : мину́та, ви́денья : виде́нья, бо́льшего : большо́го*.

[41] Там же, 83-84. Остальные тройки рифм *го́родом : го́рдом : ипподро́м* (повторено под конец), *баси́лики : ли́ки : велики́, уни́заны : ри́зный : крутизны́, гладиа́тора : теа́тра : шатра́, неви́данный : серпови́дный : видны́, зара́нее : страда́нья : воронья́, оторо́ченных : уро́чных : ночны́х, расще́лины : земе́льный : хмельны́*. Тут много рифм типа *по́чки : фо́рточки* (см. прим. 12).

[42] Шарль Вильдрак, Жорж Дюамель, Вадим Шершеневич, *Теория свободного стиха*, "Имажинисты", Москва 1920, 42-43.

[43] Курсив (предположительно с некоторыми опечатками) обозначает у Шершеневича не ударные слоги, а слоги, которые должны были бы нести ударения, чтобы получилась традиционная рифмовка. (О *кувшины́ : матершийной* см. прим. 3). Точнее третья рифма у Мариенгофа *ра́зве та́ : рассве́та*. Не совсем понятно, что здесь делает последняя рифма (неравносложная с метатезой согласных). Может быть, Шершеневич считал, что "толп" произносится "то́лап"? Во всяком случае, после этого он продолжает так: "Несомненно под его влиянием С. Есенин стал рифмовать смрада: сад, высь : лист, кто : ртом, петь: третий". Во всем перечислении нет ни одной р.р.

[44] Это правильное и тонкое замечание. Р.р. (второго, главного типа) ведет к более свободным метрическим формам (первый находится в пределах традиции, хотя и нарушает ее; третий чисто клаузулен и метрику строки как таковой не затрагивает), что́ и понятно: 'уничтожение' икта не дает установиться размерам традиционным. У Мариенгофа в ранние годы было тяготение к стиху Маяковского, потом он выработал собственный 'свободный стих', который, впрочем, в некоторых поэмах ясно тяготеет к ямбу. Однако эта ямбичность как бы заключает компромисс с р.р. Мариенгоф дробит 'первоначальную' ямбическую строку на фрагменты (вплоть до одного слога) и зарифмовывает (большею частью, разноударно) окончания этих получившихся 'новых' строк. Даже если это и 'свободный' стих, он 'вольный' в крыловско-грибоедовском смысле. В поздних стихах Мариенгоф переходит на традиционные размеры, и р.р. сразу исчезает.

[45] "Переход" Есенина к р.р. сильно преувеличен Шершеневичем. Я нашел в "Исповеди хулигана" *петь : и́споведь*, в "Кобыльих кораблях" *вы́плакать : лака́ть*, наконец в *Пугачеве гул : ка́торгу, за́мысел : съел, сообщи́ть : бунтовщики́*. Что касается других имажинистов, то у Ивнева есть *ручейки́ : вса́дники* (правда, в *Самосожжении* 1917 г., т.е., до имажинизма); у Кусикова — *ночно́й : го́рничной, бу́рок : куро́к, бере́чь : че́реп, косо́й : со́йку*, причем последние две результат метатезы, которую Кусиков культивировал в разных видах (напр., *боль : лоб*), видимо, считая это своим открытием и вряд ли зная, что это уже было у Хлебникова. За исключением Есенина в *Пугачеве*, вряд ли остальные имажинисты имитировали Мариенгофа, однако его влияние (правда, не такое уж большое) на рифму молодого, второго поколения имажинистов (можно добавить — 'несостоявшегося' поколения) несомненно. У Ройзмана находим *шары́ : бульва́ры, пала́тки : платки́, осени́ : о́сени, сего́дня : подня́в* (впрочем, он мог произносить *по́дняв*); у Н. Эрдмана *болт : болтовня́*; у Афанасьева-Соловьева *Петербу́ргу : пурго́й, осы́плется : пле́тью*; у Шмерельсона *де́вушки : у́шки*; у Полоцкого *вме́сте : шесте́ : путеше́ствовал*. Интересно, что фуисты, преподносившие себя как врагов имажинизма, старательно упражнялись в р.р., которая у них часто напоминает мариенгофовскую. См. у Перелёшина

льются : вихляются, рассвете : лети, звёзд : повязали, листкам : свист, хвост : восток, лёг : полог, вялости : пустых, кровью: головы, угрожая : вожжи, челе : пуле; у Лепока *щёки : заговорщики, тихо : этих, камень : всплесками, писк : роспись, отблеском : ком, брызги : зигзагом, озорно : грозно, посвист : лист, клянёт : слякотью*; у Решетникова *утренний гной : никну, лучей : навьючить.*

[46] Часто от проблемы отмахиваются, называя явление 'только экспериментом' (см. Томашевский, "К истории ...," стр. 269: "Я устраняю те рифмы, в которых присутствует элемент экспериментализма") и забывая при этом, что век эксперимента в русской поэзии начался Брюсовым и, судя по всем признакам, продолжается.

[47] Теоретически однако Мариенгоф ровно ничего не говорит по интересующему нас вопросу в своем единственном трактате *Буян-остров* (1920).

[48] Если не считать *приспособил : кобель*, но тут может быть и *кобель.*

[49] См. таблицу-приложение к докладу.

[50] Это первый пробовал Хлебников в поэме "Сельская дружба" (1913).

[51] Как пример, приведем рифмы, которые можно назвать рифмами ложного благополучия. В *Шершеневич : свечи* совпадает ударный гласный и получается более или менее приемлемый ассонанс (вроде *почки : форточки*), однако согласные не дают на этом успокоиться и заставляют подозревать, что дело не в ассонансе, а в разноударном диссонансе *-вич : -веч-*. То же в рифмах *любовь : обуви* и *ваши : в ушах.*

[52] Если даже просто читать списки рифм Мариенгофа, составляешь неплохое представление и о его символике и о его стилистике (что, кстати, опровергает обвинения критиков в надуманности и искусственности его поэзии).

РАЗНОУДАРНЫЕ РИФМЫ В СТИХАХ АНАТОЛИЯ МАРИЕНГОФА
(приводится дата написания и даются сведения о строфике)

Стихи в альм. Явь
ка́док : клок (1917)
кочевы́е : Пугачёва (1917)
вы́греб : в игре́ (недат.)

Стихи в альм. Конница
бурь (I)
лафа́ : Голиа́фа (1918)
жечь : сте́ржень (1918)
отца : захлебнётся (1919)
чешую́ : расчешу́ (1919)
рвы : гри́вы (недат.)

Кондитерская солнц
(10 десятистиший)
(начало /?/ 1919)
паруса́ : ру́сую
головни́ : поголо́вно
куски́ : ру́сский
псы : би́цепсы
торс : торцы́
му́зе : музея́х
ру́брикой : парики́

Магдалина (23 14-стишия и
два 13-стишия)
(начало /?/ 1919)
на́бережные : бе́режно
весну́ : ви́снут
ку́тают : ую́та
гру́ды : груди́
ды́шит : вы́кидыш
Пе́сней : ступнёй
пружи́ны : нару́жу
вине́ : ра́ковине
Заве́те : глаза́ ведь
совде́пы : депо́
тепе́рь : верте́пе
ля́жками : пля́ж ка́мни
ли́ру : рук
трико́ : крик О-о-о
о́коло : ко́локол
мотки́ : ма́тку
ду́шу : удушу́
уви́т, а не я́ : до свида́ния
любви́ Ни́ццу : дви́нется
труба́ : тру́па
каланчо́й : выкля́нчивать

Руки галстуком (1919)
(11 шестистиший)
ше́и : обрю́згшие
га́лстуком : у́хом
уме́ют : безу́мие
вышива́ть : вы́ше
бесе́д : подне́бесья
дёрн : вы́дернул
но́гу : гул
Петербу́ргу : пурго́й
зя́бли : корабли́
су́мерки : кирко́й
кривы́ми : гри́вой
кло́уна : луны́

Слепые ноги (26 четверостиший) (май 1919)
белки́ : опи́лки
у́лиц ше́и : Ни́цше
лече́бницы : гробни́цы
ковыля́х : вы́лить
Росси́я : ро́сы
глубина́ : ряби́на
згу : ви́згу
хребты́ : ле́пты
коло́да : хо́лода
и мне : огро́мней
пруды́ : гру́ды
острия́ : костра́ я
слепа́я : хле́бом
перебе́г : бе́рег
каку́ю : кухми́стерскую
ра́ди : роди́ть
лбы : разби́л бы
соба́чья : безо́блачья (в 1-ой
публикации в альм.
Плавильня слов также
упаду́ люк : вы́давлю)

Анатолеград (9 12-стиший)
(октябрь 1919)
гнию́ : ски́ния
зача́тье : косноязы́чья
у́голья : плоского́рьях
пе́пел : капе́лл
бо́ли : лик
бескре́стье : бла́говест

мешки́ : ка́мешки
сургучи́ : су́чья
пе́речень : пе́чень
револю́ции : вы́клюются
кана́тами : ко́мнаты
го́лубя : клубя́
шпа́лам : попола́м
ла́пу да́й : па́даль
ти́хое : стихи́
насле́дье : ладье́
го́рле : короле́й
сосу́ды : суда́
ра́спре : бред
асфа́льты : пальто́
оси́ : голо́сит
гло́бусы : Иису́сом
вечеро́в : чела́
лозо́й : поло́зья

Посвящение к Стихами
чванствую (15 строк)
(март 1920)
дру́жба : жбан
пе́сни : переплесни́
рты : воро́та

Встреча (4 16-стишия и
одно 12-стишие)
(март 1920)
вы́плеснет : плеснь
ру́сло : слова́
чре́во : де́рева
колыбе́ль : глы́бой
дым : иноземным
кувшины́ : матерши́ной
ка́торгу : берегу́т
ра́зве та́ : рассве́та
легла́ : стёкла
луны́ : чугу́нный
полосова́л : волоса́
колпа́к : ла́пах
животе́ : во́ете
не сня́ть : пе́сня
коню́шни : дней
коро́на : окра́ины
хлеб хозя́йский :
золоты́х языко́в
о́ргии : Сергею́
вме́сте : меси́ть

Сентябрь (май 1920)
(9 восьмистиший)
утоли́вши : ковши́
подко́вы : ковы́ль
лю́тни : мутне́й
странна́ : кра́ны
степь : пе́рстень
поля́ : оска́ля
клино́к : спозара́нок
листы́ : свист
ко́локол : кол

Тучелет (август 1920)
(4 шестистишия)
тя́жесть : жесть
по́сох : босо́й
я́блоки : легки́
ра́дости : кре́стит
лоб : приплы́ло

Кувшины памяти (1920)
(3 12-стишия и одно
11-стишие)
у́тро : труп
тишина́ : кувши́ны
стропи́ла : Пила́т
шля́пу : путь
ока́пал : бал
паркету : ко́мнату
строк : о́стров
ру́ки : други́е
легко́ : издалёка(?)
тишины́ пью :
    не́жной по́ступи

Фонтаны седины (восемь
11-стиший и одно 12-
стишие) (сентябрь 1920)
вы́черпать : тропа́
припада́й : прохла́ду
день : леденеет
котла́ : по́дло
вскипи́т : ски́петр
я мо́г : я́мой
ды́ни : дни
лу́жи : возложу́
она́ : середи́на
я́блоком : ло́кон
седины́ : середи́ну
поэ́т : пе́пел

вре́мя : реме́нь : стремена́
седо́к : су́ток
метр : ски́петр
гало́па : лба
строф : о́стров
де́вственниц : ресни́цы
лебеда́ : ле́бедя
дро́бью : бьют
ды́ни : седины́

Посвящение к Тучелету
(15 строк) (ноябрь 1920)
то́поль : пыль
очаге́ : ча́йке

*Развратничаю с вдохнове-
нием* (12 16-стиший)
(сент. 1919-нояб. 1920)
во́роги : рога́
ину́ю : лошади́ную
вранья́ : воро́ньей
вдохнове́нья : звеня́т
ту́чей : стучи́т
улюлю́ : победи́телю
ли́лии : вы́лилась
шурша́ : ча́ша
вла́гу : нага́я
и́бо : лба
язы́к : я́звы
тишины́ : ви́шня
ко́локол : молоко́
гуди́шь : гру́ди
вал : вына́шивал
Заве́та : животе́
кри́ком : старико́м
пурга́ : Петербу́рга
как жива́я : ка́жется*
зобы́ : ва́зой быть
блюсти́ : че́люсти : го́сти
го́лову : клюв : заки́нув
жо́лтому : о́мут : почему́
ло́говище : сви́щет
бряца́ет : па́льца
вью́га : не́други
слу́чкой : тако́й
пото́мство : мостовы́х
сига́ру : ру́ки
вода́ : всхо́да
руке́ : ка́торге
зёрна : черна́

поля́ : се́ятеля
весна́ : ви́снут
го́роде : сковороде́
животе́ : све́те
ста́рый : дара́ми
ковша́ : взалка́вши
ка́плю : опалю́
две́ри : вери́ги
заба́вно : в ночь
точи́ть : и про́ч.

Застольная беседа (101
строка) (январь 1921)
тишины́ : пы́шно
напо́лни : полы́нь
бубенцо́м : Лоре́нцо
дней : семидесятиле́тней
бесе́да : седа́
сгора́ем мы : боге́мы
по́лки : полки́
о́ду : году́
впереди́ : ме́дью
доха́ : стихо́в
глаз : подсказа́ла
ды́шит : щит
дно : хо́лодно
туберкулёзом : слеза́
тру́бы : губа́м
любо́вь : о́буви
вью́га : кро́вью
ладо́ни : они́
срази́л : А́зию
пламеня́т : вы́мени
пти́цу : хи́щницу
стрела́ : распростёрла
гру́стно вам : но́вые
чьи : вели́чье

Друзья (142 строки)
(март 1921)
вино́м : кувши́ны
бо́лью : прольют
же́мчуг : мчу
строк : Зарату́стра
дни : ладо́ни
песо́к : по́сох
изме́ну э́ту : мину́ту
вы́чеканил : ко́ни
ве́чером : Замоскворе́чья
зловеще : и ещё

---

* В данном случае *как жива́я* также рифмуется с *называ́ть*, а *ка́жется* с *мертвеца́*.

безды́мчатые : мчу
мосто́в : о́стров
фра́ке : в реке́
зрачка́ : на кара́чках
ва́ши : в уша́х
встре́тились : донести́ ли
ладо́ни : они́
ручья́ми : орна́мент встре́ч
каранда́ш : ла́ндыш
ковры́ : января́
во́зле : злей
Шершене́вич : све́чи
стихо́в : хворости́ной
вымпело́в : пе́ли
о́бразов : гроза́
зной : развя́зно
ле́нта : ве́рен той
лет : глаго́лет
люстр : по́люс

Разочарова́ние (134
    строки) (август 1921)
звезды́ : оде́жды (:дождь)
жеребе́ц(:ловец:сла́ва) :
    ожере́льем(:кры́лья)
со́лнце : в конце́ концо́в
арка́не : коня́
скакуна́ : стака́ном
бивуа́ком : заба́ва
не́друг : ру́ки
листво́й : пото́мство
обо мне́ : и́мени
до́черью : бере́чь
коло́нны : волна́
иностра́нец : наконе́ц
громоздя́ : мозг
собесе́дники : о́сень
не́ба : снега́
канаре́ек : реки́
ресни́ц : черни́льниц

Заговор дураков (закончен
    4 авг. 1921) (1132 строки;
    по актам I-218; II-300;
    III-364; IV-250)
по́хороны : во́ронов
ви́дела : те́ло
околева́ют : го́ловы
бальза́мом : сама́
тро́на : стране́

Петра́ : ски́петр
тре́плются : револю́ция
во́дится : я́годицы
пости́г : неблагода́рности
свечи́ : ове́чек
цыплёнка : клинки́
сорва́ть : про́рва
фельдма́ршал : ороша́л
полки́ : то́лку
жуть : ли́жут
ма́ти : па́мяти
ножны́ : жо́ны
дубы́ : за́ зубы
дураки́ : кук-карреку́
о́лово : сло́во
бока́ : соба́ка
тра́ур : дур
стихотво́рец : дворе́
сла́вы : слова́м
Долгору́ким : круги́
точи́л бы : лбы
две́ри : говори́т
стихотво́рца : во дворце́
пусть : глу́пость
во́лосы : возголоси́те
жеребе́ц : лошалю́бец

. . . . *

спра́шивай : тпру
Све́тлости : госте́й
вме́сто : мостови́н
Ми́них : мне
Яросла́ва : голова́
во́здух : звезду́
Бог : ку́бок
тя́жкую : башку́
ороша́ет : но́шу
се́мя : весьма́
голова́ : сло́во
дураки́ : ли́рике
ге́рцог : сердца́
бра́ки : дурака́
му́зыку : языко́в
ля́сы : колесо́
со́вести : прости́
крести́нах : Све́тлости
жене́ : сраже́ния
ды́ба : раба́
сватовства́ : я́ства
Вели́чества : сва́ты(:я́-то)

секре́том : сокро́вищами :
    я́щик
ду́ши : Ушако́ву
чепуха́ : ша́ха
скакуны́ : всплакну́ть
Ушако́в : кого́
пи́ром : Биро́н
Росси́и : пе́рси
ле́са : колесо́м
короля́ : са́бля
страны́ : тро́на
набра́л : рёбра
дру́ге : дураки́
досто́йную : ину́ю

. . . . *

ве́тер : ведро́
не́бо : себе́
це́рковь : кровь
копы́тах : попыта́ет
каза́рм : ярмо́
челове́чий : свечу́
мяте́ли : мсти́тель
вопро́са : о́браз
се́рдце : серди́сь
во́рога : рога́
шлем : почему́
парчо́й : горя́чее
ски́петр : ветр
стихи́й : ти́хо
све́чи : Кири́лловиче
ого́нь : то́гой
Госуда́рыни : отны́не
опо́ру : топора́
глы́ба : лба
ма́чты : мечты́
вожди́ : оде́жды
у́лей : ци́ркуля
тьма : те́мя
вожди́ : дождь
опла́чет : палача́
шею : ве́шает
о́чи : палачи́
дья́волу : обла́ве
го́рдо : кавалерга́рд
в лову́шке мы : мы́ши
жеребца́ : ожере́лье
рука́ : ро́ка
ля́сы : колесо́
ча́ша : чешуй́

го́ловы : увы́
поэ́та : золота́я

. . . .

здоро́ва : траво́й
до́кторы : ду́ры
дурачки́ : ку́рочек
безду́шный : петуши́ный
пету́х : э́ту
заткну́ть : кнута́ми
на дыба́х : сва́дьба
оле́ней : коне́й (?)
Импе́рии : звере́й
тра́вля : журавля́м
А́нны : ан не́т

Поэма без шляпы
(114 строк) (1921)
упа́ло : куполо́в
ту́фля : скуфья́
визг : виске́
грему́чие : ручьи́
доро́ге : ноге́
отдохнове́нье : вине́
кото́рой : перо́
шутя́ : осу́шит
гру́ди : по пути́
совсе́м ещё : ямщики́
родника́ми : дни
бубенцы́ : огляну́ться
неда́вно : вино́
беда́ ли : вдали́

беде́ : ле́бедь
опра́ве : брове́й
слюно́й : поля́ной
вчера́ : черни́ла
слеза́ : желе́за
ла́ндыш : ды́шит
ясне́й : пе́сней
коле́ни : дни

Одно из стихотворений в
цикле "После грозы"
(стих. датир. окт. 1922)
(24 строки)
ша́лью : алле́й
весть : и́звесть
прие́млет : земле́

COMMENTS

(Bailey) You have turned attention to some very important and at the same time some of the very neglected aspects of Russian rhyme which is now turning out to be far more complex than has usually been assumed according to the accepted textbook definition. It seems to me, however, that one must very carefully classify the different types of rhyme, and that all such classifications must be based on the relationship between the rhyme and the last ictus in the line. For **stressed rhyme**, in which the stress of the rhyming word coincides with the last ictus, we already have the categories of masculine, feminine, dactylic, and hyperdactylic. In addition, we have **unequal rhymes** with a different number of syllables (*raznosložnaja rifma*) as well as various types of **compound rhyme** (*sostavnaja rifma*) which are really a variant of stressed rhyme. Then we have two types of rhymes in which the stress does not correspond to the last ictus: unstressed rhyme and what in English is called 'wrenched' rhyme. In **unstressed rhyme**, the last ictus in the line is not fulfilled, but the stress of the word involved nevertheless corresponds with some ictus, usually the preceding one, in the line. Rhymes like *réality* and *séa* are acceptable in English and have been for hundreds of years, but they have been relatively uncommon in Russian. In **wrenched rhyme**, the stress of a polysyllabic word is non-metrical; it does not correspond to an ictus and rhythmically it seriously disrupts the meter. Chatman has found such an example in Donne: *-príson: óne*. J. Minor in his book *Neuhochdeutsche Metrik* cites numerous examples for both these types of rhymes in German. The point is that unstressed and wrenched rhymes are quite different things when one takes the

meter into consideration and in my opinion using *raznosložnaja rifma* to describe them both misses an important distinction.

The stressing *koní* occasionally occurs in folk texts. Given Xlebnikov's general penchant for employing words and forms unusual in the literary language, do you think such stressing might be possible here? The poem you cite by Ivanov in footnote 35 is written in anapest trimeter and the last ictuses are all stressed. Do you really think this is a 'lame' rhyme or could it simply be called an experimental curiosity? Belyj's poem you quote in footnote 37 is another curiosity since all the odd lines have 'normal' stressed masculine rhymes, while all the even lines have unstressed rhymes. In footnote 13 you state that verse often differs or departs from the language. We have corresponded about this subject much and undoubtedly will in the future. After much study of Russian, English, and German verse, I have realised more and more that a poet is bound to the givens of his language, that he cannot use something which does not already exist in his language. For example, it seems highly doubtful that a Russian poet could write a poem whose meter is based on length distinctions alone or on pitch distinctions alone; this is impossible because these features on a word level are not meaningful or phonemic in Russian. In performance one may distort the language, but modes of performance vary from person to person and from one period to another. The example you cite, "Išči pód stolóm, a ne ná stolé", is a clear case of contrastive stress which can be placed on any syllable of a word in Russian. Another instance would be, "Ja skazal blágodarit', and ne pódarit'". Despite all these comments, I think you have raised many pertinent points about Russian rhyme which have been all too often ignored in the past. Any future investigator of the subject will have to take them into consideration.

(Nilsson)   Mariengof's use of rhymes is, it seems to me, more complex than demonstrated on page 244. *Ruk,* for instance, rhymes not only with *grudej,* as indicated, but also (and better) with the following *žemčug,* which in its turn is connected with *mču* (as you point out). A similar example of double rhyme couplings appears later when *strok* and *pesok* form a regular rhyme while they at the same time are also combined with *Zaratustra* and *posox.*

(Pszczołowska)   I think the heteroaccentual rhyme was really used in Russian syllabic verse. It was Polish poetry which was a pattern for this verse, but not the most developed one, where paroxytonic endings were more or less strictly preserved. Russian poets of the 17th century took advantage of the second and even third class Polish poetry which kept the medieval habit of rhyming words independently of their stress. Translating or adapting Polish poems they often

put into their works whole lines or parts of them with only slight changes. It is very possible that this way the heteroaccentual rhyme might have been not only introduced but even realized in Russian verse.

In modern poetry the heteroaccentual rhyme has sometimes quite new functions. In Mariengof's poem which is quoted at the end of your paper the status of heteroaccentual rhyme is different than in the poetry you spoke about earlier. There the rhyme is part of a complicated but very delicate orchestration of the whole text, a sound net connecting words at the end of the lines as well as inside of them. In such a situation the role of end rhyme is rather weak and its heteroaccentuality is felt as an almost 'natural' feature.

Additional discussion: Hrushovsky, Issatschenko, Segal, Shapiro

AUTHOR'S REPLY

Профессор Л. Пщоловска высказала в прениях уверенность, что р.р. была реальностью в русском силлабическом стихе, так как он развивался не под влиянием развитой польской силлабики (с ее обязательной 'пароокситонной' рифмой), а был связан с более консервативной поэзией 'второго и даже третьего класса', для которой была типична средневековая, разнородная рифмовка.

Я также согласен с профессором Нилсоном (и тою же Пщоловской), что в примере из поэмы Мариенгофа рифмовка сложнее, чем показано на схеме (не говоря уже о звуковых перекличках вообще). Это согласуется с моим замечанием (сразу после примера) о 'колеблющихся' признаках и чертах.

Еще примеры русской р.р.
Брюсов
    мистрáль страстéй:реáльностей, емý ль, как всéм:бýльканьем, чушь нестú:сýщности, прóстыни:простонú, достáла яд:отстáлая (1922), весь венóк:пéсенок, вдрéбезги:ни згú (1923)
Кузмин
    пó двору велá:вы́здоровела (1917)
Шершеневич
    до воды́:дóводы, велúкий, дыши́:вы́кидыши, не мочú:нéмочи (1915?). (Следует отметить, что в *Зеленой улице* (1916) Шершеневич привел свою рифму *топорáми:удáрами* как пример "переходящего ударения").

Есенин
   голу́бчика:Губчека́ (1924)
Валерий Перелешин
   твоя:агонизи́рующая, черт возьми́:работода́тельницами (1974)
Для сравнения из нерусской поэзии:
   regréss:áccess (Dryden)

Поправка

В прим. 45 Ройзман и Н. Эрдман записаны мною во второе поколение имажинистов. Они принадлежат к первому.

METAPHOR AND SYNTAX, IN PARTICULAR IN MANDEL'ŠTAM'S POEM *GRIFEL'NAJA ODA*

JAN M. MEIJER†

I

We live in a world and we have words for it. A large number of these words is somehow stored in our memory. Looking at a thing for which we have a word we commonly have no difficulty in finding that word. Commonly also we need an appropriate situation to induce our memory to produce the needed words. We are always in a situation, only our awareness of it varies considerably.

We seldom or never think of a word in the abstract. To abstract a word from its situation requires some intellectual exertion and articulation. But even after having made this exertion, the next time we recall that word we quite likely will do so in a given situation that calls for it; we may, for example, recall the situation in which we performed the abstraction; or any other set of circumstances that called for it. It is not so that our memory stocks definite situations for each word. But commonly, if a word presents itself to our consciousness, it does so in a situation that calls for it; which, and what kind of situation is highly unpredictable. A situation implies connections with other things, that is, in our consciousness, with other words. A word, then, seldom or never occurs to us without syntactical connections.

When we speak, when we use words actively, we do so in a given situation; for our words this means: in a given context. This situation is part of our syntax and may replace what in another situation would require expression, or a different expression. In many everyday situations our syntax as expressed is defective. This is made up for by the situation. We somehow know this and make use of it. Syntax is perhaps the most normative part of language and of our speech.

As a rule we do not mark our words. We use the means of expression appropriate to the situation. If it appears that we did not make ourselves clear we start anew until we are understood.

But words have a meaning and a history. They were not made for the situations in which we use them. They have their different shades, or valencies of meaning which are never used all at the same time. There is an irreductable kernel of meaning that the lexicographer tries to define. The entry in the dictionary will often contain elementary indications concerning its syntactical possibilities. In actual use there is always a relationship of give and take with the context in which the word is used. An actualized meaning always has a syntactical component.

In the large majority of contexts the words we use will be felt to be normal. We will not mark our words without having a special reason for it. If we do mark our words and draw particular attention to them we retard the flow of information and to some extent create a new situation.

At the other side of the spectrum there is the strict requirement to avoid any markedness; this occurs in situations that tend to repeat themselves. In such situations we use symbols. They replace words and have only one syntactical function which neutralizes the opposition marked-unmarked, as for example in algebra.

II

There are several ways to mark our words. We can simply stress them, we can repeat them, use inversion, etc. Another way is to use a word in a somewhat unusual position, what traditional rhetorics calls *figurae*. The use of a *figura* gives a kind of twist to the progress of the sentence and it imparts a somewhat different meaning from what was expected. This applies in particular to the metaphor, the *figura* that interests us here. The semantic aspect of the metaphor is, or course, undeniable. Traditionally all attention has been concentrated on this aspect. But it has a syntactical aspect that is as undeniable. An example may clarify this.

In Puškin's poem of 1830, *Stichi sočinennye noč'ju, vo vremja bessonnicy*:

> Mne ne spitsja, net ognja;
> Vsjudu mrak i son dokučnyj.
> Chod časov liš' odnozvučnyj
> Razdaetsja bliz menja.
> 5   Parki bab'e lepetan'e,
> Spjaščej noči trepetan'e,
> Žizni myš'ja begotnja...
> Čto trevožiš' ty menja?
> Čto ty zračiš', skučnyj šopot?
> 10   Ukorizna, ili ropot

Mnoj utračennogo dnja?
Ot menja čego ty chočeš'?
Ty zoveš' ili proročiš'?
Ja ponjat' tebja choču,
15   Smysla ja v tebe iščju...

lines 5-7 contain metaphors for: *chod časov liš' odnozvučnyj* of line 3. This statement is a conclusion ex post facto in the sense that we do not know this at the moment we read these lines. We do know, however, that words are marked here, as we read them. Night, for example, does not sleep, nor does it tremble. This raises questions, the progress of the sentence is hampered, several possibilities offer themselves for continuing the sentence: it may hook on to any of the three words of this line. So, side by side with the clash of word meanings there arises a double- or many-tracked syntactical construction. We have to read on in order to find out which track is taken. The next line offers nothing but another metaphor. This complicates the matter still further: either the notion of life may be further elaborated upon, or the notion of universe. The two of them clash, somehow, and it is not clear which of the two will 'win', or how the combination will syntactically be accommodated. Many more syntactical loose ends are produced than would be the case with unmarked words. A syntactical construction will have to be found that solves these problems. The next line solves the larger part of this task by linking all three lines to a single subject: *ty*, when we rather expected a plural. This gives each line its syntactical position as a temporary replacement of *chod časov odnozvučnyj* (itself a worn-out metaphor). But there remains the fact that the metaphors of lines 5-7 point in different directions. This leaves some questions unanswered; the differences between them are not satisfactorily solved by the syntactical nexus formed by *ty*. A context is still required that gives each its place. As we read on we find that these uncertainties are thematized in the further lines, in the questions that they contain, and in the wish expressed in the final line to understand the *dark* language (dark being another metaphor which both answers and confirms the uncertainty of which we spoke).

This example furnishes an illustration of the syntactical aspects of metaphor. Its first syntactical property is the creation of more than one syntactical track, the possibility of more than one continuation. The result of this is a retardation of the sentence's or the context's progress and a widening of the ground it covers. The contextual functions of the metaphor can be: (a) a change in the modality of the sentence in which it occurs, for example as a result of the uncertain character of the continuation, and/or (b) a dynamization of the context, through the insistence of the questions raised by the metaphor or metaphors, and/or (c) a thematization of the double track, in the form of straight or alternative questions. All three functions can be observed in the example we have given. Not all three of them will occur with every metaphor, but it would seem that in the kind of context we have chosen at least two can be expected.

It will be clear, then, that, at least in the kind of context we have chosen, a metaphor is not a riddle that can be finally and completely solved into meaning. There always is present a syntactical aspect, that may be weaker or stronger. The semantic and syntactical aspects of metaphor must be considered as each other's complement. In fact, metaphorically speaking, we might describe the metaphor as the meeting place, within the word, of meaning and syntax, the place where the 'mass' of meaning can be transformed into syntactical 'energy', and vice versa. Or, considered from a slightly different angle, the metaphor is a word that does not quite 'fit' in the context and causes a sort of tension. The metaphor can then be analyzed into a vector of meaning and one of tension. The latter may appear as retardation or deautomatization. The result is a syntactical shift.

Little attention has been paid to this syntactical aspect of metaphor. There are several reasons for this. In order to study an object we isolate it, when we do this with the metaphor we cut off the syntactical aspects and concentrate on the semantic side. Secondly, the study of syntax has long been restricted to the individual sentence.[1] It is only in a period when text-grammars — whatever their merits to date may be — and discourse analysis have been studied that this aspect reveals itself. Further, centuries of explanation and interpretation of canonical texts have contributed their share to this concentration on semantics at the expense of metaphor.[2]

We will leave open the question of the syntactical aspects of other *figurae*. Probably they all have it, but to a different degree. The comparison, for example, is almost without it: by way of conjunctions (like, as, etc.) it is right away brought to syntactical order.

III

It is not accidental that the example which served to illustrate the syntactical aspect of metaphor was taken from literature, and in particular from the realm of poetry. It is here that its syntactical functions are strongest and most visible. This is because the work of literature creates its own context. It is independent from larger contexts and in this respect it differs from other kinds of texts. A scientific article, for example, presupposes the general rules and tenets of the discipline it concerns. The work of literature does not have this kind of dependence; it has only itself to rely on. When we say that the work of literature creates its own context, its own situation, this means two things: that everything has to be expressed and that the means of expression that are chosen have to be justified in and by the text itself.[3] This applies to metaphors as much as to other means of expression. The consequences of this will be most apparent in poetry, more so in short than in longer poems, they may be next to invisible in prose, in particular in the longer novel. The reason for this seeming contradiction is that the longer novel may contain fragments that, taken in isolation, have few or no features of an independent context; a novel may, for example, contain longer speeches, or reproduce newspaper items. It is entirely possible that in such fragments, as in any context with unmarked boundaries, a metaphor is used and exploited at once exclusively in its semantic value. A general truth, embodied in a metaphorical expression, may be used to elaborate a particular situation, accompanied by words like 'as we all know', 'as the saying goes', and the like. This can be done in any non-literary context, and is often done. This may be one more reason for the traditional stress on the semantic aspect of metaphor. It should further be borne in mind that any systematic poetics tends to influence to some extent the poetical creation of the period, so that the theory of metaphor will have influenced to some extent its practice. But it can never do away with the syntactical functions proper to metaphor.

We spoke of unmarked boundaries in relation to certain fragments in a novel. It goes without saying that the inclusion of such fragments in the novel has to be justified in and by the novel as a whole. Its boundaries are marked like those of any artistic context. When we read, normal syntax is our point of departure. If a word acts funny, syntactically speaking, we read on to know why. The reason has to be found within the given artistic context. It is within this context that the metaphor has and exercises its context-forming capacities. It cannot be replaced there by a lengthy explanatory passage – this passage itself, in turn, would have to be justified.

IV

As our subject for a further analysis of the syntactical role of metaphors we chose Mandel'štam's poem *Grifel'naja oda*. Before we do this a few preliminary remarks are in order.

(a) The syntactical 'sidestep' that a metaphor causes implies also a point of view which differs from that of the expected linear continuation of the sentence. Or, in more traditional terms: the metaphor implies a point of view on the semantic complex it stands for or alludes to. The syntactical construction of the work in its totality will have to account for all the different points of view implied and to give each of them its place in the whole. We have already indicated some ways in which this can be done, such as thematization in the form of questions. Further study will probably reveal the existence of different types of poems in regard to metaphor. One of these would be the love poem of the kind: you are a, b, ... n, in which a, b, etc. stand for different metaphors which crowd each other out, so to speak, in an effort to express the ineffable. In this type a final thematization can occur, but is not necessary.

(b) We already mentioned the general rule according to which we start to read a work of art in the 'ordinary' way until we are struck by a metaphor. We do not start by looking for metaphors unless the reigning poetics, or other works of the same poet, induce us to do so. Even in that case our looking for metaphors may lead us astray. A word which was used metaphorically in one poem may be used straight in another, and recurrent words do not by themselves imply recurrent imagery. It is in and through the individual poem that the word functions as a metaphor and has to be justified as such.

(c) Is it useful to look into the metaphors in *Grifel'naja oda* when in the poem that preceded it we find the lines:

> S čego načat'?
> Vse treščit i kačaetsja.
> Vozduch drožit ot sravnenij.
> Ni odno slovo ne lučše drugogo,
> Zemlja gudit metaforoj,[4]

This cannot be simply explained away by the fact that it occurs in another context: these words are presented as a general statement and can be considered as metapoetry. These lines bring to mind Mandel'štam's statement about the word as a *pučok, i smysl torčit v raznye storony.*[5] If we consider these statements and others on the same subject the conclusion offers itself that Mandel'štam was very conscious of what context and syntax could do to words, and the other way round. The lines quoted above are not a vote of no confidence in the word. In particular against the background of Mandel'štam's views on the word they do not argue against the approach we have chosen here.

(d) If in a poem we find quotations from or allusions to other works by the same or a different author, does the poem alluded to or quoted belong to the quoting context *in toto*? The answer to the question put in this form is clearly negative. To begin with, allusions or quotations may be unconscious or only partly conscious. Once we start looking for them, moreover, the field is in principle unlimited. Why should one not find, for example, reminiscences from

Puškin's poem *Kavkaz podo mnoju* in *Grifel'naja oda*? If the quotation is clearly conscious, the attitude towards it may vary from endorsement to parody. Not only the attitude may vary, our memory is not a formal administrator; it brings up fragments of poems in our, not necessarily in their context. In the case of *Grifel'naja oda* the references to Deržavin's last poem and Lermontov's *Vychožu odin ja na dorogu* are clearly conscious. As clearly, Mandel'štam's memory and interpretation of those poems are part of the quotation. A quotation will often be a sounding board for the words used by the quoting poet. Their being a quotation gives them a resonance that otherwise they would not have. Here again, perhaps, we might distinguish a semantic aspect and a syntactical one, in that the sounding board helps to distribute the accents in the 'sentence' of the poem. This does by no means exhaust the functions of quotations. In a recent article Ivanov has stressed the importance of quoting in twentieth century literature[6]

(e) The often heard statement that a poem is one sentence[7] is, for the time being, a metaphor. It may be helpful as a heuristic principle. A poem is a complete statement in which different elements, even if they are formally identical, like stanzas, will have different syntactical functions in the work as a whole. This does not imply, however, that we have to start our analysis from the most general aspects and work our way towards the details. We can start at either end, or in the middle, as long as we relate the various elements of the structure to each other.

(f) We do not intend to present a total interpretation of *Grifel'naja oda* in all its aspects, but only hope to point out the syntactical aspects of metaphor and the role these play in this poem.

Grifel'naja oda

Zvezda s zvezdoj – mogučij styk,
Kremnistyj put' iz staroj pesni,
Kremnja i vozducha jazyk,
Kremen' s vodoj, s podkovoj persten',
5   Na mjagkom slance oblakov
Moločnyj grifel'nyj risunok –
Ne učeničestvo mirov,
A bred ovèč'ich polusonok.

My stoja spim v gustoj noči
10   Pod teploj šapkoju ovèč'ej.

Obratno, v krep', rodnik žurčit
Cepočkoj, penočkoj i reč'ju.
Zdes' pišet strach, zdes' pišet sdvig
Svincovoj paločkoj moločnoj,
15   Zdes' sozrevaet černovik
Učenikov vody protočnoj.

Krutye koz'i goroda;
Kremnej mogučee sloen'e:
I vse-taki ešče grjada —
20   Oveč'i cerkvi i selen'ja!
Im propoveduet otves,
Voda ich učit, točit vremja;
I vozducha prozračnyj les
Uže davno presyščen vsemi.

25   Kak mertvyj šeršen', vozle sot,
Den' pestryj vymeten s pozorom.
I noč-koršunnica neset
Gorjaščij mel i grifel' kormit.
S ikonoborčeskoj doski
30   Steret' dnevnye vpečatlen'ja,
I, kak ptenca, strjachnut' s ruki
Uže prozračnye viden'ja!

Plod naryval. Zrel vinograd.
Den' buševal, kak den' bušuet.
35   I v babki nežnaja igra,
I v polden' zlych ovčarok šuby.
Kak musor s ledjanych vysot —
Iznanka obrazov zelenych —
Voda golodnaja tečet,
40   Krutjas', igraja, kak zverenyš,

I kak pauk polzet ko mne,
Gde každyj styk lunoj obryzgan,
Na izumlennoj krutizne
Ja slyšu grifel'nye vizgi.
45   Tvoi li, pamjat', golosa
Učitel'stvujut, noč' lomaja,

Brosaja grifeli lesam,
Iz ptič'ich kljuvov vyryvaja?

My tol'ko s golosa pojmem,
50 Čto tam carapalos', borolos',
I čerstvyj grifel' povedem
Tuda, kuda ukažet golos.
Lomaju noč', gorjaščij mel,
Dlja tverdoj zapisi mgnovennoj.
55 Menjaju šum na pen'e strel,
Menjaju stroj na strepet gnevnyj.

Kto ja? Ne kamenščik prjamoj,
Ne krovel'ščik, ne korabel'ščik:
Dvurušnik ja, s dvojnoj dušoj.
60 Ja noči drug, ja dnja zastrel'ščik.
Blažen, kto nazyval kremen'
Učenikom vody protočnoj.
Blažen, kto zavjazal remen'
Podošve gor na tverdoj počve.

65 I ja teper' uču dnevnik
Carapin grifel'nogo leta,
Kremnja i vozducha jazyk
S proslojkoj t'my, s proslojkoj sveta,
I ja choču vložiť persty
70 V kremnistyj put' iz staroj pesni,
Kak v jazvu, zaključaja v styk
Kremen' s vodoj, s podkovoj persten'.

V

The very title of the poem *Grifel'naja oda* presents us with a problem. One will not dispute Victor Terras's discovery that it refers to Deržavin's last poem, written on a slate, on the theme of the racing river of time. The title thus presents us with a sounding board for the poem as a whole, and only secondarily if at all for individual words. An added pointer to Mandel'štam's attitude towards the allusion might be found in his statement in *O prirode slova* that nobody today will write a Deržavin ode.[9]

The first line contains at least one metaphor: stars do not perform the actions implied by the noun *styk*. But we do not know which word is proper and which is metaphor: it can be either *kak by styk zvezdy s zvezdoj*, or *styk, kak by zvezdy s zvezdoj*. If it is the former, the stars have to be differently predicated for a normal sentence, if the latter, the status of the subject needs revision. The frequency of the word *kremen'* in the first stanza even suggests that both are true at the same time: *kremen'* and *styk* can produce stars. The mode of the first line is made unclear by the metaphor it contains.

The second line presents a second sounding board, with its reference to Lermontov's poem *Vychožu odin ja na dorogu*. It adds the notion of the stars speaking, activating another valency of that word, that of contact in a friendly sense. This is reinforced by the word *jazyk* in the third line. The word is a metaphor and it personifies both *kremen'* and *vozduch*, making these, like the stars of line 1, into potential subjects of a sentence still to be completed. The first line may also be a factual observation, through the interpretative prism of lines 2 and 3: there is contact between entities; this contact takes the form of speech. But does this go for line 4, too? This line parallels two pairs of entities, two elements of nature and two of culture. Each pair presents a contrast: hardness, fixedness, and streaming in nature, human and animal in culture, the latter metonymically. The two cultural elements have roundness in common; *podkova* receives accents from the preceding poem to the extent that it is isolated in this one. It thus heavily partakes of time. *Persten'* is the completed rounding, by contrast the human bond, almost against time.

The syntactical status of these four lines is now even less clear than before: a vision or a train of thought, subject or object — what are we to make of it? This question is not due solely to the metaphors these lines contain: somewhat similar questions are raised, for example, by Fet's poem *Šopot, robkoe dychan'e*. But the metaphors with their additional syntactical valencies, complicate the questions and make them more insistent.

The second half of the stanza imparts some structure to what is said in the first four lines. These lines contain observations and thoughts called forth by a night landscape against a background of clouds (lines 5-6). The primordial associations that it brings up (*učeničestvo mirov*) are rejected in favour of an explanation that really is not one: *bred oveč'ich polusonok*. Both lines 5-6 and lines 7-8 are conditioned by a metaphor, namely *risunok* and *bred*. Line 8, entirely metaphorical, carries the suggestion that it is the lamb clouds which dream up the landscape. But we are not entirely sure whether *oveč'i* is not a double metaphor, suggesting also the lamb-like sleep of a human observer. There is no a priori reason to exclude this possibility. In any case the many metaphors in lines 5-8 make the syntactical status of the first stanza an extremely open one, much more so than it would be after eight non-metaphorical lines. The number of possible syntactical connections is augmented by at least the number of metaphors. Each metaphor offers the possibility of continuation on the 'real' or on the metaphorical level. And as each metaphor implies a viewpoint we have only a very preliminary perspective as yet on what is described in lines 1-4. The modality of the first stanza is thereby made highly uncertain. The questions this implies may be answered in the following stanzas or may be thematized into questions.

The first two lines of the second stanza 'select' the motive of night that is implicit in the first stanza, mainly in the words *zvezda* and *polusonok*, and to some extent activate the notion of *bred*, by means of the verb *spim*. They introduce, or confirm, the presence of a human observer (*my*) and thereby stress the metaphor for clouds in *oveč'i*. The transition from the first to the second stanza is not straight, there is a syntactical shift. We will observe this phenomenon with most of the other stanzas.[10]

Lines 11 and 12 locate the observer in the landscape, obviously a mountainous one, near a source whose water disappears into the mountain with a gurgling sound that reactivates the notion of *jazyk* through *reč'*. It streams in separate rivulets that give the impression of a chain and brings froth on the water's surface. *Kremen' s vodoj* are here observed at close quarters. This second sentence (lines 11-12) shifts the preceding one to a more metaphorical position: he who sleeps cannot hear or see the water.

The second half of this stanza is again an interpretation of observations made in the first half. We have seen the same in the first stanza and will see the same in most of the other stanzas. It reactivates the metaphor of pupils we found in line 7. It stresses their lack of mastery (*sdvig*), which gives an odd, almost cubist character to the landscape the pupils drew (the same word was used in describing cubism), and also their fear. The writing utensils activate the title. The teacher, in this view of the world of stanza 1, is the streaming water. The resulting drawing is not a final one (*černovik*).

As can be expected by now the first half of the third stanza again changes the perspective. It presents a visual inventory, either of the *černovik* or of the landscape itself. Two closely connected metaphors strike us, *koz'i* and *oveč'i*. *Oveč'i* is higher and further from the viewer, in this mountainscape, than *koz'i*, and yet, somehow, more kind, more connected with life. The two times we encountered this word before it was metaphorically connected with clouds; now the human viewpoint is stressed by the metaphors with which these two words are connected: *goroda, cerkvi i selen'ja*, which are also interconnected. *Cerkvi*, moreover, combines the notions of human and of heaven. In connection with *oveč'i* as it is used both here and in the earlier stanzas two perspectives are combined, and their meeting place. The mode is not indicative, but one of possibility. All this is rendered by metaphor; there are no other, syntactical means to express this, at least not so economically.

Once more a change of perspective occurs in the second half of this stanza and once more it is an interpretation of what was seen. The elemental entities of the first stanza, and the metaphorical level of teaching that was activated by the second stanza, teaching both religiously and in a more general sense, are here combined. The mountains are the pupils, the preaching is done by the perpendicular. The water teaches, we knew that, and time, here at last mentioned, works on them too.

The air is different from the other elements: as far as it is concerned the others could as well not have been there; there are more than enough instances of the other elements in it: *presyščen vsemi*. The word *les* is in this instance (different from line 47, where it indicates part of the landscape) a metaphor. It serves to make air and space touchable, collective, to bring it nearer to the senses. This is one metaphor that receives part of its valency from sources outside this poem. *Les* occurs in other poems also, with roughly the same function, namely to 'articulate' space. Space and vast expanses rarely occur in Mandel'štam's poetry without being articulated in this sense.[11]

The fourth stanza activates the opposition of night and day. It creates syntactical connections, again by means of a change of perspective, in particular with the second stanza. Night is now *noč'-koršunnica*. Night does not fall, it rises, while *pestryj den'* is swept out (of the room in which what matters happens). The contrast of night and day is twice modulated. Night brings up the warm chalk of day and feeds this to the harder, colder slate. The active, warm and variegated day, on the other hand, drew, with this warm chalk, its impression on the backboard of night.

The second half, to which we have now progressed, reactivates the notion of pupil. Now night makes this possible (*grifel' kormit*). The blackboard, which is made to receive impressions, does not want those of day. A context is now in the process of formation in which the pupil metaphor is shared by different entities: first the worlds, then the mountains. Now there is no clear addressee for the teacher's instructions, hence the imperative takes the form of the infinitive. The teacher's role is unspecified in the first stanza, the water assumes it in stanzas 2 and 3, it is again unspecified in the fourth, but different from stanza 1. The sentence: A teaches B begins to appear as a basic syntactical unit of this context; both A and B are inanimate, hence the predicate is a metaphor. We have had in stanza 4 another change of perspective, this time from observation to imperative; we observe that in stanzas 1-4 the teaching metaphor in its different forms always appears in the second half. It thereby assumes an important organizing role, furnishing extra valencies. Thus, for example, the word *doska*, blackboard and vertical, is 'drawn into' the landscape and becomes the vertical mountainside. The adjectival metaphor *ikonoborčeskij* refers to the world of religion and preaching and relates back to: *propoveduet otves*. The word *steret'* follows from *doska* and *mel*, but the second imperative (lines 31-32) activates other notions. Impressions have developed into visions, but because of the death of day these have become diaphanous, they are both corporeal (*ptenec*, on the arm) and incorporeal. It is striking, incidentally, that the comparisons, which are hardly context-forming as we have seen, mostly refer to the animate world, whereas the context-forming metaphors animate the inanimate. The use of *ruka* is one example of this animation.

The expected change of perspective in the first half of the next stanza is a double one, both of place and of time. This part is not so much metaphorical as metonymical. It presents an inventory of the busy day in its essential aspects and parts. An association with summer and warmth is clear from the first line of this stanza (line 33). Day had its many-faceted unruly activities (*buševal*) as against the silence and wholeness of night. Children's play and pastoral activities are essential aspects of day, of how it goes its usual unruly way (*kak den' bušuet*).

The question, briefly touched upon earlier, to what extent other tropes are also context-forming, can here be developed a little for the metonym. Its general function is to refer to something larger than itself, of which it is a part or to which it is contiguous. It is arguable that the notion of day, once being made up of metonyms as it is here, does not extend its context-forming capacities but only is articulated internally; that, once the larger entity is referred to, metonyms cannot bring about further links of this larger unit with its context. This would have to be studied further. But it is demonstrated in this stanza that at least in combination with metaphor, metonym can have this capacity. An example is furnished by *zlych ovčarok šuby*. This refers back to *teploj šapkoju oveč'ej* (1. 10). The notion: belonging to sheep, thus serves to combine high and low, night and day. It has a predicative function for contrasting subjects and thus helps to create a context to which both belong.

It is striking, in contrast to both metonym and metaphor, how extremely short the syntactical 'reach' of the comparisons is. *Kak musor, kak zverenyš, kak pauk*, all referring to water, within a space of five lines, evidently are not in each other's way. Their influence is hardly felt beyond the line they are in. The character of animate which *zverenyš* and *pauk* have in common seems less important than their contrasts.

The second half of the fifth stanza brings the expected change of perspective, but it is one of time, not one of interpretation vs. observation. There is also a change of localization. The water streams downward in a non-straight way reminding one of a playful young animal. This animate character is contradicted directly in an apposition, in line 38, in connection with: *kak musor* in line 37. The water is hungry. This implies direction and wanting to appropriate. This is the same water whose teaching role was stressed in stanza 3. We thus have a text in which the water streams, teaches, is hungry and seems rejected by the icy heights from which it comes. This is due in part to the changes of perspective, which themselves are not yet explained. The only thing that can make a context out of this is questions. These duly appear, beginning with the next stanza.

But before this happens we first get another change of perspective; we focus on what appears the final point of observation, which is occupied by the *I* of the poem. It is to this point that the hungry water is directed, several of its 'legs' come together (*styk*) and in so doing reflect and fragment the moonlight. This implies another change of perspective – the *styk* is now seen reflected; we are, literally, on a double track. The use of the word here adds another predicate to those implied in the first line, without rejecting these: the contact of stars does occur, it seems to occur, and it is reflected in water. Again, this seems somehow related to, but not fully explained by the successive perspectives.

The observing *I* hears the water falling from the steep wooded mountain-side: it is the sharp sound of the slate pencil writing on the slate. It is again personified, like the blackboard (first *ikonoborčeskij*, now *izumlennyj*). Are the elements still the pupils, and are they writing now with water (the teacher), or is the water writing for them, or is the writing done upon the slate of the mountains, on the elements, that is? Combinations are suggested that raise more questions than they answer. The context now issues into a question: the teaching which is taking place – is it done by the voice of memory? The question suggests a context in which the elements not only are not impermeable data or things, but are, rather, amenable to teaching. Further, memory was at the beginning, a memory that continues to exist in today's living observer. This voice breaks the auditive unity and wholeness of night and wrings the writing utensils from the beaks of the birds of night that bring it up.[12]

After this fundamental question the context is one in which the metaphors retain their double track and at the same time reveal their context-forming capacity. The stars do make contact, air and stone do speak in a personified universe permeated by memory, a memory which was present at the creation. Before we realized this we were sleeping. Yet at the same time they cannot do so, because they are elements. This is still only a possibility, not a crystallized philosophy. We do not clearly understand yet, but we will understand, if at all, only through the voice. Only it can articulate the essential truth and our final writing (*čerstvyj grifel'*) will follow its command (lines 49-52).

The second half of the seventh stanza brings again a change of perspective.

We now concentrate on the writing *I* in action. This action is articulation for which he has to break the wholeness of night and the warm chalk it brought up from the day. In order to arrive at this articulation the *I* exchanges the undifferentiated noise (of time?)[13] for the clearer sound of what will be on target; he exchanges the (seeming) harmony for the sharp sound of the underlying disharmony and the processes that are going on: *strepet gnevnyj*.

It is striking and at the same time understandable that this questioning part of the poem shows a certain independence from the earlier part. If the metaphorical context leads to questions, these questions will concern these metaphors and therefore cannot use them in the way the earlier stanzas did. It is possible that new metaphors develop within this questioning part. When this happens they will have a smaller reach and resonance than those in stanzas 1-6. This is in fact what happens. The *I* as writing instance repeats, with a slight shift, the metaphors used earlier. But once he is 'on his own' he uses, in lines 55-56, metaphors with a different resonance and a more short-term justification. This applies to *pen'e strel*: the sound of arrows which seek a target, an exchange of arrows, a clear conflict. This metaphor combines the notions of clarity as against undifferentiatedness, target-directed as against without destination, conflict as against patching over; it thus resumes some of the notions we have found in stanzas 1-6, and adds, or clarifies, the notion of conflict. Thereby it announces the next stanza, where this notion of conflict is elaborated and where we find an echo of *strela* in the word *zastrel'ščik*.

With this stanza, the eighth, a different process sets in; the poem opens up into a wider context with: *kto ja*. The *ja*, who has noted down the sounds and visions in this landscape, and we are now concerned, for most of this stanza, with his oeuvre also. He is *ne kamen'ščik prjamoj*, not straight away the man of *Kamen'* anymore,[14] and at the same time one who does not take *kamen'-kremen'* at face value. The *krovel'ščik* has a double track also: not one to cover up, and: not one to construct a roof over this world, knowing how open it is (stanza 1). He is *ne korabel'ščik*, not to be identified with the *moreplavatel'* or the *plotnik* of the preceding poem, not one at home on the high seas. All three negations concern handiwork and together they indicate that no single predicate or kind of work describes the *I*, and hence he does not belong to one group, is without one single loyalty: *dvurušnik ja*. The decayed metaphor *dvurušnik* is thus reactivated, and its context-forming capacity partly exploited right away: *s dvojnoj dušoj*.

The three negations have the construction: I am not ... (metaphor). This amounts to: I am not what is the straight meaning of the word, *plus* I am not what is the metaphorical meaning of the word. By rejecting a meaning as applicable to a given subject, this brings an extra meaning into the context. This furnishes one more example of the context-forming capacity of the metaphor;

this use of the metaphor is fairly common, both in daily speech and in poetry.[15]

The fourth line of the eighth stanza makes the duality in which the poet lives more explicit, linking it to one more opposition found in the first part of the poem. Looking for a clear position, still being without an answer, he starts literally by counting his blessings. Blessed he is because he named stone the pupil of streaming water, because he used the voice. In this exploratory and explanatory part of the poem he refers to an earlier metaphor but demetaphorizes it: *nazyval*; the metaphor has fulfilled its function. Blessed is he who gave the foot of the mountain a fixed position on the earth by binding the strap of its sandal to the earth: this still faintly implies, in a new metaphor which derives from the world of stanzas 1-6, the possibility of movement; this is done both by using the word *podošva* and by mentioning this action as one which is necessary and blessed, and not as a factual immutable situation.

The final stanza sums up and ties up the context. Schematically speaking the context looks like this: A is both P and P´, B is (or does) both Q and Q´ (Change of perspective). What happens is that C is (or does) both R and R´, etc. (This cannot be squared). How is this? Can it be D? I am seeing this, who am I? (Non-final answer). I now study this. I want to believe.

Looking at the stanza by itself we observe that, again by a change of perspective, it combines the two groups of 'dramatis personae': the elements, and day and night. The perspective of the latter is now horizontal: *s proslojkoj t'my, s proslojkoj sveta*. The object of study is the diary of one summer's slate jottings. The use of *leto* seems to indicate that the changes of perspective were partly the result of the course of time. But this does not yet explain the contrasts. What was jotted down is the language of the elements with the layers of day and night. The two tracks of the main metaphors of this poem here combine: the dematerialization of the elements and the materialization, or mineralization (*proslojka*) of day and night.

The disharmony which finds its expression in the double tracks of the metaphors should not be a final fact. The poet cannot but observe that fact. But he wants to believe, like the unbelieving Thomas, wants to see this as a sign of a possible final harmony of the kind described by Lermontov in the poem to which the first stanza alluded. This harmony would comprise the world of culture (*podkova, persten'*) and the world of nature, dematerialized in a time perspective.

VI

Let us try to sum up our findings briefly:

(1) Metaphor has a strong context-creating ability which is most visible in short artistic texts, in particular poetry.

(2) This ability resides in the fact that metaphor creates a double syntactical track. The continuation can be predicted either on the expected or on the actually used word. The metaphorical word actually used entails a different perspective from the one which would continue the context in an unmarked way.

(3) A metaphor requires and makes possible an over-all context which accommodates both tracks. It can thereby assume various syntactical functions (e.g., expressing some forms of contrast).

(4) While a metaphor is most easily isolated and recognized semantically, its syntactical functions are, at least in artistic texts, at least as important as its semantic aspects.[16]

(5) Further study will probably reveal the existence of several types of poems, according to the way the context-forming capacity of metaphors is used in them.

(6) Mandel'štam's *Grifel'naja oda* furnishes a clear example of the context-forming capacity of metaphors.

(7) Its fundamental syntactical structure is a series of metaphorical observations, each with a non-final interpretation which in turn contains some metaphors.

(8) The modality of the observations is often unclear; the non-final interpretations issue into questions, related with the position of the final observer, the *I*.

(9) The exploration of the *I*'s position in turn does not present a final solution, but the necessity of arriving at one and the belief that this is possible.

We hope to have shown that the metaphor with its syntactical double track is a fundamental structural element of Mandel'štam's poem *Grifel'naja oda*, and, more in general, that it is a powerful element in the creation of an artistic context. In fact, further study of metaphors can help us explore the power of words in context. The point is not to deny the importance of double meanings, but to stress the fact that finding a double meaning is only part, mostly the first part of the analysis. What has to be shown also is how such a double meaning, or other way of marking the word, fits in syntactically. While *Grifel'naja oda* furnishes a clear example, this goes in principle for every poem; it may be more or less important depending on the underlying poetics — as we said, probably a typology can be constructed. The syntactical functions of metaphor seem to be exploited in particular in twentieth-century poetry, not only in Russia, but also, perhaps even mainly, outside it. In this respect also Mandel'štam belongs squarely to modern poetry.

It might be asked whether the syntactical aspect of metaphor should be reflected in a new definition. The answer, for the time being, is negative. For one thing, no definition specifically denies it; it could be quite well understood, for example, to be part of Quintilian's *cum virtute*, while on the other hand at this stage of development in contextual syntax it might be premature. If pressed for definitions of the notions of syntax and metaphor as I have worked with them, I would state that syntax is/studies the relationships of words within contexts with marked boundaries, and that metaphor is the term for a marked word which is used instead of an unmarked word or group of words and which, in the perspective it implies, has one or two semes in common with what it replaces or is felt to replace.

University of Utrecht

NOTES

[1] See for example *Grammatika russkogo jazyka*, II: *Sintaksis*, 1 (Moskva 1954), p. 6: "sintaksis – èto drugaja čast' grammatiki, (...) soderžaščaja pravila sočetanija slov i pravila sostavlenija predloženij, t. e. izlagaetsja učenie o predloženii."
[2] For a general survey of metaphor see C. F. P. Stutterheim, Jr., *Het begrip Metaphoor: Een taalkundig en wijsgerig onderzoek* (Amsterdam 1941); for a historical-rhetorical survey see H. Lausberg, *Handbuch der literarischen Rhetorik: Eine Grundlegung der Literaturwissenschaft*, 2 vols. (München 1973²), paragraphs 558-64 (pp. 285-91). See also St. Ullmann, *Semantics: An Introduction to the Science of Meaning* Oxford 1964). On the Russian metaphor in particular see Ju. I. Levin, "Struktura russkoj metafory", $\Sigma\eta\mu\epsilon\iota\omega\tau\iota\kappa\dot{\eta}$. *Trudy po znakovym sistemam* II (Tartu 1965), pp. 293-99, and his "Russkaja metafora: Sintez, semantika, transformacii", *ibid.* IV (Tartu 1969), pp. 290-305. Most interesting from our point of view is the article by N. N. Volkov, "Čto takoe metafora", *Chudožestvennaja forma, Sbornik statej*, Izdanie GAChN (Moskva n. y. [1927]), pp. 81-124. He regards the metaphor as a judgement (*suždenie*) and a relationship. If two things are in a relationship which is proper to them and does not apply to other things, these things are each other's 'interior predicate' (*vnutrennij predikat*). Two quotations may indicate his position: "Naznačenie est' dejstvitel'nyj, vnutrennij predikat vešči, zaključennyj v samoj vešči" (*o. c.* p. 115) and: "vsja tajna metafory zaključena v logičeskoj prirode vešči, 'logičeskoj', t. e. raskryvajuščej v sebe suždenie," and also:"metaforu ja ponimaju kak svernutoe suždenie, gde vešč' ili obraz zaključaet svoj vnutrennij predikat."
    Volkov thus occupies an intermediate position between the rhetorical study of metaphor in a wider sense, and philosophical and psychological studies of metaphor like those of Pongs and Werner (H. Pongs, *Das Bild in der Dichtung*, I: *Versuch einer Morphologie der metaphorischen Formen* (Marburg 1927), II: *Voruntersuchungen zum Symbol* (Marburg 1939), III: *Der symbolische Kosmos der Dichtung* (Marburg 1969); H. Werner, *Ursprünge der Lyrik* (München 1924) (his *Die Ursprünge der Metapher*, Leipzig 1919, has not been available, but see Stutterheim pp. 240-268, who also discusses Pongs on pp. 268-311). Werner stresses the relationship of metaphor and tabu, while Pongs, quoting Vico's words that every metaphor is a little myth, concludes that, "jede Metapher enthält das Weltbild

ihres Dichters" (II, p. 56) and regards "das metaphorische Bilden als die Brücke zwischen dem unsäglichen und dem sagbaren".
3 Cf. Jan M. Meijer, "Verbal Art as Interference between a Cognitive and an Aesthetic Structure", *Structure of Texts and Semiotics of Culture* (The Hague 1973), pp. 313-48.
4 This is the only time the word occurs in his poetry, as against three times for the word *sravnenie*. See *A Concordance to the Poems of Osip Mandel'štam*, edited by Demetrius J. Koubourlis (Ithaca and London 1974). A propos of relative frequency of words, in a total of 309 words we count 198 different words.
5 In his "Razgovor o Dante", *Works* II (1966), p. 413.
6 V. V. Ivanov, "Značenie idej M. M. Bachtina o znake, vyskazyvanii i dialoge dlja sovremennoj semiotiki", Σημειωτική. *Trudy po znakovym sistemam* VI (Tartu 1973), pp. 5-44. In this connection he mentions Mandel'štam "in whose creation the significance of covert quotations is very important" (*o. c.* p. 20). Cf. *ibid.*, p. 19: "Such 'collages' from quotations comparable to the cento mentioned by Bachtin, which consists of other poets' lines and halflines, have become common in contemporary prose (...), where the quotations can be regarded as metonymical replacements of an entire text". Cf. also O. Ronen, "Leksičeskij povtor, podtekst i smysl v poètike Osipa Mandel'štama", *Slavic Poetics: Essays in Honor of Kiril Taranovsky* (The Hague 1973), pp. 367-87, and his "Mandel'štam's Kaščej", *Studies Presented to Professor Roman Jakobson by his Students* (Boston 1968), pp. 252-64. He finds this metonymical character of quotations in poetry also, at least with Mandel'štam, "as the reader on the strength of the elements presented in the text has to figure out the whole (*podtekst*) from which they are taken". This is only part of the operation. It is clear from the poems as a whole that the differences between Mandel'štam and his sources are stronger than the agreements, notwithstanding his admiration for both Deržavin and Lermontov. There is as much ground to view the quotations, or rather references in this poem as indicating: an ode like, but different from, Deržavin's; a road like that in Lermontov's poem, but at the same time different from it, i.e., to view them as metaphors.
   By using the metaphor sounding board we want to indicate not so much the metaphorical or metonymical character of a quotation (depending on the case, either one may dominate), but to stress the fact that both by the referential lines it draws and by the extra accents it imparts to the words, a quotation may have a syntactical function also. (Perhaps this problem highlights also the importance of the boundaries of the work of art: what is metaphorical within one work of art may become metonymical in part in another work of art, precisely by reference to the former in the latter.)
7 Mandel'štam himself spoke of a lyrical composition as one word: "Vsjakij period stichotvornoj reči, bud' to stročka, strofa ili cel'naja liričeskaja kompozicija – neobchodimo rassmatrivat' kak edinoe slovo." *Works* II (1966), p. 413.
8 We take the text as it is printed in vol. I² (1967) of his works, i.e., including the second half of the 6th and the first half of the seventh stanza which, according to Chardžiev (*O. Mandel'štam: Stichotvorenija*. Vstup. stat'ja A. L. Dymšica, sostavlenie, podgotovka teksta i primečanija N. I. Chardžieva, izd. vtoroe, Leningrad 1973, p. 283), the author later excluded from the author's copy. This means probably the copy from which the original publication was made. We have no way of collating our text with the publication in *Vtoraja kniga*, but hold this to be identical with ours. Further, Chardžiev's editing has come in for some criticism. Moreover, the problem of variants is particularly acute for this poem and it deserves further separate study. Some of them have been published by Jennifer Baines ("Mandel'štam's *Grifel'naja oda*: A Commentary in the Light of Unpublished Rough Drafts", *Oxford Slavonic Papers* V (1972), pp. 61-82), and there are others, it seems.
9 In "O prirode slova", *Works* II (1966), p. 286. Cf. *ibid.* p. 268: 'kak trubnyj glas zvučit ugroza, nacarapannaja Deržavinym na grifel'noj doske'. Terras's article "The Time Philo-

sophy of Osip Mandel'štam" is in *Slavonic and East European Review*, xlvii (1969), pp. 344-354. D. Segal calls the poem a sustained commentary by Mandel'štam on Deržavin's lines (D. M. Segal, "O nekotorych aspektach smyslovoj struktury *Grifel'noj ody* O. E. Mandel'štama", *Russian Literature* 2 (1972), pp. 49-102). We refer to this interesting article for an approach which in many respects differs from ours.

[10] This perhaps partly accounts for the metonyms in line 4 of the first stanza. When the perspective switches it may move from metaphor, through metonym, to interpretation. The metonym would then have to be considered as an exploitation of some of the consequences or implications of the metaphor.

[11] See for example *Kogda Psicheja žizn' (poluprozračnyj les; les bezlistvennyj)*, and *Koncert na vokzale (tverd' kišit červjami; stekljannyj les vokzala)*.

[12] Ronen, *Slavic Poetics*, p. 377, has deciphered *ptičij kljuv* as 'pencil', "on the basis of the entire context in which this word is used by Mandel'štam". As we stated, we do not consider the entire context as necessarily indicating a special use in a given poem. This would imply a fixedness of vocabulary which would be exceptional. M's vocabulary shows marked developments, as Levin has shown.

[13] *Šum vremeni* is of 1925; it is possible, therefore, that we witness here the origin of that notion.

[14] Gorodeckij had called him *kamenščik* in 1913; see *Russkaja literatura konca XIX – načala XX v, 1908-1917* (Moskva 1972), p. 548.

[15] The use of proper names can be compared to this, e.g.: "Net, ja ne Bajron, ja drugoj."

[16] Viewed under the aspect of *tesnota* the metaphor could be regarded as a local overdose of *tesnota*, as a result of which two words would move one below the other.

COMMENTS

(Winner) If I may be allowed a discussion of the discussion and not the paper itself, I should like to disagree with your statement that a literary code – in contrast to a code in a metrical language – exists only when the historical period that has produced it is closed off. Your example was that the 'code' of Romanticism exists only **after** Romanticism as a way of writing literature is no longer functional.

Your postulate would assume that codes are **conscious** systems of norms and prohibitions. But they are not completely conscious, but to a very large degree subliminal, just as are the codes of language where the code (*langue*) is part of every speaker's competence, but the speaker, like M. Jourdain, is not aware of the rules which he is following. I think – though artistic codes and all secondary codes are in many ways different from the primary codes of natural language – the former are all also largely subliminal **and** in constant flux. So:

1. We cannot be sure when Romanticism ends;

2. Can we speak of a Romantic code which would unite *Sturm und Drang* and Lamartine? I think not;

3. Codes are not entirely conscious.

Additional discussion: Broyde, Nilsson, Segal, Shapiro

'Code' implies two notions:

a. a set of signs which allows of an element-by-element rendering of a message in a natural language, for example morse or military codes, and

b. a set of rules, conscious or unconscious (or partly conscious), which regulates certain kinds of actions or behaviour.

Codes can be divided into universal, or non-historical, and historical. This division does not coincide with that between a. and b. A historical code structures historical material and this material eo ipso is transient. However, the structure will have a permanence different from the historical material itself. Such a structure will at first be partly unconscious. At first it will appear as a configuration, a point of view on fundamental topical questions. It will gradually reveal a number of open spaces that can be 'filled out'. As this happens the code will become more conscious, until a stage of almost complete predictability is reached. It is only the appearance of the emergence of a new code which makes clear that this last stage is attained. It is only then, i.e., only after it has stopped functioning, that the code can be formulated comprehensively. So,

1) We cannot be sure to the day when Romanticism ends but we can be sure that by 1840 this is the case.

2) We can speak of a romantic code, the romantic code which would unite *Sturm und Drang* and Lamartine. Elements of this code would be

a) a central position of an 'I' in the world,

b) nature not as an independent entity, but more as a reflection of the hero's mood,

c) the virtual absence of two or more independent views of the hero.

ПОЛЬСКИЙ ЯМБИЧЕСКИЙ СТИХ
(В СОПОСТАВЛЕНИИ С РУССКИМ)

ЛЮЦИЛЛЯ ПЩОЛОВСКА

В настоящей работе я хочу заняться основными свойствами реализации ямбического метра в польском стихе. В польских стихотворениях метрическая схема ямба встречается в строках различной силлабической длины: от 4 до 17 слогов. Но во всём ямбическом творчестве польских поэтов чаще всего употребляется метр с 4 сильными местами, который может быть реализован в виде ямбического 8-сложника или 9-сложника, причём 9-сложник в значительной мере преобладает. Ямбический 8-сложник не выступает как единственный стихотворный размер ни в строфике, ни в астрофическом стихе; он всегда чередуется с 9-сложником или 7-сложником. 9-сложником же написаны многие отдельные строфические произведения XX столетия, в астрофическом стихе он также бывает единственным или почти единственным размером, выступая в длинных рядах. По вышеизложенным причинам ямбический 9-сложник будет главным предметом моих исследований.

В основном я буду заниматься 9-сложным ямбическим стихом междувоенного 20-летия XX века; по мере надобности буду обращаться также к более ранним и более поздним периодам его развития. Стих этот будет сопоставлен с русским ямбом. В сопоставлении такого рода интересны прежде всего сходства и различия в реализации одной и той же метрической схемы в двух славянских языках флективного строя, но с различными типами ударения. Не следует также забывать об известном факте влияния русского ямба на распространение в Польше в XX столетии ямбического 9-сложника.

Анализируя польский ямбический 9-сложник, я начну с самых общих характерных черт реализации ямбического метра в языковом материале, которые свойственны также другим силлабо-тоническим метрам, а кончу самыми специфическими чертами, касающимися только реализации метра с 9 местами.

I. Ямбический метр реализуется в различных национальных стихосложениях. Почти во всех стихосложениях нового времени ему свойствен такой способ реализации, что одному месту метра (сильному или слабому) соответствует один слог. В каждом же отдельном стихосложении ямб отличается характерными чертами реализации, зависящими, главным образом, от языковой системы и от акцентного строя текстов данного языка.

1. В польском языке самая общая черта ямбического метра, присущая также всем остальным реализованным в этом языке силлабо-тоническим метрам, состоит в том, что решительное большинство случаев реализации метра имеет парокситоническое окончание; при таком окончании последнее место реализуемого метра всегда слабое. Это свойство тесно связано с типом и местом ударения в польском языке: ударение имеет постоянное место в слове, независимо от его парадигматической формы и является парокситоническим во всех полисиллабах и в огромном большинстве полисиллабических фонетических слов.[1] Именно такие фонетические слова составляют значительное большинство всех фонетических слов в каждом тексте польского языка.[2]

2. Следующая, тесно связанная с предыдущей, черта реализации ямбического метра свойственна всем силлабо-тоническим метрам с последним слабым местом. Она состоит в том, что предпоследнему месту метра (т.е. — сильному месту) отвечает почти в 100% полноударный слог полисиллабического слова.[3] В польском языке это равнозначно во всех случаях окончанию стихотворной строки полисиллабом.

3. Когда последним местом метрической схемы является сильное место, реализация ямбического метра в польском стихе, как впрочем и всех других силлабо-тонических метров, требует в этом месте 1-сложного слова. От этого правила нет уже никаких исключений.

Преобладание парокситонических окончаний ямбических строк объясняется также в некоторой степени требованиями рифмы, которая для польского силлабо-тонического стиха является обязательным фактором. Односложные проклитики и энклитики не допускаются, в принципе, в рифменных окончаниях, а односложные полнозначные слова встречаются довольно редко в польской лексике. В связи с этим мужская рифма, которая требует окситонического окончания, является в польском стихе особо маркированной и в значительном большинстве стихотворений выступает как один из типов созвучия — рядом с женской рифмой.

Вышеупомянутые ограничения были осознаны поэтами сразу же после первых опытов введения ямба в польскую литературу. Наиболее выдающийся основоположник силлаботонизма, Мицкевич, только два

очень коротких стихотворения написал ямбическим размером с исключительно мужской рифмой. Но уже в драматическом произведении
"Дзяды" он пользуется в одной из сцен ямбическими размерами с окси-
тоническим и парокситоническим окончанием. Подобное отношение к
ямбическим размерам будет с того времени у всех поэтов XIX и XX
веков.[4]

В русском стихосложении ямбический метр с 4 сильными местами
реализуется без тенденции к преобладанию парокситонических окончаний строк. Это значит, что он выступает в форме 8-сложника или
9-сложника. В традиции русского стиховедения глубоко укоренилось
пренебрежительное отношение к этому силлабическому различию. Я не
хочу вступать здесь в спор с такой точкой зрения; в некоторой степени
она мотивирована подвижным ударением в русском языке и редукцией
безударных гласных. Но это пренебрежение к силлабическому различию между двумя реализованными формами ямбического метра
отражается на результатах исследований. Например, в подсчётах, отно-
сящихся к частотности 1-сложных слов в определённых местах ямбической схемы, не различается силлабическая длина стихотворной строки, хотя она в известной мере влияет на количество моносиллабов.

Русскими стиховедами не описано также, какой частотностью в
анализируемых ими стихотворениях характеризуются 8-сложные, а
какой — 9-сложные ямбические размеры. По наблюдениям М. Л. Гаспарова, которыми он со мной любезно поделился, в коротких строфи-
ческих стихотворениях встречается чаще всего чередование 8- и 9-
сложника. (Бывает также, что 8-сложник или 9-сложник выступают как
единственные размеры в таком стихотворении, но с одинаковой частотностью.)

В стихотворениях, написанных более длинной строфой, чем 4-стишие,
8-сложник преобладает. В длинных астрофических произведениях также
больше 8-сложников. И что самое главное для интересующих нас здесь
сравнений — бывают поэмы, написанные только 8-сложником, но не
встречаются такие, в которых единственным размером являлся бы
9-сложник.

Из описанных выше, самых общих черт реализации ямбического
метра (см. 1, 2, 3), для русского стиха характерна вторая из них. В
русском ямбе с ударением на предпоследнем слоге, как впрочем и в
реализациях всех остальных силлабо-тонических метров с таким окончанием, последнему сильному месту отвечает почти всегда ударяемый
слог полисиллаба. О том, что первая, сформулированная для польского
стиха, характерная черта в русском стихе не реализуется, я говорила

выше. Третья черта — обязательное присутствие моносиллаба на последнем месте в случае реализации метров с последним местом сильным — в русском стихе не используется, так как имеет он богатый запас полисиллабических словоформ с ударением на последнем слоге.

II. Следующие, более узкие по сфере употребления, характерные черты реализации ямбического метра в польском стихе свойственны реализации метров с простым чередованием сильных и слабых мест независимо от того, с какого — сильного или слабого — места это чередование начинается, т.е. как для ямба, так и для хорея.

1. В польском ямбическом и хореическом стихе наблюдается тенденция к группировке моносиллабов в определённых местах метрической схемы. Эту тенденцию мы постараемся определить более точно по отношению к ямбическому метру (в котором места группировки моносиллабов не во всех случаях такие же, как в хорее). Тенденция к увеличению количества моносиллабов в определённых местах ямбического и хореического метра свойственна также русским реализациям ямба и хорея.

2. В польских реализациях ямба и хорея, начиная с метра с 7 местами, имеется отчётливая тенденция к цезуре. В реализации хореических метров с 7 и 8 местами цезура выступает после 4 слога; в реализации ямбического метра с 8 местами — после 4 или после 5 слога; в реализации ямба с 9 местами — после 5 слога. В русском стихе с аналогичной структурой вышеупомянутая тенденция в основном не наблюдается.[5]

3. Третьей и главной характерной чертой реализации ямбических и хореических метров в польском стихе является запрет заполнения слабых мест слогами полисиллабов, на которые падает главное ударение. Для полного осмысления этого запрета, касающегося языковой структуры стиха, нужно ввести типологию слогов с точки зрения их отношения к словесному ударению. Я предлагаю здесь следующую типологию:

A. Слоги полисиллабов.
    1. С главным словесным ударением.
В каждом слове имеется один слог с главным ударением. Это ударение обязательно.
    2. С побочным ударением.
Побочное ударение факультативно. Оно может быть на слогах, отделённых хотя бы одним слогом от слога с главным словесным ударением.

3. Безударные.

Безударными являются прежде всего слоги, непосредственно прилегающие к полноударному слогу. Безударность таких слогов обязательна. Кроме них в длинном слове могут существовать также другие безударные слоги, прилегающие к слогу с побочным ударением. Их безударность зависит от акцентного контекста слова, и поэтому она факультативна: в другом контексте на тех же слогах может быть побочное ударение.

В 2-сложных и 3-сложных словах названные выше типы слогов размещаются по следующему принципу:

$$\overset{1}{ra}\overset{3}{nek} \qquad \overset{3}{po}\overset{1}{god}\overset{3}{ny}$$

В 4-сложных и 5-сложных словах, являющихся самостоятельными фонетическими словами, на первом слоге может стоять побочное ударение:[6]

$$\overset{2}{bły}\overset{3}{ska}\overset{1}{wi}\overset{3}{ca} \qquad \overset{2}{li}\overset{3}{te}\overset{3}{ra}\overset{1}{tu}\overset{3}{ra}$$

Когда перед 4-сложным словом находится проклитический моносиллаб, который вместе с ним составляет одно фонетическое целое, побочное ударение может стоять на этой проклитике. Например:

$$\overset{2}{ta} \ \overset{3}{bły}\overset{3}{ska}\overset{1}{wi}\overset{3}{ca}$$

То же самое касается 5-сложного слова. Но в случае, когда оно составляет одно фонетическое слово с предшествующим ему проклитическим моносиллабом, в этом фонетическом слове могут быть два побочных ударения: на проклитике и на втором слоге 5-сложного слова:

$$\overset{2}{do} \ \overset{3}{li}\overset{2}{te}\overset{3}{ra}\overset{1}{tu}\overset{3}{ry}$$

Однако побочное ударение не всегда ограничено рамками фонетического слова. Когда многосложному грамматическому слову предшествует не проклитический, но полнозначный, моносиллаб, являющийся самостоятельным акцентным целым, расположение ударений в многосложном слове может быть таким же, как в первом случае.

Сравним:

$$\overset{2}{po} \ \overset{3}{bły}\overset{3}{ska}\overset{1}{wi}\overset{3}{cy}$$

и

$$\overset{1}{tor} \ \overset{3}{bły}\overset{3}{ska}\overset{1}{wi}\overset{3}{cy}$$

или   do literatury

и   los literatury

К сказанному выше стоит еще добавить, что явление побочного ударения в какой-то степени связано с темпом речи, от которого не зависят ни главное словесное ударение, ни обязательная безударность слогов, смежных с сильноударяемым слогом.

    Б. Моносиллабы.
      1. Ударные.
      2. Безударные.

К первому типу относятся вообще так называемые полнозначные моносиллабы: 1-сложные формы существительных, прилагательных, глаголов, наречий и местоимений в именительном падеже. Ко второму — так называемые неполнозначные слова: предлоги, союзы, местоимение "się" и местоимения в косвенных падежах. Но это деление имеет иной характер, чем в случае слогов полисиллабов, и может быть принято только по отношению к моносиллабам, выступающим изолированно. В речи же ударность или безударность односложных слов зависит не столько от их значения, сколько от акцентного контекста и сильной тенденции к парокситоническому ударению, которая свойственна также во многих случаях словосочетаниям, состоящим из односложных слов.[8] Самое главное здесь то, что моносиллаб, который в одном сочетании является безударным или слабоударным, в другом — выступает как ударный:

„ta wiéś", „ná wieś", „na dóm", „dóm z kárt", „dóm ójca"

Как видно из этих примеров, это касается, в основном, как полнозначных, так и неполнозначных моносиллабов, хотя на первых чаще стоит ударение, чем на вторых.

В свете данной выше типологии слогов становится ясным, что сформулированный в II.3. запрет заполнения слабых мест ямбического и хореического метров теми слогами полисиллабических слов, которые имеют главное ударение, влечёт за собой отсутствие на сильных местах "обязательно безударных" слогов таких слов. Эти слоги находятся ведь в непосредственном соседстве со слогами, имеющими главное ударение, и в более длинных словах бывают от них отделены слогом с побочным ударением. Итак, для ямба и хорея запрет II.3. может быть формулирован также, как:

3а. Запрет заполнения сильных мест 'обязательно безударными' слогами полисиллабов.

К запрету II.3. и вытекающей из него формуле II.3а сводятся ограничения, относящиеся к реализации слабых и сильных мест ямбических и хореических метров. Это значит, что сильные места этих метров могут быть реализованы при помощи слогов с главным ударением, с побочным ударением и моносиллабов обоих типов. На слабых местах могут стоять слоги полисиллабов с побочным ударением, слоги полисиллабов 'обязательно безударные' и моносиллабы обоих типов. Следовательно, слоги полисиллабов, на которых может быть побочное ударение, и моносиллабы обоих типов эквивалентны в сфере реализации ямбических и хореических метров: все они могут заполнять как сильные, так и слабые места.

Запрет заполнения слабых мест ямба и хорея слогами полисиллабов с главным ударением касается также и русского стиха. Роман Якобсон, который сформулировал этот запрет для русского (и болгарского) стиха,[9] связывает его со словоразличительной ролью ударения в русских полисиллабах. Факт, что на слабых местах метров с простым чередованием слабых и сильных мест могут стоять ударные моносиллабы, Якобсон объясняет тем, что их ударение, не будучи фонологическим, имеет "избыточный характер, роднящий ударение моносиллабов с безударными слогами полисиллабов".[10] "Безударные" обозначает в этой цитате — не несущие на себе главного словесного ударения, так как в приведённой статье различаются только 2 класса слогов: ударные и безударные. Это кажется слишком общим различием. В реализации ямбических и хореических метров в русском стихе последствия рассматриваемого здесь запрета такие же, как и в польском: сильные места могут быть заполнены только такими слогами полисиллабов, не имеющими главного ударения, на которых может стоять побочное ударение.

В польских полисиллабах, как известно, ударение выполняет только кульминационную и демаркационную функции. Помимо того, запрет, о котором идёт речь, является существенным, как мы видели, для польских реализаций ямбических и хореических метров. В польском стихе наблюдается также реализация слабых мест при посредстве ударных моносиллабов. Может быть, языковые причины здесь такого рода: в полисиллабах имеется оппозиция между слогами с главным ударением и теми, на которых нет такого ударения. В моносиллабах такой оппозиции нет и быть не может. Их ударение имеет в огромном большинстве случаев позиционный характер, осуществляется оно или нет — зависит это от речевого контекста. Таким просодическим контекстом является также для моносиллабов и для тех слогов полисиллабов, на которых может стоять побочное ударение, метрическая схема. Её характер, конечно, иной, чем акцентный ход реального языкового соседства. Но имеется ведь в силлабо-тоническом стихе явление, называемое ритмическим импульсом. Это явление можно рассматривать со стороны воспринимающего стихотворный текст как осознанную реализацию определённого метра.

Эквивалентность моносиллабов и тех слогов полисиллабов, на которых может стоять побочное ударение в реализации как слабых, так и сильных мест ямба и хорея, является причиной некоторых метрических "расслаблений". Это может происходить особенно тогда, когда слабое место заполнено полнозначным моносиллабом, а ближайшее сильное место — неполнозначным моносиллабом, который обычно выступает в тексте как проклитика или энклитика.

Например, в ямбе:

Wiódł swą opowieść: ... no więc właśnie ...

или в хорее:

Trzeba wstawać, *choć chęć* słaba.

Подобные случаи принадлежат однако описанию конкретных способов реализации метра, которыми я в этой работе не занимаюсь.

III. Характерная черта реализации ямбических и хореических метров с 4 сильными местами.

Из рассуждений о языковой структуре стиха в I.2 и I.3 видно, что эта черта касается только парокситонических реализаций таких метров, то есть ямбического 9-сложника и хореического 8-сложника (кстати, это также самый частый хореический метр в польском стихе). Черта эта состоит в дифференциации сильных мест метрической схемы. В стихе, который реализует метр с 4 сильными местами, последнее сильное место чаще других будет заполнено слогами полисиллабов с главным ударением. За ним следует второе сильное место, на которое приходится в среднем несколько меньше таких слогов. Первое и третье сильные места отличаются значительным уменьшением частотности слогов с главыми ударением:

Ямбический 9-сложник
(по стиху поэмы Тувима "Польские цветы")

I	II	III	IV
56%	80%	38%	99%

Хореический 8-сложник
(по стихотворениям Тувима)

I	II	III	IV
34%	92%	33%	99%

Описываемая дифференциация сильных мест совпадает с дифференциацией, наблюдаемой в русском стихе (независимо от подробных различий в поэзии XVIII, XIX и XX веков). Это явление, названное К. Тарановским правилом регрессивной диссимиляции, в русской поэзии проявляется шире, чем в польской: оно охватывает также окситонические реализации ямба и хорея с 4 сильными местами.

Для сравнения с польским стихом приведу здесь результаты исследования реализации сильных мест сильноударными слогами полисиллабов нескольких сотен ямбических 9-сложников и хореических 8-сложников из русской поэзии:

Ямбический 9-сложник
(по лирике Блока 1898-1905)

I	II	III	IV
58%	81%	45%	100%

Как видно, частотность слогов полисиллабов с главным словесным ударением на очередных сильных местах метра очень похожа на то, что мы видели в польском стихе.

Хореический 8-сложник
(по лирике Блока 1898-1905)

I	II	III	IV
47%	88%	45%	100%

В русском хореическом стихе на первом и третьем сильных местах, которые в обоих языках насыщены меньше главными ударениями полисиллабов чем второе и четвёртое, мы наблюдаем больше таких ударений, чем в польском. Сопоставление расположения слогов с главным ударением в обоих языках позволяет утверждать, что в польском стихе реже встречаются строки, в которых все сильные места реализованы посредством таких слогов. Даже заполнение трёх сильных мест такими слогами в польском стихе не так часто, как в русском. Может быть, что и в этом различии играет роль характер и место ударения в польских словоформах. В языке, в котором ударение всегда стоит на предпоследнем слоге слова, бо́льшая, чем реально выступающая в стихе, частотность стихотворных строк с 4 или даже 3 сильными местами, заполненными сильноударными слогами, могла бы быть источником однообразия. Такое однообразие не угрожает русскому хореическому стиху в связи с подвижностью ударения в русском языке.

IV. Характерная черта реализации ямбических метров.

Несмотря на количество сильных мест в метре, реализации ямбических метров в польском стихе свойственна тенденция к несоблюдению на первом слабом месте запрета, сформулированного в II.3, то есть запрета реализации слабых мест слогами полисиллабов с главным словесным ударением.

Среди польских полисиллабов ударение на первом слоге имеют только двусложные слова. Поэтому вышеупомянутая тенденция неизбежно влечёт за собой реализацию следующего, сильного места метрической схемы посредством обязательно безударного слога. Мы получаем тогда, например, такую разновидность ямбического метра для 9 мест:

X́ X X X́ X X́ X X́ X   Barwa się z barwą w słońcu mieni

В польской поэзии XX века такую разновидность ямба реализует в среднем 25% 9-сложников,[11] около 16% 8-сложников и около 12-14% более коротких размеров. Но несоблюдение в начале строки правила, которое запрещает заполнять слабые места ямба слогами полисиллабов с главным словесным ударением, отмечается уже в очень ранних реализациях ямбического метра. Так построены ямбические 9, 8 и 6-сложники Мицкевича, такая тенденция выступает в ямбических стихотворениях поэтов позитивизма и модернизма.

Роль описанной разновидности ямбического стиха сводится чаще всего только к разнообразию ритмической формы стихотворения, без стилистической маркированности. Строки, начинающиеся с дисиллаба, не выполняют также в общем какой-либо композиционной функции, хотя в строфике, а также в астрофическом стихе, выступают часто поочерёдно.

Представленная выше тенденция в реализации ямба связана, наверно, с большой частотностью двусложных слов с пароокситоническим ударением в текстах польского языка, особенно в стихе, который, как известно, предпочитает короткие единицы. Но тенденция эта связана также с 'механизмами' языковой организации. В этом можно убедиться, сравнивая ямбические 9-сложники с 9-сложными отрезками прозы, структура которых отвечает чертам реализации ямбического метра, описанным в пунктах I-III. Если в этой структуре допустить появление дисиллаба в начале отрезка, окажется, что во всей совокупности прозаических отрезков[12] тенденцию к 'сильному началу' представляет 24% отрезков.[13]

В русском стихе нет тенденции к несоблюдению запрета на первом слабом месте. Запрет реализации слабых мест посредством сильноударных слогов полисиллабов соблюдается строго в XIX веке: исследователи нашли только один случай его нарушения Пушкиным и один Жуковским.[14] В начале XX века подобные случаи встречаются немного чаще, но они также воспринимаются как нарушение метрической схемы (Брюсов, Багрицкий, Цветаева и др.). Исследователи относятся к ним как к способам интонационной выделенности слова в начале строки[15] или как к "игре на ... уклонах от нормы".[16] Первое слабое место метра заполняется, таким образом, или слогом полисиллаба, на котором не стоит главное ударение, или моносиллабом.[17]

V. Характерные черты реализации ямбического 9-сложника.

1. Ощущается здесь очень сильная тенденция к словоразделу после 5 слога. Цезурная форма 5 + 4 выступает в 87%-95% строк в 9-сложнике XIX и XX веков. Причём, колебание в пределах 8% зависит не от поэтики, но от конкретного текста.

Столь выразительная тенденция к цезуре в польском 9-сложнике непосредственно связана с рассматриваемой в III. дифференциацией сильных мест метра. Акцентное выделение четвёртого очередного места (второе сильное место) при посредстве сильноударных слогов полисиллабов в языке с пароокситоническим ударением словоформ неуклонно влечёт за собой словораздел после пятого слога. Такое разделение строки является также отражением и увеличением тенденции, выступающей в 9-сложных отрезках прозы с ямбической структурой. 75% этих отрезков имеют словораздел после 5 слога.[18]

С описанной тенденцией к цезуре после 5 слога связана вторая характерная черта реализации ямбического метра с 9 местами, а именно:

2. Тяготение односложных слов к первому и шестому местам. Это представляют следующие данные (по стиху поэмы Тувима "Польские цветы"):

	1.	2.	3.	4.	5.	6.	7.	8.	9.
Моносиллабы	47%	16%	17%	20%	13%	38%	9%	1%	1%
Полнозначные	11%	10%	1%	6%	1%	10%	1%		
Неполнозначные	36%	6%	16%	14%	12%	28%	8%		

Из таблицы видно, что частотность односложных слов самая большая на первом месте: 47% слогов, заполняющих это место, является односложными словами. Но как первое, так и шестое место, где в 38% строк стоит односложное слово, явно доминируют в этом отношении над всеми остальными.

Взаимосвязь обеих особенных черт реализации ямба с 9 местами в польской поэзии имеет источником способы заполнения строк единицами ритмического словаря и структуру этих единиц. Но отдельного рассмотрения требуют здесь неполнозначные и полнозначные моносиллабы. Неполнозначные односложные слова тяготеют к первому месту именно из-за его начального характера. Подобное тяготение к началу можно наблюдать в структуре предложения, по отношению к которому стихотворная строка, особенно в силлабо-тоническом стихе, является аналогом. Тенденция к группировке односложных слов в начале строки встречается, впрочем, во всех типах польского стиха и многих иностранных. Некоторую роль здесь может играть также свойственное стиху, как языковому складу, употребление анафор, которыми особенно часто бывают односложные союзы и предлоги. В польском стихе при его заполнении в большинстве случаев 1, 2 и 3-сложными словами самым удобным местом для моносиллаба в 5-сложном полустишии с парокситоническим ударением является, конечно, начало этого полустишия. С этой точки зрения шестое место метра находится в подобном положении, как начальное: от него в огромном большинстве строк начинается второе полустишие и чаще всего перед ним проходит не только словораздел, но и раздел между фонетическими словами.

Сравнение стиха с 9-сложными отрезками прозы ямбической структуры показывает, что и в этом случае мы имеем дело с общей тенденцией, свойственной организации ряда слогов с такой силлабической длиной и таким метрическим построением. Первое место этих отрезков заполнено в 45% случаев моносиллабами (при этом 38% составляют неполнозначные, 7% — полнозначные), шестое место — в 29% (неполнозначные — 27%). Как видно, для первого места в стихе эта тенденция даже слабее, чем в прозе.

Довольно частое присутствие на первом и шестом месте полнозначных моносиллабов нельзя уже объяснять теми же причинами. Тяготение полнозначных односложных слов к шестому месту вполне понятно, так как в ямбическом метре это место сильное. Первое же место на котором так же часто или даже чаще появляются полнозначные моносиллабы, слабое. Оказывается, однако, что из 11% полнозначных моносиллабов, которыми заполнено первое место, большинство (7%) выступает перед полисиллабом с ударением на первом слоге. Например:

Kształt serca miały lub wachlarza

В польских текстах при таком столкновении двух ударных слогов ударение первого — именно моносиллаба — становится слабее, подчиняется второму.

Остальные 4% состоят из случаев, когда на сильном месте, то есть непосредственно после ударного моносиллаба, выступает слог полисиллаба, не имеющий главного словесного ударения:

*Drżąc roz*kołysał mą altanę

или же — другой моносиллаб, полнозначный либо неполнозначный:

Ksiądz rzekł: "I cóż ty, boże dzieło?"

или

Wdarł się gorący murzyn krwawy

Во втором из приведённых примеров у первого односложного слова ударение (как обычно бывает в таких словосочетаниях) несомненно более слабое, чем у второго. В первом и третьем примерах мы имеем дело с метрическим расслаблением, о котором говорилось уже в II.3.

Стоит ещё заметить, что, кроме первого места метра (слабого), полнозначные моносиллабы выступают прежде всего на сильных местах, то есть на 2, 4 и 6. На слабые места, то есть 3, 5 и 7 приходится их в несколько раз меньше (по 1%, тогда как на 2 место — 10%, на 4 — 6%, на 6 — 10%). Это доказывает, что 'акцентный потенциал' полнозначных моносиллабов используется в стихе почти так, как возможности, характеризующие в этом отношении сильноударные слоги полисиллабов. Видно также, что на те сильные места, где частотность полноударных слогов полисиллабов относительно меньшая, то есть на второе и шестое, приходится больше полнозначных моносиллабов (по 10%), на четвёртом же месте, где больше сильноударных слогов полисиллабов, реже появляются полнозначные моносиллабы (6%). Это различие можно рассматривать как явление некоторой компенсации двух разных способов реализации сильных мест метрической схемы.

Исследователи, описывающие реализацию в русском стихе ямбического метра с 4 сильными местами, считают, что отсутствует в нём какая-либо тенденция к цезуре. Действительно, по сравнению с польскими реализациями того же метра, о цезуре трудно было бы здесь говорить. Но при более тщательном разборе мест словоразделов в русских ямбических 9-сложниках оказывается, что раздел 5 + 4 выступает в 45% строк, причём никакое другое место словораздела не бывает столь частым.

С этим, вероятно, связан факт, что на 6 место метра приходится несколько больше моносиллабов, чем на остальные, за исключением, конечно, первого места, на котором частотность моносиллабов несравнимо больше, чем на всех других. Привожу данные, касающиеся участия моносиллабов в заполнении очередных мест метра для русского 9-сложника (по лирическим стихотворениям Блока 1898-1905 г.).

	1.	2.	3.	4.	5.	6.	7.
Моносиллабы	45%	10%	7%	10%	10%	13%	6%
Полнозначные	9%	7%	—	7%	1%	6%	—
Неполнозначные	36%	3%	7%	3%	9%	7%	6%

Сопоставление данных для польского и русского стиха показывает прежде всего, что в польском ямбическом 9-сложнике моносиллабы играют более значительную роль, чем в русском. Они чаще используются для построения стиха, что понятно, если мы примем во внимание различие в польском и русском ударении. Второе отличие состоит в том, что в русском стихе наблюдается выразительное тяготение моносиллабов только к первому месту. Отсутствие такой тенденции относительно шестого места связано с иными, чем в польском языке, правилами организации ритмических единиц, о чём говорилось выше. Одновременно, в русском ямбическом 9-сложнике полнозначные односложные слова заполняют (как это наблюдалось в польском стихе) кроме первого места только сильные места метра.

Из полнозначных моносиллабов, заполняющих первое место, только в половине случаев происходит ослабление ударения под влиянием смежного сильноударного слога полисиллабического слова. Половина же — это моносиллабы, после которых стоит слог полисиллаба без главного ударения или которые отделены от следующего слова синтаксическим разделом:

Змей расклубится над домами

или

Там, в полусумраке собора.

Таким образом, на первом месте процент полнозначных моносиллабов, сохраняющих своё ударение, выше, чем в польском стихе. Русским стиховедением такое 'сильное начало' ямбической строки воспринимается издавна как вполне метрическое. Однако надо помнить, что в русском ямбе не допускается на первом месте уклонение от запрета заполнения слабых мест сильноударными слогами полисиллабов. Таким образом, в сравнении с стихотворными навыками польской поэзии 'сильное начало' в русском ямбе встречается реже и, в принципе, достигается другим путём.

Варшава

ПРИМЕЧАНИЯ

[1] Под этим понятием мы имеем в виду фонетическое целое, организованное вокруг одного ударного слога; оно состоит из одной лексической единицы или из нескольких единиц (полнозначное слово плюс проклитика(и) и/или энклитика(и)).

[2] Подробные данные по этому вопросу, касающиеся как стиха, так и прозы см. M. Červenka, Z. Kopczyńska, L. Pszczołowska, K. Sgallová, A. Sławow, "Słowiańska metryka porównawcza. Słownik rytmiczny", *Pamiętnik Literacki* 1973, z. 2.

[3] В 10 рассмотренных в этом отношении выборках (по 100 слов каждая) из поэмы Тувима "Польские цветы" средняя частотность моносиллабов составляет около 1% (главные типы фонетических слов, встречающиеся в конце строк: "rad bym", "na stół", "o czym").

[4] Для этих ограничений очень показательным примером, в отрицательном смысле, конечно, является известный неоконченный перевод "Евгения Онегина" Юлиана Тувима. Знаменитому поэту, решившемуся точно передать метрическую структуру произведения, не хватало, очевидно, полнозначных слов для мужской рифмы, и он должен был довольно часто пользоваться в этом месте энклитическими формами местоимений, употребление которых в рифме он сам раньше осмеивал.

[5] О слабо проявляющемся стремлении русского ямбического 9-сложника к разделению 5 + 4 см. ниже (V).

[6] Представленная здесь характеристика побочного ударения в основном соответствует наблюдениям M. Длуской (*Prozodia języka polskiego*, Kraków 1947, 14-16 i nn.), которая дала наиболее исчерпывающее описание этого типа ударения в польском языке. Общее определение побочного ударения Длуской как связанного обязательно с первым слогом фонетического слова (стр. 16), кажется мне не совсем точным, по причинам, о которых ниже.

[7] См. Dłuska, *Prozodia ...* стр. 15.

[8] Например: а) ударение полнозначного односложного слова, стоящего перед дисиллабом, обычно подлежит ослаблению или атонизируется, б) словосочетания моносиллабов, состоящие из частицы "nie" и глагола, всегда парокситоничны, как и сочетания предлога с местоимением и многие сочетания предлога с существительным ("nie dam", "na nim", "na wieś").

[9] Роман Якобсон, "Болгарский пятистопный ямб в сопоставлении с русским", *Сборникъ въ честь на проф. Л. Милетичъ* (София, 1933), 109.

[10] Р. Якобсон, "Об односложных словах в русском стихе", *Slavic Poetics: Essays in honor of Kiril Taranovsky* (The Hague 1973), 243.

[11] Из подробных данных: Тувим ("Польские цветы") — 20%, Яструн — 20%, Слонимски — 25%, Вежински (довоенная лирика) — 31%, Херберт — 27%.

[12] Отрезки эти выбирались так, чтобы начинались от синтаксического целого и кончались фонетическим словом. Среди таким образом выбранных отрезков в среднем 1/3 составляют ямбические. Выборки из романов Жеромского.

[13] В хореическом стихе встречается также несоблюдение на первом слабом месте запрета заполнения слабых мест сильноударными слогами полисиллабов. Например:
I rozległ się śmiech murarzy
Но это очень редкие случаи в сравнении с описанным выше положением в ямбе. Например, в хореическом 8-сложнике Тувима они охватывают в среднем около 1% строк; это значит, что в большинстве произведений их вообще нет. Такие реализации хореического метра воспринимаются как его явное нарушение.

[14] Речь идёт о полнозначных словах, так как двусложные союзы и предлоги (например, *или, чтобы, между*) рассматриваются обычно отдельно с точки зрения характера ударения. Но даже и таких слов очень мало в начале ямбических строк. По неопубликованным подсчётам М. Л. Гаспарова (которые я привожу здесь, воспользовавшись любезным разрешением автора) двусложные союзы и предлоги выступают в этой позиции у поэтов второй половины XIX века в 1,2% строк.

[15] М. Л. Гаспаров, *Современный русский стих* (Москва, 1974), 196.

[16] Р. Якобсон, "Об односложных словах в русском стихе", *Slavic Poetics...*, 242.

[17] Та же регулярность касается русского хореического стиха, но здесь, в отличие от польского хорея, она реализуется с абсолютной точностью.

[18] В неямбических 9-сложных отрезках прозы раздел 5 + 4 наблюдается только в 23%.

COMMENTS

(Bailey) When Tomaševskij analyzed Puškin's iambic verse in his two articles which largely laid the foundation for the Russian linguistic-statistical method, he studied the rhythmical vocabulary of the different iambic meters and the appearance of monosyllables in each. He showed that monosyllables on the weak position of the lines essentially tend to develop in the anacrusis, after the caesura, and after a strong break in the line. Subsequent investigations have confirmed these traits. Insofar as syllabico-tonic verse is concerned, it bothers me when you use syllabic terms like 'eighter' and 'niner'. The problem is that lines with nine syllables could appear in such meters as the trochaic tetrameter with dactylic ending, iambic tetrameter with feminine ending, amphibrac trimeter with feminine ending, anapest trimeter with masculine ending, and even the three-stress *dol'nik* with two syllable anacrusis and feminine ending. On the whole, your paper shows the importance of comparative metrics because this approach is extremely helpful in more clearly elucidating the metrical structures in a given language as well as indicating how the same

meter may be realized through the linguistic givens of different languages. This especially concerns how the Polish iambic tetrameter, unlike the same Russian meter, develops non-metrical stressing on disyllabic words in the anacrusis. In this respect, you might also look at the English iambic tetrameter because one-, two-, and three-syllable words may have a non-metrical stress in the anacrusis. I am no expert in the Polish language, whose prosody differs considerably from that of Russian, but your discussion of the so-called secondary stress rather disturbs me because it seems to be so broad and flexible, and because in the final account it seems to depend mainly on performance rather than on the linguistic givens of the spoken language. The whole concept of secondary stress in English has been seriously questioned by a number of linguists. Liberman in his book *Intonation*, for example, compared secondary stressing indicated in several dictionaries and found that they often contradicted each other. At any rate, it seems to me that the main stress in a word is to a certain extent a reflection of the independence of the words, while a secondary stress is something completely different. Study of the two types of stress should be clearly differentiated. I suspect that in regard to verse rhythm, the appeal to the so-called secondary stress results from an attempt to regularize the rhythm and make it fit the meter. Reciters may or may not do this, and if this is true, then the phenomenon would really depend on the mode of performance. Have you checked recordings of Polish poems in syllabico-tonic verse to see if secondary stresses really are utilized?

(Eekman)   I would like to add a comment to your paper and ask a question about it. It struck me that, when discussing iambic verse in Russian poetry, you mention the *pobočnoe udarenie*, a secondary accent. This is neglected and ignored by most versologists. Žirmunskij in his "O nacionaľnyx formax jambičeskogo stixa" speaks of pyrrhics as a substitution for fully realized iambic feet, but does not discuss the question of secondary accents. Unbegaun in his *Russian Versification* states that "As a rule, Russian lacks the secondary stress, so frequent in English and German" (p. 16). In my *Realm of Rime* I have pointed to secondary stress in Russian rhyme (p. 38), but it also plays a certain role within the line, in places other than the clausula.

My question: is it possible to make a clear distinction between iambic and trochaic meters in, e.g., Polish and Czech verse? In Russian poetry the difference is obvious; but in a language with a paroxytonic or initial word accent, where no 'iambic' words occur, a strictly applied iambic meter would have to constantly cut through the word boundaries (as there are very many bisyllabic, 'trochaic' words) and it seems more natural to speak of trochees preceded by an anacrusis. The more so because the clausulas are so often paroxytonic. Mukařovský speaks of the 'rising intonation' of the iambic line, but what is 'rising' in a line like "O lata wzgardy, młode lata!" (Ważyk) or "v mou jeseň vešel, hřeje, voní, svítí" (Neumann)?

(Smith) I have certain doubts concerning Professor Pszczołowska's use of the syllabicity basic to the structure of Polish verse as a prime criterion in the analysis of Russian binary metres. Though her charge that Russian metrists' "calculations of the frequency of monosyllabic words ... do not distinguish the syllabic length of the line" can be countered by reference to B. V. Tomaševskij's pioneering analysis of the rhythmical characteristics of *Evgenij Onegin*, her statement is largely true of later studies, for reasons stemming from the metrical features mentioned in her reference to details received from M. L. Gasparov: in view of the normal alternation of masculine and feminine clausulae in Russian verse, the metrical basis of the line has usually been considered to exclude the clausula, alternating clausulae are not felt to disturb the homogeneity of the metre.

Are the percentages given here for the stressing of "Blok's 9-syllable iambic line" and "Blok's 8-syllable trochaic line" derived from lines extracted from works written in alternating lines of 8 and 9 syllables (i.e., with alternating masculine and feminine clausulae)?

Additional discussion: Markov, McLean, Stankiewicz

AUTHOR'S REPLY

The distinction between iambic and trochaic meters in languages with a stable place of word stress may be neglected only from the purely theoretical point of view. During the research on the realization of the iambic and trochaic meters it occurs that each of them requires a different choice of word items. E.g., in both Czech and Polish poetry the monosyllables are more frequent in iambic than in trochaic verse. The opposite situation can be found with 2-syllable words which are more numerous in trochaic poems. Moreover, in Polish iambic verse nearly ¼ of the lines realize the variant of the meter which I spoke about in my paper. This variant in any case cannot be identified with trochaic meter 'preceded by an anacrusis'.

As far as the role of syllabic length of the line is concerned I want to declare that I do not treat the syllabicity as a prime criterion in the analysis of the structure of any syllabotonic verse — neither Polish nor Russian. It is one of the constant features of this verse and its function in research depends on the problem which is to be solved. If we are interested in homogeneity of the meters, e.g., iambic ones with 4 strong positions, syllabic length of the line may be not considered. But if we want to know how these meters are realized in the material of a given language — and that was my problem — we should take into account the number of strong as well as of weak positions and their realization by the different types of syllables, the words of different length, etc.

The percentages given in my paper for the stressing and for the frequency of monosyllables in Blok's poetry are derived from lines extracted from poems written in alternating verse. Since syllabotonic lines usually constitute syntactic items (without enjambements) I think this procedure totally justified.

"JA VAS LJUBIL" REVISITED*

DANIEL RANCOUR-LAFERRIERE

Любовная лирика — вся — если не троп,
то инакоговорение.
— Viktor Šklovskij

Поэзия есть всегда иносказание.
— Aleksandr Potebnja

I. INTRODUCTORY

A. S. Puškin's masterpiece "Ja vas ljubil" has been analyzed many times in many ways. The bibliography appended to this essay should give some idea of how various have been the approaches to the poem: thematic, literary historical, sociological, biographical, linguistic, etc. The present study is psychoanalytic, but relies heavily on a knowledge of ᴛne linguistic structure of the poem, and is done with full awareness of the problems of scientific credibility which plague psychoanalysis (see: Fisher and Greenberg 1977; Rancour-Laferriere 1980). I shall therefore do a brief survey of the poem's grammatical aspects before attempting a fairly restricted psychoanalytic study of the poem. Let it be noted that "psychoanalysis" is not here used in the sense of a study of the biographical *Wahrheit* behind the *Dichtung*. Thus I am not interested, for example, in whether the poem was addressed to Anna Olenina, Karolina Soban'skaja, or Natal'ja Gončarova — all candidates who have been mentioned in the literature on the poem. Nor am I interested here in Puškin's psychological complexes or the various psychological tensions he may have been enduring on the day he wrote the poem. These are legitimate and important topics, but I will focus instead on what has been traditionally called "the poem itself" (which in this case is "zamknuto v sebe, zaveršeno" — Vejdle 1973, 166) or, on what I have argued elsewhere (1977, 17-33) is really the same thing as the sensitive reader's response to the poem in all of its linguistic richness:

(1) Я вас любил: любовь еще, быть может,
В душе моей угасла не совсем;
Но пусть она вас больше не тревожит;
Я не хочу печалить вас ничем.
Я вас любил безмолвно, безнадежно,
То робостью, то ревностью томим;
Я вас любил так искренно, так нежно,
Как дай вам бог любимой быть другим.
(*Polnoe sobranie sočinenij* III, 188)

II. GRAMMATICAL STRUCTURES

Whereas most Russian critics at least as far back as Belinskij had viewed poetry as "thinking in images" ("myšlenie v obrazax" — See Laferrière 1976, 178), a few critics recognized the existence of essentially "imageless poetry" ("bezóbraznaja poèzija" — Ovsjaniko-Kulikovskij 1923, 29; cf. Jakobson 1961, 404-5; Žolkovskij 1977-8, 271) and saw "Ja vas ljubil" as a prime example of poetry lacking in the "obraz." Setting aside the problem of just what is meant by "obraz,"[1] as well as the possibility that there may in fact exist tropes (= "obrazy" in the narrow sense) in the poem besides just the 'dead metaphor' of "$_{1-2}$ljubov' ... ugasla,"[2] we can first examine the specifically grammatical structures (what Jakobson 1961, 405 calls "grammatical figures") in the poem.

To begin with, Jakobson (*ibid.*) notices that nearly half (14 out of 29) of the inflected forms in the poem are pronouns. All three of the poem's personae are represented exclusively by means of pronouns: the male persona, "ja" *in recto,* the female persona "vy" and the third persona "drugoj" *in obliquo.* The first person pronoun, which always occupies the first syllable of a line, is always in the nominative case, and always occurs in conjunction with the form "vas," is encountered once in every distich. The second person (plural) pronoun occurs six times, always in what Jakobson elsewhere calls a [+ directional] case (dative or accusative — Jakobson 1958, 149), and always in conjunction with another pronoun. A diagram will make the consistent pairing of personal pronouns clear:

(2) | | *non-ictic* | *ictic* |
|---|---|---|
| 1 | Ja | vas |
| 2 | — | — |
| 3 | vas | ona |
| 4 | Ja | vas |
| 5 | Ja | vas |
| 6 | — | — |
| 7 | Ja | vas |
| 8 | vam | drugim |

Note that Puškin never puts the first person pronoun in an ictic position, and thus reinforces a sense of unobtrusiveness on the part of speaker (cf. Sil'man 1977, 179). The third persona, represented as the pronoun "$_8$drugim," is introduced in the last possible metrical foot, as opposed to the first and second personae, introduced in the poem's opening foot. Thus the poem is 'ringed' with pronouns:

(3) "$_1$Ja vas ... $_8$drugim"

Note also the automorphic[3] frequency distributions of the first and second person pronouns in the distichs:

(4)   *Distich*   *1st pers.*   *2nd pers.*

        I   1   1

        II   1   2

        III   1   1

        IV   1   2

Dividing the poem exactly in half yields a parallelism or proper congruence of the pronominal frequency distributions. Such a division of the poem can be made on other grounds also: 1) the alternating rhyme scheme has a natural break between the two quatrains — a b a b | c d c d; 2) each quatrain begins with the anaphoric "$_{1,5}$Ja vas ljubil;" 3) the punctuation calls for a full stop between the quatrains (but not within quatrains); 4) the poem is often mistakenly printed as two quatrains; 5) there is a progression of tenses from past to non-past elements in each quatrain (thus "$_1$ljubil," "$_2$ugasla" → "$_3$pust'... ne trevožit," "$_4$ne xoču ... pečalit'" and "$_5$ljubil," "$_7$ljubil" → "$_8$daj," "$_8$byt'" — cf. Sil'man's analysis of the poem into two "cycles," each containing a "skačok" "ot prošedšego k drugim vremenam" — Sil'man 1977, 26); 6) the first quatrain has a preponderance of stressed vowels which are back or mid, while the second quatrain's stressed vowels tend to be mid or front (in L. G. Jones' terminology, the tonality balance of the first quatrain is low [–2], while the tonality balance of the second quatrain is high [+7][4]). This last point is not exactly a "ground" for dividing the poem into two quatrains, but it is nonetheless quite interesting that the phonological progression from low-to-high tonality of quatrains is mirrored by a low-to-high progression within the thrice-occurring "key word" (Jones) "$_{1,5,7}$ljubil":

(5)   / l, u b, i l /

        tonality   —   +

        accent   —   +

This word, the first disyllable in the poem, bears a striking resemblance to "$_8$drugim," the last disyllable in the poem:

(6)   / d r u g i m /
    tonality   — +
    accent   — +
                (Jones 1965, 139)

The beginning and ending of the poem are thus tightly bound on the phonological level. But the automorphic relationship is even more extensive between opening and closing lines than had been indicated by Jones. Compare the distribution of ictic vowels in lines 1 and 8:

(7) 1 / a i o o o
     8   a o i i i /

With the vowels /i/ and /o/ being contextually opposed as [+ high tonality] vs. [— high tonality], an antisymmetrical mapping between the two lines becomes clear:

(8) line 1   line 8
     + — — — → — + + +

This is *not* a mirror symmetry, but a rare *anti*symmetry of the type I discussed in my earlier work on automorphic structures in poetry (Laferrière 1974). Further phonological similarities between the lines (e.g. — abundance of bilabial consonants) are discussed by Žolkovskij (1976c, 6) and are seen as reinforcing the exchange of roles between the first and third personae ("... vtorit obmenu roljami meždu 'ja' i 'drugim' ..."), or what might be called the oppositional equivalence between "ja" and "drugoj" (cf. the mirror symmetry of "$_1$Ja ... ljubil/$_8$ljubimoj ... drugim" — Žolkovskij *ibid.,* 4).

Not only does the poem divide into two quatrains, but the second quatrain further subdivides into two distichs, as both Jakobson and Žolkovskij have shown.[5] The resulting structure is: 4 + (2 + 2). The most obvious reason for seeing the poem this way is the formulaic anaphora "$_{1,5,7}$Ja vas ljubil" which begins each of the three units. Less obvious is the manner in which each of the three units develops a grammatical segment of the original formula. To paraphrase Jakobson (1961, 406-7): 1) the first unit develops the *predicate* of the formula "Ja vas ljubil," transforming the verb into the cognate noun "$_1$ljubov'," and introducing denials of any desire to disturb the female persona with this love at the *present* time ("$_3$No pust' ona ... ne trevožit," "$_4$Ja ne xoču pečalit' ..."); 2) the second unit develops the *subject* of the formula, describing how the male persona suffered in the *past* from love; 3) the third unit is dedicated to the *object* of the formula, concentrating on what should happen to the beloved at some *future* time.[6]

Both Jakobson and Žolkovskij pay close attention to the fact that the speaker is expressing himself in a highly ambivalent and oblique manner. For example, Jakobson notices that the auxiliary words "₁ešče," "₁byt' možet," and "₂ne sovsem" bring to naught any idea that the speaker has stopped loving the female persona ("... svodjat na net fiktivnuju temu konca" — 406). Jakobson adds that the altruistic granting of *another* lover for the female persona in the last line ("₈Kak daj vam bog ljubimoj byt' *drugim*") contradicts the earlier admission of jealousy ("₆revnost'ju tomim"). Finally, Jakobson notices that the last line can be interpreted not only as a blessing to the beloved, but also can be taken as a condemnation, as an implicit negation of altruistic feeling: "... the frozen expression 'daj vam Bog,' ... oddly displaced into a subordinate clause ..., can be interpreted as a kind of 'unreal mood' meaning that, without supernatural interference, the heroine is hardly likely to come across another such love" (407: cf. Žolkovskij 1976c, 4, 9). Even Šklovskij, in his polemic with Jakobson's grammatical approach to the poem (Šklovskij 1970, 233 ff.), agrees (237) with Jakobson's observation about the male persona's wishing an impossibility upon the female persona. Žolkovskij too notices the peculiarity of "₈daj vam bog," saying that "daj" is "ungrammatical" (1977-8, 277) in a subordinate clause, and that it is a use of the rhetorical device of *anacoluthon* (1976c, 10; cf. Slonimskij 1959, 119), i.e., a solecism whereby a syntactic sequence is broken by the intrusion of another (here imperative) syntactic sequence and never really repaired (see Lausberg 1960, I, 274, 459).[7] Žolkovskij summarizes the many peculiarities of the phrase as follows:

> ... we might note that many of the features of the last line depend on various properties of the expression *day vam bog* [God grant] — its oblique imperativeness, its unreal affirmativeness, its idiomatic tone, its syntactic governance, the stress on both monosyllables, and, of course, its (imaginary) address to God. It is so much the key to many crucial aspects of the aesthetic structure of the poem that it becomes *irreplaceable,* as it were; it turns into an image which can stand for practically the whole poem.
>
> (1977-8, 277)

Žolkovskij's summary description of the final line's overall obliqueness makes a good starting point for the psychoanalytic study which will be attempted below:

> The play with direct and oblique modes of exposition is particularly intriguing. The final admissions of love (for the heroine) and jealousy (towards *another,* who literally appears at the very last moment) are wrapped up — appropriately

for the motif of altruistic submission — in a *thick veil of obliqueness*: a subordinate clause, a full passive (with object in the nominative case and subject in the instrumental), and a dry, almost bureaucratic construction of the accusative and infinitive type ("grant to you ... to be"). The appearance of the bunch of heavy constructions has been carefully prepared for: (1) by the suppressed causal link between the third and fourth lines; (2) by the participial construction in line 6 ("... tormented"); (3) by the instrumentals of means and agent in lines 4 and 6 ("not by anything"; "by shyness"; "by jealousy"); (4) by the mirroring of "I loved" in "tormented" (assisting the changing of the active verb "to love" into a passive form "be loved"); (5) the weight of the infinitive construction is lightened by the phrasal unity and everyday idiomatic quality of the expression which governs it — "God grant."

                                                              (1977-8, 276-7)

What I want to suggest is that this "thick veil of obliqueness," which extends into other parts of the poem as well, as Žolkovskij observes, is appropriate not only to the motif of "altruistic submission," but also to a larger panorama of disturbing psychological material, conscious and unconscious, in the poem. That is, the grammatical "obliqueness" is part of the overall psychological *defense* of poetic form (Laferrière 1977, 40-47).

III. SEVENTEEN PROPOSITIONAL VARIATIONS ON "JA VAS LJUBIL"

This is not the place to do a thorough review of Žolkovskij's (and Ščeglov's) important new theory of poetics called the 'Theme–Expressiveness Devices — Text' model (for a summary, see Žolkovskij and Ščeglov 1976; also O'Toole 1978). Suffice it to say that the theory has some features in common with the combination linguistic-psychoanalytic approach to poetry that I have used in the past (see *Five Russian Poems* 1977), and that the particular realization of the theory in Žolkovskij's analyses of "Ja vas ljubil" says much that I *would* have said in this paper had I been unaware of Žolkovskij's work.[8] What I will try to do in the remarks that follow, then, is avoid repeating what Žolkovskij has said in his very extensive remarks on the poem (Žolkovskij 1976a,b,c; 1977; 1977-8), and focus instead on just one psychoanalytic task, namely, the possible unconscious propositions hidden behind the proposition "Ja vas ljubil."

    In Freud's classic study of paranoia (*Standard Edition* XII, 3-82) there is a passage in which a number of mental afflictions are analyzed as variations on the single proposition

        (14)   I (a man) love him.

For example, by defensively contradicting the verb, we get

(15) I *hate* him,

which, after exchanging subject with object, becomes

(16) *He* hates *me*,

i.e., a paraphrase of *delusions of persecution.* By changing the object of the verb in (14), the result is,

(17) I love *her,*

i.e., a paraphrase of *erotomania.* By changing the subject of the verb, one obtains

(18) *She* loves him,

i.e., a description of typical alcoholic *delusions of jealousy.* By rejecting the proposition as a whole, in effect going to

(19) I do not love anyone,

the result is characteristic of *megalomania.*

Freud's ingenious, but sketchy remarks set the stage for several other, more detailed analyses of the propositional and/or linguistic structure of the defense mechanisms (e.g.: Bruss 1976; Suppes and Warren 1975; Edelson 1972, 209; Foulkes 1978; Rancour-Laferriere 1980). It is not possible here to review all of these different structural approaches. What I will do is simply utilize the Suppes-Warren approach, since it is the one which seems most readily adaptable to the Puškin poem.

Basically, Suppes and Warren propose a system of defensive transformations which convert unconscious propositions into conscious ones. The unconscious propositions are of the form

(20) Self + Action + Object (X).

For example, an unconscious proposition of this form may be

(21) I love my mother,

but, after defensive transformation of the *action,* takes the conscious form

(22) I hate my mother,

i.e., a typical so-called *reaction formation.* Or, an unconscious proposition

(23) I am mad at my boss

becomes, after defensive transformation of the *object* (X → Y),

(24)   I am mad at my wife,

i.e., a typical instance of *displacement*. Several transformations may be combined, e.g., (23) may itself have come from

(25)   I am fond of my boss

by reaction formation, so that (24) may be the result of reaction formation *and* displacement. Thus, to start with, Suppes and Warren propose 29 possible combinations of transformations on an original proposition having the form (20). In addition, they then propose another 15 "mechanisms of identification" in which transformations substitute self for other. For example, an unconscious

(26)   *He* does it

can be transformed to

(27)   *I* do it.

on the conscious level. Altogether, then, there are 44 possible combinations of defensive transformations in the Suppes-Warren system. Obviously, these cannot all be discussed here, nor can various other details which Suppes and Warren bring up. The reader is referred to the original article of Suppes and Warren, and the reader who is not acquainted with the basics of psychoanalysis should consult a general reference on the defense mechanisms, such as Laplanche and Pontalis 1973, 234-7.

To analyze the Puškin poem by means of the Suppes-Warren model, I am going to make three basic assumptions.

The first assumption is that the reader is capable of *identifying* with the speaker. This is the fundamental identification which must always take place in order for lyric poetry to be truly appreciated (Laferrière 1977, 17 ff.). "Du gleichst dem Geist, den du begreifst," says Mephistopheles to Faust. From a linguistic viewpoint, this identification means that the first person pronominal forms do not refer to just some abstract entity ("the male persona"), nor do they refer to just Aleksandr Puškin. Rather, in the case of the particular lyric at hand, they refer to any human being who has ever experienced rejection by a beloved. And who among Puškin's readers can claim never to have suffered an unhappy love? Thus each time the pronoun "Ja" occurs, it may just as well refer to the reader as to the speaker of the "ja" in the poem. The pronoun seems to have a constant "double" reference, and is an instance of what I have elsewhere called "multiple deixis" of the category of person (1978a, 65-75; cf. Ètkind's [1978, 88-97] interesting discussion of how pronouns in poetry tend to receive a supplementary semanticization). Or, to keep to the terms of the Suppes-Warren model, it is as if the reader, after first registering the poem's repeated

(28) Я вас любил

as

(29) Он вас любил
       (the reader speaking)

then made an identification transformation on the element "Self" of (20) above:

(30) он → я

yielding

(31) Я вас любил,

i.e., exactly what the poet says, only now it is the *reader* speaking ("speaking") the words. We may say that (28) is the original message, (29) and (30) are the posited unconscious intermediaries not available in the surface, and (31) is a surface or conscious meaning that states the reader's identification and is in fact literally what the reader says to him- or herself when reading the poem. Note, however, that the reader (or Puškin himself, for that matter) is never really "locked" into the identification. That is, insofar as no *personal names* are ever mentioned in the poem, the reader is always in the safe ("well-defended," the analyst would say) position of being able to disavow the identification, to say, in effect, "èto — ne ja," "That's not me." Such safety in pronouns is of course characteristic of lyric poetry. Tamara Sil'man puts it this way: "the pronoun is a means of preserving the namelessness of the lyric subject and besides frees him from the depths of the empirical, everyday context, transforming him into a kind of 'lyric incognito' [liričeskoe inkognito]" (1977, 38).

The second assumption I am going to make is that the poem's pivotal proposition is the thrice-occurring "$_{1,5,7}$Ja vas ljubil" (which itself contains the four-fold repeated first person pronoun, the six-fold repeated second person pronoun, and the five-fold occurring verb morpheme {-люб-}). This sentence has precisely the form "Self + Action + Object" discussed by Suppes and Warren. No other sentence occurs even twice, let alone three times. All other sentences/propositions in the poem give the impression of being but a variation on or an elaboration of this "I loved you" (cf. Sil'man 1977, 179). The effect of insistently repeating this sentence is to *invite* the attribution of other meanings than *just* its surface meaning. Compare the multiplication of meanings which occurs in the following instances of token repetition:

(32)   There are Slavists and there are Slavists
       (an anonymous Slavist)

(33)   The woods are lovely, dark and deep,
       But I have promises to keep,
       And miles to go before I sleep,
       And miles to go before I sleep.
       (Robert Frost)

(34)   Свеча горела на столе,
       Свеча горела.
       (Boris Pasternak)

In (32) the repetition clearly suggests that there are two kinds of Slavist (e.g., orthodox Slavists and unorthodox Slavists). In (33) the repetition suggests that we are dealing not just with literal "miles" and "sleep," but also with a metaphorical "road of life" which ends in death ("sleep"). In (34) the repetition of "sveča" suggests that the candle is not just a literal candle, but also perhaps a symbol of "life," or perhaps a symbol of something more "Freudian" and having to do with the passion of the two lovers in this famous poem. Such lexical repetitions are part of the essential "inoskazanie" (Potebnja) or "inakogovorenie" (Šklovskij) of poetry (see epigraphs).

Finally, I am going to assume that the marked (past) tense of this proposition "I loved you" rather thinly veils a proposition in the *present* tense, namely, "I love you." That is, the love is still very much in effect. All studies of the poem (see bibliography), even the most superficial ones, agree that the poem is as much a declaration of *present* love as of past love. In any case, the removal of considerations of tense (= considerations of marked, *past* tense) corresponds well with the basic Freudian idea of the unconscious as timeless ("zeitlos").

From the viewpoint of the Suppes-Warren model, the question now becomes: Where might the poem's basic proposition

(35)   I love you

come from at deeper psychological levels? That is, what defenses might have been applied in order to arrive at this proposition? Let us first map out all of the *logical* possibilities.

For the subject of the proposition there are two possibilities: "you" and "he." That is, the male persona could, by *identification,* have replaced the other personae. For the object of the proposition there are two possibilities: "I" ("myself") and "he" ("him"). That is, the female persona could, by *projection* or *displacement,* respectively, have replaced the other personae for the speaker. Finally, for the verb, there is its opposite "hate." That is, there is the possibility that a *reaction formation* occurs. Combining all these possibilities into all possible permutations, we obtain the results indicated in Table I. As can be seen, there are $18 (= 3 \times 2 \times 3)$ possible propositions, i.e., the original "I love you" plus 17 others. The question now is: what kinds of evidence do we have that any of these transformations are in fact operating in a sensitive reading of the poem?

To begin with, it appears that the propositions which involve the *greatest* number of transformations are the *least* relevant to the poem. Thus propositions 14-17, each of which involves *three* transformations, seem utterly preposterous. There is not a shred of evidence in the poem to indicate how the third persona, who is only introduced at the last possible moment, could possibly feel ("He hates himself," "He hates me"). Nor is there any indication that the female persona could hate the third persona ("You hate him"). On the

TABLE I

Propositions from which the conscious proposition "I love you"
could have arisen by defensive transformation(s)

No.	Unconscious Proposition	Item Transformed Self	Action	Object	Number of Transformations
1	You love yourself	X			1
2	He loves you	X			1
3	I hate you		X		1
4	I love him			X	1
5	I love myself			X	1
6	You hate yourself	X	X		2
7	He hates you	X	X		2
8	I hate him		X	X	2
9	I hate myself		X	X	2
10	You love him	X		X	2
11	He loves himself	X		X	2
12	He loves me	X		X	2
13	You love me	X		X	2
14	You hate him	X	X	X	3
15	He hates himself	X	X	X	3
16	You hate me	X	X	X	3
17	He hates me	X	X	X	3

contrary, her failure to respond to the love the speaker holds for her might indicate that she loves the other man (i.e., no. 10, "You love him," which involves two transformations). As for the one other proposition involving three transformations, "You hate me," there is the remote possibility that the speaker may think it true, i.e., as a paranoid misinterpretation of her indifference. But I see no evidence in the poem for such hatred. Generally speaking, it would be difficult for any of the three-transformation propositions to be made relevant, since none of them (by definition) have the speaker as subject, a fact which contradicts the basic egocentricity of the poem.

Those propositions which are just *two* transformations away from consciousness (i.e., nos. 6-13) seem somewhat less remote from the psychological action of the poem. Thus no. 13 ("You love me") is clearly a *wish* the persona has, or at least had, though it is nowhere explicit in the poem. Indeed any propositions in which the female persona is subject will never be altogether explicit in the poem because the poem is so egocentric, that is, focused on the feelings of the speaking persona, not the other two personae. Thus the other two two-transformation propositions in which the female persona is subject ("You love him," "You hate yourself") are nowhere explicit in the poem either, though it is not completely out of the question that the male persona could have had such thoughts: the first expresses more clearly the jealousy of the speaker than the mere noun "revnost" in line 6, and the second is conceivably what the speaker wished his beloved should have felt about herself for having dared to love any other man but him.

Similarly, those two-transformation propositions in which the third persona is subject ("He loves me," "He loves himself," "He hates you") are not in the least made explicit because the poem's speaker is so egocentric. There is a sliver of suspicion that "He hates you" is a latent wish of the speaker, and there is simply no evidence on "He loves himself" and "He loves me."[9]

The remaining two-transformation propositions have the poem's speaker as subject: "I hate him," "I hate myself." The first of these is a possible implication of the speaker's jealousy expressed in line 6. As for "I hate myself," it could be regarded as an expression of the speaker's wounded pride, though there is certainly no explicit self-abnegation of *this* sort in the poem.

What now remains are the one-transformation propositions (1-5). These appear to be the propositions which are most relevant to the poem. Of the two which have someone other than the speaker as subject ("You love yourself," "He loves you"), the first would seem to be a more accurate representation of the female persona's cold indifference toward the speaker than the "You hate me" discussed above. The second, "He loves you," which can be regarded as the mirror of "You love him," is another aspect of the speaker's jealousy in line

6, and, more importantly, is a 'deimperativization' of the altruistic wish of the last line. That is, it is a statement of the third persona's love for the female persona with no marked grammatical moods or conditions attached. It comes very close to being actually explicit in the poem, and the transformation required to get from it to the "I love you" is the *identification* of the speaker with his rival, or what Žolkovskij calls an "exchange of roles" between the two males in the poem (see above, 308).

What is left are the three one-transformation propositions which have the speaker himself as subject. No. 5, "I love myself" is easily a statement of the speaker's self-pity or assuaging of wounded self-esteem which so characterizes the poem until we reach the gloriously altruistic (but also narcissistic and self-righteous) final line. No. 3, "I hate you," is quite close to the surface, i.e., is a good paraphrase of the implicit condemnation of the beloved in the last line. In effect, this proposition sums up the speaker's 'fox-and-grapes' attitude toward the lost beloved: "If loving you is of no avail, then I hate you." In wishing an *impossibility* on the female persona in the last line, the speaker is engaging in a classic Freudian reaction formation. Of course, in wishing such perfect love as his upon her, the speaker is also camouflaging his reaction formation very neatly.

The one remaining proposition, No. 4, "I love him" requires special attention. Though it is only one transformation away from "I love you," it seems, at first glance, far removed from the psychological realities of the poem. It clearly is a statement of homosexual love. Let us keep in mind that it is a statement relating to the *persona* of the poem, not necessarily to Aleksandr Puškin the man — although Puškin the man was inclined to indirectly expressing homosexual fantasies (as I have argued in *Five Russian Poems*, 48-62), and Puškin the poet at times became rather explicit about homosexuality (e.g. — *Domik v Kolomne*; see Kucera 1956, 284). In any case, any argument about the psychological reality of a proposition like "I love him" in the poem has to be made on the basis of what is actually in the poem, not on other bases. I am assuming that the reader, however sensitive, is not necessarily a connoisseur of Puškin's personal life, nor is so thoroughly acquainted with Puškin's works to remember those few occasions when male homosexuality does come close to the surface.

First of all, the speaker's love for the woman, which is everywhere apparent in the poem, is nonetheless actively pushed aside, as many scholars have observed: the verb "ljubit'" is given in the past rather than the present tense, the distant "vy" rather than "ty" is used (see Friedrich 1972), the speaker loudly declares that he does not want at present to disturb the woman in any way, and finally the jealousy hinted at in line 6 is, in the final line, ostentatiously converted to the opposite of jealousy, i.e., to what appears to be a wish for the happiness of the other two personae. The speaker 'bows out of the eternal triangle' in what appears to be a very admirable fit of generosity. The 'eternal triangle' in question would of course, in a deeper psychoanalysis of the poem than I am attempting here, be the Oedipal triangle. What I am interested in, however, is the specific manner in which the speaker 'bows out.' We have already noted the implicit condemnation of the woman in the final line, and the contrast of this condemnation with the altruism of the line. In effect, the speaker is saying:

> (36)   I hate you for not responding to my love, but I love you so much that I am giving you to another.

This formula contains two possible routes to the homosexual proposition 4, "I love him," i.e.,:

> (37)   I (a man) hate you (a woman) and therefore I love men instead,

or

> (38)   I love you so much that I put myself in your place as you are being loved by another man.

The first of these two routes strikes me as irrelevant to the poem. There would have to be in the poem a much more explicit disparaging of the woman, or of women in general (e.g., calling them all harlots), or some element of camaraderie with the other man would have to be expressed in order for such a reading to be relevant. The second route to a homosexual proposition seems valid, however. The speaker of the poem really is imagining (in a *detached* manner, as Žolkovskij says) his beloved alone with another man, and is trying to see how good a lover this other man would be from *her* viewpoint. Of course this other man should *fail* from the woman's viewpoint, but that is only the negative aspect of the poem's closing wish.[10] The positive aspect is the speaker's altruism or his empathy with the woman. He puts himself in her place. But if he really were in her place, he would be receiving love from a man, i.e., he would be in what for him is a homosexual relationship. Moreover, if she loves this other man ("You love him"), as the intense jealousy seems to indicate, then his putting himself in her position is equivalent to his giving love to a man and validates the homosexual proposition 4, "I love him." Thus there seems to be no way to avoid the homosexual overtones of his empathic identification with her at the end of the poem. My guess is that male homosexuals and women will find it easier to detect and resonate with this homosexuality than will heterosexual males.[11] Indeed, the fact that one does not *have* to be a heterosexual male to appreciate the great beauty of Puškin's poem suggests that there *ought* to be something in the poem that appeals also to male homosexuals and women. Or more precisely, Puškin's great love lyric caters not *only* to masculine, heterosexual fantasies, but to a much wider and grander range of propositions in our unconscious fantasy life.

IV. THE POETICIZATION OF JEALOUSY

Earlier (309) I stated that the various kinds of grammatical "obliqueness" in the poem, so clearly revealed in Žolkovskij's studies, are part and parcel of the defensive function of poetic form (an argument for the defensive properties of linguistic structures in poetry is developed at length in my *Five Russian Poems*, 40-47). Now, having considered some of the ego-distonic propositions buried in this particular poem, especially the homosexual proposition 4, we can see what it is that the formal properties of the poem have to defend the reader *against*. Certainly there is no pleasure to be gained for most heterosexual readers from a statement as bald as proposition 4 itself. But there is pleasure to be gained from reading the poem, which is to say that the proposition has been clothed in a sufficiently intricate and distracting linguistic structure to defend the reader against the unpleasantness of having to consciously think about the underlying homosexual proposition. Or rather, most of the poem's highly enjoyable and disarming linguistic intricacy has already occurred before the homosexual proposition is unobtrusively suggested toward the end of the poem. The homosexual proposition does not pervade the poem, but *culminates* it. Thus the underlying fantasy material might be better characterized as bisexual rather than homosexual. Frustrated heterosexual love in the past (emphasized by the repeated past tense construction "$_{1,5,7}$Ja vas ljubil") becomes a vicariously homosexual and voyeuristic look into the future love life of the beloved: "$_8$Kak daj vam bog ljubimoj byť *drugim*." The bisexual character of the poem can be contrasted with the exclusively heterosexual orientation of most of Puškin's love lyrics (e.g., "Ja pomnju čudnoe mgnoven'e," "Dlja beregov otčizny daľnoj," "Ne poj, krasavica, pri mne"), as well as with the exclusively homosexual orientation of those rare poems about young boys (e.g., "Junoša, polnyj krasy ...").

The ability to create an elaborate poetic defense in response to unpleasant semantic material is of course not something everyone has. For example, an average nineteenth century Russian gentleman who happened to lose a round in the game of love would not have been able to express his jealousy in a structure of iambic pentameter, alternating rhyme, pronominal symmetries, etc. Rather, he would have experienced his jealousy in the ordinary, universal human way. That is, he would have felt such things as the following: 1) helplessness and a sense of devastation; 2) feelings of retribution (resulting, perhaps, in a desire to do something that would make the beloved herself jealous); 3) increased sexual arousal toward the beloved; 4) a need to talk with someone about the problem; 5) intropunitiveness, i.e., feelings of guilt or anger toward one's self; 6) a need to confront the beloved and/or the inter-loper; 7) anger toward the beloved and/or the interloper; and 8) a need to create a false impression, such as indifference. These are the basic factors in jealousy which have been isolated in Bryson's (1977) experimental psycholog-ical study.

But the jealousy of Puškin's persona in "Ja vas ljubil" is not ordinary. The most striking affective feature of the poem, the altruistic giving of the beloved to another in the last line, is not even envisaged in the factor analysis of Bryson. Nor is the possibility of expressing jealousy in the form of a poem. True, the implied condemnation of the female persona in the last line is definitely a manifestation of anger (factor 7) or possibly of reactive retribution (factor 2). Also, the various forms of emotional "narastanie" in the poem which Žolkovskij studied might be tied to the feelings of helplessness (factor 1), arousal (factor 3), and anger (factor 7) — all of which seem to "grow" in the course of the poem. But the most interesting aspect of Bryson's experimental isolation of factors, from the viewpoint of Puškin's poem, is the absence of any reference to "altruistic submission" (Žolkovskij) as a possible component of jealousy. It cannot be an accident that this absence is matched by an absence of any considerations of homosexuality in Bryson's study.

V. TWO PARTING SHOTS

For the sceptical reader who still finds it difficult to imagine any homosexual overtones in Puškin's poem, I would like to offer two final arguments.

First, let that reader, if male, imagine that *he* is the lucky man who has just won the love and affection of the poem's female persona. How would he now feel if, one day, his beloved received an envelope containing Puškin's poem? Aside from just a twinge of jealousy of his own, wouldn't he also feel that this Puškin fellow is just a bit *strange*?

Puškin's contemporary Lermontov thought the poem's altruistic final cou-plet strange indeed: "... estestvenno li želať sčastija ljubimoj ženščine, da ešče s drugim? Net, pusť ona budet nesčastliva ..." (as quoted by Fedorov 1967, 55).

Second, let us consider the need to cross territorial borders. It may seem that I have introduced a lot of terribly "extrinsic" considerations (as Wellek and Warren, following Ingarden, would say) by burdening the reader with Freud's theory of paranoia, the Suppes-Warren model of defense, the Bryson study of jealousy, and other matters. Granted, I have done just that, I have crossed several boundaries between the "intrinsic" and the "extrinsic." But, as I have argued elsewhere (1977, 1-3), these boundaries are trivial and have been erected by a tradition of scholars more interested in territorial than scientific endeavor. In asserting that there is a homosexual component to Puškin's poem I have said something *new* and *falsifiable* that might never have been said without the help of all that "extrinsic" apparatus. What should now be on the agenda is not a further belaboring of the "extrinsic"/"intrinsic" dichotomy, but a plan to falsify my hypothesis. Experimental studies on the reactions of native speakers to the poem could, for example, be devised. It is only by the production and attempted falsification of new hypotheses, as Peirce, Popper, and other philosophers have argued, that science marches on.

University of California, Davis

NOTES

*   I wish to thank Barbara Milman, Daniel Rosenberg, John Robert Ross, and Savely Senderovich for their comments and encouragement. An earlier version of this essay was presented at the fourth annual meeting of the Mid Atlantic Slavic Conference of the AAASS, held at Cornell University, 21 April 1979.
[1]   At times "obraz" seems to be synonymous with "trope" (the narrow definition assumed, for example, by Žolkovskij 1977, 252), while at other times it means something much broader (e.g., Potebnja 1892; and 1905, where the term takes on both grammatical and transcendent connotations: I have discussed the meanings of "obraz" at length in Laferrière 1976).
[2]   Thus Šklovskij 1970, 239 (cf. Žolkovskij 1976b, 7) sees a *litotes* in the fact that the speaker of the poem understates and even belittles his sorrow. Žolkovskij 1976c, 5 treats the poem's last line as a *simile* ("sravnenie"), and also finds an *anacoluthon* in the line (see below, 309). I think it can be agreed, though, that there are no real metaphors or metonymies in the poem. The fact that the poem *closes* with a simile is quite characteristic of Puškin (see the interesting discussion of "simile closure" in Puškin's poetry in Proffer 1972, 190).
[3]   An automorphism in poetry is basically a structure of sameness or repetition. For a detailed classification, see Laferrière 1978a, ch. II.
[4]   The tonality balance is arrived at by adding together the number of metrically stressed (ictic) vowels which are [+ high tonality] with the number which are [- high tonality], yielding a positive or negative integer. See: Jones 1965.
[5]   The most thorough discussion of the various grounds for dividing the poem in various ways is given by Žolkovskij (1976b; and 1976c).
[6]   Note the *growing* high tonality of the three units: $-2 \rightarrow +2 \rightarrow +5$ (which can be deduced from the chart in Jones 1965, 139). This feature should be seen in connection with the numerous other instances of growth ("narastanie") which Žolkovskij describes, such as growing evidence of the speaker's *passion* through the poem, growing *submission* to the fact of not being loved in return, growing *contrast* of submission/passion, and associated syntactic-intonational patterns which

seem to 'grow' (Žolkovskij 1976b, 15-20). One particularly interesting item that Žolkovskij noticed (e.g., 1977-8, 275-276) is the fact that the stressed vowel sequence in line 6 ("To robost'ju, to revnost'ju tom*im*") is exactly the *same* as the sequence of vowels used in the rhyme scheme:

   (9)   ₁možet ~ ₃trevožit   /o/

   (10) ₂sovsem ~ ₄ničem   /e/

   (11) ₅beznadežno ~ ₇nežno   /e/

   (12) ₆tom*im* ~ ₈drug*im*   /i/,

that is,

   (13) /ó/ → /é/ (repeated) → /í/.

From the viewpoint of Jones' paper (1965), it can be said that there is a *growing tonality* from one vowel to the next. One other interesting instance of "narastanie" is the growing frequency per distich of words having secondary stress (what Avanesov would call "pobočnoe udarenie") in non-ictic position: 2 → 3 → 3 → 6.

[7]   Slonimskij says it would have been more natural to have: "Kak vas ne poljubit drugoj" (1959, 119).

[8]   In his inscriptions to my personal copies of Žolkovskij 1977 and Žolkovskij 1977-8, the author jokingly writes: "skryto-psixo-analitičeskij ètjud s negodnymi sredstvami," and "moj nedo-psixo-analitičeskij ètjud," resp. It is gratifying to see in Žolkovskij's work not a trace of the kind of knee-jerk anti-Freudianism that is present in the work of some other Soviet semioticians (see Laferrière 1978b). [This note was written before Žolkovskij emigrated from the Soviet Union — DR-L.]

[9]   Except that "He loves me" may be a wishful inversion of the homosexual proposition "I love him," which is discussed below.

[10]   In another poem ("K ***") related to the one under consideration, the negative aspect of the wish is absent. The speaker wishes

   (39)   Всё — даже счастие того, кто избран ей,
          Кто милой деве даст название супруги.
                    (cf. Blagoj 1967, 415)

[11]   I am assuming that such readers identify with the male persona of the poem. There is of course the possibility of identifying with the poem's female persona. This might be called the "minor identification" in the reading experience, as opposed to the "major identification" with the male persona.

BIBLIOGRAPHY

Blagoj, D. D.
   1967   *Tvorčeskij Put' Puškina* (1826-1830), Moscow, 413-415.
Bruss, Neal.
   1976   "The Transformation in Freud," *Semiotica* 17, 69-94.
Bryson, J. B.
   1977   "Situational Determinants of the Expression of Jealousy," paper presented at the meeting of the American Psychological Association, San Francisco.
Edelson, M.
   1972   "Language and Dreams: The Interpretation of Dreams Revisited," *Psycho-Analytic Study of the Child* 27, 203-282.
Ermakov, I. D.
   1923   *Ètjudy po psixologii tvorčestva A. S. Puškina.* Moscow/Petrograd.
Ètkind, Efim
   1978   *Materija stixa.* Paris: Institut d'études slaves.

Fedorov, A. V.
1967   Lermontov i literatura ego vremeni. Leningrad: Xudožestvennaja literatura.
Fisher, Seymour and Roger Greenberg
1977   The Scientific Credibility of Freud's Theories and Therapy. New York: Basic Books.
Foulkes, David
1978   A Grammar of Dreams. New York: Basic Books.
Freud, Sigmund
1953-65   The Standard Edition of the Complete Psychological Works of Sigmund Freud. London: Hogarth Press, 24 vols.
Friedrich, Paul
1972   "Social Context and Semantic Feature: The Russian Pronominal Usage," Directions in Sociolinguistics, ed. J. Gumperz, Dell Hymes. New York: Holt, Rinehart & Winston, 270-300.
Jakobson, Roman
1958   "Morfologičeskie nabljudenija nad slavjanskim skloneniem (sostav russkix padežnyx form)," American Contributions to the Fourth International Congress of Slavists. The Hague: Mouton, 127-156.
1961   "Poèzija grammatiki i grammatika poèzii," Poetics, Poetyka, Poètika. Warsaw: Mouton, I, 397-417.
Jones, Lawrence Gaylord
1965   "Tonality Structure in Russian Verse," IJSLP 9, 125-151.
Kucera, Henry
1956   "Puškin and Don Juan," For Roman Jakobson, ed. Morris Halle, Horace Lunt, Hugh McLean, Cornelius H. van Schooneveld. The Hague: Mouton, 273-284.
Laferrière, Daniel
1974   "Automorphic Structures in the Poem's Grammatical Space," Semiotica 10, 333-350.
1976   "Potebnja, Šklovskij, and the Familiarity/Strangeness Paradox," Russian Literature 4, 175-198.
1977   Five Russian Poems: Exercises in a Theory of Poetry. Englewood, N.J.: Transworld.
1978a   Sign and Subject: Semiotic and Psychoanalytic Investigations into Poetry. Lisse: Peter de Ridder Press.
1978b   "Semiotica sub Specie Sovietica," PTL 3, 437-454.
Laplanche, J. and J.-B. Pontalis
1973   Vocabulaire de la psychanalyse. Paris: Presses universitaires de France.
Lausberg, Heinrich
1960   Handbuch der literarischen Rhetorik. Munich: Max Hueber Verlag, 2 vols.
O'Toole, L. M.
1978   "What Price Rigor?" PTL 3, 429-435.
Ovsjaniko-Kulikovskij, D.
1923   Teorija poèzii i prozy (teorija slovesnosti). Moscow/Petrograd (5th ed.), 29-30.
Pletnev, R.
1963   O lirike A. S. Puškina. Montreal: Monastery Press.
Potebnja, A. A.
1892   Mysl' i jazyk. Xar'kov.
1905   Iz zapisok po teorii slovesnosti. Xar'kov.
Proffer, Carl
1972   "The Similes of Pushkin and Lermontov," RLT 3, 148-94.
Puškin, Aleksandr Sergeevič
1937-49   Polnoe sobranie sočinenij. Moscow: Izdatel'stvo akademii nauk SSSR, 17 vols.
Rancour-Laferriere, Daniel
1980   "Semiotics, Psychoanalysis, and Science: Some Selected Intersections," Ars semeiotica 3, 181-240.

Sil'man, Tamara
1977   *Zametki o lirike.* Leningrad, 26-27; 78; 179.
Slonimskij, A.
1959   *Masterstvo Puškina.* Moscow, 119.
Stepanov, N. L.
1959   *Lirika Puškina.* Moscow.
Suppes, Patrick and Hermine Warren
1975   "On the Generation and Classification of Defence Mechanisms," *International Journal of Psycho-Analysis* 56, 405-414.
Šklovskij, V.
1970   *Tetiva: o nesxodstve sxodnogo.* Moscow, 233 ff.
Vejdle, V.
1973   *O poètax i poèzii.* Paris: YMCA-Press, 165-167.
Vickery, Walter
1972   "'Ja vas ljubil ...': A Literary Source," *IJSLP* 15, 160-167.
Žirmunskij, Viktor M.
1977   *Teorija literatury — Poètika — Stilistika.* Leningrad, 47-48; 83.
Žolkovskij, A. K.
1976a,b,c   "K opisaniju smysla svjaznogo teksta VI," *Predvaritel'nye publikacii problemnoj gruppy po èksperimental'noj i prikladnoj lingvistike,* preprints 76, 77, 78, resp.
1977   "Razbor stixotvorenija Puškina 'Ja vas ljubil'," *Izvestija akademii nauk SSSR: serija literatury i jazyka* 36, 252-263.
1977-8 "The Literary Text — Thematic and Expressive Structure: An Analysis of Pushkin's Poem 'Ya vas lyubil ...,'" *New Literary History* 9, 263-278.
Žolkovskij, A. K. and Ju. K. Ščeglov
1976   "Poetics as a Theory of Expressiveness: Towards a 'Theme – Expressiveness Devices – Text' Model of Literary Structure," *Poetics* 5, 207-246.

ВОПРОСЫ ПОЭТИЧЕСКОЙ ОРГАНИЗАЦИИ СЕМАНТИКИ В ПРОЗЕ МАНДЕЛЬШТАМА

Д. Сегал

1. Исследование прозы Мандельштама представляет живейший интерес для *поэтического* языка, поскольку эта проза демонстрирует многие из специфических признаков, выделенных в свое время в качестве характеристики поэзии филологами, современниками Мандельштама, принадлежавшими к ценимой им формальной школе литературоведения.[1] Одновременно, для самого поэта его проза является именно прозой par excellence. Мандельштам, стремившийся преодолеть *традиционные* жанровые различия, как внутри поэзии, так и между поэзией и прозой, как никто другой четко осознавал полную автономию обеих областей словесного творчества. Для Мандельштама поэзия и проза были объединены по 'принципу дополнительности', и, если на некоем высшем уровне и можно было думать о выходе за пределы их фундаментального несходства, то только после доведения до конца всех присущих каждой из этих сфер имманентных особенностей. Поэтому так резко звучит его критика в адрес Андрея Белого, настаивавшего на поэтизации словесной ткани прозы, на перенесении в нее принципа устного произнесения: "Проза асимметрична, ее движения — движения словесной массы — движение стада, сложное и ритмичное в своей неправильности; настоящая проза — разнобой, разлад, многоголосие, контрапункт; а "Записки чудака" — как дневник гимназиста, написанный полустихами" (из рецензии Мандельштама на *Записки чудака,* том II, Андрея Белого).

Одновременно проза Мандельштама особенно сильно воспринимается как *проза поэта*. Целью настоящих заметок является показать, как Мандельштам использует при построении своих *прозаических* произведений некоторые из самых фундаментальных принципов своей поэтической семантики, выкристаллизовавшейся прежде всего в *стихе*. Кажется, что применительно к Мандельштаму справедлив в чем-то анализ соотношения стиха и прозы у Пушкина, проведенный в свое время Б. М.

Эйхенбаумом в его статье "Проблемы поэтики Пушкина". Вот некоторые из тезисов Эйхенбаума: "Интерес к сюжетным построениям привел Пушкина к прозе, а высокий стихотворный опыт сделал ее сжатой и простой. Она родилась из стиха, но не для борьбы с ним, как у Марлинского, а для уравновешения. Поэтому в ней можно узнать Пушкина — поэта, несмотря на отсутствие специфических приемов стихотворной речи. [...] Интересно поэтому, что Пушкин открывает собой развитие русской прозы, но вместе с тем не создает традиции. Пушкин и в прозе не имеет последователей. Тут дело, повидимому, именно в том, что дальнейшая проза развивается на развалинах стиха, тогда как у Пушкина она рождается еще из самого стиха, из уравновешенности всех его элементов."[2] В этом сопоставлении существенно то, что и проза Мандельштама возникла из 'самого стиха', что она не борется со стихом. Интересна и параллель к вытеснению поэзии прозой у Пушкина, начиная с 1831 года — Мандельштам пишет свои основные прозаические произведения (в том числе и 'сюжетную', "Египетскую марку") в период с 1925 по 1930 годы, то-есть когда 'стихи прекратились', по выражению Н. Я. Мандельштам. Весьма показательны и отличия в соотношении 'проза-поэзия' у обоих поэтов. Во-первых, Мандельштам обращается к прозе вовсе не из интереса к сюжетным построениям. Скорее наоборот, Мандельштам рассматривал эволюцию прозаических жанров в широком контексте взаимоотношения текста и действительности. Возможность существования повествовательной, сюжетной прозы он связывает с моделированием в общественном мировосприятии судьбы человека в истории. В статье "Конец романа" он пишет: "Все это наводит на догадку о связи, которая существует между судьбой романа и положением в данное время вопроса о судьбе личности в истории; здесь не приходится говорить о действительных колебаниях роли личности в истории, а лишь о распространенном ходячем решении этого вопроса в данную минуту, поскольку оно воспитывает и образует умы современников".

В отличие от начала девятнадцатого века, когда человек представлялся архитектором своей судьбы, двадцатый век рождает восприятие личности как зависимой от гораздо более обширных и могущественных внешних сил, как бы ни была велика роль отдельной, случайно взятой личности в комплексе исторических событий. Подытоживая этот анализ судьбы личности и судьбы прозы в двадцатом веке, Мандельштам пишет в той же статье:

"Ясно, что, когда мы вступили в полосу могучих социальных движений, массовых организованных действий, акции личности в истории падают и вместе с ними падают влияние и сила романа, для которого общепризнанная роль личности в истории служит как бы манометром, показывающим давление социальной атмосферы. Мера романа — человеческая биография или система биографий. […]

[…] Дальнейшая судьба романа будет ничем иным, как историей распыления биографии, как формы личного существования, даже больше, чем распыления — катастрофической гибели биографии.

Чувство времени, принадлежащее человеку для того, чтобы действовать, побеждать, гибнуть, любить — это чувство времени составляло основной тон в звучании европейского романа, ибо еще раз повторяю: композиционная мера романа — человеческая биография. Человеческая жизнь еще не есть биография и не дает позвоночника роману. Человек, действующий во времени старого европейского романа, является как бы стержнем целой системы явлений, группирующихся вокруг него.

Ныне европейцы выброшены из своих биографий, как шары из биллиардных луз, и законами их деятельности, как столкновением шаров на биллиардном поле, управляет один принцип: угол падения равен углу отражения. Человек без биографии не может быть тематическим стержнем романа, и роман, с другой стороны, немыслим без интереса к отдельной человеческой судьбе — фабуле и всему, что ей сопутствует. Кроме того, интерес к психологической мотивировке, — куда так искусно спасался упадочный роман, уже предчувствуя свою погибель, — в корне подорван и дискредитирован наступившим бессилием психологических мотивов перед реальными силами, чья расправа с психологической мотивировкой час от часу становится более жестокой.

Современный роман сразу лишился и фабулы, то есть действующей в принадлежащем ей времени личности, и психологии, так как она не обосновывает уже никаких действий".

Следовательно, для Мандельштама задачи прозы — существенно иные, нежели воссоздание сюжета. Мандельштам-акмеист с его постоянной привязанностью к филологии и обращенностью на язык как на самостоятельный модус культуры, видит в прозе средство для создания новых языковых орудий и, тем самым, для адекватного реагирования на новые социально-культурные ситуации своей эпохи.[3]

Во-вторых, 'дополнительность' прозаической речи по отношению к поэтической приводит к тому, что хотя проза у Мандельштама должна расти из стиха, но рост этот — в другую сторону, и нет речи об "уравновешенности всех […] элементов" стиха в прозе Мандельштама. Этим объясняются любопытные схождения и расхождения в динамических принципах построения стиха и прозы у Мандельштама, во всяком случае, достаточно четко прослеживаемые на основном корпусе поэзии и прозы, а также в теоретических суждениях поэта по поводу современной прозы. Мандельштамовский стих в огромном большинстве случаев — это стих, построенный по классическим законам русской поэтики, с употреблением канонических размеров. Сами стихотворения невелики по объему, в них, как правило, выдержано разделение на строфы, причем преобладают классические четырехстрочные строфы (в первом издании "Камня" из 23 стихотворений 18 написано четырех-строчными строфами, а в тексте "Tristia", входящем в первый том американского издания из 43 номеров — 28). Тяга к четкому строфному делению стихотворения — один из самых существенных признаков композиционной структуры мандельштамовской поэзии, и здесь мы наблюдаем ту самую уравновешенность всех элементов стиха, о которой применительно к Пушкину писал Эйхенбаум. Для мандель-штамовского стиха, принцип конструктивной симметрии ритма в ши-роком смысле слова является основоположным. Здесь уместно вспом-нить о тыняновской характеристике конструктивного фактора стиха, которая как нельзя точнее подходит именно к поэзии Мандельштама: "Таким стержневым, конструктивным фактором будет в стихе *ритм*, в широком смысле материалом — семантические группы."[4]

В противоположность этому проза Мандельштама построена на принципе *асимметрии*, отсутствия уравновешенности конструктивных элементов. Выше уже приводилась мандельштамовская характеристика прозы как асимметричной. Ритм прозы в отличие от ритма поэзии — это неправильность, разнобой. В прозе движутся 'словесные массы', то-есть упор на отсутствие строгого канона. С этим согласуется цитированное выше мнение о потере современной прозой принципа фабульности (а он мог бы выступать в качестве такого организующего канона). Отсюда уже давно отмеченная 'неорганизованность' прозы Мандельштама, ее 'фрагментарность', обилие 'ненужных', 'случайных' деталей, отсутствие завершенности, закругленности. Все эти особенности Мандельштама-прозаика находят отклики в его теоретических высказываниях о сущ-ности прозы на данном этапе литературного существования. Утрата фабулы, отход на задний план личности коррелируют с концепцией прозы как "чистого действия словесных масс" ("Литературная Москва. Рождение фабулы"). Но помимо 'отмирания' личности героя прозы отмирает, согласно Мандельштаму, и личность автора, и только в этом элиминировании автора проза получит желаемый простор для своего движения:

> "Кармен" Меримэ кончается филологическим рассуждением на тему о положении в семье языков цыганского наречья. Величайшее напряжение страсти и фабулы разрешается неожиданно филологическим трактатом, а звучит он приблизительно, как эпод трагического хора: "и всюду страсти роковые, и от судеб защиты нет". Происходило это до Пушкина.

Чего же нам удивляться, если Пильняк или серапионовцы вводят в свое повествование записные книжки, строительные сметы, советские циркуляры, газетные объявления и еще Бог знает что. Проза ничья. В сущности она безымянна. Это — организованное движение словесной массы, цементированной чем угодно. Стихия прозы — накопление. Она вся — ткань, морфология.

Нынешних прозаиков часть называют эклектиками, то-есть собирателями. Я думаю, это — не в обиду, это — хорошо. Всякий настоящий прозаик — именно эклектик, собиратель. Личность в сторону. Дорогу безымянной прозе. Почему имена великих прозаиков, этих подрядчиков грандиозных словесных замыслов, безымянных по существу, коллективных по исполнению, как "Гаргантюа и Пантагрюэль" Рабле или "Война и мир", превращаются в легенду и мир" (из статьи "Литературная Москва. Рождение фабулы").

Но если конструктивный стержень мандельштамовской прозы диаметрально противоположен его поэтической конструкции, то в чем же, все-таки, специфика его прозы как прозы поэта, почему выше мы утверждали, что она, как и проза Пушкина, вся растет из стиха? Действительно, Мандельштам стремился в своей прозе 'смоделировать' бесфабульный мир, его занимало, в первую очередь, 'движение словесной массы', более того, его проза в определенном смысле слова —'ничья', несмотря на свою сугубую автобиографичность. Однако добивается он всех этих целей иначе, чем современные ему прозаики. Совершенно невозможно себе представить, чтобы Мандельштам стал 'эклектиком' в том смысле, в каком он считал 'эклектиками' Пильняка или серапионовцев. Он совершенно чужд увлечению 'литературой факта' или 'коллажем'. Все дело в том, что в мандельштамовской прозе, в отличие от прозы Пильняка или серапионовцев, — иной конструктивный принцип; Мандельштам отмечал, что в современной ему прозе на смену фабуле пришел фольклор — сознательное закрепление, накопление языкового и этнографического материала" ("Литературная Москва. Рождение фабулы"). Конструктивный принцип — интересная история, анекдот (говоря в терминах формалистов, проза двадцатых годов — нефабульна, но сюжетна).

Конструктивный принцип прозы Мандельштама — создание семантической 'тесноты' внутри текстового массива. Иными словами то, что Тынянов считает в широком смысле *материалом* поэзии (семантические группы), в прозе Мандельштама становится *конструктивным фактором*. Материалом же его прозы (то-есть тем, что *преодолевается*, согласно теории формалистов) служит личный, повседневный опыт существования самого автора в определенной историко-культурной ситуации, связанной с данным пространством и временем. Соответственно, мандельштамовская проза, во-первых, оказывается 'поэтически организованной' на весьма низких уровнях высказывания (включая фонический уровень и уровень ядерных лексических сочетаний) и, во-вторых, преодоление поэтической личности все время придает этой прозе дополнительную, весьма важную координату *живого голоса, беседы, диалога* с читателем.

Следует, наверное, уточнить, как именно мы понимаем мандельштамовское замечание об устранении личности в прозе. В стихах Мандельштама постоянно присутствует в одной из своих граней некоторая, довольно определенно выраженная духовная и душевная позиция. От "Камня" до "Стихов 1921-1925 годов" эта позиция усложняется и приобретает все большую внутреннюю перспективу. Читатель как бы присутствует при процессе постепенного углубления и расширения *понимания, постижения, вчувствования* в мир культурно-исторического и психологически-чувственного бытия. Поэт строит перед нами свое внутреннее 'я', и чем дальше — тем более разносторонним оно становится. Это 'внутреннее я' — самоценное ядро личности — разворачивается по концентрическим кругам — от ранних психологически-метафизических стихов "Камня" ("Утро, нежностью бездонное, / Полуявь и полусон — / Забытье неутоленное — / Дум туманный перезвон...") через 'петербургские', 'описательные' ("Домби и сын" или "Мороженно! Солнце") и 'римские' стихотворения этого сборника к 'эллинским', 'петербургским' же и 'московским', а также 'гражданским' стихотворениям "Tristia" и от них к "Грифельной оде", "Нашедшему подкову" и "1 января 1924". Существенно, что в "Камне" и "Tristia" построенне поэтической личности предстает почти исключительно как Wandlung der Seele. Все берется под углом зрения этой выкристаллизовывающейся *поэтической* позиции, и в тех немногих стихах, где материалом становится опыт конкретного, бытового существования ("Золотой", "Царское село", и т.п.), он преображается так, чтобы не выходить из поэтических рамок: в вещах усматриваются более общие — эстетические или исторические — признаки, и они встраиваются в литературный ряд.

И лишь, начиная с некоторых стихотворений Tristia ("Чуть мерцает призрачная сцена", "В Петербурге мы сойдемся снова") и, особенно, со стихотворений "Кому зима арак и пунш голубоглазый" и "1 января 1924", в поэтическом творчестве Мандельштама происходит определенное расширение рамок личности. Но раздвинуть границы уже достигнутой поэтической позиции в пределах поэзии же было далее невозможно без овладения 'прозаической материей' собственного 'я'.

Это, по-видимому, и имеет в виду Мандельштам, когда провозглашает необходимость устранения личности в прозе. Примечательно, что, в отличие от других крупных русских поэтов его поколения (Маяковский, Пастернак, Ахматова), в двух первых сборниках Мандельштама совершенно не находят прямого 'отражения' биографические обстоятельства его жизни, во всяком случае, они немедленно переводятся на язык 'поэтической личности'. Видимо существовал определенный разрыв между этой личностью и повседневным, прозаическим опытом. Преодолеть этот разрыв, вместить прозаический опыт в поэзию могла только проза, но проза, близкая к поэзии по своим структурным признакам.

Показательно и другое. Поэтическая личность, постепенно складывавшаяся в стихах Мандельштама, несмотря на многообразие культурно-исторических и психологических слоев, вместившихся в нее, была чужда не только прозаическому, бытовому материалу, но и складу повседневной — не авторски-поэтической, а, пожалуй, индивидуализированно-поэтической — речи. Стихотворный строй раннего Мандельштама можно распознать сразу, в этом смысле он глубоко индивидуален, но строй этот пока не слишком восприимчив к оттенкам — фразеологическим, лексическим и стилистическим — чужого слова.

Все эти задачи была призвана выполнить проза Мандельштама. Она должна была послужить трамплином для последующего поэтического творчества, ибо невозможно было сохранить смысловые комплексы, сложившиеся в "Камне" и "Tristia", без того, чтобы не подвести под них более широкую базу. В этом смысле мандельштамовская проза ничего не 'отменяет' в его ранних стихах, не полемизирует с ними. Соотношение между этими стихами и прозой можно представить таким образом, что стихи — это непосредственный источник мандельштамовской семантики, проза его статей о литературе создает для поэтической семантики дискурсивную базу, а проза "Шума времени", "Египетской марки" должна погрузить те же, в сущности, смысловые комплексы в стихию жизни.

Овладение материей своего 'прозаического я' происходит в прозе Мандельштама не только за счет прямой реконструкции биографического опыта. Происходит развоплощение самоценной поэтической личности. Опыт подается как набор ситуаций, которые могут приписываться одновременно разным индивидуальностям с их собственными речевыми стихиями. Отсюда — смешение авторского 'голоса' с 'голосами' литературных героев, склеивание повествовательных ипостасей и сознательное выведение повествования за рамки текста. Читатель вводится в текст как полноправное действующее лицо, к нему апеллируют, от него ожидается владение тем же самым затекстовым материалом (и в том же объеме), каким владеет автор. Таким образом, на смену единой поэтической личности приходит монтаж индивидуальностей.

На уровне структуры текста проза Мандельштама построена, как уже указывалось, с учетом всего того опыта поэтической работы в области семантики, который был накоплен в его поэзии. Монтаж смысловых единиц в плане фактуры текста соответствует монтажу индивидуальностей в плане повествования. Поэзия Мандельштама, как никакая другая в русской литературе начала двадцатого века, была поэзий *семантической*. Соответствие между мандельштамовской поэтической практикой и теорией поэтического языка, разработанной специально применительно к семантике Тыняновым в его *Проблеме стихотворного языка*, представляется почти беспрецедентным.

Все признаки стихотворного языка, выделяемые Тыняновым, можно, в той или иной степени, найти в мандельштамовской прозе. Возьмем, прежде всего, три наиболее общих конструктивных признака стиха по Тынянову: *единство* стихового ряда, его *теснота* и *динамизация* в стиховом ряду речевого материала. Какой бы предполагаемый смысл слова 'стиховой ряд' мы ни имели в виду — ряд как *стихотворная строка*, ряд как слитный композиционный фрагмент стиха и/или его функциональная 'решетка', или, еще более расширительно — ряд как сфера стихотворного языка, набор стиховых явлений — в прозе Мандельштама мы обнаруживаем единство, тесноту и динамизацию слова во всех указанных планах стихового ряда. Ниже мы постараемся привести подтверждения этому тезису, здесь же укажем на чисто формальные признаки мандельштамовской прозы, связанные, по нашему мнению, с поэтическим модусом словесной семантики в ней. Часто автор отделяет друг от друга (типографским способом) прозаические строчки, создавая тем самым эквивалент стихотворной строки-ряда —, объединенного как изнутри, так и извне, ср. из "Египетской марки":

Пожары и книги — это хорошо.
Мы еще поглядим — почитаем.

Отделенность прозаических строк друг от друга создает целый ряд эффектов и среди них: возникновение ориентации на устное произношение и актуализацию латентных метрических фигур (ср. "Рысак выбрасывает бабки" — потенциальный четырехстопный ямб); концентрация семантических связей внутри строки (тыняновская теснота и

деформация вследствие единства ряда) на фоне актуализации фонологических фигур в 'стиховом ряду' — ср. строку из "Египетской марки"
"Проклятый сон! Проклятые стогны бесстыжего города", где повтор
одного и того же слова *проклятый* выступает на фоне других фоно-
морфологических повторов *(có — стó[г]н — ...сты́ — ...гó)* и приводит
к иррадиации семьи 'отрицательного' и на слово *стогны* (ср. ассоци-
ацию со *стоны*) создание 'квази-стиховых' семантических связей между
строками (как в строфе и т.п.), ср. пассаж из первой главы "Египетской
марки":

> *Последние* зернышки кофе *исчезли* в кратере мельницы-шарманки.
> *Умыкание* состоялось.
> Мервис *похитил* ее как *сабинянку,*

где между выделенными словами устанавливается связь по смысловому
признаку 'отсутствие'.

Другой способ ввода поэтической семантики — это отделение друг от
друга отдельных абзацев или более крупных пассажей. Именно такой
короткий отрывок — это основной локус семантической деформации в
прозе Мандельштама. Внутри него семантические связи носят характер
поэтических, и можно говорить о семантической тесноте внутри абзаца.
Между отдельными абзацами также можно установить постоянные
смысловые связи по второстепенным смысловым признакам и проч. В
этом смысле существенны маркированные композиционные границы
отрывков — особенно начала, которые могут быть оформлены по
стиховому принципу (анафоричность, аллитеративность), одновременно являясь своего рода стрелками вовне (ср. типичные начала абзацев из
"Египетской марки" : "Во-первых ...", "Я твердо знал ...", "А парикмахер
...", "А я бы роздал...").

Наконец, можно говорить и о стиховой тесноте прозаического текста
как целого у Мандельштама. Эта 'теснота' прежде всего проявляется в
особом, подчеркнутом внимании к уравновешиванию асимметричности
движения прозаических словесных масс за счет создания сплошной
семантической связности текста на самых разных уровнях.

2. Ниже мы попытаемся проиллюстрировать основные закономерности семантической связности в "Египетской марке" как целостном
тексте, обращая внимание и на структуру отдельных 'квази-стиховых'
фрагментов — абзацев.

В "Египетской марке" поэт обращается к 'оправданию' новой прозы:
"Железная дорога изменила все течение, все построение, весь такт нашей

прозы. Она отдала ее во власть бессмысленному лопотанью француз-
ского мужичка из Анны Карениной. Железнодорожная проза, как дам-
ская сумочка этого предсмертного мужичка, полна инструментами
сцепщика, бредовыми частичками, скобяными предлогами, которым
место на столе судебных улик, развязана от всякой заботы о красоте и
округленности".

Попробуем проследить весьма суммарно некоторые правила 'цемен-
тирования', 'сцепления' словесной массы в самой "Египетской марке",
имея в виду, что характер поэтического использования слова в мандельштамовской прозе требует несравненно более пристального и
подробного анализа, чем это возможно в рамках статьи. Речь пойдет о
правилах сцепления композиционных блоков текста, а также более
мелких его частей, правилах, оперирующих не идеологическими или
сюжетными конструкциями, а смысловыми элементами более 'низших'
уровней.

1) "Египетская марка" — произведение, нарочито лишенное 'округленности', законченности на уровне фабулы. Оно начинается со 'случайной фразы': "Прислуга-полька ушла в костел Гваренги — посплетни-
чать и помолиться Матке Божьей". Начало это никоим образом не
фабулярно: прислуга-полька (неизвестно чья — Парнока?) более не
появится в тексте, упоминание о ней имеет совершенно иные цели, не
связанные с развитием фабулы. Цели эти — семантическое скрепление
разрозненных эпизодов. Отдельные смысловые элементы начального
предложения появляются далее по ходу повести: в конце первой главы,
где впервые вводится тема смерти Бозио (правда пока без упоминания
ее имени), мы снова встречаем упоминание о костеле Гваренги: "А
потом кавалергарды слетятся на отпевание в костел Гваренги. Золотые
птички-стервятники расклюют римско-католическую певенью". В этом
же пассаже подхватывается тема католичества, затронутая вскользь в
первой фразе. В конце третьей главы возникает мотив *польского*, пере-
даваемый русской речью с польским 'акцентом' хозяйки прачечной
("Они мне всегда приносят спешку...", "Я даже в Варшаве такого не
видела", "Я не варьятка..."). Этот же мотив поддерживается самой
фигурой ротмистра *Кржижановского* с нафабренными усами. Тема
Варшавы снова повторяется уже не в фабуле, посвященной петербургским приключениям Парнока и ротмистра Кржижановского, а в авто-
биографическом отступлении: "И меня ввели в постылую варшавскую
комнату и заставили пить воду и есть лук".

И, наконец, заканчивается повесть отправлением ротмистра Кржижановского в Москву — снова возвращение 'польской' темы, с которой

как бы случайно начинается повествование.

Таким образом фабульная линия "Египетской марки" — история визитки Парнока и ее похищения Кржижановским оказывается на семантическом уровне связанной со 'случайной' фразой, с которой повесть начинается. Нарочитое отсутствие 'округленности' в фабуле как бы компенсируется возвратом на уровне более мелких смысловых элементов.

2) Неопределенность, незаконченность фабулы "Египетской марки", компенсируемая рамочной смысловой связью текста, коррелирует с неопределенным модусом многих высказываний этого текста и отсутствием нарративного перехода от одного пассажа к другому, при том что такой переход обычно осуществляется посредством установления контекстуальной смысловой связи мелких единиц.

Так во второй фразе повести "Ночью снился китаец, обвешанный дамскими сумочками, как ожерельем из рябчиков…" помимо того, что неясно *кому* 'снился китаец' (автору? Парноку?), следует отметить крайнюю 'необязательность' как самого образа 'обвешанный дамскими сумочками' так и того, с чем этот образ сравнивается ("Как ожерельем из рябчиков" — почему из рябчиков?).

Переходы от одного абзаца к другому в начале "Египетской марки" построены исключительно по принципу семантической связи на *оси комбинации*. Неслучайно в первых двух предложениях, никак не связанных фабульно, упоминаются *полька, китаец* и далее '*американская дуэль-кукушка*'. Нанизывание друг за другом слов, обозначающих национальную принадлежность, создает определенный суб-код текста, устанавливающий единство смысловой ориентации при отсутствии нарративной логической связи. Преобразование данного семантического повтора (далее поддерживаемого такими словами как *петербургской, венские, голландские* и т.п.) в суб-код становится возможным как раз вследствие необязательности, избыточности подобной 'географической' номинации с точки зрения полноты сообщения.

'Географический' суб-код обеспечивает смысловую связность всей первой главы "Египетской марки", причем эта связность в результате оказывается более прочной, чем связность фабульная. Смысловой центр прозы переходит в то, что традиционно принято было бы считать отступлением, но что у Мандельштама служит подлинным конструктивным каркасом произведения.

Прочность семантической связи обеспечивается в данном случае тем, что, начиная с определенного абзаца, географический *суб-код* становится *сообщением*. Исподволь подаваемая в отдельных словосочетаниях тема географического разнообразия, пространства, этнической и национальной принадлежности, специфичности (кроме вышеперечисленных примеров ср. такие как "Милый *Египет* вещей", "визитка на *венской* дуге", "*готическая немецкая* азбука") постепенно подводит к теме Петербурга, как особого места, где на фоне разнородных географических пластов актуализуется встреча — и контраст — российского и иностранного.

Тема Петербурга как стыка *России* и *заграницы* впервые вводится в текст в двух соседних пассажах. В первом из них речь идет о детском интересе Парнока к географической карте ("карта полушарий Ильина"), а во втором пассаже, где и происходит трансформация суб-кода в сообщение, рассказывается о "перелете певицы итальянской школы" в Америку и Россию.

В том или ином виде географический суб-код, равно как и тема "Россия — заграница" останутся одним из наиболее важных глубинных смысловых компонентов "Египетской марки" (ср., с одной стороны, постоянный рефрен о желании Парнока "поступить драгоманом в министерство иностранных дел" и рассказ о смерти Бозио в зимнем Петербурге — с другой). Любопытно, что кончается первая глава "Египетской марки" также 'географической' темой: "Дальше изображены были голландцы на ходулях, журавлиным шагом пробегающие свою маленькую страну".

3) Наряду с семантическим сцеплением осуществляемым посредством суб-кодов, проходящих через весь текст (а 'географический' суб-код — лишь один из целого набора таких суб-кодов, в число которых входит, например, суб-код музыкальный — ср. появление в самых немотивированных местах "сына Арона, ученика консерватории", "кабинетного рояля Миньон", "концертного морозца", "парадных амфилад истории и музыки", и проч.), следует отметить и другой вид сцепления: соединение двух соседних иначе несвязанных пассажей по смысловому сходству последних и первых слов абзацев, ср.:

> ... противники бьют из пистолетов в *горки* с *посудой*, в чернильницы и в *фамильные холсты*.
> *Семья моя* я предлагаю тебе герб: *стакан с кипяченой водой*.

Ср. также из второй главы:

> ... или же повести его вместе с *мученицей* — мадам Шапиро — в *Казанский собор*, где *продырявленный* воздух *черен* и сладок.
> Есть *темная*, с детства идущая геральдика нравственных понятий: шварк *раздираемого* полотна может означать честность, и холод мадеполама — *святость*.

Подобное 'точечное' сцепление словесных масс посредством сведения вместе в композиционно релевантных стыках семантически близких элементов (один из которых часто оказывается 'немотивированным' или избыточным, как *фамильные* или *темная*) приводит к актуализации вторичных смысловых признаков в контактирующих элементах. На стыке образуется связь, подобная связи слов в стихотворной строке ('теснота' по Тынянову), и фабульно несвязанные друг с другом куски текста сцепляются, пожалуй, прочнее, чем цельные фрагменты повествовательного текста.

4) Сцепление фрагментов текста может осуществляться и на фонологическом уровне. Повтор звуковой структуры целых слов ведет к их смысловому сближению и, тем самым, к установлению еще одной дополнительной координаты организованности текста. Роль фонической организации прозаического текста подчеркивалась Андреем Белым (для прозы Гоголя) и Б. М. Эйхенбаумом (для пушкинского "Выстрела"). Она тем более велика в прозе Мандельштама, полностью построенной по законам поэтического языка. Ср., в частности, такие примеры как:

> Спит! … *Шарамыжник*, на него электрической лампочки жалко!
> Последние зернышки кофе исчезли в кратере мельницы-*шарманки*.

или

> Парнок был *жертвой* заранее созданных концепций о том, как должен протекать роман.
> На бумаге *верже*, государи мои, на английской бумаге *верже* …

и далее:

> … пространство *между* Миллионной, Адмиралтейством и Летним садом им заново отшлифовано и приведено в полную готовность, как бриллиантовый *карат*.
> На такой бумаге, читатель, могли бы переписываться *кариатиды Эрмитажа, выражая* друг другу соболезнование или *уважение*."

Иногда звуковая связь определенного слова в тексте как бы восполняет смысловой пробел, и появляющийся новый гипотетический элемент служит семантическим мостиком к последующему тексту:

> Вначале был *верстак* и *карта* полушарий Ильина.

Связь *верстака* с *картой* возможна через отсутствующий, но легко достраиваемый элемент *верста*.

Звуковое подобие может приводить к смысловому сближению словарно различных смысловых единиц, особенно на фоне звуковых повторов, 'прошивающих' соседние элементы текста, ср. актуализацию внутренней формы в слове 'легкие' и, с другой стороны, иррадиацию его денотативного значения на слово 'слегка', поддерживаемые параллельным повтором звуковых групп *с...т...р...ш — т...р...х — з...т...ш — с...т...р...ш — с...п...р...ш — с...т...р...ш* в отрывке:

> "Они воняют кишечными пузырями" — подумал Парнок, и почему-то вспомнилось страшное слово 'требуха'. И его слегка затошнило как бы от воспоминания о том, что на днях старушка в лавке спрашивала при нем 'легкие' — на самом же деле от страшного порядка, сковывавшего толпу".

5) Выше уже отмечалась возвратность отдельных смысловых элементов по ходу текста. Это, пожалуй, основной прием сцепления словесных масс в повести. Подобно как в стихах Мандельштама можно проследить 'вертикальные' смысловые ряды, сложно переплетающиеся, расходящиеся, иногда дающие разветвления или образующие отдельные вкрапления, подобно 'глазкам' в породе, в "Египетской марке" можно· найти множество примеров подобного семантического 'голосоведения'. Отмеченные выше смысловые 'суб-коды' — один из примеров такого структурирования текста. Их выделение основывается на сочетании семантического повтора с семантической избыточностью, необязательностью, инконгруэнтностью.

Существуют и другие виды смысловой возвратности — повтор отдельных ситуаций, включают, например, двукратное упоминание о костеле Гваренги. Некоторые повторы гораздо обширнее. Так, в конце первой главы тема пропавшей визитки вдруг ассоциируется с литературными образами:

> "Тут промелькнули в мозгу его горячечные образы романов Бальзака и Стендаля: молодые туфли у входа в особняки, — и он отправился отбивать визитку".

Через несколько абзацев литературная реминисценция возвращается уже без всякой мотивировки, вернее с непосредственной памятью о мотивировке, приведенной выше ("Тут промелькнули в мозгу его..."):

> "У Люсьена де Рюбанпрэ было *грубое* холщевое белье и неуклюжая пара, пошитая деревенским портным...".

Повидимому, возможность закрепления в 'памяти' текста подобных мотивировок свидетельствует о стремлении автора рассматривать текст как поэтический — оказывается, что размеры прозаического текста не должны мешать его как бы одновременной, 'матричной' фиксации в памяти.

К числу наиболее выраженных повторов принадлежит тема 'зубного врача'. В ней семантический повтор сочетается с повтором фабульным и тематическим (в 'отступлении'). Начинается эта тема с первого в повести упоминания о хронологических и социальных рамках происходящего, причем это упоминание принадлежит авторской точке зрения (или объединенной точке зрения автора и Парнока):

"Стояло лето Керенского и заседало лимонадное правительство.[...]
Но уже волновались айсоры-чистильщики сапог, как вороны перед
затмением, и у зубных врачей начали исчезать штифтовые зубы".

Непосредственно после этого пассажа тема 'зубных врачей' продолжается и точка зрения становится чисто авторской с переходом к прямой речи от первого лица:

"Люблю зубных врачей за их любовь к искусству, за широкий гори-
зонт, за идейную терпимость. Люблю, грешный человек, жужжание
бормашины — этой бедной земной сестры аэроплана — тоже свер-
лящего борчиком лазуры".

Далее тема 'зубных врачей' возникает вновь лишь в первой строке следующей (четвертой) главы, где она превращается в фабульную (Парнок сидит у дантиста):

"Зубной врач повесил хобот бормашины и подошел к окну".

Любопытно, что фабульное введение зубного врача ничем не предваряется, однако смысловая связь внутри темы несомненна: подхватывается мотив *бормашины*, на котором тема остановилась в своем предыдущем появлении. Этим же мотивом прерванная тема и заканчивается через полторы страницы:

"И Парнок кубарем скатился по щербатой бесшвейцарной лестнице,
оставив недоуменного дантиста перед повисшей, как усыпленная
кобра, бор-машиной ...".

Мы закончим наш обзор семантической связности в "Египетской марке" рассмотрением некоторых сквозных мотивов, которые имеют черты, сходные с 'суб-кодами', однако не столь всеобъемлющи и глобальны.

Это — мотивы 'кипяченой воды' и 'кофе', встречающиеся на протяжении всего текста, столь же 'необязательные' как суб-коды, но более локальные, более связанные с ситуацией.

Кипяченая вода связывается в "Египетской марке" с темами семьи, детства, неприятных детских воспоминаний. Эти ассоциации носят

скорее негативный характер: кипяченая вода как знак пассивности и не-
желания, боязни столкновения с миром, стремления отгородиться от
окружающего, сохранить свой призрачный и хрупкий образ жизни ("В
резиновом привкусе петербургской отварной воды я пью неудавшееся
домашнее бессмертие"). Одновременно кипяченая вода явственно связывается с особой петербургской атмосферой бесцельной деловитости,
прозаичности и канцеляризма. Обе эти ассоциативные струи выступают
в характеристике Дворцовой площади, "где все до ужаса приготовлено к
началу исторического заседания с белыми листами бумаги, с отточен-
ными карандашами и с графином кипяченой воды".

В противоположность этому кофе всегда выступает в контексте
активного участия в жизни, как некоторый возбуждающий, экзоти-
ческий элемент (так сказать, соответственно собственным качествам
кофе), ср.:

> "И страшно жить и хорошо!
> Он — лимонная косточка, брошенная в расщелину петербургского
> гранита, и выпьет его с черным турецким кофием налетающая ночь".

Любопытно, что в конце повести обе рассмотренные темы оказываются в контекстах прямо противоположных тем, которые связы-
вались с ними в ходе повествования. Мотив кипяченой воды подается в
суб-коде 'болезни' (этот суб-код играет большую роль в смысловой
характеристике двух сближаемых автором сфер — истории и творчества) и в сочетании с другим повторяющимся мотивом — *рояля* —,
который в "Египетской марке" имеет, скорее, позитивные ассоциации:

> "Знакомо ли вам это состояние? Когда у всех вещей словно жар;
> когда все они радостно возбуждены и больны: рогатка на улице,
> шелушенье афиш, рояли, толпящиеся в депо, как умное стадо без
> вожака, рожденное для сонатных беспамятств и кипяченой воды".

Кофе, ранее связанное только с Парноком, с Н. Бруни или с
авторскими воспоминаниями, становится в конце повести поддельным,
когда его пьет ротмистр Кржижановский. При этом напиток — в
противоположность настоящему кофе, связанному с жизнью — здесь
ассоциируется со смертью:

> В Клину он отведал железнодорожного кофия, который приго-
> товляется по рецепту, неизменному со времен Анны Карениной, из
> цикория с легкой прибавкой кладбищенской земли или другой
> какой-то гадости в этом роде.

3. Таким образом, "Египетская марка" — это, прежде всего, проза
семантическая. Все, что писалось в другом месте о кардинальной роли

семиотического и *семантического* самоосознания в творчестве Ахматовой и Мандельштама, непосредственно приложимо к "Египетской марке".[5] Само собой разумеется, что основные ключи к истолкованию повести как текста, организованного по законам семантической связности, содержатся в самом тексте, в частности, в цитате о 'железнодорожной прозе', приведенной выше. Существенно, однако, и то более общее обстоятельство, что тема *языка, слова, писания* является одной из наиболее важных, структурообразующих тем "Египетской марки". Тема эта претерпевает в ходе повести существенную эволюцию, превращаясь в конце концов в *автометаописание* — рассказ о том, как пишется, по каким структурным законам построена сама "Египетская марка". При этом, повинуясь акмеистическому порыву, превращающему жизнь в текст и текст в жизнь, снимающему границу между обоими, предполагается, что пишет повесть не только автор, но и все, что составляет действительность текста — Петербург. При этом кульминация темы 'текста' наступает в конце повести, когда ее автометаописание переходит, вернее, сливается с самоописанием личности автора, и оказывается, что правила построения новой прозы — суть парадигма личности художника, личности новой, поставленной в небывало сложные обстоятельства, но способной из столкновения между этими обстоятельствами и глубинными законами своего творчества создать ценности культуростроительного плана.

Интересующая нас тема вводится исподволь, сначала в 'случайных отступлениях': в начале первой главы упоминается о — постижении "готической немецкой азбуки", затем в первом фрагменте о "певице итальянской школы" впервые возникает мотив слов, которые здесь еще *не осмысливаются*, не семантизируются, а выступают, скорее, как знаки чужого, неизвестного языка, обращается внимание на звуковой облик слов:

"Защекочут ей маленькие уши. Будет ей рот раздирать до ушей небывалый, невозможный звук 'ы'".

Обратим, между прочим, внимание на то, что в качестве типично русских согласных звуков выступают как раз те (*щ... ч... щ*), на которых построено описание самосуда толпы в четвертой главе (см. выше). Любопытно, что в двух ключевых словах этого описания ("...лица в толпе не имеют значения, но живут самостоятельно одни *затылки* и *уши*") встречается звук 'ы'.

После такого введения темы *слóва, языка, писания* она в разных ипостасях пронизывает весь текст. Встречается она и виде суб-кода, мотива, самостоятельного сообщения, фабульных фрагментов, неся на разных уровнях единство текстовой конструкции. Предварительно можно выделить следующие модификации нашей темы: 'чужое слово' и цитация, жизнь и особенно Петербург как своего рода сообщение (с обязательными 'стрелками', выводящими за пределы текста), тема единства разных коммуникативных кодов, решаемая также на фоне Петербурга, тема русской литературы и, наконец, автометаописание самой повести и автора. Само собой разумеется, что эти отдельные семантические ряды могут переплетаться и сливаться воедино.

Тема 'чужого слова' и цитации в "Египетской марке" слишком обширна, чтобы ее можно было хотя бы приблизительно разрешить в одной статье. В сущности, в каждом предложении "Египетской марки" в той или иной форме присутствует чужое слово — прямо или опосредованно. Мы же хотим затронуть лишь один небольшой аспект этой темы — авторские рассуждения по поводу вполне конкретных чужих слов, вводимых кавычками и словами типа "говорилось…" и т.п.

В большинстве случаев такие 'чужие слова' подаются через эксплицитно выраженное *другое восприятие* — либо автора, либо Парнока. И, поскольку характер трактовки чужих слов в обоих воспринимающих сознаниях сходен, возникает определенный семантический уровень, на котором автор и Парнок сливаются, отождествляются — хотя бы в некоторых аспектах своего текстового воплощения.

Первый раз остраненное чужое слово подается в детском восприятии в авторском повествовании первого лица: "О Шапиро говорилось, что он честен и 'маленький человек'. Я почему-то был уверен, что 'маленькие люди' никогда не тратят больше трех рублей и живут обязательно на Песках". Здесь, как и в дальнейшем, подчеркивается установочный, нормативный характер 'чужого слова', воспринимаемого детским сознанием — 'чужое слово' как часть внешней системы норм, которую ребенок воспринимает, не соотнося ее с языковым значением соответствующих высказываний, вернее, создавая свою систему смысловых соответствий. Знаменательно, что в качестве этих соответствий выступают определенные конкретные ситуации, воспринимаемые детским сознанием как задаваемые взрослой семантической системой, но на деле созданные ребенком ad hoc и ad hominem. Подобный способ семантизации, только систематизированный и встроенный в литературно-культурный процесс, типичен для определенных аспектов поэтики акмеизма.

Тремя абзацами ниже Мандельштам демонстрирует отчасти обратный семантический процесс: не слову приписывается значение в виде ситуации, а ситуация понимается как означающая определенное абстрактное понятие, удобнее всего описываемое одним словом: "Есть темная, с детства идущая геральдика нравственных понятий: шварк раздираемого полотна может означать честность, а холод маделолама — святость". Это — комплементарная сторона семантизации слова как ситуации.

Подобное же остраненное восприятие слова мы встречаем в семантизации имени "Николай Давыдович" Шапиро: "Мне представлялось, что Давыдович, то-есть сам Шапиро кланяется, вобрав голову в плечи, какому-то Николаю и просит у него взаймы".

Аналогичный процесс ассоциативного — детского — называния ситуации и, наоборот, осмысления слов характеризует и Парнока. Особенно это явственно в сцене самосуда, где Парнок как бы не поспевает за ходом событий и дает им то случайное, но на самом деле глубоко мотивированное (в частности на звуковом уровне) название, которое в тот исчезающе краткий момент приходит ему в голову:

"Все эти люди — продавцы щеток" — *успел подумать* Парнок.

И далее:

"Они воняют кишечными пузырями" — подумал Парнок, и *почему-то вспомнилось* страшное слово 'требуха'.

Наконец:

"И Парнок кубарем скатился по щербатой бесшвейцарной лестнице,
/.../ *вместо всяких мыслей* повторяя:
— Пуговицы делаются из крови животных!"

Обратим внимание на то, что все эти случайные ассоциации, приходящие на ум Парноку, на самом деле обладают очевидной смысловой связью: утилитарное использование туши (то-есть *трупа*) животного. На это накладывается комплекс субъективно-чувственных признаков, всегда существенный для семантики Мандельштама, в данном случае —отвращение, тошнота, дурной запах, ощущение грязи, нечистоты.

Подчеркивание случайности, непреднамеренности ассоциаций и одновременно выявление их глубинного единства имплицитно намечает существенные черты семантического порождения самой "Египетской марки".

Мотивацию названия повести мы также находим в 'чужом слове'. Парнок вспоминает клички, которыми его дразнили в детстве: "Товарищи в школе дразнили его 'овцой', 'лакированным копытом', 'египетской маркой' и другими обидными именами". Здесь возвращается мотив некоей внешней понудительной силы, связанной с 'чужим словом', мотив, который в более ослабленном виде уже встречался в том, как было введено выражение 'маленький человек'. Взрослые говорили 'маленький человек', и ребенку представлялось, что они подразумевают под этим определенную ситуацию, придуманную им самим, то-есть чужое слово обязательно связывалось с определенной реакцией, вызывало ее. 'Обидные прозвища', в сущности — словесное выражение той нормативной силы, которой обладают отношения между сверстниками.

Та же тема, но выведенная на поверхность, фигурирует в воспоминании автора о домашнем слове 'сажа' и, уже в явном виде, в воспоминании, чья субъективная модальность кажется неопределенной (автора? Парнока?) о 'домашних словечках'. В обоих случаях чужое слово вызывает воспоминание о его особой нормативной власти. Крик 'сажа!' был связан с тем, что начинала коптить керосиновая лампа, и для того чтобы проветрить помещение открывали форточку:

> *"Туда нельзя* — там форточка," — шептали мать и бабушка. Но и в замочную скважину врывался он — *запрещенный* холод — чудный гость дифтеритных пространств.

'Домашние словечки' используются как своего рода регулятор внутреннего состояния героя. К ним обращаются для того 'чтоб успокоиться'. Включают они, в частности, "отрицательные заповеди":

> "Не коверкай" — так говорили о жизни.
> "Не командуй" — так гласила одна из заповедей.

Итак, одна из функций 'чужих слов' в системе "Египетской марки" —объективация определенных ситуаций, концентрированное выражение и представление связей между вещами, которые устанавливаются ad hoc, но на манер прочных смысловых связей, существующих в 'обычном' словаре, связей, которые именно в силу своей идиосинкратичности, ориентированности на субъекта и одновременно обязательности моделируют восприятие и поведение, быть может, сильнее, чем обще-обиходные ассоциации.

Остальные случаи употребления 'чужих слов' связаны с другими модификациями общей темы 'слова', 'текста', 'писания'. Восприятие жизни как текста, речи, необходимость понимать, интерпретировать этот текст и, соответственно, возможность свободного взаимопроникновения прозы и жизни очевидны как в авторской точке зрения, так и в точке зрения Парнока. О Парноке говорится:

> "С детства он прикреплялся душой ко всему ненужному, превращая в события трамвайный лепет жизни, а когда начал влюбляться, то

пытался рассказать об этом женщинам, но те его не поняли, и в отместку он говорил с ними на диком и выспренном птичьем языке исключительно о высоких материях".

И здесь подчеркивается специфический характер парноковского осмысления событий — события как значения текста жизни, а сам текст этот, во-первых, состоит из ненужного (то-есть воспринятого как бы случайно вне утилитарных скрепляющих ассоциаций) и, во-вторых, восходит к впечатлениям детства.

"Трамвайный лепет жизни" имеет четкую пространственную прикрепленность — Петербург, с которым связаны и 'чужие слова' детства автора и Парнока, ср. в этом плане характеристику Парнока как "человека Каменноостровского проспекта", и основную черту этого проспекта: "Трамваи же на Каменноостровском развивают неслыханную скорость".

Таким же образом с самого начала связывается с Петербургом и с темой жизни как значимого текста тема 'автометаописания': во второй главе мы читаем:

"Парнок был жертвой *заранее созданных концепций о том, как должен протекать роман.*
На *бумаге верже*, государи мои, на *английской бумаге верже* с водяными отеками и рваными краями извещал он ничего не подозревающую даму о том, что *пространство между Миллионной, Адмиралтейством и Летним садом им заново отшлифовано и приведено в полную боевую готовность* как бриллиантовый карат".

Далее тема автометаописания "Египетской марки" будет все теснее сливаться с темой интерпретации Петербурга как текста, его прочтения, интериоризации, переструктирования, с темой русской литературы и с темой внутреннего состояния героя (автора, Парнока). Уже в вышеприведенной цитате мы видим отсылку во вне текста — обращение "Государи мои". Чем ближе к концу повести, тем явственнее будет звучать эта непосредственная, личная нота, вводящая читателя в текст как жизнь и приближающая рассказчика к нему — как собеседника. Тем больше будет чувствоваться вторжение рассказчика не только в текст, но и в фабулу повествования, его непосредственное присутствие на улицах Петербурга рядом с описываемыми им героями (ср. "А я бы роздал девушкам вместо утюгов скрипки Страдивария...").

В четвертой главе повести тема 'автометаописания' вводится уже более пространно как процесс писания и рисования, причем процесс улавливания случайного, ассоциативного, рисунок на 'полях черновиков'. Текст строится как собирание этих ассоциативных значений по крупице. Различные коммуникативные коды — слово, рисунок, музыка оказываются взаимно представимыми. Выявляется их смысловое единство в самом процессе писания или рисования. Особо подчеркивает Мандельштам значение пробелов в описании, пустых мест:

> "Перо рисует усатую греческую красавицу и чей-то лисий подбородок.
> Так на полях черновиков возникают арабески и живут своей самостоятельной, прелестной и коварной жизнью. Скрипичные человечки пьют *молоко бумаги.*
> Вот Бабель: лисий подбородок и лапки очков.
> Парнок — египетская марка.
> Артур Яковлевич Гофман — чиновник министерства иностранных дел по греческой части.
> Валторны Мариинского театра.
> Еще раз усатая гречанка.
> И *пустое место* для остальных".

В этом отрывке, который и графически построен как иконический знак случайного набора ассоциаций, ясно прослеживаются темы рисования портретов на полях черновиков (ср. черновики Пушкина), музыки видимой (ноты) и слышимой (валторны). Несколько мотивов ('лисий подбородок' Бабеля, "усатая красавица гречанка и греческая часть") проходят сквозным образом: маленький абзац построен в этом смысле как вся повесть в целом. В этом фрагменте мы опять встречаем упоминание о Петербурге ("Мариинский театр").

Начало пятой главы все целиком посвящено теме эквивалентности различных языков общения. Именно эта тема задает внутреннюю связность данного фрагмента повести с тем, который был только что процитирован. Речь идет о жестовой речи глухонемых, которая видится как нечто другое — непрерывное и осторожное разматывание пряжи: "В это время проходили через площадь глухонемые: они сучили руками быструю пряжу. Они разговаривали...". Этот разговор-прядение также связан с Петербургом, причем с семантически весьма отмеченным местом в нем — Дворцовой площадью. Сочетание описания Дворцовой площади как места, где "все до ужаса приготовлено к началу исторического заседания", то-есть места, связанного с *говорением*, причем говорением громким, публичным, со сценой безмолвно-бессмысленного разговора глухонемых придает особое семантическое напряжение данному исторически значимому локусу.

Собственно говоря, начиная с пятой главы все большее и большее место в повести начинает занимать тема текста, писания. Понадобилось бы процитировать целые страницы "Египетской марки" подряд, по-

этому нам придется ограничиться лишь перечислением соответствующих мест.

После пассажа о глухонемых на Дворцовой площади следует об-
ширный фрагмент о нотном письме ("Нотное письмо ласкает глаз не
меньше, чем сама музыка слух ..."). Говорится о нотном ландшафте
Моцарта, Шуберта, Бетховена, Генделя, Баха. Затем внезапно снова
вступает мотив Петербурга в связи с воспоминанием рассказчика о его
собственном обучении музыке.

Отсюда прямая связь к известному восклицанию автора: "Господи!
Не сделай меня похожим на Парнока! Дай мне силы отличить себя от
него". Чем дальше, тем теснее сливаются смысловые характеристики
рассказчика и Парнока: оба — завсегдатаи петербургских концертов,
оба противопоставлены страшному миру самосуда и жестокости. Чем
дальше — тем более отрывисто письмо мандельштамовской прозы, и
вот опять отрывок о том, как она пишется, отрывок, выглядящий как
графическое изображение прозаической манеры автора:

> "Я не боюсь бессвязности и разрывов.
> *Стригу* бумагу длинными ножницами.
> Подклеиваю ленточки бахромкой.
> Рукопись — всегда буря, истрепанная, исклеванная.
> Она — черновик сонаты.
> *Марать* — лучше, чем писать.
> Не боюсь швов и желтизны клея.
> Портняжу, бездельничаю.
> Рисую *Марата* в чулке.
> *Стрижей*".

Здесь принцип смысловой связи по звуковому подобию особенно
прозрачен.

Эта манера воспринимается автором как противодействие обще-
принятому в то время 'телеграфному стилю', который навязывается сам,
помимо воли:

> "Не повинуется мне перо: она расщепилось и разбрызгало свою
> черную кровь, как бы привязанное к конторке телеграфа — публич-
> ное, испакощенное ерниками в шубах...".

В этом фрагменте впервые вводится тема русской прозы. Мандельштам полемически противопоставляет свою прозу 'бессвязности и
разрывов' глубокомысленным попыткам создать 'прозу двадцатых
годов'.

В этом отрывке реализуется скрытая стилистическая фигура: 'теле-
графный стиль' приобретает ситуационную реальность (конторка теле-

графа) и выступает в виде прямых телеграфных цитат: 'скучаю', 'целую'. И еще одна деталь: писательское ремесло оказывается тесно связанным с мотивом шубы. Эта связь прослеживается в других прозаических вещах Мандельштама ("Шум времени" и "Четвертая проза").

В конце пятой главы тема русской литературы и Петербурга выделяется в самостоятельный фрагмент ("Скандалом называется бес, открытый русской прозой или самой русской жизнью в сороковых что ли годах...").

Фрагмент этот близок по стилю главке "В не по чину барственной шубе" из "Шума времени". Пожалуй, его специфичность заключается в использовании 'петербургского' кода для подачи темы литературы. Сам мотив 'скандала' с его генезисом у Достоевского возвращает читателя к петербургской теме (см. ниже о 'родословной' Парнока — "капитан Голядкин"). Здесь же упоминание об Ипполите и даче в Павловске и квартире на Разъезжей. Тема отрицательного, насмешливо-презрительного отношения к 'литературе' продолжается ("пропала крупиночка [...] в те отдаленные времена [...] — эта дробиночка именовалась честью", "однажды бородатые литераторы, в широких, как пневматические колокола, панталонах, поднялись на скворешню к фотографу и снялись на отличном дагерротипе. [...] Все лица передавали один тревожно-глубокомысленный вопрос: почем теперь фунт слоновьего мяса?"), причем, так же как во фрагменте о "перелете певицы итальянской школы" здесь подчеркивается связь русской 'интеллигентской' традиции в жизни и литературе со скукой, серостью, пошлостью. Мандельштам спорит и с восприятием Петербурга этой традицией: "Они не видели и не понимали прелестного города с его чистыми корабельными линиями".

Чем ближе к концу повести, тем теснее сплетаются вместе различные 'голоса' темы 'слова, писания'. Тем больше роль этой темы в общей структуре повести, тем больше места ей отводится в словесной ткани. Фабула все больше отходит на задний план, уступая место описанию точки зрения (ср. из шестой главы: "Дворцы стояли испуганно-белые, *как* шелковые куколи. Временами белизна их *напоминала* выстиранный с мылом и щелоком платок оренбургского пуха").

Автометаописание "Египетской марки" начинает обретать черты автоописания субъекта текста (от Парнока — к первому лицу), процесс творения текста сближается с описанием самоощущения его создателя, а это самоощущение, в свою очередь, подается как черта, внутренне присущая городу и истории. Шестая глава вся посвящена 'памяти' — воссозданию воспоминаний детства, связанных с Петербургом, ощущений, ассоциируемых со значением. В седьмой главе автор открыто провозглашает принцип своей прозы: осознание ассоциативной структуры 'точки зрения' рассказчика, который тут же показывает действие этого принципа: "В *моей восприятии* Мервиса просвечивают образы: греческого сатира, несчастного певца кифареда, временами маска еврипидовского актера, временами голая грудь и покрытое испариной тело растерзанного каторжанина, русского ночлежника или эпилептика".

Соположение разных исторических культурных пластов по принципу вневременной смысловой связи обнажается здесь таким образом, что древнее, античное, принадлежащее *культурной традиции* оказывается родственным самым 'низким' слоям *жизни*, лишенным, казалось бы, какой-либо связи с культурой.

Знаменательно, что этот отрывок непосредственно переходит в автоописание, причем смысловая связь устанавливается по напряженности эмоций, их накалу, трагизму:

"Я *спешу* сказать *настоящую правду. Я тороплюсь.* Слово, как порошок аспирина, оставляет привкус меди во рту.

Рыбий жир — смесь пожаров, желтых зимних утр и ворвани: вкус вырванных лопнувших глаз, вкус *отвращения, доведенного до восторга*".

Итак — основа творческого состояние — спешка, лихорадка — то-есть нечто близкое болезни. В дальнейшем именно код болезни будет суммировать все 'голоса' темы писания. С другой стороны, упоминание о творческой спешке, лихорадке приводит к убыстрению самого ритма мандельштамовской прозы и к появлению различных модификаций этого мотива в последующих частях повести. Вот отрывки из пассажа, непосредственно следующего за только что процитированным: "Книги тают, как ледяшки, принесенные в комнату. Все *уменьшается.* [...] Все *уменьшается.* Все *тает.* И Гете *тает. Небольшой* нам отпущен срок."

Здесь тема 'текста', 'книги' метафорически представлена в суб-коде мороза, льда. Сразу же вслед за этим наступает инверсия кода и сообщения и город зимой оказывается книгой, причем в контексте *уменьшения времени:*

"*Все трудней* перелистывать страницы мерзлой книги, переплетенной в топоры при свете газовых фонарей.

Все, дровяные склады — черные библиотеки города — мы *еще* почитаем, поглядим".

Далее метафорическая тема *города-книги* переходит в тему *книг, библиотек* (реальных) *в городе,* при этом тема творческой лихорадки, данная в автоописании, переходит в болезнь, болезнь реальную, а точнее — детскую:

"Некоторые страницы сквозили как луковичная шелуха.
В них жила корь, скарлатина и ветряная оспа".

Заканчивается седьмая глава псевдо-цитатой: рассказом о болезни и смерти Бозио в Петербурге.

Восьмая и последняя глава начинается с образа Петербурга — текста ("он получил обратно все улицы и площади Петербурга — в виде сырых корректурных правок, верстал проспекты, брошюровал сады"), сразу переходящего в Петербург-болезнь ("Он думал, что Петербург — его детская болезнь, и что стоит лишь очухаться, очнуться — и наваждение рассыплется: он выздоровеет, станет как все люди..."). Это — болезнь субъекта текста. Она прямо связана с темой русской литературной традиции ("Все эти люди, которых спускали с лестниц, шельмовали, оскорбляли в сороковых и пятидесятых годах..."), которую следует пережить и превзойти, снять:

"Надо лишь снять пленку с петербургского воздуха, и тогда об-нажится его подспудный пласт. Под лебяжьим, гагачьим, гага-ринским пухом — под тучковыми тучками, под французским буше умирающих набережных, под зеркальными зенками барско-холуй-ских квартир обнаружится нечто совсем неожиданное.
Но перо, снимающее эту пленку — как чайная ложечка доктора, зараженная дифтеритным налетом. Лучше к нему не прикасаться".

Весь конец "Египетской марки" посвящен теме 'писания', 'болезни', 'лихорадки', теме 'прозы', ее собственного метаописания и описания состояния автора. Приведем лишь некоторые самые показательные места: "Страшно подумать что наша жизнь — это повесть без фабулы и героя, сделанная из пустоты и стекла, из горячего бреда одних отступ-лений, из петербургского инфлуэнцного бреда".

Состояние пишущего подобно состоянию описываемых им вещей: "Знакомо ли вам это состояние? Когда у всех вещей словно жар; когда все они радостно возбуждены и больны. ... Тогда, признаться, я не выдерживаю карантина и смело шагаю, разбив термометры, по зараз-ному лабиринту...". В начале повести, как уже было сказано, шла речь о том, что "температура эпохи вскочила на тридцать семь и три".

Таким образом, оказывается, что на определенном уровне субъект, объект и история объединены в некотором смысловом субстрате, по-строенном по правилу соположения случайного и выявления внутренней семантической близости. Переход к прозаическому творчеству ("выход из карантина") явно связан и с личностной самореализацией автора. Это, в частности — преодоление в прозе определенных ограничений на тематику и средства выражения, свойственных стихотворному творчеству Мандельштама до периода 1930 года. Это и преодоление границ собственной личности во внетекстовом плане. Автометаописание текста оказывается парадигмой нового типа личностного поведения. Это справедливо как для прозы Мандельштама, так и для прозы Ахматовой, ср. из "Египетской марки":

> "Страх берет меня за руку и ведет. Белая нитяная перчатка. Митенка. Я люблю, я уважаю страх. Чуть было не сказал: "с ним мне не страшно!".

Принципы семантической связности и автометаописания текста, которые мы старались проиллюстрировать на примере "Египетской марки", находят отражение в других прозаических произведениях Мандельштама. В другом месте мы сравним семантическое строение "Египетской марки" с "Четвертой прозой" и некоторыми другими прозаическими вещами Мандельштама. Здесь же ограничимся указанием на некоторые особенности смысловой композиции "Египетской марки", важные как проявление действия поэтической семантики в прозе. Эти же особенности будут позднее характерны для "Четвертой прозы", "Разговора о Данте", "Путешествия по Армении". По мере движения текста от начала к концу можно констатировать следующее:

1) уменьшается роль 'фабулы' (либо внетекстовой событийной цепи — в очерке);

2) соответственно, возрастает асимметричность 'словесных' масс, усиливается 'разорванность' письма; абзац все более тяготеет к замкнутости; увеличивается композиционная нагрузка семантических скрепов;

3) увеличивается смысловая нагрузка на фонологический уровень;

4) увеличивается 'семантическая теснота' в композиционно-маркированных частях текста (границы абзацев, главок);

5) возрастает роль смыслового ритма;

6) на первый план выходят темы автометаописания текста и самосознания авторской личности;

7) увеличивается число 'степеней свободы' на нарративном уровне, текст развивается к концу 'конусообразно'.

Иными словами, мандельштамовская проза обнаруживает своеобразную динамику: степень овладения 'поэтической' семантикой в прозе становится по мере развития текста все большей, но одновременно текст становится более прозой в смысле Мандельштама (асимметричное движение словесных масс). Выдвижение на первый план субъекта (обнажение лирического начала) сопровождается тенденцией к обнажению и прозаизации авторской речи. Овладение материей авторского 'я' приводит к большей свободе от него и позволяет в далнейшем включить эту материю в стихи.

The Hebrew University

ПРИМЕЧАНИЯ

[1] Ср., например, "Опыт последних лет доказал, что единственная женщина, вступившая в круг поэзии на правах новой музы, это русская наука о поэзии, вызванная к жизни Потебной и Андреем Белым и окрепшая в формальной школе Эйхенбаума, Жирмунского и Шкловского" (из статьи "Литературная Москва 1").

[2] Б. М. Эйхенбаум, "Проблемы поэтики Пушкина", в сборнике Б. М. Эйхенбаум, *Сквозь литературу,* перепечатка в серии *Slavistic Printings and Reprintings,* XXVI ('s-Gravenhage, Mouton, 1962), стр. 167-68.

[3] Ср. "… в России ломают головы, как вывести на живую дорогу освобожденную от лирических пут независимую прозаическую речь" (из рецензии на *Записки чудака,* т. II, Андрея Белого).

[4] Ю. Тынянов, "Литературный факт", в сб. *Texte der russischen Formalisten,* B. I. (München, Fink Verlag, 1969), стр. 408.

[5] См. Ю. И. Левин, Д. М. Сегал, Р. Д. Тименчик, В. Н. Топоров, Т. В. Цивьян, "Русская семантическая поэтика как потенциальная культурная парадигма", *Russian Literature,* No. 7-8, pp. 47-83.

COMMENTS

(Winner) You brought up an important problem of the poetics of prose, especially of contemporary prose: the breaking up of the semantic space by the seemingly random distribution of semantic and formal elements: semantic units, images, epithets, etc., thereby creating new, and striking, equivalences. It is true, as Hrushovsky has just remarked, that this feature is also found in 19th-century prose — in Mandelštam it is actualized, as it is also in other modern prose writers, Joyce (as Hrushovsky has just mentioned), but also Robbe-Grillet and Ladislav Fuks. (I have written about this facet in the latter writer.) It would seem to me that this is closely connected with the poetics of modern painting, i.e., the breaking up of spaces in cubist painting and also in surrealist painting.

Additional discussion: Hrushovsky, de Mallac, Nilsson, Shapiro, van der Eng.

THE EVALUATIVE COMPONENT
IN A THEORY OF POETIC LANGUAGE

MICHAEL SHAPIRO

Theories of poetic language abound. Unfortunately, those which are explicitly structuralist in substance — for instance, Jakobsonian 'linguistic criticism' — have failed to make the quantum leap beyond articulating a kind of *catalogue raisonné*, beyond the mere parsing of grammatical elements and categories whose interplay constitutes the linguistic texture of poetry.

The chief impediment to the creation of a genuinely explanatory theory of poetic language has been the banishment of **value** from the purview of linguistic theorizing about verse structure.[1] This situation appears to have arisen as a consequence of an unfortunate dichotomy between what has been characterized (Stankiewicz, 11) as the external vs. internal properties of poetic texts. We can understand such a conjuncture if only from the realization that the very phrase 'value judgment' conjures up precisely the constellation of putatively extra-literary (hence 'external') criteria which make reference to a psycho-social adstructure rather than to the poetic structure sensu stricto. While accepting the caveat that poetics (like linguistics) should eschew heteronomous explanation whenever possible, we must at the same time reexamine the methodological legitimacy of excluding the axiological (value) component from a theory of poetic language.

There is a sense of the term 'value' which is appropriate to an inquiry into the linguistic structure of poetry and simultaneously pregnant with a fructiferous explanatory potential toward the solution of age-old problems of poetics. It is the "valeur linguistique" of Saussure's *Cours* (1960; Part Two, Chapter IV), better known and more extensively developed in the Praguean guise — that of **markedness**.[2] Saussure represented the sign or *signum* as consisting of two conjugate aspects, the perceptible *signans* and the translatable *signatum*.[3] What he apparently did not do, however, was colligate his notion of *valeur* with a bipartition of the linguistic sign. Saussure's fundamental explanatory insight — "la langue ne peut être qu'un système de valeurs pures" (1960:155) — remains inchoate as a direct result.

The signans/signatum structure of the sign is inherent in the **conceptualization** of reality evinced by all human semiotic systems, and this applies equally to external apperception as to introspection. Conceptualization, notably, cannot proceed without a simultaneous **evaluation**. In language, whose structure is defined by the network of relationships underlying its phonological and grammatical **oppositions** and the rules of their combination/concatenation, a sign cannot subsist in vacuo. It exists only in virtue of being paired with its opposite term. And it is this semiotic duple that necessarily encompasses the evaluative aspect — markedness. The latter, being a purely formal entity, can furthermore be defined as itself the signans of the meaningful relationship — termed **signification** — obtaining between the perceptible *signans* and the translatable *signatum*:

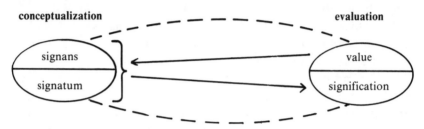

This is a rather complex set of relationships, whose comprehension may perhaps be facilitated by juxtaposing the above exposé with Charles Sanders Peirce's notion of **interpretant**. Peirce defines the latter variously as the "cognition produced in the mind" (1.372),[4] "the idea to which [the sign] gives rise" (1.339), and "that determination of which the immediate cause, or determinant, is the Sign" (6.347). He regards the interpretant as itself a sign (2.303). This scheme, then, corresponds exactly to the relationship between the conceptual unit — the sign — and the interpretive value — the markedness value — which, in turn, stands itself as signans to a complex signatum, the signification.

Every phonological and grammatical opposition — in short, all oppositions — in language have a semiotic superstructure composed on the two polar values (**marked** vs. **unmarked**) of the markedness relation that are inalienable attributes of a given opposition's terms. The markedness relation constituted by its polar values inheres in the form of language and not in its substance.[5] As the dominant axiological principle governing conceptualization in human semiotic systems, markedness must not be identified (*pace* Jakobson 1971a, 1971b:218) with quality, since the latter belongs to substance while markedness is a formal universal.

It is, in fact, an **asymmetric** relation.[6] Of the two terms that define it, the one labeled 'marked' represents a formally more complex or narrowly-defined value, whereas the other term, labeled 'unmarked', represents a formally less complex or less narrowly-defined value.

Reentering the domain of poetic language, we should continue by observing that any theory of its structure must, as a cardinal concern, attempt to explain whether — and if yes, then how — the patterning of sound and meaning is systematically manifested. Traditionally, investigations of the sound–meaning nexus in poetry have conceived their task to be a search for direct cohesions and congruences between the phonic texture of (chiefly lyric) verse and the generalized semantic purport.[7] This endeavor has been carried out in parallel to studies constituting a massive literature on sound symbolism,[8] which chronicle the repeated attempts of psychologists, linguists, ethnologists, and literary scholars to establish a language-specific as well as a universal basis which would explain the implementation of certain sounds with certain allegedly cooccurrent meanings. Ultimately, this kind of research has been directed toward verifying a hypothesis, viz. that sounds have inherently expressive values. This hypothesis is disconfirmed by comparative evidence[9] which leads to the conclusions that (1) "a phoneme (or phoneme sequence) can be invested with expressive value only with reference to a given phonological system"; and hence (2) "any phoneme (sequence) can be endowed with expressive value" (Andersen 1968:181). The consequences of these conclusions have yet to be fully appreciated by poeticists.[10]

Since, for the most part, the linguistic structure of verse utilizes the means already present in ordinary language, we must — in order to define the special role of poetic language and the pattern of organization which underlies this role — begin with a clear understanding of the structure of phonology and grammar. At this juncture we are better served by limiting our aperçu to phonology, as this sector is much more amenable to a rigorous exposition.

Despite decades of accumulated insight into the structure of sound patterns, it is only in the last few years that a coherent understanding of phonology as a **semiotic system** has begun to emerge.[11] The most important corollary of such an understanding is a view of the terms of phonological oppositions as signs, articulated by a palpable (perceptible, material) signans — the **distinctive feature specification** — and having a unique, purely diacritic, signatum 'otherness' (cf. Jakobson 1962:304).[12] Each phonological opposition is to be construed as a minimal (i.e. binary) **paradigm**, since the relation between the two terms of the opposition is such that the presence of one implies the absence of the other. The two signs constituting each such minimal paradigm are defined by the perceptual parameters of their sign vehicles (signantia). It is the condition of mutual exclusion obtaining between these two signs in the paradigm that defines them as distinct from each other and invests them with their meaning of phonemic otherness.

Terms of phonological oppositions cannot occur singly; they require a domain simultaneously comprised by other oppositions. These are the smallest simultaneous sign complexes of language, conventionally called phonemes. Actually, phonemes are **syntagms**, that is to say they are hierarchical structures organized in such a way that their immediate constituents are rank ordered. In this respect, phonemes share the chief principles of organization with their isomorphic counterparts in grammar. Unlike the latter, however, wherein hypotactic relations can subsist along with paratactic relations, phonological syntagms are purely hypotactic structures. Relations of subordination are determinative in assigning relative importance to any pair or set of features.

The signans/signatum relation (signification) in phonology while being unique in its purely diacritic function is nevertheless subject to the same evaluative interpretation as are all signs in human semiotic systems. Given an inventory of distinctive features and the ways in which they are combined into simultaneous syntagms (phonemes), we must further have recourse to the evaluative superstructure which endows the hierarchy of distinctive feature relations with their semiotic form, i.e. to markedness values. For it is the markedness value that gives definition to and determines the **form of the meaning**.

This brings us to the crux of the matter as regards the sound/meaning nexus in poetic language. Sounds — whether they be considered in a phonological or a purely phonetic perspective — have no inherent meaning. They are capable only of distinguishing meaning (the diacritic function). Repeated attempts to assign meaning to sounds via their cooccurrence with certain semantic purports have invariably been flawed by the high risk of subjectivity, impressionism, and downright capriciousness. For every textual fragment cited in support of a particular assignment of meaning to a particular sound,[13] it is not difficult to find counterexamples (cf. Šengeli, 262-3). The reason for the ultimate failure of the synaesthetic approach can be perceived in the logical mistake of juxtaposing, in an unmediated fashion, signs which have a purely diacritic function (sounds) and can be expressed only asynthetically, with signs (morphemes, grammatical categories) that can be expressed either synthetically (morphemes) or asynthetically (grammatical categories).

The evaluative component is just the medium by which purely asynthetic signs are conjoined or integrated with synthetic/asynthetic signs into a pattern exhibiting coherent principles of organization. Since each phonological opposition has, besides the plus/minus feature specification attaching to its two terms, the two concomitant and inherent markedness values marked/un-marked, it is these markedness values (and only these!) of sounds that can be juxtaposed to the markedness values of the morphological and lexical entities with which the sounds cooccur. Methodologically, the sound/meaning nexus becomes a patterned relationship just in case there are congruences between the markedness values of the sounds in a poetic text and the markedness values of all other (i.e. non-phonic) elements, viz. morphological, lexical, syntactic, and (even) metrical.[14]

It should be emphasized that congruences between phonic and non-phonic markedness values are particularly frequent in lyric and shorter folk poetry, largely absent from larger genres, and, in fact, need not be present at all, regardless of genre. At the same time, it should also be understood that mere repetition of certain sounds, without any discernible and semiotically patterned connection to the other linguistic levels of the text, betokens a relation between signans and signatum that can be called 'automorphic', or following Jakobson (1971b:704-5), **introversive semiosis**, wherein a message signifies itself and whereby poetry and music achieve their greatest tangency. This notion comports neatly with Jakobson's well-known definition (1960:356) of the poetic function as "focus on the message for its own sake". This kind of automorphic repetition in modern Russian poetry need not be accompanied by any ascertainable synaesthetic effects, as in the following excerpts:

у буржуа на полках книжных
стоит веленевый Верлен
(Евтушенко)

Сидишь, одергиваешь платьице,
И плачется тебе, и плачется ...
(Вознесенский)

Лебедь уплыл в полумглу
Вдаль, под луною белея.
Ластятся волны к веслу,
Ластится к влаге лилея.
(Бальмонт)

Милиция, улицы, лица
Мелькали в свету фонаря.
Покачивалась фельдшерица
Над склянкою нашатыря.
(Пастернак)

An admixture of onomatopoeia or kinaesthesia can render the automorphism less introversive, as in:

И ни души. Один лишь хрип,
Тоскливый лязг и стук ножовый,
И сталкивающихся глыб
Скрежещущие пережевы.
(Пастернак)

The poetic function can, of course, be fulfilled by paronomasia:

Из недр и на ветвь — ры́сями!
Из недр и на ветр — свистами!
(Цветаева)

The sound pattern can also implement the phonic structure of a so-called 'summative' (key) word (Hymes 1960:118). The most straightforward application of this device is illustrated by the anagrammatization of answers to Russian verse riddles in the riddles themselves[15]:

Бык — на дворе,
Рога — до берега.
(*Дорога* со двора)

Узелок, Кузьма,
Развязать нельзя;
Имечко хорошо:
Алексеем зовут.
(*Замок*)

На потолке,
В уголке,
Висит сито,
Не руками свито.
(*Паутина*)

In these examples the purely automorphic function has been attenuated or significantly subordinated to what can be called the **iconic function**, by which is meant specifically the diagrammatization of relations obtaining between and amongst units of the expression plane on the one hand; and between units on the content and the expression plane, on the other. The cohesiveness inherent in iconicity is illustrated in a most striking fashion by the humorous Russian proverb[16]:

Табак да баня,
Кабак да баба —
Одна забава.

There is an obvious parallelism; but this is merely a mask for the systematically much more cogent and pervasive **asymmetry** characteristic of poetic language as a whole (Shapiro 1976). But this thema of asymmetry informing the schema cannot be revealed, specifically as it concerns the phonic texture, except by recourse to the valorizations attaching to the phonemes which comprise the lexical entities. If we juxtapose, in order, the vertical and the horizontal duples in virtue of which the proverb is structured, we note that there is simultaneously a **similitude** and a **dissimilitude** of elements on the syntagmatic axis, elements which are thus in a relation of complementarity — i.e. in an asymmetric relation — to each other[17]:

1. *t*abak / ba*n*'a	/t/	= [U nas] [U cmp]	/n'/	= [M nas] [U cmp]
2. *t*abak / *k*abak	/t/	= [U cmp] [U str]	/k/	= [M cmp] [U str]
3. *k*abak / *b*aba	/k/	= [M cmp] [U str]	/b/	= [U cmp] [U str]
4. ba*n*'a / *b*aba	/n'/	= [M nas] [U cmp]	/b/	= [U nas] [U cmp]
5. *b*aba / zaba*v*a	/b/	= [U nas] [U cmp]	/v/	= [M nas] [U cmp]
6. o*d*na / za*z*ava	/d/	= [U cmp] [U str]	/z/	= [U cmp] [M str]
7. od*n*a / za*b*ava	/n/	= [M nas] [U cmp]	/b/	= [U nas] [U cmp]

The complementarity displayed by the markedness values of the sounds is mirrored by a consistent series of complementarities in the non-phonic aspects of this proverb. As correctly perceived by Jakobson (1970:306), the substantives are clearly metonymies. *Tabak* is an instrument; *kabak* a location. Both words are substituted for materials taken into the human body orally. This common channel — the mouth — facilitating a resultant pleasure stands itself in a synechdochic (hence metonymic) relation to the rest of the body. Similarly, *banja* is a locational metonymy, and *baba* an instrumental one. In this latter case, the order of metonymies is reversed in comparison to the first pair: location precedes instrument. And this reversal instantiates yet again the theme of complementarity informing the structure of the proverb. Finally, there is an alternation of the grammatical markedness values with respect to the categories of gender and animacy in the several substantives. *Tabak* and *kabak*, being masculines, are unmarked for the feature of gender, whereas *banja, baba* and *zabava*, being feminine, are marked for gender. At the same time, *baba*, being (the sole) animate, is marked for the feature of animacy, while all other substantives in the proverb are inanimate, hence unmarked for animacy. It is to be noted that the rhyme of the punch line, *baba / zabava*, places *baba* at the semantic pivot of the entire proverb, and this focal function is mirrored by the fact that the double sequence /ba/ is the sole common denominator binding all five substantives. The culminative, equational function of *baba* thus leaves no room for any interpretation other than that *odna zabava* means 'the same fun' (*contra* Jakobson 1970:305).

What transpires from an analysis such as the above is the ultimate interpretation of poetic structure that is quite at odds with a canonic Jakobsonian approach. The pervasive parallelism comes to be understood as a decidedly subsidiary phenomenon, necessarily present only as a frame whereby the oppositive units and their values are juxtaposed. The primary structural pattern is constituted by dissimilitude, which does not exclude similitude but nonetheless dominates it hierarchically. This asymmetry is implemented in the workings of the evaluative component: the complementarities manifested by the phonic texture are diagrammatically mirrored (in the Peircean sense) by those of the non-phonic texture.

The transparency of formal structure characteristic of folk genres such as the proverb should not cause us to assume that the kinds of cohesions of markedness values at the several levels cannot be found in imaginative lyric verse. Since a lyric is almost never as condensed as a proverb or riddle, when we speak of patterned relations between form and meaning we must limit our scope to particular verses or strophes whose position in the poem is functionally and compositionally significant. Thus, typically, the initial, penultimate, and final strophes are marked units in lyrics with several strophes (as will be illustrated below); the same applies to lines within short(er) non-strophic poems. This does not, of course, exclude the possibility of odd strophes or lines occurring with a perspicuous cohesion of phonic and non-phonic values, but this would then be well-motivated functionally in terms of the overall progression or dynamic design of poetic form and meaning.

Methodologically, investigations of the phonic texture ('orchestration') of Russian verse have been characterized by an openly atomistic approach which focuses either on the patterning of (chiefly stressed) vowels or on that of consonants. I know of no study (including those, e.g. Taranovsky and Jones, which utilize distinctive features) that even attempts systematically to integrate the organization of both vocalic *and* consonantal patterns into a unitary framework. To be sure, when the focus is on one of these two major classes of sound, supporting evidence from the organization of the other major class is adduced whenever possible (Taranovsky 1965:118). But the procedure is quite ad hoc and adventitious.

Furthermore, there is a tacit assumption that the phonological system of Moscow Russian as we know it today is identical with that of Pushkin's day. That there is no warrant for such an assumption as regards vowels I have attempted to demonstrate in two recent studies (Shapiro 1974a, b).[18] The relevance of these findings, if correct, cannot be underestimated in the study of poetic language, since the markedness values, given the same inventory of vowel phonemes, are different in Old Muscovite (OM) from those of contemporary standard Russian (CSR).[19]

TABLE 1

OM VOWEL SYSTEM

	DIFFUSE	COMPACT	FLAT
/a/	U	M	U
/i/	M	U	M
/u/	M	U	U
/e/	U	U	M
/o/	U	U	U

CSR VOWEL SYSTEM

	DIFFUSE	COMPACT	FLAT
/a/	M	U	U
/i/	U	M	M
/u/	U	M	U
/e/	M	M	M
/o/	M	M	U

In the light of this systematic difference, one must at the very least urge caution in accepting analyses of poems which assume the language of Russian poetry to be essentially an undifferentiated continuum from the 1730's to the present day. One cannot simply put Pushkin and Blok under the same microscope and expect to arrive at a valid perception of the structure of their poetry. The principles of organization informing the work of both poets are *sensu lato* the same; but the spectroscopic apparatus must be calibrated differentially.

It is, naturally, the preponderant occurrence of one particular sound or class of sounds that gives rise to atomistic analyses. To take a well known lyric from Pushkin,[20] the ubiquitousness of /u/ in the initial strophe invites some sort of synaesthetic interpretation:

> Брожу ли я вдоль улиц шумных,
> Вхожу ль во многолюдный храм,
> Сижу ль меж юношей безумных,
> Я предаюсь моим мечтам.

The stressed vowel pattern numbers 9 /u/'s out of a total of 12:

u	u	u
u	u	a
u	u	u
u	(i)	a

If we were to adopt the criteria enunciated by Taranovsky (1965:118-9), we should expect the preponderance of /u/ to instantiate the emotion summarized by the term 'instability'. But one would have to do a lot of semantic stretching in attempting to incorporate the purport of the Pushkin strophe under analysis into a synaesthetic scheme; and what is worse, the attempt would fail.

The theory of poetic language I am advancing herein asserts that whatever congruences there are — of any kind, not merely phonological — manifest themselves as cohesions of markedness values. Leaving aside the vowels for the time being, an examination of the consonants reveals a consistent relationship between feature values. Among obstruents, fricatives and affricates are invariably marked for either or both of the (syncategorematic) features abrupt/nonabrupt and strident/mellow, whereas stops are invariably unmarked for both of these features:

FRICATIVES [16]
š/ž [M str]   x [M abr]
s/z [M abr]   f [M str]

AFFRICATES [2]
c   [M str]   č [M str, M abr]

STOPS [2]
p/b   [U str, U abr]
t/d   [U abr, U str]
k/g   [U str, U abr]

Now, to get to the sonorants, of which there are thirty in this strophe (13 nasals, 9 liquids, 8 glides), it should be noted at the outset that glides appear to play no role whatever (other than a possible automorphic one), and this is due to the systematic fact of their not being distinguished by either of the features of stridency or abruptness (/j/ is [+ acu], hence [M acu]; /v/ and /v́/ are [− acu], hence [U acu]). In the case of all other sonorants (for that matter — all other consonants!), stridency and/or abruptness are distinctive: the nasals are [− str], hence [M str]; /r ŕ/ and /l ĺ/ are, respectively, [+ abr] and [− abr], hence [M abr] and [U abr]. The numerical distribution of consonants in the first strophe is charted in the following table:

TABLE 2

Line	p/t/k	l	r	m/n	v/j	š/ž	s/z/f	c/č	x
1	2	3	1	2	1	2	1	1	1
2	2	2	1	4	2	1	1	0	2
3	1	1	0	4	2	3	2	0	1
4	3	0	0	3	4	0	2	1	0
Totals	8	6	2	13	9	6	6	2	4

[NB: p/t/k includes b/d/g]

Taking the liquids into account (but not the glides), we get a ration of 33:14, (70%) marked consonants to unmarked; without them, the ratio increases to 31:8 (80%). The consonantal patterning is thus rendered abundantly clear.

In order to escape the atomistic approach it is precisely at this juncture in the analysis that the consonant pattern must be understood as being in a coherent relationship with the vowel pattern. Given the phonological relations which I assume to have prevailed in Muscovite speech around Pushkin's time (v. Table 1 above), the predominant vowel /u/ was evaluated as [M dif], as was /i/. These two sounds differed from each other with respect to their values for the flatness feature: /u/ was (and remained) [U fla], while /i/ was (and remained) [M fla].

Methodologically, what is important here is the status of the **absent** sound /i/ as well as the present sound /u/. Based on a fairly extensive analysis sample which cannot be presented in its entirety here, it can be (at least provisionally) asserted that absent sounds play no role, even indirectly, in determining the linguistic structure of verse. Thus, in the Pushkin example, we need not take into account the fact that /i/ is also [+ dif], hence [M dif], i.e. identical in value to the predominant /u/. We need only concentrate on the relations contracted by /u/ vis-à-vis the remainder of the actually occurring sounds.

With this qualification in mind we can proceed to consider the [M dif] of /u/ as paramount vocalically and to see how the recurrence of this value coheres with other values within the framework of the entire strophe. Specifically, the cohesion is expressed by the fact that an overwhelming number of consonants (80%) are marked for abruptness or stridency, while the predominant vowel is also marked. This kind of congruence between the two major classes of sound in a poetic text should be distinguished **in principle** from the mere repetition of one or another sound (automorphic function). The latter device can occur at random, but the sort of tight cohesion illustrated by the Pushkin strophe will tend to occur in functionally prominent positions. This is most emphatically NOT to say that it will always occur in these positions; but its occurrence is limited to them. Thus, in the remainder of the poem, no such congruences are to be found again, not excepting the functionally prominent last strophe:

> И пусть у гробового входа
> Младая будет жизнь играть,
> И равнодушная природа
> Красою вечною сиять.

TABLE 3

Lines	p/t/k	l	r	m/n	v/j	š/ž	s/z/f	c/č	x
1	5	0	1	0	2	0	1	0	1
2	6	1	1	2	1	1	1	0	0
3	3	0	3	2	2	1	0	0	0
4	2	0	1	1	4	0	2	1	0
Totals	16	1	6	5	9	2	4	1	1

It is interesting and significant to discover (Blagoj 1973:124-6) that Pushkin's "Станцы", as this poem was called when first published (in "Литературная газета", 6.1.1830), went through a series of revisions and alterations before assuming its final form. Pushkin began with an incomplete first strophe which, however, already adumbrated the contrastive, contrapuntal nature of what was to evolve:

> Куда б меня мой < > мятежный
> Не мчал по < > земной —
> Но мысль о смерти неизбежной
> Везде б < > всегда со мной

This fragment then takes on a much less amorphous shape:

> Кружусь ли я с толпой мятежной,
> Вкушаю ль сладостный покой —
> Но мысль о смерти неизбежной
> Везде б <лизка>, всегда со мной.

Thus it stands through numerous revisions of the remainder of the poem, which in its final pre-publication form is dated by the author as having been completed on December 26, 1829. But Pushkin sensed an inappropriateness about the first strophe which he remedied by striking it out in toto and composing two entirely new strophes in its stead, in which form the poem is known.

It does not take a detailed analysis of the rejected first strophe to perceive its lack of phonic structure. This perception is strengthened, of course, by a comparison of the rejected and the ultimate versions of the first strophe. Conversely, too, the tight structure of the final version becomes even more palpable thereby.

The methodological validity of the analysis presented above can be tested in a number of ways. Consider Lermontov's well known lyric "Молитва":

[I]   В минуту жизни трудную
      Теснится ль в сердце грусть:
      Одну молитву чудную
      Твержу я наизусть.
[II] Есть сила благодатная
      В созвучье слов живых,
      И дышит непонятная,
      Святая прелесть в них.
[III] С души как бремя скатится,
      Сомненье далеко —
      И верится, и плачется,
      И так легко, легко ...

The functionally prominent strophes are the first and the third, the second playing a patently transitional role. The initial strophe has the following inventory of consonants:

TABLE 4

Line	p/t/k	l	r	m/n	v/j	š/ž	s/z/f	c/č	x
1	2	0	1	4	2	1	1	0	0
2	3	1	2	1	0	0	3	0	0
3	3	1	0	3	2	0	0	1	0
4	2	0	1	1	2	1	2	0	0
Totals	10	2	4	9	6	2	6	1	0

The consonantal pattern of the final strophe, on the other hand, is:

TABLE 5

Line	p/t/k	l	r⁻	m/n	v/j	š/ž	s/z/f	c/č	x
1	6	0	1	1	0	1	2	2	0
2	2	1	0	3	1	0	1	0	0
3	1	1	1	0	1	0	0	5	0
4	4	2	0	0	0	0	0	0	2
Totals	13	4	2	4	2	1	3	7	2

The patterns of stressed vowels, when juxtaposed, are:

[I]	u	i	u	[III]	i	e	a
	i	e	u		e	–	o
	u	i	u		e	–	a
	u	(a)	u		a	o	o

Note that [I] has, with the exception of a functionally irrelevant /a/ in the final line, a consistently [+ dif] character, that is to say it is summatively characterized with respect to vowels as [M dif]. Strophe [III], on the other hand, with the exception of the initial vowel of the first line /i/, is characterized by the feature term [– dif], hence the value [U dif]. At the same time, note that the consonantal pattern of [I] evinces almost double the number of [M abr] / [M str] phonemes (22:12). The congruence between consonants and vowels is thus indubitable. In [III] the number of consonants marked or unmarked for abruptness/stridency is exactly equal (17:17) if we count liquids and just about equal if we do not (15:13). This means that while the consonantal patterning is neutralized, the vocalic remains clear when juxtaposed to that of [I]. Specifically, the two patterns are opposed to each other as [M dif] : [U dif]. This opposition, it is obvious, is coherent with the strongly oppositive cognitive and affective content of the two (initial and final) strophes in question.

Exigencies of space and time constrain me from adducing further examples.[21] I have concentrated, in the main, on attempting to demonstrate the methodological inexcludability of 'value' from a theory of poetic language. In the process, certain cohesions in the phonic structure of poetic texts have been exploited as evidence of immanent principles of linguistic organization informing poetry. A fuller explication of these principles would have to muster a more extensive array of systematic cohesions between the phonic structure and the grammatical categories actually occurring in given pieces of poetry. Syntactic, lexical, and intonational phenomena would then be investigated with an eye towards ascertaining whether the system of congruences embraces all relevant structural components seriatim. By 'structural components' I mean to include those which articulate the purely conventional (rhyme, meter, etc.) as well as the purely linguistic, cognitive, and affective facets of poetic structure.

The chief claim of the theory of poetic language advanced hereinabove is that the sole explanatory medium through which the conventional and linguistic structures (and their interconnection) can be educed is the evaluative component of language — markedness. A richer elaboration of both the theory and the claim underlying it defines, in my opinion, a fruitful research program for poetics in the immediate future.

University of California, Los Angeles (written in 1974)

NOTES

[1] Cf. Stankiewicz 1961:11: "The study of poetic language must, then, also be detached from the concept of values, which depends ultimately on extra-literary considerations."
[2] I am, of course, making a possibly gratuitous attribution. But cf. Burger 1962:67.

[3] The adjectives modifying the two components of the sign are borrowed from Jakobson 1971b:274.

[4] In citing from Peirce 1965-66, the accepted practice is to refer to volume and paragraph number. For an analysis of Peirce's semiotic, see Fitzgerald 1966 and now Greenlee 1973.

[5] Cf. Andersen 1974:893: "It should be noted that markedness relations pertain to the form of language. They should be consistently distinguished from such notions as relative articulatory complexity, relative optimalness, or relative text frequency, which are facts about the substance of language. For even though it is often the case that, for instance, the unmarked term of an opposition involves less articulatory complexity and occurs more frequently than the corresponding marked term, this is not necessarily so. Markedness is a matter of conceptual complexity and as such is to a significant extent independent of the substance of language."

[6] This is the asymmetry characteristic of polarity in human semiotic systems and not the one associated with the mathematical or physical notion of polar opposites. Cf. Shapiro 1976.

[7] Studies utilizing the more modern notion of distinctive features, e.g. Jones 1965, Taranovsky 1965 and 1970, have also proceeded on the assumption of an unmediated referability of sound and meaning.

[8] The major works in the field are Delbouille 1961 and Fónagy 1963. For extensive bibliographical information, see Dombi 1974 and Žuravlev and Orlov 1971; cf. Hymes 1960, Ivanova-Lukjanova 1966, Orlova 1966, Panov 1966, and Crockett 1970. A handy typology of 'sound effects' in poetry is given by Šengeli 1960:262-9.

[9] Andersen 1968:181 cites "initial z in English or French, z before vowel or sonorant in Lithuanian, or after short vowel in North German; č before front vowel in Lithuanian, ʒ and g in Ukrainian, back vowels after palatal consonants in Czech, initial ñ in French or Italian, geminates at various stages of the development of Germanic languages, etc., etc."

[10] Or by linguists; cf. Jakobson 1969:372-3.

[11] See Andersen 1974; cf. Shapiro 1974d and the references therein.

[12] For a fuller exposition, see Andersen 1975.

[13] I have in mind particularly the seeming arbitrariness of Taranovsky 1965.

[14] This thesis is developed in my book *Asymmetry: An Inquiry into the Linguistic Structure of Poetry*.

[15] The examples are drawn from Gerbstman 1968; cf. Jakobson 1970.

[16] Cf. Jakobson's analysis (1960:305-6).

[17] The markedness assignments are made on the basis of certain formal universals, as delineated in Shapiro 1972.

[18] The consonantal subsystem remains the same as between OM and CSR. I have utilized the markedness values established in Shapiro 1974a for both vowel systems.

[19] Implicit in my analysis is the premise that Pushkin, while adhering to many 18th century poetic conventions, implemented in speech and poetry the phonological system of his own time and locus, viz. the innovating Moscow dialect which took the shape we know it in by the 1830's.

[20] Cf. the analysis of Blagoj 1973:124-29.

[21] These (including non-Russian ones) are to be found in my *Asymmetry*.

REFERENCES

Andersen, Henning
    1968   "IE *s after *i, u, r, k* in Baltic and Slavic", *Acta Linguistica Hafniensia*, 11:171-90.
    1975   "Markedness in Vowel Systems", *Proceedings of the Eleventh International Congress of Linguists* (Bologna, 1972), edited by Luigi Heilmann. Bologna: Il Mulino.
Blagoj, D. D.
    1973   "Mysl' i zvuk v poèzii", *Slavjanskie literatury (VII Meždunarodnyj s'ezd slavistov, doklady sovetskoj delegacii)*, 99-130. Moscow: Nauka.

Burger, A.
1962   "Essai d'analyse d'un système de valeur", *Cahiers Ferdinand de Saussure*, 19:67-76.
Crockett, Dina B.
1970   "Secondary Onomatopoeia in Russian", *Word*, 26:107-13.
Delbouille, Pierre
1966   *Poésie et sonorités: La critique contemporaine devant la pouvoir suggestif des sons*. Paris: Société d'Édition "Les Belles Lettres".
Dombi, Erzsébet P.
1974   "Synaesthetia and Poetry", *Poetics*, 11:23-44.
Fitzgerald, John J.
1966   *Peirce's Theory of Signs as Foundation for Pragmatism*. The Hague: Mouton.
Fónagy, Ivan
1963   *Die Metaphern in der Phonetik*. The Hague: Mouton.
Gerbstman, A. I.
1968   "O zvukovom stroenii narodnoj zagadki", *Russkij fol'klor*, 11:185-97.
Greenlee, Douglas
1973   *Peirce's Concept of Sign*. The Hague: Mouton.
Hymes, Dell
1960   "Phonological Aspects of Style: Some English Sonnets", in Sebeok, 109-31.
Ivanova-Lukjanova, G. N.
1966   "O vosprijatii zvukov", in Vysotskij, 136-43.
Jakobson, Roman
1960   "Closing Statement: Linguistics and Poetics", in Sebeok, 350-77.
1962   *Selected Writings, I: Phonological Studies*. The Hague: Mouton.
1970   "Subliminal Verbal Patterning in Poetry", *Studies in General and Oriental Linguistics*, edited by R. Jakobson and S. Kawamoto, 302-8. Tokyo:TEC.
1971a   "Krugovorot lingvističeskix terminov", *Fonetika Fonologija Grammatika*, 384-7. Moscow: Nauka.
1971b   *Selected Writings, II: Word and Language*. The Hague: Mouton.
Jones, Lawrence G.
1965   "Tonality Structure in Russian Verse", *IJSLP*, 9:125-51.
Orlova, E. V.
1966   "O vosprijatii zvukov", in Vysotskij, 144-54.
Panov, M. V.
1966   "O vosprijatii zvukov", in Vysotskij, 155-62.
Peirce, Charles Sanders
1965-66   *Collected Papers*, 8 vols. in 4, edited by C. Hartshorne et al. Cambridge, Mass.: Harvard University Press.
Saussure, Ferdinand de
1960   *Cours de linguistique générale*, 5th ed. Paris: Payot.
Sebeok, Thomas A. (ed.)
1960   *Style in Language*. Cambridge, Mass.: MIT Press.
Shapiro, Michael
1972   "Explorations into Markedness", *Language*, 48:343-64.
1974a   "Alternative Feature Ranking as a Source of Phonological Change", *Scando-Slavica*, 20:117-28.
1974b   "O nekotoryx fonologičeskix opredeliteljax èvoljucii russkoj rifmy", *Russian Linguistics*, 1:151-62.
1974c   "Sémiotique de la rime", *Poétique*, 20:501-19.
1974d   "Tenues and Mediae in Japanese: A Reinterpretation", *Lingua*, 33:101-14.
1976   "Deux paralogismes de la poétique", *Poétique*, 28:423-39.

Stankiewicz, Edward
    1961   "Poetic and Non-Poetic Language in their Interrelation", *Poetics Poetyka Poètika,*
           11-24. Warsaw: Państwowe Wydawnictwo Naukowe.
Šengeli, G. A.
    1960   *Texnika stixa.* Moscow: GIXL.
Taranovsky, Kiril
    1965   "The Sound Texture of Russian Verse in the Light of Phonemic Distinctive Features",
           IJSLP, 9:114-24.
    1970   "Zvukovaja struktura stixa i ee vosprijatie", *Proceedings of the Sixth International
           Congress of Phonetic Sciences* (Prague 1967), edited by B. Hála et al., 883-5. Prague:
           Academia.
Vysotskij, S. S. (ed.)
    1966   *Razvitie fonetiki sovremennogo russkogo jazyka.* Moscow: Nauka.
Žuravlev, A. P., and Ju. M. Orlov
    1971   "Priznakovoe semantičeskoe prostranstvo russkix glasnyx", *Razvitie fonetiki sovremen-
           nogo russkogo jazyka: Fonologičeskie podsistemy,* edited by S. S. Vysotskij et al.,
           209-228. Moscow: Nauka.

COMMENTS

(Bailey) You are quite right in emphasizing the role of the dissimilar in poetic structure, but I wonder if, in reacting to Jakobson's concept of 'pervasive parallelism', you have not gone to another extreme. For one thing, how can something be perceived as being dissimilar if there is not an already existing background of similarity? At any rate, I do not at all agree with your statement that "the primary structural pattern is constituted by dissimilitude". In the Russian proverb you cite, "Tabák da bánja, Kabák da bába — odná zabáva", there is a great deal of parallelism in addition to the asymmetry you point out. The lines each consist of a parallel phrase, each has five syllables, each has stresses on the second and fourth syllables (xx́xxx́–iambic dimeter), the lines all exhibit the same vowel harmony (all lines have stressed *á*), and the lines, at least from a twentieth-century standpoint, rhyme, a feature typical of folk *skazovyj stix.* All of these symmetrical parallel features impose a definite restriction on the selection of vocabulary in the proverb. One could rewrite this miniature piece of folk poetry by utilizing other words which would maintain the semantic axis, but which would disrupt the orientation toward the poetic function: "Maxórka da vinó, Kafé da bába — odnó utešénie." If a poet decides to use a meter in a poem, he at the same time accepts the givens or limitations that meter places on his selection of vocabulary; furthermore, he largely must place his words in such a way that their stresses correspond to the ictic positions which emerge through the pervasive parallelism of lines throughout the poem. As Tomaševskij long ago demonstrated in his article on Puškin's iambic verse, every meter and every ictus in each meter imposes a

selection of vocabulary. Only words of a certain rhythmical shape, that is, number of syllables and place of stress, may be used; all others are automatically excluded. Let us take, for example, the word *blagoslovénie* which consists of six syllables and has a stress on the fourth (xxxx́xx). Taking into account that the last ictus in Russian meter is a constant or is always stressed, this word may not be used in the iambic trimeter (xxxxx́x); it is also excluded from the iambic pentameter with caesura (xx́xx́ / xx́xxx́); it may be employed in the iambic pentameter without caesura only when its stress corresponds either to the second or third ictuses (xx́xxx́xx́xx́); and in the iambic hexameter with caesura it can be selected only when its stress coincides with the first ictus (xx́xxx́ / xx́xxx́). The point of all this is that it is precisely the pervasive parallelism of the meter which imposes a **prior** selection of verbal material. If a poet also chooses to use rhyme and a stanzaic form, he even further accepts a restriction on vocabulary.

(Birnbaum) I would tend to agree with the speaker's suspicion regarding 'linguistic overkill' when it comes to some aspects of analysis and interpretation in poetics. Still, like Shapiro, I feel that the introduction and application of **some** linguistic terminology and underlying notions in the field of poetics, whose object after all is a particular — viz., 'poetic', i.e., aesthetically motivated — usage of **language** can be most fruitful indeed. One such powerful notion is precisely that of markedness values (Russian *značimost'*). You will agree, I think, that markedness values, as you conceive of them, are not absolute (i.e., language-universal — only the features that in a given system can be marked or unmarked are presumably invariants), but always **relative** (i.e., language-specific), namely, relative to the whole linguistic system or, in our case, the poetic-linguistic subsystem (subcode) within which these values operate. Cf. in this connection the emphasis on **relationships** (rather than on material or substance invariance) not only by Saussure, referred to in the paper, but even more so by Saussure's most consistent follower and heir, Louis Hjelmslev. By way of example, see his claim concerning the 'translatability', as it were, of any language (say, Danish) into some other semiotic system (including non-linguistic sign-systems) with preservation of the pertinent relationships (on a one-to-one basis) — but not of the substance — leaving the fundamental structure ('form') of the particular language intact.

One footnote: Granted the novelty of asserting the parallelism between the paradigmatic unit of the phoneme ('bundle' of coexistent distinctive features) and the axiomatically syntagmatic syntagm ('phrase') as concerns their respective structural hierarchies, are you familiar with some fairly similar ideas advanced by Kuryłowicz in his 1949 paper "La notion de l'isomorphisme" (reprinted in his volume *Esquisses linguistiques*)? There Kuryłowicz not only compares (and largely equalizes) the hierarchical structure of such units of the expression and content planes as, on the one hand, the syllable and, on the other, the syntagm (including, in his as well as others' opinion, also the sentence or clause, i.e., the predicative syntagm *par préférence*) but, moreover, he also conceives of a parallelism obtaining between the hierarchical structure of syntagms and the relative place (what in German would be called *Stellenwert*) of individual phonemes within the hierarchically defined correlations by which these phonemes form classes and subclasses of phonemes.

(Kjetsaa) I agree with Professor Shapiro that sounds have no inherent meaning, but this does not mean that they do not have certain expressive values. Thus it has clearly been shown by psycholinguistic experiments that certain sounds are often associated with certain categories, e.g., *a* with 'greatness', *i* with 'smallness', *l* with 'tenderness', and *r* with 'aggressiveness'. For further information, see Iván Fónagy, "Communication in Poetry", *Word* 17 (1961), and my paper "Lomonosov's Sound Characteristics", *Scando-Slavica* XX (1974).

(Nilsson) Your model seems to work with examples from Romantic poetry. But it should also, I think, be tested with Symbolist and Post-symbolist poetry. Pasternak especially should be a case in point. Have you tried to apply your model to him?

Additional discussion: Abernathy, Broyde, Segal, Stankiewicz

AUTHOR'S REPLY

(to Birnbaum) Yes, indeed, the importance of Hjelmslev's thought cannot be overestimated. Having recently reread his *Prolegomena*, I find his distinction between content-form and expression-form to be particularly fruitful. It seems to me that the neo-structuralist notion of markedness is tangent with if not identical to Hjelmslev's content-form.

As regards phonological syntagms and the provenance of the concept, I am familiar with Kuryłowicz's work but do not believe that his 1949 paper even adumbrates the concept. My understanding of the phoneme as a hierarchically arranged syntagm of distinctive features derives from Henning Andersen. It should be noted, incidentally, that Andersen rightly calls attention to the necessarily hypotactic structure of the phoneme, a structure obscured by Jakobson's term 'bundle' (of distinctive features).

(to Kjetsaa) I am grateful to Professor Kjetsaa for the references but remain unconvinced, even if one substitues 'expressive values' for 'inherent meaning'. Psycholinguistic experiments are notoriously factitious, and my review of the available literature inclined me to take the data and the conclusions with a barrel of salt (not excluding Fónagy's numerous pieces).

The problem of sound symbolism may perhaps be thought of in a broader context, namely that of the 'meaning of music'. From time immemorial, it has been common to ascribe some sort of meaning to music, whereas I think it is now clear that music in and of itself has no meaning. To be sure, no one would deny that music evokes a whole range of emotions in listeners. Precisely to what extent that emotive reaction is systematic is in dispute.

(to Nilsson) I have indeed applied my model to Pasternak. My tentative conclusion is that he, like many other twentieth-century Russian poets, utilizes sounds in their purely 'automorphic' function. Perhaps the Acmeists would be more likely to have produced poetry in which the sound structure is integrated with the grammatical structure in the way I have indicated for Pushkin in my paper (also Fet; see my *Asymmetry: An Inquiry into the Linguistic Structure of Poetry*, in the North-Holland Linguistic Series). I think the program of research and the methodology outlined in my paper would be particularly appropriate and timely for Mandel'štam scholarship.

THE VERSIFICATION
OF V. F. XODASEVIČ 1915-39

G. S. SMITH

> ... исследование творчества немыслимо вне
> исследования формы. С анализа формы
> должно бы начинаться всякое суждение об
> авторе, всякий рассказ о нем.
>
> В. Ф. Ходасевич, *О Сирине* (1937)

1. INTRODUCTION

This paper will not attempt an exhaustive study of Xodasevič's versification; it is based exclusively on an analysis of the most substantial—but by no means complete—collection of the poet's work,[1] and omits certain levels of metrical analysis. In his preface to the 1927 collection of his verse, Xodasevič rejects his first two volumes[2] as 'juvenile' and clearly implies that his poetic maturity should be dated from 1915. The versification of the two early collections, of the poems omitted from the 1961 volume,[3] and of Xodasevič's numerous translations[4] will form essential components in a complete discussion of the characteristics and evolution of this poet's metrical style; in the present study, attention will be concentrated on the mature period, and contrastive material will be drawn from the work of other contemporary poets rather than from the earlier works of Xodasevič himself.

For the purposes of this study Xodasevič's verse of 1915-39 has been divided into four groups on a chronological basis; this grouping corresponds largely, but not exactly, to the internal divisions of *SS,* three of which bear the titles of books first published as separate collections.[5] The four groups are:

1. December 1915-June 1920 ("Putem zerna"); the last period of the poet's life in his native Moscow. The upper limit of this period is defined by the onset of illness, which prevented Xodasevič writing any verse between July 1920 and January 1921.

2. January 1921-June 1922 ("Tjaželaja lira"). During this time the poet lived in Petrograd.

3. July 1922-spring 1926 ("Evropejskaja noč'"); Xodasevič emigrated in June 1922 and lived in Berlin, Prague, and Italy before settling in Paris in 1927.

The poetry of this period was first collected in the 1927 edition.
4. Summer 1926-1939. The publication of the 1927 edition marked
Xodasevič's swansong as a poet; after this date he was to work almost entirely
as a critic. The verse of this period was first collected in *SS*.
The method of analysis used below is based most directly on the work of K.
F. Taranovsky[6] and James Bailey,[7] and concentrates on metrical and rhythmical analysis at the level of the verse line; for reasons of economy of space,
levels below the line, and of rhyme and stanza form, will not be discussed.[8]

2. METRICAL AND RHYTHMICAL TYPOLOGY

2.1 *General Metrical Groups*

An analysis of the 136 poems in *SS* according to metrical groups yields the
following results (percentages are of the total number of 136 poems):

Metrical Group	Iambic	Trochaic	Ternary	Others
	76.5	11.0	5.1	7.4

A distribution of this kind is idiosyncratic in the extreme in the context of
Russian verse of Xodasevič's time. M. L. Gasparov's general metrical typology[9] provides the following comparative data (percentages are of the total
number of poems studied):[10]

	Iambic	Trochaic	Ternary	Others
Russian verse 1890-1924	49.5	19.5	14.5	16.4
Russian verse 1925-1935	34.0	25.0	15.0	26.0

Compared with the average for 1890-1924, Xodasevič has about 27% more
iambic poems, 8.5% less trochaic poems, 9.4% less in ternary metres, and 9%
less in the non-classical metres. In his concentration on binary metres and his
exclusion of the *dol'nik* and accentual verse, Xodasevič has in effect rejected
the metrical innovations characteristic of Russian poetry from 1890 to 1925;
his additional neglect of the ternary metres means that he has gone back to a
metrical repertoire reminiscent of Russian poetry in the third decade of the
nineteenth century. In fact, Xodasevič's typology exhibits a striking similarity
to those produced by Gasparov for the two decades 1811-1830 (percentages
are again of the total number of poems studied):[11]

	Iambic	Trochaic	Ternary	Others
Russian verse 1811-1820	79.5	10.5	6.0	4.5
Russian verse 1821-1830	77.0	12.0	8.5	2.5

This comparison provides a quantified justification of the commonplace observation that Xodasevič's poetry represents a return to classicism, Puškinian norms, and the like.[12] This, however, is at the level of metrical typlogy at its most abstract, and stands in need of scrutiny in much greater detail. A refinement of this assertion will be attempted below in terms of rhythmical variations, but at least the levels of rhyme and stanza form will also need to be incorporated before statements about the Puškinian nature of Xodasevič's verse can be made with any confidence on formal grounds.

The significance of Xodasevič's metrical typology is amplified when seen against the background of Russian émigré verse. As a very broad, and perhaps misleading, approximation to such a background, an analysis has been made of two sections of the most substantial anthology of modern Russian émigré verse.[13] The first section collects the work of the older generation of émigré poets, who left Russia already fully formed as poets; Xodasevič's own work has of course been excluded from this material. The second section collects the work of 37 'Paris poets', "some of whom had been writing already in Russia, but who fully expressed themselves abroad".[14]

	Iambic	Trochaic	Ternary	Others	Total poems
Older generation	53.6	5.8	14.5	26.1	69
Paris poets	47.6	16.2	25.7	10.5	191

To generalise on the basis of these figures is of course risky, since they are based on an extremely small number of poems, whose metrical characteristics may be influenced by the personal taste of the compiler, himself a prominent émigré poet. However, it is clear that Xodasevič's typology differs markedly on this showing from those of the older generation of émigrés and his younger companions. While the proportion of trochaic verse composed by the older generation is on this evidence remarkably small, the proportion of their work in non-classical metres (26.1% of poems) reflects the metrical experimentation characteristic of Russian poetry during their formative period, the twenty years preceding the Revolution. The figure for works in ternary metres of the older generation, 14.5%, it will be noted, corresponds exactly to Gasparov's figure for this category for Russian poetry 1890-1924. The younger generation of émigré poets give firm indications of a turning away from the non-classical

metres, but the proportion of iambic metres in their work actually drops
compared with the figure for the older generation. The distribution of metrical
groups attested by Gasparov's typology and that of *Na zapade* indicate that
within his historical context, Xodasevič was a poet of marked metrical
originality.

Gasparov's typology is at an extremely high level of abstraction, and makes
no distinction between the work of poets of different schools. In order to place
Xodasevič's typology in a more sharply focussed context, a summary comparison will be made with three contemporary first-rank poets, Blok, Mandeľštam, and Cvetaeva.

	Iambic	Trochaic	Ternary	Others	Total lines
Blok (monometric lyrics 1898-1921)[15]	54.0	13.7	19.3	13.0	22806
Mandeľštam[16] 1908-1925	67.5	16.9	6.2	9.4	2995
Cvetaeva (monometric lyrics 1908-1939)	27.5	19.9	27.4	25.2	16373
Xodasevič 1915-1939	82.0	8.0	4.2	5.8	3030

Certain incompatibilities are inherent in the terms of this comparison, since
the figures for Blok and Cvetaeva cover the whole of their careers and exclude
polymetrical works, while the figures for Mandeľštam exclude the last period
of his creative life. But even allowing for distortions, it will be seen that while
Xodasevič's metrical typology has a good deal in common with that of
Mandeľštam, Xodasevič is an 'iambic poet' to an extraordinary degree; he
rejects not only the non-classical metres in his mature work, but rejects the
ternary metres even more firmly.

Xodasevič's metrical typology will now be examined in terms of the four
chronological periods mentioned above.

	Iambic	Trochaic	Ternary	Others	Total poems
1.	74.2	8.6	2.9	14.3	35
2.	70.0	25.0	5.0	—	40
3.	84.1	5.3	5.3	5.3	38
4.	78.3	—	8.7	13.0	23
Total poems	104	15	7	10	136
%	76.5	11.0	5.1	7.4	100.0

The iambic metres thus remain dominant in all four periods, never falling below 70% of all poems composed in the period; of the other metrical groups, only the trochaic ever rises beyond 15%, and this only during the second period. The rise of the trochaic metres at this time is at the expense of the non-classical metres, which are eliminated entirely. The iambic preference is at its strongest during the first emigration period. This tendency must be seen as an emphatic rejection of contemporary trends in Russian versification; to push the implications further than this would be unwise on the basis of formal factors alone. In fact, Xodasevič's metrical typology anticipates in an extreme way the "reaction against modernist tendencies" discerned by Gasparov in Soviet poetry after 1935,[17] though there is absolutely no analogy to his complete abandonment of the trochaic metres, and as will be seen below, to his continuing neglect of the dol'nik.

2.2 Individual Metrical Groups

The metrical groups presented in the various tables above will now be discussed separately, and their constituent metres examined. A distinction will be drawn between homogeneous metres, where the lines of a poem are entirely of the same type and number of feet; mixed metres, in which the lines all employ the same type of foot, but in numbers which vary according to a regular pattern; and free metres, in which the number of feet to the line varies irregularly.

2.2.1 Iambic Metres
2.2.1.1 Homogeneous

	I2		I3		I4		I5		I6	
	Poems	Lines	Poems	Lines	Poems	Lines	Poems	Lines	Poems	Lines
1.	1	20	2	42	3	36	2	28	1	12
2.	—	—	—	—	23	370	3	23	—	—
3.	—	—	1	12	27	766	2	26	—	—
4.	—	—	—	—	10	213	1	19	1	12
Totals	1	20	3	54	63	1385	8	96	2	24

This evidence permits the first refinements to be made to the remarks above concerning the relation of Xodasevič's metrical typology to that of his contemporaries. Gasparov has shown[18] that within the iambic metres, the pentameter has steadily gained ground since 1890 and in the thirty years before

1968 actually supplanted the tetrameter as the most frequently used iambic metre in Russian verse. The verse of the émigré poets mentioned above shows the same tendency in even greater relief:

	I3	I4	I5	I6	Total lines
Older generation	7.2	48.2	37.0	7.6	502
Paris poets	3.4	29.3	66.4	0.9	1525

In respect of the tetrameter and pentameter, Xodasevič is returning to a distribution characteristic not so much of the Puškin period as of the eighteenth century, before the incursion of the pentameter as a viable metre in Russian poetry. The low prominence of the hexameter, however, is in accord with the virtual disappearance of this metre from Russian poetry since 1925.[19] However, these tendencies will have to be more fully discussed on the basis of an examination of all types of iambic metre rather than the homogeneous types alone.

The dimeter, trimeter, and hexameter, used in one,[20] three,[21] and two[22] poems respectively, are clearly minor among the homogeneous iambic metres, and their rhythmical characteristics will not be examined here.

The iambic tetrameter (I4) is Xodasevič's cardinal metre. Its rhythmical characteristics will first be examined according to the four chronological periods.

	Ictus	I	II	III	IV	Av.	Total lines
Period	1.	75.0	83.3	38.8	100.0	74.3	36
	2.	78.9	86.5	38.9	100.0	76.1	370
	3.	71.9	84.9	30.1	100.0	72.4	766
	4.	76.5	82.1	45.5	100.0	76.0	213
							1385

These figures will be compared with Taranovsky's for I4 of the eighteenth century, the nineteenth century, and 1890-1920,[23] and with Gasparov's for the older generation of Soviet poets:[24]

	I	II	III	IV	Av.
18th cent.	93.2	79.7	53.2	100.0	81.5
19th cent.	82.1	96.8	34.6	100.0	78.4
1890-1920	83.5	87.4	49.1	100.0	80.0
Older Soviet poets	81.4	87.5	45.2	100.0	78.5

Xodasevič's I4 has three individual characteristics: low stressing of the 1st ictus, low stressing of the 3rd ictus (except for the fourth period), and low average stressing for all ictuses. Taranovsky has shown that the bipartite structure characteristic of I4 since Puškin was weakened by a tendency among poets of the period 1890-1920 to level out the strength of the first two ictuses in the line. Gasparov has shown that among older Soviet poets this tendency was retarded, but that the younger generation of Soviet poets has tended to "return to the eighteenth century" by consistently weakening the second ictus in the line and strengthening the first. In the context of this general evolution, Xodasevič can again be seen to be moving against the prevailing currents of his time. Not too much value should be placed on the figures quoted above for the first period, since the number of lines involved is so small; what is most striking is Xodasevič's evolution towards a clearly bipartite structure in the third period. Here the second ictus is 13.2% stronger than the first, and the third ictus is weakened to the very low figure of 30.5%, producing a clearly bipartite structure reminiscent of the poets of the 1820s and 1830s. The poet with whom Xodasevič's I4 of the second and third periods has most in common is Vjazemskij:[25]:

		I	II	III	IV	Av.
Vjazemskij	1820-22	79.3	85.2	49.7	100.0	78.6
Vjazemskij	1826-27	77.5	86.6	48.9	100.0	78.3

Though the general shape of Xodasevič's I4 is reminiscent of that of the Puškin era, the low average level of stressing in the modern poet is a significant point of difference. The most fully developed bipartite structure of nineteenth-century I4, in which the second ictus becomes an actual or near constant, is not characteristic of Xodasevič. The stressing for the second ictus never reaches higher than 86.5% in any of the four periods; in this respect, Xodasevič is in accord with the general movement of his time. Taranovsky's figures for nineteenth-century poets and the period 1890-1920 show a drop from 96.8% to 87.4% stressing for this second ictus—though, of course, Xodasevič does not share the concomitant tendency to strengthen the first and third ictuses. Only one of the late nineteenth- and early twentieth-century poets studied by Taranovsky shows stressings as low as the 72.9% for the first ictus and 30.5% for the third; this poet is Belyj, whose I4 has been studied by Taranovsky in a special article.[22] After experimenting with an archaic 18th-century structure in his lyrics of 1904-5, Belyj in 1906 invented a completely idiosyncratic I4 structure, then used these two types concomitantly, then returned to the 18th-century structure, and eventually in 1916-22 "returned to the bipartite structure of the iambic tetrameter with strong ictuses in the fourth and eighth syllables".[27] Taranovsky's article concludes with a comparison between Belyj's I4 and the rhythmical structures attested in Xodasevič's first two collections, and establishes a clear case of the direct rhythmical influence of Belyj's work on that of Xodasevič. In his lyric *Sicevoe carstvo* (1909), Xodasevič imitated Belyj's unique rhythmical structure with third ictus stronger than second. However, Xodasevič's use of this structure was an isolated example; it is not attested in any of the poems written after 1915. But Xodasevič can in some sense be said to have followed Belyj in returning to the bipartite structure, though he never pushes this tendency as far as Belyj:

	I	II	III	IV
Belyj 1916-1918	68.2	94.2	35.1	100.0
Xodasevič 1922-5	72.9	86.1	30.5	100.0

In Belyj's bipartite structure, the second ictus is stronger than the first by 26%, where in Xodasevič the difference is only 13.2%, in Belyj the third ictus is weaker than the second by 59.1%, where in Xodasevič the difference is 55.6%, also extremely marked, but not so much as in Belyj. The key to the difference is clearly the relative weakness of the second ictus in Xodasevič.

Limitations of space preclude anything but the most summary presentation of the rhythmical tendencies masked by the overall period figures given above. At the level of the individual poem, four fairly clear defined rhythmical types emerge. These will be called types A, B, C, and D. Type A (24 poems)[28] is the bipartite structure with stronger second and weaker first and third ictuses; type B (ten poems)[29] is the 'eighteenth-century' structure with stronger first than second, and stronger second than third ictuses. Types C (fifteen poems)[30] and D (fourteen poems)[31] could be seen as variants of a single structure; type C has first and third ictuses of approximately equal strength, but third ictus of below 35% stressing; type D differs from C only in respect of its third ictus, which has stressing of above 35%. (The first two of these types correspond to types A and B in Taranovsky's analysis of Belyj's I4). The overall stressing for the four types is as follows:

	I	II	III	IV	Av.	Total lines	Total poems
A	68.3	90.4	31.6	100.0	71.4	647	24
B	79.0	72.0	45.5	100.0	74.1	200	10
C	78.8	84.1	23.1	100.0	71.5	246	15
D	78.4	82.2	45.5	100.0	76.5	292	14
						1385	63

The relative distribution of the four types within the four periods of Xodasevič's work is as follows (percentages are of the total number of I4 lines for the
period):

	Period			
	1	2	3	4
A	—	46.5	56.6	19.7
B	—	19.4	10.4	22.5
C	33.3	14.6	21.0	8.9
D	66.7	19.5	12.0	48.8
Total lines	36	370	766	213

The bipartite structure thus dominates the second and third periods, and is
then demoted to third position behind the B and D types in the fourth period.
The prominence of the B and D types in the fourth period accounts for the
unprecedentedly heavy stressing of the third ictus at this time.

The foregoing analysis obviously does no more than scratch the surface of
the problems presented by Xodasevič's I4. Further analysis will be necessary
in order to determine the linguistic factors underlying the rhythmical characteristics of this metre, and also the range of semantic associations of the four
rhythmical groups.

The iambic pentameter (I5) is a marginal form among the homogeneous
iambic metres used by Xodasevič; it was pointed out above that this is one
aspect of his metrical originality. Only 8 poems (96 lines) are composed in this
metre.[32] Of these, only three were composed after the cut-off date (1922) of
James Bailey's major examination of this metre, and the overall picture of the
rhythmical characteristics of Xodasevič's I5 for 1915-1939 does not differ
significantly from the one given by Bailey for Xodasevič's rhymed I5 for
1914-23:[33]

	I	II	III	IV	V	Av.	Total lines
1915-39	84.3	73.9	81.2	47.9	100.0	77.5	96
1914-23	86.4	76.3	82.2	40.7	100.0	77.1	118

2.2.1.2 Mixed Iambic Metres (MI)

Ten poems (312 lines) are composed in MI. Xodasevič does not favour any
particular arrangement of lines; no form is used for more than two poems. Six
poems of this kind are found in the first period;[34] none in the second period;
only two in the third period.[35] One of the latter is "S berlinskoj ulicy", which
has isosyllabic lines of six syllables, and through the use of alternating dactylic

and masculine rhyme achieves a popular-style metrical effect uncharacteristic
of Xodasevič's verse as a whole:

С берлинской улицы
Вверху луна видна.
В берлинских улицах
Людская тень длинна.

The longest of Xodasevič's poems in MI is the 156-line narrative ballad *Džon Bottom*. The 14 lines of this work have a clearly bipartite structure, whose second ictus is significantly stronger than in the homogeneous lyrics using this metre (Type A above):

Ictus	I	II	III	IV
Times stressed	51	76	27	78
%	78.2	97.4	34.6	100.0

The trimeter lines of *Džon Bottom* give this metre a place among the constituent MI metres that far exceeds its importance among the homogeneous iambic metres: percentages are of the total number of 312 MI lines:

I2	I3	I4	I5	I6
11.9	34.3	37.8	15.4	0.6

2.2.1.3 Free Iambic Metres (FI)

The presence or absence of FI is one of the most important formal factors in respect of which the four periods of Xodasevič's mature work contrast. These metres are defined here in absolute terms, that is, the threshold for considering a metre as free has been lowered to zero; using currently accepted standards in this matter, certain poems included below in this category would be considered homogeneous, since a single line length account for over 90% of all lines in the poem. They have been kept together here as a group because of their similarity in terms of genre. FI will be analysed in two categories according to the presence or absence of rhyme.

With seven poems (442 lines), FI is the dominant metrical type of the first period. These poems will be listed and the constituent line lengths given as percentages of the total number of lines in the poem:

(Blank FI)	I1	I2	I3	I4	I5	I6	Total lines
Epizod	1.3	2.6	—	—	79.0	17.1	76
Polden'	1.8	3.6	—	—	76.4	18.2	55

Vstreča	—	4.2	—	—	95.8	—	48
2-go nojabrja	—	—	—	1.2	91.9	6.9	86
Obez'jana	—	—	5.3	1.7	86.0	7.0	57
Dom	—	1.4	—	—	87.8	10.8	74
Muzyka	—	—	—	—	87.0	13.0	46
Total lines		14			381	47	442
%		3.2			86.2	10.6	

This restriction of the component line-lengths virtually to two, I6 and I5, and the overwhelming predominance of I5, represents a further stage in the consistent evolution that has been demonstrated by P.A. Rudnev in his discussion of Bloks' FI with relation to 19th century poetic tradition.[36] The rhymed FI of the first period show the following distribution of component line-lengths:

(Rhymed FI)	I5	I6	Total lines
"O esli b v ètot čas ..."	68.8	31.2	16
Zoloto	50.0	50.0	14
Išči menja	83.3	16.7	12
Lastočki	75.0	25.0	12
Total lines	37	17	54
%	68.5	31.5	

In the rhymed type of FI, the variety of line lengths has been reduced therefore to I6 and I5 alone, but the proportion of I6 lines is just over 20% greater than in blank FI. The rhythmical characteristics of both types of I5 have been investigated in Bailey's article.[37]

Blank FI disappear from the poetry of the second period, and there are only two short poems in this period using the rhymed type; again, only I5 and I6 are employed:

(Rhymed FI)	I5	I6	Total lines
Sumerki	46.2	53.8	13
"Ne materju, no tul'skoju krest'jankoj"	86.1	13.9	36
Total lines	37	12	
%	75.5	24.5	

Neither the rhymed nor the blank type of FI is attested in the first émigré period. As will be seen fully below, this means that I5 has been virtually eliminated from the metrical typology at this stage.

Both types of FI reappear in the fourth and final period. One poem uses the blank type: the unfinished fragment of 1925/7 'Net ničego prekrasnej i privoľ- nej", of whose twenty lines 19 are pentameters. Two poems use rhymed FI, and in contrast to this type in the first period, they introduce lines of other lengths than pentameter and hexameter:

	I3	I4	I5	I6	Total lines
(Rhymed FI)					
Peterburg	5.0	55.0	40.0	—	20
Noč'	—	43.7	50.0	6.3	16
Total lines	1	18	16	1	36
%	2.8	50.0	44.4	2.8	

Noč' is a borderline case between FI and MI; the order of line lengths is: 5454 4554 5454 5564. The predominance of tetrameter in *Peterburg* and the three constituent lines of these two poems make them unique among Xodasevič's FI poems, they could be said to represent a return to early 19th century norms, but the extremely small number of lines involved makes it difficult to press this assertion with confidence.

To complete this schematic examination of Xodasevič's iambic metres, the proportions of iambic lines of all the three metrical types discussed above will be assembled. Percentages are of the total number of iambic lines for the period.

Period	I1	I2	I3	I4	I5	I6	Total
1	0.3	6.9	7.0	8.2	66.9	10.7	729
2	—	—	—	83.7	13.6	2.7	442
3	—	1.7	3.4	91.8	3.1	—	830
4	—	—	17.7	66.9	12.5	2.9	480

The crucial relationship is the one between the two major line-lengths, tetrameter and pentameter: I5 dominates the first period, drops by over 50% in the second period, and is virtually eliminated in the third; I4 in the first period is less favoured even than I6, but leaps up by over 70% in the second period and accounts for over 90% of all iambic lines in the third. The less concentrated poetic work of the fourth period sees a retreat from the extreme distribution of the third period towards a more even distribution closer in type to that of the first period.

2.2.2 *Trochaic Metres*

2.2.2.1 Homogeneous

The trochaic metres form a minor group within Xodasevič's repertoire, and are concentrated in the second period. Apart from a single poem in T3,[38] the tetrameter, used in thirteen poems,[39] is the only homogeneous trochaic metre represented. This predilection for T4 is another respect in which Xodasevič's practice runs counter to contemporary trends; as can be seen from the comparative figures below, Xodasevič is returning to a distribution of the trochaic metres characteristic of the second decade of the 19th century:

	T3	T4	T5	Others	Total poems
Russian poetry 1811-20	7.0	76.0	—	17.0	54
1890-1924	3.5	41.0	23.0	32.5	362
1925-35	5.0	34.0	37.0	24.0	233
Older émigrés	—	50.0	50.0	—	4
Paris poets	6.5	25.8	51.6	16.1	31
Xodasevič 1915-1939	7.1	92.9	—	—	14

Xodasevič's neglect of T5 goes against a consistent trend in Russian poetry which has led to a situation where after 1925 T5 supplants T4 as the most popular of the trochaic metres.[40]

Since the number of lines involved is relatively small, and hardly any significant rhythmical differentiation is involved, the rhythmical structure of all Xodasevič's homogeneous T4 lines will be examined together:

Ictus	I	II	III	IV	Av.	Total lines
Times stressed	111	181	96	200		
%	55.5	90.5	48.0	100.0	73.5	200

This, of course, is the clear bipartite structure characteristic of this metre since its inception in Russian poetry.[41] Among the homogeneous T4 poems, only one has a rhythmical structure that differs significantly from the bipartite shape: this is "Tak byvaet počemu-to", where the first ictus is stronger than the second.[42]

2.2.2.2 Mixed trochaic metres (MT)

A single poem, "Obo vsem v odnix stixax ne skažeš'", is composed in regularly alternating trochaic lines; its stanza form is T5656; the six pentameter lines of this poem are the only T5 lines attested in the poems studied.

2.2.2.3 Free Trochees (FT)

There is no example of this type of metre in the poetry studied.

2.2.3 *Ternary Metres*

Only homogeneous ternary metres are attested in the poetry studied; they include dactylic tetrameter (three poems),[43] amphibrachic trimeter (one poem),[44] and anapaestic trimeter (three poems).[45] The rhythmical structures of these metres are in no way remarkable; there is the normal practically constant fulfilment of ictuses except for the initial ictus of the dactylic metre, and the normal tendency for the first syllable of the anapaestic lines to attract hypermetrical stressing:

D4 Ictus	I	II	III	IV	Av.	Total lines
Times stressed	26	30	29	30		
%	86.6	100.0	96.6	100.0	95.8	30

An3 Ictus	I	II	III	Av.	Total lines	First syllable
Times stressed	53	50	53			16
%	100.0	94.3	100.0	98.1	53	30.2

The weakened middle ictus and the relatively high stressing of the initial syllable of the An3 are accountable to the famous lyric *Pered zerkalom*:

> Я, я, я. Что за дикое слово!
> Неужели вон тот — это я?
> Разве мама любила такого,
> Желтосерого, полуседого
> И всезнающего, как змея?

2.2.4 *The dol'nik*

2.2.4.1 Homogeneous

The *dol'nik* is weakly represented in the metrical typology of the first, third, and fourth periods, and absent in the second; it accounts for a total of six poems (110 lines). Three types of metre are attested, with three-ictus (three poems), [46] four-ictus (one poem),[47] and six-ictus (two poems)[48] lines. The three-ictus *dol'nik* is of a different type in each of the three poems. *Slezy Raxili* has a disyllabic anacrusis in all but two lines; the first interval is disyllabic in two thirds of the lines, and the second interval disyllabic in 62.5% of the lines; in Gasparov's typology for this metre, [49] the distribution of line-types is: type III, 9; type II, 8; and type I, 7; that is, the distribution characteristic of the

'Gumilev type' of three-ictus *dol'nik*. "V zabotax každogo dnja" uses types II and III only, and with a monosyllabic anacrusis. The isolated later example of three-ictus *dol'nik, U morja* 4, is characterised by the omission of the middle ictus in 11 of the 28 lines, and a disyllabic anacrusis in all but one of the lines. The two poems in 6-ictus *dol'nik* are both imitations of classical metres. "Sladko posle doždja", according to the author's note, uses as a basis the metre of *Exegi monumentum*:[50]

> Сладко после дождя теплая пахнет ночь.
> Быстро месяц бежит в прорезях белых туч.
> Где-то в сырой траве часто кричит дергач.

Daktili combines three elegiac distichs into a six-line stanza:

> Был мой отец шестипалым. По ткани, натянутой туго,
> Бруни его обучал мягкой кистью водить ...

2.2.4.2 Mixed *dol'nik*

One poem, *Okno vo dvor*, consists of three quatrains of four-ictus *dol'nik* interspersed with five quatrains in which there is an alternation of three- and four-ictus *dol'nik* lines. All the lines of this poem have a strongly marked amphibrachic cadence, there being only 6 monosyllabic intervals in the entire 32 lines, and only 7 lines with disyllabic rather than monosyllabic anacrusis.

2.2.4.3 Free *dol'nik*

One late poem, "Skvoz' nenastnyj zimnij denek" (1927), is composed in mixed three- and four-ictus *dol'nik* lines. The poem is ohly ten lines long.

2.2.5 *Accentual Metres*

The entire corpus of verse written by Xodasevič after 1915 includes only one poem in accentual verse of a conventional kind, "Milye devuški, verte" (1916). The poem is in strict accentual verse with four stresses to the line, with stem lengths ranging between nine and twelve syllables.[51] It is significant that seven lines of this poem were written in 1912, the final five having been added in 1916; these final five lines are significantly more highly regulated, i.e. *dol'nik*-like, than the lines written earlier.

One further poem is perhaps best categorised as accentual: this is the metrical tour de force *Poxorony* (1928), a sonnet in one-syllable lines.

3. CONCLUSIONS

At the end of his historical survey of the metrical typology of Russian verse which has been frequently referred to above, M. L. Gasparov offers a six-stage periodisation of the history of Russian verse on metrical grounds. There could be no more impressive illustration of Xodasevič's metrical idiosyncracy than to say that his practice goes against *every single one* of the distinguishing features that Gasparov lists for the relevant period: 'The 'modernist period (1890-1924)' is a time of the renovation of the metrical repertoire: non-classical metres are feverishly assimilated, and at the same time experiments are conducted 'on the periphery' of the traditional syllabo-tonic system (long lines, expansion and contraction at the caesura). Under the onslaught of the non-classical metres, it is above all the ternary metres that give ground, and trochaic metres again come to the fore. Within the trochees the pentameter develops as swiftly as before, and within the iambic metres it is also the pentameter that develops".[52]

Further detailed work on the metrical repertoire and rhythmical styles of Xodasevič's contemporaries will reveal more precisely the extent to which he was an isolated reactionary rebel; but on the evidence offered above, he can be seen to have rejected the accentual verse most strongly associated with Maja-kovskij and the Futurists, and equally strongly to have rejected the *dol'nik*, the Symbolist metrical innovation that was adopted by the Acmeists. Xodasevič's 'return to Puškinian norms' is substantially demonstrable at the level of metre, but less so at the level of rhythm. The problems of rhyme and stanza form remain to be investigated. No attempt will be made here to explore the complex aesthetic, ideological, and personal reasons lying behind the metrical choices in Xodasevič's mature poetry; there can be little doubt, however, that he defined the essence of these reasons in the last stanza of his renowned poem on the iambic tetrameter, where he says of this meter:

Ему один закон — свобода,
В его свободе есть закон.

NOTES

[1] Vladislav Xodasevič, *Sobranie stixov (1913-1939)*. Redakcija i primečanija N. Berberovoj (New Haven, 1961). This edition will be referred to below as *SS*, with page number.
[2] *SS*, 7. The two collections were *Molodost'* (1908) and *Sčastlivyj domik* (first edition 1914, second revised and enlarged edition 1921).

3   A few poems from the collections *Putem zerna* (first edition 1920) and *Tjaželaja lira* (1922) were excluded from the respective sections of the 1927 volume and not restored in *SS*; eight poems, four of them unfinished, were first published in *Vozdušnye puti*, aľmanax 3 (1963), 16-18, and aľmanax 4 (1965), 120-5. These poems have been excluded from analysis, as have the lyrics *Akrobat* and "So slabyx vek", included in *Putem zerna* and *SS* but dating from 1913/1914, and "Za oknom — nočnye razgovory" (1915), included in the second edition of *Sčastlivyj domik*.

4   On the translations from Yiddish, see Luis Bernxard, "V. F. Xodasevič i sovremennaja evrejskaja poezija", *Russian Literature*, 6 (1974), 21-31.

5   These sections are: *Putem zerna*; *Tjaželaja lira*; *Evropejskaja noč*"; and *Stixotvorenija, ne vošedšie v sobranie stixov 1927 g.*

6   K. F. Taranovsky, "Stixosloženie Osipa Mandeľštama (s 1908 po 1925 god)", *International Journal of Slavic Linguistics and Poetics*, V (1962), 97-123.

7   James Bailey, "The Metrical and Rhythmical Typology of K. K. Slučevskij's Poetry", *International Journal of Slavic Linguistics and Poetics*, XVIII (1975), 93-117.

8   Of the growing number of metrical typologies for Russian poets (see e.g. those listed in my "Bibliography of Soviet Publications on Russian Versification since 1958", *Russian Literature Triquarterly*, 6 (1973), 679-94), none have so far included metrical and rhythmical analysis at both line and stanza level.

9   M. L. Gasparov, *Sovremennyj russkij stix: Ritmika i metrika* (Moscow, 1974), 39-75. This book will be referred to below as *SRS*, with page reference.

10   *SRS*, 51.

11   *SRS*, 51.

12   This assertion has been made most categorically by Vladimir Markov: Xodasevič "defiantly based his poetry on almost a letter-perfect imitation of Puškin. The miracle was that he managed to create great and original poetry in this way, a poetry whose mystical content is even more poignantly apparent because of a strict classical form" (*Preface*, in *Modern Russian Poetry*, London, 1966, lxiv-lxv). In his review of *Tjaželaja lira*, Andrej Belyj wrote that "Iz Xodaseviča zrejut znakomye žesty poèzii Baratynskogo, Tjutčeva, Puškina ..." (quoted in Gleb Struve, *Russkaja literatura v izgnanii*, New York, 1956, 141); and Mandeľštam asserted that "Ego mladšaja linija — stixi vtorostepennyx poètov puškinskoj i poslepuškinskoj pory — domašnie poèty-ljubiteli, vrode grafini Rostopčinoj, Vjazemskogo i dr." ("Burja i natisk", *Sobranie sočinenij v trex tomax*, II, New York, 1971, 339-51, esp. 345).

13   Ju. P. Ivask (compiler), *Na Zapade: Antologija russkoj zarubežnoj poèzii* (New York, 1953).

14   Ivask, *op. cit.*, 7.

15   Based on P. A. Rudnev, "Metričeskij repertuar A. Bloka", *Blokovskij sbornik* 2 (Tartu, 1972), 218-67, esp. 267.

16   Taken from K. F. Taranovsky, *op. cit.* (Note 6), 98, 112.

17   *SRS*, 53.

18   *SRS*, tables on 54 and 56-7.

19   *SRS*, 54-6.

20   *Smolenskij rynok* (1916).

21   *V Petrovskom parke* (1916); *Anjute* (1918); "Ni rozovogo sada" (1922).

22   *Putem zerna* (1917); *Na smerť kota Murra* (1931).

23   K. F. Taranovsky, *Ruski dvodelni ritmovi* (Belgrade, 1953), 84, Tabela III; id., "Ruski četvero-stopni jamb u prvim dvema decinijama XX veka", *Jugoslovenski Filolog*, XXI, 1-4 (1955/6), 15-43.

24   *SRS*, 76-125.

25   K. F. Taranovsky, *Ruski dvodelni ritmovi*, 81-4, Tabela III.

26   K. F. Taranovsky, "Četyrexstopnyj jamb Andreja Belogo", *International Journal of Slavic Linguistics and Poetics*, X (1966), 127-47.

27   *Loc. cit.* (Note 26), 132.

[28] Period 2: *K Psixee, Iskušenie,* "Ljublju ljudej, ljublju prirodu", *Lida, Elegija,* "Gorit zvezda, drožit èfir", *Avtomobiľ,* "Druzja, druzja!", *Perešagni.* Period 3; "Boľšie flagi nad èstradoj", "Ni žiť, ni peť", *U morja* I, "Net, ne najdu segodnja pišči ja", *Pod zemlej, Berlinskoe, Xranilišče,* "Poka duša v poryve junom", *Afrodita, Zvezdy, Iz dnevnika, Sorrentijskie fotografii.* Period 4: "Net, ne šotlandskoj korolevoj", *Pamjatnik, K Lide.*

[29] Period 2: *Iz dnevnika* ("Mne každyj zvuk terzaet slux"), *Iz okna* 2, *Beľskoe usťe, Ulika.* Period 3: "Vstaju rasslablennyj s posteli", "Vdrug iz-za tuč ozolotilo", *An Mariechen,* "I veselo, i tjaželo". Period 4: "Poluzabytaja otrada", "Ne jambom li četyrexstopnym".

[30] Period 1: *Ručej.* Period 2: *Psixeja,* "Puskaj minuvšego ne žaľ", *Gostju,* "Ne verju v krasotu zemnuju", "Pokrova Maji potaennoj". Period 3: *U morja 3,* "Živ Bog! Umen, a ne zaumen", "Trudoljubivoju pčeloj", "Skvoz oblaka fabričnoj gari", *Vodopad, Pan, Ballada.* Period 4: "Kto sčastliv vernoju ženoj" (unfinished), "Skvoz dikij golos katastrof" (unfinished).

[31] Period 1: *Bez slov, Variacija.* Period 2: *Den',* "Smotrju v okno — i preziraju", "Kogda b ja dolgo žil na svete", "Igraju v karty, p'ju vino", *Žizeľ.* Period 3: *Stansy,* "Gljažu na grubye remesla", *U morja 2,* "Vesennij lepet ne raznežiť". Period 4: "Kak boľno mne ot vašej malosti" (unfinished), *Ja, Prinošenie R. i M. Gorlinym.*

[32] Period 1: *Pro sebja,* 1 and 2. Period 2: *Duša, Porok i smerť, Mart.* Period 3: "Vse kamennoe ...", *Dačnoe.* Period 4: "Velikaja vokrug menja pustynja" (unfinished).

[33] James Bailey, "The Evolution and Structure of the Russian Iambic Pentameter from 1880 to 1922", *International Journal of Slavic Linguistics and Poetics,* XVI (1973), 119-46.

[34] (14242) *Utro, U morja*; (15352) *Na xodu*; (15454) *Stansy*; (15552) *Sny*; (15552 (5563, 5562)) *Xleby.*

[35] (12323) "S berlinskoj ulicy"; (14434) *Pesnja turka.*

[36] Rudnev, *op. cit.* (Note 15), 243-4.

[37] Bailey, *op. cit.* (Note 33), 139, 141.

[38] *Meľnica.*

[39] Period 1: "Brenta, ryžaja rečenka"; Period 2, "Tak byvaet počemu-to", *Burja, Iz okna* 1, *Probočka, V zasedanii,* "Na tusknejuščie špili", *Vakx,* "Ledi dolgo ruki myla", *Večer,* "Starym snam zaterjan sonnik"; Period 3: *Slepoj, Romans.*

[40] *SRS,* 61.

[41] Taranovsky, *Ruski dvodelni ritmovi,* 58-66, Tabela I.

[42] On this rhythmical structure in Cvetaeva, see James Bailey, "The Basic Structural Characteristics of Russian Literary Meters", in C. Gribble (ed), *Studies Presented to Professor Roman Jakobson by his Students* (Cambridge, 1968), 17-38, esp. 27.

[43] Period 1: *Šveja*; Period 2: "Strannik prošel"; Period 3: "Bylo na ulice polutemno".

[44] Period 2: *Ballada.*

[45] Period 3: *Pered zerkalom;* Period 4: *Bednye rifmy,* "Skvoz ujutnoe solnce...".

[46] Period 1: *Slezy Raxili,* "V zabotax každogo dnja"; Period 3: *U morja,* 2.

[47] Period 1: *Po buľvaram.*

[48] Period 1: "Sladko posle doždja ..."; Period 4: *Daktili.*

[49] M. L. Gasparov, "Russkij trexudarnyj doľnik XX v.", *Teorija stixa* (Leningrad, 1968), 59-106, esp. 70.

[50] *SS,* 213.

[51] On this verse type, see *SRS,* 331-9; James Bailey, "The Development of Strict Accentual Verse in Russian Poetry" (1974, unpublished).

[52] *SRS,* 74.

COMMENTS

(Bailey)   Your paper demonstrates how intuitive assessments of a poet's versification need to be verified by precise analysis. One has long heard comments about how Xodasevič imitated Puškin's verse, but now you have factually shown how true this is. His case is a clear instance of how a poet may return to and revive archaic features in poetry, and how important a role tradition often plays in poetic technique. You also once again show how one poet may 'hear' and then reproduce the various rhythmical structures elucidated through statistical analysis. Rhythmical variants in a meter are quite real for a poet. I know that you did not attempt to go into the thematic associations for the four types of rhythmical structures you found in Xodasevič's iambic tetrameter, but can you even so offer some remarks or impressions on this subject? Are there any similar genre or thematic associations in his poems written in trochaic tetrameter?

(McLean)   Would you consider the epithet *reakcionnyj* appropriate as qualifying the metrical practise of Xodasevič? (This formulation sounds facetious, and was perhaps intended as such; but it nevertheless contains a serious core — a question about the nature of 'forward' and 'backward' motion in the history of metrical systems, Russian in particular.)

Additional discussion: Broyde, Issatschenko, Stankiewicz, Terras, Vickery.

AUTHOR'S REPLY

I was certainly not trying to be facetious in using this epithet; in retrospect I regret using it because it's such a loaded word. It was the most concise way I could think of to characterise the practice of a poet who rejects contemporary innovatory trends and develops a metrical typology reminiscent of a past epoch. I have in mind purely formal factors; the wider-ranging implications of Xodasevič's metrical choices, their relations with theme and style, is a subject I intend to discuss elsewhere. However, I doubt if 'backward' movement is possible, since what intervenes between an original occurrence and a revival cannot be cancelled out, and the ends will be new even though the means be old.

THE AESTHETIC CATEGORIES
OF *ASCENT* AND *DESCENT*
IN THE POETRY OF VJAČESLAV IVANOV

VICTOR TERRAS

I

Many Western aestheticians today will agree with Benedetto Croce who banned the so-called 'aesthetic categories' from his phenomenology of art.[1] At the same time the concepts of eighteenth-century British sensualist aesthetics, which Croce likewise dismisses out of hand,[2] are at the core of modern structuralist poetics. Regularity, symmetry, proportion, and order are the terms in which it seeks to capture the essence of poetic creation. Also, while the old aesthetic categories (such as the Beautiful, the Sublime, or the Tragic) rarely appear in literary analysis, at least in the West, new polarities such as 'Apollonian : Dionysian', 'static : dynamic', and 'line : color', are commonly used as 'distinctive features' in scholarly descriptions of works of literature.[3] A discussion of the polarity 'ascent : descent', which plays a focal role in Vjačeslav Ivanov's philosophy of art, does not seem to be too extravagant an undertaking.

Ivanov's aesthetic theory and poetic practice must be viewed against the background of his philosophy.[4] Ivanov believed that poetry is an immediate revelation of the highest truth[5] and regarded it as a mystical activity, a means of revealing in words the divine essence of the universe.[6] One may speak in Ivanov's case of 'aesthetic mysticism', since it is precisely the artist to whom it is given to perceive and to express truth. "God is an artist, and His judgment, it would seem, will be the judgment of an artist", Ivanov once wrote.[7] Art is an energy which produces a quintessence of being.[8] Ivanov is very much a Platonist in that he believes that poetic creation is an act of atavistic *anamnesis* which allows men to become once more aware of the World Soul.[9] Ivanov's conception of poetic vision often assumes Orphic traits.[10]

The so-called theurgic function of poetry is seen as a "release of true Beauty from under the coarse covers of matter",[11] a Neoplatonic conception. At the same time, Ivanov always insists that, while a mystic, he is also a realist and that his poetry is to lead *a realibus ad realiora*.[12] Poetry is to him a quintessential, potent, and sacred form of the word, Ivanov's conception of reality is thus hierarchic.[13]

Ivanov is resolutely opposed to subjective idealism (to which he refers as "idealism", while his own objective idealism is called "realism"): "It is the artist's highest duty to refrain from imposing his will upon the surface of things, and rather to recognize and to pronounce with gratitude the hidden will of essence itself. Like a midwife who eases the process of birth, he must help things to reveal their beauty".[14] The danger of "idealism", says Ivanov, lies precisely in its leading toward subjective "creation", rather than to a faithful revelation of truth, in its tending to convert the artist into a "deceitful Sirene, a sorcerer who creates his illusions at will".[15] Hence Ivanov's ideal of art is "earthly" rather than "heavenly".[16] It is stated with overwhelming simplicity in one of his last poems:

> Вы, чьи резец, палитра, лира,
> Согласных Муз одна семья,
> Вы нас уводите из мира
> В соседство инобытия.
> И чем зеркальней отражает
> Кристал искусства лик земной,
> Тем явственней нас поражает
> В нем жизнь иная, свет иной.
> И про себя даемся диву,
> Что не приметили досель,
> Как ветерок ласкает ниву
> И зелена под снегом ель.
>
> ("Свет вечерний", стр. 172)

Ivanov's mysticism can thus be reduced to what he calls the "inner canon", meaning "the law which says that the human individuality is structured according to universal norms", so that an intensification of human existence means an "enlivening, strengthening, and growing awareness of the bonds and interrelationships between individual existence on the one side, and communal, universal, and divine existence on the other".[17] The "inner canon" of the human soul is projected upon the "inner canon" of the work of art. This explains the striking chains of identities found in Ivanov's poetry, such as the identity of the inner heavens of the soul and the starry sky above us.[18]

With the content of art eternally and absolutely identical, it is clear that the artist's creative role is limited to discovering forms that are adequate to this content.[19] The work of art, insofar as it owes its existence to the artist, is *forma formata,* while the creative process is *forma formans.*[20] Ivanov refuses to consider form independently of content: any play or ornamental use of words, arbitrary neologisms, conscious pursuit of sound symbolism and euphonic patterning as a mere display of the poet's virtuosity is to him a violation of the sanctity of the word.[21]

It is obvious that all of these positions are reformulations (and often mere repetitions) of the Neoplatonic philosophy of art based on the eighth chapter of Plotinus's fifth *Ennead* and found in, to name only authors who had a direct influence on Ivanov, Goethe, Schelling, Apollon Grigor'ev, Tjutčev, Foeth, and Vladimir Solov'ev.[22] Ivanov's aesthetic thought acquires some interest through the fact that his poetry offers a massive corpus of apt illustrations of his theoretical positions. There is no easy or immediate explanation for this phenomenon, although Ivanov himself would of course advance the familiar organicist notion that philosophy and poetry are but different avenues to the same truth. I shall try to approach this question in connection with some observations regarding certain specific elements of Ivanov's philosophy which, like his more general ideas, are perfectly mirrored in his poetry.

One meets in Ivanov's philosophy several dichotomies which can be understood as additions to the set of commonly known aesthetic categories. Thus, Ivanov distinguishes between artists who are 'mystifiers' (*oblačiteli*) and artists who are 'demystifiers' (*razoblačiteli*). The former create riddles, mysteries, and masks, the latter reveal the truth of life and tear off masks.[23] Another dichotomy often encountered in Ivanov's thought is that of the artist who creates from hunger, and the artist who creates from plenitude and generosity.[24] It is with this dichotomy that Ivanov himself links that of ascent (*vosxoždenie*) and descent (*nisxoždenie*).[25] All three dichotomies mentioned here are prominent in Nietzsche, with whom Ivanov is connected by strong and multiple ties.

Ascent is, first of all, the upward striving of the soul, and descent the condescension of the divine. "Therefore", says Ivanov, "our sensation of Beauty is composed at once of a sensation of a winged victory over earthly heaviness and a sensation of return to the womb of the Earth".[26] (Here it must be kept in mind that Ivanov, a Neoplatonist, conceives of the Divine as immanent in the human soul). Hence ascent is linked with the male principle, and descent with the female, Apollo and Aphrodite respectively. (Dionysus stands for chaos and is androgynous).[27] Ascent and descent are thus concepts which belong, first and foremost, to the religious sphere:

> In terms of religious thought, descent is an act of love and a sacrificial introduction of divine light into the darkness of the lower sphere seeking enlightenment. To man, righteous descent means, first and foremost, to bow down before what

is lowly in all Creation and to serve it (as indicated by the symbolic washing of feet), to lower oneself voluntarily at the urging of an individual sense of duty before those who have served one's exaltation.[28]

On the divine level this is of course the mystery of God's second *persona*, that of the Son.[29] In a concrete historical context, Ivanov sees a tendency toward spiritual descent as a trait of the Russian national character.[30] He also suggests, precisely in this context, that ascent and descent may be manifestations of the 'laws' of self-preservation and self-destruction (Eros and Thanatos), respectively.[31]

With specific reference to art and the creative process, Ivanov links the dichotomy of *ascent : descent* with the familiar dichotomy of *poet : artist*: "As a man, the artist must ascend, as an artist he must descend".[32] This means that the artist's intuition, like any other man's, should point him heavenward (this is the 'poet' in him, in organicist parlance), while his craftsmanship gives the ideal an earthly form (the 'artist's' task).[33] Among all the forms of verbal art, lyric poetry is the one in which the need for descent is felt least. Therefore, Ivanov concludes somewhat surprisingly, there is less 'pure art' in lyric poetry than in other art forms.[34] Carin Tschöpl has pointed out, no doubt correctly, that the emphasis of Ivanov's creativity shifted gradually from mystic ascent to artistic descent.[35]

Ivanov conceives of the creative process as of a movement up and down a vertical axis with these principal stages (in ascending/descending order): earthly objective reality → subjective mirroring of the Self → the desert beyond the Self → the point of transcendental contemplation of a reality-to-be-overcome → intuitive grasp of a higher reality (various stages, after the highest of which the descent begins) → "Apollonian contemplation of the apogees of ascent" → objective artistic incarnation.[36] Ivanov recognizes that the principal stages along this vertical are also those of religious experience. As he puts it, "God is on man's vertical".[37] He thus takes for granted that great art is always religious art.

It is important to note that Ivanov realizes the scheme of *ascent : descent* in his dramatic poems *Tantalus*[38] and *Prometheus,* and quite consciously so. A diagram to this effect is found in Ivanov's preface to *Prometheus.*[39]

II

I now proceed to a description of Ivanov's last collection, *Svet večernij* ("Vespertine Light", Oxford, 1962), in terms of *ascent : descent* and some related features. Selection of this particular volume (a presentation of the entire corpus of Ivanov's poetry being out of the question) was motivated by the following considerations. *Svet večernij* is artistically the finest of Ivanov's collections. The poetry here is less motivated by Ivanov's theoretical thought than the poetry of earlier collections. It is thus closer to an ideal of 'pure poetry'. Certainly only few of the poems of *Svet večernij* would seem to be directly connected with Ivanov's theoretical treatises dealing with *ascent : descent*. Finally, examination of Ivanov's earlier collections suggests that the points made here are even more apparent there. Yet the poetry of *Svet večernij* is as much as ever before in Ivanov's career an effort to fulfill the poet's mission as he conceived of it:

> Nudus salta! Цель искусства —
> Без покровов, без оков
> Показать, кто ты таков,
> Темные поведать чувства
> Заповедных тайников —
> ("Свет вечерний", стр. 123)

A significant trait of Ivanov's poetry, fully borne out by *Svet večernij*, is the prevalence in it of elementary imagery. While the human soul is the subject of most of these poems, its essence is revealed in images of air, water, earth, and fire, heaven and nether world, light and darkness. There is, if we disregard inevitable exceptions (the volume includes the cycles *Roman Sonnets* and *Roman Diary,* where the eternal city will occasionally appear quite plastically), little of the historical and regional flavor which we find in Mandel'štam, little of Axmatova's personal flair, few sacrifices to the 'great God of details' which make Pasternak so unique. Ivanov deals in poetic universals, not to say in poetic clichés. Ivanov's description of Novalis is also a self-portrait:

> Он был из тех певцов (таков-же был Новалис),
> Что видят в снах себя наследниками лир,
> Которым на заре веков повиновались
> Дух, камень, древо, зверь, вода, огонь, эфир.
> ("Свет вечерний", стр. 93)

Ivanov's elementary imagery may very well be one aspect of his 'pure lyricism': lyric poetry has, it seems, an inherent tendency toward a certain vagueness and abstractness, as Emil Staiger has pointed out, among others.[40] It is precisely in this sense that Gumilev, a fine critic, understood this trait of Ivanov's poetry.[41] Ivanov's frequent cosmic ecstasies may be but another side of the same phenomenon.[42] It must not be overlooked, though, that a tendency toward elementary imagery is characteristic of Symbolist poetry at large.

But in none of the Russian symbolists does it appear quite as massively as in Ivanov.

Significantly, heaven and earth prevail among Ivanov's imagery, both in variety and in number of images. Unlike in many poets with a great deal of airborne imagery, earth is in balance with heaven. The heavens (*nebo, nebesa, èfir, lazur'*) appear most often as the cloudless dome of azure, or as "the sky", without a qualification.[43] But the starry sky appears almost as often.[44] Accordingly, the frequent appearances of the Sun[45] are almost matched by the Moon, the signs of the Zodiac, and astrological imagery.[46] Dawn and dusk are approximately in balance.[47] The recurrent image of the music of the spheres seems to refer to the diurnal sky in most instances.[48]

Earth appears both without a qualification and as Mother Earth (*zemlja rodnaja,* and such).[40] There is a great wealth of subterranean imagery. The nether world (*nedra, glub', preispodnja, ad, čistilišče*)[50] and cave imagery (*peščera, labirint, grob, mogila*)[51] appear as often as sky imagery. The salient point is that in a great many instances the sky and the earth, the nether world and the heavens appear in the same poem, creating the vertical dynamics so characteristic of Ivanov.[52]

Water imagery is somewhat less common in Ivanov's poetry. There is a great deal of 'flowing water' imagery, but this is largely accounted for by the fact that a whole cycle of sonnets is devoted to the fountains of Rome.[53] The river of time (it occurs quite often) would seem to be a metaphor rather than an image in its own right in most instances.[54] There is a good deal of ocean imagery, almost always dynamic, as Tschöpl has observed.[55]

Finally, there is an impressive array of fire imagery.[56] It could be enlarged if the Sun (in particular the frequent fiery sunset images) and a number of striking images of single stars are assigned to this element.[57]

This extraordinarily massive accumulation of elementary imagery is interesting as such. What makes it even more interesting is the fact that in a great many instances these elementary images are explicit projections of the states of the poetic persona's soul, so much so that one is inclined to consider even Ivanov's 'nature poetry' as descriptions of an 'inner' landscape. There are numerous examples of the 'inner sky' (*vnutrennee nebo*), all more or less in accord with the image created in a sonnet of that title (p. 91).[58] Somewhat more surprisingly we find as many instances of an 'inner sea' as we find of an 'inner sky'.[60] Also, the 'bark of the soul' is a recurrent image.[61] Lastly, in a striking image, the soul becomes the fiery, whirling wheel of Ixion, and an 'inner Sun' also appears.[62] Such projections are psychologically motivated by the exceedingly frequent side motifs of 'sleep', 'dream', and 'night'.[63]

We may now proceed to a description of the dynamic aspect of Ivanov's imagery. What movement there is in the poems of *Svet večernij* tends to be vertical or airborne. The horizontal movement of the wayfarer on the road (Goethe's *Wanderer*) is uncharacteristic of Ivanov. Among the 260 poems in *Svet večernij*, 199 feature a dynamic vertical image or images which, in my judgment, may be said to dominate the poem in question. In some of these instances several such images appear. My count is based on the one image which I consider to be the dominant. Obviously other readers of the same poem may have a different impression.

Among these 199 dominant images, there are a total of 27 which can be defined as horizontal flight (12), soaring (8), or floating (7), where no vertical movement can be discerned.[64]

Ascent and *descent* are almost as equally balanced as *heaven* and the *nether world* are among Ivanov's static images. Among images of ascent one may distinguish images of anastasis,[65] various cosmic images (such as the ascent of heavenly bodies),[66] mythological images (including Christian),[67] images featuring ascent to the summit of a mountain,[68] and vertical movement involving stationary vertical objects such as towers, trees, and the Cross.[69] The most important category of ascent is of course 'ascent of the soul' which dominates 15 poems.[70] In all, at least 40 of the poems of *Svet večernij* can be called 'ascent poems'.

Among images of descent the following may be distinguished. There is some water imagery here, and in particular the image of the descending river of time.[71] Cosmic imagery (descent of heavenly bodies and such) is well represented.[72] But more often descent is symbolic. It may be the descent of a vision, of the Light, or of the word.[73] It may also be the descent of peace, of love, of the Divine, or of death.[74] Finally, there is a great deal of religious-mythological imagery, including descent *ad inferos*.[75] The descent of the soul understandably appears less often than its ascent (5 times).[76] In all, I counted 72 'descent poems'.

Another body of poems combines ascent and descent. There are, again, cosmic images.[77] Also, descent : ascent (or *vice versa*) of a vision,[78] or in religious-mythological images.[79] Descent : ascent between heaven and earth may be considered a special category.[80] Finally, the human soul is involved in 22 'ascent : descent poems'.[81] There are 49 'ascent : descent poems' in all. Ivanov's cosmos resembles that of Foeth's famous poem "Na stoge sena nočju južnoj". The sky can turn into a bottomless abyss: *struj èfirnyx glubina* (7: 3). Conversely, the Sun may rise "from the depths": *A v nedrax — Solnca, solnca roždestvo!* (100: 8).

There remain 11 poems which I can only classify as being structured around movement on a vertical axis.[82] In addition to the large number of poems which explicitly deal with the descent and/or ascent of the soul, there are others which express the movements of the soul in metaphoric terms. These instances are not included in my count.

It is then true of Ivanov's imagery at large that it is dominated by elementary images, that its movement proceeds on a vertical axis, and that it is often symbolic of the attitudes and movements of the soul. It must be noted that many of the poems that do not fall within this description are relatively trivial, incidental pieces. There are not many great poems that must be excluded from these generalizations.

III

How is one to account for this peculiar nature of Ivanov's poetry? To begin with, Ivanov's elementary imagery and its symbolism follow ancient traditions. To mention only the less obvious instances, both the 'inner sky' and the 'inner sea' images go back as far as classical antiquity.[83] They appear, specifically, in German romantic poetry.[84] The labyrinth of the heart is an ancient conceit,[85] while the cry of the soul from the depths is of course biblical (Psalm 130). In effect, Ivanov uses a great deal of biblical, classical, and other (Indian, Teutonic, Slavic) elementary imagery throughout his poetry.

In a beautiful poem, Ivanov singles out Tjutčev, Foeth, and Vladimir Solov'ev as his masters.[86] Obviously their imagery largely coincides with Ivanov's. Tjutčev in particular has a similar emphasis on the heavens, the starry sky, the inner sky, sky and earth, music of the spheres, flight imagery, the inner sea, the lower depths, etc.[87]

Airborne imagery as well as images suggesting movement along a vertical axis are likewise easily found in the poetic tradition upon which Ivanov's opus rests. To begin with, the ascent and descent of the human soul on a ladder which extends from the lower depths to exalted moral perfection and heavenly bliss is an ancient cliché of mystic poetry and prose. We find it in St. John of the Cross (e.g., in his poem "En una noche obscura") to whom Ivanov devotes one of the most moving poems of his "Roman Diary".[88] The descent of the Divine (as the Holy Ghost, beauty, grace, etc.) is likewise a mystic cliché. Significantly, this particular image is characteristic of Nietzsche, Ivanov's master: "Wenn die Macht gnädig wird und herabkommt ins Sichtbare, Schönheit heisse ich dieses Herabkommen" (*Also sprach Zarathustra*, "Von dem Erhabenen"). Images of ascent (to the sky, to the summit of a mountain, to a tower, etc.), of the upward surge of flocks of birds, smoke, architectural structures, and of the imagination dominate Nietzsche's poetry, as Gaston Bachelard has shown.[89]

Descent to the nether world is another classical cliché. It may be mentioned that Orpheus appears repeatedly in *Svet večernij*, as do other denizens and visitors of Hades and other underground caverns: Persephone, Ariadne, Heracles, Tantalus, and Sisyphus.

The heaven-earth axis, so characteristic of Ivanov's poetry, is also a most common cliché of romantic poetry, German as well as Russian.[90]

Ivanov is one of the few Russian poets who consistently and successfully cultivated the sonnet, a poetic form the structure of which is traditionally associated with a pattern of ascent : descent.[91] Even in Petrarch's sonnets (to whose spirit and form Ivanov's are close) this pattern often corresponds to a perfectly literal ascent to and/or descent from heaven.[92] The ascent : descent pattern (or descent : ascent, or variations of either pattern) certainly prevails in Ivanov's sonnets. It is observed in every single one of the sonnets of the cycle "De profundis amavi": note how the last line of each of them features a vertical image: *Ljubit' iz preispodnej byl moj dar — Svergalsja zolotom bezlikix livnej — Rassekla Smert' sekiroj bespoščadnoj — Net igl ostrej Ljubovi dikix ternij! — I molot po serdcu udarit vdrug — I žarkij lob dyxan'em tonkim studit — Za tiximi sozvezd'jami tonu — L'ju žarkix žil ostatočnuju krov'...* (pp. 102-105).

An explanation of the idiosyncrases of Ivanov's poetry in terms of poetic traditions is unsatisfactory, because Ivanov is clearly an original poet.[93] The three basic traits of his poetry (elementary imagery, ascent : descent, and direct projection of both upon the states of the soul) are so strong that they demand an intrinsic explanation even if they were induced by the influence of an existent poetic tradition.

Ivanov believed that his poetry was the vehicle of a Platonic *anamnesis*,[94] an expression of the identity of the world soul and the human soul:

> Будит звездное служенье
> В нас ответное движенье.
> Миг — и в нашей келье тесной
> Свод вращается небесный,
> Запредельные пустыни
> Веют ужасом святыни,
> Ночь браздят светил орбиты ...
> ("Свет вечерний", стр. 146)

The identity of the cosmic sky and the 'inner sky', as discovered by the poet's intuition, is therefore to be taken quite literally:

Когда б лучами, не речами
Мы говорили; вещих дум
Наитье звездными очами
С небес в неумствующий ум
Гляделось, а печаль, уныла,
Осенним ветром в поле выла,
И пела в нас любви тоска
Благоуханием цветка:
Тогда бы твой язык немотный
Уразумели мы дыша
Одною жизнию дремотной,
О, мира пленная душа!
                    ("Свет вечерний", стр. 118)

From Ivanov's point of view, then, the visual images of ascent : descent in his poetry are not so much metaphors of some psychic movement, as they are symbols of it, that is, expressions of a psychic reality. By the same token, these images are not 'illustrations' of Ivanov's metaphysical ideas, but each is a different expression of the same movements of the soul.

It is in this context that Gaston Bachelard's phenomenology of imagination can be applied to Ivanov's poetry. Bachelard treats the poetic image not so much as a symbol of a structure (like some literary critics), but would like to observe it *per se*, phenomenologically.[95] The underlying objective notion is the Jungian,[96] that certain dream images, which tend to appear in poetry also, are primary psychic phenomena, preceding sensory experience and thought: they are immediate experience, on whose basis thought can develop.[97] Hence Bachelard emphasizes that certain basic images ought to be understood in terms of their generation by the human psyche, rather than in terms of a reception of impressions from the outside world.[98]

Bachelard's conception of the generation of poetic images essentially coincides with the Plotinian *endon eidos* and with Ivanov's version of the same.[99] As Pire has pointed out, Bachelard also continues the tradition of Rimbaud ("on me pense"), the automatism of the Surrealists, and similar notions, all based on the supposition that cosmic rhythms are dormant in the human subconscious.[100] The distinction which Bachelard makes between imaginative powers (*forces imaginantes*) nurtured by the novelty of experience, and imaginative power generated by the inner depths of the human soul, is more specifically relevant to Ivanov and his poetry.[101] If this is a true distinction, Ivanov's imagination is a very pure example of the latter type. His imagery is dreamlike, vague, and to an extent rarely met in other poets, elementary. The substance of Ivanov's imagination persistently assumes the elementary form of air, water, earth, and fire, rather than the form of well-defined and structured objects of pragmatic experience.

Bachelard has pointed out how one or the other element dominates in the imagination of certain poets. Nietzsche is of course the aerial poet *par excellence*.[102] Despite his dependance on Nietzsche, Ivanov does not share this quality with him, the 'inner sea' is as prominent in his imagination as the 'inner sky'. The earth and the depths of the nether world are as important for him as are the heavenly bodies. Ivanov's *imagination matérielle* is rather evenly balanced.

Another distinction made by Bachelard is even more relevant to Ivanov's imagination: *imagination matérielle : imagination dynamique*.[103] To put it concretely, Nietzsche is a *poète aérien* in the context of *l'imagination matérielle*; he is a *poète vertical* in the context of *l'imagination dynamique*. (Similarly, Jung's archetypes are not only images but also foci of energy). Ivanov also makes such distinction, as he sees myth as the 'dynamic mode' of symbol.[104] In the context of *imagination dynamique*, again, the experience of movement (such as airborne ascent) is seen as primary, and its metaphysical, religious, moral, or simply pictorial equivalents as secondary. Thus, Nietzsche, *poète ascensionnel*, precedes Nietzsche, *moraliste du surhumain*.[105] In fact, Bachelard goes as far as to claim that every statement of value is a verticalization to begin with.[106]

It would seem that the dynamic component of Ivanov's imagination is, like Nietzsche's, vertical. The movement characteristic of his imagery is not that of the march, or of the dance, of floating on the gentle waves of a quiet sea, or even in the gentle breeze of the ether. In Ivanov's poetry, the movement is vertical, and almost always it also stands for a movement of the moral substance of the soul.

Ivanov, it would seem, was a greater lyric poet than playwright, philosopher, or prophet. The poetry of *Svet večernij* rings true, and probably will, so long as the language in which it was written will live. Meanwhile most of Ivanov's dramatic, theoretical, and polemic works lack this ring of truth. Yet they all say essentially the same thing. It is, then, not too farfetched to assume that Ivanov's Neoplatonic philosophy is a projection upon an intellectual plane, of movements of the soul more directly and forcefully expressed in his poetry. 'Ascent' and 'descent' are, then, true aesthetic categories, highly relevant to a description of the deep structure of his poetry, rather than mere poetic 'themes' or 'motifs', or even 'metaphors'.

Brown University

NOTES

1   Benedetto Croce, *Aesthetic as Science of Expression and General Linguistic* (New York, 1966), 87.

2   Croce, 259-60.

3   Ivanov assumes that art fluctuates between static and dynamic manifestations of its energy. See V. Ivanov, "Predčuvstvija i predvestija: novaja organičeskaja èpoxa i teatr buduščego", *Po zvezdam* (St. Petersburg, 1909), 189-219. Yet the same terms are also used by the Russian Formalists.

4   This has been done, with considerable success, by Carin Tschöpl, *Vjačeslav Ivanov: Dichtung und Dichtungstheorie* (Munich, 1968).

5   See C. M. Bowra's introduction to *Svet večernij*, xv.

6   Bowra, xix.

7   V. Ivanov, "Sporady", *Po zvezdam*, 344.

8   The Plotinian *dynamis*, Goethe's *Kraft*. Ivanov speaks of "energy whose name is Art". See "Predčuvstvija", 199-200.

9   See, for instance, V. Ivanov, "Drevnij užas", *Po zvezdam*, 394.

10   See, for instance, "Poèzija", *Svet večernij*, 3, or "Pamjati Skrjabina", *ibid.*, 92-3.

11   V. Ivanov, "Dve stixii simvolizma", *Po zvezdam*, 284.

12   For a discussion of Ivanov's interpretation of 'realism', see James West, *Russian Symbolism: A Study of Vyacheslav Ivanov and the Russian Symbolist Aesthetic* (London, 1970), 153-80.

13   See, for instance, Vjačeslav Ivanov, "Granicy iskusstva", *Borozdy i meži* (Moscow, 1916), 220-21.

14   V. Ivanov, "Dve stixii", 250.

15   *Ibid.*, 254-55.

16   Vjačeslav Ivanov, "Mysli o simvolizme", *Borozdy i meži*, 158.

17   Vjačeslav Ivanov, "Granicy iskusstva", 210.

18   "Est' Mlečnyj Put' v duše i v nebesax; / Est' množestvo v obeix six vselennyx: / Odin glagol dvux knig zapečatlennyx" (*Cor ardens*, I, 61). Cf. Tschöpl, 104.

19   Vjačeslav Ivanov, "Granicy iskusstva", 211.

20   See Aleksis Rannit, "Vyacheslav Ivanov and his *Vespertine Light:* Notes from my Critical Diary of 1966", *Russian Literature Triquarterly*, 4 (1972), 268.

21   V. Ivanov, "Sporady", 351.

22   A philosophy of art, moreover, which had been current in Russia for a long time. See Victor Terras, *Belinskij and Russian Literary Criticism: The Heritage of Organic Aesthetics* (Madison, 1974).

23   V. Ivanov, "Sporady", 345-46.

24   *Znaet Boga serdce veščem gladom / Za stolami polnoty* ("Bogopoznanie", *Svet večernij*, 78).

25   *Brat' i davat'* — *v obmene ètix dvux ènergij sostoit žizn'. V duxovnoj žizni i dejatel'nosti im sootvestvujut* — *vosxoždenie i nisxoždenie* ("Granicy iskusstva", 197).

26   V. Ivanov, "Simvolika èstetičeskix načal", *Po zvezdam*, 29.

27   *Ibid.*, 29-30.

28   V. Ivanov, "O russkoj idee", *Po zvezdam*, 329-30.

29   *Ibid.*

30   *Ibid.*, 332-34.

31   *Ibid.*

32   V. Ivanov, "Granicy iskusstva", 210.

33   Cf. Tschöpl, 177.

34   V. Ivanov, "Granicy iskusstva", 208.

35   Tschöpl, 172.

36   Vjačeslav Ivanov, *Borozdy i meži*, 194, 218.

37   *Ibid.*, 163.

38 See Armin Hetzer, *Vjačeslav Ivanovs Tragödie "Tantal": Eine literarhistorische Interpretation* (Munich, 1972), 141-83.

39 V. Ivanov, *Prometej: Tragedija* (St. Petersburg, 1919), xxiv.

40 Cf. Ivanov's above mentioned remarks on the 'ideal' nature of lyric poetry.

41 *Neizmerimaja propast' otdeljaet ego ot poètov linij i krasok* [...] *Ix poèzija — èto ozero, otražajuščee v sebe nebo, poèzija Vjačeslava Ivanova — nebo, otražennoe v ozere. Ix geroi, ix pejzaži — čem žiznennee, tem vyše; soveršenstvo obrazov Vjačeslava Ivanova zavisit ot ix prizračnosti* (Nikolaj Gumilev, review of *Cor ardens, Sobranie sočinenij*, 4 vols. (Washington, D.C., 1964-1968, IV, 266).

42 Cf. Tschöpl, 134. Some examples from *Svet večernij*: "Garmonija sfer" (4-5), "Lira i os'" (16-18), "Rimskij dnevnik", January, No. 11 (118), and November, No. 2 (164-165).

43 (I am listing page and lines in *Svet večernij*:) 7: 1ff., 8: 1ff., 12: 1, 24: 1 ff., 33: 18-20, 92: 12-18, 94: 1-6, 96: 3-4, 102: 27-28, 104: 21-25, 105: 15-16, 106: 19-20, 109: 19-28, 110: 23-28, 120: 13-16, 132: 11-12, 147: 17-25, 153: 13-14, 154: 25-26, 155: 5-12, 158: 8-9, 162: 27-30, 163: 1-4.

44 3: 10, 3: 21-28, 13: 23, 33: 30ff., 37: 7-8, 38: 32, 59: 19-21, 59: 23-31, 65: 3-8, 78: 25, 79: 26-33, 81: 8-13, 81: 21-30, 85: 8, 86: 4, 89: 5, 92: 1, 105) 14, 140: 3, 145: 18ff., 149: 8ff., 151: 13ff., 162: 25.

45 6: 25, 14: 19-21, 16: 7-21, 18: 9-14, 24: 11-13, 32: 15-16, 43: 5-6, 59: 14, 61: 5, 69: 23, 89: 4, 97: 2, 100: 8, 105: 15-16, 110: 15-16, 122: 26-29, 142: 2ff., 149: 5, 155: 27-28, 166: 7-9.

46 17: 31-33, 26: 13-14, 96: 4, 98: 15, 99: 1, 101: 9, 103: 15-16, 148: 11-12, 151: 13-14, 161:13, 169: 26, 174: 2.

47 3: 19, 5: 10ff., 13: 29ff., 25: 18, 29: 5ff., 29: 21ff., 30: 13ff., 69: 14-15, 93: 25, 99: 13-14, 102: 27-28, 162: 1, 162: 28ff., 166: 7-11, 166: 16-19.

48 3: 12-13, 4: 24ff., 11: 6-7, 15: 1ff., 16:29ff., 17: 30-31, 81: 1ff., 95: 21-22, 115: 9, 122: 21, 128: 3-4, 130: 10-12, 140: 3-4, 142: 5-10.

49 4: 5, 25: 20, 27: 1ff., 43: 2, 44: 1ff., 84: 1ff., 95: 13ff., 98: 4, 117: 1, 119: 20, 123: 27-28, 128: 6, 141: 24-27.

50 *nedra*: 4:13-15, 6: 26-27, 61: 10, 79: 1, 89: 30, 100: 8, 119: 11-12 (*tajnik rodimyj*), 123: 5 (*zapovednyx tajnikov*), 142: 7, 149: 4; *glub', glubina, bezdna*: 3: 24, 52: 32, 78: 1, 92: 17, 95: 16, 106: 1, 149: 2, 160: 3, 164: 20; *preispodnja, ad, čistilišče*: 13: 9ff., 71: 9ff., 77: 27ff., 79: 3ff., 96: 17, 102: 14, 105: 20, 123: 20, 133: 9-12, 138: 2, 140: 19-20, 165: 38; *omut, bezdna morskaja*: 123: 6-7, 171: 19-20; *Lethe*: 6: 26-33, 130-132 ("Lethaea"), 155: 12.

51 *grob, mogila, rov, sarkofag*: 12: 10, 24: 9, 38: 13ff., 39: 7ff., 40: 11, 42: 17, 44: 2, 62: 6, 64: 20, 66: 12, 73: 5, 85: 1ff., 92: 7ff., 97: 8, 101: 27-28, 114: 14, 116: 29-30, 129: 5-8, 140: 32, 148: 6, 148P 21-22, 150: 10, 152: 22, 161: 19, 163: 14-16, 167: 21, 168: 17, 168: 38; *peščera, vertep, berloga*: 61: 15, 81: 18ff., 83: 5ff., 100: 15-17, 104: 16; *labirint*: 14-16, 71: 23, 89: 2.

52 3: 18ff., 4: 8ff., 17: 21, 24: 1ff., 25: 15ff., 29: 11-12, 33: 17ff., 41: 1ff., 72: 22ff., 84: 1ff., 95: 11ff., 122: 22, 138: 4, 139: 1ff., 140: 21-28, 155: 27-28, 162: 27ff., 171: 6.

53 "Roman Sonnets", 106-10.

54 38: 24-25, 42: 14ff., 50: 7-8, 54: 15-21, 60: 26ff., 113: 7, 128: 12, 140: 1-2.

55 Tschöpl, 110. Examples: 10: 3ff., 22: 1-4, 23: 1-8, 23: 9ff., 25: 1ff., 29: 5-16, 90: 1-14, 117: 15-23, 139: 1-12, 143: 17-27, 151: 8-9, 154: 18-22, 171: 15-18.

56 4: 18-19, 14: 16-17, 40: 3, 65: 21ff., 68: 9-12, 77: 10, 92: 28-30, 95: 22, 97: 10, 98: 14, 99: 28, 100: 23-27, 106: 19-38, 139: 24, 151: 18ff., 152: 27-29, 161: 18, 173: 6.

57 5:4, 5: 16, 28: 23-29, 46: 19-20, 94: 19, 107: 14, 115: 5-16, 171: 7ff.

58 3:10, 3:27-29, 11: 10-13, 15: 6-7, 17: 29-31, 26:24-27, 37: 8-9, 59: 5, 65: 5-9, 80: 13-16, 91: 7-31, 104: 15-28, 115: 11-12, 118: 9-12, 128: 8, 139: 1-16, 146: 3-14, 154: 25-26.

59 71: 9ff., 77: 27ff., 96: 17, 102: 14, 106: 1, 160: 3.

60 3:16-17, 3: 19ff., 8: 7-12, 9: 6-7, 10: 1ff., 37: 1ff., 62: 1-7, 89: 17-18, 90: 1-2, 91: 23ff., 92: 27-28, 139: 10-12, 142: 13-14, 143: 16ff., 146: 2, 148: 22-26, 154: 18-22, 171: 15-20.

61 37: 1ff., 89: 19-20, 98: 9-10, 122: 1-12, 125: 16-19.

62 61: 5-6, 122: 26-29.

[63] *sleep, dream:* 4: 16ff., 13: 21ff., 25: 28ff., 31: 1-8, 45: 18ff., 40: 6ff., 47: 26ff., 59: 12ff., 66: 24ff., 89: 16ff., 106: 21, 113: 10, 114: 9ff., 117: 4-6, 125: 15ff., 127: 21-24, 148: 22ff., 161: 12, 166: 23, 167: 30ff., 169: 6-8; "Life is a dream": 60: 6ff., 101: 15-28, 102: 1-14, 102: 23-28, 144: 25ff., 171: 21-22.
[64] *flight, aerial view:* 26: 17ff., 37: 1ff., 62: 1ff., 66: 24ff., 71: 5-6, 77: 1ff., 94: 7ff., 96: 1-14, 126: 21-24, 132: 5-12, 132: 19-20, 141: 16ff., 159: 16-17; *soaring (ether):* 31: 18ff., 94: 1-3, 101: 9-11, 118: 1ff., 123: 25-26, 145: 4-5, 168: 3-5; *floating (waves):* 25: 7-8, 89: 19-20, 90: 23ff., 122: 1ff., 125: 17-18, 143: 17, 154: 18-22.
[65] 21: 23, 38: 15ff., 45: 25ff., 52: 34, 92: 16-18, 103: 22-23, 106: 18-20, 117: 7-8, 119: 20-22, 156: 24ff., 157: 22-24, 161: 8 (6 of these were counted as 'dominants').
[66] 5: 3-4, 59: 12ff., 115: 2-4, 115: 844., 149: 8ff., 153: 13-20, 162: 23-26, 166: 7-11, 169: 21-22 (9 'dominants').
[67] 9: 11ff., 51: 21ff., 128: 27ff. (3 'dominants').
[68] 21: 19-21, 150: 16ff., 152: 9ff., 156: 14, 167: 13ff. (1 'dominant').
[69] *Stolp, bašnja:* 94: 20, 97: 14, 104: 7, 105: 11, 108: 7-8; *šater, šalaš:* 11: 22ff., 30: 8-11, 33: 7, 68: 10, 79: 33, 81: 5, 105: 2, 128: 7, 130: 6, 162: 11; *trees:* 3: 2-3, 21: 1ff., 21: 30-31, 22: 26-27, 27-32 ("Serebrjanyj bor"), 53-56 ("Derev'ja"), 60: 7-8, 61: 24, 67: 17ff., 84: 1ff., 106: 22, 116: 3, 117: 15, 124: 18, 142: 15ff., 149: 4, 150: 25, 165-166 ("Kiparisy"), 167: 23-24, 169: 9ff.; *the Cross:* 92: 8, 128: 26, 139: 17ff., 152: 9, 153: 3, 156: 26-27, 170: 23 (5 'dominants').
[70] 59: 4ff., 63: 10ff., 64: 1ff., 64: 19ff., 77: 20ff., 82: 1ff., 83: 29-33, 85-86, 91: 7ff., 92: 1-6, 100: 27-28, 106: 1-9, 123: 1ff., 139: 1-16, 154: 23ff., 172: 9ff.
[71] 38: 24-25, 54: 13-20, 61: 2-6, 113: 7ff. (4 'dominants').
[72] 5: 9ff., 24: 1ff., 22: 25ff., 33: 14-15, 34: 1ff., 38: 26ff., 110: 15ff., 117: 1-14, 118: 9-20, 122: 13ff., 147: 17-25, 151: 13-16, 158: 21ff., 161: 13ff. (14 'dominants'). In five of the 'fountain poems' (107-10) the image of descending water appears to be the 'dominant'.
[73] 3: 18ff., 3: 7ff., 11: 5ff., 11: 22ff., 13: 23ff., 27: 14-18, 37: 26ff., 5-: 5-8, 59: 21ff., 69: 4ff., 81: 1ff., 98: 28, 124: 5ff., 128: 1-4, 160: 6 (15 'dominants').
[74] 40: 6ff., 41: 5ff., 41: 14ff., 42: 1ff., 45: 6ff., 70: 7ff., 126: 9ff., 134: 19-28, 136: 6-7, 139: 27-28, 140: 7-8, 168: 22-23, 170: 27-29 (13 'dominants').
[75] 7: 8ff., 7: 26ff., 26: 4-6, 102: 27-28, 121: 9-16, 130: 11-22, 140: 21-24, 148: 6-9, 158: 1ff., (9 'dominants'); *descent ad inferos:* 13: 17-20, 13: 24-25, 130: 20-23, 131: 9-12, 131: 21ff., 138: 20-21, 163: 13-16 (7 'dominants').
[76] 72: 1ff., 72: 20ff., 119: 11-12, 160: 3-4, 162: 7-8.
[77] 100: 5ff., 145: 18ff., 146: 15ff., 148: 23ff., 164: 17ff. (5 'dominants').
[78] 99: 5-14, 103: 1-14, 114: 9-17 (3 'dominants').
[79] 6: 9ff., 14-16, 21: 24ff., 60: 6ff., 119: 23ff., 150: 10-11 (6 'dominants').
[80] 25: 14ff., 33: 16ff., 42: 14ff., 81: 18ff., 95: 11ff., 129: 21ff., 138: 1-6, 142: 1-14, 155: 27-30, 162: 27ff., 170: 24ff. (11 'dominants').
[81] 22: 17ff., 41: 5ff., 45: 18ff., 59: 21ff., 79: 1ff., 89: 1ff., 90: 1ff., 92: 7ff., 97: 1-14, 97: 15-28, 101: 15-28, 102: 1-14, 103: 15-38, 104: 15-28, 105: 1-14, 105: 15-28, 118: 21ff., 121: 9-16, 126: 1-4, 144: 21-24, 154: 5ff., 156: 5ff., 157: 13ff. (24 'dominants').
[82] 16-18 ("Lira i os'"), 21: 1ff., 67: 17ff., 79: 25ff., 84: 1ff., 95: 1-10, 142: 15ff., 148: 14ff., 160: 17ff., 165: 7ff., 171: 7ff.
[83] See E. R. Curtius, *Europäische Literatur und lateinisches Mittelalter* (Bern, 1948), 136-38 ("Schiffahrtsmetaphern") and 46-47, 118, 121, 128, 181, 197, 362-363 ("Himmelsreise").
[84] Novalis, in particular, has many striking examples, e.g., "Tiefgerührt von heilger Güte / Und versenkt in selges Schauen / Steht der Himmel im Gemüte, / Wolkenloses Blau", (Novalis, *Werke und Briefe* [Munich, 1962], 297); "Eine göttlich tiefe Trauer / Wohnt in unser aller Herzen, / Löst uns auf in eine Flut. / Und in dieser Flut ergiessen / Wir uns auf geheime Weise / In den Ozean des Lebens / Tief in Gott hinein" (*ibid.,* 299).
[85] It appears in German romantic poetry as well, e.g., "Labyrinth der Brust" in Goethe's "An den Mond".
[86] *Svet večernij,* 162.

[87] See F. I. Tjutčev, *Lirika*, 2 vols. (Moscow, 1965), I, 9, 46, 216 (music of the spheres), 16, 63 (sky and earth), 17, 26, 46, 66 ('inner sky'), 29, 51, 137, 195 ('inner sea'), 57, 118 ('inner chaos').

[88] "Todo nada" (*Svet večernij*, 156-57). It is quite likely that the Socratic *katabasis* of the soul into Hades as a step to its *epanodos* from the day that is night to the true day (in Plato's *Republic*) is one of the sources of Ivanov's *ascent : descent* imagery. On this and other Platonic traits in Symbolism, see Miroslav John Hanak, *Maeterlinck's Symbolic Drama: A Leap into Transcendence* (Louvain, 1974), 45-55.

[89] Gaston Bachelard, *L'Air et les Songes* (Paris, 1943), passim.

[90] Joseph von Eichendorff's famous "Es war als hätt' der Himmel die Erde still geküßt" appears in many variations in Tjutčev, Xomjakov, Foeth, Majkov, a.o.

[91] See Johannes R. Becher, *Das poetische Prinzip. Mit einem Anhang: Philosophie des Sonetts oder kleine Sonettlehre und "Ein wenig über vier Seiten"* (Berlin, 1957), 420-21. His terms are "Gefälle" and "Aufstieg".

[92] Some typical ascent poems: "Levommi il mio pensèr in parte ov'era", "Quel sol che mi mostrava il camin destro", or "I'pensava assai destro esser su l'ale".

[93] Cf. Gumilev's assessment of Ivanov, quoted note 41 above.

[94] Cf. Heinrich Stammler, "Vjačeslav Ivanov's Image of Man", *WSJ*, XIV (1967/68), 139.

[95] See François Pire, *De l'imagination poétique dans l'œuvre de Gaston Bachelard (Paris, 1967), 30*.

[96] See Pire, 49. Bachelard himself quotes Jung often.

[97] In other words, Bachelard assigns to *le signifiant* a full existence quite independent of *le signifié*. So then: "Le rêve avant la réalité — le cauchemar avant le drame — le terreur avant le monstre —la nausée avant la chute" (*L'Air et les Songes*, 119).

[98] Cf. Pire, 115.

[99] Plotinus's concept of creation 'from inside' (*endon eidos*) corresponds to Bachelard's concept of the imagination. Cf. the chapter "Innere Form" in Franz Koch, *Goethe und Plotin* (Leipzig, 1925), 128-83.

[100] Pire, 126-27.

[101] Gaston Bachelard, *L'Eau et les Rêves: Essai sur l'imagination de la matière (Paris, 1943), 1*.

[102] Bachelard points out Nietzsche's criticism of Wagner's music: rather than inviting man to march or to dance, it invites him to just float along on its waves. To the aerial poet Nietzsche, aerial music is infinitely superior to water music (*L'Air et les Songes*, p. 152).

[103] See Pire, 96.

[104] Vjačeslav Ivanov, "Zavety simvolizma", *Borozdy i meži*, 129.

[105] Pire, 105.

[106] Gaston Bachelard, *L'Air et les Songes*, 18.

COMMENTS

(de Mallac) Professor Terras' **explication** of Ivanov's aesthetic categories in terms of their Plotinian, Goethean, Novalisian and other resonances is a fascinating one indeed.

Especially in view of the fact that the majority of Slavic scholars have failed so far to acquaint themselves with Bachelard's theory of the poetic imagination, it is particularly fortunate for us to have the extremely thoughtful analysis by Mr. Terras of Ivanov's categories in terms of Bachelard's theory.

I would be grateful to Mr. Terras for commenting on the following points:

(a) the extent of the inspiration which Ivanov may have derived from Baudelaire (whether or not this is explicitly acknowledged by him); and

(b) the extent to which, specifically, the poem "Elévation" in *Les Fleurs du mal* could have had a direct bearing upon Ivanov's conception of the categories of **ascent** and **descent**.

(Winner) I would like to express a disagreement with the historical-methodological remarks with which you open your written paper. You speak of the concepts of 18th century aesthetics: regularity, symmetry, proportion, and order as being at the core of modern structuralist poetics. I think it is very important to note, and I am sure that this was intended by you, though not expressed, that structural poetics sees the essence of poetic creation not only in the elements of regularity and symmetry, but also in their opposite. Structural poetics is concerned with both symmetry *and* non- or anti-symmetry, with norm and anti-norm, and the tension between them.

Additional discussion: Green, Hrushovsky, Markov, Segal

AUTHOR'S REPLY

I am very grateful to Professor de Mallac for pointing out a parallel of which I was not aware. It can be taken for granted that Ivanov was familiar with Baudelaire's "Elévation" in *Les Fleurs du mal*. But it is not very likely that this poem triggered Ivanov's poetic and theoretical preoccupation with ascent and descent. If there was any such direct and identifiable stimulus, it must have been Plato (in his *Phaedrus*, for example). I believe that the ascent/descent of the soul is a human universal, whose poetic expression may occur spontaneously, but in many cases will be triggered or enhanced by earlier examples. My essay is concerned with Ivanov's creative *Gestalt*, rather than with an investigation of diachronic connections between his opus and that of earlier poets and thinkers. Hence my allusions to descent/ascent in some other poets, quite sketchy, to say the least, merely serve the purpose of suggesting that we are dealing here with a very widespread phenomenon. Professor de Mallac's remark strengthens this contention.

I fully agree with Professor Winner's remark. The matter which he touches upon is obviously merely a part of my preamble and has no bearing on the substance of my paper. Hence I believe I can allow my paragraph to stand as is. My readers will surely read this paragraph the way Professor Winner did.

МЛАДОЙ ПЕВЕЦ И БЫСТРОТЕЧНОЕ ВРЕМЯ
(К ИСТОРИИ ОДНОГО ОБРАЗА
В РУССКОЙ ПОЭЗИИ ПЕРВОЙ ТРЕТИ XIX ВЕКА)

В. Н. ТОПОРОВ

Речь идет об одном образе русской поэзии, утвердившемся в ней в начале XIX в., быстро ставшем ходячим и разошедшемся позже и по частям на штампы из репертуара позднеромантической традиции, как она представлена у эпигонов и ниже — в массовой традиции альбомов провинциальных барышень. Тем не менее, и в начале XX в. известны случаи, когда этот образ освобождался от клише и тем самым от автоматизма восприятия, оживлялся и актуализировался; правда, всегда это достигалось за счет создания такого контекста, в котором этот образ становился в отношение реминисценции к образу-источнику.

Разбираемый здесь образ представляет собой микросюжет, который выражается в двух формах — ипостасной (условно — 'младой певец') и концептуально-философической (условно — 'быстротечность времени'). Обе эти формы соотнесены друг с другом и в значительной степени изоморфны, но первая из них специфичнее, индивидуализированнее и в силу этого более открыта внетекстовым влияниям; именно через нее и осуществлялась прежде всего связь образа с внеположенной реальностью, происходило перераспределение содержания между тем и другим и вырабатывался текст того порядка сложности, когда он становится самодовлеющим (т.е. когда он не может уже рассматриваться т о л ь к о как образ внеположенного и, наоборот, приобретает силу вызывать изменения во внеположенном). Различия между названными двумя формами таковы, что они могут соединяться друг с другом в одном и том же поэтическом тексте, не создавая тавтологии; обычно распределение функций таково: 'младой певец' — сюжетная конструкция, 'быстротечность времени' — ее идея, смысл, интерпретация, внутренняя форма.

Обращение к этому образу (поневоле краткое и суммарное; излагаемой ниже — не более, чем с х е м а с заполнением ряда ее блоков лишь ч а с т ь ю имеющегося в распоряжении автора материала) объясняется в первую очередь тем, что на его примере особенно рельефно можно показать, как в рамках русской поэзии осуществлялся переход от

подражания, учения, игры, 'искусства' (*И здесь кончается искусство
…*) к созданию текстов исключительной сложности (в указанном выше
смысле), синтезирующих свое и чужое, личное и сверхличное, текстовое
и внетекстовое, и далее — к 'почве' и 'судьбе' (*И дышит почва и судьба
…*).

Место и время создания этого образа — поэзия Жуковского 1802-1811
гг. (с дальнейшими уточнениями, вариациями, повторениями), прежде
всего "Сельское кладбище", "Вечер", "Певец". Источниками образа для
Жуковского, его предшественников и последователей, если говорить в
общих чертах, послужили многочисленные и довольно однообразные
обращения к теме в р е м е н и в русской поэзии 70-90-х годов XVIII в. (с
некоторыми исключениями); мотивы о с е н и и к л а д б и щ а постоянные
в 90-1800-х годах; поэтические тексты з а п а д н о е в р о п е й с к о й литературы, разрабатывающие те же темы и известные в России непосредственно или в переводах (французская и особенно английская
поэзия XVIII в.-самого начала XIX в.); некоторые события в н е л и т е-
р а т у р н о г о ряда, пересекшиеся с поэтическим рядом. Каждый из этих
источников требует разъяснений, которые здесь по необходимости
минимальны. Только при знании фона и учете его изменений можно
оценить структурные составляющие разбираемого образа. Тема в р е-
м е н и в русской поэзии XVIII в. ориентирована на подчеркивание мотивов *премены,* регулярности и извечной закономерности временных
циклов, б ы с т р о т е ч н о с т и времени. Отсюда — тема всевластия, мо-
гущества времени, нередко соединенная с удивлением перед этим его
свойством. Философско-экклезиастическая позиция приводит к идее
с у е т н о с т и всего, что помещено во времени (напр., жизни), горацианско-
эпикурейская позиция, напротив, подчеркивает комфортность, п р и я т-
н о с т ь жизни, поскольку последовательность временны́х циклов с неиз-
бежностью предполагает приятные периоды и состояния (юность,
любовь, дружба и т.п.). Первая позиция оказалась более богатой продолжениями: *премена,* изменчивость, непостоянство жизни и ее носи-
теля человека как результат обусловленности их свойствами времени
породили семантические цепи, образовавшие целый комплекс, который
и можно считать итогом 'разыгрывания' темы времени в русской поэзии
XVIII в.:

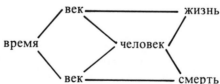

Помня, что "Всякое стихотворение — покрывало, растянутое на остриях нескольких слов. Эти слова светятся, как звезды. Из-за них существует стихотворение" (Блок, *Записные книжки*, 84) и в целях экономии, уместно привести ряд наиболее показательных контекстов XVIII в. о времени с подчеркиванием тех элементов, которые (содержательно и/или формально) имели продолжение в образе времени, оформившемся в начале XIX в. Ср.: *Так малая премена,* | *... Хоть мучит и немало,* | *Будь терпеливый.* || *Что в мире постоянно?* | *... Не всё ли есть превратно?* | *Кой цвет не вянет?* | *Весну сжигает лето,* | *Осень то пременяет;* | *... Зима...* || *В счастьи много несчастья* || *... То стоит, то восходит,* | *Сие тут пребывает;* | *Глядишь, другое сходит,* | *Иное пропадает* | *В ничто глубоко!* || *Словом, нет и не будет* | *Ничего, кроме Бога* | *... Что б было вечно* || *... Сего должно едина* | *Повиноваться воли:* | *... Примем сердечно* || *Что б от него не было;* || *... В тебе мне есть всё благо* ... (Тредиаковский, "Ода о непостоянстве мира", 1730; ср. также изд. 1752 г. и франц. вариант — "Та же самая ода по-французски", 1730);

— *Почто печалится в несчастьи человек?* | *Когда веселый век, как сладкий сон, протек,* | *Пройдет печаль, и дни веселы возвратятся.* || *Жизнь человеческу цветку уподобляй,* | *Который возрастет весной и расцветет;* | *Но воздух к осени как станет холодняй,* | *Валится, вянет лист, иссохши пропадает.* || *И лето жаркое весне вослед идет,* | *Как придет осень, тут зима год совершает,* — | *Жизнь человеческа подобно так течет:* | *Родится он, взрастет, стареет, умирает.* || *И счастие судьба пременно наш дала;* | *Как свет пременен сей, и наша жизнь пременна ...* || *Премены ждав бедам, в несчастье веселись,* | *С часами протечет напасть и время грозно.* | *Умерен в счастье будь, премены берегись,* | *Раскаянье в делах уже прошедших поздно* (Ржевский, "Станс", 1760); *Прошли драгие дни ...* | *Минувшие часы я стану вображать...* ("Элегия", 1760); *Судьба всё превращает,* | *Течет в пременах свет,* | *То здеся погибает,* | *Другое там растет.* || *... Сперва весну встречаем,* | *Там лето вслед течет,* | *Там осень ожидаем,* | *Зима год пресечет.* || *... Настав, прейдет ненастье,* | *Наступит свет опять ...* || *Всё с временем согласно,* | *Себе премены ждет ...* ("Стансы" 1, 1761);

— *... "Всего дороже время"* | *... Напрасно ищешь ты без времени затей ...* | *Потребно ко всему и время и труды* | *...И все во всем от времени плоды.* | *От времени забава,* | *От времени и слава ...* | *И благо всякое, какое только есть ...* (Сумароков, "Время", впервые —

1781); *Время проходит,* | *Время летит* ... | *Счастье, забава,* | *Светлось корон,* | *Пышность и слава,* | *Всё только сон* ... ("Часы", 1759); *Во всем на свете сем премена* | *И всё непостоянно в нем,* | *И все составлено из тлена:* | *Не зрим мы твердости ни в чем;* | *Пременой естество играет* ... || *Почтем мы жизнь и смерть мечтою;* | *Что мы ни делаем, то сон* ... || *От смерти убежать не можно,* | *Умрети смертным неотложно,* | *И свет покинуть навсегда.* | *На свете жизни нет миляе,* | *И нет на свете смерти зляе;* | *Но смерть последняя беда* ("Ода к М. М. Хераськову", 1763);

— *Всё на свете сем превратно,* | *Всё на свете суета;* | *Исчезает невозвратно* ... | *И минется, яко сон.* || *Всякой вещи в Свете время* ... || *Ах! о время дней кратчайших* ... | *Сколь ты скоро протечешь,* | *И что в жизни нам приятно,* | *Ты с собою невозвратно* | *Всё во вечность увлечешь* ... (Майков, "Ода о суете мира", 1775); *Как в бурный океан втекают быстры воды* | *И исчезают в нем,* | *Сему подобяся, летят во вечность годы,* | *Стремяся день за днем.* | *В природе всё, что есть рождается и вянет:* | *Минул прошедший год и боле не настанет,* | *Настал теперь другой, но сей, как тот, минет* ... | *А прочее их всё по смерти их минет,* | *И всё во вечности безвестно пропадет* ... ("Стихи на 1777 год");

— *Зияет время славу стерть:* | *Как в море льются быстры воды,* | *Так в вечность льются дни и годы;* | *Глотает царства алчна смерть.* || ... *Приемлем с жизнью смерть свою,* | *На то, чтоб умереть, родимся.* || ... *Куда, Мещерской! ты сокрылся?* | ... *Где ж он?* — *Он там.* — *Где там?* — *Не знаем* ... || ... *Сегодня Бог, а завтра прах;* | ... *А завтра: где ты человек?* | *Едва часы протечь успели,* | *Хаоса в бездну улетели.* | *И весь, как сон, прошел твой век* || ... *Вы все пременны здесь и ложны:* — | *Я в дверях вечности стою* ... || ... *Почто ж терзаться и скорбеть,* | *Что смертный друг твой жил не вечно?* | *Жизнь есть небес мгновенный дар;* | *Устрой ее себе к покою* ... (Державин, "На смерть кн. Мещерского", 1779); *Река времен в своем стремленьи* | *Уносит все дела людей* | *И топит в пропасти забвенья* | *Народы, царства и царей.* | ... *То вечности жерлом пожрется* | *И общей не уйдет судьбы!* (1816);

— *Всё подвластно перемене, что на свете сем ни есть:* | ... *И на что мы ни взираем,* | *Перемену примечаем.* | *Всё, что есть,* — *всё исчезает безвозвратно навсегда.* | ... *Всё, что есть, одно другому должно место уступать,* | *И без сей премены миру часу бы нельзя стоять* (Хемницер, "О перемене"); *Такого состоянья нет,* | *Где б суета не пребывало* ... | *Всё за собой ее влечет,* | *Она в сем свете*

управляет, | *Одна рождает, созидает,* | *Она одна сей движет свет.*
("Стансы на суету");

— *О смерть! предел неизбежимый!* || *... Тебя повсюду мы сретаем,* | *Тебя нигде мы не уйдем!* | *Всем вестна ты; но мы не знаем,* | *Когда, и как, и где умрем ...* || *Сей сон — мгновенна скоротечность,* | *Пред вечностию — жизнь ничто.* | *Смерть нас предводит в бесконечность,* | *От ней не скроется никто.* (Княжнин, "Стансы на смерть", 1790 /?/);

— *"Не льстись ничем ты вечным в свете"* — *Твердит тебе то год, и час,* | *И миг, что в молненном полете* | *Крыло времен несет от нас.* || *... Кто весть, угодно ли судьбине* | *Прибавить к нашей жизни миг?* (Капнист, "Суетность жизни", 1801-1805); *Неприметно утекают* | *Воскрыленные года* | *... И прогнать не могут мимо* | *Смерти ввек неумолимой.* || *... Все мы так, как тень, пройдем ...* ("Время", 1791);

— *На быстрых времени крылах* | *Часы, дни, годы улетают;* | *Едва родятся — исчезают,* | *Теряясь вечности в волнах.* || *... Что жизнь? — Мгновенье, слаба тень.* | *Едва родимся — умираем ...* (Клушин, "Всё пройдет", 1793);

— *Дни счастливы миновались,* | *Дни приятные мечты* || *... Дней прошедших вспоминанье ...* || *Всё в природе сохранилось,* | *Нет премены никакой ...* (Нелединский-Мелецкий, 1796); *Вспоминанье прежних дней ...* ("Мысль, мучительна и слезна");

— *Летит, мой друг, крылатый век,* | *В бездонну вечность всё валится,* | *Уж день сей, час и миг протек,* | *И вспять ничто не возвратится ...* || *Где ныне сладостны часы ...* (Радищев, "Ода к другу моему", 1, впервые — 1807);

— *Природа нам напоминает,* | *Что быстро время угрожает,* | *В ничтожество всё обратить,* | *Что всё исчезнет, прекратится ...* || *Приятны летни дни проходят,* | *И за собой они выводят* | *Угрюмости осенних туч ...* (Тучков, "Ода на человеческую жизнь", 1789); *Но скучно время се приходит,* | *И вечер жизни настает!* || *... Дни все минутся,* | *Как сонны мечты,* | *Смертью прервутся* | *Все суеты* ("Ода суетности", 1817) и т.д., включая сюда и сходные образы из переводных стихотворений: Увы! проходит век крылатый (Поповский, *Из Горация,* Кн. II, ода XIV) или переводы Пниным (1798) и Н. Радищевым (1804) оды А.-Л. Тома́, "Время" и др., ср. также, "Adieux à la vie", Вольтера (1778).

— Среди этого довольно однообразного материала выделяются версии темы времени у пятерых писателей — Д е р ж а в и н а как лучшего выразителя трагического аспекта этой темы *en majeur*; Х е р а с к о в а, наиболее точно и полно синтезировавшего как раз те мотивы, которые были усвоены XIX-ым веком[1]; Радищева с его "Осмнадцатым столетием" (1801), где впервые разворачивается тема исторического времени в коллизии с трагической судьбой индивидуума (и намеком на тему искупления в истории); Карамзина, подчеркнувшего нравственный аспект времени (невечный и смертный человек соразмеряет вечное время с масштабом своих духовных (и физических) возможностей и верит, что нравственная жизнь, даже будучи конечной, не может прийти в противоречие с бесконечным временем)[2]; и, наконец, Муравьева, оказавшегося и в этом отношении предшественником русского преромантизма и повлиявшего в трактовке образа времени и на Карамзина, и на Батюшкова и даже на позднего Хераскова ("Прошедшее"), о чем писалось в другом месте. За эпикурейско-горацианскими ходами, нередко используемыми Муравьевым, зреет тема обусловленности смысла жизни смертью, растет ощущение субъективности времени, его органической укорененности в личности, от которой оно может зависеть. В поэзии Муравьева с 70-х годов XVIII в. начинает складываться тот фонд поэтической фразеологии на тему времени (в частности, и прежде всего — его быстротечности), который, будучи введенным в общие рамки иной традиции, составил основу соответствующего словаря образов в поэзии Жуковского и других авторов его круга[3]. Несколько примеров:

> И, затем воспоминая,
> Скоротечность дней своих,
> Не достигнувши до края,
> О цене помысли их.
> День, который улетает,
> Крылий вспять не обращает
> И скрывается навек ...
> Жизнь — мечтание прекрасно:
> То минутный утра сон.
>
> Протекло, что было прежде:
> Ты живешь всегда в надежде
> Быть счастливей, чем теперь.
> Ах! живи, не медля мало.
> Половина — дел начало,
> И ты времени не верь.
> Наше счастье к нам столь близко ...
>   "Скоротечность жизни" (1775).

Сей понт есть нашей жизни время,
И наша жизнь есть наше бремя ...
Едва родимся мы, уж стонем
И прежде в бедствиях потонем,
Чем будем помнить мы себя;
А время, невозвратно время,
Бежит и косит смертно племя,
Их тлен и память потребя ...
"Ода шестая" (1775).

... Невольным манием предстанет перед очи
Мгновенье, в кое я из света выду вон.
Ужасный переход и смертным непонятный!
Трепещет естество, вообразив сей час,
Необходимый час, безвестный, безвозвратный, —
Кто знает, далеко ль от каждого из нас? ...
Гоняясь пристально за радостью мгновенной,
Отверстой пропасти мы ходим на краю.
Цвет розы не поблек, со стебля сриновенный, —
Уж тот, кто рвал ее, зрит бедственну ладью.
На долгий жизни ток отнюдь не полагайся,
О смертный! Вышнему надежды поручив
И помня краткость дней, от гордости чуждайся.
Ты по земле пройдешь — *там* будешь вечно жить.
"Неизвестность жизни" (1775).

Постойте, вобразим, друзья, бегуще время ...
Счастлива жизнь! увы! ти бросилась в забвенье.
Не сон ли целый век?
Во времени одну занять мы можем точку.
Минута, кою жил, длинняе году сна ...
Мгновенье каждое имеет цвет особый ...
Для доброго — златой.
Все года времена имеют наслажденья:
Во всяком возрасте есть счастие свое ...
"Время" (1775).

Бежит, друзья, бежит невозвратимо время ...
Проходит скоро год, — да скоро возвратится,
Увядший цвет теперь раскинется весной;
А смертный человек уж младостью не льстится ...
Погаснут страсти в нас, которыми пылаем,
И склонимся ко сну.
Сон будет ли тогда иль вечно разбужденье?
Ах! пусть то будет сон, коль страшно нам восстать! ...
Однако ж, о судьбы! коль буду я порочен,
О милосердии к вам дланей не простру,
Да рок мой ни на миг не будет мне отсрочен,
Пускай я млад умру.
"Ода" (1776).

Медлительней текут мгновенья бытия
                    "Ночь" (1776).

Мгновенье, в кое нас приготовляют годы ...
Не мчись ты от меня, едва успев родиться,
И дай мне от твоих мечтаний насладиться, —
Иль жребий от меня мой будет похищен? ...
Любовь! я не умру, тобой не насыщен.
                    "В горящей юности ..." (1778).

Ах! несмотря, что скоро время мчится,
Мгновенья есть, когда оно влачится ...
                    "Товарищи, наставники ..." (1779).

Почто я вас узнал, минуты восхищенья,
Когда вы от меня так быстро унеслись?
                    "Я был на зрелище ..." (1770-е годы).[4]

В этой связи уместно напомнить, что Муравьев был автором стихотворного послания к В. П. Петрову — "Успех бритской музы", где особо
выделил (наряду с традиционно упоминаемыми Шекспиром, Мильто-
ном, Попом) Томсона (*Что есть прекраснее Томсоновых картин...*),[5]
одну из ведущих фигур английской сентиментальной поэзии, который
вместе с Юнгом и Греем сыграл такую значительную роль в создании
пререромантического пейзажа, усвоенного Карамзиным и его продол-
жателями и эпигонами. Именно томсоновские "Времена года" и юнгов-
ские "Ночные мысли", многократно переводившиеся на русский язык,
начиная с 70-80-х годов XVIII в. (в частности, А. М. Кутузовым,
Карамзиным, Дмитриевым, и др.),[6] соединили для русского читателя
тему времени с темами смерти, кладбища, осени, уединения, тоски. Эти
последние, как уже говорилось, также были одним из основных источников рассматриваемого образа. В данном случае это утверждение не
нуждается в доказательствах. Существенно лишь назвать несколько
образцов, которые (независимо от поэтического уровня) показательны
для разработки этих тем на рубеже XVIII и XIX вв. К теме осени ср.:
Карамзин "Осень" (1789), Красовский "Осень" и "Осеннее чувство"
(1802), Грамматин "Осень" (1810), Кюхельбекер "Осень" (1816), и др.[7]; к
теме кладбища ср.: Карамзин "Кладбище" (1792; переработка стихотворения Козегартена), Каменев "Кладбище" (1796), Милонов "Уны-
ние" (1811; подражание Томсону) и многочисленные переводы и пере-
работки греевской "Elegy Written in a Country Churchyard" (1750),
начавшиеся с 1784-1785 г.[8] (вплоть до Жуковского). Нередко обе эти
темы равноправно соединяются, как в "Элегии" (1802) Андрея Тургенева.

Ядром описываемого здесь образа, оказавшимся весьма устойчивым и способным к вхождению в разного рода контексты, или — при другой установке — наиболее диагностической частью образа являются построения типа:

> Прошли, прошли вы, дни очарованья! ...
> ... Вам след в одной тоске воспоминанья! ...
> ... Несчастие об вас воспоминанье! ...
> Мне умереть с тоски воспоминанья! ...
>   Жуковский "Воспоминание" (1816).

Они постоянно воспроизводятся и у самого Жуковского (ср.: *Минувших дней очарованье,* | *Зачем опять воскресло ты?* | *Кто разбудил воспоминанье* ... "Песня", 1818),[9] и его младших современников (ср. *Протекших дней очарованья,* | *Мне вас душе не возвратить!* Дельвиг, "Разочарование", (1824), и значительно позже — вплоть до блоковских образов — *Прошедших дней немеркнущим сияньем* | *... тоскующим дыханьем* | *... Воспоминаньем дальним и прекрасным* (I, 46; 1900).[10] В русской поэзии начала XIX в. ядро образа, функционально равноценного микромотиву (или, точнее, серии весьма сходных микромотивов, соответствующих единой схеме), составляли следующие элементы:

> *миновать (пройти, пролететь, улететь, промчаться, удалиться, пронестись, протечь, исчезнуть и т.п.);*
> *дни (лета, годы, век, жизнь, молодость, юность, любовь, надежда и т.п.);*
> *очарованье (обаянье, мечта и т.п.);*
> *воспоминанье (память, мечта, сон, надежда и т.п.);*
> *тоска.*

К указанным элементам примыкали другие, менее обязательные:

> *быстро (скоро, неизбежно, неотвратимо и т.п.);*
> *милый (золотой, светлый, юный и т.п.);*
> *весна (утро, юность, веселье и т.п.);*
> *цвет (цвести);*
> *увядать (угасать, блекнуть, валиться и т.п.);*
> *след*[11]; *глас (голос) и др.*

Когда ядро обрастало этими дополнительными элементами, почти автоматически — с известного времени — имплицировались еще два микромотива — юноша (часто — *певец, поэт* и т.п.) и смерть (*умереть, могила*), которые, сочетаясь друг с другом, порождают третий (но уже зависимый) мотив преждевременности — тем более существенный, что для предшествующей эпохи подчеркивалась именно в е ч н о с т ь времени. Следует заметить, что в поэзии начала XIX в. отмечены разные способы упорядочения перечисленных элементов в единый мотив. Два полюса — н у л е в а я степень упорядоченности (или близкая к ней), предполагающая близкое соседство в стихах всех этих элементов или их существенной части при отсутствии сколько-нибудь выявленной схемы зависимостей между ними (сюжетной, синтаксической, семантической и т.д.), и м а к с и м а л ь н а я степень упорядоченности, при которой перечисленные элементы включаются в сюжетную схему, ставшую одним из наиболее ходких и модных клише в поэзии того времени.

Максимально упорядоченная схема элементов предполагает среди прочих такие операции, как возможность включения в о п р о с а (иногда удвоенного): *Куда?; Зачем?; Где?*, связанного с глаголом группы *миновать* в 3-м лице[12] прошедшего времени, относящегося к субъекту из группы *дни*. Вместе с тем элемент этой группы *дни* часто имеет при себе двойное определение: первое из группы *милый* и/или из группы *миновать* с трансформацией вида Vb. → Adj^{Vb}. (*миновать* → *миновавший*), второе — родительный падеж элемента из группы *очарованье* (между прочим, при всех вариантах конкретной реализации существенно наличие отглагольного имени на *-ание/-анье*, ср. далее *воспоминаний/воспоминанье*). Оформленный таким образом минимальный мотив [(?) & *дни* ((& *милые* $\vee$ *минувший* &/ $\vee$ *очарованья*)) & *миновать*] уравновешивается обычно другим мотивом, характеризующимся антитетичностью по отношению к первому в заданных пределах: (*дни миновали*), но осталось *воспоминанье* (: *очарованье*), *тоска воспоминанья*[13] об этих минувших днях очарованья, единственный *след* которых сохраняется в памяти. Но это *воспоминанье* обычно гибельно (*Мне у м е р е т ь с тоски воспоминанья!*)[14] несчастно (*Н е с ч а с т и е об вас воспоминанье!*) или, по крайней мере, бессмысленно, напрасно (*Зачем опять воскресло ты? | Кто разбудил воспоминанье ...*).[15] При выборе того продолжения схемы, которое связано с появлением элемента *умереть,* чаще всего возникает побочный мотив в двух вариантах — с м е р т ь ю н о ш и / п е в ц а и увядание ц в е т (к) а / п а д е н и е л и с т ь е в. Иногда антитетичность отношения двух названных мотивов заметно сглаживается. Обычно это происходит при трансформации глагольной конструкции в именную (ср. *Прошли, прошли вы, дни очарованья!* — но: *Минувших дней очарованье ...*), которая не дает возможности закончиться мотиву в ее пределах и влечет за собой группу глагола, нередко расширенную вопросом (*Зачем опять воскресло ты?*). Естественно, что во многих случаях подобная схема представлена лишь частично или с некоторыми осложнениями и видоизменениями разного рода.

Весьма важно подчеркнуть, что сама эта схема или отдельные ее части требуют для их опознания и идентификации некоего более расширенного контекста, в котором содержатся те или иные указания на этот счет. Поэтому майковское *Минул прошедший год* (и далее: *и боле не настанет,* 1777) лишь материально совпадает с элементами схемы; концептуально и стилистически же эти мотивы включаются в совершенно иной круг образов; их устойчивость и формульность, скорее, способствовали консервации подобных способов выражения в пределах данной традиции, чем облегчали их использование и преобразование в рамках других направлений. Не единственным но исключительно важным средством создания этого нового контекста было введение элемента группы *воспоминание.* В плане содержания речь идет о появлении мотива воспоминания, памяти, мечты и т.п. в сцеплении с мотивом м и н о в а т ь & в р е м я. На формальном уровне существенно появление слова ритмической структуры ∪ ∪ ∪ – (∪) ∪, обычно — *воспоминáние, воспоминáнье,* распределение которых регулируется правилом: *воспоминáние* не может кончать стих, *воспоминáнье* тяготеет к маргинальной позиции — чаще всего в конце стиха, реже — в его начале. Иногда вместо *воспоминáние (-ье)* выступает слово той же структуры *очаровáние (-ье),* которое и семантически в подобных контекстах сильно сближается со словом *воспоминáние* (ср. *воспоминание об очаровании, очарование воспоминания* и т.п.), нередко трактуемым как п а м я т ь ✕ о ч а р о в а н ь е. Еще реже на месте *воспоминáние (-ье)* выступает слово *мечтáние (мечтáнье),* реализующее усеченный вариант ритмической схемы. Указанный критерий дает исследователю хорошие возможности разобраться в генеалогии этой части схемы и отделить ходы типа приведенного выше майковского от тех, которые могут считаться действительными источниками образа, как, например, *Жизнь — мечтание прекрасно:* | *То минутный утра сон.* | *Протекло, что было прежде* и под. у Муравьева или *Дни счастливы миновались,* | *Дни прелестнейшей мечты ...* | *Прошлых дней воспоминанье* ...; *Воспоминанье прежних дней* ... у Нелединского-Мелецкого.[16] Еще более близкая вариация, бесспорно последняя перед Жуковским и несомненно учтенная им позднее, засвидетельствована в "Элегии" (1802) Андрея Тургенева — *Воспоминание минувших дней блаженных,* включенное в контекст, характеризующийся почти всеми признаками разбираемой схемы. Ср.: *Всё жило, всё цвело, чтоб после умереть;* — *Но ты во цвете лет сраженная Судьбою,* | *Приди, приди сюда беседовать с тоскою*[17]; — *Ни юность, для других заря прекрас-*

ных дней; — В чьих горестных сердцах умолк веселья глас[18]; *— И должен лишь в прошедшем жить, | В прошедшем радость находить | ... Утро ясно | Блаженных детских дней! ... | Зачем так быстро ты? | ... Живи хоть в памяти моей ...* (последняя цитата — из "И в двадцать лет уж ...") и др.[19] Мотивы осени и кладбища в "Элегии",[20] довольно близко воспроизведенные вскоре Жуковским, образуют естественный переход к теме с м е р т и, соотнесенной с осенью. Вместе с тем смерть внезапна, преждевременна, неотвратима. Хотя и разрозненно, возникают мотивы ю н о с т и, б е д н о г о с т р а д а л ь ц а, соотнесенные с образом автора-поэта и, следовательно, имплицирующие на следующем шаге образ с т р а д а л ь ц а - п о э т а, б е д н о г о п е в - ц а, ю н о ш и, который и явился последним завершающим звеном схемы.[21] Но у Тургенева в поэтических текстах этот процесс кристаллизации схемы останавливается на предпоследнем этапе. Ср.: *Всё жило, всё цвело, чтоб после у м е р е т ь*[4] *— ... Воспоминание минувших дней блаженных! | Ах! только им одним с т р а д а л е ц и живет! | ... Но ты, во цвете лет с р а ж е н н а я Судьбою ...; — Ни ю н о с т ь, для других заря прекрасных дней, | ... Ничто, ничто Судьбы жестокой ни смягчило; — Хотела вечно жить для счастья, для него; | Хотела — гром гремит — ты видишь г р о б его; — Уже сокрылось всё, чем б е д н ы й веселился* и др. К этому же кругу тем Тургенев обратится еще не раз: *А вы, которы в нем отраду находили, | ... Проститесь с ним навек! С поникшими очами | Вы будете стоять на месте, где он цвел, | Вы вспомните о нем, и, может быть, с слезами, | Но он для ваших глаз опять не расцветет | И только прах один печальный здесь найдет* (1802)[22]; *— Погаснет жизни луч в очах, | ... И взор твой будет на гробах* ("Мой друг", 1803). Одновременно с "Элегией" появляется перевод греевского "Сельского кладбища", где Жуковский прикасается к той же теме преждевременно погибшего юноши, нежного сердцем, чувствительного душой и любящего: *Ах! может быть под сей могилою томится | Прах с е р д ц а н е ж н о г о, у м е в ш е г о л ю б и т ь; — Взошла заря — но он с зарею не являлся, | Ни к иве, ни на холм, ни в лес не приходил ... | На утро пение мы слышим гробовое ... | Несчастного несут в могилу положить ...* И самое интересное в том, что косвенно выступающая тема п е в ц а, отсутствующая, кстати, в подлиннике (ср.: *А ты, почивших друг, п е в е ц уединенный, | И твой ударит час, последний, роковой | И к гробу твоему ...*), явно обнаружится в заключительной эпитафии, из которой выясняется, что умерший юноша — п о э т:

Здесь пепел ю н о ш и безвременно сокрыли;
Что слава, счастье, не знал он в мире сём;

Но Музы от него лица не отвратили,[23]
И меланхолии печать была на нём ...,

хотя мотив поэта в таком явном виде отсутствует в "Elegy" Грея.[24] Так или иначе, к самому началу XIX в. практически сложилась разбираемая тема. Порознь все её компоненты были воспроизведены уже не раз. Менее четко выкристаллизовывалась тема безвременной смерти юноши-поэта: она встречалась нечасто, во-первых, и воплощалась несколько абстрактно, с недостаточно определенными сюжетными связями и мотивировками, во-вторых. Собственно говоря, "Элегия" Тургенева и "Сельское кладбище" были первыми серьезными попытками соединить этот мотив с остальной частью схемы, которая могла уже считаться в принципе оформленной. Внезапная смерть двадцатидвухлетнего Андрея Тургенева в 1803 г., предсказанная им в стихах последнего года его жизни, оказалась той критической точкой, после которой кристаллизация схемы стала неотвратимой. Так, впервые в русской поэзии внутритекстовое событие соотнеслось как причина и пророчество с внетекстовым событием с тем, чтобы последнее определило структуру целого класса последующих текстов, характеризующихся названной схемой. Впервые ряд поэтический и ряд внетекстовый, событийный соединились и — более того —стали в отношение причины и следствия, дав начало образованию того исключительной сложности текста, который может быть выделен внутри русской поэзии.

У начала этого текста стоял Жуковский,[25] и Владимир Соловьев был прав, назвав "Сельское кладбище" "родиной русской поэзии".[26] Именно Жуковскому выпало на долю синтезировать схему в ее целостности и установить тот особый род отношений между поэтическим текстом и сферой внеположенного, о котором говорилось выше. Только Жуковский сумел выразить этот мотив в такой ритмической схеме, которая впоследствии с теми или иными вариациями не раз воспроизводилась в русской поэзии в связи как раз с этим кругом образов.[27] Жуковскому же принадлежит и другое достижение, значение которого имеет общий характер: он сумел построить схему (как в принципе и все свои поэтические тексты) таким образом, что семантическая индивидуальность каждого элемента оказалась несколько подавленной, менее определенной и однозначной и, наоборот, были актуализированы общие черты в этих элементах (прежде всего на уровне эмоциональных ореолов). В результате нюансы и переходные состояния получили преобладание над исходными лексическими значениями,[28] что открыло в дальнейшем путь к перестановкам элементов в схеме.

Уже в "Вечере" (1806) тема ранней смерти приурочена к юноше, другу, образу Тургенева (что удостоверяется записью Жуковского — "... Утро — Пришествие весны — весна все оживляет — Разрушение и жизнь А ... краткость его жизни — гроб его — надежда пережить..."). В "Вечере" эта тема введена в уже вполне сложившийся контекст схемы: *К протекшим временам лечу воспоминаньем* ... | *О дней моих весна, как быстро скрылась ты* ‖ *Где вы, мои друзья, вы, спутники мои?* ‖ ... *О братья! о друзья! где наш священный круг?* ‖ ... *Один — минутный цвет — почил, и непробудно,* | *И гроб безвременный любовь кропит слезой.* ‖ ... *Блажен, кому дано цевницей оживлять* | *Часы сей жизни скоротечной!* ‖ ... *Так, петь есть мой удел... но долго ль? ... Как узнать? ...* | *Ах! скоро, может быть, с Минваною унылой* | *Придет сюда Альпин в час вечера мечтать* | *Над тихой юноши могилой!*[29] Апофеоз этой темы — стихотворение "Певец" (1811), внутренне относимое к Андрею Тургеневу и — хотя и в разной степени — суммирующее соответствующие образы "Элегии" Тургенева и "Сельского кладбища":

> ... На ветвях лира и венец ...
>   Увы! друзья, сей холм — могила;
>   Здесь прах певца земля сокрыла;
>   Бедный певец!
>
> Он сердцем прост, он нежен был душою —[30]
> Но в мире он минутный странник был;
> Едва расцвел — и жизнь уж разлюбил,
> И ждал конца с волненьем и тоскою;
>   И рано встретил он конец ...
>
> Он дружбу пел, дав другу нежну руку —
> Но верный друг во цвете лет угас ...
> · · · · · · · · · · · · · · · · · · ·
>   Ты спишь; тиха твоя могила,
>   Бедный певец!
>
> · · · · · · · · · · · · · · · · · · ·
>   Погибло все, умолкни, лира ...
> Что жизнь, когда в ней нет очарованья?
>
> · · · · · · · · · · · · · · · · · · ·
> И нет певца ... его не слышно лиры ...
> Его следы исчезли в сих местах ...

И далее не раз возникает образ погибшего певца. Ср.: *Ветр осенний бушевал,* | *И приютный лист опал.* | *Здесь нередко по утрам* | *Мне певец встречался,* | *И живым его струнам* | *Отзыв откликался ...* | *Нет его, певец увял;* | *С ним и отзыв замолчал* ("Песня", 1815);

Минувших дней очарованье, | *Зачем опять воскресло ты?* || *... Не узрит он минувших лет;* | *Там есть один жилец безгласный* | *... Там вместе с ним все дни прекрасны* | *В единый гроб положены* ("Песня, 1818) и др., причем тема постоянно варьируется.[31] Иногда аналогичная схема не заполняется образом юноши, но содержит параллели человек — цветок, смерть — увядание и т.д. (ср. "Цветок", 1811: *Минутная краса полей,* | *Цветок увядший, одинокий ...* || *Увы! нам тот же дан удел ...* | *С тебя листочек облетел —* | *От нас веселье отлетает.* || *... Смотри ... очарованья нет;* | *Звезда надежды угасает ...* | *Увы! кто скажет: жизнь иль цвет* | *Быстрее в мире исчезает?*).

Мотив преждевременной смерти юноши-певца очень скоро получает широкое распространение и обнаруживает тенденцию к дальнейшим вариациям, в частности, к соотнесению его с самим автором, что обычно влечет за собой 'Ich-Erzählung' (ср., впрочем, уже в XVIII в.: *Пускай я млад умру*).[32] Несколько примеров помогут дать представление о развитии этого образа: — *Хочу я завтра умереть* | *... Прости навек, очарованье* | *... Приближьтесь, о друзья мои* | *... Певец решился умереть.* | *... В последний раз мою цевницу ...* | *В последний раз, томимый нежно* | *Не вспомню вечность и друзей ...* | *Простите, милые друзья ...* | *И пусть на гробе, где певец* | *Исчезнет в роще Геликона,* | *Напишет беглый ваш резец:* | *"Здесь дремлет юноша-мудрец,* | *Питомец нег и Аполлона"* (Пушкин, "Мое завещание", 1815); *Вздохнули ль вы, внимая тихой глас* | *Певца любви, певца своей печали?* | *Когда в лесах вы юношу видали,* | *Встречая взор его потухших глаз —* | *Вздохнули ль вы?* ("Певец", 1816; с явными следами влияния одноименного стихотворения Жуковского); *Я видел смерть ...* | *Я видел гроб; открылась дверь его;* | *Душа, померкнув, охладела ...* | *Покину скоро я друзей,* | *И жизни горестной моей* | *Никто следов уж не приметит* | *... И всё ... прости в последний раз.* | *... Прости! миную всё ... Уж гаснет пламень мой,* | *Схожу я в хладную могилу ...* ("Элегия", 1816); *Медлительно влекутся дни мои* | *... О жизни час! лети, не жаль тебя* | *... Пускай умру, но пусть умру любя!* ("Желание", 1816); *Туманные сокрылись дни разлуки* | *... Ушла пора веселости беспечной,* | *Ушла навек ...* | *... Всё кончилось ...* | *... Минувших дней погаснули мечтанья,* | *И умер глас ...* | *... Опали вы, листы вчерашней розы! ...* | *Умчались вы, дни радости моей,* | *Умчались вы, — невольно льются слезы,* | *И вяну я на темном утре дней* ("Элегия", 1817); *В последний раз, быть может, я с тобой* | *... Где вы, лета беспеч-*

ности недавной? | ... *Они прошли, но можно ль их забыть?* | *Они прошли* ... | *Один, с тоской, явлюсь я, гость угрюмый,* | *Явлюсь на час — и одинок умру.* | ... *Ужель моя пройдет пустынно младость?* ... ("Послание к кн. А. М. Горчакову", 1817); *Но всё прошло — и скрылись в темну даль* ... | *Пускай не будут знать, что некогда певец,* | *Враждою, завистью на жертву обреченный,* | *Погиб на утре лет,* | *Как ранний на поляне цвет* ... | *И гроб несчастного, в пустыне мрачной дикой,* | *Забвенья порастет ползущей павиликой!* ("К Дельвигу", 1817) и т.д.; — *Пробьют урочные часы* | *И низойдет к брегам Аида* | *Певец веселья и красы.* || *Простите, ветренные други* ... (Баратынский, "Элизийские поля", 1827); *Когда твой голос, о Поэт,* | *Смерть в высших звуках остановит,* | *Когда тебя во цвете лет* | *Нетерпеливый рок уловит* ... || *И тихий гроб твой посетит* ...; — *Любви дни краткие даны,* | *Но мне не зреть ее остылой;* | *Я с ней умру, как звук унылый* ... (Дельвиг, "Романс", 1824)[33]; — *Бедное сердце! Рано для юноши осень настала* ... | *Други! Я умер душой — нет уж прежних восторгов,* | *Нет и сладостных прежних страданий: всюду молчанье,* | *Холод могилы!* (Кюхельбекер, "Осень", 1816); *Цвет моей жизни, не вянь!* ...... *зачем же* | *Я на заре не увял* ... | *В памяти добрых бы жил рано отцветший певец!* ("Элегия", 1817); — *Сбылись пророчества поэта,* | *И друг в слезах с началом лета* | *Его могилу посетил.* | *Как знал он жизнь, как мало жил!* (Веневитинов, "Поэт и друг", 1826-1827); — *Но час настал, меня во гроб сокрыли,* | *Мои уста могильный хлад сковал* | ... *где прах певца лежал* ... | *И сладкий глас попрежнему звучал* (Хомяков, "Сон", 1826) и т.д. Ср. в иной, более поздней традиции хлебниковское *Нет уже юноши, нет уже нашего* ...

В этой связи особого внимания заслуживают элегии В. Ф. Раевского, прежде всего "Элегия I" (1819?):

> Раздался звон глухой ... Я слышу скорбный глас,
> Песнь погребальную вдали протяжным хором,
> И гроб, предшествуем бесчувственным собором.
> Увы! То юноша предвременно угас!
> Неумолимая невинного сразила
>   Зарею юных дней ...
> Останется в удел одно воспоминанье! ...

с необычными продолжениями:

> Почто же человек путем скорбей, страданья,
> Гонений, нищеты к погибели идет?
> Почто безвременно смерть лютая сечет

Жизнь юноши среди любви очарованья?
Почто разврат, корысть, тиранство ставят трон
На гибели добра, невинности покою?
Почто несчастных жертв струится кровь рекою
И сирых и вдовиц не умолкает стон?

и далее почти в духе лермонтовских инвектив в "Смерти поэта"[34]; эта тенденция еще очевиднее в "Элегии на смерть юноши" (между 1812 и 1816), где элегическое начало сильно оттеснено.[31]

Естественно, что в связи с описываемой схемой нельзя пройти мимо стихотворения Мильвуа "La chute des feuilles", многократно переведенного и вызвавшего целый ряд подражаний в русской поэзии. Популярность этого стихотворения в России 10-20-х годов XIX в. вне всякого сомнения. Ранняя смерть Мильвуа (34 лет), вскоре после появления стихотворения в печати ("Élégies", 1812-1814) и в год появления первого русского перевода его,[36] позволяла видеть в "La chute des feuilles" (и некоторых других стихотворениях Мильвуа) пророчество. Но главная причина успеха заключалась все-таки, видимо, в том, что это стихотворение не могло не восприниматься как идеальная реализация анализируемой здесь схемы. Читательское восприятие было не только вполне подготовлено, но и, будучи в отношении этих образов и всей схемы активным, готово к включению этого стихотворения в определенную традицию русской поэзии и даже к ряду трансформаций и своего рода 'постредактированию'. Ядро стихотворения, действительно, исключительно близко к текстам того же рода в русской поэзии, упоминавшимся выше (осень, роща, обнаженные леса, желтизна, падающие листья и т.п. как существенные элементы пейзажа, общее настроение и т.п.):

De la dépouille de nos bois
L'automne avait jonché la terre;
Le bocage était sans mystère …
Triste, et mourant à son aurore,[37]
Un jeune malade,[38] à pas lents,
Parcourait une fois encore
Le bois cher à ses premiers ans.
— "Bois que j'aime! adieu … je succombe.
Ton deuil m'avertit de mon sort;
Et dans chaque feuille qui tombe
Je vois un présage de mort …
Tu m'as dit: "Les feuilles des bois
A tes yeux jauniront encore;
Mais c'est pour la dernière fois …
Plus pâle que le pâle automne,
Tu t'inclines vers le tombeau.

Ta jeunesse sera flétrie ...
Et je meurs! De sa froide haleine
Un vent funeste m'a touché,
Et mon hiver s'est approché
Quand mon printemps s'écoule à peine ...
Mais vers la solitude allée
Si mon amante désolée
Venait pleurer quand le jour fuit,
Eveille par un léger bruit
Mon ombre un instant consolée",
Il dit, s'éloigne ... et sans retour
La dernière feuille qui tombe
A signalé son dernier jour.
Sous le chêne on creusa sa tombe ...

Соответствующая схема русской поэзии была достаточно влиятельной, чтобы определять ряд важных изменений в переводе. Здесь достаточно указать на два нововведения, имплицированных соответствующими элементами схемы. Преромантический вступительный пейзаж, как правило, предусматривал мотив реки, источника, вод.[39] У Мильвуа его нет, но в переводах он весьма част: *Ручей свободно зажурчал* и *Простите рощи и долины,* | *Родные реки и поля* (Батюшков, "Последняя весна", 1816), *Брега взрывал источник мутный* (Баратынский, "Падение листьев"),[40] *Прости, шумливая река* (Туманский, "Падение листьев", 1823). Мильвуа называет героя стихотворения *un jeune malade* (в другой редакции *un jeune habitant*; в очень близком стихотворении "Priez pour moi" (1816) с той же схемой — *un pauvre malade, le jeune malade*[41]). Лучший русский перевод — вопреки Мильвуа и в соответствии с описанной выше схемой — говорит *о младом певце: На преждевременный конец* | *Суровым роком обреченный,* | *Прощался так младой певец ...* (Баратынский, "Падение листьев", 1823), ср. и у Батюшкова: *Певец любви, лишь ты уныл!* | *Ты смерти верной предвещанье* | *В печальном сердце заключил....*[43] Эти изменения, конечно, не случайны, и именно они дали начало традиции (ср. также: Дон Гуан — п о э т из всей дон-жуанской традиции только у Пушкина, о чем писала уже Ахматова). Точно так же закономерно появление в переводах "La chute des feuilles" и других элементов из схемы, не находящих соответствий в тексте Мильвуа или представленных там в существенно приглушенном виде. Не касаясь здесь некоторых второстепенных деталей,[43] нужно особенно подчеркнуть отличия от Мильвуа в разработке образа времени.[44] Если французский поэт предпочитает цветовые характеристики изменений от весны к осени (*L'automne avait jonché la terre; Les feuilles des bois* | *A tes yeux jauniront encore; Plus pâle que le pâle automne; Mais ma languissante verdue | Ne laisse après elle aucun fruit)* и лишь однажды непосредственно вводит мотив у в я да н и я (*ta jeunesse sera flétrie...*), русские переводчики усиленно подчеркивают именно этот последний мотив, хорошо знакомый им по схеме. Ср.: *Ты первые увидишь розы | И с ними вдруг увянешь ты. | Уж близок час ...Цветочки милы, | К чему так рано увядать?; в Полях цветы не увядали ...* (Батюшков); — *Лежал поблекший лист кустов; Долин отцветших созерцатель ...* (Милонов); — *И вяну я ...* (Баратынский); — *Листы поблекшие опали; Узришь ты рощи увяданье; Увянешь ты во цвете дней* (Туманский).[45] Соответственно этому и смерть юноши изображается как у гасание: *А бедный юноша... погас!* (Батюшков); *На утро — юноша погас* (Туманский). Итог совершившегося кодируется глаголом *сбылось: Сбылось! Увы! судьбины гнева ...* (Баратынский); *Сбылось! своим дыханьем хладным ...* (Туманский): Уместно вспомнить, что этот глагол в русской поэзии 10-20-х годов связывался с поэтом и/или его смертью, ср.: *Сбылись поэта сновиденья!* (Пушкин, "Послание к Юдину", 1815); *Сбылись пророчества поэта! | И друг его с началом лета | Его могилу посетил. | Как знал он жизнь, как мало жил* (Веневитинов). Повторение общего элемента в разных текстах поэтического ряда и смерть Веневитинова[46] еще одним узлом связывают оба эти ряда.

Особого внимания заслуживают некоторые другие филиации образа времени, которые в ряде случаев так или иначе связаны с находками А. И. Тургенева и Жуковского и обнаруживаются в переводах Мильвуа и во многих других текстах, давших начало самостоятельной традиции в развитии этого образа. Речь идет об образе, увековеченном Пушкиным в элегии Ленского: *Куда, куда вы удались, | Весны моей златые дни?* Не следует упускать из виду, что эти слова принадлежат юному поэту накануне его безвременной гибели (*Его уж нет. Младой певец | Нашел безвременный конец! | Дохнула буря, цвет прекрасный | Увял на утренней заре ...; Друзья мои, вам жаль поэта: | Во цвете радостных надежд ... | Увял! ...*).[47] *Младой певец* Баратынского ("Падение листьев") говорит, по сути дела, то же, что и Ленский: *Вы улетели сны златые | Минутной юности моей!* (вместо: *Quand mon printemps s'écoule à peine...*).[48] Тот же образ повторяется и в других переводах из Мильвуа: *И сном неясным, безотрадным | Промчалась молодость моя* (Туманский) и особенно: *Как призрак легкий улетели | Златые дни весны моей* (Милонов),[49] являющееся непосредственным источником фразы Ленского (Пушкина), не говоря о второстепенных переводах Степанова (1825) и Глебова. Полностью или частично этот образ укореняется и вне переводов из Мильвуа, а иногда и до появления самого стихотворения Мильвуа. Ср. у Жуковского: *О счастье дней моих, | Куда, куда стремишься? | О дней моих весна, | Как быстро скрылась ты* ... ("Вечер"); — *Где вы, дни радости, восторгов, упоенья? | Сокрылись ... и мечты вы унесли с собой* (В. Л. Пушкин, "Элегия", 1816); *Веселья, счастья дни златые, | Как быстрый вихрь промчались вы* ("К жителям Нижнего Новгорода", 1812) — *Погибла для меня делам и жизни сладость, | Воспоминания дней юности златой* (Гнедич, из черновиков стихотворения на смерть Г. И. Бужинской, 1819); — *На крыльях времени безмолвного летят | ... Как у весны цветы, у нас младые годы!* ("Осень", 1819); — *Было время! где вы, | Годы золотые* ... (Дельвиг, "Песня", 1820, уже вне элегической традиции); — *Быстро, быстро пролетает | Время* ... | *Ах! давно ль весна златая | Расцветала на полях? — | Час пробил* ... | *И сокрылася опять. | Ах, одно мне утешенье — | О тебе воспоминать* (Ъ — Ъ, — "Галатея" 1829, №5, стр. 196-97); — *Юности беспечной младость | Счастье прежних бывших дней... | Миновалось, миновалось! | Цвет увял души моей* (Мотыльков / = С. Д. Пономарева/, — "Благонамеренный" 1824, ч. XXV, №5, стр. 352-53); — *Где вы, лета беспечности недавной?... | Они пришли, твои златые годы | ... Они прошли, но можно ль их забыть?* (А. С. Пушкин. "Послание к кн. А. М. Горчакову"); *Где ж детства ранние следы? | Прелестный возраст миновался, | Увяли первые цветы!* ("Послание к Юдину"), *Минуты счастья золотые...* (Там же); *Ушла пора веселости беспечной... | Умчались вы, дни радости моей...* ("Элегия"); *Златые дни, златые ночи...* ("Друзья"); *Как век весны промчался ясной* ("Элегия"); *Забуду ли то время золотое* ... ("Сон"); *... Где рано в бурях отцвела | Моя потерянная младость, | ... Подруги тайные моей весны златыя* ... ("Погасло дневное светило", 1820) и др.[50] ср. *златая младость, юность, золотые часы, время* и т.д.: — *Промчалось ты, златое время* ... (Баратынский, "Стансы") и т.д. Достаточно рано отмечен подобный образ у А. И. Мещерского: *Так быстро пронеслись златые счастья дни!* ("На смерть В. А. Габбе", 1814)[51] и целого ряда менее талантливых поэтов-эпигонов (у которых — правда, позже — образ начинает уже частично разрушаться.[52] Учитывая многочисленность подобных примеров, в частности и в особенности у Пушкина лицейского периода,[53] можно высказать мнение, что *Куда, куда вы удалились, | Весны моей златые дни?* представляет собой не только ироническую реплику на шаблоны элегической поэзии начала века, но и отчасти едва ощутимую автопародию. Впрочем, постоянство с которым Пушкин обращался и к близкой теме преждевременной смерти юноши (-певца) в эти годы и степень индивидуализации темы дают повод думать не только о литературной основе соответствующих образов в юношеский период творчества.

Те же мотивы широко воспроизводятся в стихах других поэтов пушкинской поры, причем часто в вариантах довольно точно соответствующих схеме. Ср. у К о з л о в а: *И кто ж весну свою забыл?* | *... Кто не живет воспоминаньем?* | *И я его очарованьем ...* | *И память прежних светлых дней*[54] | *... Ах, для чего же молодое,* | *Мое ты счастье золотое,* | *Так быстро, быстро пронеслось!* ("К другу В[асилию] А[ндреевичу] Ж[уковскому]", 1822); *Прекрасный друг минувших светлых дней ...* | *Не зреть мне дня с зарями золотыми,* | *Ни роз весны ...* | *Всегда со мной очарованье* ("Чернец", 1825); *Там певца воспоминанье ...* | *Там любви очарованье* | *С отголоском прежних дней* ("Венецианская ночь", 1825); *Зачем ...* | *Ты льешь очарованье,* | *И оставляешь ... светлых дней* | *Одно воспоминанье!* | *Минувшее ...* ("К радости", 1824); *Там твое воспоминанье* | *... Для сердец очарованье* | *И прекрасного завет* ("К княгине М. А. Голицыной", 1825) и др.; — у Б а р а т ы н с к о г о: *Товарищ радостей минувших,* | *Товарищ ясных дней ... ужель минувших дней ...* ("Послание к барону Дельвигу"); *А прошлых лет воспоминанья* ("Запустение")[55]; *Как сладкое душе воспоминанье ...* | *Какое-то влечет очарованье ...* ("Она"); ср. дальнейшие вариации с постепенным размыванием образа: *Разочарованному чужды* | *Все обольщенья прежних дней* | *... Слепой тоски моей не множь ...* | *Забудь бывалые мечты* ("Разуверение"), *О наслажденьях прежних дней* | *... Что было цветом бытия!* | *... Забудь печальные мечты* ("Утешение"); *Напрасно я себе на память приводил* | *И милый образ твой и прежние мечтанья:* | *Безжизненны мои воспоминанья* | *... Но годы долгие в разлуке протекли ...* ("Признание") и др.; — у Я з ы к о в а: *Воспоминанья прошлых дней,* | *Воспоминанья золотые*[56] | *... Но где ж они,* | *Мои пленительные дни* ("А. А. Воейковой", 1826) и т.д.

Характерно, что в наиболее полном виде эта образность продолжает сохраняться в 30-40-е годы (а иногда и позже) у поэтов-эпигонов. Наиболее же значительные поэты этого времени (Лермонтов, Тютчев, Фет, Григорьев и др.), не говоря уже о тех, кто начинал в 10-20-е годы и продолжал работать и в следующие десятилетия, пытаются строить новые ряды образов, исходя из отдельных, порознь взятых элементов исходной схемы, последовательно уклоняясь от синтезирования всей схемы в целом. Показательно, что и разработка этого круга образов в западноевропейской поэзии практически перестает привлекать внимание русских поэтов. Это относится и к тем случаям, когда западноевропейские поэты обращались к той же самой теме времени или даже когда и там и здесь шли параллельные поиски.[57] Более поздние схождения и пересечения русской и западноевропейской поэзии в разработке образа времени носили уже совсем иной характер (ср. Ахматова и Элиот).

Одним из важнейших результатов эволюции описанной схемы было выделение из всего комплекса мотивов, ее составляющих, мотива с м е р т и   п о э т а. При этом смерть становится знаком особой отмеченности поэта, его избранности, связи с судьбой. И уже перед поэтом не быстротечное время, несшее гибель *младому певцу,* а куда более страшная сила. Рылеев, Грибоедов, Дельвиг, Пушкин, Лермонтов увидели ее, и в этом смысле их смерть иная нежели у Андрея Тургенева или даже Веневитинова, хотя все они умерли молодыми. Чем дальше, тем теснее переплетаются ряд поэтический и ряд жизненный, тем больше разнородного материала втягивается в этот уже почти единый поток. "Элегия" Тургенева и его смерть,[58] "Сельское кладбище (< Грей) и "Певец" Жуковского, "Падение листьев" (< Мильвуа) Баратынского, Милонова, Батюшкова, юношеские предчувствия Пушкина, элегия Ленского и его гибель, смерть Пушкина и лермонтовское "Смерть поэта" (с отсылкой: *Как тот певец, неведомый, но милый ...*) и его видения в "Сне" (*В полдневный жар в долине Дагестана...*), гибель Лермонтова и шевыревское "На смерть поэта" и далее — как итог векового пути и пророчество одновременно — *Тёмен жребий русского поэта,* | *Неисповедимый рок ведет ...* и *Но не дано Российскому поэту* | *Такою светлой смертью умереть ...*[59] — лишь вехи на этом пути. Но не всякая безвременная смерть поэта включается в этот путь. Шенье и Мильвуа, Вакенродер, Новалис и Клейст, Байрон, Шелли и Китс умерли молодыми, но тот двуединый текст со столь легко исполняющимися пророчествами, о котором говорится в этой статье, не был создан ни во французской, ни в немецкой, ни в английской поэзии.

Москва

ПРИМЕЧАНИЯ

¹ Ср.. *Где* прошедшее девалось?
Всё, как *сон, как сон прошло*;
Только в *памяти* осталось ...
Будущее настает —
Где ж оно? Его уж нет! ...
Всё, как молния *мелькает*,
Будто на крылах *летит*;
Ах! *летит* невозвратимо,
Как река, проходит *мимо*,
И реке возврата нет —
К вечности она *течет* ...
Жизни вечером *увяли*,
Будто утренни *цветы* ...

Все тщета в подлунном мире,
Исключенья смертным нет ...
Жизнь, как ветерок, провеет,
Всё разрушится, истлеет ...
Что меня ни утешало,
Время, время всё *умчало*;
Жизни сей кратка стезя
И продлить ее нельзя.
Что такое есть — родиться?
Что есть наше житие?
Шаг ступить — и возвратиться
В прежнее небытие.
        "Прошедшее", 1806.

Ср. также "Стансы" (1760), представляющие собой перевод из Руссо ("Stances": *Que l'homme est bien durant sa vie ...*) и поэму "Вселенная" (о времени).

² Ср. в "Послании к Дмитриеву" (1794):

Конечно так — ты прав, мой друг!
Цвет счастья скоро *увядает* ...
Но *жизни* алая *весна*
Есть *миг* — увы! *пройдет* она,
И с нею мысли, чувства наши ...
Надежды и *мечты златые*,
Как птички, быстро *улетят* ...
Орудием небесным быть
И в *памяти* потомства жить,
Казалось мне всего славнее ...
Но *время*, опыт разрушают
Воздушный замок юных лет;
Красы волшебства *исчезают*
Теперь иной я вижу свет ...
И мрачный свет предать на волю
Судьбы и рока; пусть они,

Сим миром правя искони,
И впредь творят, что им угодно
А мы ...
Мой друг! не мы тому виной.
Мы слабых здесь не угнетали,
И всем ума-добра желали:
У нас не черные сердца!
И так без трепета и страха
Нам можно ожидать конца
И лечь во гроб, жилище праха.
Завеса вечности страшна
Убийцам, кровью обагренным ...
В ком дух и совесть без пятна,
Тот с тихим чувствием встречает
Златую Фебову стрелу ...

(ср. в "Стансах к Н. М. Карамзину" |1793| Дмитриева: *Утро дней моих затмилось*, | *И опять не расцветет*; | *Сердце с счастием простилось* | *И мечтой весенних лет*. || *... Вы цветете... мы увяли!* | *Дайте старости покой*). Заслуживают внимания и стихи из раннего письма к И. И. Дмитриеву (1787):

Но что же скажем мы о времени прошедшем? ...
Мы *жили, жили* мы — и более не скажем,
И более сказать не можем ничего ...
Но всё, мой друг, мне всё казалось время сном
Бывали страшны *сны*, бывали и приятны;
Но значат ли что *сны*? Не суть ли только дым?

Ср. еще: *... сокрылось*! | *Среди весенних ясных дней в жилище мрака преселилась!* ("Послание к женщинам", 1795). Карамзин, кажется, был первым, кто позволял себе шутку в связи с темой времени: *Все вещи разрушает время ...* || *Нам, право согласиться, должно* | *Ему таким же злом платить* | *И делать всё, чем только можно* | *Его скорее погубить* ("Время" [Подражание], 1795).

³ Об образе времени в поэзии Батюшкова, усвоившего лучше других уроки Муравьева, писалось раньше.

⁴ Сходные образы неоднократно встречаются и в других стихотворениях. Ср.: ... *Не зрела всех времен непостоянна света,* | *Цветок, что только цвел во утренни часы,* ... | *И лучше так увясть, как увядают розы* ... | *И помни, что к бедам родился человек* ("Письмо к А. М. Брянчанинову", 1775); *Прости, спокойный град, где дни мои младые* | *В сени семейственной вкушали сны златые* | ... *Ах! память жизни сей* ... ("Путешествие", первая полов. 1770-х годов); *Но скорые года без пользы прокатились,* | *С мечтами вы ушли и вспять не возвратились!* | ... *Вы, младости мечты, я в вас паду назад* ... ("Жалобы музам", 1776), ср. "Оду третию" (1775, о суете), и т.п.

⁵ Ср.: *Природу возлюбив, природу рассмотрев,* | *И вникнув в круг времен, в тончайшие их тени,* | *Нам Томсон возгласил природы красоту,* | *Приятности времен* ... (Карамзин, "Поэзия", 1787). Ср. там же: *О Йонг, несчастных друг, несчастных утешитель!* ... *И с смертию дружа, дружишь ты нас и с жизнью* ... или у Каменева: *О Юнг! Философ, утешитель!* | *Подай мне силы, будь учитель!* | *Да песни грустных усладят* ... ("К П.С.Л.Р.", 1796).

⁶ См.: Ю. Д. Левин, "Английская поэзия и литература русского сентиментализма", *От классицизма к романтизму* (Ленинград, 1970), стр. 195-297.

⁷ Но не "Осень" и "Осень во время осады Очакова" Державина, "Осень" (1801) Ключарева и под., принадлежащие к другой традиции (то же относится к разработке этой темы у Ржевского, Тучкова и ряда других поэтов XVIII в.).

⁸ Ср.: "Покоящийся трудолюбец" 1784, ч. 1; 1784, ч. 4, и др. Любопытно, что эта элегия привлекла внимание и в противоположном лагере — П. И. Голенищев перевел ее в 1803 г. и был похвален за это А. С. Шишковым, о чем сообщает С. П. Жихарев в *Записках современника*.

⁹ Ср.: *Что жизнь, когда в ней нет очарованья* ("Певец"). Иной поворот темы: *Не умерло очарованье! Былое сбудется опять* ("Я музу юную бывало ...", между 1822 и 1824). Ср. те же образы в другой аранжировке: *Но для меня твой вид очарованье;* | *В твоих листах вся жизнь минувших лет;* | *В них милое цветет воспоминанье* ("Цвет завета", 1819); *Цвет жизни был сорван, увяла душа* | ... *Пред ним оживились минувшие дни,* | *Давно улетевшая младость* ... ("Теон и Эсхин", 1814); *Ты унываешь о днях, невозвратно протекших* | ... *Легким полетом несутся дни быстрые жизни* ("К самому себе", 1813); *О время прежнее, о время незабвенно?* | *Или веселие навеки отцвело,* | *И счастие мое с протекшим протекло?* | ... *Как часто о часах минувших я мечтал* | ... *Так, мнится, юноша цветущий исчезает* ("К Филалету", 1808); *О! не бывать минувшему назад!* | *Сколь весело промчалися те годы* ... ("Тургеневу", 1813); *К протекшим временам лечу воспоминаньем* ... | *О дней моих весна, как быстро скрылась ты* ... ("Вечер", 1806); *О дней моих весна златая,* | *Постой ... тебе возврата нет* ... | *Летит* ... | *О! Где ты, луч путеводитель* | *Веселых юношеских дней?* ("Мечты", 1812) и др.

¹⁰ Ср.: *Не жди былого обаянья* (I, 47) при *Прошли, прошли вы, дни очарованья* у Жуковского.

¹¹ Помимо *Ваш след в одной тоске воспоминанья!* ср. еще у Жуковского: *В его глазах развалины унылы:* | *Один его минувшей жизни след* ("Тургеневу") и др. Эта образность была рано усвоена Пушкиным, ср.: *И жизни горестной моей* | *Никто следов уж не приметит* ... ("Я видел смерть ..."); ... *я радость ненавижу;* | *Во мне застыл ее минутный . след* ("Опять я ваш ..."); *Украдкой радость отлетает,* | *И след ее — печали след* ... ("Наслажденье"); *Позволь в листах воспоминанья* | *Оставить им минутный след* ("В альбом"); *И жизни горестной моей* | *Никто следов уж не приметит* ("Элегия"); *Где ж детства ранние следы?* | *Прелестный возраст миновался* ... ("Послание к Юдину"), и др.

¹² С возможностью трансформации Vb. (3 л.) → Vb. (2 л.) и одновременно Nominat. *(дни)* → Vocat. *(дни)*.

¹³ Ср. "Тоску припоминания" у Анненского.

[14] Появление инфинитива (или целой их серии) в этом месте схемы вполне закономерно и может быть проиллюстрировано многими примерами.

[15] Впрочем, есть и оптимистичесие вариации: *В них милое цветет воспоминанье* ...

[16] Иногда сходные образы появляются и у Дмитриева ("Стансы к Н. М. Карамзину").

[17] Ср.: *Прошли, прошли вы* ... у Жуковского или — с переносом удвоения на вопрос — *Куда, куда вы удалились* ... У Пушкина (ср. иную аранжировку: *Ушла пора веселости беспечной,* | *Ушла навек* ... "Элегия" ["Опять я ваш, о юные друзья!"], 1816; *Умчались вы, дни радости моей!* | *Умчались вы* ... Там же).

[18] Ср. у Пушкина в другой ритмической схеме: *Что смолкнул веселия глас* ... ("Вакхическая песня", 1825) и — что существеннее — *Слыхали ль вы за рощей глас ночной* | *Певца любви, певца своей печали?* и *Вздохнули ль вы, внимая тихий глас* ... ("Певец", 1816), сильно зависящее от одноименного стихотворения Жуковского, посвященного А. И. Тургеневу и воспроизводящего многие образы и мотивы "Элегии" (ср. *Он пел любовь — но был печален глас.* Жуковский). Сходные употребления слова *глас* неоднократны, как у Жуковского (ср.: *Денницы тихий глас; Их сердце милый глас в могиле нашей слышит; ... из гроба важный глас* | *Давно минувшего внимает; Я в сердце твой приемлю глас; И сердца глас в нее проник; ... и глас певца* | *Бессмертно дело освятило* и т.д.), так и у Пушкина (*И тихой глас простой свирели* | *С улыбкой дружества внимать; Я звал ее — и глас уединенный* | *Пустых долин* ...; *Внемлите мой печальный глас* ...; *И тайный глас мечты моей* ..., и др. Ср. также у Пнина *Мне мнится, что еще сей твой я слышу глас* ("Плач над гробом друга моего сердца", 1805; учитывая, что стихотворение имеет автобиографический характер, нельзя игнорировать его, рассматривая тему *младого певца*), у Туманского ... *Как глас изменивший надежды* и *Глас нежныя дружбы, отрады сердец* ... ("Больной певец", 1824) и др.

[19] Анализ "Элегии" А. И. Тургенева см. Ю. М. Лотман, "Поэзия 1790-1810-х годов", *Поэты 1790-1810-х годов* (Ленинград, 1971), стр. 35-36. Подробнее о влиянии Тургенева на Жуковского см. в другом месте.

[20] Ср.: *Угрюмой Осени мертвящая рука* | *Уныние и мрак повсюду разливает;* | *Холодный, бурный ветр поля опустошает* ... | *Поблекшие леса в безмолвии стоят.* | *Туманы стелются над долом, над холмами.* || *Где сосны древние задумчиво шумят* | *Усопших поселян над мирными гробами* ... | *На камне гробовом печальный, тихий Гений* | *Сидит в молчании* ... Ср. здесь же характерный мотив к о л о к о л а (*Лишь колокол нощной один вдали звучит,* | *И медленных часов при томном ударенъи* ...), повторенный потом многократно. Интересно, что он отсутствует в первом переводе "Сельского кладбища", но появляется во втором переводе — *Колокол поздний кончину отшедшего дня возвещает (The curfew tolls the knell of parting day* ...), в редакции 1801 г.: *Вечерний колокол печально завывает (раздается)*; ср.: ... *Ударил колокол* ... у Голенищева-Кутузова. Этот мотив (бой часов, удары колокола как знак приближения к смерти, конца) в русской поэзии восходит, кажется, к Сумарокову ("Часы"):

Как ударяет	Смертный, будь ниже
Колокол час,	В *жизни* ты сей;
Он повторяет	Стал ты поближе
Звоном сей *глас:*	К *смерти* своей.

И далее — "Ода на смерть князя Мещерского" (1779): *Глагол времен, металла звон* ... и т.д.; "Водопад" (1791-1794): *Не слышим ли в бою часов* | *Глас смерти, двери скрып подземной?* у Державина и "Вселенная" (1790-1791) — о времени: *Являя острие искривленной косы,* | *Имеет на главе летучие часы;* | *Держаще звон в руке, звучанье производит* ... у Хераскова.

[21] Ср. уже у Муравьева: *Да рок мой ни на миг не будет мне отсрочен* | *Пускай я млад умру* ("Ода" ["Бежит, друзья, бежит ..."], 1776), откликнувшееся в пушкинском стихе *Пускай умру, но пусть умру любя!* ("Желание", 1816), ср. *Умру любя* в "Цыганах" и

т.д., видимо, восходящее к карамзинскому *Люблю — люблю — умру любя!* ("Отставка", 1796).

[22]   В дневнике Тургенева стихотворение предваряется записью: "До́рогой мне пришло на мысль написать песнь н е с ч а с т н о г о п р и п о г р е б е н и и".

[23]   Ср. выше: *Дары небесных М у з гордыне посвящать… (… and pride | With incense kindled at the M u s e' s flame).* Ср. также: *Their name, their years, spelt by th' unletter'd M u s e* или *Or waked to extasy the living l y r e.*

[24]   Ср.: *Here rests his head upon the lap of earth | A y o u t h, to fortune and to fame unknown; | F a i r s c i e n c e frown'd not on his humble birth | And melancholy mark'd him for her own.* Еще определе-нее сформулирована тема поэта в переводе 1839 г.: *Ю н о ш а здесь погребен, неведомый счастью и славе; | Но при рожденьи он был небесною м у з о й присвоен …*

[25]   Об отношении поэтического текста и событийного ряда (минимальность интервала между жизненными переживаниями и их поэтическим изображением) см. автора, "Из исследований в области поэтики Жуковского" (в печати).

[26]
Не там, где заковал недвижною бронею
Широкую Неву береговой гранит,
Иль где высокий Кремль над пестрою Москвою,
Свидетель старых бурь, умолкнувший, стоит,

А там, среди берез и сосен неизменных,
Где в сумраке земном на небеса глядят,
Где праотцы села в гробах уединенных
Крестами венчаны, сном утомленных спят, —

Т а м н а з а к а т е д н я, осеннею порою
Она, волшебница, явилася на свет

. . . .

На с е л ь с к о м к л а д б и щ е явилась ты недаром,
О гений сладостный земли моей родной!

. . . .

. . . . но первым лучшим даром
Останется та грусть, что на кладбище старом
Тебе навеял Бог о с е н н е ю п о р о й.
                                     ("Родина русской поэзии", 1897).

[27]   В частности, *блаженных* в цитированном стихе Тургенева, резко отличающееся ритмически от содержательно сходных образов 10-20-х годов, было решительно изъято из схемы этого образа в творчестве последующих поэтов в то время, как *Воспоминание минувших дней* (и с инверсией: *Минувших дней воспоминанье*) стало поэтическим дости-жением начала XIX в. Изъятие *блаженных* тем более показательно, что *блаженный, блаженство* — излюбленные слова в поэзии Тургенева. Ср. в "Элегии": *Вы, кои в мире сем простилися навек | Б л а ж е н с т в а с милою, прелестною мечтою; Придите — здесь еще б л а ж е н с т в о есть дня вас!; И время быстрое б л а ж е н с т в а твоего; Не будет для тебя б л а ж е н с т в о м добродетель!* Ср. также в других стихотворениях: *И светлые лучи б л а ж е н с т в а …; И счастлив их б л а ж е н с т в о м; Во злодеяниях найти б л а ж е н с т в о мнит; Ах! Если б знал ценить свое б л а ж е н с т в о он …; Погибель за тебя — б л а-ж е н с т в о; … Утро ясно | Б л а ж е н н ы х детских дней …; забудем здесь искать б л а-ж е н с т в а; Б л а ж е н с т в о вольности, любви, уединенья; Б л а ж е н с т в о м на земле ласкаться …* Соответствующий образ существенно отличает поэзию Тургенева от воплощений описываемой схемы, что, впрочем, не означает отсутствия этого мотива у Жуковского, ср.: *О дней моих весна, как быстро скрылась ты | С твоим б л а ж е н с т в о м и страданьем!* ("Вечер") и др.

[28]   Иначе говоря, аспект непрерывности получил преобладание над аспектом дискрет-ности.

²⁹ Ср. также обращение к Андрею Тургеневу в одной из ранних редакций 13-й строфы "Вечера" (*Почто, мой Лизидась, с тобой я разлучен!* ...).

³⁰ Ср. в "Сельском кладбище": *Он кроток сердцем был, чувствителен душою* и *Прах сердца нежного, умевшего любить* ...

³¹ Ср.: *Заснув на холме луговом* ... | *Я унесен был легким сном* ... ‖ *Но я проснулся, наконец* | ... *Дорогой шел младой певец* | *И с пеньем удалялся* ... ("Сон", 1816) и даже *А юноши нет и не будет уж вечно* ("Кубок", 1831, из Шиллера) и др.

³² В несколько ином плане и с иными мотивировками этот мотив настойчиво повторяется Сумароковым: *Когда зла смерть!* ... *и я, и я тогда умру.* | *Такою же сражусь, такою же судьбою* ("В болезни страждешь ты ..."); *Не можно больше жить с толикою тоскою;* | *Подай мне руку, смерть, и приведи к покою* ("Отчаянье мой дух как фурия терзает"); *Теперь приходит смерть и дух мой гонит вон* ... ‖ *Родился, жил в слезах, в слезах и умираю* ("Сонет"); *И если их уже ничто не отвратит;* | *Отваживайся! смерть их вечно прекратит* ("Терпи, моя душа ..."), и т.п.

³³ Ср.: *Умру — и скоро все забудут о поэте!* ("Тихая жизнь"), а также: *Как бы предчувствием столь раннего конца* ... | ... *она несчастлива была* ("На смерть***, 1823).

³⁴ См. Л. Г. Фризман, "Эволюция русской романтической элегии (Жуковский, Батюшков, Баратынский)", *К истории русского романтизма* (Москва, 1973), и след.

³⁵ Уместно напомнить о сходного рода трансформациях и других тем, вошедших в схему, в стихотворениях В. Ф. Раевского. Ср. "К сельскому убежищу" (1810-е годы) или "Осень" (1810-е годы), которой в этом отношении противостоит, действительно, элегическое начало "Элегии II" (конец 1810-х-начало 1820-х годов): *Шумит осенний ветр, долины опустели!* | *Унынье тайное встречает смутный взор:* | *Луга зеленые, дубравы пожелтели* ...

³⁶ "Последняя весна" Батюшкова (*Вестник Европы* 1816, №11). В примечаниях к другому переводу из Мильвуа ("Гезиод и Омир — соперники") Батюшков писал: "Эта элегия переведена из *Мильвуа*, одного из лучших французских стихотворцев нашего времени. Он скончался в прошлом году в цветущей молодости. Французские музы долго будут оплакивать преждевременную его кончину ...".

³⁷ Ср. в поздней редакции — *Mourant à la fleur de son âge* ...

³⁸ Другой вариант — *Un jeune habitant du vallon* ...

³⁹ Ср.: *И грозно пенится ревущая река* (Тургенев); *Шумящие стада толпятся над рекой; Чуть слышно там плескает в брег струя* (Жуковский) и т.п.

⁴⁰ И далее: ... *Вдоль незабвенного ручья* и ... *На берегах Стигийских вод*, чему нет соответствий в тексте Мильвуа.

⁴¹ Ср.: *Dans la solitaire bourgade,* | *Revant à ses maux tristement,* | *Languissait un pauvre malade* | *D'un long mal qui va consumant.* | ... *Vous direz: "Le jeune malade* | *Est délivré de tous ses maux!"* ‖ ... *Le terme approche, je l'attends.* | *Il fut court, mon pèlerinage!* | *Je meurs au printemps de mon âge* ...

⁴² Ср. *страдалец молодой, юноша* и *страдалец* у Туманского; *страдалец юный, юноша* у Милонова ("Падение листьев", 1819).

⁴³ Ср. мотив холма у Баратынского и Туманского *(Вались, вались, мой холм могильный; На холм заветный, в тихий час* ...; *Засыпь, сокрой мой холм приютный* ...) и др.

⁴⁴ Разбирая этот вопрос, нельзя игнорировать и более периферийные (для русской поэтической традиции) линии в разработке сходного круга тем — Шенье и Парни.

⁴⁵ Ср.: *Тронитесь, Камены, любимым певцом* | *Он вянет, недугом сраженный* | ... *Он вянет, ...и А ты увядаешь!* — *Где пламя в очах?* ... в элегии Туманского "Больной певец" (1824), которая в сочетании с его переводом из Мильвуа как бы синтезирует всю схему. Интересно словоупотребление в сходном образе (ср. у Мильвуа *Et dans chaque feuille qui tombe* | *Je vois* ... ‖ *Tombe, tombe, feuille éphémère* ...) у русских переводчиков, связываемое с предшествующей традицией (примеры выше): *И с стебля сельный цвет свалится; Вались, валися, лист мгновенный* (Милонов); *Шуми, валися лист*

минутный, | *Шуми, вались с родных ветвей* (Туманский). Наконец, здесь же можно упомянуть и другие образы мимолетного времени, данные в растительном коде, — веточка, цветок, листок (уменьшительная, как правило, форма этих слов, относящихся к зрелым и относительно большим частям растения (осенняя пора), моделирует именно мимолетность, малость перед лицом вечности). И в этих образах, быстро приобретших популярность (вплоть до превращения их в клише), чужое быстро становится своим, а свое нередко облегчало эту адаптацию. Достаточно напомнить две пары примеров — "Image de la vie" (1735) Грессе (*... Vous voyez un faible rameau | Qui, par les jeux du vague Eole, | Enlevé de quelque arbrisseau, | Quitte sa tige, tombe, vole* ...) и "Веточка" (перевод Веневитинова (1823), включающийся и в серию подобных образов в русской поэзии); "La feuille" (1815) Арно (*De ta tige détachée, | Pauvre feuille desséchée, | Où vas-tu? ... | Je vais où le vent me mène* ...) и многочисленные русские переводы этого стихотворения (в том числе Жуковским, Козловым), его переработки, предвосхищения и продолжения (включая лермонтовское "Дубовый листок оторвался от ветки родимой ..." (1841), тема которого возникла еще в 1829 г.).

[46] Ср. "Поэт и друг":

... И их пророчества мне ясны.
Душа сказала мне давно:
Ты в мире молнией промчишься!
Тебе всё чувствовать дано,
Но жизнью ты не насладишься ...
Тому, кто жребий завершил,
Потеря жизни — не утрата:
Без страха мир покинет он.
Судьба в дарах своих богата,
И не один у ней закон:
Тому — процвесть с развитой силой
И смертью жизни след стереть,
Другому — рано умереть,
Но жить за сумрачной могилой.

[47] Другой предсмертный вопрос Ленского *... но ты | Придешь ли дева красоты, | Слезу пролить над ранней урной* ... совпадает с желанием *un jeune malade* (следанного певцом у Баратынского и Батюшкова) из элегии Мильвуа —*Mais vers la solitude allée | Si mon amante désolée | Venait pleurer* ... Совпадения шли и дальше: ...*Не долго плакала она.* | *Увы! Невеста молодая | Своей печали не верна* ... при: *Mais ce qu'il aimait ne vint pas | Visiter la pierre isolée (Не приходила дева к ней!* —, как скажет Баратынский); *И Делия не посетила | Пустынный памятник его | Но, с скорбию в душе своей, | Подруга к ней не приходила* (Милонов); *И с милой лаской на устах | Туда не приходила дева* (Туманский). Подобное словам Ленского мог бы сказать и его творец, вышедший на роковой поединок в день, некиим образом соотнесенный с днем гибели Ленского. Интересно, что элегия Ленского своего рода пародия на целый класс текстов, основанная на суммировании характерных микрообразов. Не случайно, что здесь обнаруживаются реминисценции из ряда поэтов, в их числе — А. Тургенев и М. Милонов.

[48] Упущенное Баратынским *mon printemps* как бы восстанавливается Пушкиным: *Весны моей* ... Характерно, что Батюшков в своем переводе вообще заменяет осень на весну ("Последняя весна"). Ср. характерные для французской элегической традиции ходы типа *O jours de mon printemps ... | A votre fuite en vain un long regret s'oppose* ... (Шенье).

[49] Ср. там же: *Твоя весна скорей промчится* ..., а также: *Протекших дней воспоминанье* ... ("К сестре моей", 1812).

⁵⁰ Ср. В. В. Виноградов, *Стиль Пушкина* (Москва, 1941), стр. 172-73. В этом смысле *О, где ты, юность золотая* (Белый, "К Меттнеру") и даже *Опять, как в годы золотые* (Блок, "Россия") представляют собой далекий отголосок старой традиции.

⁵¹ В этом круге образов у Мещерского немало и других перекличек с Жуковским. Ср. *В тени дубрав, окинутых молчаньем, | Твой слышу глас* ("Присутствие милой", между 1815 и 1818); *Где звезда-путеводитель?* ... ("Пловец", между 1815 и 1818) — в стихотворении, которое многими мотивами перекликается с "Пловцом" Жуковского (1812). Ср., в частности, *В тучах звездочка светилась | Не скрывайся! я взывал* (Жуковский), а также образ путевой звезды, звезды-путеводителя (стихотворения, дневниковые записи, например, от 4 февраля 1812 г., письма).

⁵² От этого последнего случая нужно, разумеется, отличать такие, в которых основная схема только еще нащупывается. Ср. у П. И. Шаликова: *О роща! время протекло, | Весны дыханье оживило | Тебя... | Ты прошлою, мой друг, весною | ... И дни во мгле мои текут!* ("Роща", 1797), и др.

⁵³ Следовательно, задолго до зимы 1818 г. и июня 1819 г., когда тяжелая болезнь могла дать поэту основание соотнести реальные опасения с поэтическими образами.

⁵⁴ Ср. у Лермонтова: *И прежних лет восторг священный, | Воспоминаньем оживленный* ... в стихотворении, посвященном двоюродной сестре И. И. Козлова, А. Г. Хомутовой (1841). Ср. и более ранние заготовки типа: *Не льстит мне воспоминанье дней минувших* ("К***", 1831); *Я б много припомнил минут пролетевших, | А я не люблю вспоминать* ("Романс", 1831); *И не изгладишь ты никак из памяти своей | ... минуты прежних дней* ("Романс", 1831); *Я памятью живу с увядшими мечтами, | Виденья прежних лет толпятся предо мной* ("Сонет", 1832); *Не обнажай минувших дней* ("К*", 1832), и др.

⁵⁵ Ср. там же: *Толпою полетят виденья прежних дней...; Что ж? пусть минувшее минуло сном летучим!* Ср.: *Но пролетели дни младые* ("Старик").

⁵⁶ Ср. тютчевское: *Я помню время золотое...* (1836), перекликающееся с поздним *Я вспомнил время золотое* ... (1870), которое своим заключением возвращает нас к исходной схеме:

Тут не одно воспоминанье,	И то же в вас очарованье,
Тут жизнь заговорила вновь,	И та ж в душе моя любовь! ...

("К Б. Я встретил вас ...")

Ср. также: *И на земле ей дико стало, | Очарование ушло* ... (1851).
Однако те же образы, что и в схеме, сложившейся на 50-60 лет ранее, объединяются теперь для воспроизведения совершенно иной ситуации. С этими поздними филиациями, отмечаемыми у Тютчева, Фета, В. Соловьева и др., так или иначе связаны раннесимволистские реминисценции, обнаруживающие также (например, у Блока) явные следы влияния Жуковского (ср. автора, "Блок и Жуковский" (в печати).

⁵⁷ Достаточно напомнить о тютчевском мотиве отраженном в таких стихах, как *Помедли, помедли вечерний день, | Продлись, продлись, очарованье* ("Последняя любовь", 1853(?), с включением ряда элементов схемы) или *О время, погоди!* ("Так в жизни есть мгновения ...", 1855), в связи с той же темой у Ламартина: *"O temps, suspends ton vol, et vous, heures propices, | Suspendez votre cours"* — "Le lac", 1820 (интересно, что Фет, переводивший это стихотворение в 1840 г., обращается к репертуару схемы: *"О время, не лети! Куда, куда стремится | Часов твоих побег?"*). Ср. далее: *Mais je demande en vain quelques moments encore, | Le temps m'échappe et fuit; | Je dis à cette nuit: "Sois plus lente"* ... (у Фета: *... Я говорю: о ночь, продлись!* ...) и др. Ср., впрочем, уже в "Больном певце" Туманского: *Останься, не мчися в безоблачный рай, | Крылатая гостья неволи!* (о жизни).

⁵⁸ Справедливости ради здесь уместно вспомнить эпитафию Карамзина на смерть его

друга А. А. Петрова (1766-1793), помещенную в "Московском журнале" (I, 23), ср. особенно: *Под камнем сим лежит сокрыто бренно тело,* | *Останок юноши, достойного любви.* | *Он умер, испытав печали и надежду...* В связи с темой поэзии (*Поэзия — цветник чувствительных сердец*) ср. в "Протее" (1798):

> Но горестных картин и ужасов о с е н н и х
> В унылых рощах, где в а л и т с я ж е л т ы й лист
> На ж е л т у ю траву. . . . .
> Там ю н о ш а стоит над шумною р е к о й
> И, зря печальный г р о б натуры пред собой,
> Так мыслит: прежде всё здесь жило, зеленело,
> Ц в е л о для глаз; теперь уныло помертвело!
> И я душою ц в е л, и я для счастья жил —
> Теперь навек у в я л и с счастием простился!
> Ничто ж мне жизнь? — сказал ... в волнах реки сокрылся ...
> О нежные сердца! сей юноша любил ...

Ср. также "Стихи на смерть Пелского" (1803), "Весеннюю песнь меланхолика" (1788, особенно ее конец), и отдельные образы в других стихотворениях: *Нет Альциндора!...* *Тисы над гробом* | *Юного друга томно шумят* или: *Куда, Элиза, ты сокрылась* | *... Быв в цвете майских дней своих ...* (в приписываемых Карамзину текстах).

[59] Впрочем, см. уже у Кюхельбекера: *Горька судьба поэтов всех племен;* | *Тяжеле всех судьба казнит Россию ...* ("Участь русских поэтов", 1845). Тем интереснее связи Кюхельбекера с началом этой традиции. См. *Дневник* (Ленинград 1929), стр. 63 (об "Элегии" Тургенева): "Еще в лицее любил я это стихотворение, и тогда даже больше 'Сельского кладбища', хотя и был тогда энтузиастом Жуковского. Окончание Тургенева элегии бесподобно". Ср. также *Могилу тихую певца* у А. Бестужева-Марлинского ("Шебутуй", 1829) и несколько раньше "Тень друга" (1824) Ив. Бороздны.

SEMANTIC DYNAMICS IN
NARRATIVE TEXTS

JAN VAN DER ENG

In this paper I will deal with certain aspects of semantic dynamics in narrative texts, that is of dynamics as they are actualized during the process of reading. To begin with, I shall give a provisional description of a motif as a dynamic element in narration. Then I shall go into the various devices that may be used to render a motif dynamic. In the first place I shall distinguish different types of internal semantic relations between text parts containing one or more motifs and belonging to the same narrative. Secondly, I wish to deal with the significance of extratextual semantic relations, that is relations between a part of the text to be described and another text. Finally I shall make some remarks about the sometimes very great importance of these external relations when the relation is one between a text or part of a text on the one hand, and conceptions of human reality on the other hand. External relations with other texts and with what we call 'human reality' may have a profound influence on the various types of internal relations.

We must not forget the fact that quite often one motif or a group of motifs establishes several types of internal relations at the same time: these relations may refer to different thematic aspects, for instance, both to the action and the characterization. This multi-functional aspect of motifs, this capacity of forming different types of relation at different thematic levels, will be further discussed in connection with some other important aspects of narrative dynamics. But now I will first try to shed some light upon the concept of the literary motif. Tomaševskij's definition of a motif is that it is the smallest semantic unit of all the thematic data. He distinguishes free motifs, which can be left out without damaging the totality of the causal and temporal course of events, and fixed motifs which cannot be left out without invalidating the causal and temporal course of events.[1]

There seems to be an analogy between fixed motifs and, what I call, motifs as dynamic elements in narration. In the latter case, however, the motif is not only determined by its relation to action moments (that is, the causal and temporal course of events) but also by data belonging to the characterization and the setting. A useful starting point, however, is Tomaševskij's description of the motif as an element in relation to the theme.

I suggest that we assign the thematic data to various levels, connected with and implying one another: the level of characterization, both physical and psychological, the action level denoting every action the characters undertake, both in words and in fact, including everything that happens to them, and lastly the level of the geographical and social setting. We might add a fourth level that explicitly states what is only implied in the aforementioned levels: that is, general statements about the characters (or even about man in general), about the actions and events connected with the characters (or with man in general), and about the geographical and social setting of the characters (or man in general).

The interrelations between the various levels and the fact that each level implies the other, often boils down in fact to the dominance of one of them over the others: it may be that the action is determined by the psychological qualities of the characters, that the setting, both geographical and social, bears the trademark of the intellectual and emotional traits of the characters.

On the other hand, certain restrictions, taboos, regulations and other aspects of the setting may influence or even determine a character and his actions (as, for instance, occurs clearly in the naturalistic novel).

Actions too, may predominate, in which case the characters may possess only enough individuality necessary to initiate the unfolding of an action-pattern according to its own, usually stereotyped rules of adventure. Geographical and social details in these cases function only in a subordinate relation to the action, endangering it, making it possible or hindering it.

The dominance of one of the thematic levels is determined by the narrator's attitude or, in those cases where he switches continuously from one point of view to another, by that viewpoint which bears most weight. The narrator's attitude is marked by two important factors:

a) the degree of knowledge as shown by the amount and the quality of the information given to the reader;

b) the emotional and intellectual approach to the narrated facts.

Under a) we can distinguish between narrators who possess omniscience, restricted omniscience (for instance, the narrator's knowledge is adapted to the here + now perspective of one of the characters) and knowledge of a specific kind (for example, when a narrator refers to sources of information as for instance in chronicles). The possible variations in the amount of information are unlimited, and in addition, the author can use mixed forms, varying from omniscience to restricted omniscience and to no knowledge at all.

The emotional and intellectual approach too permits of all kinds of gradation: emotionally cool and distant, and intellectually superior; sensitive to the feelings of a particular character, and intellectually reserved; an emotional and intellectual symbiosis with the emotions and intellect of a character; feelings of breathless admiration, associated with intellectual inferiority etc. It goes without saying of course, that here, too, all kinds of mixed forms may occur with interchanging emotional and intellectual attitudes.

Sometimes an author conceals for a long time the amount of information he possesses; he administers his information carefully and selects varying degrees of knowledge, understanding and evaluation. In an article on the first part of *Crime and Punishment* I have tried to show that the dominating level varies several times as a result of changes in the narrator's attitude — at first the text exhibits mainly an adaptation in knowledge and approach to the perspective of Raskol'nikov; later on, however, we see, in combination with this, an authoritative evaluation on the part of the narrator. In this way, data, which seemingly belonged to the action-level exclusively, turn out to be more symptomatic of Raskol'nikov's pathological condition.[2] In other words the dominant thematic significance of motifs is *not* invariable: it may at first be related principally to the action level and then to the characterization level: consequently, one particular motif may have different dominant thematic functions, which take one another's place in the course of the story. One of these functions, however, in the end will turn out to be the most prevalent one and the ambiguity as to which is dominant will be resolved.

In its relationship to the thematic levels, a motif, as a dynamic element in narration, might be called an incomplete datum, which becomes more complete as the story unfolds. In any given construction (a sentence, a paragraph and the like) a motif appears in the first place as a datum referring to either characterization, event or situation; the semantic structure of a motif, however, is determined by this construction only to a very limited extent. To determine its semantic structure, a 'filling-in' from the preceding and following texts is necessary, a 'filling-in' even from other texts, and from reality. Because of this filling-in, this relating the motif to preceding and following motifs or groups of motifs, an event datum may become primarily important for the characterization of a character, a datum of the setting may become primarily important for the action, and a detail of the characterization may become significant for the presentation of a social class and so forth. In its relation to the preceding and following text a motif often acts as a "thematic chameleon": it may be linked up with motifs of these text fragments on the basis of dominant (or temporarily dominant) and subordinated (or temporarily subordinated) thematic levels: the corresponding thematic features on both sides can belong to the dominant or subordinated level, or one can be dominant, the other subordinated. Hence the same motif can be linked to several others at different thematic levels and now set off features of characterization, then of action and so forth.

As an example of filling-in from other texts I refer to Vinogradov's article on Gogol's novella *The Nose*. In his article Vinogradov shows the connection with Sterne's *Tristram Shandy* and with various specimens of journalistic writings about noses.[3] The relation with another text may be important for the semantic completion of the motifs, because the related fragment of external text is semantically linked up with the whole structure of this external text; in other words it is filled-in already. It may happen, for instance, that certain motifs in an action-moment in a detective story strongly remind the reader of a corresponding action-moment in another detective story. This corresponding feature in the two stories will extend to the consequences the action-moment had in the other story. The reader will project both that action-moment and its consequences on to the story he is reading and they may have a strong influence on his expectations regarding its further development. Essential in this respect is that in this way the author has a large range of possibilities at his disposal of assigning an additional meaning to certain motifs in his text, either throughout it or for a longer or shorter period only.

He may also create a range of possibilities by making use of specific relations with existing conceptions of human reality. Implicit references to human reality, to an anthropological structure are to be found in every story, because of the fact that the correlation of a text with reality is a condition for its comprehensibility. In addition to this there are textual indications forcing the reader to make comparisons with his own conceptions of reality. This type of reference may be established even by using such ordinary words as 'normal', 'extremely', 'strange', etc. Think for instance of Gogol's stories.

A very distinct way of forcing the reader to make comparisons occurs for instance in a story by Robert Penn Warren, when he addresses the reader as follows: "You have seen him a thousand times. You have seen him standing on the street corner on Saturday afternoon, in the little county-seat towns. He wears blue jean pants, or overalls washed to a pale pastel blue like the colour of the sky after a shower in spring...",[4] etc. At the end of *The Nose,* too, we find this emphatic address to the reader: "Vot kakaja istorija slučilas' v severnoj stolice našego obširnogo gosudarstva! Teper' tol'ko po soobraženii vsego vidim, čto v nej est' mnogo nepravdopodobnogo. ... A vse odnako že, kak porazmysliš', vo vsem ètom, pravo, est' čto-to. Kto čto ni govori, a podobnye proisšestvija byvajut na svete; redko, no byvajut."

Of the three types of relations I have mentioned, the most important are the internal relations between motifs belonging to the same narrative text. The external relations in fact function only to add nuances to the internal relations, even though this may go very far indeed. There exist certain types of internal relations we shall call oppositions from now on. These opposition types spring from a specific relation of dissimilarity and similarity between significant elements of the story, making possible a comparison between the motifs of two parts of the text. These motifs, placed in opposition to one another, are compared with each other at one thematic level. They may pertain to the dominant or subordinated level in each text fragment in which they occur.

The specific relationship between the similarities and dissimilarities is centred on the dominance of either the former or the latter. It is, of course, the narrator who decides which data will be given the greater prominence. The narrator, too, decides on the exact nature of those prominent similarities or dissimilarities. He may for instance reduce the dissimilarities to mere modifications of the basic idea, or he may lend them an antinomic quality. This becomes very obvious when for instance two different narrators at different moments of the story expose the same fact and are, in their evaluation of it, in diametrical opposition with one another. The same effect will be achieved by one and the same narrator varying the amount and quality of his information as well as his emotional and intellectual approach. The narrator decides also in which text part which motifs in the opposition will be dominant. In cases where the hero is comparable with a secondary character, the opposition, as a rule, will function to set off the hero; the text fragment in which the hero is spoken of is given semantically a greater weight by the opposition than the fragment centred round the secondary character. In other words, the reader's attention is drawn towards those motifs in the fragment which are filled in by the preceding text to the greatest extent and which to the greatest extent require to be filled in by the following text. In most cases these motifs will be the motifs in the last text fragment to have been read but not necessarily so: the last text fragment may refer to a secondary character and it may show a narrative perspective that is inferior (in knowledge etc.) to the narrative attitude in the preceding fragment.

However important the role of the narrator is for the determination of the opposition-type and for its further evaluation, it is the reader's perception that, in a great many cases, is conclusive for constituting the opposition: very often there is no direct causal relation between the text fragments in opposition. Sometimes even the causal relation is completely absent, for instance when fragments about totally unconnected events, characters, or social settings are compared.

Although the number of opposition-types is limited, their differentiation on the basis of fillings-in from the given text, from other texts and from conceptions of reality is probably infinite. The determination of an opposition-type occurs in the first place on the basis of the dissimilarities or similarities that are given a dominant position in the two text fragments. If they concern essential aspects of the thematic level that is dominant in both fragments, the opposition may be rendered in words partly coinciding with the textual data. I say partly, because a certain abstraction is inevitable.

A greater abstraction will be found when the data are less essential to the dominant thematic level, still greater even when they belong to a subordinated thematic level. Those similarities or dissimilarities that remain in the background may be only partly or even not at all expressed in the oppositional fragments. The preceding text quite often should be taken into consideration to grasp features of similarity or dissimilarity that are kept in the background but nevertheless constitute necessary components for comparison. It goes without saying that filling-in, based on earlier narrative data, scattered over many pages, as a rule necessitates the greatest degree of abstraction, though most of the information in these pages will be irrelevant for the opposition in question.

Four frequently occurring opposition types are: parallelism, antithesis, analogy and variation. The principal elements in parallelisms are dissimilarities, set off against the background of similarities; in antitheses the dissimilarities develop and increase in an antinomic way against the background of similarities, in analogies the main elements are similarities against the background of dissimilarities, in variations we find differentiations of one basic idea. The latter opposition type may require some further explanation: in variations the differentiation of one basic idea may be effectuated with the help of phraseological diversity in the wording of essentially synonymous data, or by introducing 'deep-lying' significant elements into the text, which form the basis for data having ostensibly nothing or very little in common with one another, even belonging to different thematic levels.

A rough outline of these opposition-types at the characterization level might look for instance like this:

parallelism — a devoted, undemanding love versus an exacting love with the lover willing to go far, without, however, totally committing himself. In such a case background details may be supplied in other parts of the text, for instance corresponding data such as high class setting, wealth, intelligence and artistic interests.

antithesis — love versus hate. We may find the same background details (partly) in other sections of the text as in parallelisms.

analogy — love versus love. Here the background information derived partly or wholly from preceding parts of the text may denote an incongruence in intelligence, artistic interests and so forth.

variation — love versus love. Features of dissimilarity (indispensable to analogies) do not occur or more correctly they are reduced to phraseological differences, representing of course different voices speaking about the same. There is, however, the second type of variation, opposing apparently uncomparable thematic data: love making its appearance through words of tenderness versus love behind actions opposing a person's ambitions, leanings and so forth.

Variations of this second type play an essential part in the dynamic construction of a story: they form the basis of series of the same type of opposition that express the development of a specific thematic aspect. We can think of a series of antitheses, which expresses the shaping of two antinomical characters, a series of parallelisms, which elucidates the changes in successive stages of an intrigue etc. The part of the variation in these series of antitheses, parallelisms etc., consists in the recurrence of an 'underlying' set of significant elements, partly implied in the oppositional text fragments, partly inserted into them. This set is dynamically established by force of the semantic connections between the oppositional text fragments of the series: as a rule only some significant elements of the set are implied in each of these fragments and from one fragment to another the implied features will partly differ. Other features of the set will be inserted into a passage of the series as a consequence of its coherence with previous and subsequent oppositional text fragments.

The set may contain more or less puzzling significant elements, i.e. such features which require further information. The occurrence of such fragmentary and until further notice rather ambiguous features often leads to a junction with a subsequent series supplying the needed information most often in combination with new riddles.

In the succession of series a hierarchical order is established: the higher a series ranks the more it imparts information to the solution of riddles introduced into previous series and the more it makes enigmas to be solved in forthcoming series. In this respect propounding a riddle makes more impression on the reader than solving one. As a rule every new series brings more answers and questions than the previous one. But this is of course not necessarily so.

I shall now go into some important aspects of some of the opposition series in the story *Pchenc* by Sinjavskij.[5] This will give me the opportunity to demonstrate the significance of the narrator's attitude for determining the type of the opposition to be used, for modifying it into a series of variations, and for adding further nuances by means of relations to extratextual elements. It will also give me the opportunity to examine overlapping series and series which succeed one another and the hierarchical relationship between them: the multi-thematic functionality of motifs will be demonstrated in connection with all this.

Pchenc may be divided into different parts, each part being characterized by a continuity of place, person and action. One of these parts concerns a number of amorously tinted scenes in which the 'I' and Veronika are confronted with one another. These scenes include both moments of action and observations about details of the scene together with 'I''s reflections on these details. The same holds true for observations about Veronika. All the details of the scene, the reflections on them and the reported thoughts about the girl's character and intentions form part of the framework of the action-moments.

Here we find a series of the type I have described in another article as an encircling or framework series, that is a series in which the data on place and persons are characterized by continuity and synchronism and the actions of the characters depicted in their mutual confrontations are characterized by continuity and causality.[6]

All the thematic levels play a part in framework series. One level dominates and the data of other levels are considered relevant only in as far as they set off the dominating level. This particular relevance is, as a rule, very great. There may be, however, text fragments which have hardly any relevance to the dominant thematic level. They fulfull an important thematic function, though. We shall see this in *Pchenc*.

The 'I' imparts his information to the reader in such a way that the framework series consists of parallelisms at the dominant action-level. Specific to this series are the advances of Veronika related by the 'I' as far as not revealed by the girl's own words, and the parrying reactions of the 'I', including his subsequent observations and reflections. Some background correspondences in these parallelisms are specified in passing both before and during these series: a mutual need for contact, a mutual enemy in the I's landlady who is also Veronika's mistress, a mutual love of cactuses. The advances and subsequent retreats which take place against this common background may be reproduced from one text moment to another as follows:

a) The 'I' tells how Veronika approaches him with an invitation for dinner / The I by way of diversion begins to talk about their mutual enemy: the landlady (this conversation develops as follows: Veronika mentions certain steps the authorities plan to take against the 'I', whereupon the 'I' says he will call in the police and further reflects on the dangers of having again the police's attentions fixed on him).

b) Veronika says she will take all the blame (for the mess in the bathroom) and then the 'I' tells of her attempt to touch his hand / The 'I' jumps backwards to avoid this, saying he is not ill and does not have a temperature, and then suggests they sit down at table.

c) The (unspoken) observations of the 'I' about the nasty smelling food, and his unspoken reflections on 'culinary sadism': the disgusting structure of scrambled eggs and sausages, the brutal treatment of corn; his again unspoken question regarding the effect the appearance of a writer or an engineer as a course on the menu would have are followed by Veronika's insistence on his eating and once again the soothing assurance that she will take all the blame for the bathroom.

d) Veronika tries to worm out information regarding the 'I''s friends, wife and children / The 'I' keeps stirring his tea and answers that for him she had supplanted all his friends and that an old hunchback is no good companion for a woman. In a comment which he does not speak aloud he says he sincerely wants to keep her from a confession of love. His main consideration seems to be that sexual pretensions on her side might ruin their alliance against malicious neighbours. He adds that to prevent the disaster (of a confession and sexual pretensions) he would be willing to pose as a criminal or as a paederast etc. He rejects this idea as too dangerous because of the intriguing splendour that might be connected with it.

e) Veronika says that he is too generous, that he is too much afraid of being a burden on others, and that it is not pity that is moving her but that she loves cactuses and that he resembles a cactus. He relates how she touches his hand with her burning fingers / The 'I' shrinks back as if from fire. The compassion of Veronika, who thinks he must be ill because his temperature is so low, becomes unbearable. Claiming a headache the 'I' asks her to leave.

f) Waving her hand like a little girl, Veronika disappears, saying "see you tomorrow" and adding the instruction to present her with a cactus on the morrow / Thereupon the 'I' reflects on Veronika's imperative tone and on the tyranny of lovers who demand recompense for their love. He sighs wistfully how good it would be should nobody love him.

The dissimilarities in these parallelisms may be reduced to the following different stages of the coupling of advances and retreats:

a) an invitation for dinner on the one hand, diversions by talking about social difficulties on the other;

b) Veronika's alleviating these difficulties plus her familiar touching of the body as opposed to the 'I''s recoiling from her touch and his emphatic denial of being ill as an explanation for this behaviour plus finally his suggestion to sit down at table as a means of diverting her attention;

d) attempts to indulge in confidential talk against acknowledgement of friendship and rejection of the possibility of a love-relationship with a hunchback;

e) an implicit confession of love and the touching of the 'I''s hand in contrast to his shrinking back as if burnt and his request that she leave on the pretense of illness;

f) amorous gestures and pretensions on the one hand, and reflections on the tyranny of love on the other.

(c has been omitted as it refers to data which have nothing or little to do with the series of parallelisms at the action level).

The set of significant components on which the series rests may be described as: intimacy versus distance / desire for physical contact versus aversion / thoroughness versus clumsiness / frankness versus reservation.

It will be clear from the above reproduction of the text-moments and from the differences in advances and retreats, that these significant data are not realized in all the oppositional parts. In a) for instance, we do not find the aversion against physical contact. This element, however, may be implied in the distracting manoeuvre. In b) there are no attempts to evoke confidences, but we may connect Veronika's intimate gesture towards the 'I''s body with such an attempt. In f) we do not see any readiness to defend someone in trouble but this thoroughness, as an implicit element, is characteristic of the whole relationship. There is both a backward and forward projection of significant data on to the various elements in the series of parallelisms where these data are not implied (or not explicitly expressed) in the parallelisms themselves.

The growing intensity in the variations of the parallelism seems to me unmistakable. The clumsiness of the 'I', for instance, shows a certain progression and even leads to a sort of impasse in which he can only think of a rather poor excuse (that is: illness) to send Veronika away — a poor excuse because he had emphatically denied the very same thing just a bit earlier.

It is easy, too, to distinguish a gradation in the growing resourcefulness with which Veronika sets out to reach her goal. The frankness and outspokenness of Veronika and the fact that the 'I' is hiding something are indicated more and more clearly. These aspects are also brought out by the growing vagueness, secrecy and strangeness which come to be characteristic of the reticence of the 'I'. There are moments one thinks he is in hiding from the police and is seeking help from the girl for certain things he does not wish to reveal. Such ideas are however shattered when the 'I' refrains from using various possibilities to keep the girl at arm's length: he does not wish to play the criminal, the paederast or the madman because this might lend him a dangerous allure. All this makes the question as to what exactly causes him to be so incommunicative or, put differently, what exactly motivates him in his relationship with Veronika, more forceful.

A description of the phraseological construction of the gradation does not fall within the scope of this short discussion. I wish to round off this subject with some remarks on overlapping series, on the hierarchical order between them, on the factor that determines the sequence of series and, finally, on the hierarchy between series succeeding one another. In the framework series of parallelisms at the action-level, it is easy to detect two constituent series of parallelisms at the same level, that is, Veronika's advances on the one hand and the parrying reactions of the 'I' on the other. Each of these series of parallelisms is based on its own set of features. Both sets are dynamically reconstructed and form, either implied or inferred from backward and forward projections, the basis of all the passages in opposition in each of the series: in both cases these sets are varied in the oppositional fragments. Of the two series in question, the one connected with the 'I' (the parrying reactions) is hierarchically the principal one. This is not only because the narrator and the 'I' are one and the same, but also for another reason that determines the hierarchy in a much more general sense. A series will predominate when, in relation to the preceding and especially to the following text, it is least complete, that is, when it raises the most questions. The 'I''s stand-offishness gives rise to several questions, esp. his inadequate physical reactions. His secrecy may lead one to suppose that he is a criminal or a spy or something equivalent. At the same time these suppositions are curtailed by his own observations (for instance when he says that he could pretend to be a criminal, etc.). The question of his identity, however, remains as intriguing as ever. This question comes to the fore particularly forcefully in a part of the text where the 'I' shows hardly any parrying reactions towards Veronika, that is, in the passage with his observations on culinary sadism. As far as the action of the 'I' is concerned this fragment hardly belongs to the series of parallelisms. The central element in this part of the text is the question of the identity of the 'I': that is, his psychological identity, a question which is raised by the 'I''s indignation about the suffering inflicted on corn. The alert reader may even at this stage already be wondering about the 'I''s physical identity.

From this moment onwards the question of the 'I''s identity is irrevocably linked with all the instances in which his parrying reactions occur. We may even say that from here on these passages are read in the first place with a view to obtaining information on the 'I''s personality: the thematic dominance in this constituent series begins to change. The other constituent series becomes primarily a catalyst, continually directing the reader's attention to the 'I''s mysterious personality. We should keep in mind here that Veronika's advances frequently are not put in her own words but related from the 'I''s point of view.

This means that within the framework series the coupling of advances and retreats basically functions to set off the mysterious personality of the 'I' again and again. In other words: in a system of series, a framework series and its constituent series, the predominant one is the series of which the motifs in the oppositional text parts are semantically least complete, leave a great deal open for guesswork, and require the most amount of additional information. This series determines in the end the dominant thematic level.

The series that most needs additional information also determines the rise of a following series in which more mysterious, paradoxical and absurd elements may be added to the same thematic material and where at the same time 'filling-in' may begin to take place, that is, the completion of information in relation to the preceding series.

This second series will then become of greater importance hierarchically as a result of the already mentioned increase in the mystery etc. on the one hand and of the partial revelation of earlier puzzling moments on the other. Various examples are to be found in *Pchenc*. For instance, in a series of confrontations between the 'I' and a hunchback, more and more becomes clear about the former's physical, psychological and social identity, but at the same time more and more mysterious data about him are brought into the story.

Other series also spring out as a result of the necessary completion of the information on the 'I'. These series may differ as regards the type of opposition and thematic level (that is, the level more close to the surface), but the core of each of them consists in the unravelling of the riddle of the 'I''s identity: throughout all the series a set of features is to be varied at the characterization level of the 'I'. Consequently, the dominant level in the story is the characterization; all the events, all the actions, all the data regarding geographical and social setting finally turn out to be above all symptomatic of the identity of the 'I'.

I think I should add a final word about the gradation of oppositions by means of their relationships to other texts and to reality. As I have said before, the gradation may be a strong one. A great many passages in *Pchenc* for instance, while focusing the reader's thoughts over and over again on the mysterious physical and psychological identity of the 'I', acquire a paradoxical quality as a result of the relations to human reality that are indicated by the text.

Let me give one example: it concerns a passage in which the unusual physical and psychological identity of the 'I' is implicitly stated in some observations on the human body and some possible ways to improve its disgusting form a little. The first words of the text fragment, *no bud' ja na ich meste...*, literally establish a link with the standard image of the human body. Following these words the 'I' suggests, if he were a human being, he would have his legs shortened by plastic surgery and would have himself fixed up as a real hunchback, etc. When these, to us, eccentric opinions about a physical form that would be less disgusting are projected on to our conceptions of reality, they give the passage a paradoxical quality.

The question of what exactly the 'I' looks like is, of course, brought strongly to the fore. Any filling-in on our part from our conceptions of reality produces only a negative image: the 'I' rejects normal, well-proportioned legs, the shortening of them in his opinion only lessens their repulsive appearance, it certainly has no harmonizing effect. As regards relationships with other texts, Sinjavskij's story might be linked up with patterns of science fiction. Robinson Crusoe is mentioned as a person the 'I' more or less identifies with. There are indications for relations with propagandist journalism, for instance in the passage where the letters of the word *čelovek* occur in various combinations: *čelovek..., vekočel..., čekelov..., kevoleč....* Though the word here also becomes devoid of meaning, this is accomplished in a different way from the journalistic propagandist writings, where it is merely brought about by the frequent use of the word in question. By means of this playful raillery on word-mongering some specific aspects of non-conformist isolation are added to the abnormal psychological identity of the 'I'.

University of Amsterdam

NOTES

[1] Cf. B. Tomaševskij, *Teorija literatury. Poètika* (Moskva-Leningrad, 1928), p. 137.
[2] Cf. "Le procédé du suspense dans la première partie de *Crime et châtiment*", *Russian Literature,* 4 (The Hague, 1973), pp. 72-86.
[3] V. V. Vinogradov, *Èvoljucija russkogo naturalizma: Gogol' i Dostoevskij* (Leningrad, 1929), pp. 7-88.
[4] Opening lines of the story *The Patented Gate and the Mean Hamburger.*
[5] Abram Terc [Andrej Sinjavskij], *Fantastičeskie povesti: V cirke; Ty i ja; Kvartiranty; Grafomany; Gololedica; Pchenc; Sud idet. Ljubimov. Čto takoe socialističeskij realizm* (New York, 1967), pp. 175-95.

[6] "Priem: central'nyj faktor semantičeskogo postroenija povestvovatel'nogo teksta", *Structure of Texts and Semiotics of Culture,* ed. by Jan van der Eng and Mojmír Grygar (The Hague-Paris, 1973), pp. 29-58.

COMMENTS

(Meijer)   1. On p. 441 of your paper, you state that "the ambiguity as to which [function] is dominant will be resolved". Is that always so, is it not possible that this ambiguity will remain even after reading the novel is completed?

2. You stated in your resume that by using the word 'strange' an author refers the reader to his own world, i.e., to the world outside the story. But does such usage not rather indicate a line drawn within the story, between normal and strange behaviour?

Additional discussion: Eekman, Hrushovsky, Nilsson, Segal, Terras, Winner

AUTHOR'S REPLY

1. The dominant thematic function of motifs will vary in the course of a story. This phenomenon is closely connected with changes in the approach and in the knowledge of the narrator (and the reader) that take place while the story continues.

An important question is whether structure in a story can exist without a hierarchical arrangement of the changes in thematic dominance, the changes in the principal relevance of motifs of either the action, or the characterization, or the social setting. When we distinguish for instance picaresque novels, psychological novels and social novels, the distinctions will be based on this primary relevance (cf. also Muir's classifications: novel of action, novel of character and so on).

Since a primary relevance of one thematic level often presupposes a secondary relevance of the other levels, there will always be a certain ambiguity. The important thing is to discover the hierarchical arrangement of the various changes, not to remove every possible ambiguity.

2. An author will sometimes use adjuncts like 'strange' and 'normal', without creating a specific intra-textual opposition. We refer to our example of the opening lines in Robert Penn Warren's story, where instead of 'normal' the wording 'a thousand times' appears and where the reader is directly

challenged to compare the narrative statement with his own experience: "You have seen him a thousand times", etc. Another instance is to be found in the opening paragraphs of F. Scott Fitzgerald's story *The Curious Case of Benjamin Button,* where the narrator declares that he will stick to the amazing facts and will leave it to the reader to form an opinion about these facts. If adjuncts like 'strange' and 'normal' create an intra-textual opposition, this opposition will stand out only against the background of reality: without reality the notion would be unintelligible. Consequently, when authors try to restrict the number of words they use, when they leave things unmentioned or half-mentioned, they are appealing to the reader's conception of reality, forcing him to supply the necessary complementary information from it.

In a great many cases the reader will first of all compare certain textual elements with the accepted code of life and will perceive the intra-textual opposition only later on: this will happen when oppositions occur in text parts separated from one another by other text parts.

Postscript

I would like to point out the principles of dynamic narrative construction which I discussed in this paper. First of all I have tried to give a provisional description of the narrative motif. I have called it an incomplete thematic element referring primarily to one of the thematic levels: characterization, event of social setting. Let me add that this incomplete element may consist of one word, a group of words or a short sentence. When it consists of one word or a group of words it acquires significance by its position in the sentence: a sentence is often marked by an emotional and/or intellectual approach of the speaker. If the sentence is neutral in this respect, it will be part of a paragraph which shows the speaker's attitude. A motif does not exist outside the sentence: outside this phraseological entity it would be just a word or a group of words which has no relation whatsoever with a speaker/narrator and his text. When the word (or group of words) is not embodied in the sentence or paragraph, it will designate a textually undetermined element of either characterization, action or setting. Embodied in a sentence/paragraph the same word (group of words) will function as a motif, i.e. it will be significant on more than one thematic level: as an element of the outer or inner characterization it may also pertain to the action and possibly to the social setting. Its significance on one of the thematic levels will be dominant, however, and it will have a subordinate semantic relevance for the other levels. Dominance and subordination, however, tend to be fluctuating. The semantic structure of a motif is not only determined by its place in the sentence, but also by its connection with several other motifs throughout the text. These relations with other text parts may influence the dominant thematic significance of the motif within the text. It may change as to its dominant thematic relevance. Such a change may occur more than once.

The relation to another text part I have designated as an opposition. The opposition of a fragment to a second textual part (both of them consisting of one or more motifs) takes place on one thematic level: that is, only features of the characterization, or the action, or the social setting are singled out, though each of the oppositional parts may have relevance to more than one thematic level. The relationship brings to the fore, however, one thematic point of comparison. The essential condition for every opposition is that the opposed fragments must show similar and dissimilar features. Either the dissimilarities or the similarities will be dominant. By his presentation of the facts the narrator makes clear which are prevalent. The nature of the dominant similarities or dissimilarities determines the type of opposition. I have distinguished several types: analogies (the dominant features in oppositional groups of motifs are similarities); parallelisms (dissimilarities as dominant features); antitheses or contrasts (dominant dissimilarities, antinomic in character); variations (identical facts, presented in phraseological different ways in accordance with different points of view of one or more speakers/narrators).

Oppositions of one type are often grouped together in a series which sometimes forms a continuous flow of textual sections, sometimes constitutes a chain of remote fragments scattered all over the text. Such a series informs the reader of a specific process or pattern of the action, the characterization or the setting: in other words all textual sections of the series pertain to complementary data on a common dominant thematic level. The connections between all the fragments of the series are based upon a set of semantic components of the deep structure. This set of basic constituents is generated in a dynamic way, i.e. by the connections between the fragments of the series: some features may be reinforced by the relation of a textual section to one or more oppositional sections; others may be progressively or regressively actualized by the connections of a text part with previous or following oppositional fragments. All this is closely connected with what I have called gradation in series: in a succession of text fragments the set of features will acquire a growing complexity, acuteness and expressiveness.

The dominant thematic level in a series may change in the process of the narrative construction. This change is the result of certain gaps in the information about the circumstances and developments on the dominant thematic level. The reader's wish for these gaps to be "filled in" may divert his attention to facts of another thematic level: thus an actional scheme may come to be more intriguing, more significant for the mental condition of the character behind the action than for the stages and the final outcome of the course of action.

In every narrative we find a succession of series. The rise of each new series is the result of the need for extra information (to solve contradictions, unriddle mysteries, etc.). Most of the time this will be done in combination with an attempt to complicate old issues by adding new, puzzling elements to them: thus the rise of yet another series will be guaranteed.

The successive series and their dominant thematic levels are hierarchically arranged. The more complementary information (from the preceding and the following context) a series needs, the higher it ranks in this hierarchy. Its place in the hierarchy is also connected with the information (both the quantity and the quality of it) it gives about mysterious elements in the preceding text. The hierarchical organization of all the thematic patterns which were dominant for a longer or shorter stretch of the text, will be finally established at the end of the narrative, when the process of thematic construction is completed, when construction has become structure. It will be possible to trace some constant features in all text sections. A kind of superseries will be composed of fragments of all the other series. Thus in Sinjavskij's story the essence of the main character's identity shows through the textual sections, through the succession of event-sequences and through the specific presentation of the social environment.

The factors (discussed in the above) determining the dynamic semantic construction of narratives can be listed as follows:
a) the gradual semantic completion of motifs by means of oppositions of several types;
b) the formation of series of oppositions of one type on one dominant thematic level;
c) the gradation in the series;
d) the change of thematic dominance in a series;
e) the hierarchical arrangement of all the series.

Amsterdam 1981

PROBLEMS IN PUŠKIN'S FOUR-FOOT IAMBS

WALTER VICKERY

I. MASCULINE AND FEMININE ENDINGS

In his article, "Slučajnye četyrexstopnye jamby v russkoj proze", V. E. Xolševnikov gives the results of a study of random four-foot iambs taken from six different prose writers.[1] The six samples together yield the following stress pattern (figures for the fourth ictus are omitted in the present study since they invariably equal 100):

I	II	III
71.3	72.5	38.1

Other studies, based on various prose writings and using a variety of approaches, including and emphasizing the construction of 'theoretical' models, have given roughly similar results. For comparative purposes they are here reproduced:

N. Ryćkova	77.9	66.6	52.1
A. Proxorov	78.2	61.3	45.1
K. Taranovsky	78.8	61.3	44.9
M. Gasparov	79.7	60.3	41.8[2]

An interesting feature of the figures given by Xolševnikov is the division into eight- and nine-syllable groups, i.e., into masculine and feminine endings. Breaking his figures down into masculines and feminines, we obtain the following:

M.	68.3	74.3 (+2.8)	34.7
F.	72.9 (+4.6)	71.5	40.0 (+5.3)[3]

We see that the feminines have a higher stress percentage than the masculines on the third ictus, a lower percentage on the second ictus, and a higher percentage on the first ictus. Xolševnikov sees the higher stress percentage of the feminines on the third ictus as a confirmation of his *a priori* assumption that the feminine third-ictus stress will be stronger because in the feminines only a four-syllable word will automatically eliminate the third-ictus stress, whereas in the masculines a third-ictus stress will automatically be eliminated by either a three- or four-syllable word. We may add that at least in prose, a stress on the third ictus will decrease the probability of a stress on the second ictus, and the absence of a stress on the second ictus will increase the probability of a stress on the first ictus. Given, therefore, the greater strength of the feminines on the third ictus, the pattern of greater masculine strength on the second ictus and greater feminine strength on the first ictus is logical. It follows the principle of compensation.

The six prose writers used in the study reported by Xolševnikov include Puškin and Lermontov. Separating Puškin and Lermontov from the remaining four and from each other, we obtain the following patterns:

Puškin	M.	80.0 (+6.0)	76.0 (+4.1)	34.0
	F.	74.0	71.9	38.4 (+4.4)
Lermontov	M.	68.5	83.6 (+17.5)	43.8
	F.	86.4 (+17.9)	66.1	51.7 (+7.9)

Clearly, though the spread in his figures is greater, Lermontov follows the combined stress pattern of the six-writer group. Puškin does not. In Puškin the masculines are stronger on the first ictus.

The question naturally arises as to whether the differences in Puškin's and Lermontov's prose stress profiles, i.e., differences in masculine and feminine endings, will be reflected in their verse. And, in general, since the differences between masculine and feminine lines have received little attention, what differences of this type will appear between the verse of the two poets.

Since the main subject of our inquiry is Puškin, and since Lermontov's prose profile is 'logical', we take Lermontov first. We examined 600 lines from *Demon* and 400 lines from *Tambovskaja kaznačejša*. The results were:

Demon	M.	85.4	92.4 (+1.4)	37.2
	F.	87.3 (+1.9)	91.0	45.5 (+8.3)
Tamb. kaz.	M.	81.6	94.7 (+6.3)	39.3
	F.	86.6 (+5.0)	88.4	52.3 (+13.3)

And the two samples combined:

	M.	83.7	93.4 (+3.4)	38.2
	F.	87.0 (+3.7)	90.0	47.0 (+8.8)

We note in passing that for the first two icti the spread in the figures is considerably less in the verse than in the prose, and that the spread in the figures for the third ictus is considerably greater in *Tambovskaja kaznačejša* than in *Demon*. Meanwhile, the main point is that Lermontov's verse profile, based on our two samples, is in accord with his prose profile, based on the figures presented by Xolševnikov.

For Puškin we first examined the lyrics from 1814-1836 (3,721 masculine and 3,705 feminine lines).[4] Our composite totals are:

		I	II	III	Stress loads	
M.		87.4 (+1.1)	92.0	40.8	80.0	80.2
F.		86.3	92.4 (+0.4)	42.6 (+1.8)	80.3	

The spread between the figures for masculine and feminines for the individual icti is small. But the sample is large. On the basis of our composite totals we note that Puškin's stress profile follows *neither* his own prose profile, where the masculines are stronger on the second ictus, *nor* the profile of Lermontov or the six-writer group, where again the masculines are stronger on the second ictus and, additionally, weaker on the first.

More clearly interpretable results are obtained by breaking Puškin's lyrics down into years and periods.[5] We show this breakdown:

		I	II	III	Stress loads	
1814	M.	95.0 (+1.8)	87.8	49.2	83.0	84.0
	F.	93.2	90.5 (+2.7)	56.3 (+7.1)	85.0	
1815	M.	96.2 (+4.6)	92.2 (+2.1)	38.8 (+2.2)	81.8	80.7
	F.	91.6	90.1	36.6	79.6	
1816	M.	90.7	91.2	37.9 (+3.3)	79.9	79.9
	F.	91.3 (+0.6)	93.3 (+2.1)	34.6	79.8	
1817	M.	89.6	87.7	41.7 (+9.8)	79.8	79.4
	F.	90.8 (+1.2)	93.9 (+6.2)	31.9	79.1	
1818	M.	84.1 (+0.8)	92.1	36.5 (+6.2)	78.2	77.7
	F.	83.3	95.5 (+3.4)	30.3	77.3	
1819-20	M.	87.1 (+0.1)	87.6	31.3	76.5	77.4
	F.	87.0	89.4 (+1.8)	37.0 (+5.7)	78.4	
1821	M.	82.7	91.3 (+1.2)	47.4 (+0.9)	80.4	80.1
	F.	82.7	90.1	46.5	79.8	
1822	M.	82.6	89.9	34.2	76.7	78.6
	F.	85.4 (+2.8)	94.4 (+4.5)	42.4 (+8.2)	80.6	

1823	M.	84.0	88.8	42.4	78.8	
						80.4
	F.	85.1 (+1.1)	95.9 (+7.1)	47.1 (+4.7)	82.0	
1824	M.	88.5 (+2.7)	94.3 (+0.8)	44.3 (+4.3)	81.8	
						80.8
	F.	85.8	93.5	40.0	79.8	
1825	M.	81.7	89.4	45.1	79.0	
						79.5
	F.	83.2 (+1.5)	90.8 (+1.4)	46.2 (+1.1)	80.0	
1826	M.	81.4 (+4.3)	92.2	44.3	79.5	
						80.4
	F.	88.2	92.5 (+0.3)	44.7 (+0.4)	81.4	
1827	M.	88.1 (+4.3)	93.2	38.1	79.8	
						79.8
	F.	83.8	93.6 (+0.4)	41.6 (+3.5)	79.8	
1828	M.	83.1 (+0.1)	94.6 (+0.7)	33.8	77.9	
						78.9
	F.	83.0	93.9	42.6 (+8.8)	79.9	
1829	M.	87.4 (+8.9)	86.7	38.6	78.7	
						78.5
	F.	78.5	89.6 (+0.6)	45.2 (+6.6)	78.3	
1830	M.	82.5	94.9 (+1.3)	37.2	78.6	
						80.7
	F.	83.0 (+0.5)	93.6	54.5 (+17.3)	82.8	
1831-36	M.	89.5 (+5.4)	95.8	46.7 (+0.1)	83.0	
						82.4
	F.	84.1	95.9 (+0.1)	46.6	81.6	

Before discussing the relationship between masculine and feminine lines, we have the following general comments on these rhythmical patterns:

1) The average stress load for 1814 is significantly higher than for other years or periods (84.0% against a total average stress load of 80.4%). In speaking of Puškin's early five-foot iambs, V. B. Tomaševskij noted a similar phenomenon and attributed it to the inclination of the beginner to stamp out clearly for himself the beat of the meter, the inclination to 'scan'.[6] Tomaševskij's observation applies equally well to Puškin's 1814 four-foot iambs. By

1815, the average stress load is down to 80.7%, and it does not reach 80% again until 1821 (80.1%).

2) The 1831-1836 period shows an average stress load of 82.4%. Though well below the 1814 84.0%, this is a high figure. Obviously, the explanation for the high 1814 percentages cannot be applied to 1831-1836. Had Puškin lived longer, 1831-1836 could conceivably have heralded an evolution toward higher average stress loads. Such speculation would involve us in the larger question of the effects of theme and style on rhythmic patterns. This problem will be discussed below in Section II.

3) The atypically high average stress load for 1814 is in part due to the high percentage for the third ictus — 52.8%, when we combine masculines and feminines. After 1814 the third ictus drops rapidly in strength. During 1815-1820 it averages 36.3%. In 1821 it rises again — to 47.0%, and thereafter seldom falls below 40% (in 1822, a small-sample year, 38.2%, in 1827, 39.8%, and in 1828, 38.1%). In spite, then, of subsequent fluctuations, 1821 marks something of a turning point for the third ictus.

4) In the early years there is considerable fluctuation in the relationship between the first and second icti. In 1814-1815 (again combining masculines and feminines) the first ictus is clearly the stronger. In 1816-1817 the second ictus takes a narrow lead. In 1818, a small-sample year, the lead is greater. But not until 1821 does the second ictus clearly establish an ascendancy which it never thereafter relinquishes. Our observations on the first and second icti, as well as those above on the 1814-1821 third ictus, are in general accord with the evolutionary pattern established by K. Taranovsky.[7]

Turning now to the respective roles of the masculine and feminine lines, we note:

1) While 1821 is seen (above) as marking a step in the evolution of the third ictus in terms of combined (masculine and feminine) percentages, a change occurs at about the same time in the relative strengths of the masculine and feminine lines for this ictus. In 1814 the feminines clearly have the upper hand (56.3% against 49.2%). From 1815 through 1818 the masculines are dominant. But in the 1819-1822 period, the feminines take over and, though not with perfect consistency, remain stronger than the masculines to the end. The one year that runs significantly counter to this pattern is 1824, when the masculines prevail over the feminines by 44.6% to 39.9% in a sample of 332 masculine and 338 feminine lines. It is of course the sudden surge of strength in the masculines in 1821 (47.4%) which enables us to say that this is a significant year. But overall it is the feminines, particularly in the post-1821 years, which provide the greater strength to the third ictus.

2) Worthy of note, however, is the gain in absolute terms in the strength of

the masculines in the final 1831-1836 period. While in the 1825-1830 period the masculines show only 39.2% against 46.1% for the feminines, in the 1831-1836 period the masculines rise to 46.6%, the feminines holding steady at 46.7%. Here again, as in 1821, it is the masculine surge which produces the relatively high overall figure for the third ictus. And in the 1831-1836 period it is the masculine surge which largely accounts for the high average stress load mentioned above. This masculine surge will take on greater significance when we note (below) the figures for *Mednyj vsadnik,* where the masculines are significantly stronger than the feminines.

3) The masculines and feminines again play separate and distinctive roles in the development of the stress patterns for the first and second icti. If we think in terms of the evolution of Puškin's rhythmic pattern *away from* eighteenth-century norms *in the direction of* nineteenth-century norms, i.e., toward the establishment of the supremacy of the second ictus over the first, we see that the feminine role is the more progressive. The figures given below show the differences between the percentage figures for the masculines of the first ictus and the masculines of the second ictus, and similarly, the differences between the feminines of the first ictus and the feminines of the second ictus. The fourth column shows combined differences, without distinction between masculines and feminines, thus permitting us to observe the overall evolution of the rhythm in terms of the relationship to each other of the two icti:

		I	II	M/F	Second Ictus Leads First Total
1814	M.	95.0	87.8	—7.2	
	F.	93.2	90.5	—2.7	—4.9
1815	M.	96.2	92.2	—4.0	
	F.	91.6	90.1	—1.5	—2.8
1816	M.	90.7	91.2	—0.5	
	F.	91.3	93.3	—2.0	—1.3
1817	M.	89.6	87.7	—1.9	
	F.	90.8	93.9	—3.1	—0.6
1818	M.	84.1	92.1	—8.0	
	F.	83.3	95.5	—12.2	—10.1
1819-20	M.	87.1	87.6	—0.5	
	F.	87.0	89.4	—2.4	—1.4

1821	M.	82.7	91.3	—8.6	—8.0
	F.	82.7	90.1	—7.4	
1822	M.	82.6	89.9	—7.3	—8.2
	F.	85.4	94.4	—9.0	
1823	M.	84.0	88.8	—4.8	—7.7
	F.	85.1	95.9	—10.8	
1824	M.	88.5	94.3	—5.8	—6.7
	F.	85.8	93.5	—7.7	
1825	M.	81.7	89.4	—7.7	—7.6
	F.	83.2	90.8	—7.6	
1826	M.	81.4	92.2	—10.8	—7.6
	F.	88.2	92.5	—4.3	
1827	M.	88.1	93.2	—5.1	—7.4
	F.	83.8	93.6	—9.8	
1828	M.	83.1	94.6	—11.5	—11.2
	F.	83.0	93.9	—10.9	
1829	M.	87.4	86.7	—0.7	—6.5
	F.	78.5	89.6	—11.1	
1830	M.	82.5	94.9	—12.4	—11.5
	F.	83.0	93.6	—10.6	
1831-36	M.	89.5	95.8	—6.3	—8.2
	F.	84.1	95.9	—11.8	

In the early years of first-ictus supremacy, followed by the years of fluctuation, i.e., 1814-1817, the feminine lines emerge as the more progressive in the sense that in 1814-1815 the second-ictus feminines trail their first-ictus counterparts by less than the second-ictus masculines trail their first-ictus counterparts, and in 1816-1817 the second-ictus feminines lead their first-ictus counterparts, while in the masculines the relationship between the first and second icti is in a state of flux. In 1818, a small-sample year, both masculines and feminines show a surge of strength. This surge is not sustained in 1819-1820, though both masculines and feminines (the former only marginally) have stronger second than first icti. From 1821 on, the supremacy of the second ictus is assured, and the margin of supremacy is normally greater in the feminines than in the masculines (in 1829, a small-sample year, the masculine second ictus is actually slightly weaker than the masculine first ictus).

4) Out total figures for the lyrics of 1814-1836 bear out Xolševnikov's *a priori* assumption that the feminines will be stronger than the masculines on the third ictus (42.6% against 40.8%). However, if we look at the figures for individual years, particularly in the 1815-1819 period, we recognize that linguistic factors, while encouraging a tendency, constitute no very severe constraint in this matter. We note in this context that Lermontov's *Mcyri,* where the four-foot iambs are exclusively masculine, receives from Taranovsky the comparatively high figure of 45.1% for the third ictus.[8]

5) Compensation does not seem to be a significant factor for Puškin. In his prose, as sampled by Xolševnikov, the masculines were stronger than the feminines on the first ictus. In his verse the significant fact is that in spite of the greater strength of the feminines on the third ictus, the feminines are again (though only by the slim margin of 0.4) stronger on the second ictus. Here too, there are considerable fluctuations in individual years. And here too, linguistic factors do not constitute an inhibiting constraint.

Above, in connection with the comparatively high average stress load of the 1831-1836 lyrics, we mentioned briefly the problem of theme or subject-matter. The question arises whether genre or theme significantly affects rhythmic patterns. We therefore examined samples of Puškin's narrative poetry to see if the same masculine-feminine patterns would hold good there, and/or if additional insights could be obtained. We examined the first 500 lines of *Ruslan i Ljudmila*; *Kavkazskij plennik* (734 lines); *Cygany* (533 lines); *Graf Nulin* (370 lines); the first canto (408 lines), the first 300 lines of the second canto, and the last 292 lines of *Poltava* (in all, 1000 lines); *Mednyj vsadnik* (481 lines); the first 400 lines of the second chapter and the first 400 lines of the sixth chapter of *Evgenij Onegin* (800 lines).[9] The percentages follow:

R. i L.	M.	89.6	91.6 (+1.6)	45.2	81.6	82.2
	F.	92.4 (+2.8)	90.0	48.8 (+3.6)	82.8	
K. pl.	M.	89.6 (+2.4)	90.4	45.2	81.3	81.6
	F.	87.2	93.6 (+3.2)	46.9 (+1.7)	81.9	
Cyg.	M.	89.8 (+10.2)	90.2	43.9	81.0	81.4
	F.	79.6	91.4 (+1.2)	55.4 (+11.5)	81.8	
Gr. N.	M.	81.9	86.8	53.3 (+3.6)	80.5	80.9
	F.	87.8 (+5.9)	87.8 (+1.0)	49.7	81.3	
E. On.	M.	83.3	88.6	42.5	78.6	79.4
	F.	85.5 (+2.2)	91.3 (+2.7)	45.1 (+2.6)	80.5	

Poltava	M.	85.9 (+1.0)	93.2	43.8	80.7
	F.	84.9	95.1 (+1.9)	44.8 (+1.0)	81.2

81.0

M. vsad.	M.	84.1	96.4	43.8 (+2.5)	81.1
	F.	84.3 (+0.2)	97.8 (+1.4)	41.3	80.9

81.0

The combined totals are:

M.	86.3 (+0.4)	91.1	44.5
F.	85.9	92.8 (+1.7)	47.0 (+2.5)

We note:

1) The combined totals follow the rhythmic profile already observed in the lyrics. The feminines are stronger on the third ictus, stronger on the second, and weaker on the first than the masculines. On the third ictus, the feminines show slightly greater relative strength than in the lyrics (+2.5 against +1.8). Also on the second ictus (+1.7 against +0.4). The masculine lead on the first ictus has declined (+0.4 against +1.1).

2) Here, as with the lyrics, linguistic factors cannot be seen as imposing constraints, merely as promoting tendencies. Thus, for the third ictus, the masculines are stronger than the feminines in *Graf Nulin* and *Mednyj vsadnik.* The first ictus shows considerable fluctuations — with the masculine clearly dominant in only one sample, *Cygany.*

3) There are indications of possible evolution in the relationship of masculines to feminines on the first ictus. If we looked only at *Ruslan i Ljudmila, Kavkazskij plennik,* and *Cygany,* we might be tempted to assume that the masculines had come from behind to establish ascendancy. The figures for the three works show for the masculines: —2.8, +2.4, and +10.2. But there the rising curve ends. In only one sample after *Cygany* (*Poltava*: +1.0) do the masculines lead. If we take the first ictus percentages for all samples up to and including *Cygany,* including our first *Evgenij Onegin* sample, and compare them with the percentages for our post-*Cygany* samples, we obtain:

	1817-24	1825-33
M.	88.4 (+2.0)	84.3
F.	86.4	85.2 (+0.9)

But these figures cannot be used for prognostic purposes. If they indicate anything, it is probably less a trend toward feminine superiority, more a trend toward a leveling out of the respective strengths.

II. STYLISTIC AND THEMATIC FACTORS
AND THEIR RELATIONSHIP TO STRESS PATTERNS

In discussing the four-foot iambs of Soviet poets, Gasparov observes the presence of two familiar rhythmic tendencies — the eighteenth-century rhythmic pattern and the nineteenth-century bipartite structure. He comments: "The average figures for the rhythmic curve [in Soviet poets] are only a result of their interaction," i.e., of the interaction of the two tendencies.[10] Puškin started writing during the 1814-1820 second stage of the period of transition from the eighteenth century.[11] It is not therefore surprising that his four-foot iambs reflect the rhythmic patterns of both centuries. But more than that. If we look at the rhythmic patterns of individual lyrics or of specific samples taken from his narrative verse, we frequently encounter a wide diversity which cannot be neatly equated with either eighteenth- or nineteenth-century patterns. Elsewhere we demonstrated the diversity of the rhythmic patterns in Puškin's lyrics written in five-foot iambs. We did not regard these fluctuations as purely random, as resulting solely from the smallness of the samples. We attributed them at least in part to differences in style based on differences in the lyric genres.[12] Much earlier, Tomaševskij was adopting the same approach when he noted the strength of the fourth ictus of Puškin's 1823-1825 epigrams written in five-foot iambs, and tentatively linked this strength with the influence of J. B. Rousseau's epigrams.[13] The attempt to link stress patterns with themes (tematika) goes back to Andrej Belyj.[14] What is involved is, in effect, the carrying one step further of the conventions of Greek and Roman poets who adopted specific meters (and sometimes dialects) for specific themes and genres.[15]

Clearly, differences in rhythmic pattern are less clearcut and these differences less easily related to theme and genre than is the case with differences in meter. We shall start by demonstrating the wide diversity of the rhythmic patterns of individual lyrics. We take as an example the 1831-1836 period. The number of lines for each lyric is shown:

Lyric	Lines	I	II	III	Stress load
"Pered grobniceju"	30	83.3	100	63.3	86.7
"Bor. godovščina"	90	92.2	98.9	50	85.3
"Čem čašče"	40	90	100	50	85.0
"V trevoge"	10	90	90	50	82.5
"V al'bom Abamalek"	9	88.9	88.9	11.1	72.2

"Krasavica"	16	68.8	100	25	73.4
"V al'bom"	8	100	75	87.5	90.6
"Želal ja"	8	100	100	12.5	78.1
"Gusar"	116	87.1	94.8	56.0	84.5
"Kogda b ne"	8	100	100	37.5	84.4
"Carej potomok"	12	66.7	75	41.7	70.8
"Stoju pečalen"	14	85.7	92.9	14.3	73.2
"Kto iz bogov"	29	96.6	100	34.5	82.8
"Ja dumal"	8	62.5	100	12.5	68.8
"K kastratu"	10	100	100	60	90
"V moji osennie"	28	85.7	89.3	39.3	78.6
"Kogda vladyka"	35	82.9	97.1	25.7	76.4
"Davydovu"	14	78.6	100	50	82.1
"Al'fons saditsja"	45	82.2	93.3	57.8	83.3

These nineteen samples, when taken together (530 lines, 285 M., 245 F.), give the following percentages and stress load:

87.0   95.8   46.6   82.4

The diversity (scatter) in the individual samples is clear at first glance. This can be shown by: 1) the standard deviations derived from the total percentages (i.e., 87.0, 95.8, 46.6); 2) the standard deviations derived from the means of the individual percentages; 3) the averages of deviation from the means (i.e., from 87.0, 95.8, 46.6):

1)	11.0	7.9	20.8
2)	11.0	7.8	20.0
3)	8.5	5.8	16.7

These figures merely confirm what was already clear. They also show that the third ictus is the least stable, the second the most stable.

Looking back to the nineteen samples, we note: 1) the smaller samples give the wildest figures, i.e., the greatest amount of scatter (e.g., 11.1, 12,5 and 87.5 for the third ictus); 2) nevertheless the larger, though still small samples differ significantly from each other (e.g., 25.7, 34.5, 56.0, and 63.3 for the third ictus) and from the mean figures.

Our approach to the sample figures is as follows: 1) very small samples are statistically unreliable in terms of general rhythmic tendencies; 2) but the percentage figures for very small samples *do* have meaning in any discussion of the individual poems; 3) the larger samples shown are not large enough to be statistically significant in terms of general rhythmic tendencies; 4) our larger samples are, however, large enough to justify the question whether the scatter is purely random or whether it is related to stylistic and thematic factors. It is to this question that we turn.

None of our nineteen 1831-1836 samples comes close to approximating the rhythmic pattern represented by the figures (87.0, 95.8, 46.6) to which, taken together, they average out. If they come close for one ictus, then they violate the pattern of one or both of the other icti. They also show wide divergencies in average stress loads. Since our samples are too small to justify conclusions, we shall not confine ourselves to these samples (nor attempt to discuss all of them individually), but shall use some of them as springboards in our attempts to establish connections between styles and rhythmic patterns.

For example, the average stress load (84.5%) for "Gusar" is high. This is not surprising. A high average stress load can only be produced by a high incidence of short words (stress groups). And a high incidence of short words is to be expected in a *skaz* poem whose tone is conversational. Following this approach, we shall examine samples, along with "Gusar", of Puškin's dialogue verse. There is (at least in much poetry) an indistinct border between conversational speech and lyric or elevated speech. Examples of the latter are the dialogues in *Kavkazskij plennik* and Aleko's eulogy of the simple non-urban life in *Cygany*. These are not included among our samples. Our samples aim, with only partial success, at conversational speech.

Two relatively large samples, "Pered grobniceju svjatoj" (30 lines) and "Borodinskaja godovščina" (90 lines), belong to the tradition of the patriotic ode. They also have high average stress loads. To these two samples we shall add further examples of Puškin's odaic style in order to discover what rhythmic patterns emerge. Here again, genre borderlines are by no means always distinct.

The epigram is not represented in our nineteen samples. But the very small sample, "K kastratu" (10 lines), has stylistic affinities with the epigram. It also has a high average stress load. The fact that the epigram sets much store by pithiness and scansion encourages the hypothesis that epigrams have high average stress loads. We will examine a number of epigrams to test this hypothesis — and to see if further characteristics are to be found.

Four of our nineteen samples may be classified as 'album-type' verse (*al'bomnye stixi*). We will examine these and other *al'bomnye stixi*. To be included in this category a poem is not required to have been physically written in someone's album. In fact, most of our samples were. More important, however, is that the poems be complimentary and lightly amorous without their expressing deep emotions.

Only one of our samples can be classified as love poetry, "Krasavica". We will take this and other examples to see if any characteristic rhythmic patterns emerge. Here too, borderlines are blurred. Love poems are so often so intimately interwoven with emotional reactions related to the poet-narrator's experiences and Weltanschauung that at one end of the spectrum love poetry merges with what may be loosely termed the 'philosophical'. At the other end of the spectrum, love poetry merges with *al'bomnye stixi*. We have in fact included "Krasavica" in both categories.

We will also examine examples of Puškin's poems reflecting a Biblical style.

Dialogue. Our percentages:

Poem[16]	Lines	I	II	III	Stress load
Cygany	214	89.7	87.9	59.3	84.2
Gr. Nulin	36	88.9	88.9	63.9	85.4
E. Onegin	314	89.8	91.7	55.1	84.2
Poltava	198	85.4	94.4	62.1	85.5
M. vsadnik	14	88.2	91.7	58.2	84.5
"Gusar"	116	87.1	94.8	56.0	84.5
Totals	892	88.2	91.7	58.2	84.5

We note: 1) The figures for the individual samples, even the small samples, are strikingly consistent, i.e., they show a very small amount of scatter about the mean figures; 2) The average stress loads and the third-icti figures are, predictably, very high; 3) The relative strengths of the first and second icti show a tendency to level off — as compared with the more familiar mature Puškin pattern with a weaker first and stronger second ictus. The relative decline in the strength of the second ictus is to be explained primarily by the great strength of the third ictus. In this category (notwithstanding the relatively short stress groups), the third ictus appears sufficiently strong to exact compensation. The relative increase in strength of the first ictus is a part of the overall high stress load resulting from shorter-than-normal stress groups.

Odaic Style. Under this heading we have included poems dealing with civic and patriotic themes:

Poem[17]	Lines	I	II	III	Stress load
"Voľnosť"	96	93.8	91.7	31.3	79.2
"Olegov ščit"	16	81.3	100	56.3	82.8
Poltava	165	88.5	95.2	38.2	80.5
"Pered grobniceju"	30	83.3	100	63.3	86.7
"Bor. godovščina"	90	92.2	98.9	50	85.3
M. vsadnik	82	84.1	98.8	41.5	81.1
Totals	479	88.9	96.2	41.8	81.7

1) There is considerably less consistency than with the dialogue verse, i.e., the amount of scatter is greater.

2) The total average stress load is high for Puškin, but not remarkably so — certainly nowhere as high as the figures for "Pered grobniceju svjatoj" and "Borodinskaja godovščina" (in our nineteen samples) might have led us to expect.

3) The total average stress load and the total percentage figure for the third ictus would have been considerably higher, had "Voľnosť" and the *Poltava* sample not been included. The mere fact that "Voľnosť" was written in 1817 suggests that time (i.e., Puškin's epithet-laden style of writing in much of his earlier poetry) could be a factor. In the case of *Poltava,* written in 1828, the time factor cannot at first sight be pressed into service. However, the odaic style was infrequently employed in Puškin's four-foot iambs, and it is not unreasonable to posit regression. But in this case, we have to explain the strong third icti and high average stress loads in our other odaic samples. Such an explanation is far from impossible. For certain stylistic changes (irrespective of meter and genre, and possibly connected with Puškin's work in prose) are discernible in Puškin's poetry from around 1830. This requires much further study. But we will raise the question again in our summation.

Meanwhile, we digress to discuss yet another question — the relationship of the eighteenth-century Lomonosov ode to "Voľnosť" and, in part, to the *Poltava* sample. The tradition of the eighteenth-century ode would lead us to look in Puškin's odaic style for a strong first ictus, a weaker-than-normal second ictus, and a stronger-than-normal third ictus. In "Voľnosť" this is reflected only palely in the comparatively strong first ictus (93.8%), its greater strength than the second ictus, and the fairly low figure for the second ictus (91.7%). The third ictus shows no hint of eighteenth-century strength. The weak second ictus and strong third ictus of the eighteenth-century ode is dependent not only on shorter stress groups, but on a different word order than that which characterizes most of Puškin's verse, and specifically "Vol'-nost'". For the sake of comparison, we take Lomonosov's 1747 "Oda na den' vosšestvija na vserossijskij prestol Elisavety Petrovny" (240 lines). A preliminary investigation indicates that the following are some of the rhythm-producing differences:

a) The incidence of line-ending noun-adjective combinations (including adjectival pronouns) which *eliminate* the third-ictus stress is far higher in "Vol'nost'" than in the "Oda". This is shown in the following percentage table, in which we include the *Poltava* sample for comparison. The first column shows the percentage of lines where the third ictus is not stressed (III Unstressed). The second column shows the percentage of unstressed third icti where lack of stress is caused by noun-adjective combinations (III Unstressed: N-A):

	III Unstressed	III Unstressed N-A
"Vol'nost'"	68.7	45.5
"Oda"	52.9	26.8
Poltava	61.8	29.4

Thus, in "Vol'nost'" nearly half of the lines missing stresses on the third ictus end in noun-adjective combinations, in the "Oda" slightly over a quarter do. In *Poltava,* while the percentage of missed stresses is high, this is not accounted for to any great extent by noun-adjective combinations.[18] Further study of the other factors producing a weak third ictus in *Poltava* is required.

b) Lomonosov makes greater use of short-ending adjectives and predicative adjectives.

c) Lomonosov interposes words between the component parts of his noun-adjective combinations more frequently than does "Vol'nost'". This has the effect of preserving the stress on the third ictus and, more often than not, of eliminating the stress on the second ictus, e.g., "Gde *merzlymi* borej *krylami".*

4) Three of our six samples (one only 16 lines) show considerable strength on the third ictus.

5) All samples except "Vol'nost'" show greater strength on the second than on the first ictus — in keeping with the nineteenth-century stress profile.

The Epigram:

Title	Lines	I	II	III	Stress load
"Zautra ..." (1816)	6	100	100	33.3	88.9
"Èp. na smerť ..." (1813-17)	4	100	100	75	93.8
"Dobryj čelovek" (1817-20)	6	100	100	50	87.5
"Xoť vpročem" (1821)	5	80	80	100	90.0
"Maľčiška ..." (1829)	12	91.2	100	50	85.4
"Moe sobranie" (1829)	14	85.7	85.7	35.7	76.8
"K bjustu" (1829)	8	87.5	100	37.5	81.3
"Nadejas ..." (1829)	12	83.3	83.3	66.7	81.3
"Ne to beda ..." (1830)	6	100	100	83.3	95.8
"Ne to beda ..." (1830)	5	80	100	100	95
Totals	78	89.7	93.6	56.4	84.9

Our samples are extremely small. But the figures are sufficiently striking to be regarded as significant. They speak for themselves. Clearly, they have little effect on larger statistical averages. The epigram provides one example of a widespread phenomenon — rhythmic clustering, i.e., the tendency for a rhythmic drive to sustain itself over a short number of lines. This occurs in longer poems. But it is more visible in short poems. The great amount of scatter in short poems is not only random, i.e., the result of the smallness and lack of statistical significance of the sample. It is also often the result of deliberate artistic intent. We cannot forbear to reproduce one *outre tour de force*: "Cyklop" (1830):

> Jazýk i úm terjája rázom,
> Gljažú na vás edínym glázom:
> Edínyj gláz v glavé moéj.
> Kogdá b suďbý togó xotéli,
> Kogdá b imél ja stó očéj,
> To vsé by stó na vás gljadéli.

Average stress load: 100

Al'bomnye stixi:

Lyric	Lines	I	II	III	Stress load
"V al'bom" (1817)	6	100	100	66.7	91.7
"Golycynoj" (1817)	8	100	87.5	25	78.1
"M. A. Golycynoj" (1823)	16	100	93.8	31.3	81.3
"M. Èjxfel'd" (1823)	8	100	100	62.5	90.6
"A. N. Vul'f" (1825)	6	83.3	100	100	95.8
"K Zine" (1826)	5	80	100	20	75
"K Timaševoj" (1826)	12	91.7	91.7	50	83.3
"Volkonskoj" (1827)	15	80	93.3	26.7	75
"Akafist" (1827)	10	90	90	20	75
"Ty i vy" (1828)	8	87.5	100	41.7	84.4
"Ee glaza" (1828)	17	94.1	100	29.4	80.9
"Portret" (1828)	8	87.5	87.5	25	75
"Sčastliv ..." (1828)	8	100	100	12.5	78.1
"Otvet A. I. G." (1828)	16	81.3	93.8	25	75
"Uvy! Jazyk" (1828)	20	70	100	40	77.5
"Ušakovoj" (1829)	20	85	95	35	78.8
"Ja vas uznal" (1830)	16	50	100	25	68.8
"V trevoge" (1832)	10	90	90	50	82.5
"Kogda-to ..." (1832)	9	88.9	88.9	11.1	72.2
"Krasavica" (1832)	16	68.8	100	25	73.4
"Gonimyj ..." (1832)	8	100	75	87.5	90.6
Totals	242	84.7	95.0	34.3	78.5

1) The samples are short and show a considerable amount of scatter; 2) Our comments on the tendency in small samples for the rhythmic drive to sustain itself apply here as for the epigram; 3) The scatter does not conceal the obvious prevalent tendency toward a low average stress load and a weak third ictus.

Love Poetry

Lyric	Lines	I	II	III	Stress load
"Grečanke" (1822)	31	80.6	100	22.6	75.8
"Inostranke" (1822)	12	75	83.3	33.3	72.9
"K ..." (1825)	24	75	100	29.2	76.0
"Kogda v ob"jatija" (1830)	20	80	95	30	76.3
"Proščanie" (1830)	15	80.1	93.3	46.7	80
"Zaklinanie" (1830)	24	87.5	100	45.8	83.3
"Dlja beregov" (1830)	24	83.3	95.8	47.8	81.3
"Krasavica" (1832)	16	68.8	100	25	73.4
Totals	166	79.5	97.0	34.3	77.7

1) The samples are small; 2) However, in stress profile they are remarkably consistent, both with each other and with the total average figures, i.e., the amount of scatter is small. Only the dialogue, among the types of verse sampled above, shows a comparable consistency; 3) In all cases the second ictus has the ascendancy over the first, a typical nineteenth-century rhythmic pattern; 4) The low overall average stress load and the low total percentage for the third ictus bring the profile closer to Jazykov (1823-1831) than to what we normally expect in Puškin. So also the high average percentage (97.0) for the second ictus.[19]

Poetry reflecting a Biblical style:

Title	Lines	I	II	III	Stress load
"Podražanija Koranu"					
I	16	93.8	93.8	37.5	81.3
II	20	95	95	20	77.5
III	28	78.6	89.3	46.4	78.6
IV	14	100	78.6	64.3	85.7
V	16	68.8	93.8	56.4	79.7
VI	20	75	100	30	76.3
"Prorok"	30	83.3	100	46.7	82.5
"Ančar"	36	91.7	86.1	36.1	78.5
Totals	180	85.6	92.2	41.1	79.7

1) The composite percentages and average stress load for these samples show no very unusual features, reproducing not only the general stress profile that we might expect, but, specifically, figures which would be acceptable for almost any post-1820 larger sample of Puškin's verse; 2) The individual samples show differences in rhythmic profile which are extremely interesting and merit more detailed study than is here possible. They represent a mixture of eighteenth-century, transitional-period, and nineteenth-century tendencies. "Podražanija" I and II, with equality for the first and second icti, and a weak third ictus (in II too weak for the purposes of our statement) are reminiscent of transitional-period patterns. "Podražanija" III, V, and VI, and "Prorok" show (notwithstanding the weak first ictus and strong third ictus in V) acceptable patterns for the nineteenth century. "Podražanie" IV and "Ančar" show (notwithstanding the unacceptably low 36.1% for the third ictus in "Ančar") strong affinities with the eighteenth-century rhythmic drive. This is not surprising in view of thematic and stylistic links with eighteenth-century verse paraphrases of the Bible. We recall, however, that eighteenth-century thematic links failed to produce eighteenth-century patterns in both our composite percentages and individual-sample percentages for the odaic style. Although, then, our individual samples are too small to be statistically significant, their rhythmic patterns are relevant and essential for any detailed stylistic analysis of the artistry of these poems.

SUMMATION

We have offered examples of different categories of Puškin's verse. We will now attempt to sum up some of the problems and to balance the ledger in terms of what we believe has and has not been done — and what remains to be done.

In Section II we speak loosely of theme and style. The two often go hand in hand. but they are by no means identical. A poet's style may change even as he continues to treat the same theme. And his style may remain the same even though the themes he treats are different. It is the first of these two possibilities which, as we suggested above, probably accounts for the rhythmic heterogeneity we encountered in discussing Puškin's odaic style.

Themes too present a problem. The basic problem is one of clear demarcation. Should we make a distinction between social-political protest, which is the theme of "Voľnosť", and the patriotic theme, which characterizes the other samples placed in the category of odaic style? And if we take a reasonably long sample, we can hardly expect it to present a cohesive homogeneous whole, either thematically or stylistically. Thus, we offered 165 lines from

Poltava as a sample of the odaic style. These lines are far from homogeneous. Their common denominator is that they describe the battle. This gives them a lexical kinship. But syntactically, many of the lines are 'neutral' — in the sense that their syntactic ordering is not specifically odaic, but could serve many purposes, in the present case narrative. And this is reflected in the rhythmic patterns. This is not to remove narrative from the ode, for narrative is a familiar part of the ode. We will take from the *Poltava* sample one small hyperodaic (but also narrative) sample:

> Togda-to svyše vdoxnovennyj
> Razdalsja zvučnyj glas Petra:
> "Za delo, s bogom!" Iz šatra,
> Tolpoj ljubimcev okružennyj,
> Vyxodit Petr. Ego glaza
> Sijajut. Lik ego užasen.
> Dviženʼja bystry. On prekrasen,
> On vesʼ, kak božija groza.
> Idet. Emu konja podvodjat.
> Retiv i smiren vernyj konʼ.
> Počuja rokovoj ogonʼ,
> Drožit. Glazami koso vodit
> I mčitsja v praxe boevom,
> Gordjasʼ moguščim sedokom.

The figures obtained from this 14-line sample are far closer to our preconceived idea of odaic patterns than are those of the larger sample:

> 100   92.9   57.1

We are not suggesting that passages can be hand-picked to produce satisfactory figures. Samples taken from eighteenth-century odes also show lack of homogeneity and differences in rhythmic pattern. We merely wish to call attention to the problem of demarcation.

Genre is a term that can be used appropriately in the context of the present study. But it must be used with caution. Neither genre nor theme nor style can be equated. To take one obvious example: within the genre of the narrative poem we can have a variety of themes and of styles. And the genre of the narrative poem can and does include, for example, the dramatic and lyric genres.

We spoke just above of the possibility of a poet's style remaining the same even while he treats different themes. We must go one step further by recognizing that there need not be a correlation between rhythmic patterns and styles or themes. Speaking of Soviet poets, Gasparov comments: "Differences in genre and the factor of evolution produce relatively insignificant changes in the four-foot iambs of individual poets." He goes on to qualify this statement by giving specific examples of change.[20] In Puškin's case we have, we believe, assembled sufficient materials to state categorically that differences in rhythmic pattern can be related to differences in theme and style.

Much remains to be done. Further samples can be added to the categories examined here to determine whether our patterns hold. Other categories can be studied. A major task, not undertaken here, concerns the roles of masculine and feminine lines. In Section I we dealt with their respective roles mainly in terms of chronological evolution. In Section II we avoided mention of masculines and feminines. The study of masculines and feminines within the framework of different themes and styles offers a promising field for investigation. For example, in our samples representing the odaic style, the masculines are stronger than the feminines on the third ictus by 43.4% to 39.8%. This runs significantly counter to the general pattern of greater feminine strength on the third ictus. What is the explanation?

Some of the phenomena observed in this study are self-explanatory, e.g., the high average stress load in dialogue. In some cases we have attempted to provide tentative explanations for our findings. But much remains to be done to provide systematic detailed explanation for the facts.

Our study has been devoted to Puškin. It does not claim to be exhaustive. What applies to Puškin may or may not apply to other poets — and in varying degrees. But our study justifies one theoretical statement. Changes in rhythmic patterns can be studied in terms of chronological evolution (e.g., in Puškin, the drop in the average stress load after 1814). But in one sense time is a redundant factor. Changes may occur in time, but there is normally some factor other than time to account for them. For example, the change in Lomonosov's rhythmic patterns between 1741 and 1747 is explained by the change in his theoretical approach to the pyrrhic foot. The change from the eighteenth-century to the nineteenth-century rhythmic structure is explained by Taranovsky as due to the influence of the five-foot iamb. Changes in rhythmic structure may be due to the influence of prose or to changes in the literary language. And changes in the literary language may be produced by changes in Weltanschauung and by changed priorities in terms of genre and theme. Notwithstanding the reservations expressed above regarding the difficulties of establishing a neat equation between rhythmic patterns on the one hand and themes and styles on the other, by and large rhythmic patterns are influenced by thematic and stylistic factors. Rhythmic patterns and changes in rhythmic pattern should therefore always be studied with due regard to thematic and stylistic factors.

University of North Carolina

NOTES

[1] The study was made by N. D. Klimovec. See Xolševnikov's article in *Slavic Poetics: Essays in Honor of Kiril Tarnaovsky* (The Hague: Mouton, 1973), pp. 549-57.

[2] See Xolševnikov, *op. cit.* Also M. L. Gasparov, *Sovremennyj russkij stix* (Moscow: 1974), p. 79.

[3] The figures in parentheses are given for convenience to show at a glance the differences in stress strength between masculines and feminines for each ictus.

[4] Not included are: 1) lyrics not assigned in the 10-volume Academy edition to specific years; 2) four-foot iambs which appear in poems written in iambs of varying length (*vol'nye jamby*) — this because syntax is significant and syntactic arrangement is affected by the length of the line; 3) lyrics of four lines or less; 4) incomplete lines in which missing words made it impossible to assign stresses. Incomplete lines where stress can be determined are included, e.g., "Ja? ja ... češu".

[5] Lines examined for individual years: 1814 — 181 M., 190 F.; 1815 — 449 M., 464 F.; 1816 — 227 M., 240 F.; 1817 — 163 M., 163 F.; 1818 — 63 M., 66 F.; 1819-20 — 217 M., 216 F.; 1821 — 312 M., 312 F.; 1822 — 149 M., 144 F.; 1823 — 125 M., 121 F.; 1824 — 332 M., 338 F.; 1825 — 235 M., 238 F.; 1826 — 167 M., 161 F.; 1827 — 176 M., 173 F.; 1828 — 278 M., 265 F.; 1829 — 127 M., 135 F.; 1830 — 234 M., 235 F.; 1831-36 (when Puškin's output in four-foot iambs was drastically reduced) — 285 M., 245 F. It must be borne in mind that the samples vary in size. Since smaller samples are for present purposes less reliable, caution should be observed in dealing with samples taken from 1818, 1823, and 1829.

[6] *O stixe* (Leningrad: 1829), pp. 234-35.

[7] *Ruski dvodelni ritmovi* (Beograd: 1953), pp. 76-84. See also his Tables II and III.

[8] Taranovsky, Table III.

[9] The samples divide into masculines and feminines as follows:

	M	F
R. i L.	250	250
K. pl.	374	360
Cygany	264	269
Graf N.	182	188
E. On.	456	344
Poltava	511	489
M. vsadnik	251	230
Totals	2,288	2,130

[10] Gasparov, p. 92.

[11] As defined by Taranovsky, pp. 74-79.

[12] Val'ter Vickeri, "K voprosu o ritme cezurnogo pjatistopnogo jamba Puškina", *International Journal of Slavic Linguistics and Poetics* XIV, 134-75.

[13] Tomaševskij, pp. 156-57.

[14] *Simvolizm* (Moscow: 1910), p. 263 and ff. Belyj was actually more interested in equating and distinguishing between individual poets and periods on the basis of rhythmic structure. Belyj's attempt to use rhythmic patterns to characterize and distinguish individual poets was of course anticipated by Sievers and others who applied statistics to Old German poetry to determine authorship and dating. See Eduard Sievers, *Zur Rhythmik des germanischen Alliterationsverses*

(New York: Stechert, 1909). This is pointed out by V. Žirmunskij, *Vvedenie v metriku* (Leningrad: 1925), p. 41. Extremely revealing and heartwarming from our standpoint is Žirmunskij's concern that Belyj's findings are vulnerable to and may be distorted by random deviations caused by differences in genres which may have "their own rhythmic peculiarities". This is precisely our hypothesis.

[15]   See Edward Stankiewicz, "Structural Poetics and Linguistics", *Current Trends in Linguistics* (The Hague: Mouton, 1974), XII, p. 641: "The choice of language is sometimes used to distinguish entire genres or to mark poetry in opposition to prose (e.g., the choice of different dialects for different genres in Greece, the use of a superdialectal *koine* in Serbo-Croatian epic poetry, the special languages of the Icelandic and Irish poetic guilds)". Stankiewicz also points out that "Aristotle maintains that 'Nature herself teaches us to choose the appropriate meter' (*Poetics*, 1460a). The use of the 'discursive' iamb in dialogues alternates in the Greek theater with the use of anapests in the appearances of the chorus, while the hexameter, or 'heroic meter' is the 'natural' meter of the Greek epic tale" (p. 647). See also similar connections in Tomaševskij, "O strofike Puškina", *Puškin: Issledovanija i materialy*, II. Also Taranovsky, "O vzaimootnošeniji stixotvornogo ritma i tematiki", *American Contributions to the Fifth International Congress of Slavists* (The Hague: Mouton, 1963) I, 287-322.

[16]   In the *poèmy* our samples are taken from the following passages: *Cygany* — lines 42-67, 267-298, 302-439, 468-486, 510-520; *Graf Nulin* — 147-168, 326-339; *Evgenij Onegin* — Chapter III, first two stanzas, dialogue in third and fourth stanzas, stanzas xvii-xix, and first 4 lines of stanza xx, last 7 lines of stanza xxxiii, and stanzas xxxiv-xxxv; Chapter IV, stanzas xii-xvi, stanza xlviii and first 10 lines of xlix; Chapter VII, stanza xli, and first 12 lines of xlii; Chapter VIII, last 7 lines of xlii, and xliii-xlvii; *Poltava* — II, 16-118, 181-236; III, 367-406; *Mednyj vsadnik* — I, 49-62.

[17]   In the *poèmy* our samples are: *Poltava* — III, 153-317; *Mednyj vsadnik* — "Vstuplenie", 1-42, 67-91; II, 150-164.

[18]   Noun-adjective combinations ending the line and eliminating the third ictus are only a part of a more general syntactic pattern first described by Osip Brik. The pattern consists of three stress groups (e.g., noun plus adjective plus noun; or adjectival pronoun plus adjective plus noun, e.g., "Krasa polunočnoj prirody" or "Moi studenčeskie gody") which normally eliminate the third ictus. See "Ritm i sintaksis", *Novyj Lef,* 1927, No. 3-6.

[19]   Taranovsky's figures (Table III) for Jazykov are:

	I	II	III	Stress load
1823-24	84.8	99.2	24.6	77.2
1825-28	80.7	96.7	26.3	75.9
1829-31	77.3	98.7	33.2	77.3

[20]   Gasparov, p. 95.

COMMENTS

(Lilly)   Did you detect any correlation between the rhythmic patterns of the stanzaic verse and the arrangement of the clausulae?

(Smith)   Professor Vickery's paper is a stimulating and pioneering essay in the use of linguistic-statistical analysis at micro-level; this type of study becomes more and more necessary now that the method has fixed so much information at higher levels (periods, rhythmical characteristic of poets' complete works). "Much", indeed, "remains to be done." But rather than

adding further samples, the ones presented here could be further analysed: firstly, with reference to the constituent line-types of the various groups in horizontal axis (using the standard six or Tomaševskij's 35); second, by incorporating the factor of word boundary; and thirdly, by using a more delicate index than the binary 'stress vs. unstress' in rhythmical analysis, perhaps along the lines suggested recently by V. S. Baevskij and M. L. Gasparov.

Additional discussion: Bailey, Pszczołowska.

AUTHOR'S REPLY

(to Lilly)   Not so far. I have tested AbAb stanzas against aBaB stanzas. Also (not for Puškin) in the 10-line odaic stanza I have tested the feminine rhymed couplets (lines 5 and 6) and the dEEd final quatrain. but these probes have to date been too limited to justify conclusions — one way or the other. Certainly too limited to indicate that there is no correlation. I think that this approach is promising, and intend to work further along the lines suggested by your question.

(to Smith)   Your points are well taken. Your first point is dealt with in part in my reply to Professor Lilly, and I agree that in that type of work which (as indicated) is only in its preliminary stages due consideration should be given to rhythmic figures. Also to word-boundaries, and in that connection I can say that I have started work on the grammatical categories of words ending the line in relation to their length, seeking a correlation between the grammatical category and the last word-boundary in the line. The results could, hopefully, yield insights into stylistic questions as well as stress patterns. I agree with your third point relating to degrees of stress, but at this stage in my work there are already enough unknowns to make me reluctant to further complicate my inquiries. If I am to tie together satisfactorily my two problems (1. masculines versus feminines, 2. genre influences on stress patterns) I believe I will have to add further samples, and have started work along the lines indicated on Lomonosov and Deržavin.

SOME VISUAL ASPECTS OF POETRY
AND THEIR CORRELATES*

DENNIS WARD

1

While Roman Jakobson has observed that "a poetic work is not confined to aesthetic function alone, but has in addition many other functions. Actually the intentions of a poetic work are often closely related to philosophy, social didactics, etc." (Jakobson, 1971:83) and Ju. Lotman has been at pains to consider the poem in its aesthetic and cultural context (see Lotman, 1968), neither scholar, nor indeed any contemporary student of structuralist poetics, would deny the validity of the analysis of a poem as a 'non-contextual entity'. In fact much attention has rightly been devoted by poetics in the last half century and more to the analysis of poems as non-contextual entities.

Since a poem is a verbal object, analyses of it as a 'non-contextual entity' may be concerned at some point with the phonic substance and with form, "the organization of the substance into meaningful events" (Halliday, 1961:243), i.e. with grammar and lexis. To expand this, poetics studies not merely the paraphraseable content of a poem but also its phonetic texturing, its grammatical structures and their arrangement, and lexical interrelations, implications, networks, auras which are not immediately apparent from the paraphraseable content. Poetics reveals moreover that sound and grammar may have iconic function in the poetic text.

There is, however, another aspect of poems to which little attention has been devoted, exception being made for certain poems and types of poems. This is the visual aspect. It may well be considered that the visual aspect — or the various visual aspects of poetry are of marginal interest to the poeticist and therefore almost or even entirely negligible. Yet in Slavic poetics and in the poetics of other languages too we are — most of us and for the most part — dealing with printed texts. We are literate and not only do we hear poems, we also read them. Indeed it is probably true to say that we read poems far more often than we hear them performed or perform them ourselves. We can capture the phonetic texturing of a poem without hearing it and may also be aware of some iconic function that the phonetic texture may have. Certainly we do not need to hear a poem in order to analyse and appreciate its lexical attributes and its grammar, together with any possible iconic function that the latter may have. Not only, however, do we read a poem — we also *view* it. We see a poem as an object on a page and some of the visual features of the object we see are features of graphic substance with conventional linguistic meanings, some are clues to the nature of the verse, some may be clues to performance, and it may be that some have or appear to have no or only marginal linguistic function, versificational function or performance function. In any event visual features make the shape — that of an aesthetic object — which we view, and moreover visual features may have an iconic function.[1]

The question of 'poet's choice', that is of accident *versus* design, has been put and answered by Jakobson in the following way: "Are the designs disclosed by linguistic analysis intentional and premeditated in the creative work of the poet? A calculus of probability as well as an accurate comparison of poetic texts with other kinds of verbal messages demonstrates that the striking particularities [of the poetic texts] cannot be viewed as negligible accidentals governed by the rule of chance. Any significant poetic composition, whether it is an improvisation or a fruit of long and painstaking labour, implies a goal-oriented choice of verbal material" (Jakobson, 1970:302). I suggest that visual features other than those with normal conventional linguistic significance should be regarded as equally premeditated even though it may not always be possible to determine what the poetic intention was.[2] In the following sections we shall be primarily concerned with aspects of the linear disposition on the page of a poem, though this will lead to a brief consideration of non-linear disposition of certain entities. Examples are taken from Russian poetry, with references to the work of some English and French poets, but remarks and such conclusions as are drawn are relevant to poetry in other languages, including other Slavic languages.

2

The indentation of lines is a typographical device common to both prose and poetry. In prose it commonly marks the beginning of a paragraph and also dialogue, functions which it may have in verse, where however it has other functions. It is some at least of these other functions to which remarks and illustrations below are devoted. Attention is directed first to 'simple indentation' — in the meaning of the indentation of single and/or matched lines in a set of lines (whether or not the set constitutes a stanza) and the contrast with neighboring lines which are not indented. In simple indentation there may be

— and often is — only one degree of indentation, i.e. all indented lines are indented to the same distance.[3] There may be further degrees of indentation, which, if necessary, may be called 'secondary', 'tertiary', etc. indentation. Simple indentation does not here embrace, however, either *lesenka* or 'progressive indentation', wherein two or more successive lines are progressively indented by the same measure. Both *lesenka* and progressive indentation are discussed below. Simple indentation, if it has any discernible function, is associated with prosodic (metrical and rime) features, and sometimes with 'theme'.

Simple indentation to mark nothing but rime is a not uncommon device, wherein rime-matched lines ranged full out left are contrasted with riming lines indented and ranged. The function of indentation *versus* non-indentation in such a case will be called 'rime-correspondence'. Verses with one type of rime throughout are not common but examples are not difficult to find. One such example of uniform type of rime with simple indentation is provided by Lermontov's *Pocelujami prežde sčital* (Lermontov, 1940:89), where all the rimes are masculine, or the same poet's *Pesn' barda*, also with masculine rimes throughout:

(1) Я долго был в чужой⋅стране,
       Дружин Днепра седой певец,
     И вдруг пришло на мысли мне
       К ним возвратиться наконец.
                    (Lermontov, 1940:213)

More common are rime-schemes in which the type of rime varies (masculine-feminine, masculine-dactylic, feminine-dactylic), as in Lermontov's *Trostnik*:

(2) Сидел рыбак веселый
       На берегу реки,
     И перед ним по ветру
       Качались тростники.
                    (Lermontov, 1940:228)

Here, indentation marks[4] not only the matching of riming syllables but also the matching of masculine with masculine, and feminine with feminine, as it does in the same poet's *Pesn'* — '*Ne znaju ...*' (1940:72-73), '*Xot' davno ...*' (1940:163), *K D. —Bud' so mnoju ...*' (1940:64-65), etc. In verse-arrangements such as these, where lines with masculine endings are indented, the indentation corresponds with the lines which are, by one syllable, shorter. This is regarded here as an instance of rime-correspondence and not 'meter-correspondence' (see below).

Similarly, the indentation of masculine-rimed lines contrasted with the non-indentation of dactylic-rimed lines is regarded as an instance of 'rime-correspondence'. Examples of such rime-correspondence are provided by

Lermontov's *Svidan'e* (Lermontov, 1940:255), or Baratynskij's *Ljubov'* (Baratynskij, 1945:65) or his *Dve doli*:

> (3) Дало две доли провидение
>   На выбор мудрости людской:
>   Или надежду и волнение,
>   Иль безнадежность и покой.
>   (Baratynskij, 1945:47)

In Kirsanov's *Sumčatost'* indentation marks both alternating rime and, as it happens, alternation of various types of rime:

F(eminine) M(asculine):

> (4) Авоськи — дело!
>   И может быть —
>   Придется к телу
>   их приживить.
>   (Kirsanov, 1972:224)

D(actylic) M:

> (5) Ему — распихивать
>   толпу у касс,
>   ему — запихивать
>   в суму запас!
>   (*ib.*: 224)

and

D Hd (hyperdactylic) and F D:

> (6) И этим многое
>   они выгадывают:
>   четвероногие
>   из сум выглядывают,
>   экономично,
>   тепло и правильно,
>   гигиенично
>   и комфортабельно.
>   (*ib.*: 233-34)[5]

Indentation may fulfil the function of rime-correspondence even in a partly rimed poem, such as Polonskij's *Lebed'*:

> (7) Пел смычок, — в садах горели
>   Огоньки, — сновал народ, —
>   Только ветер спал да тёмен
>   Был ночной небесный свод.
>   (Penguin:188)

These trochaic tetrameters with truncated fourth foot in the even lines are rimed masculine in those same even lines. Indentation *versus* non-indentation therefore correlates with rime *versus* absence of rime and, incidentally, with masculine *versus* feminine ending.

If indentation occurs in unrimed verse it cannot — to state the obvious — have the function of rime-correspondence. It may instead have a function which will be called 'meter-correspondence', and this correlation may be one which centers upon the character of the feet or upon the number of feet. Examples of the former correlation are to be found, for instance, in the Russian version of unrimed hexameters such as Puškin's *Carskoseľskaja statuja* (Puškin, 1949:III, 182), *Otrok* (III, 192), *Rifma* (III, 191), *Trud* (III, 181). In all these poems the odd lines are typical 'Russian' hexameters, having five dactyls and a final trochee replacing the classical spondee. The 'permitted' substitution of dactyl by trochee within the line occurs in *Otrok* (1. 1), *Rifma* (11. 3 and 5), and *Trud* (11. 1 and 5). The even lines of these poems are also basically dactylic (*Rifma* 1. 2 has an initial trochee), with six beats, but the third and sixth feet are truncated, consisting simply of one (stressed) syllable, e.g.

(8)   Дева печально сидит, праздный держа черепок.
       . . . .
       Дева, над вечной струей, вечно печальна сидит.
                              (Puškin, 1949:III, 182)

Since the even lines are indented, indentation then correlates with foot-variation and, incidentally, with variation in the number of syllables.

Much more common is a correlation of indentation with the length of lines in the sense of number of feet. Unrimed verse gives such examples as Karamzin's *Osen'*:

(9)   Веют осенние ветры
       В мрачной дубраве;
       С шумом на землю валятся
          Желтые листья.   (Karamzin, 1966:79)

Section 5 of Axmatova's *Luna v zenite* shows slight assonance at the end of some lines but it is hardly enough to be called rime:

(10)   Как ни стремилась к Пальмире я
          Золотоглавой,
       Но суждено здесь дожить мне
          До первой розы.
       Персик цветет и фиалок дым
          Черно-лиловый ...
       Кто мне посмеет сказать, что здесь
          Злая чужбина?   (Axmatova, 1967:I, 270)

Indentation with the function of meter-correspondence is found in partly rimed verse, as in Kirsanov's *Stroki v skobkax*. While there is assonance in some line-endings, regular rime conjoins only lines 2 and 6 of each stanza:

> (11)   Жил-был — я.
>   (Стоит ли об этом?)
>   Шторм бил в мол.
>   (Молод был и мил ...)
>   В порт плыл флот.
>   (С выигрышным билетом
>   жил-был я.)
>   Помнится, что жил.
>   (Kirsanov, 1972:83)

If the even lines of this poem are taken to be trochaic trimeters, with truncated final feet in lines 4 and 8, and the odd lines consist of three beats with no intervening slacks (in classical terms, three 'monomacers'), then indentation correlates with a difference in meter.

In Martynov's *'Nikogo...'*, where most of the lines are rimed, the single-beat lines are indented, while the two-beat lines are set full out left. So too are the three monosyllabic lines, consisting respectively of two words which are stressed only for emphatic purposes (*on, no*) and one which is never stressed (*ved'*).

> (12)   Никого,
>   Ничего!
>   Ручеек пересох.
>   Только в русле его
>   Серебрится
>   Песок.
>   Он
>   Клубится слегка...
>   (Martynov, 1972:120)

In fully rimed verse, indentation with the function of meter-correspondence may correlate with the rime-pattern, in the sense that only equimetrical lines are rimed, or it may not. Cvetaeva's *'Tebe — čerez sto let'*, for example — one of her rare poems with indentation — has three pentameters followed by an indented trimeter, with the rime-scheme aFbMaFbM

> (13)   К тебе, имеющему быть рожденным
>   Столетие спустя, как отдышу, —
>   Из самых недр, — как нá смерть осужденный,
>   Своей рукой — пишу:
>   (Cvetaeva, 1965:151-52)

The basic pattern of Lermontov's *Poslednee novosel'e* is similar, with one more foot per line (3 hexameters + 1 tetrameter), and it is this basic pattern which leads Obolensky (Penguin: 164-68) and the editor of the *Slovo* edition (Lermontov, 1921:II, 297-300) to set the poem in stanzas and indent all fourth lines.[6] Èjxenbaum (1940:197-98), breaking the poem not into stanzas but into three sections, adheres closely to the association of indentation with shorter line, so that he does not have a completely uniform pattern of three lines full out left followed by one indented (in one or two places he appears to break his own 'rule'). The setting adopted by Andronikov and Oksman (1964:106-108) — and earlier by Andronikov, Blagoj and Oksman (1957:63-65) — is very similar to that of Èjxenbaum — but not entirely identical. Thus it is at once evident that both poets and editors are aware of the meter-correspondence of indentation and that the poet's variations of a basic pattern may — and do — provide editors with problems.

A constant rime-pattern is maintained in the four quatrains of Kirsanov's *Odno iz nabljudenij* — aMbFaMbF — where the three short lines are well indented and ranged, while an exceedingly long line, occupying a different position in each quatrain (such that the typographical layout renews its impact with each quatrain) is set full out left:

(14)　　　Отцом среди своих планет
　　　　　и за Землей следя особо —
　　　　　распространяло Солнце свет
　　　(но чувствовалось, что оно поеживается от озноба).
　　　　　　　　　　　　　(Kirsanov, 1972:149)

These illustrations of meter-correspondence of indentation partly associated but not entirely coinciding with rime-correspondence are concluded with some brief remarks on significant secondary indentation and further degrees of indentation. Karamzin's *Gimn slepyx* has two pentameters (lines 2 and 4), rimed M and ranged full out left, two tetrameters (1 and 3), rimed F, primarily indented and ranged with two tetrameters (6 and 8) which are rimed M and F with two trimeters (5 and 7), F and M, these trimeters being secondarily indented. The pattern therefore is (where $>$ indicates primary and $>>$ indicates secondary indentation) $>$aFbM$>$aFbM$>$$>cF>dM>$cF:

(15)　　　Владыко мира и судьбины!
　　　　Дай видеть нам луч солнца твоего
　　　　　Хотя на час, на миг единый,
　　　　И новой тьмой для нас покрой его,
　　　　　　Лишь только б мы узрели
　　　　　Благотворителей своих
　　　　　　И милый образ их
　　　　　Навек в сердцах запечатлели.
　　　　　　　　　　　　(Karamzin, 1966:97)

An example of significant tertiary indentation is Puškin's *Razluka* (Puškin, 1949:259), entirely iambic, with lines of the following number of feet: 5545443333555566466. Both F and M rimes occur, hexameters are ranged full out left, pentameters primarily indented, tetrameters secondarily and trimeters tertiarily indented, producing a pattern >aF>bM>>bM>aF>>aF >>cM>>>dF>>>cM>>>dF>eM>aF>aF>eMfFgM>>gMfFgM. Further degrees of indentation, with meter-correspondence, are rare but not unknown, — in 'Pindaric' verses, for instance. In Krylov's fables, which often have three indentations, even four (e.g. *Orel i kury*) and five (e.g. *Volk na psarne*) degrees of indentation occur.[7]

Examples of complete coincidence of meter-correspondence with rime-correspondence, i.e. where equally ranged lines are equimetrical and rimed, are numerous. Simply to illustrate such coincidence, reference may be made to Puškin's *Obval* and *Èxo* (Puškin, 1949:III, 136-7 and 227) both with masculine-rimed iambics throughout each stanza — 4-4-4-2-4-2 — and patterned aaa>ba>b; his *Na xolmax Gruzii* (III, 112),. with alternation of six and four iambs, patterned aM>bF, etc.; Jazykov's *K Rejnu* (Penguin:125-128), also with alternation of six and four iambs, but patterned aF>bM, etc.; Grigor'ev's '*O, govori xot' ty so mnoj*' (Penguin:214-215), alternating four and three iambs, patterned aM>bD, etc.; and Bal'mont's *Akkordy* (Penguin:243), with stanzas of anapestic lines throughout — 2-2-3-2-2-3, and patterned >aD>aDbM>cD>cDbM.[8] Many other patterns can be found.

Indentation may occur with no apparent prosodic correlation of any import. Little purpose is served, for instance, by indenting the first line of each of the riming hexameter couplets of Al. Tolstoj's *Knjaz' Mixajlo Repnin*, at least when the couplets are in any case separated by spaces (Penguin:172-75). Similarly, as has been implied above, the indentation of the first lines of quatrains in some editions of Lermontov's *Poslednee novosel'e* has little if any prosodic function. Otherwise indentation is, in the first instance, a simple signal that ranged lines have something in common. In the case of rime-correspondence alone, indentation is no more than a simple signal.[9] In the case of meter-correspondence, whether or not it coincides with rime-correspondence, indentation is iconic. It is not, however, an image but a diagram, in that the indentation of a line corresponds with the fact that it is shorter, in number of feet, or in number of syllables: the relation of the positions of the left hand ends of lines is analogous to the relation of the length of the lines — 'the further in, the shorter the line'. It is, however, not unknown for the longer line to be indented, as in Pasternak's *Matros v Moskve*:

(16)   Я увидал его, лишь только
        С прудов зиме
        Мигнул каток шестом флагштока
        И сник во тьме.

                              (Pasternak, 1961:87-90)

In such a case as this indentation cannot be considered diagrammatic on the principle just described.

3

In the majority of the poems in Kirsanov's volume *Lirika* (1962), all the lines except the first are indented and ranged, a device which may more conveniently be described by saying that the first lines are 'reverse indented'. Were it not for the uniformity of the device one would be tempted to ascribe to the reverse indentation in one or two of the poems the function of isolating the first word or words in order to identify or underscore a theme, as in *Rabota v sadu*, a poem with language as its theme, beginning

(17)   Речь — зимостойкая семья.
        Я, в сущности, мичуринец.
        Над стебельками слов — моя
        упорная прищуренность.

                              (Kirsanov, 1962:21)

If any function could be attributed to the reverse indentation in this volume it would be a 'negative function', in that when it does *not* occur it signifies that all the poems in a particular section are to be regarded as a unit — a cycle with a unifying theme. However, poems from Kirsanov 1962 which were in *Četyre tetradi* (Kirsanov, 1940), such as *Četyre soneta* (1940:54ff., 1962:89ff.) and *Poslednee maja* (1940:77ff., 1962:92ff.) are not set with initial reverse indentation in the earlier volume (*Četyre soneta*, moreover, has all the sonnets after the first indented and ranged, a device which is not adopted in the later volume). It may therefore be that reverse indentation in Kirsanov 1962 is merely an editor's or compositor's idiosyncrasy, with or without the poet's recognition, and of no poetic significance.

'Theme-correspondence' as a function of indentation is perhaps more likely in Martynov's *Voda*, each stanza of which begins with an indented line consisting of one word, whereas other single-word lines in the poem are not indented. The indentation isolates the theme, water:

(18)   Вода
        Благоволила
        Литься!

                              (Martynov, 1972:71)

which is then repeated in the pronouns at the head of each stanza (*Ona/Ej/ Ej/Ej*). While the third and fifth stanzas of the same poet's *Nočnye zvuki* (Martynov, 1972:111) also begin with single-word indented lines, it cannot be said that these words establish or isolate a theme.

The theme of Kirsanov's *Smerti boľše net* is given in just these words, the first line of the poem. The line is repeated and then progressively 'decapitated' and indented thus:

(19) Смерти больше нет.
  Смерти больше нет.
    Больше нет.
    Больше нет.
      Нет. Нет.
        Нет.
      (Kirsanov, 1972:8)

This arrangement is better described as right ranging and its obvious effect is to put increasing weight on the negative (cf. below remarks on the ultimate point of the same poet's *Ad*). In performance the ever-shortening sentences and the increasing weight on *net* could be brought out but the right ranging produces an additional visual impact which left ranging would not give: shaped as it is, the stanza demands constant re-reading — and viewing.

Kirsanov provides the single instance of apparently significant stanza-indentation which will be commented on in this connection. His poem *Dve gorstki zvezd* falls into three parts, each consisting of a couplet followed by two short-line quatrains. The last quatrain in each part is indented as a whole, quatrains preceding the last being secondarily indented. Thus the couplets are ranged, the final quatrains of each part are ranged, and the intervening quatrains are ranged: there is therefore structural and visual similarity of the three parts and this similarity parallels that of the content. Moreover, the singly inset final quatrains of each part are identical in grammatical structure, differentiated only by the pronoun which ends each line:

(20) Альфа —я,   ...ты,   ...мы,
  Бета —я,   ...ты,   ...мы,
  Гамма —я,   ...ты,   ...мы,
  Дзэта —я... ...ты... ...мы.
      (Kirsanov, 1972:169-70)

In this poem, then, the poet has visually integrated parts and sub-parts by indentation and ranging.

It is Kirsanov who also provides us with examples of what may be called 'reverse *lesenka*'. Normal *lesenka* is achieved by breaking a line into hemistichs disposed one below another and, by irregular indentation, so setting them that the first symbol of each hemistich after the first is ranged with the last symbol of the preceding hemistich. Its function may be to indicate rhythmic or stress units, or — if the whole line is a 'unit of attention' — to create 'sub-units of attention'. In reverse *lesenka* the first hemistich is 'stepped' as in normal *lesenka* but each succeeding hemistich has its *last* symbol ranged with the *first* symbol of the preceding hemistich, as in

(21)   смутно чувствуют:
                           дверь,
                     кресла,
              угол стола,
        пустота!

                                   (Kirsanov, 1972:178)

Another example in the same poem (*Zerkala*) occurs at 184, and examples can be found in *Tvoja poèma* (Kirsanov, 1962), at 45, 49, sometimes with normal *lesenka* to produce a zig-zag pattern (57), which is also achieved with overlapping hemistichs (53, 63, 64, etc.). Left ranging of indented lines, sometimes after a normal *lesenka*, occurs as at 45:

(22)   сорвал
        с календаря
                     листок,
              даря
        запекшиеся в ночь слова.

Other variations of indentation occur and not all of them, nor all of those described above can be attributed to the need to accommodate a *lesenka* without line turnover. Occasionally a function can be detected in these variations in irregular indentation, such as the vertical alignment of grammatically identical syntagmas, to underscore their parallel meanings, as in

(23)   — А ты смотри
                     живи,
        еще Володька есть ... —
              И в бред,
        в дыханье,
        в хрип,
        в — дышать всю ночь
                     (Kirsanov, 1962:51)

and

(24)   Губой
                        ресницы трогаю,
                        пою:
        ты мне нужна,
        ты мне мила ...
                                    (Kirsanov, 1962:52)

Apart from such few instances as these one can only conclude that 'Kirsanov's acrobatics' (Voznesenskij, 1970:156) are either simply that or are deliberate variations on *lesenka* in order to refurbish the device by making it strange.

4

So far we have examined some aspects of irregular indentation, however briefly, and before that regular but simple indentation and ranging of matched lines. In 'progressive indentation' several lines in sequence are indented by regular but successively greater distances. There is no ranging of matched lines, nor of terminal symbols as in *lesenka* or reverse *lesenka*. An example from Axmatova's *Poèma bez geroja* is:

(25)   А во сне все казалось, что это
       Я пишу для кого-то либретто,
       И отбоя от музыки нет.
                        (Axmatova, 1968:II, 123)

and it is aspects of the function of progressive indentation in this poem and in two poems of Voznesenskij that will form the subject of these paragraphs.

K. Verheul has amply explored and demonstrated not only the theme of time in Axmatova's poetry in general and particularly in *Poèma bez geroja*, but also the 'concentric development and linear progression' of this poem (Verheul, 1971:180-98). The concern with the three phases of time — past, present, future — and their constant interflux is most evident in Part I of the poem, which contains too the turmoil of the masquerade. It is this part which is, of the three parts, most abundant in words and phrases designating or evoking concepts of time and sequentiality. Part I also has six digressions, while Part II has none and Part III one only. These digressions, ranged left and printed in italics, are typographically distinguished from the rest of the poem, just as in content they are 'outside' the flow of the poem.[10] Moreover, while Part II has quite regular triplet-sestet structure and Part III has possibly one slight departure from regularity in this respect, Part I has some thirty 'irregularities' in the sense of expansion of the basic triplet to four, five and up to eight lines. It is these features of Part I which mark the distinctness of its mood from that of Parts II and III where, after Part I, there is a 'lowering of tension'.[11]

The peculiar 'rotating movement' of the double triplets is fundamental for the development of the themes of the poem, as Verheul observes (Verheul, 1971:198). Verheul does not refer to the visual presentation of the cyclical structure. Since the (basic) pattern is *aabccb* one might have expected, if indentation were to be used at all, that paired adjacent riming lines would be ranged full out left, with the third and sixth riming lines indented and ranged, since this in fact more clearly underscores the rime-pattern.[12] Instead, one has the progressive indentation of each triplet,[13] which does not (completely) 'lay bare the device'. However, the chosen typographical pattern reveals more immediately the organization of the textual content. Each 'saw-tooth' or pair of 'saw-teeth' is a sense-group: indeed most of them are sentences. Beyond this, however, is the purely visual impression of an endlessly unrolling scroll of time and experience and memory, so that while the basic function of the indentation of the triplets is to mark 'stanza/sentence' division it has another function — and both operate through visual channels.

The eight progressively indented lines to be found in Voznesenskij's *Latyš-skij èskiz*[14] (Voznesenskij, 1966[1]:92) have an obviously 'cumulative' effect, parallel to the cumulation of the four thousand days of the prisoner's sentence. Progressive indentation, up to five units, coupled with a shift back to full left, in Section VI of Voznesenskij's *Oza* (Voznesenskij, 1966[2]:24), has yet another function. Each part of the dialogue in this poem begins with a line full out left which is then followed by a heavily indented line, this being the first of several progressively indented lines. The progressive indentation continues until the end of a sentence is reached, when the next line is again set full out left. In all but one instance (where the réplique has not ended) the next line contains the phrase uttered by the 'black raven'. By means of the progressive indentation the eye is made to track steadily down and right, before being suddenly switched back full left and thrust repeatedly on the phrase *A na xuja*.[15] The shock effect is reinforced by visual presentation — line manipulation.

5

The various kinds of line indentation so far discussed do not result in the creation of blocks of print which could be enclosed within a regular geometrical shape, except perhaps accidentally. Indentation not infrequently results in the creation of almost symmetrical shapes but these are irregular and also accidental. Lines can however be apparently so indented and reverse indented as to produce regular and symmetrical geometrical shapes. In fact the effect is achieved by centering (disposing about a vertical central axis) of lines whose length is deliberately calculated to produce vertical symmetry, assisted when necessary by word and letter spacing.

Such is the device employed by Dylan Thomas in his cycle of twelve poems *Vision and Prayer* (Thomas, 1952:137-48), wherein the first six poems, relating to *Vision*, are cast in the form of a rhombus (diamond, lozenge) and the second six, relating to *Prayer*, in the form of 'Easter wings', as D. Holbrook puts it (Holbrook, 1972:183). It seems unlikely, on the fact of it and in the knowledge of Thomas's poetry, that these shapes are simply geometrical figures:

It is possible to believe that the second figure, that of the *Prayer* sequence, is a rough representation of a St. Andrew's cross. More likely is that the figure of the second set is achieved by inverting the upper and lower halves of the rhombus. In that event the shape of the second set is a 'response' to the shape of the first set, as the poems of the second set are a response to the *Vision* of the first set. Holbrook pursues a similar idea and notes that the first poem of the cycle begins at the upper apex with

Who
Are   you ...

while the last poem has at its very centre the single-word line 'I'. In other words the visual shapes result in enormous weight on 'Who?' and 'I' in these poems which are part of Thomas's "attempt to ask and answer the question, which is King Lear's question, 'Who is it that can tell me who I am?'" (Holbrook, 1972:183).

A similar effect of weight upon a single word is achieved by Kirsanov in his rhombus poem *Ad* (Kirsanov, 1972:40-41), which has no respondent figure. The fifty progressively expanding and then contracting lines of this poem are constructed with such skill that it is only towards the end of the second half that resort has to be made to word spacing in order to maintain the steady decrease in line-length. Is this poem more than just a startlingly impressive feat and an impressively startling shape, which in itself would be a remarkable poetic device? The verbal material leads me to correlate the increasing line-length of the first part with the cumulative depiction of the horrors and torments of Hell. The second half, with its more broken rhythms, describes the poet-narrator's personal torment in Hell and is also cumulative, in a different sense — in the sense that it descends deeper and deeper into the narrowmost pit and ends with the single word *ad* — *Hell* (note how the poem also begins at a point — the point of entrance to Hell: *Idu/v adu*). In terms of this interpretation the shape of the poem is iconic — it is a metaphor, which may be expounded thus: as the lines cumulate in length so the depicted horrors of Hell cumulate, and as the uttermost physical point of the poem is reached so too is the uttermost point of a personal Hell.

More 'ambitiously' shaped, if in some respects more naive poems are those whose verbal material is so disposed on the page as to take on the delineation of a physical object. Such shaped poems have a long tradition in western literatures, beginning in Classical Greek literature with the so-called *texnopaignia*.[16] Baroque poets of the sixteenth and seventeenth centuries wrote shaped poems, George Herbert's *The Altar* and *Easter Wings* being two of the best-known examples of the art (Herbert, 1941:26, 43; Summers, 1954:123-46). The *texnopaignia* are now printed with normal horizontal lineation, which usually renders unrecognizable their pictural intention (Legrand, 1927: cf. 225 with 230-31, 'The Egg'; and 226 with 228, 'The Ax'), and the same is true of Herbert's *Easter Wings* (see Sparrow, 1969:3, for an illustration of the poet's intention). In all these poems the verses are so constructed as to create the required shape. In Lewis Carroll's *Alice in Wonderland* the verses of 'Fury's Tail' are simply made to fit into the shape of a curly, tapering tail, without regard to the length of the verses themselves. This poem, the *texnopaignia* and the Baroque shaped poems are clearly icons, specifically images, in that the shapes created simply delineate the outlines of physical objects. Pictural, supposedly, are the eleven pages of Mallarmé's *Un Coup de Dés*, though it is difficult to discover the "appropriate ideogram" for each page, as Mallarmé's editor observes, even *with* the aid of the text (Cohn, 1951:34-35; Cohn, 1966:89-111). Many of Apollinaire's *calligrammes*, on the other hand, are quite recognizable 'pictures' (Apollinaire, 1966:162, 174-5, 176-7, 182, 186, 189, 192, etc.).

Though some of Apollinaire's *calligrammes* contain lines of verse, normally set, in addition to the pictural element, they are not *derived* from other poems, whereas at least two of Voznesenskij's recent set of picture-poems in Russian *are* derived from other poems by the same poet (Voznesenskij, 1970:161-66). Among these *izopy* (presumably an acronym of *izobraziteľnye poèmy* — or of *izopoèmy*?) *Boj petuxov* (164-65) consists of seven and a half lines of the poem on 73-74 set in normal linear fashion, together with the words of part of the remaining text so disposed on the page as to depict a fighting cock (or is it two fighting cocks?) and a severed head. These pictural elements can be 'deciphered', with the aid of the text, but cannot be read as text: they are little if anything more than 'drawing with words'. *Xoždenie po vodam* (163) consists of three words, *čajka plavki boga*, — disposed in the shape of a seagull — taken from the last two lines of the 59-line poem *Obščij pljaž No. 2* (24-27). Whereas the picture-poem *Boj petuxov* can be said to represent the 'core' of the textual poem *Boj petuxov*, the same cannot be said of *Xoždenie po vodam* — it represents the core of the last two lines only of *Obščij pljaž No. 2*, though it must be said that Voznesenskij claims that the textual poem sprang from the picture-poem: *S ètogo načalis' stixi. Èto metaforičeskij genezis stixa* (159).

The picture-poem *Paroxodik* (162), deriving from no textual poem,[17] can be read easily as text and at the same time is a simple picture of a steamer and its spreading wake. *Most* (161) is also original (non-derived), though Voznesenskij gives (158) at least the beginning of what might have been a textual poem on the same theme (the only common element in the picture-poem and the textual poem is the morpheme *id-*, occurring once in the textual poem and many times in the picture-poem). This picture-poem cannot be read as sentences, nor even as syntagmas but only as separate words or vocables and their inversions. The lower part of this picture-poem is meant to represent the reflection in a river of the upper part (strictly speaking, not all the letters are true mirror-images, but this is a triviality). The four picture-poems discussed are simply pictures of objects, halted — it is true — in the train of some action. They are icons in the sense of images. The picture-poem (and palindrome) *A luna kanula*, consisting just of these three words and having no textual equivalent, is not entirely in the same category, for it is meant to represent an event in process, namely a flight to the moon and back — as Voznesenskij says (160).[18]

The enlarged letters *a* may be considered to be images of earth and moon. The letters distributed in an arc between them may constitute an image — of a spaceship at different stages of its flight — or may be seen rather to constitute a diagram, the distribution of the letters being roughly analogous to the complete flight of a spaceship between the two bodies. As Peirce observes (Peirce, 1933:260), one cannot understand the purport of a diagram without a clue. Voznesenskij's explanation could clue to a diagram or an image and it is not in itself detrimental to the quality of this picture-poem of Voznesenskij's that it has to be clued. All of his picture-poems are in fact clued but it is surely essential that the clue to the icon of a picture-poem should be manifest in the verbal material and this cannot be said to be so of all of Voznesenskij's *izopy*.

While admitting that "the instrument with which both Mallarmé and the lapidary writers were in their different ways experimenting [was] one that [was] capable of producing, within a limited range, subtle and even moving effects", J. Sparrow concludes that "the literary effect that can be achieved by visual presentation is limited, and their efforts to go beyond its limits were a failure" (Sparrow, 1969:143 and 144). Similarly, Legrand, à propos the *texnopaignia*, writes: "The figured poems ... have hardly any other value than that of curiosities ... their literary merit is slender, if not null" (Legrand, 1927:226-27). While not wishing to dismiss Mallarmé's *Un Coup de Dés* in this fashion, we may be more inclined to do so with Apollinaire's *calligrammes* or Voznesenskij's *izopy*, though we should not lose sight of the latter's remarks on the contemporary importance of the visual medium (156-57) and the concluding remarks of his introduction to the *izopy*: "I foresee accusations of lack of seriousness, of fun and games, of playing with words. I do not think that poetry should definitely 'have to be a little bit stupid' but why should it not sometimes be frivolous?" (160).[19]

Examination of one typographical device, indentation, led to the attribution to this device of the functions of rime-correspondence and meter-correspondence and in the latter case an iconic function was proposed. The ostensible absence of either rime-correspondence or meter-correspondence led to the suggestion that indentation may sometimes perform the function of theme-correspondence. More elaborate typographical dispositions of the lines of poems and the iconicity of such dispositions was then briefly discussed and this led finally to remarks on the images of picture-poems, in which the linear conventions of typesetting are ignored. In the scope of this paper it was not possible to comment on the visual aspect of stanza-division or of punctuation — and the absence thereof.[20]

University of Edinburgh

NOTES

* I wish to thank A. D. S. Fowler, Professor of Rhetoric and English Literature, University of Edinburgh, for bibliographical help; J. M. Davidson, Production Manager, Edinburgh University Press, for advice on terminology and printing practice; and G. Smith, Department of Russian Language and Literature, University of Birmingham, for bibliographical guidance and helpful answers to my questions about metrics.
[1] Three types of signs are distinguished by C. S. Peirce: "A sign is either an *icon*, an *index*, or a *symbol*" (Peirce, 1932:170). An index simply indicates by its presence the presence or existence of something else, with which it has an actual connection — thus smoke is an index of fire and a rolling gait may be an index that a man is a sailor — or drunk. A symbol is a purely conventional

sign, the meaning of which must be learnt. An icon "represent[s] its object mainly by its similarity
... an iconic representamen may be termed a *hypoicon*" (Peirce, 1932:157), of which there are three
types: *image, diagram,* and *metaphor*. An *image* contains the simple qualities of the thing it
represents, thus a picture of an object is an image. In a *diagram* the relations of the parts of the
signatum are represented by analogous relations between the parts of the *signans*. "Many
diagrams resemble their objects not at all in looks; it is only in respect of their parts that their
likeness consists" (Peirce, 1932:159). A *metaphor* displays neither the simple qualities of the thing
it represents — it is not a 'picture' — nor are its parts in a relationship analogous to that of the
parts of the object it represents, rather the *signans* exhibits a parallelism to the *signatum*. The
fulcrum of a metaphor is 'as if'. See also Shapiro, 1969:7.

[2] In saying this, however, I make due allowance for editorial interpretation or, in the worse case,
interference — and touch upon this matter at points below.

[3] Indication of the distance by which a line is indented is not given in ems but, where necessary,
in approximate terms.

[4] 'Indentation' will henceforth be used either merely in the sense of 'indentation' or, when
convenient, in the sense of 'indentation *versus* non-indentation'.

[5] In the first stanza of this poem indentation does not entirely correspond to matching rime-
types, since — as in each stanza — even lines are indented, yet the rime-scheme is 1aD 2bM 3aD
4a(?)D 5bM. Thus:

> Среди рисунчатых
> зверей и змей —
> семейство сумчатых
> не хуже, в сущности,
> других семей.

> (Kirsanov, 1972:223)

It may therefore be that indentation in this poem is a more or less meaningless device — even lines
are indented, odd lines are not. In this connection note that in stanza 2 *all* the rimes are dactylic.

[6] Obolensky indents equally the first and fourth lines, so that indentation apparently signifies
'first or last line of quatrain', while *Slovo* indents first lines and secondarily indents fourth lines.
Hence the primary indentation of *Slovo* must presumably signal 'first line of quatrain' while the
secondary indentation signals '(generally) shorter line', i.e. meter-correspondence.

[7] These two fables are so set in Pares' bilingual edition (Krylov, 1943:12 and 17 respectively),
whereas the former has three indentations, the latter four in Krylov 1859:184-85 and 200-201
respectively (second edition — first edition not available to me).

[8] It seems to be the most reasonable course to describe the structure of this poem so, with
extra-metrical stress on the first syllable of 2.5, 3.2, 3.4. Less convincing would be to allow these
three lines to 'dictate' the analysis and arrive at trochee + 2 dactyls for lines 1, 2, 4 and 5 of each
stanza. Indentation would then signal variation in the character rather than the number of the feet
and the indentation of the initial lines would be unusual. The analysis adopted here associates
indentation with the metrically shorter lines.

[9] Unless it is a rather 'vague' metaphor: 'the difference and similarity of the indented and
non-indented lines is parallel to the difference and similarity of their rimed endings'.

[10] V. Poluxina notes (private communication) that the epigraphs — outside the body of the
poem — are italicized too.

[11] V. Poluxina (private communication).

[12] This is in fact how Obolensky sets an extract from the poem:

> Были святки кострами согреты,
> И валились с мостов кареты,
>   И весь траурный город плыл
>   По неведомому назначенью
>   По Неве иль против теченья
>   Только прочь от своих могил.   (Penguin: 323)

[13] Verheul rightly dismisses the suggestion that Axmatova's stanza structure may be derived from that of a cycle of poems by Kuzmin (Verheul, 1971:196, n. 23). A double triplet, rimed *aabccb*, set with exactly the same indentation as *Poèma bez geroja*, but in syllabic verse of seven syllables, was used by Trediakovskij in *Prošenie ljubve* —

Покинь Купидо стрелы:
уже мы все не целы
но сладко уязвлены
любовною стрелою
твоею золотою;
все любви покорены:
(Trediakovskij, 1963:74)

I am not suggesting that Axmatova 'found' her stanza in Trediakovskij.

[14] This *is* presumably the title of the poem. In Voznesenskij 1964 and 1966[1] it is so entitled though in the contents list of the former it appears as *Latyšskaja saga* and Flegon in Voznesenskij 1966[2] has it as *Latyšskij nabrosok*.

[15] The phrase *na figa* in the Soviet edition is quite clearly *not* what Voznesenskij wrote and I have therefore used the phrase reinstated by Blake and Hayward and adopted by Flegon (see Voznesenskij, 1966[2]:24-25, especially the note on p. 25).

[16] A brief, lucid account of *texnopaignia*, with some illustrations, is to be found in Legrand, 1927:220-35.

[17] As far as I have been able to determine.

[18] "Since the foot of man has touched the Moon, the Moon as a myth, as a sentimental legend, irreality, has disappeared. The picture-poem *A luna kanula* is read from left to right and back again. The reader, as it were, follows with his eye a flight to the moon and back". Without this explanation, I, for one, would not have understood the picture-poem properly. Indeed, on first reading it, without having read Voznesenskij's introductory remarks, I took it to signify either moon-rise or moon-set — though the words implied the latter and yet read upwards instead of downwards — *and* were in the wrong quadrant for moon-set....

[19] More recently, the title-pages — on Voznesenskij's direction, one presumes — of two sections of his 1972 volume of poems have been set so as to represent recognizable objects — a human figure (5 — *S uma by ne sojti*) and a sail-boat (113 — *Avos*).

[20] Since this paper was written the following relevant data have come to my attention. (a) The extracts from Kirsanov quoted as examples (22), (23), and (24) are set slightly differently, though still not as 'regular' *lesenka*, in Semen Kirsanov, *Sobranie sočinenij, 1, liričeskie proizvedenija* (Moscow, 1974). See pp. 112, 119, and 119-20 and cf. note 2 above. (b) Examples of shaped poems in Russian can be found in *Russkaja sillabičeskaja poèzija XVII-XVIII vekov[2]* (Ed. A. Pančenko), *Biblioteka poèta, bol'šaja serija* (Leningrad, 1970), 39-40 and facing 97. (c) Remarks on Voznesenskij's *izopy*, in part similar to those in this paper, can be found on pp. 170-71 of V. P. Grigor'ev, "Grafika i orfografija u A. Voznesenskogo", in *Nerešennye voprosy russkogo pravopisanija*, ed. L. P. Kalakuckaja (Moscow, 1974), 162-71. The bulk of this article is devoted to an examination of punctuation as a meaningful device in Voznesenskij's poetry. (d) Since the appearance of his *izopy*, Voznesenskij has been experimenting with moveable letters on blackboards to create entities similar to the *izopy* but which he calls *maga* (see Herbert R. Lottman, "Work in progress — Voznesensky magic", *Intellectual Digest*, IV, 3, Del Mar, California, Nov. 1973, 8-12).

BIBLIOGRAPHY

Apollinaire, G.
    1966   *Œuvres complètes de Guillaume Apollinaire — Alcools, Calligrammes, Poésie, Théâtre, Critique*. Paris.

Axmatova A.
1967/68   *Sočinenija* (Eds. G. P. Struve, B. A. Filippov), 2 vols. Inter-Language Literary Associates.
Baratynskij, E.
1945   *Stixovorenija* (Ed. I. Medvedeva). Moscow.
Cohn, R. G.
1951   *L'œuvre de Mallarmé — Un Coup de Dés.* Paris.
1966   *Mallarmé's Masterwork — New Findings.* The Hague and Paris.
Cvetaeva, M.
1965   *Izbrannye proizvedenija.* Moscow-Leningrad.
Halliday, M. A. K.
1961   "Categories of the Theory of Grammar", *Word,* 17, 3 (Dec. 1961), 241-92
Herbert, G.
1941   *The Works of George Herbert* (Ed. F. E. Hutchinson). Oxford.
Holbrook, D.
1972   *Dylan Thomas — The Code of Night.* London.
Jakobson, R.
1970   "Subliminal Verbal Patterning in Poetry", *Studies in General and Oriental Linguistics Presented to Shiró Hattori* (Eds. R. Jakobson, Shigeo Kawamoto), 302-8. Tokyo. [French version, "Structures linguistiques subliminales en poésie", in R. Jakobson, *Questions de Poétique,* Paris, 1973, 280-92].
1971   "The Dominant", *Readings in Russian Poetics* (Eds. L. Matejka, K. Pomorska), 82-87. Cambridge, Mass., and London. [French version, "La Dominante" in R. Jakobson, *Questions de Poétique,* Paris, 1973, 145-51].
Karamzin, N.
1966   *Polnoe sobranie stixotvorenij* (Ed. Ju. Lotman). Moscow-Leningrad.
Kirsanov, S.
1940   *Četyre tetradi.* Moscow.
1962   *Lirika.* Moscow.
1972   *Zerkala²*. Moscow.
Krylov, I.
1859   *Polnoe sobranie sočinenij I. Krylova ..., II: Stixotvorenija i basni²*. St. Petersburg.
1942   *Russian Fables of Ivan Krylov,* with verse translation by Bernard Pares. Harmondsworth.
Legrand, Ph. E.
1927   *Bucoliques Grecs, II: Pseudo-Théocrite, Moschos, Bion, Divers.* Paris.
Lermontov, M.
1921   *Polnoe sobranie sočinenij.* 4 vols. Berlin.
1940   *Stixotvorenija, tom pervyj* (Ed. B. M. Èjxenbaum). Leningrad.
1957   *Sobranie sočinenij M. Lermontova, I: Stixotvorenija* (Eds. I. L. Andronikov, D. D. Blagoj, Ju. G. Oksman). Moscow.
1964   *Sobranie sočinenij M. Lermontova, I: Stixotvorenija* (Eds. I. L. Andronikov, Ju. G. Oksman). Moscow.
Lotman, Ju.
1968   *Lekcii po strukturaľnoj poètike: Vvedenie, teoriia stixa (= Brown University Slavic Reprint, V).* Providence.
Martynov, L.
1972   *Vo-pervyx, vo-vtoryx i v-treťix — stixi raznyx let.* Moscow.
Pasternak, B.
1961   *Stixotvorenija i poèmy.* Moscow.

Peirce, C. S.
1932   *Collected Papers, II: Elements of Logic* (Eds. C. Hartshorn, P. Weiss). Cambridge, Mass.
1933   *Collected Papers, III: Exact Logic* (Eds. C. Hartshorn, P. Weiss). Cambridge, Mass.
Penguin Book of Russian Verse. Ed. D. Obolensky, Harmondsworth, 1962.
Puškin, A.
1949   *Polnoe sobranie sočinenij.* Moscow-Leningrad.
Shapiro, M.
1969   *Aspects of Russian Morphology: A Semiotic Investigation.* Cambridge, Mass.
Sparrow, J.
1969   *Visible Words: A Study of Inscriptions in and as Books and Works of Art.* Cambridge.
Summers, J. H.
1954   *George Herbert: His Religion and Art.* London (123-46, Ch. VI, "The Poem as Hieroglyph").
Thomas, D.
1967   *Collected Poems, 1934-1952.* London.
Trediakovskij, V. K.
1963   *Izbrannye proizvedenija*[2] (Eds. L. I. Timofeev, Ja. M. Stročkov). Moscow-Leningrad.
Verheul, K.
1971   *The Theme of Time in the Poetry of Anna Axmatova.* The Hague-Paris.
Voznesenskij, A.
1964   *Antimiry.* Moscow.
1966[1]   *Axillesovo serdce.* Moscow.
1966[2]   *Moj ljubovnyj dnevnik.* London.
1970   *Ten' zvuka.* Moscow.
1971   *Vzgljad. Stixi i poèmy.* Moscow.

THE PRAGMATICS OF THE LITERARY ARTS: THE LANGUAGE OF LITERATURE AND THE DECODING OF LITERARY TEXT[1]

THOMAS G. WINNER

The study of the verbal arts is a time-honored discipline, reaching back to Aristotle's descriptive poetics. Nevertheless, it is, as Gerald Manley Hopkins has remarked, a "baby science," for it has yet to find firm methodological grounding. Its many schools have, throughout the centuries, twisted and turned in many directions, and many have reduced literature to, or attempted to explain it entirely by, external systems, or have recounted the history of a text, examined the "influences" of authors and schools upon each other, or attempted various kinds of taxonomies by period, genre, etc. or they have presented close readings. In the last decades, hermeneutic schools have called for dense readings of closed texts, echoing Hopkin's call for the study of poetry "with the microscope and the dissecting knife." There have been numerous efforts to provide poetics with a precise scientific methodology, and many of these new directions, particularly those labelled structuralist, have applied to the study of literature the methods of linguistics; but the limitation of the problems of poetic texts to those of texts of natural language, and thus those of poetics to those of linguistics, have frequently misled the researcher.

In sum, the study of literature has been traditionally split into two seemingly mutually irreconcilable camps, that of extrinsic and that of intrinsic approaches, to use Wellek's and Warren's terms.[2] The former includes studies relating the work of literature to society, economic systems, philosophy, *Geistesgeschichte,* and psychology, as well as the comparative movement, concerned with the problem of "influences" within and across cultures, while the latter encompasses the many schools of close reading, hermeneutics, *explication de texte,* the programs of the Russian Formalists, the Anglo-Saxon New Critics, and the attempts of some French structuralists to derive the grammar (*langue*) of a genre, period, etc. from the comparison and abstraction of formal properties of individual texts. The bipolarity of extrinsic and intrinsic has, in general, paralleled the opposition content/form.

In the early thirties, the Prague Linguistic Circle began to address itself to this bifurcation. The extension of the field of semiotics from the area of language to that of the arts in general and to the verbal arts in particular, paved the way for a global approach to aesthetic objects which would marshal a program to conjoin the many disparate perspectives of poetics into a comprehensive theory that would bridge the form/content opposition, thus heuristically relating not only text to code and synchrony to diachrony, but also the entire literary series and its individual texts to other systems in culture and their individual manifestations. A fundamental assumption of the Prague Circle was that literary art is a system related to other systems, and that its full description must encompass all the complexities of the specifics of each system, the unifying invariants and all the interaction between the various related systems and subsystems. Only then can the literary text be fully understood.

Thus, semiotics of literature, as it was first developed in Prague in the 1930s, has provided hope for fresh and nonreductive syntheses of former problem areas the application of which is still in its early stages. Among the regions in which the semiotic approach has furnished original methodologies and procedures bridging former gaps are those relating the artistic text to its agents, that is the domain of the pragmatics of the literary text: the age-old question of how the text relates to its producer (that is the problem of the author in his various guises) and its many real and potential receivers (that is the problem of text reception, of text analysis, multiple readings, etc.).

The domain of pragmatics is the most complex dimension in the interpretation of the literary text. Charles Morris identified three spheres of semiotic activity inseparably related: 1) the syntactic sphere which investigates the relationship of the signs of a text to each other and asks questions about the inner structuration of the text; 2) the semantic sphere which investigates the relation of the given text to its designata and subsumes the syntactic realm; and 3) the pragmatic sphere which is concerned with the relation of the sign or sign text to the producer and receivers of the text. This latter region subsumes the first two, thus dealing with the greatest number of systems and possessing the most complex metalanguage.[3] Since aesthetic texts are dynamic structures that incorporate norm-violations as basic structural features and organizing themes; furthermore, since semiotic-structuralist interpretation is itself a pragmatic activity, a reconstruction similar, as Cesare Segre[4] has noted, to a reading where the text is perceived in linear-temporal fashion but where it is rearranged achronically in memory; therefore pragmatics is a crucial and highly complex area; and it is small wonder that the literary analyst was often tempted to define art in so limited a fashion that the pragmatic sphere was not taken into account. Thus, traditional aesthetic theories have frequently ignored the problem of the author and the receivers (e.g. the various Formalist theories, including the Russian Formalists and the Anglo-American New Critics), or they have reduced the work to its creator or to its reception. In either case, theory is impoverished. Some recent theories of text reception (e.g. the German theories of *Textrezeption* of Iser and Jauss) have examined the problem of the reception of a text, but they have generally neglected the addressor and the context, including the relation of the text to other culture texts, artistic or not. On the other hand, the so-called "history of reception," once so popular in comparative literature, has dealt with the problem in a manner that frequently ignored the text itself.

An approach to this problem which eschews reduction and relates the producers and users of the text to the text itself as well as to complex contextual configurations and entire cultural world views has been developed by modern semiotics which has moved persistently from the predominantly formal to the predominantly meaningful levels of the text and, in ever expanding circles, to the relation of the text to other systems, including its agents. Basically, the new approaches are founded on the postulate of the autonomous (not immanent) nature of the aesthetic text, which is seen as only semi-closed and into which elements may enter through the mediating role of the creating and interpreting subject. Underlying much of modern aesthetic pragmatics is Jakobson's thesis of the fundamentally antithetical character of the process of encoding and decoding, the latter being based, in part, on statistical probabilities and stochastic processes.[5] But we must also note that, because of the norm-violating character of artistic texts, the jumps, gaps, reversals, and new juxtapositions of heterogeneous elements of such texts can not, in fact, be dealt with by consideration of the purely statistical and stochastic probabilities posited by Jakobson for natural language in its nonaesthetic functions. The stochastic processes which apply to referential texts have only limited applicability to aesthetic texts and can be applied primarily to linear-temporal processes where the receiver sequentially decodes partial meanings. A work of literature is, however, not entirely a linear-temporal structure, since it also is constructed atemporally, paradigmatically; hence the importance of metaphor, semantic and formal parallelisms, basic symbols, transformations, etc.

Semiotics takes into account complex networks of relationships between the texts of the literary series and those of other series. Aesthetic texts are thus never seen as closed systems, but always as partially open, yet autonomous, systems of signs, related — but never reduceable to — other systems of culture: language, social hierarchies, cultural values, as well as individual psychologies. How these extratextual systems enter into relation with the autonomous text is a complex issue pertaining to the pragmatic domain; for it is through the mediation of the sending and perceiving subject that these systems penetrate the artistic text, which is, however, not reduceable to these stimuli.

The creation and reception of poetic texts may be seen as proceeding in the following linear sequence: An author, consciously or unconsciously utilizing various cultural codes at his disposal (language, poetic codes, and many other cultural codes), creates a text which is then decoded by a receiver who is again guided in this process by an unconscious or conscious awareness and utilization of the cultural codes of his own time and cultural environment, and sometimes, but by no means always, by a partial knowledge of the multiple codes of the author's time and ambience. Thus we can construct the following schema, where A = addressor, T = text, and $R_1 \ldots R_n$ = the totality of possible receivers of the text:

$$A \rightleftharpoons T \rightleftharpoons R_1, R_2, R_3, \ldots R_n$$

$$A \text{ codes (CA)} \quad \begin{array}{c} R \text{ codes (CR)} \\ (A \text{ codes}) \end{array}$$

The double directional arrow between the text and its agents indicates that neither the process of text production nor that of text reception is unidirectional. The addressor frequently takes on the role of a receiver, as when he stops and reads what he has written and rewrites it; and the act of reception is not a passive process. For during the act of reception the receiver projects upon the text his own psychological energy. And in this mutual communicative act, in which author and reader "collaborate" in the textual creation, cultural codes impinge upon the process both on the author's side and on that of the many receivers who, through the ages, receive and perceive the text and make it concrete. Thus the author is conditioned by other culture codes of his time and place, social and artistic, and each generation of receivers partakes of the codes of their time and place, but must have a minimum knowledge also of some codes of the addressor's time and ambience. Thus the communicative links existing between an author and those he consciously or unconsciously addresses are complex and dynamic. For the communication to be complete, there must be a channel that permits the message to proceed from A to R. And this channel can be faulty and it can distort (e.g. a badly copied or partially decomposed manuscript in the case of a written text, a palimpsest, etc.). There must also be partially overlapping codes; the many interrelated codes of the addressor must be, at least partially, comprehensible to the various generations of receivers, or communication will not take place. Because of the anti-normative character of artistic texts, the overlap may be slight. Artistic communication then may involve misunderstandings or reinterpretions not only based on faulty channels, but also — and more importantly — on the minimal overlap in aesthetic texts between A codes and R codes.

In this complex process, the roles of addressor and decoder may be partially reversible. Thus Mukařovský called art an uninterrupted dialogue between all those who successively create art and all those who successively perceive it.[6] The relation between author and reader has been well described by Lotman as a battle between an encoder and all decoders, all attempting to shape the text.[7] The receiver is thus also an encoder, a co-creator of the work of art which he "translates" into his code and interprets in the context of his own cultural experience, that is in the environment of all the cultural codes that make up the many semiotic systems of the receiver's culture. Moreover, some of these interpretations become part of the artistic tradition, helping to shape creations of other artists, or even of the same artist in later works.[8] The structure of the work as it appears during the act of perception is thus formed through the cooperative action of both poles of the artistic communication process, the addressor and receiver. The reader and the author jointly create the work by accepting or rejecting it or its parts and by imbuing it with a final meaning.

The Role of the Author in Cultural Context

As we have noted, in the history of aesthetic and literary theory attempts to solve the problem of relation of author to text have frequently had recourse to two extreme positions: 1) the work of art is seen as a reflection of the author, his psyche and biography, or 2) in reaction to 1) — the work of art is seen as a closed system from which the creative personality is excluded. From the perspective of semiotics we can approach the work of art as a system which encompasses both the author and receivers as components of the communication process, and as firmly implanted in cultural context, without reducing the work to any of these systems external to it. While the relation of the work of art to its author is ambiguous, the author is nevertheless always present in his work and the intensity and closeness of this relation varies from work to work, from author to author, from period to period and from genre to genre. A work of art is forever distinguished from aesthetically perceived natural phenomena by the very fact of its source of creation, the author whom the perceiver always senses behind the text. But the intensity of this perception varies, because the role of the author is historically changeable. There are periods in which the author's role is highly marked, and others when it is not. Thus in the Middle Ages the concept of literary authorship was of only slight cultural importance, hence the profusion of anonymous works emanating from that period. The fifteenth century saw the concept of *homo faber* grow in importance and, while the author was generally known, it was his craftsmanship and technical prowess which was important and not his creative originality. It was only in the sixteenth century that the individuality of the author became a subject of conscious interest, and this concern increased until it crested in the age of Romanticism to diminish again in the age of Realism and to rise again in the poetry of the Symbolists. Different genres also vary in the distance perceived between text and author. Thus, as Jakobson has remarked, the lyric begins with the first person singular and the present tense of the verb, and thus the author appears to be immediately perceived in the lyric, unlike the epic, which takes its beginning with the third person singular and the past tense of the verb. While a direct and necessary identification of the first person and the present tense of the text and the psychological state and life experience of its author should not be advanced, the latter is usually felt more intensely in lyrical works than in epic novels. (In oral art, which we are not considering here, the relation of author to text is less direct than in "high" art, since the performer, rather than the anonymous author, is felt as a presence within the text.)

The author's psychological and biographical experience and make-up, while related to the text, can never be identified with it; because the author's life experiences — no matter how realistically presented — are doubly transformed: first by being introduced into the total structural context of the work and by receiving numerous symbolic reinterpretations and, second, by the process of text reception, where the receiver recreates the work by virtue of his own intentional energy.

The semiotic problem of the place of the author in his work in the theory of poetic texts as cultural sign systems is a complex one in which oversimplification is especially dangerous.

The Reception of Poetic Texts

The problem of the reception of poetic texts is one of the most challenging, but also one of the most neglected, areas of poetic theory. As the whole sphere of pragmatics of poetic texts, the area of text reception involves all aspects of the poetic communication: the text itself, the real and implied author as he is manifested in the text, the creative process in general, the intention of the receiver, the teleology and ontology of the text itself, the evolution of artistic forms, styles and genres, as well as cultural context of all kinds — linguistic, aesthetic, social, spatio-temporal, etc., which have been partially outlined by me in the original paper presented at the conference which resulted in this volume.[9] As we have already seen, the production of literary texts is in a sense a collaborative enterprise, since art is an intersubjective communication. Thus the question of semiotic reception is essentially a question of how meanings are produced by, and for, the text, and how the reader contributes to the text. The underlying assumption of text pragmatics must be the denial of the formalist belief that the text alone is the basic, knowable, permanent, immutable, independent component of the poetic act. But in arguing for the reader's interpretive role we need not resort to total relativity and to subjectivity. For just as encoding proceeds in at least partial accordance with codes (literary, linguistic, and other), so also the decoder is hardly a completely free agent who can interpret arbitrarily; for he is in some measure bound to, and formed by, the many cultural codes impinging upon him, and by the material of the text itself. The relation of the receiver to codes is even more complex than that of the author, since the consumer also partially grasps the codes that have influenced and informed the author's creation of the text.

Text reception is thus a complex interpretative process since a multitude of codes impinge upon the reader and upon those aspects of the author's codes which overlap with those of the readers. Hence the perception of an aesthetic text is a process of reconstruction, it is in the truest sense a transcoding, a translation from one set of codes (those of the addressor) to another set of codes (those of the receiver).

Basing ourselves on Jakobson's six-factor, six-function model of communication, we can hold that all communications in culture are polyfunctional, with functions arranged in fluctuating hierarchies. The intentionality of the receiver may alter the hierarchical structure of functions of the addressor of the text. Thus while the encoder may have created a text dominated by a utilitarian function, for the receiver such a text may become dominated by an aesthetic one, i.e. it may become predominantly self-oriented. For example, a utilitarian object may be enshrined in an art museum and considered as an aesthetic object by later generations; homilies with a dominant referential or metacultural function at encoding may be read as art; myths and historical legends, which function as explanations in various referential ways especially in pre-literate cultures, can be perceived by other cultures as dominantly aesthetic in orientation; similarly jokes which may be first dominated by the phatic function (as a way of establishing contact and diminishing psychological distance) may be read as a form of mini-art; even mnemotechnic rhymes, which have a dominantly utilitarian function, may be dominated by the aesthetic function in the decoder's perception. Conversely, texts encoded as artistic works may be read with another controlling function: *Le rouge et le noir* may be read for social and historical information; *Beowulf,* the *Nibelungenlied,* and the *Igor Tale* may serve as linguistic documents.

Artistic texts are polysemic and therefore present problems of yet another kind to the reader, that of a certain diffuseness of meaning. The self-orientation and self-directedness of the aesthetic text accounts for its attenuated relation to the *denotatum,* thus focussing the attention of the reader upon the internal structuration of the text. The ambiguity of the sign–object relation in the aesthetic text impels the reader to interpret the text both objectively and subjectively. The peculiar polysemy of the artistic text leaves many indefinite aspects or empty spaces, many passages, images, characters, that appear to have shifting meanings. And it is, as the Polish philosopher Ingarden has noted almost half a century ago, a task of the reader to make concrete (*konkretisieren*) these ambiguities.[10] Their concretization is naturally based largely, but not exclusively, on the cultural codes of the receiver.

Thus it is that the aesthetic text is unstable to the extreme: because of its polysemy every text admits of many kinds of concretizations, in fact such plural interpretations are often required by the very nature of the text. We have therefore the contradictory situation that every text represents many texts. Each text admits of many meanings and thus a poem is a somewhat different text every time it is read not only by different generations of readers, but by different readers in the same generation and culture. Even each individual reading of a text by the same reader creates a partially new text. But, as we have noted, this does not imply complete relativism and unchecked subjectivity: for, as we have seen, the reader is only the co-creator of the work; he does not create it himself. The reader is always part of a community of art-producers and art-receivers, and thus he always partakes of the author's code — even if only through a minimal affinity of codes.

Literary texts are dominantly self-oriented and norm-violating, thus drawing attention to their structuration. Norm violations are of course not limited to artistic discourse. Also in non-artistic texts, every *parole* violates the *langue* and, by feedback, these alterations in turn gradually alter the code. In fact, we know that no cultural act can adhere completely to the norms, for if culture completely reproduced itself, it would be devoid of information, thus becoming non-culture.[11] But norm-violation may be a marginal phenomenon in non-artistic texts, whereas it represents an essential condition of the aesthetic functioning; and this presents an additional problem to the decoder. But whereas other interpretive difficulties increase over the ages, since CA and CR overlap less as the time distance between A and R increases, the obstacles created by norm-violation may diminish as the time span between encoding and decoding increases for reasons which will be discussed below.

The problem of text reception must be studied both synchronically and diachronically. This opens a whole theoretical area that needs further investigation. This essay will treat only a small section of this problem.

Synchronically we may examine the problems inherent in one reading of the text and relate this to the codes of the specific reader and his knowledge of the codes of the author. Or we may take a time-slice (the present time will present the least difficulties) and create a taxonomy of readers, as Lotman[12] has attempted. We may thus posit four types of readers, or four types of readings: 1) the naive reader, who is interested only in raw content, for whom it is sufficient to know "what happens" in *War and Peace*. Such a reader may be thrown off balance by norm violations perpetrated by the author which may make the text partially incomprehensible, or evoke responses such as "people don't act that way", "this is wrong grammar", or simply "this is boring, it can be skipped since it contributes nothing to the content". 2) The second type is the sophisticated reader who grasps the construction of the work and the interaction of its levels, the relation of the expression and content plane to each other, and understands in varying degrees the relations of textual levels to extratextual codes. 3) The third type is the scholarly reader who extrapolates one level of the work and examines it (e.g. the meter, language, imagery, etc.), relating it to other textual levels and extratextual structures. 4) The fourth type of reader is one who uses the text for a purpose fundamentally different from that for which it has been constructed. Such a reader may read *War and Peace* as an historical document and *Crime and Punishment* as a philosophical treatment of certain aspects of Christian ethics. From the point of view of synchrony, we must also remember that each historical period "reads" differently. Thus in all historical periods, different relations between reader and text are normative. For instance, in the Middle Ages, reading was ritualistic and based on generally accepted cultural maxims and symbols, whereas the Romantics demanded a highly individualized reading.

In the realm of diachrony, we observe first of all that reception by the same reader varies during different readings of one and the same text, each reading presenting a new interpretation, but each reading also partially overlapping with all previous readings. Since memory makes reception a durable process, a previous reading is still in the reader's mind during a second reading, and all the previous readings form a complex memory structure during the nth reading.

Such a process becomes more complex in oral art and in the performing arts, where each perception confronts a text altered by different text performers.

Differences in readings are also affected by different artistic macrotexts or cultural world views which inform different attitudes of the reader. For example, a reader and author are separated by temporal and cultural distance, by centuries and/or continents. Indeed, the problem of the distance between A code and the R codes may be overwhelming; and this problem is accentuated in the verbal arts because of the necessity of deciphering the primary linguistic code as well as the artistic codes. Thus a Shakespearean text assumes a knowledge of the English of the late 16th century. For instance the word *nunnery* in Hamlet's injunction to Ophelia ("get thee to a nunnery ..." (III,1)) originally denoted not only a convent, but also a brothel; and without this information the perception of Shakespeare's words is changed, since the reader did not understand the pun.

How far can the reader be aware of ever-changing codes? The history of a work of art is one of constant modification of its concretization, for each reader is a product of his own time, and different artistic conditions contributing to the aesthetic perception and valuation of a given work, undergo radical changes in the course of time. The reader's codes become a prism through which a received text is refracted. It is then interpreted in codes with which the reader is familiar. Thus, we face a seeming contradiction. While the material qualities of the work of art remain relatively constant through the ages, the perceivers' codes change and different generations of readers are informed by different codes. Thus the relatively stable material level of the artistic construct, which functions as its signifier, is united to different sets of signifieds, depending on different cultural contexts. Here much depends on the acquaintance of the reader with the A code. As an example of the reader with minimal acquaintance, we might consider a modern reader of a medieval text who is not aware of medieval symbolism. For him confusion replaces the ambiguity that the text would create for a medieval, or informed contemporary, reader.

In contrast, there is the informed reader who attempts to reconstruct the medieval A code, which is very distant from his CR. For such a reader the task becomes that of accounting for all elements of the text in the original cultural context. The sophisticated decoder reads the original work not only through the prism of his knowledge of earlier artistic codes, but also through his awareness of his own codes which, in turn, are a synthesis of all the accumulated cultural information at his disposal since the time of encoding.

Thus a sophisticated twentieth century reader of a poem by Puškin will not consider Puškin's five-foot iambic line and his enjambement as norm-violations, although both features were revolutionary when used by Puškin. Such an educated reader will read Puškin's poem not only as measured against the poetic code of Puškin's time, but also with the knowledge of poetic codes of intervening systems and impinging cultures, for he is aware also of those of Tjutčev, Fet, Baudelaire, Rilke, Majakovskij, etc., as well as with the CAs antecedent to Puškin (Chaucer, Shakespeare, Goethe, etc.). This has been noted by many scholars.[13]

I have tried to show that the complex area of text pragmatics is related to many other areas of traditional concern to poetics: to the text itself, its manifold meanings and its relation to the plethora of codes of the cultures of both poles of the pragmatic axis. It is a dynamic field which takes into account both the synchronic and the diachronic dimensions of the text in their complex relationship. In examining this important domain, we should not reduce; nor, however, can we be prey to total relativism.

Barnet, Vermont
December 1980

NOTES

[1] The paper which was actually presented at the poetics conference in 1976 has since been published ("On the Decoding of Aesthetic Texts", *Studia semiotyczne* (Warsaw), vol. IX (1979), pp. 43-62). The present essay reflects the development of the author's thought since then.

[2] René Wellek and Austin Warren, *The Theory of Literature*, New York (Harcourt Brace), 1956.

[3] For a discussion, cf. Jerzy Pelc, "Poetics and Logical Semiotics," *Poetics and Theory of Literature*, 4/1 (1979), p. 82.

[4] Cesare Segre, *Structures and Time: Narration, Poetry, Models.* Translated by J. Meddemmen. Chicago, 1979. p. vi.

[5] Roman Jakobson, "Zeichen und System der Sprache. Schriften zur Phonetik," *Sprachwissenschaft und Kommunikationsforschung.* Berlin, IV (1962). Cited from *Selected Writings*, II, pp. 272-79.

[6] Mukařovský, "Problémy individua v umění", *Cestami poetiky a estetiky.* Praha, 1971, p. 53.

[7] J. M. Lotman, *Lekcii po strukturaľnoj poètike,* Moscow, 1964. Reprinted as *Brown University Slavic Reprint,* edited by T. G. Winner, Providence (Brown University Press), 1968, p. 169.

[8] Cf. Mukařovský, "La norme esthétique", *Travaux du IXe Congrès International de Philosophie.* Paris, 1937. Cited from Mukařovský, *Studie z estetiky.* Praha, 1.

[9] T. G. Winner, *op. cit.*

[10] Roman Ingarden, *Das literarische Kunstwerk,* Tübingen 1965, pp. 261-70. (Original edition, Halle [Saale], 1931).

[11] For a discussion of the information character of culture, cf. B. A. Uspenskij *et al.,* "Theses of the Semiotic Study of Culture (as applied to Slavic Texts)," Jan van der Eng and M. Grygar, eds., *Structure of Texts and Semiotics of Culture.* Paris–The Hague (Mouton), 1973, pp. 1-28.

[12] J. M. Lotman, *Struktura xudožestvennogo teksta. Brown University Slavic Reprint IX,* ed. by T. G. Winner, Providence, 1971, pp. 44-52.

[13] B. A. Uspenskij, "K issledovaniju drevnej živopisi", Preface to L. F. Žegin, *Jazyk živopisnogo proizvedenija,* Moscow, 1970, p. 4. P. Zumthor, *Essai de poétique médiévale,* Paris (Seuil), 1972, p. 20.

ON 'RHYME' IN THE RUSSIAN LAMENT

DEAN S. WORTH

Studies of Russian rhyme have dealt almost exclusively with literary rather than with folk genres, while investigations of folk verse have been concerned more with metrics than with rhyme.[1] The obvious reason for this is that much folk poetry, unlike most literary verse since the advent of syllabo-tonicism, does not have regularly recurring, predictable rhyme patterns. 'Rhyme' in the *bylina* and *pričitanie* occurs irregularly, unpredictably, and usually as a secondary, almost chance result of syntactic and grammatical parallelism. Consider, for example, the opening lines of a daughter's lament for her dead mother, collected by Barsov:[2]

> Я сидѣла нонь, печальна, призадумалась;
> В эвтот час, бѣдна горюша, во минуточку,
> Допустила злодий — скорую смерётушку
> До родителя — желанной своей матушки.
> Я бы видѣла злодийку душегубицу,
> Со оружия, лиходийку, застрѣлила бы,
> С пистолета я, злодийку, запалила бы;
> Она крадчи шла, злодийка, лиходѣица,
> Ко крылечку вѣдь она не подходила,
> За витó она колечко не гремѣла;
> Малой пташечкой в окошко залетѣла
> И впотай она родитель уносила;
> Укатилося великое желаньице,
> Оно в водушки, желанье, во глубокии,
> В дики темныи лѣса да во дремучии,
> За горы́ оно, желанье, за толкучии,
> Быдто рыбинку спустила я в синё море,   61

Here we see 'rhymes' which conform to the canons of classical literary verse, including one perfect *a b b a* quatrain: *застрѣлила бы | запалила бы, подходила | не гремѣла | залетѣла | уносила, дремучии | толкучии* as well as less precise correspondences like *минуточку | смерётушку | матушки* which would occasion little surprise in the verse of a twentieth-century poet. However, rich as these sound correspondences often are in the Russian lament, they are not regular, and since they do not recur in predictable patterns, they cannot fulfill that 'organizing function' which Žirmunskij took to be the very essence of rhyme.[3] In this sense, 'rhyme' in the *pričitanie* is not really rhyme at all. And yet there are good reasons for studying these rhymes (having made our demurrers, we abandon the quotation marks), both for their own sake, as an important albeit secondary poetic device in this type of folk verse, and because of their relation to the rhymes of literary verse, in particular to seventeenth-century syllabic verse on the one hand and to the 'new rhyme' of the twentieth century on the other.

We shall begin with a taxonomy of end-rhymes. In considering their variety, it is important to bear in mind both the irregularity with which they occur and the fact that they result in most cases from morphological and syntactic structures which, rather than rhyme itself, are the cardinal organizing principle of the lament.

The rhyme classification below illustrates the *types* of rhyme which occur in the Russian lament, without pretending to exhaust the tokens of each type; the illustrations are taken primarily from the first hundred pages of Barsov's texts. We describe first the affixally more complicated nominal (= substantival and adjectival) rhymes and then the simpler verbal types; within each group we deal first with those rhymes which conform to the classical canons (merely as a convenient classificatory framework) and then with those rhymes which are richer and poorer than canonical rhyme respectively.

Canonical nominal rhyme is only rarely non-affixal, but cf. *волосу / голосу* 54. Adjectival and diminutive substantival suffixes account for most rhymes of this type. One finds adjective-forming suffixes {ov}, e.g. *рядовыи / торговыи* 25, *дубовыя / кленовыя* 48, *о Христовъ дни / о Петровъ дни* 133; {ov,#n} *духовныи / церковныи* 49; {,iv} *спѣсивая / брословая* 82; {,in} *гусиныи /лебединыи* 112; frequently the diminutive (= attenuating) adjective suffix {ošon,#k}, e.g. *тихошенько / низешенько* 21, *ранешенько / поздешенько* 19, *скорешенько / частешенько* 125 (note the antonymy and synonymy of the lexical morphs in the last two examples; a major function of lament rhyme is precisely the creation of such lexical appositions). Deverbative (participle- and gerund-type) adjectives occur with {uč} *дремучии / толкучии* 61, *сыпучие / катучие* 55, *потѣшаюци / надрываюци* 76; {,on} *спрошоная / застрочоная* 63, *золоченыя / спасеныи* 28 (we assume that the variant nom. pl. spellings are due to the intrusion of literary orthography and irrelevant for pronunciation); {,im} *родимая / любимая* 42. The only substantival affixes occurring in our material are diminutive, viz. {anjic}, {enjic} and {,inoč#k}, e.g. *причитаньица / безталаньица* 10, *маханьицо / ходаньицо* 69, *воспѣваньица / жупляньица / спорыданьица / разставаньица / выставаньица* 126, *прегрѣшеньицо / неможеньицо* 13, *доли-*

ночки / третиночки 72, *сиротиночки / сѣмяниночки* 71, *деревиночкъ / осиночкъ* 102, this last example representing a mixed type in which the rhyme segment is derivational in one member of the pair and lexical in the other.

Rich rhyme among substantives and adjectives can be both non-affixal (or mixed), e.g. *голодная / холодная* 2, *работушку / заботушку* 56, *поталанње / пожеланнње* 89, *безподсудная / безрозсудная* 45 (NB the additional *po... po* and *bez... bez* in the last two exx.; this *'левизна'* will be discussed below), and with the same kinds of suffixes as occurred in the canonical rhymes above, e.g. *грановитыя / красовитыя* 49, *дурливыи / хлопотливыи* 17-18, *щепливой / уцьливой* 38; *свѣтлешенько / теплешенько* 50, *смѣлешенько / веселешенько* 42, *ранешенько / познешенько* 65 (cf. *поздешенько* above); *отъѣданьица / повиданьица* 53, *благословеньицем / надѣленьицем* 77, *третиночка / частиночка* 50. Only in a few rare cases is the rhyme attained by tautology, e.g. *Соловеюшко садился под окошечко / Как орел да эта птича на окошечко* 26; *Человѣка, што ни лучшаго / Человѣка самолучшаго* 46.

Poor nominal rhyme is not easy to define. Morphological parallelism between neighboring lines, and the often only partial phonological similarity between, say, two diminutive suffixes, can result in line ends whose sound correspondences are clearly greater than those of pure chance, but still hardly great enough, or regular enough, to be termed even poor rhyme. For example, the following pairs are given in order of what might be called diminishing rhyme intensity, ranging from obvious though poor rhyme to a (near-) non-rhyme: *духовныи / церковныих* 16, *щелковыи / пуховую* 104, *времячка / семеюшка* 7, *головушка / окошечком, широкая / торнешенька* 1, *складено / скованы* 52. Quite arbitrarily, we shall define poor rhyme as line ends with sound correspondences less than those of the literary canon, but with obligatorily identical stressed vowels; corresponding segments with differing stressed vowels will be termed 'sub-rhyme' and treated separately.

There are three types of poor rhyme in the lament, since the non-corresponding segments can occur in the grammatical endings, in the preterminal (lexical and/or derivational) morphs, or in both terminal and preterminal positions. Examples where only the **grammatical endings differ:** *духовныи / церковныих* 16, *шелковыи / пуховую* 104, *звѣриная / лошадиныи* 39, *высокую / глубоку бы* 39; *понизешеньку / веселешенько* 43, *потихошеньку / холодешенько* 72; *плавлены / славлен* 95; *скотинушку / перинушки* 115. In a fair number of cases it is **only** the grammatical morphs which differ: *родителей / родители* 84, *головушки / головушка* 37, *обидушки / обидушку* 54, *дороженьки / дороженька* 25, *вербу золо-*

чоную / *верба золочоная* 109, *плотников-работников* / *плотники-работники* 100; cf. the 'included' rhyme *вольныи* / *довольную* 16. The opposite situation obtains when the grammatical endings are identical but the **preterminal morphs differ:** *прохожиим* / *убогиим* 4, *со чистá полѣ* / *со синя́ морѣ* 6, *создана* / *послана* 3-4, *полюшках* / *полосушках* 6, *обидушкой* / *кручинушкой* 53, *здоровьицо* / *усторонъицо* 65, *ластушка* / *матушка* 131, *стрым заюшком* / *горносталюшком* 19; this type is more frequent with verbal forms, e.g. *поглядывать* / *посматривать* / *выспрашивать* 85. In the examples just adduced the non-corresponding segments were located primarily or exclusively in the lexical morphs, but this is not always the case, cf. *в замолотчики* / *во работники* 32. Substantially rarer is a kind of poor rhyme caused by transposing segments, e.g. *все браныя* / *сахарныя* / *медвяныя* 27. The weakest type of poor rhyme occurs in cases where **both the terminal and the preterminal morphs differ.** Occasionally the final vowel which is potentially and sometimes actually phonologically although not metrically stressed, is identical: *голóвушка́м* / *смерётушка́* 4, *дѣвушка́м* / *бесѣдушка́х* 124, *спорядóвыйм* / *молодóй вдовѣ* 21; more often, however, it differs, e.g. *времячко* / *денечка* 101, *головушка* / *окошечком, золота* / *волосы* 108, *кудреватыя* / *булатное* 107, *Онегушкѣ* / *головушка* 6. Occasionally the same lexical morph recurs with different derivational suffixes, e.g. *Как ходили по крестьянской по работушкѣ* / *Мы за шуточки работу работали* 106, *Я ходила на родину свою родинку* / *Ко желанным ли родителям* / *Ко свѣтушку ли братцу я родимому* 89. Finally, there are some poor rhymes in which the number of non-corresponding segments is so large that one may well question whether they are felt as rhyme at all, for example: *прокладбище* / *свадебка* 132, *родителей* / *дѣвичествѣ* 8. On the other hand, there are a good many cases where the total sound correspondence is far larger that the term 'poor rhyme' would imply. It is hard to imagine that the mourner who sings

> Рóдима моя матушка!
> Наталья свѣт Ивановна?
> Тебѣ добро принять, пожаловать,
> Стакан да пива пьянаго,
> Чарочку да зелена вина
> От меня от бѣдной сироты!   79

is insensitive to the concatenations of *iva — ovna — ova — iva — avi* etc. that make a type of almost-quatrain out of the central four lines of this passage. This and similar passages pose a tantalizing problem for the analyst: their richness cannot be described in traditional rhyme terms, although rhyme is a part of this richness, nor can other statistical methods be employed — at least not mechanically — because of the irregularity with which these phonologically cohesive passages occur.

Nominal **sub-rhyme** repeats some of the poor-rhyme types illustrated above, with the difference that the dactylic stress falls on lexical or derivational morphs with differing vowels. In some cases the entire remainder of the words is identical, e.g. *сирочествѣ / вдовичествѣ* 35, *головушек / сдержавушек* 13, *матушки / дѣтушки* 2, while in others the posttonic segments also differ, e.g. *сусѣдушко / сдержавушкѣ* 16, the latter occurring most often with identical derivational morphs surrounded by differing lexical morphs on the left and grammatical endings on the right, e.g. *батюшка / личюшко* 5, *вѣкушко / головушек* 13, *ноченькой / птиченьки* 26. Occasionally one encounters identical endings and similar but non-identical derivational morphs: *годышок / дѣтушек* 12, *кустышка / камешка / батюшка* 57. Finally, in some cases the disparity between the adjacent line ends is so great that their status even as sub-rhymes is due less to their own phonology than to the preceding morphological and phonological correspondences which as it were 'suggest' that the line ends too may be related to rhyme types: in the lines

> Будет уличка — ходить да не широкая,
> Путь дорожинька вот им да не торнешенька   1

the line ends *широкая / торнешенька* would hardly be felt as related in any way to rhyme were it not for the immediately preceding *да не / да не* and the lexical parallelism *уличка / путь дорожинька* which bind the two lines into a sort of couplet. Similarly, in the lines

> Со укла́ду сердце складено,
> Со желѣза груди скованы   52

it is not only the *sk ... n / sk ... n* of the line ends, but also the preceding *so +* genitive constructions and the lexical parallelism of *сердце / груди* which bind the forms *складено / скованы* into a related pair.

Verbal rhymes show a restricted range of variation compared to nominal rhymes, for the obvious reason that intra-verb affixation is restricted to a few tense, mood, person etc. forms, most of which are terminal; in other words, the greater variety of nominal rhyme types is due to the greater variety of derivational types among nouns and adjectives. **Canonical verbal rhyme** can be illustrated by *укатится / отшатится* 8, *нагибаются / растилаются* 65, *сражаешься / отправляешься* 92, *снаряжаетесь / сподобляетесь* 120, *угощаюся / обливаюся / забавляюся* 40-41, *потрудилися / не лѣнилися* 49, *не будила бы / не пустила бы* 129, *трога́тися / терятися* 51, *положите-тко / помяните-тко,* in all of which the abundance of clitics serves only to create the necessary dactylic clausulae. **Rich verbal rhymes** usually owe their richness to the imperfectivizing suffix {va}, e.g. *одѣвали | отпѣвали* 111, *подѣватися | украватися* 17, *свиваемся | раставаемся* 100-191, *не давайте-ткось | не разбивайте-ткось* 28, less frequently to phonologically similar roots as in *годилася | родилася* 99, *приютитися | пришатитися* 113, *забрякали | защолкали* 76 (NB the identical prefixes in the last two exx.). There is one case of 'included' rhyme, *не ладится | не гладится* 47, and several of rich rhymes built on identical roots with differing prefixes, e.g. *прискинули | откинули* 50, *не заводили бы | да не вводили бы* 43, *приубавила | поприбавила* 54, *предъявилося | объявилося* 27. **Poor rhyme** in verbs can be due to differing lexical morphs as in *воротятся | расходятся* 19, *не выписать | не вычитать* 12, *похаживать | поглядывать | посматривать* 5, *повыстань-ко | повыглянь-ко* 98, *повыгощу | повызову* 51, to non-correspondences between terminal morphs as in the examples *свидались бы | срѣталися* 15, *не молилися | не просили мы* 13, *почитали | убоялись* 33, *хвастати | похвастаю* 52 or between non-terminal grammatical morphs if the endings are identical, e.g. *водится | родятся* 48, *выростала бы | разцвѣтали бы* 20, *разливается | обливаюся* 42, *не ставишься | не сдаваешься* 9; finally, the differing segments can occur in more than one morph, as in the cases *не водится | не воротятся* 4, *да поразойдется | да поразольются* 6, *обвиватися | посматривать* 66, and there are the expected cases bordering on non-rhymes, e.g. *засыпайся-тко | управлять надо* 24. All in all, as has been noted repeatedly ever since the eighteenth century, verbal rhymes are not very interesting. That is, they are not very interesting **as rhymes**; in another way, however, they are not entirely without importance.

The verbal rhymes we have just been examining, and in particular the poor verbal rhymes, show an unusually high degree of phonological correspondence to the left of the rhyme itself. This can create rich rhymes as in *не заводили бы | да не вводили бы* 43, but is much more frequent with poor rhymes, in which cases it forms the left-hand 'compensation' Žirmunskij noted e.g. in Deržavin's verse.[4] This left compensation is sometimes only hinted at, as in *торговыя | гербовыя* (org | ger) 5, but is most often due to identical verbal prefixes as in *разгоряется | раскипляется* 64, *воспѣвает | возжупляет* 106, *повыстань-ко | повыглянь-ко* 98, to such negative and emphatic clitics as *не* and *да*, e.g. *не придет | не выдет* 11, *не молилися | не просили мы* 13, *да одѣватися | да намыватися* 23, *да пошаталися | да роспаялися* 96 (we include canonical rhymes with left compensation, as the principle involved is the same as with poor rhyme), and often by some combination of a prefix and a clitic (or, occasionally, an adverb), as in the cases *да приоббают / да приласкают* 25, *да не сжидает / да не срѣтает* 92, *не заносило бы / не залило бы* 20, *да все не старuют / да все не ржавиют* 31, *теперь да коротается / теперь да преклоняются* 11. Similar left compensation occurs with nominal rhymes, e.g. *поталаннѣе / пожеланнѣе* 89, *за дыбучима / за дремучима* 141, *да все рублевыя / да все шелковыя* 13, etc. etc. The function of these added clitics appears to be primarily metrical; they 'fill out' the obligatory metrical pattern of the line without significantly affecting its semantics. But they also perform an important secondary function, one which is relevant specifically to our topic. By increasing the morphological, and hence the phonological similarity of adjacent line-ends, they throw the remaining *dis*similar segments into sharper contrast. The more nearly identical is the sound shape of adjacent lines, the more deliberately salient is the semantic confrontation of their non-identical parts. The morphemes {star} 'old' and {ržav} 'rusty' share a secondary semantic feature 'deterioration', 'inability to perform one's function', which is brought to the foreground and emphasized when the surrounding phonetic identity forces them into an ad hoc equation:

> Знать за тридевять за крѣпкима замками,
> Сторожа стоят вѣдь там *да все не старuют,*
> Как булатнии замки *да все не ржавиют;*   31

Similarly, it is the surrounding [dəfs,o … ovyjə] that emphasizes the common semantic feature 'high quality, valuable' of the morphemes {rubl,} 'ruble' and {šolk} 'silk' in the lines:

> Мы не ставили свѣщи *да все рублевыя,*
> Мы не клали пелены *да все шелковыя,*   13

In contradistinction to literary verse, where it is the phonologically similar segments (rhymed words etc.) which are thrust into semantic juxtaposition, in folk verse this semantically organizing function is assumed by the phonologically dissimilar segments. In other words, in folk verse the function of phonological similarity and contrast is the mirror image of that of literary verse.

In reading the laments, it soon becomes apparent that the 'foregrounding function' of phonologically identical or very similar line-parts is not restricted to line-end position. On the contrary: the left-enriched line-ends we have just been discussing are but one positional variant of a technique used throughout the line. Before continuing the discussion, therefore, it will be useful to examine briefly the metrical and syntactic structure of the lament line, if only rather superficially.[5]

Most lament lines (91% of the 339-line sample studied here) are in trochaic hexameter with dactylic clausulae; the 2nd, 4th and 6th feet (i.e., the 3rd, 7th and 11th syllables) are obligatorily stressed, while stress on the odd feet (i.e., the 1st, 5th and 9th syllables) is optional. The even-foot stress sometimes requires unusual word stress (in other words, the metrical stress overrides the word-stress rules), e.g. *стàла хóрошо ходùть да одѣвáтися* 23. Typical lament lines are:

Тỳт повы́йдем на могѝлушку умéршую 225

Погляжý на вàс, побѣ́дная голóвушка 125

Я̀ путём идỳ ширóкоей дорóженькой 35

This pattern is maintained in 71% of the 13-syllable lines examined, while the other 29% are defective, either omitting one syllable (rarely, two), e.g. (× marks omissions):

Знàть, не ýчастью-талáном награждáли × 8

× За лѣ́сушка онò да за дремýчии 1

Ты со вòлостью × ϶́той красовѝтою 9

or in rare cases adding a syllable, e.g.

Я̀ не пó часту к тебѣ̀ да вѣдь ухáживаю
Я̀ не пó долгу горю́шица усѣживаю 29

Syntactically the lines are organized around the focal points of the three obligatory stresses; the latter act, so to speak, as the pegs upon which the syntagmas are hung. The most frequent syntagmatic division (61% of our sample) is into syntagmas of 5 + 3 + 5 syllables, e.g.:

Впереди меня / злодийка / уродилася
Впереди меня / в купѣли / окрестилася 8

Хоть я пóдолгу / горюша / снаряжалася
Хоть я спóтиху / побѣдна / сподоблялася 141[6]

In another 26% the border between the second and third syntagmas occurs one syllable farther to the right, giving a 5 + 4 + 4 division, e.g.:

Не сходили мы / во улички / рядовыя
Не дошли да мы / до лавочки / торговыя 5

Мы не ладно-то / лебедушки / удумали
Мы не хóрошо / побѣднушки / уладили 215

The fact that 87% of our examples are of the 5 + 3 + 5 and 5 + 4 + 4 types shows that the first, five-syllable syntagma is relatively stable, whereas the border between the other two is less rigidly fixed.[7] Put another way, this means that the basic division is into two cola of five and eight syllables respectively, with the second colon subdivided into three-plus-five or four-plus-four syllables respectively. Lines in which the first syntagma has only four syllables are much rarer, namely 7% with 4 + 4 + 5 division, e.g.:

Оны рады / мужиченка / во котлѣ варить
Оны рады / вѣдь живóва / во землю вкопать 285

and 5% with 4 + 5 + 4, e.g.:

> Я глядѣла / во косѣвчато / окошечко
> Я смотрѣла / на дороженьку / широкую   138

One percent of the 13-syllable lines are of unclear (perhaps 5 + 2 + 6, perhaps inaccurately transcribed) structure.

The few nonasyllabic lines in our small sample (9%) are divided equally between 5 + 4 and 4 + 5 structures, e.g.:

> Не учесана / головушка
> Не укатана / рубашечка   57

> Призавие / буйным вѣтрышком
> Призагрие / красным солнышком   258[8]

The phonological similarity or identity which serves to foreground dissimilar segments can occur in any one of the three cola of which the lament tricolon is composed, or it can occur in more than one of these cola.

Rhyme-type correspondences occur in but ten percent of the initial cola of the lament.[9] Onset cola show lesser variety of rhyme-types than line-ends, and the phonological constraints on initial cola seem fewer; for example, whereas absolute identity is extremely rare at line-end, it is frequent in onsets:

> Впереди меня / злодийка уродилася,
> Впереди меня / в купѣли окрестилася   8

> Со кручинушки / смерётушка не придет,
> Со кручинушки / душа с грудей не выдет   11

> Ты поро́скажи / крестовой — милой кумушко
> Ты поро́скажи / Бладыкѣ многомилосливу   292

> Буде нé любо / братцам сдвуродимым
> Буде нé любо / племянничкам любимым   243

One also finds exact rhyme, e.g.

> По роду́ мнѣ-ка / желанной родной дядюшка
> По кресту мнѣ-ка / крестовой этот батюшка   165

and various combinations of rich and poor rhyme, e.g.

> Снаряжались вы / голубонько скорёшенько
> Поѣзжали вы / со братцем веселёшенько   200

> Какой нрав то / у братцев у родимыих
> Какой разум / у сестриц да богоданыих   226

but in the great majority of cases the function of rhyming segments is clearly to set off those morphs which differ in their sound structure; rhyme is but one part of the total morphosyntactic identity which provides the background against which differing morphs stand out so sharply. In fact, it hardly seems to matter whether the stressed 3d-syllable vowels are identical, creating a rhyme, as in

> Ушибать стане / — великая тоскичюшка,
> Унывать стане / ретливое сердечюшко   6

> Я бы по́ часту / туда стала учащивать,
> Я бы по́ долгу / вѣдь там стала усѣживать   20

or whether these obligatorily-stressed vowels differ, creating what we have termed 'sub-rhyme', as in

> Изнавѣшена / была я цвѣтным платьицом,
> Изнасажена / была я скатным жемчугом   8

> Вы обуйте / столько рѣзвы мои ноженьки,
> Вы одѣньте / столько бѣлы мои плечушки   32

In all cases the function of the phonological (as of the other) correspondences is to bring into confrontation the differing morphs {šib}:{noj}, {čast}:{dolg}, {věs}:{sad}, {-uj}:{děn}.

The semantic relations established by this foregrounding technique would require detailed study beyond this article's scope. A preliminary survey of confronted pairs indicates that there are three types of semantic confrontation: (1) (partial or full) synonymy, e.g.

> *Поглядѣла* бы / во бѣло его личушко
> *Посмотрѣла* бы / во ясны ему очюшки   152

> Он не *вор*, кажись, / был не мошенничек
> Он не *плут*, кажись, / был не разбойничек   251

> Я не *нищиим* / вѣдь есть да не прохожиим
> Я не *бѣдныим* / не брезгую убогиим   4

> Што за *чюдушко*-то / мнѣ да причюдилося?
> Што за *дивушко*-то / мнѣ-ко предъявилося?   27

(2) somewhat less frequently, antonymy, e.g.:

> Хоть по *утрышку* / приди да ты ранёшенько
> Хоть по *вечеру* / родитель ты познёшенько   65

> *Впереди* оно / безсчастье не укатится
> *Позади* оно / злодийно не останется   63

> Вы во *зимное* / гумно да в замолотцики
> Вы во *лѣтныи* / меня да во работники   32

(3) various kinds of synechdochic and metonymic pairs, e.g.:

Всѣ *поля* да / со насѣвами
Всѣ *луга* да / со покосами   48

Они *голосом* / ведут по тихошеньку
Они *слóвечко-* / то скажут полегошеньку   243

Не под *лицё* мнѣ / красной дѣвушкѣ
Не под *плечо* мнѣ / молодёхонькѣ   78

Стала *клубышком* / во ноженьках кататися
Стала *червышком* / побѣднушка свиватися   259

Во *дворъ* держать / горюшицу коровницей
Во *избы* держать / побѣдную подворницей   227

Similarly confronted semantic pairs obviously occur elsewhere as well, e.g. in the above examples, the line-ends *личушко : очюшки, мошенничек : разбойничек, ранёшенько : познёшенько, замолотцики : работники,* etc.; space prevents our pursuing this topic here.

The medial colon is the least structured of all three. One does find repetition, e.g.

Чего нá слыхе- / то вѣк было / не слыхано
Чего нá виду- / то вѣк было / не видано   289

Много множество / е в мирѣ / согрѣшения
Как больши того / е в мирѣ / огорченья   291

and occasional semantic oppositions of the type so frequent in the initial colon, e.g.:

Он затопае / *ногама* / во дубовой пол
Он захлопае / *рукама* / о кленовой стул   283

Я ходила бы / *побѣдна* / любовалася
Я смотрѣла бы / *несчастна* / красовалася   153

but in general phonology is less at the service of morphological oppositions in the medial colon than elsewhere. One notes, for example, that the syntactic role of words occurring in the medial colon is less central to the sentence structure than are those of the initial and terminal cola (cf. the frequent appositive qualifiers like *побѣдна, несчастна* above). Segments in the medial colon, more often than anywhere else, are added in order to fill out the metrical requirements of the line, as demonstrated e.g. by the fact that the particle да occurs in the eighth syllable, i.e. at the end of the medial colon, far more frequently than in all other syllables taken together.[10]

So far we have seen that rhyme at the line-end has a dual function: on the one hand, it serves to join neighboring lines into couplets and quatrains (although much less regularly than in literary verse), and on the other hand, it serves to foreground the non-corresponding segments, creating ad hoc semantic oppositions. In the initial colon, this foregrounding function becomes predominant, although a certain 'organizing' function of phonological correspondences can still be detected. In the medial colon, the functional load of rhyme is lower than in either the initial or the final colon; neither the metrically organizing nor the semantic foregrounding function appears with any regularity.

Finally, one other function of rhyme should be noted: phonological correspondences (hand-in-hand with morphological and syntactic ones, as always in the lament) organize adjacent lines into at times quite complex sets of couplets, quatrains, etc.; furthermore — and in this the lament differs totally from all known types of literary verse — these 'stanzaic' patterns are not the same in the initial, medial and final cola. Consider the lines:

Впереди да шло	/ безсчастье	/ ясным соколом
Позади оно	/ летѣло	/ черным вороном
Впереди оно	/ безсчастье	/ не укатится
Позади оно	/ злодийно	/ не останется
Посторóнь оно	/ злодийно	/ не отшатится
Кругом—около	/ безсчастье	/ обстолпилося
Всѣм беремечком	/ злодийно	/ ухватилося 8

Within the initial cola, the interleaved *впереди* and *позади* form an *a b a b* quatrain phonetically bound together by the rich rhymes [d,í — d,í — d,í — d,í] and subsequent [ló — nó — nó — nó], the latter reflecting in mirror image the [nó — ló] of lines 5-6, otherwise opposed to lines 1-4 by their stressed third-syllable [ó] in *Посторóнь онò : Крỳгом óколо*. The parallel nominal clausulae of lines 1-2 (*ясным соколом : черным вороном*) form a couplet opposed to the following five verbal lines, while the negative particles opening the final cola of lines 3-5 form a central tristich opposed both to the nominal 1-2 and, by the non-past — past opposition, to lines 6-7; the central tristich itself is bound together by the left-enriched canonical rhymes [n,e ... át,itsa : n,e ... át,itsa] flanking the assonant [n,e ... án, etsa]. The medial cola, with their interleaved *безсчастье* and *злодийно*, tie all seven lines into a *a b a c c a c* pattern repeated nowhere else in the lines. While the clausulae of lines 6-7 form a perfect rhyme [ílosa : ílosa], the initial cola of these lines are totally different (*Кругом около : Всѣм беремечком*), as if the initial colon were already 'moving on' to some different structure and different topic, while the final colon still rests in the structure and content of the preceding lines; the tension created by such combinations of identity and difference within different cola of adjoining lines is an important structural function of the sound pattern of these lines.

Although the foregoing remarks have of necessity been rather impressionistic, we hope that they may nonetheless have indicated at least some of the functions of rhyme-type sound correspondences in the Russian lament. In many cases, our comments have only been suggestive, and would require a much more thorough statistical underpinning in order to be considered as demonstrated fact.

University of California, Los Angeles

NOTES

[1] On rhyme in folk genres (but not in the lament), see R. Jakobson, "Vlijanie narodnoj slovesnosti na Trediakovskogo", *Selected Writings*, IV (The Hague-Paris, 1966), 619 et seq.; V.M. Sidel'nikov, *Poètika russkoj narodnoj liriki* (Moscow, 1959), 121-28; P. G. Bogatyrev, *Voprosy teorii narodnogo iskusstva* (Moscow, 1971), 489ff.; D. Samojlov, "Nabljudenija nad rifmoj", *Voprosy literatury*, 1970, No. 6, 160-77, and in his *Kniga o russkoj rifme* (Moscow, 1973), 29ff.; M. Štokmar, "Stixotvornaja forma russkix poslovic, pogovorok, zagadok, pribautok", *Zvezda vostoka*, 11, 1965, 149-63; I. M. Kolesnickaja, "O nekotoryx drevnejšix formax narodnyx pesen (pesnja v skazke i rodstvennye ej pesennye vidy)", *Russkij fol'klor*, 12 (1971), 31; K. Hartmann, *Volksepik am Weißen Meer* (München, 1974), 31-40; V. Žirmunskij, *Rifma, ee istorija i teorija* (Pb., 1923), 336-37; M. Shapiro, "Inexact rhyme in Russian proverbs and riddles", *Studia Linguistica A.V. Issatchenko... dedicata* (in press); L. V. Mukovozov, "O russkoj rifme", *Russkaja reč'*, 1971, No. 3, 29-38. Among works on the lament (but not dealing with its formal structure), see A. G. Vasil'ev, "Kompozicionnye osobennosti poxoronnyx pričitanij (po materialam fol'klornyx èkspedicij v novgorodskuju oblast')", *Russkij fol'klor*, 12, (1971), 91-101; N. P. Kolpakova, "Nekotorye voprosy sravnitel'noj poètiki (pričet' i pesnja)", *Sovetskaja ètnografija*, 1967, No. 1, 41-53; K. V. Čistov, "Russkaja pričet'", *Pričitanija* (*Biblioteka poèta*, b.s.) (Leningrad, 1960), 5-46; —, "Pričitanija", *Russkoe narodnoe poètičeskoe tvorčestvo*, II, 2 (Moscow-Leningrad, 1956), 12-192; M. K. Azadovskij, "Lenskie pričitanija", reprinted in his *Stat'i o literature i fol'klore* (Moscow-Leningrad, 1960), 114-74; V. G. Bazanov, "Pričitanija russkogo severa v zapisjax 1942-1945 godov", *Russkaja narodno-bytovaja lirika* (Moscow-Leningrad, 1962), 3-44; P. Arant, "Alliteration and repeated prepositions in Russian traditional lament", *Slavic Poetics: Essays in honor of Kiril Taranovsky* (The Hague-Paris, 1973), 1-3.

[2] E. V. Barsov, *Pričitanija severnogo kraja*. Čast' I: *Plači poxoronnye, nadgrobnye i nadmogil'nye* (Moscow, 1872).

[3] V. Žirmunskij, *Rifma, ee istorija i teorija* (Petersburg, 1923).

[4] *Ibid.,* 189-90.

[5] These remarks, which must be considered tentative and treated with caution, are based only on the 329 highly-structured lines which clearly participate in line-end, rhyme-type 'couplets'. Whether or not the less highly structured lament lines also show the same dependence of syntax on metrics will be investigated in a separate article. K. V. Čistov, "Russkaja pričet'", *Pričitanija* (*Biblioteka poèta*, b.s.) (Leningrad, 1960), 41, underestimates the formality of lament structure in speaking of the "relatively free arrangement of stressed and unstressed words" between the two (or three) obligatory stresses of the lament line. A more scientific survey is found in R. Jakobson,

"Slavic epic verse", *Selected Writings,* IV (The Hague-Paris, 1966), 430-33. On lament metrics generally see K. Taranovski, *Ruski dvodelni ritmovi* I-II (Beograd, 1953), 356, 369.
[6] It frequently occurs that the eighth syllable is occupied by the clitic да, e.g.:

> Стала хо́рошо ходить да одѣватися
> Стала до́ бѣла она да намыватися   23
>
> Нѣту душеньки его да во бѣлой груди
> Нѣту зрѣнья у его да во ясных очах   248

In such cases it might at first glance seem possible to attribute the да to the third rather than the second syntagma, resulting in a 5 + 2 + 6 division. However, there is no independent evidence for the existence of a 5 + 2 + 6 type (the only examples would come from such lines with ∂a), so it seems reasonable to attribute the ∂a to the middle syntagma, giving the 5 + 3 + 5 type for which there is massive independent evidence. Cf. Note 10 below.
[7] Indeed, in a few cases one could assume either a 5 + 3 + 5 or a 5 + 4 + 4 division, e.g.

> Со полосыньки / у вас да / я / долиночки
> Не со поженки / у вас да / я / третиночки   32

We assume in such cases that the syntagmatic division follows (actually, motivates) the lexico-grammatical parallelism, e.g. in the given lines we divide 5 + 4 + 4.
[8] The fact that the 4 + 5 nonasyllable is isomorphic with neither the first and second, nor the second and third syntagmas of the high-frequency thirteen-syllable types (5 + 3 + 5, 5 + 4 + 4) is evidence that the nonasyllable is an independent structural type and not merely an abbreviated thirteen-syllable line.
[9] There are 64 rhyme-type onsets in the 1188 lines of Barsov's first long *Plač po muže.*
[10] The distribution of the 267 occurrences of ∂a is as follows:

syllables:	1	2	3	4	5	6	7	8	9	10	11	12	13
no of да:	12	0	0	90	2	3	0	156	3	1	0	0	0
% of ∂a:	4.5	0	0	33.7	.7	1.1	0	58.4	1.1	.4	0	0	0

I.e., ∂a occurs after the second and the first obligatory stresses, but as a proclitic is totally excluded from the clausula, where its role is filled by unstressed derivational suffixes, by the clitics -*ся* and -*тко*, and by extended (old longform?) endings like -*ыим,* -*ыих.*

COMMENTS

(Bailey)   Your paper is probably the first in which someone has endeavored to analyze the usage of 'rhyme' in Russian folk narrative verse since Žirmun-skij published his book *Vvedenie v metriku* in the 1920's. I have only a few general comments and not really questions about this complex subject. One should always have a certain amount of 'healthy' skepticism about published folk texts because far too often collectors and editors consciously or uncon-sciously tend to tilt the special poetic language of folklore toward the standard literary language. One of the problems is how much the dialectical elements in the language of a singer should be normalized so that an average reader can easily understand the text. The problem is that when one is dealing with texts

which have to some extent been 'cleansed' phonetically, how can one for certain deal with the phonetics of folk rhymes? This is a difficulty for which there probably is no easy answer, but is must be born in mind. I wonder if you could not find a more suitable term for 'poor rhyme', because it may tend to imply an evaluative attitude more characteristic of literary poetry, that is, good and bad rhymes. As Jakobson pointed out, *da* may be either a particle or conjunction; if it is a particle, it may be either an enclitic or proclitic, but if it is a conjunction, then it is a proclitic. In folk trochaic verse I would not regard iambic lines as being 'defective' simply because they are a common reflection of standards which are looser than those in literary use. The same should be applied to lines which have a feminine or hyperdactylic ending in a song which otherwise has dactylic clausula. I would be hesitant to ascribe all unusual word stresses in folk texts merely to metrical requirements because many unusual stresses are in fact archaic, dialectical, or even traditional in folk songs. Besides this, some purely 'arbitrary' stresses may arise from a singer's attempt to make the musical rhythm and linguistic rhythm coincide. One would expect to find less 'rhyme' in songs with a dactylic ending; it might be profitable for you to study the feminine rhymes which, for example, are relatively speaking far more numerous in the many recordings of the ballad "Mat' knjazja Mixajla ubivaet ženu ego". Although it is true that the best epic performers tend to avoid using particles in the dactylic clausula, some singers do this fairly often, especially Marfa S. Krjukova who I believe does also employ *da* in this position.

Additional discussion: Hrushovsky, Markov, Segal, Shapiro, Stankiewicz, Timberlake

ВЛАДИМИР МАЯКОВСКИЙ И СТИХ XX ВЕКА
(К ПОСТАНОВКЕ ВОПРОСА)

А. Л. ЖОВТИС

Стих Маяковского начиная с 20-ых годов и до наших дней изучался преимущественно в двух аспектах.

Первый — определение системности, принципов организации стихотворного стиля художника, яркое новаторство которого было столь же очевидно для современников, как очевидно и для нас. Здесь выстраивается длинный ряд работ, начиная с известных страниц книги "О чешском стихе" Р. Якобсона и кончая последними статьями М. Гаспарова и Б. Гончарова.[1] Это, так сказать, направление *вглубь* — от констатации акцентности как основополагающего принципа стиха Маяковского до выяснения структурной роли пауз и статистики междударных интервалов в конкретных произведениях.

Второе направление исследований связано со стремлением литературоведов осмыслить влияние системы Маяковского на другие литературы, в особенности на литературы народов СССР. Констатировались прежде всего внешние признаки этого влияния, начиная со знаменитой лесенки, которая появилась, кажется, во всех литературах — молдавской, украинской, казахской и т.д. Маяковского много переводили. Поиски метроритмических аналогов приводили поэтов к разным решениям; ими использовались разнообразные ресурсы ритмической выразительности и средства национальных поэтик. Естественно, что переводческий опыт также изучался. Можно назвать (как одну из ранних), например, работу Масгуда Расули о переводах Маяковского на узбекский язык[2].

Есть однако ещё один аспект возможного изучения новаторства стихотворной системы и реализовавшегося на основе этой системы стихотворного стиля. Стих Маяковского необходимо изучать в глобальном масштабе как явление, характерное для XX века, изучать не имманентно (в пределах текста), а с точки зрения общей эволюции поэтических форм в мировой литературе. Иначе говоря, система должна быть осмыслена в контексте всего литературного развития и сопоставлена с другими фактами, быть может, прямо и не связанными с творческой деятельностью В. В. Маяковского, но представляющими собой проявление той же тенденции (или — тех же тенденций). Естественно, что такая постановка вопроса требует предварительного накопления материала. Надо знать, как организуется современный стих в разных литературах, когда и в каком направлении началась его деканонизация, какова роль в нём 'свободных' и 'освобождённых' форм и т.д. Обобщение на этом уровне вовсе не просто. Настоящий доклад представляет собой только попытку постановки вопроса.

Начнём с нескольких любопытных фактов. В стихах Назыма Хикмета двадцатых годов ощутимы признаки стиховой организации, ведущие к Маяковскому. Классическая форма разрушена. 'Столбичное' построение, использование строчных букв вместо заглавных, строк длинных и коротких (отнюдь не всегда представляющих собой метрические звенья силлабического стиха), свобода рифмовки и новаторские тенденции в рифме — всё это, казалось бы, позволяет говорить о влиянии великого революционного поэта. Так обстоит дело в оригинале. Уже Багрицкий и Дементьев в своих переводах подчёркивали сходство:

> Тот, кто не знает,
> пускай узнает,
> вы нарумяненный шарлатан,
> вы, прикрывая кинжал в кармане,
> нам продавали в караван-сарае
> гнилые французские ткани,
> сотню на сотне беря за обман[3].

Это из стихотворения "Восток и Запад". Другие переводчики также ориентируются на такой стихотворный стиль (П. Железнов, М. Павлова, и даже гораздо менее чуткий к стиховой фактуре В. Журавлёв). Переводческая интерпретация кажется оправданной и потому, что очевидно сближаются общественные позиции писателей и идейная направленность их творчества. Вспомним также, что Хикмет учился в Советском Союзе, знал русский язык и высоко ценил Маяковского. Это ли не достаточные основания для того, чтобы утверждать плодотворное влияние Маяковского на молодого турецкого поэта, взрывавшего канон изысканного и обусловленного множеством правил классического стиха? Литературоведы так и поступали. Однако недавно стали известны свидетельства самого Хикмета о том, что в двадцатые годы он имел слабое представление о творчестве Маяковского, не читал его, так как ещё плохо знал русский язык. По словам Назыма Хикмета, его стихи 20-ых годов просто не могли нести на себе никаких влияний с этой стороны.

Сходные черты стихотворного стиля (черты, перечисленные выше) характеризуют творчество замечательного латышского поэта Александра Чака. Здесь влияние Маяковского и факт перенесения некоторых его принципов в национальную поэзию бесспорен. Чак объяснял это влияние и не раз мотивировал его своими поисками в области формы. Можно сказать, что строчная буква в латышской поэзии как средство 'демонтажа' классической строки появилось в значительной мере благодаря заимствованию Александра Чака у раннего Маяковского. Таков второй факт.

Факт третий. В англоязычных литературах честь введения той же строчной буквы принадлежит имажистам. Как и Маяковский, они входили в литературу накануне первой мировой войны (или чуть раньше). Для них характерна была гипертрофия образного начала в лирике и особое внимание к проблемам стиховой формы. Задачи поэзии Ф. Флинт сформулировал так: установка на образность, свободный нерифмованный стих, внутренний ритм и музыкальность. Р. Олдингтон (начинавший как поэт), Эзра Паунд, Хильда Дулитл, Эми Лоуэлл — все они боролись с *традиционализмом формы*, и все они использовали строчную букву в начале строки. Английский литературовед пишет, что строчная буква стала у них знаком, говорящим читателю: это стихи имажистов.[4] Маяковский на них бесспорно не влиял; их творчества он тоже не знал.

У нас принято считать, что указанный графический принцип введён в русскую литературу именно им. Это верно, хотя до Маяковского строчная буква в начале строки (или подстрочия) встречается по крайней мере у трёх поэтов — А. Белого, З. Гиппиус и П. Потёмкина.[5]

Если один из трёх приведённых фактов подтверждает прямое и непосредственное влияние Маяковского на иноязычного поэта (Чака), то два других говорят о 'самозарождении' сходных тенденций в разных контактировавших в этом случае литературах.

К. Д. Вишневский в своей работе о русском стихе XVIII века не без остроумия замечает, что с создателями первых русских силлабо-тонических стихов Глюком и Паусом "произошло нечто, напоминающее судьбу многочисленных изобретателей пароходов и паровозов; немало талантливых мастеров не только придумывали, но даже строили различные 'самобеглые' механизмы; иные из этих машин даже двигались. Но изобретателями в глазах человечества оказались те, кто, так сказать, 'внедрили' свое открытие в быт современников. Разумеется, для этого необходимы были определённые условия. Но разве не так было со стихом?"[6] На этот вопрос можно, разумеется, ответить положительно.

Так было со стихом не только в петровскую эпоху — так бывало всегда.

Конечно, любопытно, "кто первый сказал Э", но для науки гораздо важнее выяснение тех внутренних предпосылок и условий, благодаря которым новые приёмы и средства выразительности берутся литературой на вооружение. История поэзии знает множество приходивших не вовремя Ползуновых и Можайских. Стихам одних из них, "как драгоценным винам", наставал "свой черед", другие остаются в распоряжении историков литературы и лишь изредка становятся предметом удивления, когда, например, оказывается, что Шевырёв за 80 лет до Хлебникова "пустил ходить по вольной" хореи и ямбы в своём переводе строф "Освобождённого Иерусалима",а первые опыты создания верлибра принадлежат А. П. Сумарокову.

О Маяковском писали, что он: (1) ввёл акцентный стих в русское стихосложение, (2) разработал систему неточной рифмовки, (3) широко использовал полиметрию (В. М. Жирмунский в последней своей работе говорил об амбивалентности его стиха), (4) разработал новую графическую систему. Но сразу же выяснилось, что все эти структурные признаки стиха наличествовали в письменной или устной русской поэзии задолго до него (тонический или чисто тонический стих объяснял уже Востоков, а дольники внедрялись на протяжении долгих десятилетий — от Державина до Блока; неточная рифма была в фольклоре и постепенно завоёвывала позиции в поэзии XIX века; в "Современниках" Некрасова торжествует принцип полиметрии; о графике предшественников Маяковского говорилось выше). Однако органичное *сочетание* упомянутых признаков действительно даёт представление о стихе Маяковского как о системе, а аналогия этих признаков и их сочетаний в иноязычных литературах позволяет говорить о 'сходстве' и 'влиянии'. В приведённых трёх примерах мы видели — в одном — 'влияние', в двух других (если отвести влияние) — 'сходство'. И, что самое важное, самое существенное — *полные или частичные аналогии оказываются возможными только при сопоставлении принципов построения стиха Маяковского и других поэтов XX века*.

Здесь уже нельзя ограничиться синхронным рассмотрением национальных просодий и их модификаций в XX веке. Необходимо сопоставление истории стиховых систем. Наиболее простой случай такого сопоставления — русский и английский классический и современный стих (в обоих случаях господствует силлабо-тоника).

Беглый взгляд на английский стих обнаруживает, что акцентная система появилась в нём в 80-ые годы XIX века в творчестве Джеральда Хопкинса, но расцвела в XX веке, что неточная рифма разрабатывалась

Р. Броунингом.[7] Однако объединение этих формантов (плюс новая графика) произошло в 10-20-ые годы, когда свершилось генеральное 'раскрепощение' классической метрики, а литературное наследие Хопкинса стало оказывать влияние на современную поэзию (сходной оказалась посмертная судьба польского поэта Циприана Норвида). Была здесь и существенная разница — господствующим стал у англичан и американцев верлибр, который в русском стихосложении не занял сколько-нибудь значительного места.

Если мы обратимся от силлабо-тонических систем к силлабическим, то аналогии станут менее броскими, но не менее убедительными. Окажется, что и в тех литературах, где многовековая традиция диктовала строгую, жёсткую структуру, обуславливала число слогов, положение цезур и звеньев, характер и расположение рифм и т.д. *происходили процессы деканонизации классической метрики*. То же самое происходило и в младописьменных литературах едва успевших выработать свои нормы и создать свои размеры и лирические жанры. Примером может послужить хотя бы якутская поэзия.[8]

Оценивая такие факты, литературоведы, как будто договорившись друг с другом, стали писать о разрушении национальных традиций, о непродуктивном заимствовании у чужеземных поэтов, о небрежности и нетребовательности, о нигилизме, о необходимости бороться с разрушением формы. Так говорили японцы, англичане, азербайджанцы и даже французы, создавшие национальную форму верлибра 90 лет назад.[9]

Спору нет — везде происходит деканонизация классического стиха, но наряду с этим в поэзии всех народов происходит *формирование новой системности*, причём при всей разнице просодических возможностей и традиций в этих системах, противопоставленных классике, наблюдается и вырисовывается *нечто общее*. Все они находятся в одном отношении к предшествующему этапу развития 'своей метрики'.

Каково же это отношение и в чём стих Маяковского является отражением глобальных тенденций литературного развития? Ответ на этот вопрос требует попутного внимания к проблеме верлибра.

Верлибр в нашей концепции — это нерегулярный неметрический стих, система, 'стиховность' которой держится на ничем *не регламентированных повторах фонетических сущностей, на смене мер повтора*.[10] Стих Маяковского описывался нами как система, к которой неприложимы определения 'акцентный стих' или 'рифменный стих' и которая не может описываться и как 'хореи и ямбы' (пусть вольные, бесцезурные, но всё-таки хореи и ямбы). Основное в этой системе — множественность (плюрализм) и относительность (релятивность) её определителей. Это значит, что в пределах одного произведения **меняется** принцип организации стиха, причём в одних случаях на участке текста кристаллизуется равноударность (акцентный стих), в других ведущей формантой (структурной доминантой) может стать рифма, в третьих — строгая силлаботоничность. Эти признаки могут сочетаться и сходиться в метроритмическом построении, ослабляться или усиливаться (вплоть до характерного для раннего Маяковского использования полноударных четырёхстопных ямбов) и т.д.[11]

Мы не вправе говорить о полиметрии его построений, потому что этой системе присуще корреспондирование рядов не только на уровне метра, но и на других уровнях (фонетическом и, реже, синтаксическом). Теоретически же стих Маяковского допускает и включение в него кусков верлибра. Принципиальная разница между стихом Маяковского и собственно верлибром в том, что Маяковский использует только *первичные* ритмообразующие признаки стиха, а верлибр уравнивает функцию признаков *первичных* и *вторичных* (или — по Томашевскому — побочных).

Нас не должна смущать строгость многих построений Маяковского, особенно последнего периода. Это — не безусловная строгость классического стиха, а *условная*, могущая в любой точке построения сменить свои структурные определители.[12]

Отличие стиха Маяковского и верлибра от классического — не в акцентности, не в качестве рифмы, и не в графике наконец. Использование этих формантов является лишь отражением свойств более общего порядка.

В классическом стихосложении канонизировалась **симметрия** в построении рядов и канонизировался принцип **монометрии** как задания, сквозного повтора как средства материализации установки на симметрию. Отсюда — нормативность построения на всех уровнях, от характера рифмы до строфики. Не суть важно с этой точки зрения, что нормы тюркского стихосложения были одни, а русского другие. *Симметрия* и *монометрия* господствовали. Стих был однородным, или *гомоморфным*.

Поэзия XX века десимметризировала стих на всех его уровнях. Полиметрия — лишь частное проявление новой установки — на гетероморфность, на свободу использования приёмов связывания параллельных строк, на смену структурной доминанты. Гетероморфность и асимметрия пришли на смену гомоморфности и симметричности.

Проследить этот процесс можно на самом разном материале, причём везде обнаруживается: (1) период, предшествующий канонизации симметричных и гомоморфных структур, (2) период победы их (классическое стихосложение) и, наконец, (3) новый период — как бы возвращение к некоторым принципам народного стиха. Приведем несколько примеров.

Классический японский стих. По характеристике Н. Конрада отличается строжайшей силлабической организованностью. В XX веке (в *синтайси*) в нём появляется 'свобода метрического размера', существовавшая в народной поэзии.[13] Компоненты метрической формы остаются, но эквивалентность параллельных рядов исчезает. Далее появляется *дзюиси* (верлибр).[14]

Киргизский стих. Уже фольклорные формы его, по словам Кулана Рысалиева, симметричны, что — добавим — свидетельствует об относительно позднем их создании (это развитый народный стих). Период классического стиха сменяется формой *зркин ыр*. "Ритмические части его не знают симметрии", но это не верлибр, а структура, в которой усиливается ритмообразующая роль ритмических частей и отмечается выровненность их по синтаксическому построению.[15] В последнем случае вырисовывается верлибристская тенденция (вторичные ритмообразующие признаки выступают на передний план).

Тюркологи (М. Хамраев и другие) говорят о свободном метре в тюркских просодиях — *чачма шеир* (иначе — *зркин вазн*) как о структуре, восходящей к далёкому прошлому, к древнейшему стиху, в котором не было равносложности, вернее, она "колебалась в очень широких рамках" (Жирмунский). Таким образом, и в этом случае речь идёт о народном творчестве, об истоках.[16]

Интересно, что с появлением в национальных системах стихосложения разного рода асимметричных форм ('освобождённых' и 'свободных') после обычных атак на них традиционалистов критики с удивлением обнаруживают их 'исконность'. В недавно вышедшей работе Л. Черкасского "Новая китайская поэзия" (20-ые—30-ые годы) автор пишет: "Некоторые китайские учёные утверждали, что новая поэзия '4 мая' свободной рифмовки, ритма, интонации близка не 'стихам нового стиля' (речь идёт о системе, утвердившейся в 7-10 вв. н.э., т.е. в эпоху Тан. — А. Ж.), а 'стихам старого стиля' (т.е. системе, господствовавшей до эпохи Тан, но сохранившейся на периферии литературы на протяжении многих веков. — А. Ж.). Но даже если считать китайскую поэзию XX века преемницей 'стихов старого стиля', нужно отметить, что традиционность не помешала ей обрести такие черты, которые лишь в самом общем виде напоминали прародителей."[17]

В литературах, проходящих ускоренный путь развития и сохранивших по каким-либо причинам элементы гетероморфности и асимметрии в построении стиха, можно заметить два направления движения — к канонизации и кристаллизации жёстких форм (одно направление) и к созданию форм 'освобождённых'. Так, якутский стих, не прошедший ещё эпохи метрического нормирования, в творчестве поэта начала века Кулаковского кристаллизовался как 'аллитерационный свободный', в котором строфика эмбриональна, рифма эпизодична и несистематизирована (на 1000 строк, по подсчётам Г. Васильева зарифмовано 493), местами встречаются чётко выделенные синтаксические конструкции и т.д. Это — живая предыстория метрического письменного стиха. Другой поэт, Платон Ойунский, уже в 20-ые годы явился канонизатором строгой силлабической системы. Современная же якутская поэзия вернулась в значительной части своих произведений к гетероморфному (в нашей терминологии) стиху и к использованию верлибра, сочетающего архаическую традицию с новейшими 'модерными' тенденциями литературного развития.

Десимметризацию стиха и использование гетероморфных структур можно было бы показать на примере множества систем стихосложения, не соприкасавшихся друг с другом. Н. Мухамедов, анализируя стихи Али Сардар Джафри на урду и описывая раскрепощённую форму *азадназм*, показывает, как начинает меняться количество слоговых звеньев ('стоп') в пределах полустишия классического ряда и колебаться размеры самих 'стоп'.[18] В европейских литературах — это французский 'освобождённый стих' (*vers libéré*), а затем полное торжество принципа —в *vers libre,* в немецкой — *freie Rhythmen*, существующие с XVIII века, но получившие особенное распространение в XX (Арно Хольц, Бехер), и т.д. Генеральное наступление верлибра в англоязычных литературах Африки, испаноязычных — Южной Америки, наконец, в славянских литературах связано с победой того же принципа, вернее, с одной из возможностей его реализации.

Как в европейских литературах, так и в младописьменных можно указать на существование полярных форм стиха — и жёстко метрических (верметра), и верлибра. В вышедшей недавно антологии современных поэтов Ганы, пишущих по-английски, классическая силлаботоника мирно соседствует с верлибром, очевидно зависимым от опыта Уитмена, Сэндберга, Т. Элиота, и других.[19]

Такова общая картина эволюции стиховых систем в последние 50-60 лет.

Чем вызвано это явление в мировом масштабе, явление, в русской литературе особенно ярко демонстрируемое на материале творчества Маяковского? Однозначный ответ здесь невозможен. Важнейший момент, обусловивший эту эволюцию, отметил Д. Лихачёв, говоривший о том, что именно в нашем столетии формальная внешняя организованность литературы сменяется более глубокой и более органичной внутренней организованностью.[20]

Немаловажную роль играет и победа реалистических принципов в искусстве, борьба против стереотипов и всяческого рода нормированности. Наконец, изучение жанровой и видовой локализации несимметричных стиховых форм в разных литературах приводит к заключению, что они преобладали там, где начинают доминировать говорные или ораторские интонации. В этом плане 'столбичная' или 'лестничная' разбивка текста даже метрически строго организованного стиха способствует деформации его монотонных интонаций, вводит новые приёмы делимитации строки. Говоря о поэтике Маяковского, Н. Гей справедливо отмечает (вслед за Л. И. Тимофеевым и другими авторами): "… это поэтика публицистической, авторской обращенности к читателю, а вернее к многоликой аудитории живых слушателей поэтического слова, живой импульс непосредственного воздействия на третье лицо, находящееся вне стихотворного текста, осуществляемая в каждой интонации стиха."[21] Песенные интонации, естественно, не нуждаются в десимметризации.

Новые принципы организации художественного материала не отменяют прежние. Назым Хикмет в своих композициях широко использовал классические метры, но эти метры перестают быть единственной возможностью и не прогнозируются в тексте так, как в традиционных формах. Их движение нарушается (может быть нарушено) в любом пункте построения. Происходит диффузия форм — не только стиховых, ибо в наше время смешанные композиции стиха и прозы — не редкость. Они были уже у Маяковского (поэма "Человек"), а если говорить о литературах Востока, то это сочетание для них — вообще не новость.

Важнейшее качество поэзии XX века — усиление "корреляции чувства и стиха".[22] Диффузия формы помогает решению этой задачи.

Решение Маяковского — не единственное. Не только для иноязычных литератур, на которые он может оказывать непосредственное влияние, но и для русской. Продолжение его стихотворческой традиции — это поиски новых возможностей *сочетания симметричных и асимметричных построений*, стиха однородного и неоднородного. Величие его как революционера формы именно в этом, а не в 'открытии' ударника или неточной рифмы. Воспроизводить его стиховые формы нетрудно, но это путь эпигонства. Продолжать его традицию — значит искать новые пути сочетания формантов в целях выразительности, в целях мотивировки каждого компонента формы оттенками содержания.

Алма-Ата

ПРИМЕЧАНИЯ

[1] М. Л. Гаспаров, "Вольный хорей и вольный ямб Маяковского", *Вопросы языкознания* 1965/3; его же, "Акцентный стих раннего Маяковского", *Труды по знаковым системам* III (1967); Б. П. Гончаров, "О паузах в стихе Маяковского", *Русская литература* 1970/2; его же, "Интонационная организация стиха Маяковского", *Русская литература* 1972/2; его же, "Об изучении стиха Маяковского", *Поэт и социализм: К эстетике Маяковского* (Москва: Наука, 1971).

[2] М. Расули, *Поэзия В. В. Маяковского на узбекском языке (К вопросам поэтического перевода),* автореферат диссертации ... (Ташкент: АН Узб. ССР, 1969).

[3] Н. Хикмет, *Избранное,* изд. иностранной литературы (Москва 1953), стр. 43.

[4] J. Hollander, "From the viewpoint of literary criticism", *Style in Language* (New York, 1960), p. 405.

[5] См.: А. Белый, *Золото в лазури* (Москва 1904); З. Гиппиус, *Собрание стихов* 1 и 2 (Москва 1904-1910); П. Потёмкин, *Смешная любовь* (Санкт-Петербург 1908).

[6] К. Д. Вишневский, "Русская метрика XVIII века", *Вопросы XVIII века* (= *Труды кафедры русской и зарубежной литературы, Учёные записки,* 123, Серия филологическая) (Пенза 1972), стр. 138.

[7] C. M. Bowra, "The futurism of Vl. Mayakovsky", *Creative Experiment* (New York 1949), p. 101; B. J. Pendlebure, *The Art of the Rhyme* (London 1971).

[8] Г. М. Васильев, *Якутское стихосложение* (Якутск: Якутское книжное изд., 1965), разд. "Развитие литературного стихосложения".

[9] См. в нашей статье "О критериях типологической характеристики свободного стиха", *Вопросы языкознания* 1970/2.

[10] См. наши работы: "Границы свободного стиха", *Вопросы литературы* 1966/5; "От чего не свободен свободный стих?", *Стихи нужны ... : Статьи* (Алма-Ата: Жазуши, 1968); "О критериях типологической характеристики свободного стиха", *Вопросы языкознания* 1970/2; "Свободный в выборе...", *Вопросы литературы* 1972/11; "Свободный стих или верлибр", *Краткая литературная энциклопедия* 6 (Москва 1971); и др. См. также ряд других исследований, авторы которых подходят к проблеме со сходных позиций, напр.: Z. Czerny, "Le vers libre français et son art structural", *Poetics, Poetyka, Поэтика* I (Warszawa: PWN, 1962); B. Hrushovski, "On free rhythms in modern poetry: Preliminary remarks toward a critical theory of their structures and functions", *Style in Language,* ed. by Thomas A. Sebeok (New York-London: J. Wiley, 1960); Vl. Streinu, "Versificația modernă", *Studiu istorie și teoretie asupra versului liber* (București 1966).

[11] См. нашу статью "Освобождённый стих Маяковского", *Русская литература* 1971/2.

[12] См. там же.

[13] Н. Конрад, "О японской поэзии", *Японская поэзия; Сборник,* перевод с японского, стр. 11.

[14] А. И. Мамонов, *Свободный стих в японской поэзии* (Москва: Наука, 1971).

[15] Кулан Рысалиев, *Киргизское стихосложение,* автореферат диссертации... (Фрунзе 1965), стр. 62 и 64.

[16] М. Хамраев, *Очерки теории тюркского стиха* (Алма-Ата: Мектеп, 1959), гл. 3: "Чачма теир"; В. М. Жирмунский, "Огузский героический эпос и 'Книга Коркута'", *Книга моего деда Коркута* (Москва-Ленинград: изд. АН СССР).

[17] Л. Е. Черкасский, *Новая китайская поэзия (20-30-ые годы)* (Москва: Наука, 1972), стр. 192.

[18] Н. Мухамедов, *Али Сардар Джафри и его поэзия* (Ташкент: Фан, 1969).

[19] *Messages: Poems from Ghana* (Ibadam 1971).

[20] Д. С. Лихачёв, "Будущее литературы как предмет изучения", *Новый мир* 1969/9.

[21] Н. К. Гей, "Художественная форма и национальные традиции", *Проблемы художественной формы социалистического реализма* 2 (Москва: Наука, 1971), стр. 25.

[22] Vl. Streinu, "Versificaţia modernă" (Bucureşti 1966), p. 17.

PARTICIPANTS

Robert Abernathy
University of Colorado

James Bailey
University of Wisconsin

Henryk Baran
State University of New York
at Albany

Henrik Birnbaum
University of California, Los Angeles

Marianna Birnbaum
University of California, Los Angeles

Steven Broyde
Amherst College

Guy de Mallac
University of California, Irvine

Thomas Eekman
University of California, Los Angeles

Michael Flier
University of California, Los Angeles

M. L. Gasparov
Institute of World Literature, Moscow

Joan Grossman
University of California, Berkeley

Michael Green
University of California, Irvine

Kenneth E. Harper
University of California, Los Angeles

Michael Heim
University of California, Los Angeles

Benjamin Hrushovski
Tel Aviv University

†A. V. Issatschenko
University of Klagenfurt/
University of California, Los Angeles

Vjač. Vs. Ivanov
Slavic and Balkan Institute, Moscow

Lawrence G. Jones
Boston College

Geir Kjetsaa
University of Oslo

Ian K. Lilly
University of Auckland

V. F. Markov
University of California, Los Angeles

Jiří Marvan
Monash University, Clayton, Australia

M. R. Mayenowa
Polish Academy of Sciences, Warsaw

Hugh McLean
University of California, Berkeley

†Jan M. Meijer
University of Utrecht

Victor Terras
Brown University

Nils Åke Nilsson
University of Stockholm

Alan Timberlake
University of California, Los Angeles

Lucylla Pszczołowska
Polish Academy of Sciences, Warsaw

V. N. Toporov
Slavic and Balkan Institute, Moscow

Daniel Rancour-Laferriere
University of California, Davis

Jan van der Eng
University of Amsterdam

D. Segal
The Hebrew University, Jerusalem

Walter Vickery
University of North Carolina

Stanislav Segert
University of California, Los Angeles

Dennis Ward
University of Edinburgh

Michael Shapiro
University of California, Los Angeles

Thomas G. Winner
Brown University

G. S. Smith
University of Birmingham

Dean S. Worth
University of California, Los Angeles

Edward Stankiewicz
Yale University

A. L. Žovtis
University of Alma Ata